SPECIAL NEEDS
OFFENDERS in
CORRECTIONAL
INSTITUTIONS

To my sons Jonathan and Eithan
May you have the insight
to be tolerant and understanding to the needs of others

—L. Gideon

SPECIAL NEEDS OFFENDERS in CORRECTIONAL INSTITUTIONS

Lior Gideon

John Jay College of Criminal Justice

EDITOR

Los Angeles | London | New Delhi
Singapore | Washington DC

Los Angeles | London | New Delhi
Singapore | Washington DC

FOR INFORMATION:

SAGE Publications, Inc.
2455 Teller Road
Thousand Oaks, California 91320
E-mail: order@sagepub.com

SAGE Publications Ltd.
1 Oliver's Yard
55 City Road
London EC1Y 1SP
United Kingdom

SAGE Publications India Pvt. Ltd.
B 1/I 1 Mohan Cooperative Industrial Area
Mathura Road, New Delhi 110 044
India

SAGE Publications Asia-Pacific Pte. Ltd.
3 Church Street
#10-04 Samsung Hub
Singapore 049483

Copyright © 2013 by SAGE Publications, Inc.

A catalog record of this book is available from the Library of Congress.

978-1-4129-9813-0

Acquisitions Editor: Jerry Westby
Publishing Associate: MaryAnn Vail
Production Editor: Eric Garner
Copy Editor: Diane DiMura
Typesetter: C&M Digitals (P) Ltd.
Proofreader: Laura Webb
Indexer: Sheila Bodell
Cover Designer: Candice Harman
Marketing Manager: Lisa Sheldon Brown
Permissions Editor: Karen Ehrmann

12 13 14 15 16 10 9 8 7 6 5 4 3 2 1

Contents

Preface

Offenders with special needs have always been part of the criminal justice system. However, up until recently their visibility in correctional institutions was very low. For several decades, not much attention was given to anyone who harmed society; they were considered castaways, people society was better off without. Usually they were sentenced to jail or prison, and that was it—justice was served. Recent years, however, have seen a fresh interest in what is going on inside our prisons, and in particular how offenders are (or are not) being rehabilitated. This interest followed a period of what could be called an obsession with crime, during which the number of people sentenced to do time steadily increased, and convicted criminals were simply "warehoused," shut away from society behind massive walls and barbed wire. The policy was little more than "lock them up and throw away the key."

In addition, people finally came to understand that about 90% of these incarcerated people would inevitably be released and return to the communities from which they originally came. This sparked an interest in understanding these populations, what was being done for them while they were behind bars, and how society could better prepare to handle these masses of released offenders. Once more, rehabilitation—along with its associated terms, reentry, and reintegration—became the buzzword of correctional practice. With that, scholars began to understand that simply incarcerating people does not make society any safer, and in many cases, it even causes more harm than good, by harming the offenders, their families, their communities, and society as a whole. Consequently, evidence-based research began to form around the question of just what are the best correctional and rehabilitation practices for reducing recidivism and promoting public safety. Such endeavors led scholars to understand that because not all individuals are the same, it would stand to reason that the same is true for incarcerated individuals. This in turn led to the development of intake methods that focus on identifying risks and needs for each incarcerated individual upon admission to a correctional institution, and often even earlier, during the sentencing stages.

This book focuses on offenders who have special needs within the corrections system—special groups with particular concerns and needs, or who present certain challenges to prison staff. What are their experiences behind bars, and how do these experiences contribute—or not—to the rehabilitative efforts made by correctional institutions? Each chapter of the book identifies and describes the characteristics of a particular group and explains why it should be considered a *special needs* case. The author then discusses the challenges such offenders face as inmates, as well as the challenges they pose to correctional management and the daily routine of the facilities. When relevant, such discussions turn to efforts at rehabilitation and preparations for the inevitable reentry and reintegration. At the end of each chapter, the authors suggest guidance for related policy, which may also be used by readers as further points of discussion.

The book has a total of 17 chapters, including the introduction. These are designed to fit a semester-long course, so this may also be used as a primary textbook. Or it can be used as a supplemental textbook for students to focus on a specific group of inmates (or several), as each of the chapters functions on its own, using original and up-to-date data and research. All chapters are followed by discussion questions to promote critical thinking and class discussion, as well as a list of supplementary suggested readings and websites to feed curiosity.

Astute readers will also notice the thread that flows through the pages of the book, guiding readers to think about rehabilitation, reentry, and reintegration of special needs offenders. Chapters of the book are ordered in such a way that more visible groups of inmates are presented and discussed first (Chapters 2–6); Chapters 7–10 deal with groups of inmates that have always been present in correctional facilities but have received very little attention; and the last chapters, Chapters 11–15 deal with smaller, less visible special needs inmates that are often left out of the correctional discussion. Finally, an examination of substance abusing inmates, a well-documented and researched group, is presented in Chapter 16. Ending the book this way seems fitting, as inmates with substance problems are in fact the majority of incarcerated offenders, so their needs are quite urgent.

A key feature of the book is an integrative conclusion that brings together the policy recommendations of each of the chapters. It is within this context that a theoretical model is presented to illuminate the need to assess each and every individual offender before he or she is sentenced and processed into the correctional system. It is hoped that this theoretical model will further the discussion on special needs offenders and the manner in which their multifaceted characteristics will be addressed. The goal is to provide not just much-needed intervention, but also a just form of punishment, one that is proportional to the offense and fits the offender without causing further and unnecessary damage that might prevent him or her from successfully reintegrating.

—*Lior Gideon*

Acknowledgments

A s I taught a number of introductory and advanced courses in corrections, it became apparent that our system does not live up to society's expectations of *correction*. Offenders go in and come out in the same state, and at times in even worse condition. That led to the examination of rehabilitation, reentry, and reintegration, and ultimately to a previous book published on this topic: *Rethinking Corrections: Rehabilitation, Reentry, and Reintegration* (with Hung-En Sung). Through the pages of that book, a recurring theme was the need to individualize corrections-based intervention. Thus, to supplement this first discussion of the later phases of the corrections process, it was almost a natural step to initiate a discussion of the special needs of offenders earlier in the process, starting with sentencing and intake, and to acknowledge that although they committed a crime, they are still individuals, and as such have special needs.

Colleagues who teach corrections supported this initiative commenting on the almost complete absence of material in a single collection. Accordingly, it made perfect sense to compile the accumulated knowledge into one book. The process was invigorating and provided me with the amazing opportunity to work with ambitious individuals in the corrections field, both as practitioners and scholars (and a few who work as both). Each and every one of them was a true inspiration, and taught me a great deal about the topic thanks to their different approaches and perspectives. Yet, we all share a common notion and understanding that inmates are individual people, and although they must pay for their wrongdoing and crimes, something must be done to address their particular needs—not just for their sake, but for the sake of those who serve them, and above all, for the sake of public safety.

Equally important to this project are the people how provided us with valuable support and feedback. I would like to thank Jerry Westby, Sage's executive editor, and his assistant, Erim Sarbuland, as well as the editorial team for their impeccable work. Both Jerry and Erim were my control tower in sometimes very dark skies; Jerry also helped navigate and overcome the unexpected winds that blew away some of the initial contributors. He was always available and willing to give a guiding hand to find a replacement for lost or otherwise off-the-radar contributors, and also to offer good advice and reassurance whenever the need arose. But above all, Jerry believes in my work and in the success of this project, and this is the best one can ask for. Erim seems to be always on the other end of the line (or web) and was very quick to respond and provide assistance and solutions. I was truly blessed to have the wonderful opportunity to work with a great copy editor, Diane DiMura, who was highly devoted to this project. Diane's very precise, and punctual work without doubt improved this manuscript, and for that I am grateful. Appreciation is also extended to dear colleague, Staci Strobl, for her useful comments and support on the first draft of the proposal to this book. I would also like to express my gratitude to my personal editor, Zora O'Neill, for being critical of my work, revising my writing, and on top of it all making my ideas clear to others. Thank you!

Bringing different contributors into a new project is not an easy task, and at times it may also be a challenge. Each one writes in a different style and introduces a unique spin on things, which can make reviewers somewhat unhappy! By now I believe I was able to navigate through these reviews successfully, but not without the help of the wonderful contributors, as well as my colleagues who shared their ideas and criticism (sometimes unstintingly), with one aim in mind: to improve this project. Indeed, their input was often insightful and provided contributors with necessary direction and advice on how to revise their work while aligning the chapters in a coherent fashion. I would like to extend my gratitude to Elizabeth Dretsch (Troy University–Dothan), Shannon Hankhouse (Tarleton State University), Robert Michels (Santa Clara University), and Vanessa Woodward (University of Southern Mississippi) who provided the project with some highly valuable insights. This book is a result of a truly peer-reviewed effort, and for this we are all grateful.

As always, I reserve special thanks for those who inspire me the most—my family. Both my sons, Jonathan and Eithan Gideon, spent hours doing what they like the most, surfing the Internet, but with one aim: to help me design the cover for this book. Their many suggestions, discussions, and insights on each and every picture and design were truly remarkable. Gideon boys, you are the best team ever!

CHAPTER 1

Introduction: Special Needs Offenders

Lior Gideon

In the past two decades, the human landscape in correctional institutions has shifted significantly from its known historical image of young offenders in their prime years, in good mental and physical health. In fact, due to mandatory sentences, "three strikes" laws, truth in sentencing, states abolishing parole, and a general get-tough-on-crime approach, correctional institutions are facing new challenges that stem from the fact that increasing segments of the prison population do not comply with the traditional image, and so incarceration cannot be an equal punishment or treatment to all. It is within this context that the current text discusses the issues and challenges surrounding incarcerated offenders with special needs, and the ways in which such challenges may be addressed by policy makers in the corrections field. Specifically, the aim of this book is to examine the different populations under correctional supervision, and in particular those incarcerated. Such an examination is relevant and important because these populations pose a variety of challenges to the system and require special attention. Consequently, they place different demands on correctional facilities, requiring institutions to address different risk challenges and meet diverse rehabilitative needs.

BACKGROUND

There are more than 9 million people imprisoned worldwide (Dammer & Fairchild, 2006), with the United States being the leading nation in incarceration (Gideon & Sung, 2011; Jacobson, 2005; Petersilia, 2003; Tonry, 2006; Travis, 2005). In fact, according to the 2011 Bureau of Justice Statistics, at year-end 2010, state and federal prison authorities had jurisdiction over 1,605,127 prisoners, with local jails holding 748,728 (at midyear 2010) persons. Such high numbers are a direct product of a "getting tough on crime" attitude, which increased dramatically in recent decades. This attitude inspired such sentencing trends as mandatory sentencing, truth in sentencing, "three strikes" laws, and mandatory minimum sentences, and as a direct consequence, new populations were introduced to the prison and jail environments, creating new challenges for prison administrators and the correctional system as a whole, and in particular, resulted in the impediment of rehabilitation programs and preparation of these offenders for release.

Considering the fact that more than two-thirds of offenders sentenced to jails and prisons have histories of substance abuse (Chaiken, 1989; Chavarria, 1992; Gideon, 2010; Inciardi, 1995; Inciardi, Martin, Butzin, Hooper, & Harrison, 1996; Welsh, 2011), reentry, and reintegration practices become even more of a challenge. Nevertheless, this is not the sole problem that current correctional institutions and practitioners face. A worrisome increase is observed in convicted inmates under the age of 18 (Seiter, 2008; Sickmund, 2003; Snyder & Sickmund, 2006). Many scholars have noted with alarm that the juvenile offender population is growing in correctional facilities, especially in adult correctional facilities (Bilchik, 1998; Griffin, Torbet, & Szymanski, 1998; Kuanliang, Sorensen, & Cunningham, 2008). Another noticeable growing population in correctional facilities is convicted female offenders (Morash & Schram, 2002; Pollock, 1998, 2001, 2004). In fact, Stohr, Walsh, and Hemmens (2009) argue that "the number of incarcerated and supervised women under the correctional umbrella has never been larger" (p. 570). Female offenders pose new challenges to current classification practices (see Van Voorhis & Presser, 2001). For example, Baunach (1992), Henriques (1996), and Rocheleau (1987) addressed the challenges presented by incarcerated mothers and the social consequences of their incarceration for broader social issues (Dodge & Pogrebin, 2001; Pollock, 2004).

An equally important growing challenge in recent years is that of senior inmates (Aday, 1994, 2003; Aday & Webster, 1979; Kerbs & Jolley, 2009; Moritsugu, 1990). Scmalleger and Ortiz-Smykla (2009) have observed an increase of 85% in elderly inmates in the nation's correctional facilities since 1995. Many of these inmates require expensive medical treatment. Drummond (1999) questions whether it is necessary for such offenders to remain in custody after they become old and frail, and indeed according to Clear, Cole, and Reisig (2009), newly released inmates are now not only older and have served longer periods of imprisonment, but they also have higher levels of substance abuse and other medical issues that require community monitoring.

Hammett, Roberts, and Kennedy (2001) examined the health-related issues in prisoner reentry and demonstrated the need for adequate health care for those inmates with infectious diseases that can threaten the community. Specifically, Hammett, Kennedy, and Kuck (2007) discuss the potential harms of infectious diseases such as HIV/AIDS: more than 23,000 infected inmates were documented at year-end 2004, with an estimated 10% more that are not confirmed. Other diseases the researchers identified as significant were tuberculosis as well as sexually transmitted diseases such as syphilis, gonorrhea, chlamydia, genital herpes, and hepatitis. A study conducted on Rikers Island in New York found that the rates of the above diseases increased during 2000, and in particular, among females and juveniles detention centers (Brown, 2003). Corzine-McMullan (2011) argues that such health challenges need to be addressed as do mental health issues of incarcerated inmates, as these inmates pose new challenges for correctional officials as well as for those interested in reintegration.

In addition to inmates with health issues, there are other significant segments of the prison population that are being overlooked by current research and available textbooks. For example, Knickerbocker (2006) estimates that based on the last national census of 2000, more than 8.7 illegal immigrants entered the United States. The U.S. Border Patrol union reports a much higher number of between 12 million and 15 million. Such numbers are sure to be reflected in our prison system, resulting in a new breed of inmates that require special attention. For example, Seiter (2011) notes that 9,720 people were held in U.S. Immigration and Customs Enforcement facilities at year-end 2007. Recent estimates from the state of California indicate that the number of illegal immigrants currently incapacitated by the prison system is about 19,000 (Aviram, 2010). This is a unique population in any country's prison system; they are not documented and often do not speak the local language.

Although small in numbers, those convicted under the U.K. Terrorism Act and its equivalents around the world are an incarcerated population that poses many challenges. For example, Israeli prisons hold more than 10,000 inmates on charges related to national security and terrorism (Israeli Prison System, 2009). This category of inmates has received little attention, but it is becoming more visible in correctional settings. In the United Kingdom, recent data provided by the British Ministry of Justice (personal correspondence April 15, 2009) indicate that there are currently 132 incarcerated offenders convicted under the Terrorism Act, with the majority convicted under recent terrorism legislation. The American Federal Bureau of Prisons is also holding an increasing number of inmates convicted under similar legislation. Actual numbers for this population are constantly changing and increasing, and thus it becomes essential to examine the extent to which such offenders are represented in the correctional system. Several different congressional committees have focused on the issue of radicalization in prisons, thus reflecting the fear of what may emerge from this growing population.

Distinct from the previous groups are those inmates who have served in the military. Mumola (2000) states that with more than 25,062,400 veterans in the U.S. population, a staggering number of 225,700 veterans were held in the nation's prisons and jails as of 1999. That is an increase of more than 50% in incarcerated veterans since 1985, with majority of them doing time for violent offenses. More recent data by Mumola and Noonan (2008) estimates that the number of veterans incarcerated in local jails, state, and federal facilities had increased to 228,700 at year-end 2007. This population poses many social challenges that are external to our correctional system. With the return of all American soldiers from Afghanistan and more recently from Iraq at the end of 2011, this population will likely increase, as thousands of soldiers have come home to a tough economic climate, social upheaval, and a difficult job market.

Based on the above examples, we can understand that special-needs offenders are those offenders, both men and women, with unique requirements within the corrections system. Anderson (2008) describes these populations as "those incarcerated . . . with unusual or unique requirements stemming from their physical or mental age or other disabilities" (p. 361).

Other prison populations that demonstrate special needs include sex offenders, homosexual inmates, and inmates under protective custody. It is in this context that the current book aims to expand and supplement existing knowledge.

EFFECTS ON CORRECTIONAL MANAGEMENT

The mosaic of incarcerated offenders poses new challenges to jail and prison staff. Different offenders with diverse needs, along with a rising incarcerated population, make it difficult for correctional administration not only to address offender's needs but also to achieve their own mandate of administering and implementing court-prescribed sentences while maintaining safety and well-being of the staff, inmates, and the general public. Such variation in the prison population also impedes corrections from achieving its other goals of treatment, rehabilitation, surveillance, and control of its many inmates.

In order to address this, more emphasis should be given to the intake process, during which a prisoner's specific needs and risks can be more accurately identified. This will enable correctional managers to better allocate resources while addressing pressing issues that may threaten the security of the facility and its mode of operation.

It is important to keep in mind that any institution is the sum of all of the people who operate within its walls. That is, jails and prisons are not a reflection just of the staff, but even more so of the inmates who reside within their walls. Different populations thus require different attention and resources. For example, elderly and chronically ill inmates pose less of a risk for violent behavior compared with mentally ill and active, non-treated substance abusers. As such, they require more medical attention and treatment but less control. On the other hand, mentally ill offenders pose a greater challenge and risk to other inmates, staff, and themselves, and thus require more attention and a different organizational strategy. Inmates of different religions, gay and lesbian inmates, and chronically ill incarcerated offenders all add another dimension to the multifaceted prison environment. Each group is a test of the system's tolerance and the boundaries of safety versus security of the facility, as well as court-protected constitutional rights. Their unique needs also challenge institutions' surveillance and control abilities, which can be an impediment that may provide a fertile ground to the development of hazardous behaviors that may affect public safety, while at the same time prevent those who need treatment from receiving it. Each of the following chapters focuses on a specific segment of these special needs offenders, while emphasizing each group's distinctive characteristics and the challenges they present to correctional administration and staff. At the end of each chapter, a policy section is presented to enable readers to contemplate specific policies that may assist in managing such populations. It is through those sections that readers can turn their attention to prospects of rehabilitation and future reintegration of such offenders.

REHABILITATION AND REINTEGRATION OF SPECIAL NEEDS OFFENDERS

One of the many goals of correction is to rehabilitate offenders and prepare them for reentry. This goal has been contested in recent decades, as research on the effectiveness of correctional treatment became available. While studies in the 1950s and

1960s provided evidence that correctional treatment is effective in reducing recidivism rates (Bailey, 1966; Logan, 1972), later studies suggested that with very few and isolated evidence some correctional interventions work to some extent, while others simply do not work (Martinson, 1974). Politicians translated Martinson's study to simply "nothing works," and this doctrine paved the way for decades of change in correctional policies, which became more punitive and focused more on the goal of public safety through incapacitation. At the same time, competing criminological theories, as well as various attempts to explain social deviance, governed the discussion over the causes of crime and criminal behavior for several decades. Such cacophony led in turn to the development of different punitive approaches, some of which assume the criminal's rationality and others assume the offender to have a personality defect.

But the correctional pendulum, swinging between punishment and rehabilitation, did not stop, and unsurprisingly, the controversy led further to direct attention to matching treatment with distinct typologies of offenders (Ashford, Sales, & Reid, 2001). In fact, criminal justice and correctional scholars began to focus on developing methods for identifying the needs of offenders in specific categories, and for assessing their reaction to institutional treatment. Andrews, Bonta and Hoge (1990) developed the risk-needs assessment tool, which identifies static and dynamic factors that help classify offenders and thus determine the level of service they should be exposed to. As Jeglic, Malie, and Calkins-Mercado (2011) point out, "this resulted in the development of the risk-need-responsivity (RNR) model for evaluating program effectiveness" (p. 37).

The development of the RNR model should not have come as a surprise to those researchers dealing with the rehabilitation of offenders. About five decades earlier, Sutherland (1939) observed that the key to effective delivery of correctional intervention is individualization of treatment, as no two men are alike. Such an observation remains highly important and especially relevant when dealing with special needs offenders.

According to Sung and Gideon (2011), it appears that case management programs specifically designed for offenders with targeted special needs "produce much better outcomes than generic programs serving a wide variety of offenders" (p. 91). In fact, studies have shown that case management in which the specific offender's needs are addressed leads to a better rehabilitation process and as a result to reduction in recidivism (Longshore, Turner, & Fain, 2005; Loveland & Boyle, 2007). A case management approach that takes into consideration the offender's criminogenic traits as well as other personal characteristics (e.g., gender, age, mental well-being, sexual and religious orientation, and past history) has a better chance of modifying the factors contributing to the development of delinquent behavior and of reducing repeated incarcerations (Ashford et al., 2001).

Despite all this, there is still a dire shortage of adequate research that focuses directly on special needs offenders and what sort of treatment they require. The current book is thus a first attempt to concentrate on such populations and place them on the emerging rehabilitation and reintegration research agenda. The remainder of this chapter will briefly present each population, as a means of introducing the reader to some of the issues that this book will cover.

Juvenile Offenders

Many of the juveniles entering the criminal justice system are very young, some less than 15 years old. As with adult offenders, most are boys, but unlike the adult population, which is majority African American, most are White or Hispanic, and only 29% are Black/African American (Schmalleger & Ortiz-Smykla, 2009). According to the Federal Bureau of Investigation (2007), law enforcement agencies place about 1.6 million juveniles into correctional custody. Juveniles accounted for more than 15% of all arrests, with about 16% of arrests for violent crimes. In fact, the FBI reported that juveniles were responsible for 42.8% of index crimes (i.e., 16.5% violent crimes and another 26.3% for property crimes). This harsh reality suggests that juvenile presence in correctional institution may be on the rise. Juveniles entering the criminal justice system are poorly integrated into the normative society; often they suffer from social isolation and emotional neglect. These tend to associate with lack of family bond and support, as well as deteriorating social cohesion. Not surprisingly, some develop substance dependency, while others exhibit mental issues and violent behavior. Recent cases demonstrated that more and more cases are waived from juvenile courts to adult courts, where juveniles are sentenced as adults. According to Seiter (2011), "the past twenty years have seen an increase in the number of waivers of jurisdiction form juvenile to adult court" (p. 280). Such a trend is evidence that many states are departing from their philosophy of rehabilitating juveniles and turning to a more punitive philosophy.

Regardless of their incarceration status, however, juveniles are still regarded as a special needs inmate population, as they require special attention whether incarcerated in a juvenile facility or an adult one. This is mainly due to the fact that young inmates tend to be more violent, have more difficulties adjusting to the prison environment, and may also have a higher risk of being victimized by other inmates. Such conditions are not conducive to treatment and rehabilitation, and consequently, may have a negative effect on reintegration. Chapter 2, by Quarles Emeka and Walters, discusses the needs, risks, and challenges of juvenile offenders behind bars, while presenting the historical and contemporary development of juvenile representation in the American criminal justice system.

Female Offenders

Female incarceration rates have risen dramatically since the 1990s, and have now even surpassed the rate of male incarceration. Many of the incarcerated women are mothers to minor children (Glaze & Maruschak, 2010) who are left behind in foster care or cared for by grandparents—a situation that can result in parents losing custody and children being neglected—which may in turn worsen the consequences of incarceration. The needs of incarcerated mothers thus require different and specialized attention from a correctional standpoint, as they need to address issues of separation while also prepare them for reintegration and the time when they will attempt to regain their children's trust and legal custody.

This requires special parenting programs, as well as family intervention initiatives, which at times may be very difficult to achieve as most incarcerated females are being cut off from their families during the incarceration period. Both Chapter 3, on incarcerated females, and Chapter 4, an analysis of pregnancy and motherhood behind bars, discuss the challenges of incarcerated females. In Chapter 3, Pasko and Chesney-Lind present a general description of the challenges of incarcerated females, and focus on their unique characteristics. Chapter 4, by Henriques and Gladwin, focuses on a specific challenge, one unique to females, and often linked to their mental well-being: being a mother and the potential loss of connection and guardianship. It delves further into the unique situations of giving birth while incarcerated and the implications of such a scenario on both mother and newborn.

Chronically Ill Inmates

As noted earlier in this chapter, the stereotypical image of a strong, young male inmate is no longer the reality of today's prison environment. Many incarcerated offenders have practiced unhealthy and risky behavior by abusing alcohol and substances, smoking, or engaging in unprotected sex, often with multiple partners. These behaviors, combined with lack of health insurance and regular physical checkups, often result in deteriorated health conditions. Accordingly, the rate of sexually transmitted infections (STIs), hepatitis, tuberculosis, asthma, hypertension, diabetes, and other illnesses is evident in correctional facilities in rates that are much higher than in the general population. Indeed, research indicates that those entering correctional facilities are characterized by higher rates of chronic medical conditions (Freudenberg, 2001). Wilper et al. (2009) found that about 39% of federal inmates and a similar percentage of local jail inmates have at least one chronic illness. In state prisons, the researchers found this percentage to be even higher, at about 43% of all state inmates.

Such medical conditions pose a major impediment for successful rehabilitation and reintegration and may also affect the inmate during the course of incarceration. Infectious diseases (e.g., hepatitis, HIV/AIDS, tuberculosis, and other STIs) are also a challenge for correctional administrators and pose great risk to other inmates and the staff. In Chapter 5, Dretsch provides a thorough account of chronically ill inmates behind bars, while discussing the challenges associated with the daily routine of and interaction with those inmates, as well as assessing what is currently available and offered to inmates who need medical attention.

Mentally Ill Inmates

Historically, many mentally ill people were confined to prisons and jails simply because no other social reaction was available to their behavior. With the deinstitutionalization movement of the 1950s and 1960s, many facilities for the mentally ill reduced the number of beds available for the hospitalization of such people, leaving many of them drifting and roaming the streets of big cities. This situation led to increased encounters with law enforcement and subsequently to arrests of more mentally ill individuals. According to Torrey and colleagues (2010), by incarcerating mentally ill people in higher numbers, the American correctional system has returned to the conditions that characterized prisons more than 200 years ago, when a large number of mentally ill were also placed behind bars. It's not surprising that many scholars refer to modern prisons and jails as the *new asylum* (Arngo, 2002; Fagan & Ax, 2011; Wynn, 2011).

Such an increase in mentally ill inmates requires a high level of professionalism to detect and assess different issues and how they can be addressed while the inmate is incarcerated. Moreover, mentally ill inmates are often more difficult to handle, as they tend to be more violent and also tend to have more disciplinary infractions. Consequently, offenders sentenced to jail or prison must be evaluated in an intake process, and be screened for mental illnesses. Most intakes are based on self-report by the offenders on previous mental health conditions; this could be problematic, as some may not report their true conditions. Such a situation can place the psychological staff at an initial disadvantage that may result in erroneous assessment of the offender's needs and risk and may also impede the ability of correctional authorities to tailor an appropriate treatment and reentry plan.

Another important consideration is the fact that most mentally ill offenders tend to be violent and as such pose more risk to jail and prison staff and other inmates. Such a risk usually requires a higher level of security, which in turn typically places many mentally ill offenders with other high-risk offenders who are not mentally ill. In a recent study, the author of this chapter found that about 77% of incarcerated offenders in New York State supermax facilities and special housing units (SHUs) suffered from some form of mental illness, and that such a condition was associated with the decision to place the inmate in these highly secure and restrictive environments. Placement in high-security institutions poses additional challenges for mentally ill offenders, and often the conditions of their incarceration are not conducive to their desired treatment. Nevertheless, most inmates with identified mental health issues do receive some level of treatment, usually provided by the institutional psychologist. Chapter 6, by working correctional psychologists Nicholas and Bryant, discusses the challenges of treating mentally ill inmates behind bars.

Older and Geriatric Inmates

While the general population of the United States is aging, the average age of incarcerated offenders also increases. An aging incarcerated population is also the result of mandatory sentences, "three strikes" laws, and longer sentences, all of which results in more offenders spending longer periods of time behind bars. Data from the Bureau of Justice Statistics indicates that an increase of more than 40% in male inmates over the age of 50 was documented between 1998 and 2009. For incarcerated females over age 50, the increase is much more acute, at 139% over the same time period. Such statistics provides a clear picture according to which the average age of the American prison population is increasing and as a result presents correctional administrators with a host of new challenges.

According to Seiter (2011), one of the most pressing issues that results from this condition is the high cost of medical care associated with elderly inmates, who present a number of illnesses and health problems due to both general aging and particular lifestyle choices. Older inmates' health problems are different from those shared by younger inmates, which puts jail and prison clinics at a major disadvantage as health care providers. Many services that are available to the elderly population outside the prison walls may not be as accessible inside the prison. In addition, many facilities are not geared to deal with chronically ill inmates and many of the infectious diseases found among the incarcerated. As noted earlier, prisons were not designed to hold ill and dependent populations. Most facilities are designed to hold young and physically active inmates who can work and be involved in prison routine and activity. The cells, beds, and other facilities are designed for inmates with good physical stamina. Imagine, for example, an older inmate who has difficulty walking being placed in a cell block on the second or third floor. This inmate must share a cell with another person, and may even be required to sleep on the upper bunk of an already small bed. While most elderly offenders tend to be compliant with prison rules and regulations, they also tend to be easy prey for younger and violent inmates. Such conditions are not optimal for rehabilitation and preparation for reentry and reintegration. And many older inmates have spent long years behind bars, and when they are about to be released back to the community, they have very little knowledge of how to seek and receive the care they need. Consequently, the level of attention directed at managing the elderly inmate population has increased while efforts by correctional administrators and facilities are slowly catching up. In Chapter 7, Aday and Krabill focus on older and geriatric inmates behind bars and the challenges they pose to prison officials and management. The chapter also discusses the issues around the managing and treatment of such population.

Gay and Lesbian Inmates

In the general population, homosexuality is now accepted or at least tolerated, but inside correctional facilities such behavior is forbidden and considered a violation of prison rules and regulations. This is mainly due to the potentially coercive and problematic nature of such relations and the problems they may cause in controlling the inmate population and the operations of the facility. Although it is difficult to identify the actual scope of sexual activity in prison, and homosexual activity in particular, such behavior exists. In fact, all prisons have policies against any type of sexual behavior between inmates, and if caught inmates are punished.

Inmates are typically expected to be tough and demonstrate self-control. But openly homosexual inmates can be perceived as weak and may become the target of harassment and victimization (as can straight inmates, for that matter). For any inmate, fears of being sexually assaulted during incarceration are not conducive for successful rehabilitation and later reentry and reintegration. Inmates who have been sexually assaulted during their incarceration take this horrific experience with them when they leave prison. Some may have even contracted sexually transmitted diseases as a result of their attack, and will be exporting them back to the community upon release.

Consequently, homosexuality behind bars, and gay and lesbian inmates specifically, has received increased attention in recent years, particularly after the passing of the Prisoners' Rape Elimination Act (PREA) of 2003. However, incarcerated homosexual behavior fascinated researchers decades prior to the PREA. In Chapter 8, Hensley, Eigenberg, and Gibson discuss homosexuality behind bars while providing a thorough examination of gay and lesbian inmates and coercive sexual conduct among inmates. In their discussion, they provide a unique opportunity to examine the challenges these inmates pose to the system, as well as the challenges they have to face once sentenced and how the system reacts to their needs.

Inmates Under Protective Custody

Although it varies by state and facility, most jails and prisons have the ability to assign specific inmates to protective custody (PC), a type of segregation within the facility that is designed to address the unique security needs of inmates. In these units, inmates are separated from the general population on the basis of a threat, or to prevent potential victimization. Not all inmates can stand the harsh isolation of protective custody, and many experience deterioration in health. Usually conditions in protective custody units are much harsher than in the rest of the facility, and inmates are not just isolated, but also supervised almost 24/7. Such conditions of segregation can damage inmates' well-being and provoke symptoms of anxiety and depression, among a host of many other mental problems. This may impede attempts at rehabilitation and later reintegration. Chapter 9, by Miller and McCoy, describes the conditions of protective custody, the needs of those inmates assigned to PC, and the policies that need to be developed to address such needs.

Sex Offenders

Sexual offenders are a unique category of inmates that requires specific attention. Not only are they considered by other inmates to be of low status, but often they are ridiculed, harassed, assaulted, and even sexually victimized by other inmates (Palermo, 2005). For this reason, many of the offenders convicted and sentenced as sexual offenders try to mask their crimes and avoid the stigma. Correctional staff should be aware of these concerns, as they can put those inmates at a disadvantage, making them weak and thus easy prey for other inmates.

On the other hand, when sexual offenders try to escape the stigma of their crime, they may not receive appropriate treatment. In fact, some convicted sexual offenders may choose not to attend sexual-offender treatment to avoid being recognized by other inmates. Lack of appropriate intervention during incarceration is not desired and should be addressed, targeted, and mandated early in the intake process. Prior research proves that treatment of sexual offenders is effective in reducing sexual offense recidivism (Palermo, 2009), and that the rate of recidivism of treated sexual offenders is relatively very low (about 5.3%), in comparison with other offenses, particularly in comparison with substance-use-related offenses (Gideon, 2011).

Unfortunately, as Maile, Calkins-Mercado, and Jeglic state in Chapter 10, treatment for these offenders is not mandated at present. This means that some sexual offenders can be released back to society untreated for their problem, and thus increase the risk of reoffending.

Inmates of Different Religions

Religion is an important part of rehabilitation. Thus, it is not surprising that many inmates discover or rediscover religion and strengthen their faith. For many inmates, life behind bars is gray, gloomy, and hopeless; religion can fill the gap, providing inmates the warmth and support they need. Accordingly, research on faith-based initiatives in prisons has flourished in recent years. Such studies have focused on examining the potential benefits of introducing religion as part of the rehabilitation effort—an idea that was initially introduced by the Quakers in the 18th century. Today, American prisons must comply with the provisions of the First Amendment and allow their inmates freedom of religion. Inmates can identify as Christian, Muslim, Jewish, Native American, Sikh, Rastafarian, Wiccan, or part of any other religious group, and can request special considerations that will comply with their beliefs. By law, states are mandated to the best of their ability to provide religious services and accommodate the spiritual needs of incarcerated offenders.

But it is at times difficult to provide the ideal conditions of worship and guidance to every religion. Security requirements, as well as the safety of the staff and other inmates, are of prime concern and may present conflicting agendas. Budget constraints, as well as the ability to recruit suitable chaplains, are another barrier to insuring such services are available and provided to inmates. Furthermore, some religious groups require special diets or ceremonies that may be in violation of facility rules and regulation, and may not be understood by the staff and administration. These may cause friction between inmates and staff that at times lead to violent eruptions and prison riots. In Chapter 11, Zaitzow and Jones discuss the power of faith-based programming behind bars—its strengths, weaknesses, and implications—while also providing an in-depth account of the challenges and corresponding policies that should be examined to improve religious services to those inmates who need it. The reader should also relate the religious discussion presented in Chapter 11 to that of Islamic radicalization of inmates presented by Rappaport, Veldhuis, and Guiora in Chapter 15.

Incarcerated Veterans

Inmates with a history of military service have typically been neglected in the correctional setting. A report by Noonan and Mumola (2007) states that although their proportional representation in American correctional facilities has been steadily decreasing after a peak following the Vietnam War, their absolute numbers in state and federal facilities actually rose by 58% between 1985 and 2000. However, the above report relies on data collected up till 2004, and hence fails to represent recent developments in regard to this important segment of inmates. Unfortunately, recent American military involvement in Afghanistan and Iraq and the subsequent return of many war veterans will likely increase the visibility of this population in American correctional facilities. In fact, slightly less than a quarter of a million military veterans can be found in jails and prisons, most of them having served in wars and many of them suffering from a host of physiological and psychological problems (although not disproportionately compared with nonveterans), including posttraumatic stress disorder (PTSD), substance use, and alcohol addiction.

Not much research is available on this inmate population; however, available data by the Bureau of Justice Statistics suggests that the majority of incarcerated veterans are males and that "more than half (57%) of veterans in state prison were serving time for a violent offense, including 15% for homicide and 23% for sexual assault, which included rape. Among nonveterans, less than half (47%) were in state prison for a violent offense; one in five were held for homicide (12%) or sexual assault (9%)" (Noonan & Mumola, 2007, p. 1). Most of the violent behavior was directed toward females and minors. As a result, these inmates' sentence length is much longer on average despite the fact that their criminal record is often not as long as nonveterans. In addition, veteran inmates are overall older and better educated than other state and federal prison inmates. In Chapter 12, Rosenthal and McGuire show how these unique characteristics of veterans behind bars present prison officials with specific challenges, and how this can be further complicated by the fact that many correctional staff members are veterans themselves.

Inmates on Death Row

Capital punishment is reserved for those offenders who did the unspeakable. Many times, offenders sentenced to death are those who took life, were found guilty of treason, or committed the most heinous crime one can possibly imagine. Such acts are defined by law and may vary by state and jurisdiction. The majority of death row inmates are housed in only three states: California, Florida, and Texas. However, except for five states, all other states hold inmates on death row.

Despite the attention given to high-profile death penalty cases, the number of inmates on death row is relatively small, and these inmates do not exhibit any significant differences from other incarcerated offenders, except for the capital crime they committed and have been convicted of. According to the Death Penalty Information Center (2012), almost all the inmates on death row are male, with females accounting for less than 2% of the population. In terms of education, about 40% of death row inmates completed high school or GED, and about 51% did not complete 12 years of education; the rest had some college or graduated from college. Such educational data may also be connected to research that found death row inmates to have on average lower IQ scores (Cunningham, Sorenson, Vigen, & Woods, 2011; Cunningham & Tasse, 2010; Cunningham & Vigen, 1999; Frierson, Schwartz-Watts, Morgan, & Malone, 1998). As Cunningham states in Chapter 13, in which he examines the special needs of death row inmates, these characteristics prevent many of them from engaging in meaningful solitary intellectual pursuits.

Death row inmates are usually segregated from other inmates and are mostly left idle. These conditions not only burden the facilities but also affect inmates and staff. Contrary to the usually vicious criminal behavior for which they were convicted, death row inmates tend to be less problematic when it comes to prison regulations. Schmalleger and Ortiz-Smykla (2009), relying on previous studies, argue that death row inmates "seldom exhibit disciplinary problems" (p. 592) and that regardless of their incarceration conditions, they are the least likely to cause any problems or engage in any serious violent activity during their incarceration. Their compliance with prison rules and regulation may be associated with their older average age, length of incarceration, and prior experience in being incarcerated, as well as the high levels of supervision in the facilities that hold such inmates. It goes without saying that those sentenced to death do not receive any form of rehabilitative treatment or participate in work programs; they are mostly confined to their cell 23 hours a day. The majority of inmates are not allowed visitors or any of the other privileges that many other inmates enjoy such as recreation. Such limitations, along with the finality of their sentence, results in the isolation of many death row inmates, who are also not allowed to associate with other inmates. Chapter 13, by Cunningham, provides a thorough account of death row inmates and their characteristics, while also raising some questions as to the effectiveness of the conditions of their incarceration.

Illegal Immigrants as Inmates

Not much is known about the number of illegal immigrants that are currently behind bars in American facilities. However, evidence shows that such cases exist and that the numbers of illegal immigrants housed in American correctional facilities is on the rise. In fact, in their discussion of this segment of the prison population in Chapter 14, Weiss and Vasquez state that there is a "surprising variability in criminal justice data on immigrants" behind bars. The range of reported immigrants and illegal immigrants in prison is very big, estimated to be anywhere from 48,000 to more than 220,000 people. Such a spread is a result of different types of data collection and focuses of attention, and it may not even account for immigrant detainees. Nevertheless, these numbers reflect American immigration policy and may also take into account the large number of offenses committed by immigrants. Stana (2005) reported that illegal immigrants were arrested 459,614 times and were charged with no less than 691,890 different offenses. Furthermore, 97% of aliens in prison had more than one arrest. With new homeland security and migration policies, the endless battle against drugs and human trafficking along the Mexican border, and others infiltrating the country for various reasons, the immigrant population is likely to increase and become more visible in our correctional system. In fact, data shows that over 80% of immigrants were arrested in only three states: Arizona, California, and Texas.

Such a population becomes problematic to manage, as many of them have no English proficiency and may have very little funds, if any, to pay for their legal representation. Such barriers may impede the correctional professionals from adequately identifying their needs and assessing their actual risk, which may in turn affect their classification and eligibility for programming. Consequently, many are left idle for long periods of time, and, as Weiss and Vasquez describe in their chapter, many do not have an actual release date or the knowledge of what will happen to them. This problem is more evident for those who were arrested for entering the country illegally and are awaiting deportation. In such cases, many are placed with convicted criminals that will take advantage of and victimize them. Chapter 14 also presents the historical development of American immigration policies and how they have affected the criminal justice system, and in particular, jails and prisons (both state and federal). The chapter also discusses the challenges and abuses of this population within the criminal justice system, and their vulnerability once placed behind bars.

Radicalization and Terror-Related Inmates

Following the attacks of September 11, 2001, prison officials as well as policy makers began turning their attention to a growing segment of the prison population: inmates converting to Islam and becoming more radicalized. Converting to Islam and strengthening religious beliefs was always part of prison reality, a way to search for meaning, protection, and redemption (as discussed by Zaitzow and Jones in Chapter 11). However, the moral panic associated with recent events and the notorious Al-Qaeda terror group has turned the spotlight on Islam and provoked the fear that inmates could be radicalized and prepare for committing acts against their countries.

Not much is known about this population or how many inmates are actually radicalized while incarcerated. However, their presence poses a new challenge to correctional administrators, as well as to public safety after release. Further, attempts at rehabilitating and reintegrating such inmates may become an even bigger challenge, as faith-based organizations and activities are often used as a rehabilitation method. Thus, when it comes to dealing with inmates who were radicalized while incarcerated, how will such religious initiatives promote reintegration and public safety, if at all? Chapter 15, by Rappaport, Veldhuis, and Guiora, focuses on the scope and challenges of this population, while offering comparative wisdom acquired from other countries and how their correctional systems have dealt with inmate radicalization.

Substance-Abusing Inmates

The presence of inmates with substance dependency poses a major problem for correctional officials and incarcerated individuals. Almost 70% of jail and prison inmates are known to have some sort of drug or alcohol dependency (Gideon, 2011).

However, only a small percentage receives any treatment to address their need and thus reduce their recidivism. For example, studies suggest that only 15% to 18% of substance-abusing inmates in jails receive any treatment for their addiction (La Vinge, Solomon, Beckman, & Dedel, 2006; Welsh, 2011), and in state prisons, a similarly small percentage receives such treatment (Gideon, 2011; Prendergast & Wexler, 2004). Further, a 1996 study completed by the National Center on Addiction and Substance Abuse at Colombia University found that 70% to 85% of state prison inmates were in need of some level of substance abuse treatment, but only 13% actually received any treatment (Gideon, 2011). Because most incarcerated offenders do suffer from some form of drug or alcohol dependency, and these same offenders are highly associated with mental illness, these facts should place this population at the top of the priority list for all incarcerated inmates. Such a reality should really force policy makers to focus on a less punitive approach toward such offenders, while aiming at treating and rehabilitating them as an alternative to incarceration. Chapter 16 provides a detailed description and account of the scope of substance-abusing inmates in jails and state and federal facilities, while also offering an examination of what is currently done to address this issue within the limits of those institutions.

POLICY IMPLICATIONS

With more offenders being sentenced and for longer periods of time, the inmate climate is rapidly changing its human landscape. It is crucial to recognize that a society cannot simply lock up its members as the only social reaction to crimes committed. It is vital for correctional scholars and practitioners to address the growing challenges presented by the inmate population with special needs. Many of these special needs are strongly associated with social changes in the general population, so they won't be disappearing any time soon. These are particularly important as most incarcerated inmates will leave prison at one point and return to their home communities. If left untreated, their integration may not be as successful as society wants and hopes for, and further issues of public safety may surface and increase concern.

While prisons are places of punishment, the level of punishment experienced by different offenders may be unusual and at times cruel if the needs of inmates are ignored or neglected. Simply placing people behind bars may not be the optimal social reaction to crime and social delinquency. Consequently, and as will be discussed through the chapters of this book, each individual inmate should be assessed for needs and risk, as well as more general status, in order to tailor a punishment that fits the crime, while also increasing the likelihood of rehabilitation that will lead to successful reentry and reintegration. Addressing the different needs and backgrounds of incarcerated offenders is of extreme and vital importance, not just for the inmates, but also for the correctional facility and staff. When special needs are met, facilities can better manage the inmate population, and at times may even do so with less expense. For example, and as will be discussed by Cunningham in Chapter 13, death row inmates do not require 23 hours of lockdown, and are proven to be able to integrate with the general prison population. Other offenders may be better off not being placed in a correctional environment if they suffer from mental illness, as discussed by Nicholas and Bryant in Chapter 6, because they are less likely to comply with rules and regulations of the facility and thus find themselves locked in special housing units (SHUs).

Additionally, identifying and addressing the needs of inmates may also benefit the rehabilitation, reentry, and eventual reintegration process. As will be discussed in this book, incarceration conditions for special needs offenders often are not conducive to these offenders' rehabilitation efforts. For example, gay inmates cannot benefit from treatment if they are living in fear of being sexually assaulted and victimized. Similarly, sex offenders who are afraid of being identified by other inmates may not wish to take part in treatment, which can be detrimental to their rehabilitation process.

To that end, the following chapters of this book present different categories of special needs offenders, their needs, and the challenges they present. Of course, many other categories of incarcerated offenders can be discussed under the title of *special needs*, but this is the first attempt at mapping some of them as well as the system's reaction to them. Each chapter ends with a section on policy implications that summarizes the challenges and potential strategies for dealing with that specific category of special needs inmates. It is hoped that such strategies and recommendations will inform policy makers and consequently find their way into future policies as they are being developed for the benefit of all.

DISCUSSION QUESTIONS

1. Who are the special needs offenders, and what are some of their challenges?

2. Why should scholars and policy makers care about the topic of special needs offenders?

3. Why is a focus on special needs offenders so important when discussing rehabilitation, reentry, and reintegration?

4. What are some of the challenges special needs offenders pose to correctional management and to the routine of the jail or prison?

5. What other categories of special needs offender can you think of that are not covered by this book? Discuss why you think they should be considered as special and what their specific needs and challenges are.

REFERENCES

Aday, R. H. (1994). Golden years behind bars: Special programs and facilities for elderly inmates. *Federal Probation, 23*, 162–172.

Aday, R. H. (2003). *Aging prisoners: Crisis in American corrections.* Westport, CT: Praeger.

Aday, R. H., & Webster, E. L. (1979). Aging in prison: The development of a preliminary model. *Journal of Offender Rehabilitation, 3*(3), 271–282.

Anderson, J. C. (2008). Special needs offenders. In P. M. Carlson, & J. S. Garrett (Eds.), *Prison and jail administration: Practice and theory* (2nd ed.). (316–372). Sudbury, MA: Jones & Bartlett.

Andrews, D., Bonta, J., & Hoge, R. (1990). Classification for effective rehabilitation: Rediscovering psychology. *Criminal Justice and Behavior, 17*(1), 19–52.

Arngo, B. (2002). Transcarceration: A constructive ethnology of mentally ill offenders. *The Prison Journal, 81*(2), 162–186.

Ashford, J. B., Sales, B. D., & Reid, W. H. (2001). *Treating adult and juvenile offenders with special needs.* Washington, DC: American Psychological Association.

Aviram, H. (2010). Commentary: Defining the problem. *Hastings Race and Poverty Law Journal, 7,* 161–175.

Bailey, W. C. (1966). Correctional outcomes: An evaluation of 100 reports. *Journal of Criminal Law, Criminology, and Police Science, 57,* 153–160.

Baunach, J. P. (1992). Critical problems of women in prison. In I. L. Moyer (Ed.), *The changing role of women in the criminal justice system: Offenders, victims, and professionals* (99–112). Long Grove, IL: Waveland Press.

Bilchik, S. (1998, May). A juvenile justice system for the 21st century. *Juvenile Justice Bulletin.* Washington, DC: U.S. Office of Juvenile Justice and Delinquency Prevention.

Brown, K. (2003). Managing STIs in jails. *Infectious Diseases in Corrections Report.* Providence, RI: Brown University. Retrieved February 24, 2012, from http://www.idcronline.org/archives/april05/article.html

Bureau of Justice Statistics. (2011). Correctional populations in the United States, 2010. Washington, DC: U.S. Department of Justice. Retrieved from http://bjs.ojp.usdoj.gov/index.cfm?ty=pbdetail&iid=2237

Chaiken, M. R. (1989). *In-prison programs for drug-involved offenders.* Rockville, MD: National Institute of Justice.

Chavarria, F. R. (1992). Successful drug treatment in a criminal justice setting: A case study. *Federal Probation, 56,* 48–52.

Clear, T. R., Cole, G. F., & Reisig, M. D. (2009). *American Corrections* (7th ed.). Belmont, CA: Thomson/Wadsworth.

Corzine-McMullan, E. (2011). Seeking medical and psychiatric attention. In L. Gideon & H. E. Sung (Eds.), *Rethinking corrections: Rehabilitation, reentry, and reintegration* (253–278). Thousand Oaks, CA: Sage.

Cunningham, M. D., Sorensen, J. R., Vigen, M. P., & Woods, S. O. (2011). Life and death in the lone star state: Three decades of violence predictions by capital juries. *Behavioral Sciences & the Law, 29* (1), 1–22.

Cunningham, M. D., & Tassé, M. (2010). Looking to science rather than convention in adjusting IQ scores when death is at issue. *Professional Psychology: Research and Practice, 41*(5), 413–419.

Cunningham, M. D., & Vigen, M. P. (1999). Without appointed counsel in capital postconviction proceedings: The self-representation competency of Mississippi death row inmates. *Criminal Justice and Behavior, 26*(3), 293–321.

Dammer, H. R., & Fairchild, E. (2006). *Comparative criminal justice systems.* Belmont, CA: Thomson/Wadsworth.

Death Penalty Information Center (2012, January 23). Facts about the death penalty. Washington, DC. Retrieved from http://www.deathpenaltyinfo.org/documents/FactSheet.pdf

Dodge, M., & Pogrebin, M. R. (2001). Collateral costs of imprisonment for women: complications of reintegration. *The Prison Journal, 81*(1), 42–54.

Drummond, T. (1999, June 21). Cellblock seniors. *Time, 60*.

Fagan, T. J., & Ax, R. K. (Eds.). (2011). *Correctional mental health*. Thousand Oaks, CA: Sage.

Federal Bureau of Investigation. (2007). *Crime in the United States, 2006*. Washington, DC: U.S. Department of Justice.

Freudenberg, N. (2001). Jails, prisons, and the health of urban populations: A review of the impact of the correctional system on community health. *Journal of Urban Health, 78*(2), 214–235.

Frierson, R. L., Schwartz-Watts, D. M., Morgan, D. W., & Malone, T. D. (1998). Capital versus noncapital murderers. *Journal of the American Academy of Psychiatry and Law, 26*, 403–410.

Gideon, L. (2010). *Substance abusing inmates: Experiences of recovering drug addicts on their way back home*. New York, NY: Springer.

Gideon, L. (2011). Corrections in an era of reentry. In L. Gideon & H. E. Sung (Eds.), *Rethinking corrections: Rehabilitation, reentry, and reintegration* (1–17). Thousand Oaks, CA: Sage.

Gideon, L., & Sung, H. E. (2011). *Rethinking corrections: Rehabilitation, reentry, and reintegration*. Thousand Oaks, CA: Sage.

Glaze, L. E., & Maruschak, L. M. (2010). *Parents in prison and their minor children*. Washington, DC: Bureau of Justice Statistics.

Griffin, P., Torbet, P. M., & Szymanski, L. A. (1998). *Trying juveniles as adults in criminal court: An analysis of state transfer provisions*. Washington, DC: National Center for Juvenile Justice.

Hammett, T. M., Kennedy, S., & Kuck, S. (2007). *National survey of infectious diseases in correctional facilities: HIV and sexually transmitted diseases*. Rockville, MD: National Institute of Justice.

Hammett, T. M., Roberts, C., & Kennedy, S. (2001). Health-related issues in prisoner reentry. *Crime & Delinquency, 47*(3), 390–409.

Henriques, Z. (1996). Imprisoned mothers and their children: Separation-reunion syndrome dual impact. *Women and Criminal Justice, 8*(1), 77–95.

Inciardi, J. A. (1995). The therapeutic community: An effective model for corrections-based drug abuse treatment. In K. C. Haas & G. P. Alpert (Eds.), *The dilemmas of corrections: Contemporary readings* (3rd ed.). (406–417). Prospect Heights, IL: Waveland.

Inciardi, J. A., Martin, S. S., Butzin, C. A., Hooper, R. M., & Harrison, L. D. (1997). An effective model of prison-based treatment for drug-involved offenders. *Journal of Drug Issues, 27*(2), 261–278.

Israeli Prison System (2009). Security prisoners prisons. Retrieved from: http://www.ips.gov.il/Shabas/PRISON/Shabas+Mission/בתי+רהוס+לאסירים+בטיחונים.htm

Jacobson, M. (2005). *Downsizing prisons: How to reduce crime and end mass incarceration*. New York, NY: NYU Press.

Jeglic, E. L., Maile, C., & Calkins-Mercado, C. (2011). Treatment of offender populations: Implications for risk management and community reintegration. In L. Gideon & H. E. Sung (Eds.), *Rethinking corrections: Rehabilitation, reentry and reintegration* (37–70). Thousand Oaks, CA: Sage.

Kerbs, J. J., & Jolley, J. M. (2009). A commentary on age segregation for older prisoners: Philosophical and pragmatic considerations for correctional systems. *Criminal Justice Review, 34*(1), 119–139.

Knickerbocker, B. (2006, May 16). Illegal immigrants in the US: How many are there? *The Christian Science Monitor.* Retrieved from http://www.csmonitor.com

Kuanliang, A., Sorensen, J. R., & Cunningham, M. D. (2008). Juvenile inmates in an adult prison system: Rates of disciplinary misconduct and violence. *Criminal Justice and Behavior, 35*(9), 1186–1201.

La Vigne, N., Solomon, A. L., Beckman, K. A., & Dedel, K. (2006). Prisoner reentry and community policing: Strategies for enhancing public safety. U.S. Department of Justice Office of Community Oriented Policing Services. Retrieved from http://www.urban.org/UploadedPDF/411061_COPS_reentry_monograph.pdf

Logan, C. H. (1972). Evaluation research in crime and delinquency: A reappraisal. *Journal of Criminal Law, Criminology, and Police Science, 63*, 378–387.

Longshore, D., Turner, S., & Fain, T. (2005). Effects of case management on parolee misconduct: The Bay Area services network. *Criminal Justice and Behavior, 32*, 205–222.

Loveland, D., & Boyle, M. (2007). Intensive case management as a jail diversion program for people with a serious mental illness: A review of literature. *International Journal of Offender Therapy and Comparative Criminology, 51*, 130–150.

Martinson, R. (1974). What works? Questions and answers about prison reform. *The Public Interest, 35*, 22–54.

Morash, M., & Schram, P. J. (2002). The prison experience: Special issues of women in prison. Prospect Heights, IL: Waveland.

Moritsugu, K. (1990). Inmate chronological age versus physical age. *Long-term confinement and the aging inmate population.* Washington, DC: Federal Bureau of Prisons.

Mumola, C. J. (2000). *Veterans in prison or jail: A special report.* Washington DC: Bureau of Justice Statistics.

Mumola, C. J., & Noonan, M. E. (2008). *Justice-involved veterans: National estimates and research resources.* Paper presented at the meeting of the U.S. Department of Veterans Affairs, Baltimore, MD.

Noonan, M. E., & Mumola, C. J. (2007). *Veterans in state and federal prison, 2004.* Washington, DC: Bureau of Justice Statistics. Retrieved from http://www.bjs.gov/content/pub/pdf/vsfp04.pdf

Palermo, G. B. (2005). Prisonization and sexual offenders: A compounded problem. *International Journal of Offender Therapy and Comparative Criminology, 49*(6), 611–613.

Palermo, G. B. (2009). Reintegration and Recidivism. *International Journal of Offender Therapy and Comparative Criminology, 53*(1), 3–4.

Petersilia, J. (2003). *When prisoners come home: Parole and prisoner reentry.* New York, NY: Oxford University Press.

Pollock, J. M. (1998). *Counseling women in prison.* Thousand Oaks, CA: Sage.

Pollock, J. M. (2001). *Women, prison, and crime.* Belmont, CA: Wadsworth.

Pollocak, J. M. (2004). *Prisons and prison life.* Los Angeles, CA: Roxbury.

Prendergast, M. L., & Wexler, H. K. (2004). Correctional substance abuse treatment programs in California: A historical perspective. *The Prison Journal, 84*(1), 8–35.

Rocheleau, A. M. (1987). *Joining incarcerated mothers with their children: Evaluation of the Lancaster visiting cottage program* (Pub. No. 14,886–149–250–6-24–87). Milford, MA: Massachusetts Department of Corrections. Retrieved February 24, 2012, from http://www.mass.gov/eopss/docs/doc/research-reports/inmate-eval/eval-309B.pdf

Schmalleger, F., & Ortiz-Smykla, J. (2009). *Corrections in the 21st century* (4th ed.). New York, NY: McGraw-Hill.

Seiter, R. P. (2008). *Corrections: An introduction* (2nd ed.). Upper Saddle River, NJ: Prentice Hall.

Seiter, R. P. (2011). *Corrections: An introduction.* (3rd ed.). Upper Saddle River, NJ: Prentice Hall.

Sickmund, M. (2003). *Juvenile offenders and victims—National report series: Juveniles in court.* Rockville, MD: Office of Juvenile Justice and Delinquency Prevention.

Snyder, H. N., & Sickmund, M. (2006). *Juvenile offenders and victims: 2006 national report.* Washington, DC: Office of Juvenile Justice and Delinquency Prevention.

Stana, R. M. (2005). *Information on certain illegal aliens arrested in the United States* (GAO-05–646R). Washington, DC: U.S. Government Accountability Office.

Stohr, M. K., Walsh, A., & Hemmens, C. (2009). *Corrections: A text/reader.* Thousand Oaks, CA: Sage.

Sung, H. E., & Gideon, L. (2011). Major rehabilitative approaches. In L. Gideon & H. E. Sung (Eds.), *Rethinking corrections: Rehabilitation, reentry, and reintegration* (71–95). Thousand Oaks, CA: Sage.

Sutherland, E. H. (1939). *Principles of criminology* (3rd ed.). Chicago, IL: J. B. Lippincott.

Tonry, M. (2006). *Thinking about crime: Sense and sensibility in American penal culture.* Oxford, U.K.: Oxford University Press.

Torrey, E. F., Kennard, A. D., Eslinger, D., Lamb, R., & Pavle, J. (2010, May). *More mentally ill persons are in jails and prisons than hospitals: A survey of the states.* Arlington, VA: Treatment Advocacy Center & National Sheriffs' Association.

Travis, J. (2005). *But they all come back: Facing the challenges of prisoner reentry.* Washington, DC: The Urban Institute Press.

Van Voorhis, P., & Presser, L. (2001). *Classification of women offenders: A national assessment of current practices.* Rockville, MD: National Institute of Justice.

Welsh, W. N. (2011). Prison-based substance abuse programs. In L. Gideon & H. E. Sung (Eds.), *Rethinking corrections: Rehabilitation, reentry, and reintegration* (157–192). Thousand Oaks, CA: Sage.

Wilper, A. P., Woolhandler, S., Boyd, J. W., Lasser, K. E., McCormick, D., Bor, D. H., & Himmelstein, D. U. (2009). The health and health care of US prisoners: Results of a nationwide survey. *American Journal of Public Health, 99,* 666–672.

Wynn, J. (2001). *Inside Rikers: Stories from the world's largest penal colony.* New York, NY: St. Martin's Griffin.

CHAPTER 2

Juveniles Behind Bars

Traqina Quarles Emeka and
Nelseta Walters

Johnny, 15, breathed a sigh of relief as he stood before the judge in a juvenile courtroom. He narrowly avoided being certified as an adult for his role in the aggravated robbery of a store clerk in his poverty stricken neighborhood. The judge took into account that Johnny is a first-time offender and committed him to a juvenile facility for 12 months. Johnny's mother, Shirley, sat in the back of the courtroom with her head held low during the hearing. She is a single, working mother with four children. At the time of the incident, Shirley was at her part-time job. Johnny was to babysit his siblings, but he chose to sneak out to visit with friends.

He reflected on the events that led to his involvement with the juvenile justice system. He was visiting with friends when one suggested that the group rob the food mart around the corner, using a stolen gun purchased from one of the many available sources in the neighborhood. At first, Johnny said *no*; but, with prodding and pressure from his friends, he decided to join the group. The plan was to enter the store, take the money, run away, and split the stolen currency. However, when the group of four entered the store to commit the crime, the store clerk attempted to take the gun away from Johnny's peer. In an instant, the gun fired hitting and severely wounding the store clerk. In a panic, Johnny and his friends fled the scene. The juveniles were caught a short while later by police. Johnny is confused and afraid; he wishes he could erase this life changing event.

INTRODUCTION

A juvenile in the United States is defined as an individual who falls within a specified age range and is subject to the jurisdiction of the juvenile court. Thus, the only difference between a juvenile and an adult is chronological age: and similarly, age is the only difference between a delinquent and a criminal. It must be noted that policies regarding processing of juveniles differ across states, and juveniles in some states are given rights (e.g., the right to a trial by jury) that are not constitutionally guaranteed.

Juvenile court jurisdiction is based mainly on the age of the offender, however, each state legislature determines the minimum and maximum age at which a person is considered a juvenile. The most common **maximum age of a juvenile court jurisdiction** is 17, meaning that in states that classify 17 as the maximum age of juvenile court jurisdiction, a 17 year old who commits an offense should be processed in juvenile court. The maximum age of jurisdiction in three states (Connecticut, New York, and North Carolina) is 15. In Texas, and nine other states the maximum age of jurisdiction is 16, meaning that a 17 year old in Texas who commits an offense will be tried in the adult court. On the other hand, if the same juvenile travels to Florida and commits the same offense while still 17 years of age, the individual will be handled in juvenile court. The variation in the laws shows that there is no magic age at which an individual becomes a mature adult, capable of making adult decisions. In addition, mandatory laws across states allow juveniles to be processed as adults before they reach the maximum age of juvenile court jurisdiction.

While every state has a maximum age of juvenile court jurisdiction, not every state has a specified **minimum age of juvenile court jurisdiction.** Figure 2.1 shows the minimum age of juvenile court jurisdiction by state. Individuals who are younger than the minimum age of juvenile court jurisdiction are believed to lack the ability to develop intent and to know right from wrong. These individuals cannot be processed in the juvenile justice system, regardless of the act they commit. States that set a minimum age of juvenile court jurisdiction usually set the age

Figure 2.1   Minimum Age of Juvenile Court Jurisdiction by State

Age	State
6	North Carolina
8	Arizona
10	Arkansas, Colorado, Kansas, Louisiana, Minnesota, Mississippi, Pennsylvania, South Dakota, Texas, Vermont, Wisconsin
No minimum age specified	Alabama, Alaska, California, Connecticut, Delaware, District of Columbia, Florida, Georgia, Hawaii, Idaho, Illinois, Indiana, Iowa, Kentucky, Maine, Michigan, Missouri, Montana, Nebraska, Nevada, New Hampshire, New Jersey, New Mexico, North Dakota, Ohio, Oklahoma, Oregon, Rhode Island, South Carolina, Tennessee, Utah, Virginia, Washington, West Virginia, Wyoming

Source: Howard N. Synder and Melissa Sickmund. *Juvenile Offenders and Victims: 1999 National Report*. Washington, DC. U.S. Department of Justice, Office of Juvenile Justice and Delinquency Prevention, 1999.

between 6 and 10 (Snyder & Sickmund, 1999). For example, the minimum age of juvenile court jurisdiction in Maryland, Massachusetts, and New York is 7, while the minimum age in 10 states such as Arkansas, Mississippi, and Texas is 10. North Carolina has the lowest age of juvenile court jurisdiction—6 years of age. In states that set a minimum age of juvenile court jurisdiction, individuals younger than the minimum age are not subject to juvenile court jurisdiction and thus cannot be processed in juvenile court or held liable for their actions, regardless of the offense committed. Thus, a 9-year-old juvenile in Texas who commits murder would not be incarcerated for the offense, but would be released to the custody of his or her parents. If the parents are deemed unfit, the child could be removed from the parents and home, but the juvenile court could not confine the individual for the action.

Despite the contradiction in age of accountability and responsibility across states, juveniles, because of their chronological and mental age, are viewed as individuals with special needs. Their immaturity identified them as lacking the *mens rea* or criminal intent that is needed to commit a crime. In the case of nondelinquents they are viewed as minors in need of supervision, and thus should not be incarcerated or held in secure confinement.

HISTORY

Juvenile delinquency is a relatively new phenomenon; childhood is a social creation in which societal changes and contexts have enabled us to define and address the issues surrounding childhood. Acts that we now label as deviant have been in existence for thousands of years. Preindustrialized societies addressed deviant acts informally because a formal means was not deemed necessary nor was it of particular use in primitive society. The Dark Ages was a period of extreme hardship as life expectancy was tremendously low. Given such, it should be of no surprise that there were typically no strong emotional ties to children: their life expectancy was so low and an effective coping mechanism would suggest that limited attachment would provide an increased ability to cope with death. Children were typically seen as tools for economic gain and for carrying on the family name or heritage. Children were treated as little adults and received the rite of passage to adulthood through apprenticeship. Until the 18th century, the behavior of children was controlled through physical punishment.

The Renaissance period changed the portrayal of children from little adults to those of innocents. The view was that juveniles should be given guidance and direction. The improvements in medicine that accompanied the Renaissance period most likely resulted in lower mortality rates as well as familial attachment to children. The church, the Industrial Revolution, and the Renaissance were instrumental to incorporating a strict work ethic, purity, and obedience to ensure that children were disciplined and directed in the proper manner (Empey, 1978). The school, church, and family were all informally responsible for ensuring that children were raised properly.

Industrialization and urbanization prompted critical changes. As society became more socially organized, age stratification occurred. There were deliberate intentions to separate children from adults. Children were viewed developmentally different than adults and this belief encouraged a structured education system and increased parental responsibility. Behavior defined as "acceptable" was extremely narrow as more acts were defined as deviant. *Delinquency* was a term coined in response to the greater discipline and control deemed necessary to change the behavior of children.

Policy, culture, and social institutions in the 20th century United States led to defining, or rather creating, a stage between childhood and adulthood. The transition from childhood to adulthood was elongated to slow the process of childhood to prepare children to enter adulthood (Furstenberg, 2000). As a means for preparing children to enter adulthood, adolescence became a distinct life stage. The prevention of delinquency was formed to create and maintain a utopian sense of social order. Those with political power, wealth, and prestige possessed the ability to maintain and control the actions and behaviors of juveniles. Institutions such as houses of refuge, reformatories, and industrial schools (to be discussed later in the chapter) were created to regulate the behavior of children.

THE DEVELOPMENT OF THE JUVENILE JUSTICE SYSTEM

The juvenile justice system was created in the late 1800s with the intent to reform U.S. policies regarding young offenders. Prior to this, children who broke the law in 18th century America were treated like adults. Parents were responsible for controlling their children, and parental discipline was very strict and punishments were harsh. The laws made no distinction based on the age of the offender, and youths who committed crimes were treated like adult criminal offenders and could be subjected to prison sentences, whippings, and even the death penalty. No provisions were made to account for the age of offenders; there were no separate laws or courts, and no special facilities for the care of children who were in trouble with the law.

A number of developments during the 19th century paved the way for a separate system of justice for juveniles. An increase in birthrate and an influx of immigrants to America brought a new wave of growth to the American cities. With this growth came an increase in the numbers of neglected and dependent children. Youth living in urban areas were thought to be more prone to deviant and immoral behavior than other youths. Early reformers who were members of the Society for the Prevention of Pauperism expressed their dissatisfaction with the practice of placing children in adult jails and workhouses. They called for institutions that would instruct delinquents in proper discipline and moral behavior (Mennel, 1973).

In the 19th century, a shift in society's views on juvenile delinquents was advanced by the actions of political and social reformers as well as the research of psychologists. Early reformers who were interested in rehabilitating, rather than punishing children, built reformatories such as the **House of Refuge** in New York in 1825, to house juveniles who earlier would have been placed in adult jails. Operating under a new-found conviction that society had a responsibility to recover the lives of its young offenders, the juvenile justice system exercised its authority within a *parens patriae* (states as parent of guardian) role. The *parens patriae* doctrine meant that state assumed the responsibility of parenting children until they were "cured" or began to exhibit positive changes or became adults. Youth were no longer tried and punished as adults offenders, rather their cases were heard in an informal court, with the judge as the "wise parent," and often without the assistance of attorneys. The judge focused not only on legal factors surrounding the delinquent behavior, but also on extenuating evidence such as the social background of the juvenile.

The doctrine of *parens patriae* was first tested in the Pennsylvania Supreme Court case of *Ex parte Crouse* in 1838. The father of Mary Ann Crouse argued that his daughter was illegally incarcerated without a trial. The Court denied his claim, stating that the Bill of Rights did not apply to juveniles. The Court stated that when parents are found to be "incompetent" in their parental duties, the state has the right to intervene and provide the child with guidance and supervision. The Crouse ruling was based on what the court believed was the best interests of the child and the entire community, with the assumed intentions that the state could provide the proper education and training for the child. As states intervened in more juvenile cases, especially ones involving minor misbehaviors, the concept of *parens patriae* would later meet more legal challenges.

The first juvenile court was created in Cook County, Illinois, in 1899 (Snyder & Sickmund, 1999). The juvenile court's mission was to provide individualized care to all youth. Important to the formation of the court was the notion that youths were victims of society's problems and therefore were not entirely responsible for their behaviors. Reformers rejected the idea of dealing with juveniles in a punishment-oriented adult system and treatment of juveniles came under the supervision of juvenile courts and included a wide range of dispositions from probation to institutionalization. A unique feature of the juvenile court was the **indeterminate sentence**. Under the indeterminate sentence structure, the youth would remain under the juvenile court and its agencies until he or she was cured. By the 1960s, juvenile courts had jurisdiction over all cases involving persons under the age of 18 and transfer into the adult criminal system was made only through a waiver of the juvenile court's authority. However, the civil proceedings in the juvenile court did not afford youths who were facing a potential loss of liberty the due process of law rights explicated by the 5th and 14th Amendments.

Landmark U.S. Supreme Court Cases in Juvenile Justice

Compared to the criminal justice system, relatively few juvenile court cases have been heard before the Supreme Court. Prior to the 1960s, juvenile justice operated under the medical model, and the goal of juvenile proceeding was to "cure" the wayward juvenile, and so juvenile proceeding was more of a civil nature. Thus, the Supreme Court adopted a hands-off approach to juvenile justice, except during the due process revolution of the 1960s. Four landmark U.S. Supreme Court decisions mandated fundamental due process in juvenile justice. These cases clarified the due process and rights of juveniles by outlining what form the process would take as well as the rights juveniles accused of a crime would be afforded.

Kent v. United States was the first U.S. Supreme Court case in which it was ruled that juveniles facing waiver to adult court are entitled to some basic due process rights. Kent was 14 years old when he came into contact with the juvenile court of the District of Columbia in 1959. He was charged with several burglaries and robberies and was placed on probation. At age 16, and still on probation, Kent was again arrested and charged with burglary robbery and rape. The court decided to waive Kent to the adult court for criminal proceedings without holding a hearing, conferring with Kent, his parents, or his lawyer, publishing any findings or statement of the facts, and without giving a reason for the waiver. Kent was convicted on six counts and was sentenced to serve 5 to 15 years on each count for which he was found guilty.

The U.S. Supreme Court decided that the District of Columbia Juvenile Court Act entitled Kent to certain fundamental due process. In addition to the right to a waiver hearing, the Court held that juveniles are entitled to certain due process rights when facing possible transfer to adult court: (1) the right to be represented by counsel, (2) the right to access records considered by the juvenile court in determining waiver, and (3) the right to hear a statement of the reasons in support of waiver. The *Kent* guidelines require the juvenile court judge to consider several factors, such as the seriousness of the offense, the degree and quality of the evidence, the sophistication and maturity of the juvenile, and the *prospect* of adequate rehabilitation when making a waiver decision. While the *Kent* case marked the first time the Court was willing to extend due process rights to juvenile proceedings, the rights given in *Kent* were only applicable in waiver proceedings; as a result the decision was limited in scope.

In re Gault, a 1967 decision by the U.S. Supreme Court, is noted as the most important case decided by that court in the area of juvenile justice. In *Gault,* the Court affirmed the necessity of requiring courts to respect due process of law rights of juveniles during adjudication proceedings. This ruling was a result of Arizona's decision to confine Gerald Francis Gault. Gault, aged 15, was placed in detention for making an obscene phone call to a neighbor while on probation. The Arizona juvenile court decided to place Gault in the State Industrial School until he became an adult (age 21) or was "discharged by due process of Law." The question of the Supreme Court in the *Gault* case was, "Does a juvenile have due process rights during the adjudication stage of a delinquency proceeding?" The Supreme Court decision emphasized that juveniles had a right to receive fair treatment under the law and highlighted the following basic rights to minors at adjudication:

- the right to obtain legal counsel
- the right to receive notice of the charge
- the privilege against self-incrimination
- the right to confront and cross-examine witnesses

These due process requirements would introduce more order, formality, and in some cases, aspects of the adversarial system, but it did not specifically grant juveniles all the procedural rights given to defendants in criminal proceedings. Thus, while the *Ex parte Crouse* decision is viewed as one of the first challenges of *parens patriae* doctrine, critics believed that the *Gault* decision signaled the end of the traditional model of juvenile justice by formalizing the juvenile court and making it more similar to the adult court.

The *Gault* case instituted fundamental due process rights to juveniles at adjudication. However, many of the rights outlined in the U.S. Constitution and applied to criminal proceedings had not been specifically applied to juveniles. In 1970, the standard of proof necessary for conviction was incorporated into juvenile proceedings in the case of *In re Winship*. Winship, age 12, faced a delinquency hearing in a New York Family Court because he stole money from a woman's purse in a locker. The juvenile court judge found that Winship had engaged in delinquent conduct and committed him to a training school for 18 months, subject to extension under New York law. With the case of *In re Winship*, the U.S. Supreme Court ruled that when a juvenile is faced with a proceeding where incarceration might result, the standard of proof should be "beyond a reasonable doubt" instead of "preponderance of the evidence" which is used in civil court proceedings. It must be noted that the court did not extend this level of proof to all juvenile proceedings, but only to delinquency proceedings where incarceration might be the result.

In 1971, one year after the *Winship* decision the U.S. Supreme Court applied another constitutional right to juvenile proceedings in the case of *Mckeiver v. Pennsylvania*. In 1968, Joseph Mckeiver, age 16, was charged with robbery, larceny, and receiving stolen goods. He was adjudicated in the juvenile court and was represented by counsel at his delinquency proceedings. Mckeiver requested a trial by jury but his request was denied, and the judge adjudicated Mckeiver a *delinquent* and placed him on probation. He appealed his case and the U.S. Supreme Court refused to apply right to a jury trial to juvenile proceedings. The Court stated that its decisions thus far on juvenile justice had already formalized and protected juveniles, and that jury trial would put an end to the idealistic prospect of informal, protective proceedings for juveniles. In addition, it was noted that jury trial would not greatly strengthen the fact-finding function of the juvenile court and to grant jury trials would end the distinctions between the criminal and the juvenile systems. The decision in *Mckeiver* showed that the Court was not ready to eliminate the juvenile justice system entirely.

Another U.S. Supreme Court decision that applied a fundamental right to juvenile proceedings was the case of *Breed v. Jones* in 1975 (see Table 2.1). In *Breed*, juveniles were granted constitutional right against double jeopardy. Today, several landmark U.S. Supreme Court juvenile cases fundamentally transformed the traditional juvenile justice system and instituted a variety of procedural and substantive rights for juveniles. These cases serve as the foundation of juvenile justice procedure and law.

| Table 2.1 | U.S. Supreme Court Decisions in Juvenile Justice |

Cases	Decisions
Kent v. United States, 383 U.S. 541 (1966)	Juveniles must be given due process rights when transferred from juvenile to adult court.
In re Gault, 387 U.S. 1 (1967)	Juveniles in delinquency proceedings that can result in confinement in an institution where their freedom would be curtailed are entitled to the essential of due process.
In re Winship, 397 U.S. 358 (1970)	Proof beyond a reasonable doubt, instead of preponderance of the evidence, is required in juvenile adjudication in delinquency cases.
McKeiver v. Pennsylvania, 404 U.S. 528 (1971)	Juveniles are not entitled to trial by jury even in delinquency cases where the juvenile faces possible incarceration.
Breed v. Jones, 421 U.S. 517 (1975)	Juveniles are protected against double jeopardy by the U.S. Constitution.

Juveniles in Correctional Institutions (1800s–1980s)

At the beginning of the 19th century, delinquent, neglected, dependent, and runaway children in the United States were treated the same as adult criminal offenders. Similar to the practice in England, children convicted of crimes received harsh sentences like those imposed on adults. During the first half of the 19th century, urbanization, the child saving movement, and a growing interest in the concept of *parens patriae* triggered the development of institutions for the care of delinquent and neglected children. Youth in urban areas were viewed as susceptible to the influences of their decaying environment. The children of the so-called dangerous classes were viewed as a group that might be "saved" by a combination of state and community interventions (Platt, 1969). Intervention into the lives of these children became acceptable for wealthy, civic-minded citizens, and vagrant children were housed in *settlement houses* or shelters, and nonsecure facilities.

In the early 1800s, legislation was introduced to humanize criminal procedures for children and to help young people avoid imprisonment. Despite these measures, no official facilities existed for the care of youths in trouble with the law. Youths who committed petty crimes, such as stealing and vandalism, were viewed as wayward children or victims of dependency and neglect and were placed in community asylums or homes. Youths who were involved in more serious crimes were subject to the same punishments as adults—imprisonment, whipping, or death.

The Society for the Reformation of Juvenile Delinquents in New York advocated for the separation of juvenile and adult offenders (Krisberg, 2005), and in 1825 the New York House of Refuge was established to take in dependent, neglected, and delinquent youths. Other houses of refuge in Boston and Philadelphia were soon established, and these were followed shortly thereafter by reform schools for vagrant and delinquent juveniles. Contrary to popular belief, many of the youths housed in the reformatories were petty offenders, orphans, and homeless children, and, according to Schlossmann (1977), belonged to the wayward, incorrigible, or vagrant class. State reform schools opened in Massachusetts in 1847, in New York in 1853, in Ohio in 1857; and the first State Industrial School for Girls was opened in Massachusetts in 1856. Unlike the houses of refuge, where the daily routine was based on hard work, discipline, religion and self-denial, the reformatories focused on educating youth, while seeking to instill good habits through hard work. In response to overcrowding, deplorable conditions, and reports of brutality in the houses of refuge, training schools were developed in the mid-19th century. Training schools were meant to be different from reformatories and houses of refuge; they focused on training not discipline. Structure was replaced with freedom of the "yard," recreation time, and sports. The classification system was used to sort different types of youths and their problems, and the educational and vocational programs were used to help give the youths a marketable skill upon release.

Juveniles in Correctional Institutions (1980s–present)

Following the U.S. Supreme Court decisions and the federal guidelines that occurred in the 1960s and 1970s, the pendulum began to shift toward law and order and control of juveniles. In response to public perceptions that serious juvenile crime was increasing and the system was too lenient with offenders, punitive laws were passed to remove juvenile offenders charged with serious crimes from the juvenile system. Some juveniles now face mandatory or automatic waiver, and, in some states, the prosecutors can use their discretion to file certain cases directly in criminal court (Snyder & Sickmund, 2006).

Today, correctional facilities or state schools are used to house serious, violent, or chronic offenders. These are juveniles who may be transferred to the adult correctional system—based on split sentencing or mandatory sentence structure. Juvenile delinquents in these facilities live in strict, secure environment where they are separated from other juveniles and society. There is less of an emphasis on rehabilitation, and juveniles within this setting may find that participation in programs such as education and counseling is secondary to the main focus of control—strict intense supervision.

JUVENILE PROCESS AND DYNAMICS

Delinquency Theory

There are numerous theories that purport to explain juvenile delinquency and behavior; explanations range from sociological, psychological, and biological influence. The **Classical School of Criminology** assumes that all individuals are rational beings who exercise free will. Rational choice theories suppose that all individuals choose to engage in delinquent or criminal acts. This body of theories would likely support the notion that juveniles should be punished because they freely choose to engage in delinquent acts. Further, juveniles should be punished for crime and delinquency in order to prevent future offending. The **Positivist School of Criminology** and the introduction of the social sciences as a discipline prompted the foundation of a juvenile court as a viable option to address the social and behavioral issues of juveniles. In recent years, such views have been criticized that informal treatment does not adequately address handling serious offenses that would be felonies if committed by adults.

Psychological theories tend to focus on the individual and target those factors that predispose some individuals toward crime. Most psychological theories distinctly hold that human behavior is not determined by biological factors but, rather, through development and socialization. **Social learning theories** explain how learning from the social environment can shape behavior. Behaviorist theorists, such as B.F. Skinner, suggest that aggressive behavior can be learned through punishment and reinforcements; conformity and deviance can both be learned through interactions with others and their responses to behavior. Given such, if a juvenile is rewarded for deviant behavior, the juvenile may respond to the positive reinforcement by continuing deviant behavior. **Differential association theory** posits that criminals are not different from noncriminals as there is no distinct personality, learning pattern, or thinking pattern that distinguishes the two. Hence, learning to commit crimes is the same as learning any other behavior (Williams & McShane, 1998). Differential association theory suggests that primary learning occurs in the association of others and within the associations with significant others; individuals generally adapt to the norms and values of their social environment.

The Chicago School focuses on the structure of society and not the individual. Social disorganization theory suggests that crime and delinquency are the result of a breakdown of community control, thus weak informal social control. Social disorganization offers that crime is a result of the physical environment and may offer opportunities for crime regardless of residents. **Social control theory** does not explain delinquent offending, but instead focuses on those who conform to the norms of society. Attachment, commitment, involvement, and belief are key elements that bond an individual to society. Social control theory posits that strong bonds lead to conforming behavior. In essence, juveniles with strong bonds to the family, peers, school, and other institutions of social control are less likely to engage in delinquent behaviors.

Strain theory focuses on the structure of society and explains crime and delinquency as a response to the lack of opportunities to attain wealth. Merton created five modes of adaptation by which individuals deal with strain: conformity, innovation, ritualism, retreatism, and rebellion. The theory supposes that class division creates individual strain through unequal access to achieve the goals of society. Miller's **Focal Concerns Theory** (1958) posits that the lower class culture evolved from conflict with middle class culture. Lower class culture continues to possess more and more members as the gap between the *haves* and the *have-nots* continues to grow.

JUVENILE RISK FACTORS

Gender

Female offenders represent a smaller number of the juvenile population than do their male counterparts. However, female offending has been on the increase (see Chapter 3 by Pasko & Chesney-Lind). The literature has provided a body of work illustrating the unique factors that have been associated with female risk. Females are more likely than males to be abused and they are more likely to suffer from family-related problems and trauma. Emeka and Sorensen (2009) suggest that a gender-specific risk instrument should be used to assess female risk and identify potential risk factors for proper programming and treatment. According to Hartwig and Myers (2003), there are problems with many correctional programs given that most female delinquency programs are designed for males. The authors cite that gender roles are reinforced; whereas, females who are seen as passive and submissive are rewarded for such behaviors. Also, females may be punished for possessing or exhibiting traits thought to be associated with males. Specifically, Hartwig and Myers (2003) noted five points in which females receive differential treatment from males:

- Females are more likely to be referred to psychiatric treatment rather than offender treatment.
- Gender bias suggests that females are at a lower risk of delinquency than their male counterparts.
- Females tend to be charged for status offenses at a higher rate than males.
- Male delinquency is seen as behavioral and female delinquency viewed as a conduct disorder (psychiatric disorder).

If risk factors that may most influence female offending are not identified, female offenders may not be able to receive adequate treatment, successfully reintegrate, and will continue to offend. Without the adequate support and programming, female offenders may remain in the juvenile justice system.

Family, School, and Community Factors

Family, peers, school, and community factors have all been considered as both risk factors and protective factors. Risk factors influence or perpetuate antisocial and delinquent behaviors (see Table 2.2). Protective factors are those that contribute to prosocial or positive behavior; protective factors can also work as interventions to risk factors. Although there are numerous risk factors that contribute to delinquent offending, each juvenile is different and must be assessed individually to address specific risk factors.

Communities, families, and schools can together address the juvenile violence problem to reduce juvenile offending (Heide, 1999). Communities can participate by

Table 2.2 Risk Factors for Delinquency and Future Violent Juvenile Offending

Family Factors

- Parenting
- Maltreatment
- Family violence
- Divorce
- Parental psychopathology
- Familial antisocial behavior
- Teenage parenthood
- Family structure
- Large family size

Peer Factors

- Association with deviant peers
- Peer rejection

School and Community Factors

- Failure to bond to school
- Poor academic performance
- Low academic aspirations
- Living in a poor family
- Neighborhood disadvantage
- Disorganized neighborhoods
- Concentration of delinquent peer groups
- Access to weapons

Source: Adapted from R. Loeber and D. P. Farrington (Eds.). 2001. *Child Delinquents: Development, Intervention, and Service Needs.* Thousand Oaks, CA: Sage.

providing mentors, developing programs within the community to encourage positive behavior, and offering safe recreational centers and sport facilities. Family dynamics are important to offenders as supportive networks. Families can contribute to reducing juvenile offending by setting limits, being involved, being positive role models, and listening to children. Healthy, intact families are those that help juvenile with their needs, have clear well-defined boundaries, and provide communication, problem-solving, and support for offenders. Dysfunctional families lack the ability to provide healthy support for juveniles; they may pose a risk for juvenile delinquency. Schools are critical to reducing juvenile offending and should have consistent discipline policies, provide information about healthy families and environments, make appropriate referrals, and serve as positive role models to juvenile offenders.

JUVENILE OFFENDER TYPES

Drug and Alcohol Issues

It is essential to understand the unique characteristics of juvenile drug offenders. According to Alexander and Pratsinak (2002), there are six indicators for juveniles who abuse drugs. These juveniles are more likely to do the following:

1. Exhibit problem behaviors rather than signs of drug abuse

2. Progress from use to dependency quicker than adults

3. Abuse more than one substance

4. Remain in the denial phase longer than adults

5. Receive reinforcement from peers

6. Have slowed development and impaired abstract thinking

The goal of drug education programming is to ensure that juvenile drug offenders will make the successful transition to a drug-free life. The ethnicity and culture of juveniles must be taken into consideration to better understand their demeanor and values.

The premise of drug classes is to help drug addicts consider the consequences of their actions to themselves and to loved ones. Social interaction between family and children can be important for both offenders and families as it may act as a motivating factor. It is important to examine antisocial behaviors and personalities because true antisocial individuals tend to be risk takers and sensation seekers. When treating such individuals, providers should point out the punishment that may occur rather than emphasizing the feelings of others; antisocial individuals are generally more concerned with satisfying their own needs before the needs of others.

Mental Issues

The deinstitutionalization movement of the 1970s prompted the diversion of many mental patients from residential institutional facilities to community programs to receive treatment. Inadequate funding resulted in many mentally ill patients lacking appropriate medication or self-medicating themselves. Therefore, the criminal justice system was charged with housing those mentally ill offenders who lacked placement in facilities that addressed mental disorders (see Chapter 6 by Nicholas & Bryant). Although the study of mentally ill juveniles is still in its early stages (Boesky, 2002), the research suggests that juveniles with mental disorders are more involved in the juvenile justice system than youth without mental disorders. The lack of adequate resources to address juvenile mental disorders is reminiscent of the 1970s deinstitutionalization movement because changes in healthcare reduced the length of stay in residential facilities. Also, the considerable reduction in residential treatment options for serious mental disorders has resulted in limited options for said youth.

Early intervention is critical to prevent juveniles from entering the juvenile justice system as those youth with serious mental problems and comorbidity issues are more likely to be refused treatment. Refusal of treatment results when serious mental offenders may be viewed as security threats to treatment facilities (Alexander, 2000). Further, many treatment facilities are not equipped to treat juveniles with serious disorders and offending patterns. Also, limits on the types of services provided by treatment programs may lead juveniles with serious disorders to be placed in detention facilities. Hence, the underlying problem of mental illness and similar disorders are underexplored and unrecognized.

Violent Offenders

Male offenders are more likely to engage in violent offenses and drug offenses than females. Further, males are more likely commit violent offenses such as homicide and aggressive behavior. Juveniles who commit homicide resulting from conflict are more amenable to treatment than those resulting from psychosis and crime (Alexander, 2000). Teenage murderers may kill based on responses to perceived environmental situations and constraints (Heide, 1999). Youth under 13 years of age represent a small percentage of juvenile homicide offenders. Preadolescent youth typically act impulsively without clear goals. Youth under 9 years of age typically do not have a clear concept of death and may not understand the finality of death.

Juvenile homicide remains an important issue because juvenile killers come from varying backgrounds, ethnicities, and races. The victims of juvenile homicide range from strangers to acquaintances and from children to senior citizens. Although most of the juvenile homicide offender literature focuses on males, female homicide offenders are worth noting (Heide, 1999). Female offenders who murder are more likely to kill someone they know and use an accomplice to complete the act. When male juveniles commit homicide against a single individual, it is most likely to be an acquaintance. However, the juvenile offender is more likely to be a stranger when multiple victims are killed. Juvenile homicide offenders are most likely to kill in groups and are most likely to use a firearm. Many juvenile homicide offenders are come from dysfunctional families, with a prior arrest record, drug and alcohol abuse, and violence within the home (Heide, 1999). Similarly, most juvenile homicide offenders do not have mental deficiencies or psychoses, are not model students in the classroom, and do not come from a healthy home life environment.

Treatment in correctional institutions is deemed essential for juvenile violent offenders. Problems evident within prisons, such as the availability of drugs and alcohol, the threat of violence, homosexual activity, and theft, do not appear to offer an environment conducive to rehabilitative treatment. Myers (2002) noted four reasons for the success of treatment programs within institutions to include: developing cognitive and emotional growth (maturation), containment in a prosocial environment, nature of the offense (homicides are atypical), and positive effect of programming. These successes suggest that treatment and rehabilitation can help juveniles reenter society with emotional and developmental skills to prevent recidivism. The multisystemic treatment (MST) model has been shown to have high rates of success. MST treatment is based on including the family, peers, schools, court, and juvenile justice system to reduce juvenile delinquency. Behavioral change within the natural environment is thought to have a long-lasting effect on the behavior of juveniles.

Chronic Offenders

The Wolfgang, Sellin, and Figlio (1972) birth cohort study was the first of its kind to conduct a longitudinal study to measure delinquency. The birth cohort study tracked all boys born in Philadelphia, Pennsylvania, in the year 1945. School records, police contact information, and selective service registration information were the means used to follow the cohort subjects. The research was conducted to detect the age of onset of delinquency and the age of desistence or progression.

The birth cohort study revealed that 35% of the boys were brought into the criminal justice system at least once (Wolfgang, Sellin, & Figlio, 1972). Sixty-five percent of the boys did not come into contact with the criminal justice system. Regarding race, 28.6% of Whites were classified as offenders and 50.2% of non-Whites were classified as offenders. Fifty-four percent of the boys were of higher socioeconomic status (26.5% classified as delinquent) and 46% of the boys were of lower socioeconomic status (44.8% classified as offenders). Race and socioeconomic status were strongly related to delinquency.

Non-Whites were more likely to be processed through the criminal justice system. According to the authors, non-White delinquent boys were most likely to be from lower socioeconomic status, have lower achievement levels, lower I.Q. scores, lower amounts of formal education, and high rates of school and residential mobility. Non-Whites were also more likely to be classified with serious offenses, use of physical violence, and as chronic offenders. Whites of high socioeconomic status were more likely to be one-time offenders and be classified with less serious offenses.

Results of the cohort study suggest that a small amount of delinquents (approximately 6%) were responsible for a majority of the delinquent acts. The study found that there was no specialization as offenses increased in number. Delinquents labeled chronic offenders were those who committed more than four offenses. Implications of the cohort study suggest that delinquency prevention would be more effective when used on those juveniles after the third offense is committed because 46% desist after the first offense with 35% to follow after the second. Thus, the timing of intervention is critical to reducing delinquency. Although several cohort studies have followed, the Wolfgang and colleagues cohort study has been used as a standard regarding chronic juvenile offending.

JUVENILE COURT PROCESSES

Juveniles who come in contact with the law can either be processed formally or informally. Table 2.3 shows the different steps in processing a juvenile. Most juveniles who are incarcerated are processed in the juvenile or adult court. These are juveniles who have committed delinquent acts or are chronic status offenders. At the intake stage, these juveniles receive a delinquency petition—a formal request by a prosecutor asking the juvenile court to adjudicate the youth a delinquent—or a waiver petition where the youth is referred to the adult court for processing. Report shows that approximately 50% of delinquents are petitioned and about 1% are waived to the adult court (Puzzanchera & Snyder, 2008).

Table 2.3   Steps of the Juvenile Court Process

Adult	Juvenile
Crime	**Delinquency:** Acts or conduct in violation of criminal laws **Status offense:** Behavior that is considered an offense only when committed by a juvenile
Arrest	**Summons:** A legal document ordering an individual to appear in court at a certain time on a certain date
Initial Appearance	**Initial hearing:** An often informal hearing during which an intake decision is made
Bail	**Detention:** Holding a youth in custody before case disposition
Charging	**Intake decision:** The decision made by juvenile court that results in the case being handled either informally at the intake level or more formally and scheduled for an adjudication hearing **Nonpetitioned:** Cases handled informally by duly authorized court personnel **Petition:** A document filed in juvenile court alleging that a juvenile is delinquent or a status offender and asking that the court assume jurisdiction over the juvenile
Preliminary Hearing	**Conference:** Proceeding during which the suspect is informed of rights and a disposition decision may be reached
Grand Jury	Not applicable
Arraignment	Occurs during the conference
Evidence	Juveniles have the same constitutional protections as adults with regard to interrogation, and unreasonable search and seizure
Plea Bargaining	**Plea bargaining:** Formal and informal discussions resulting in juvenile's admitting guilt
Trial	**Adjudicatory hearing:** Hearing to determine whether a juvenile is guilty or not guilty
Sentencing	**Disposition:** A court decision on what will happen to a youth who has not been found innocent **Placement:** Cases in which juveniles are placed in a residential facility or otherwise removed from their homes. **Probation:** Cases in which juveniles are placed under informal/voluntary or formal/court-ordered supervision **Dismissal:** Cases dismissed (including those warned, counseled, and released) with no further disposition anticipated **Other:** Miscellaneous disposition including fines, restitution, and community service
Appeal	**Appeal:** Request that a higher court review the decision of the lower court

Adjudication and Disposition

The adjudicatory hearing is used in delinquency cases as a fact finding hearing to determine whether the allegations in the delinquency petitions are valid. Although the U.S. Supreme Court has extended the legal principles of due process to delinquents at the adjudication stage, not all rights granted by the constitution and the amendments have been extended to juvenile justice system. For example, in 1971, the court held that juveniles had no constitutional rights to jury trial because the juvenile proceedings were not viewed as a criminal prosecution within the meaning and reach of the Sixth Amendment (*Mckeiver v. Pennsylvania*, 1971). The U.S. Supreme Court, however, held that when the state undertakes to prove a juvenile delinquent guilty of committing a criminal act, it must do so beyond a reasonable doubt (*In re Winship*, 1970). The standard for other categories of juveniles such as deprived, abused/neglected, and dependent is usually the civil standard of preponderance of the evidence or clear and convincing evidence.

The dispositional hearing focuses on the alternatives that are available to meet the needs of the juvenile. For the delinquent juvenile, The Uniform Juvenile Court Act (sec. 31) states that the court may use any disposition best suited to the juvenile treatment, rehabilitation and welfare (National Conference of Commissioners on Uniform State Laws, 1968). Thus, juveniles may receive probation, may be placed in an institution or other facility for delinquents, or be committed to the state institution. The most severe dispositional alternative available to juvenile court judge considering a case of delinquency is commitment to a correctional facility. The general trend in juvenile court is to refrain from committing all categories other than delinquents, to juvenile correctional institutions unless the child in need of supervision warrants such action after other alternatives have failed. In addition, most juvenile courts provide for transferring juveniles exhibiting mental retardation or mental illness to the appropriate authority within the state. Most states now specify the maximum amount of time for confinement of a juvenile. This practice reflects a shift from indeterminate to determinate sentences, which is fostered by mandatory sentences. However, the court may, under some circumstances, terminate its dispositional order prior to its mandated date if it appears that the purpose of the order has been accomplished.

Juvenile Waiver/Certification

Juvenile courts acts contain provisions for waiver of the juvenile court's jurisdiction over certain offenses committed by minors of certain ages. Policies regarding transfer of juveniles to the criminal justice system differ across states and include statutory exclusion, judicial waiver (discretionary, mandatory, and presumptive), prosecutorial (direct file, concurrent jurisdiction), and legislative (statutory exclusion, once an adult always an adult). In states using exclusion statutes, state legislators identify certain categories of juveniles (i.e., those who commit violent offenses and those who are habitual, serious offenders) to exclude from the juvenile court jurisdiction. Under concurrent jurisdiction, the prosecuting attorney has the discretion of filing certain types of cases in adult or juvenile court. Judicial waiver allows the transfer by the juvenile court judge (Office of Juvenile Justice and Delinquency Prevention, 2003). The main purpose of waiver was to allow for greater flexibility in dealing with serious and violent juveniles by imposing longer and harsher sentences. It allows the prosecutors and judges another option to deal with chronic offenders and to purge the juvenile justice system of those who have exhausted and would not benefit from rehabilitative alternative.

JUVENILES IN PREADJUDICATION PLACEMENT

Nondelinquents Behind Bars

Prior to the 1970s, nondelinquents such as status offender, dependent and neglected juveniles, the mentally ill, and juveniles addicted to drugs or alcohol could be held in secure institutions with delinquents. In 1968, the Juvenile Delinquency Prevention and Control Act, developed by Congress, recommended that juveniles charged with noncriminal or status offenses be removed from formal adjudication and commitment to detention centers and juvenile institutions. The supporters of such practices argued that involvement in status offenses was a slippery slope leading into delinquency, and early intervention might prevent serious delinquency. On the other hand, those who were against locking up status offenders, noted the unfairness of punishing juveniles for minor deviant behavior and expressed concerns about the negative effects on status offenders housed with older, chronic, juvenile delinquents. The Juvenile Justice and Delinquency Prevention Act (JJDPA) was passed in 1974 and was amended to include other requirements for the safety and protection of juveniles (see Table 2.4). In this act, Congress required the Deinstitutionalization of Status Offenders (DSO) as well as the sight and sound separation of juvenile delinquents from adult offenders. Part of the rationale behind the separation of juvenile and adult offenders was evidence that delinquent juveniles learned criminal behavior from older inmates. The JJDPA was amended in 1980, whereby it required that juveniles be removed from adult jails and lockups; and in 1992, states were required to address the issue of disproportionate minority confinement. States could choose to participate or not, but would run the risk of losing federal grant money if they did not (Holden & Kapler, 2005).

Following the JJDPA in 1974, most states were in compliance with the JJDPA mandate, and fewer status offenders were held in secure detention before adjudication because state laws prohibit such practices. The *parens patriae* doctrine holds that the juvenile justice process should avoid stigmatizing the juvenile when possible. This meant that juvenile detention centers in the past were used as a last resort, even for serious offenders, because of the potential for the detained juvenile to be branded or victimized as a "criminal." Today *parens patriae* has faded and despite the mandates of JJDPA, juveniles are being held in detention centers for various reasons. The erosion is best demonstrated by a U.S. Supreme Court case which held that preventive detention is constitutional, implying that juvenile detention could be used not just to protect juveniles but also to protect society (*Schall v. Martin*, 1984).

Table 2.4	Core Requirements of the Juvenile Justice and Delinquency Prevention Act

Year*	Major Requirements of the Juvenile Justice and Delinquency Prevention Act
1974	The "deinstitutionalization of status offenders and non-offenders" requirement specifies that juveniles not charged with acts that would be crimes for adults "shall not be placed in secure detention facilities or secure correctional facilities."
1974	The "sight and sound separation" requirement specifies that, "juveniles alleged to be or found to be delinquent and [status offenders and non-offenders] shall not be detained or confined in any institution in which they have contact with adult persons incarcerated because they have been convicted of a crime or are awaiting trial on criminal charges." This means that juvenile and adult inmates cannot see each other and no conversation between them is possible.
1980	The "jail and lockup removal" requirement states that juveniles shall not be detained or confined in adult jails or lockups. Exceptions: juveniles being tried as a criminal for a felony or who have been convicted as a criminal felon; six-hour grace period to temporarily hold juveniles until other arrangements can be made; jails in rural areas may hold delinquents up to 24 hours.
1992	The "disproportionate confinement of minority youth" requirement specifies that states determine the existence and extent of the problem in their state and demonstrate efforts to reduce it where it exists.
1996	Regulations modify the Act's requirements: (1) In nonresidential areas in jails, brief, accidental contact is not a reportable violation; (2) permit time-phased use of nonresidential areas for both juveniles and adults in collocated facilities; (3) expand the six-hour grace period to include six hours both before and after court appearances; (4) allow adjudicated delinquents to be transferred to adult institutions once they have reached the state's age of full criminal responsibility, if such transfer is expressly authorized by state law.

Source: Adapted from Snyder and Sickmund, 2006, p. 97.

*The years the requirement was first included in legislation.

In *Schall,* the court recognized that while detention is potentially harmful and stigmatizing to the juvenile, in some cases the potential harm to society as a result of pretrial crime outweighed the liberty interest of juveniles.

Some critics argued that status offenders are being "bootstrapped" (moving from the status of status offender to delinquent offender) because of violation of court order (Holden & Kapler, 2005) and are held in secure confinement. Proponents argue that it is not effective to release certain types of status offenders, such as runaways and those with behavioral and emotional problems as required by JJDPA. Other nondelinquents are being held in mental hospitals or substance abuse treatment facilities. Feld (2003) referred to these juveniles as "hidden delinquents" because they are captured in the "hidden system." While these forms of institutions do not violate the mandates of JJDPA, youth in these institutions are usually afforded less due process rights than delinquents, yet their freedom is being taken away. Controversy over this form of institutionalization is heightened by the Supreme Court decision of *Parham v. J. R.* (1979), where the Court held that parents may commit their child to a mental hospital as long as a neutral fact finder finds "evidence" of mental illness (*Parham v. J. R.*, 1979). In this situation, the child may be held indefinitely until the parents request that their child be released or when there is evidence that the child no longer suffers from a mental illness.

Juveniles in Detention Centers and Adult Jails

Historically, juveniles who were held in detention centers were there to ensure their appearance in court or, in cases where the youth did not have parents or guardians to care for him or her, until the adjudication hearing. However, over time, the purpose of detention has changed to ensure the safety of the juvenile who may pose a threat to himself or herself, and to prevent potential subsequent crime.

Juveniles awaiting adjudication can be held in detention centers or jails. Detention centers hold juveniles at many points in the juvenile justice process and in different situations. However, most juveniles are not held in detention center from delinquency referral to final disposition. Although most juveniles are not detained (on average, 20% of juveniles are detained until final disposition), detention caseloads have increased 48% between 1985 and 2005 (Puzzanchera & Snyder, 2008). The largest relative increase was for person offenses at 144%, with drug offenses increasing 110%, and public order offenses up by 108%. In contrast, cases involving detention for property offenses decreased and while the proportion of drug offense cases involving detention peaked to 35% in 1990; by 2005 it had declined by 18%.

Detention trends between 1985 and 2005 relating to age, gender, and race can be summarized as follows:

- **Age:** Overall, older juveniles (16 or older) are more likely to be detained than younger juveniles for cases involving both males and females. Likewise, between 1987 and the mid-90's, for both age groups, drug offense cases were more likely to involve detention than were other offense cases. In 2005, 16-year-olds accounted for 25% of cases that involved detention, a larger percentage of cases than any other single age group.
- **Gender:** In 2005, male juveniles charged with delinquency offenses were more likely (22%) than females (17%) to be held in secure facilities while awaiting disposition. While the number of cases resulting in detention is increasing at a faster rate for females than for males, approximately 80% of detained juveniles are males.
- **Race:** African American youth are overrepresented in detention caseloads. While they represented 33% of the overall delinquency caseload in 2005, they made up 42% of the detention caseload. Between 1985 and 2005, African American youth were overrepresented in detention caseloads for drug, person, property, and public order offenses. The greatest overrepresentation was for drug offense cases—31% of all cases involving drug offense violations but represented 49% of such detained cases (Puzzanchera & Snyder, 2008).

Although **jails** are intended for adults, juveniles are held in adult jails despite the mandate of the federal Juvenile Justice and Delinquency Prevention Act (JJDPA) of 1974. Two of the requirements of JJDPA were sight and sound separation of juveniles from adults and the removal of juveniles from adult jails and lockups. Despite evidence that the practice of housing juveniles in adult jails is waning, in 2004, juveniles were still being held in adult jails. A report from the Bureau of Justice Assistance, *Juveniles in Adult Prisons and Jails: A National Assessment,* reported that in 2000, approximately 9,100 juveniles under 18 were being held in adult jails (Austin, Johnson, & Gregoriou, 2000). Similarly, a 2004 report from the Office of Juvenile Justice and Delinquency Prevention, *Juveniles in Corrections,* stated that 7,600 youth under 18 were held in adult jails. These juveniles include youths under 18 who are considered adults by state law but still counted as juveniles by researchers. It is believed that only about 20% of juveniles in adult jails are being held in violation of the JJDPA requirement.

JUVENILES IN POSTADJUDICATION PLACEMENTS

Secure Confinement

Juveniles who are held in postadjudication placements are typically in secure confinement in diagnostic and transfer facilities, stabilization facilities, state schools and juvenile correctional facilities, and transition facilities. Adult prisons are also used for delinquents who have been waived and convicted in adult court or those who have been sentenced under blended sentencing statutes.

A 2005 report titled *Juvenile Court statistics 2005,* revealed that while the number of out-of-home placements increased by 69% between 1985 and 1997, there was a decrease of 23% through 2005 (Puzzanchera & Snyder, 2008). Dispositions reflecting out-of-home placements between 1985 and 2005 relating to gender, race, and age can be summarized as follows:

- **Age:** In each year from 1996 to 2005, cases involving juveniles age 16 or older that were adjudicated delinquents were more likely to result in out-of-home placements than were cases involving juveniles age 15 or younger regardless of the offense. Likewise, the likelihood of out-of-home placements declined more for younger than for older juveniles.
- **Gender:** For each year between 1987 and 2005, cases involving males adjudicated delinquents were more likely to result in out-of-home placements than were cases involving females. For males, in 2005, person offenses (27%) and public order offenses (25%) cases adjudicated delinquents were most likely to result in out-of-home placements, followed by property cases (23%) and drug offense case (20%). For females, public order cases (20%) were more likely to result in out-of-home placements, followed by person cases (18%), property cases (15%) and drug offenses (13%).
- **Race:** In 2005, the likelihood for adjudicated juveniles to be placed in out-of-home placements was greater for African American youth and Native American (25% each), than for White (21%) or Asian juveniles (22%). In each year between 1992 and 2005, drug offense cases involving African American youth adjudicated delinquents were more likely to result in out-of-home placements than were drug cases involving juveniles of any other race. (Puzzanchera & Snyder, 2008).

Diagnostic and Transfer Facilities

A **diagnostic facility** is the first stop for adjudicated and institutionalized juveniles. At this stage, juveniles are assessed, classified, and assigned to the most suitable placement in the state juvenile correctional facilities. The juveniles undergo a battery of tests, including psychological, intelligence, and physical. In addition, social workers complete a social history report, detailing the juvenile's background with the court, family history, prior drug or alcohol abuse, school progress, and other extenuating factors that may be beneficial to the rehabilitation plan. **Transfer facilities** are short term and secure. They are used to hold adjudicated juveniles until a room becomes available in state school. Most states do not have a separate, state-operated transfer facility, and therefore adjudicated juveniles are typically held in the county detention center until a room is available at the state school.

Stabilization Facilities

Juveniles in stabilization facilities are mentally ill and/or emotionally disturbed. They are referred from other secure facilities such as a diagnostic facility or state school. Youth in these facilities are given a mental health evaluation. These juveniles are often determined to be a danger to themselves and others, or have deficiencies in day-to-day functioning due to psychiatric disorders. They exhibit suicidal behaviors, self-mutilation (i.e., cutting) and other emotional disorders such as schizophrenia. It is estimated that about 20% of all youths in the juvenile justice systems have serious emotional disorders (Teplin, 2001).

State Schools and Juvenile Correctional Facilities

State schools or juvenile facilities are locked, secure, and long term, and are viewed as prisons for juveniles. More than one third of juveniles in residential placements are there for person-related offenses such as homicide, sexual assault, and aggravated assault and approximately 48% for property, drug, or public order offenses. A 2004 report written by Sickmund of the Office of Juvenile Justice and Delinquency Prevention (OJJDP) provides the following summary for juveniles in corrections:

- Juvenile facilities reported more juvenile delinquents in placement in 1999 than any time since 1991.
- The offense profiles were similar for those held in public facilities and those held in private facilities.
- Person offenders were 35% of juvenile offenders in custody nationwide; drug offenders were 9%.
- Minority youth accounted for 7 in 10 juveniles held in custody for a violent offense in 1999.
- In nearly all states, a disproportionate number of minorities were in residential placement in 1999. Nationally custody rates were highest for African Americans.

- Females make up a small portion of the juveniles in custody, but require unique programming.
- Seven in ten juveniles offenders in custody were held in locked facilities rather than staff secure facilities.
- On June 30, 2000, 7,600 youth younger than 18 were held in adult jails nationwide.
- Most youth sent to adult prisons are 17-year-old males, minorities and person offenders

Transition Facilities

A transition facility or a "halfway house" placement is typically used for juveniles who have completed their sentence in state school and are determined to need structure before returning to the community. Juveniles sent to transitional facilities include special needs youth such as sex offenders, violent offenders, and high-needs, chemically-dependent juveniles. Placement of juveniles in these settings is not meant to ensure extra supervision for punishment, but is seen as benefiting the juveniles with respect to their future reintegration.

Adult Correctional Institutions/Adult Prison

Some juveniles who are processed in adult court are likely to be convicted and sent to adult prisons. A 2000 report by the Bureau of Justice Assistance, *Juveniles in Adult Prisons and Jails: A National Assessment,* revealed that approximately 5,000 juveniles are in adult prisons (Austin, Johnson, & Gregoriou, 2000). Seventy-five percent of these juveniles were sentenced as adults, and 23% were held as adjudicated juveniles. In addition, the report shows that almost 60% of juveniles held in adult prisons were sentenced for person offenses, 21% for a property offense, and 1% for a drug-related offense. African Americans constituted 55% of juveniles in state prison, and the age of juveniles sent to adult prison ranged from 13 to 17, with 80% of juveniles being at least age 17. Males made up approximately 96% of all juveniles in adult prison. Overall, the typical juvenile sent to adult prison was an African American male, age 17 or 18, who had committed a person offense (Sickmund, 2004).

Juveniles Life Without Parole

All states have established mechanisms for transferring or waiving jurisdiction to the adult court. Once this transfer occurs, the accused juvenile loses all special rights and immunities and is subject to most of the full range of adult penalties for criminal behavior. For example, in the past, juveniles could be provided an "absolute" sentence such as life without parole (Cothern, 2000); however, U.S. Supreme Court decision in *Graham v. Florida* (2010), no longer allows a life sentence for youth who have not committed homicide. In addition, in 2005, the Supreme Court held in

Roper v. Simmons that states cannot execute offenders who are under the age of 18 at the time of the offense. The ruling stipulates that juveniles are not as culpable as adult criminals and executing juveniles would violate both the Eighth and the Fourteenth Amendments. At the time, the ruling affected 72 juveniles in 12 states.

JUVENILE REENTRY AND REINTEGRATION

Juvenile reentry and reintegration after incarceration and institutionalization is a critical issue facing the juvenile justice system. There are many juvenile reentry and reintegration programs, but the success of such programs requires support from federal, state, and local governments. The goal of juvenile reentry and reintegration programming is to rehabilitate juveniles and equip them with the necessary skills to become law-abiding, productive citizens. Effective reentry and reintegration programs should address issues to reduce recidivism and enable juveniles to achieve success. The public generally supports rehabilitation, reentry, and reintegration programs for juveniles as many believe juveniles are malleable and amenable to treatment and rehabilitation. Further, the public appears to believe most juveniles will desist from delinquent offending and most will eventually be released back into the community.

Although the goal of juvenile reentry and reintegration is rehabilitation, high caseloads, limited resources, and a lack of specialized training greatly impact the effects of a successful transition into society (Byrnes, Macallair, & Shorter, 2002). Juveniles released from institutional commitments are likely to face numerous challenges to include: lack of educational options, lack of housing options, limited skills and education, gang affiliations, institutional identity, substance abuse problems, mental health problems, lack of community support and role models, and legislative barriers (p. 9).

Many juveniles are not released to family members but, rather, are placed in residential or transitional housing. Dysfunctional families are typically unable to provide adequate role models and, likewise, communities plagued by poverty provide inadequate support to juveniles. Many juveniles incarcerated in juvenile justice detention institutions have been affiliated with gangs. Gangs may serve as surrogate families for those juveniles who come from dysfunctional families. Juveniles who are incarcerated for long periods of time are subjected to institutionalization; the structure and routine of institutional life becomes commonplace in the lives of many offenders. Juveniles with institutional identity are typically ill-equipped to handle a life of independence, which requires internal discipline. Many juveniles who are released from juvenile institutions are at the age of majority and therefore, public education laws do not apply. Both substance abuse and mental health problems exist in high numbers in juvenile detention facilities.

Legislative barriers are key challenges that juveniles released from detention placement must face. Juvenile offenders, convicted of certain offenses, may be restricted from some government services provided for the needy. Federal education grants, welfare, food stamps, public housing, and certain types of jobs (i.e., childcare, nursing, etc.) prohibit some offenders with certain felony offenses from participation in such programs (Byrnes, Macallair, & Shorter, 2002). For example, there is a lifetime ban on those convicted of felony drug offenses to receive food stamps and welfare. Likewise, Supplemental Security Income (SSI) recipients may lose benefits if they violate certain parole conditions.

Juvenile reentry and reintegration programs generally offer both concrete skills such as practical life skills as well as effective communication skills to prepare them for a successful transition into society. Successful programming provides a balance between self-sufficiency and healthy, emotional well-being (Propp, Ortega, & Newhart, 2003). It is critical for juveniles making the transition from institutionalization to society to maintain effective communication and connections with the community. In many cases, juveniles are offered both tangible and intangible skills within independent living and community programs (Propp et al., 2003). Mentoring has proven important to provide direction and support to address the immediate needs of juveniles in transition (Davis & Barnett, 2000). Social support, such as communication and connections, help to ease the stigma associated with juvenile parolees. Likewise, relationships with family members and caseworkers can prove invaluable as juvenile parolees may experience some crises during transition. Strong relationships between case managers and juveniles are deemed necessary to build trust and a genuine concern and interest for the well-being of juveniles in transition (Davis & Barnett, 2000).

Comprehensive follow-ups for juveniles who have completed reentry programs are necessary to measure the effectiveness and long-term outcomes of such programs. Services such as vocational training, drug treatment, mental health treatment, and counseling can help to further offer successful outcomes. Adequately trained juvenile justice professionals are critical to ensuring that juveniles in transition fully benefit from reentry programs. Aftercare services are in place to offer ongoing support for juveniles leaving transitional programs.

JUVENILE AFTERCARE

Institutionalization is used for juveniles whom the court deems need secure placement and limited freedom. Aftercare, also known as parole, is a conditional release from an institution. Juveniles who are released from institutions receive corrections aftercare support. These juveniles may require more support than those juveniles who were allowed to remain in the community after adjudication. Aftercare may be revoked when the youth cannot function in the community or if the youth commits a serious offense.

Protection of society and the adjustment of youth are considered the two primary goals of aftercare. Juvenile aftercare officers are typically charged with providing rehabilitative and social services to juveniles. The primary tasks of juvenile aftercare officers include intake, investigation, and supervision. Aftercare functions to allow the youth to remain in the community while providing programming to help facilitate rehabilitation. However, large caseloads coupled with a lack of corrections training may impede rehabilitation. While in the institution, parole officers initiate services such as education classes, counseling, and classification. Juveniles are released from custody dependent upon their progress or rehabilitation.

POLICY IMPLICATIONS

The perception of juvenile institutionalization as a critical social problem continues to be an ever-existent area of concern. According to Zimring (1998), there have been two occurrences within the last 30 years in which juvenile crime has been considered a crisis. The first began around the mid-1970s and ended around the late 1970s. The second began in the early 1990s and continues today. The perception of youth violence was the same in both occurrences with respect to the belief that juveniles are a new 'breed' of offender than in the past and that lenient treatment of juveniles resulted in increased juvenile crime and violence. The idea that juveniles are more vicious than in the past offers credence to the notion that more punitive sanctions are necessary. Also, terms such as *accountability* and *consequences for actions* represent a distinction between children and juveniles. The distinction appears to offer maturity and justify juvenile institutionalization and the waiver of juveniles to criminal court.

The current belief of juvenile crime is that juvenile violence will continue to increase in the coming decades. As a result, public fear of crime and the get-tough ideology has prompted local governments to implement juvenile regulatory measures to reduce juvenile crime. Many juveniles have been institutionalized and transferred to adult court as a means to address the juvenile problem. Longer sentences, special enforcement, increased public access to juvenile proceedings, and blended sentencing provide examples of get-tough strategies. Legislation to address the youth crime problem has been adopted in almost every U.S. state. Due concern has not been given to the assumption that the underlying problems of juvenile crime have not been explored. Instead, much criticism has been given to the juvenile court for failing to reduce juvenile crime. However, such criticism is baseless, because juvenile courts cannot solve social problems as the juvenile justice system responds to the back end of social problems.

A large number of juveniles participate in some form of violence during their adolescent years, however, only a small percentage become chronic offenders. Although a small group of chronic offenders are responsible for most violent offenses, it is sometimes difficult to identify these juvenile offenders and provide programming to address their individual needs. Côté, Vaillancourt, Barker, Nagin, and Tremblay's (2007) study of physical aggression during childhood suggests that early education should be considered in an attempt to prevent youth violence. The longitudinal research suggests that at two years of age, physical aggression may be detected in children. Early quality childhood education could likely reduce the physical aggression of developing children. It has been long understood that prevention and intervention strategies have proven effective in reducing juvenile delinquency. Future responses to the delinquency problem should include examining evidence-based programs that have reduced juvenile recidivism.

Out-of-home placement facilities can provide treatment and direction as they address the myriad of issues facing individual juveniles. The Colorado Division of Youth Services, for example, developed five key strategies to address juvenile programs (Estrada, 2011). The five strategies are as follows: the right services at the right time, quality staff, safe environments, proven practices, and restorative community justice. The right services at the right time addresses programs that fit the unique circumstances of individual juveniles. Assessing juvenile needs, determining their motivation, and providing support during the transition from state schools to the environment at the right time are key factors in measuring offender success (Estrada, 2011). A quality staff must be in place to ensure that juveniles in residential placement receive all of the services provided in their individual plans. Staff should be adequately trained and understand the crucial roles they play in juvenile success and within the institution. Safe environments allow for the safety and security of juvenile facilities for both the juveniles and staff. Evidence-based practices should be implemented to provide the most up-to-date proven strategies for success in out-of-home placement reentry. Restorative justice has been traditionally used in community-based corrections. However, future research should assess how the restorative justice model can be used with juveniles who are in transition to the community. Restorative justice works to restore peace to society by involving the offender, victim, and community in the process. The idea suggests that reconnecting youth to the community will involve personal accountability, acceptance into the community and victim empathy.

Rehabilitation has been the foundation of the juvenile justice system since the creation of the first juvenile court. Rehabilitation is, indeed, a realistic and practical goal. Rehabilitation is important because most juveniles in out-of-home placement will, at some point, be released to the community. In the community, juveniles will be accountable for their actions and behaviors.

DISCUSSION QUESTIONS

1. Discuss the role of delinquency theory in explaining juvenile offending. Which of the theories do you feel best explain juvenile delinquency?

2. The Eighth Amendment of the U.S. Constitution prohibits cruel and unusual punishment. Define cruel and unusual punishment. What are some punishments that courts have considered cruel and unusual for juveniles?

3. Discuss the roles of a transitional facility. Why is it important to operate transitional facilities for juveniles?

4. What was the justification for subjecting nondelinquents to the same procedures and outcomes as delinquents in the 1970s? What are some of the adverse effects of this practice?

5. What is the role of aftercare in the juvenile justice process? In what ways does aftercare prepare juveniles for reintegration into the community?

SUGGESTED READINGS

Abbott, D. E. (1991). *I cried you didn't listen: A survivor's exposé of the California Youth Authority.* Los Angeles, CA: Feral House Press.

Bullis, M., Yovanoff, P., Mueller, G., & Havel E. (2002). Life on the 'outs': Examination of the facility-to-community transition of incarcerated youth. *Exceptional Children.* 69(1), p. 7–23

Del Carmen, R., Parker, M., & Reddington, F. (1998). *Briefs of leading cases in juvenile justice.* Cincinnati, OH: Anderson.

Feld, B. C. (1997). Abolish the juvenile court: youthfulness, criminal responsibility, and sentencing policy. *Journal of Criminal Law and Criminology, 88*(1), 68–136.

Howell, J. C. (2003). *Preventing and reducing juvenile delinquency: A comprehensive framework.* Thousand Oaks, CA: Sage.

Humes, E. (1997). *No matter how loud I shout.* New York, NY: Simon & Schuster.

Kempf-Leonard, K., Tracy, P., & Howell, J. C. (2001). Serious, violent, and chronic juvenile offenders: The relationship of delinquency career types to adult criminality. *Justice Quarterly, 18,* 449–478.

Loeber, R., & Farrington, D. P. (2001). *Child delinquents: Development, intervention, and service needs.* Thousand Oaks, CA: Sage.

McShane, M., & Williams, F. P. (Eds.). (2007). Youth violence and delinquency: Myths and monsters. *Juvenile Treatment and Crime Prevention*: Vol. 3. Westport, CT: Praeger.

Mennel, R. M. (1972). Origins of juvenile court: Changing perspectives on the legal rights of juvenile delinquents. *Crime and Delinquency, 18,* 68–78.

Parsell, T. J. (2006). *Fish, a memoir of a boy in a man's prison.* Cambridge, MA: Da Capo Press.

Roberson, C. (2000). *Exploring juvenile justice* (2nd ed.). Incline Village, NV: Copperhouse.

Santos, M. G. (2007). *Inside: Life behind bars in America.* New York, NY: St. Martin's Griffin.

Sutton, J. (1998). *Stubborn children: Controlling delinquency in the United States, 1640–1981.* Berkeley: University of California Press.

Watkins, J. C. (1998). *The juvenile justice century: A sociolegal commentary on American juvenile courts.* Raleigh, NC: Carolina Academic Press.

WEB RESOURCES

- Uniform Juvenile Court Act, on the disposition of a delinquent child
  http://www.legis.nd.gov/cencode/t27c20.pdf

- Juvenile Court Statistics
  http://www.ojjdp.gov/ojstatbb/njcda/pdf/jcs2005.pdf

- Conditions of confinement in juvenile detention and correctional facilities
  http://www.ojjdp.gov/publications

- National report in support of state JJDPA compliance
  http://www.juvjustice.org/announcement_140.html

- The National Reentry Resource Center
  http://nationalreentryresourcecenter.org/

- OJJDP Evidence Based Prevention Model Programs Guide
  http://www.ojjdp.gov/mpg/programTypesDefinitions.aspx

- OJJDP Juvenile Offenders and Victims 2006 report
  http://ojjdp.gov/ojstatbb/nr2006

- Texas Criminal Justice Coalition
  http://www.criminaljusticecoalition.org/juvenile_justice

REFERENCES

Alexander, R. (2000). *Counseling, treatment, and intervention methods with juvenile and adult offenders.* Belmont, CA: Wadsworth.

Alexander, R. B., & Pratsinak, G. J. (2002). *Arresting addictions.* Lanham, MD: American Correctional Association.

Austin, J., Johnson, K., & Gregoriou, M. (2000). *Juveniles in adult prisons and jails: A national assessment.* Washington, DC: U.S. Department of Justice, Bureau of Justice Assistance.

Boesky, L. M. (2002). *Juvenile offenders with mental health disorders: Who are they and what do we do with them?* Lanham, MD: American Correctional Association.

Breed v. Jones, 421 U.S. 517 (1975).

Byrnes, M., Macallair, D., & Shorter, A. D. (2002). *Aftercare as afterthought: Reentry and the California youth authority.* Prepared for the California State Senate Joint Committee on Prison and Construction Operations. San Francisco, CA: Center on Juvenile & Criminal Justice.

Côté, S. M., Vaillancourt, T., Barker, E. D., Nagin, D., and Tremblay, R. E. (2007). The joint development of physical and indirect aggression: Predictors of continuity and change during childhood. *Development and Psychopathology, 19*(1), 37–55.

Cothern, L. (2000). *Juveniles and the Death Penalty.* Rockville, MD: U.S. Department of Justice, Office of Juvenile Justice and Delinquency Prevention.

Davis, R. K, & Barrett, C. T. (2000). Bridges for former "systems" youth. *Families in Society, 81*(5), 538–543.

Emeka, T. Q., & Sorensen, J. (2009). Female juvenile risk: Is there a need for gendered assessment instruments? *Youth Violence & Juvenile Justice, 7,* 313–330.

Empey, L. (1978). *American delinquency: Its meaning and construction.* Homewood, IL: Dorsey Press.

Estrada, A. J. (2011). The Colorado division of youth corrections' five key strategies. *Corrections Today, 73,* 28–31.

Ex parte Crouse, 4 Whart. 9 (PA.1838).

Feld, B. C. (2003). *Juvenile justice administration in a nutshell.* St. Paul, MN: West.

Furstenberg, F. F. (2000). The sociology of adolescence and youth in the 1990s: A critical commentary. *Journal of Marriage and the Family, 6,* 896–910.

Graham v. Florida, 08–7412 (2010).

Hartwig, H. J., & Myers, J. E. (2003). A different approach: Applying a wellness paradigm to adolescent female delinquents and offenders. *Journal of Mental Health Counseling, 25*(1), 57–75.

Heide, K. (1999). *Young killers: The challenge of juvenile homicide.* Thousand Oaks, CA: Sage.

Holden, G., & Kapler, R. (2005). Deinstitutionalization of status offenders: A record of progress. *Juvenile Justice, 2,* 3–10.

In re Gault, 387 U.S. 1, 87 S. Ct. 1428 (1977).

In re Winship, 397 U.S. 358, 90 S. Ct. 1068 (1970).

Kent v. United States, 383 U.S. 541 (1966).

Krisberg, B. (2004). *Juvenile justice: Redeeming our children.* Thousand Oaks, CA: Sage.

McKeiver v. Pennsylvania, 403 U.S. 528, 91 S. Ct. (1971).

Mennel, R. M. (1973). *Thorns and thistles: Juvenile delinquents in the United States, 1815–1857.* Syracuse, NY: Syracuse University Press.

Miller, W. (1958). Lower class culture as generating milieu of gang delinquency. *Journal of Social Issues, 14,* 5–19.

Myers, W. C. (2002). *Juvenile sexual homicide.* San Diego, CA: Academic Press.

National Conference of Commission on Uniform State Laws. (1968). Uniform juvenile court act. Philadelphia, PA: Author.

Office of Juvenile Justice and Delinquency Prevention (2003, June). State statutes define who is under juvenile court jurisdiction. *National Report Series.* Washington, DC: Office of Juvenile Justice and Delinquency Prevention. Available at http://www.ncjrs.gov/html/ojjdp/195420/page3.html

Parham v. J. R., 442 U.S. 584 (1979).

Platt, A. M. (1969). *The child savers: The invention of delinquency.* Chicago, IL: University of Chicago Press.

Propp, J., Ortega, D. M., & Newhart, F. (2003). Independence or interdependence: Rethinking the transition from "ward of the court" to adulthood. *Families in Society, 84,* 259–266.

Puzzanchera, C., & Snyder, H. N. (2008). *Juvenile court statistics 2005* (32–35). Pittsburg, PA: National Center for Juvenile Justice.

Roper v. Simmons, 543 U.S. 551 (2005).

Schall v. Martin, 104 S.Ct. 2403 (1984).

Schlossmann, S. L. (1977). *Love and the American delinquent: The theory and practice of "progressive" juvenile justice, 1825–1920.* Chicago, IL: University of Chicago Press.

Sickmund, M. (2004). Juveniles in corrections. *National Report Series.* NCJ 202885. Washington, DC: U.S. Department of Justice, Office of Juvenile Justice and Delinquency Prevention. Available at http://www.ncjrs.gov/html/ojjdp/202885/contents.html

Snyder, H. N., & Sickmund, M. (1999). *Juvenile offenders and victims: 1999 national report.* Washington, DC: U.S. Department of Justice, Office of Juvenile Justice and Delinquency Prevention.

Snyder, H. N., & Sickmund, M. (2006). *Juvenile offenders and victims: 2006 national report.* Washington, DC: U.S. Department of Justice, Office of Juvenile Justice and Delinquency Prevention.

Sutton, J. (1998). *Stubborn children: Controlling delinquency in the United States, 1640–1981.* Berkeley: University of California Press.

Teplin, L. A. (2000). *Assessing alcohol, drug, and mental disorders in juvenile detainees.* NCJ 200102. Washington, DC: U.S. Department of Justice, Office of Juvenile Justice and Delinquency Prevention. Available at http://www.ncjrs.gov/pdffiles1/ojjdp/fs200102.pdf

Williams, F., & McShane, M. (1998). *Criminological theory.* New York, NY: Prentice Hall.

Wolfgang, M. E., Sellin, T., & Figlio, R. (1972). Delinquency in a birth cohort. In J. E. Jacoby (Ed.), *Classics of criminology* (pp. 58–65). Prospect Heights, IL: Waveland Press.

Zimring, F. (1998). *American youth violence.* New York, NY: Oxford University Press.

CHAPTER 3

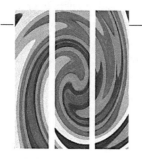

Incarcerated Female:
A Growing Population

Lisa Pasko and Meda Chesney-Lind

More than one million women in the United States are under some form of criminal justice supervision (Glaze & Bonzcar, 2007). By 2009, the number of women imprisoned in the United States increased 800% over the past three decades, bringing the number of women behind bars to over 105,000 (West, 2010). From 1995 to 2009 alone, the number of women behind prison bars increased 87%, and women now account for nearly 7% of the total prison population (see Table 3.1; Stephan, 2008; West, 2010). Over a third of them served time in the nation's three largest jurisdictions: Texas, California, and the federal system (West, 2010; see also Chesney-Lind, 2002, pp. 80–81). Currently, women also account for 23% of the

Table 3.1 Number of Female Prisoners Under the Jurisdiction of State or Federal Authorities, December 31, 2000–2009

Year	Total	Federal	State	Percent of sentenced prisoners
2000	85,044	8,397	76,647	6.4%
2001	85,184	8,990	76,194	6.3
2002	89,066	9,308	79,758	6.5
2003	92,571	9,770	82,801	6.6
2004	95,998	10,207	85,791	6.7
2005	98,688	10,495	88,193	6.7
2006	103,343	11,116	92,227	6.9
2007	105,786	11,528	94,258	6.9
2008	106,358	11,578	94,780	6.9
2009	105,197	11,780	93,417	6.8

Source: West & Sabol (2010). *Prisoners in 2009.* Washington, DC: Bureau of Justice Statistics.

probation population, 12% of the jail population, and 12% of the parole population in the United States (Glaze & Bonzcar, 2007).

Increases in the number of women in prison surpassed those of men over this period, as well. The number of women in prison has increased at nearly double the rate of men since 1985 (Sentencing Project, 2007). A similar pattern can be found in the number of women in jail, where a 32% increase was seen between 2000 and 2009; for men, the increase was 22% (Bureau of Justice Statistics, 2010a, 2010b).

The soaring numbers of women under lock and key are not simply products of the increasing reliance in the United States on imprisonment, although that has played a role in the pattern. Nationally, the rate of women's imprisonment is also at an all-time high. In 1925, women's rate of incarceration was 6 per 100,000. In 2001, the rate climbed to 58 per 100,000 and by 2009, the rate had reached an historical high of 67 per 100,000, with Hispanic and African American women experiencing even higher rates of incarceration (see Table 3.2). Taken together, these figures signal a major policy change in society's response to women's crime—one that has occurred with virtually no public discussion

So, as the number of people imprisoned in the United States continues to climb, our nation has achieved the dubious honor of having the highest incarceration rate in the world, with Russia following as a distant second (Mauer, 1999, 2006). Along

Table 3.2 Estimated Number of Sentenced Prisoners Under State or Federal Jurisdiction Per 100,000 U.S. Residents, by Sex, Race, Hispanic Origin, and Age, December 31, 2009

Age	Female Prisoners			
	Total	White	Black	Hispanic
Total	67	50	142	74
18–19	23	17	42	24
20–24	109	86	186	124
25–29	149	115	287	164
30–34	188	155	361	178
35–39	206	164	426	187
40–44	172	131	360	171
45–49	94	67	205	107
50–54	45	32	101	60
55–59	22	18	42	29
60–64	11	9	22	22
65 or older	3	2	6	4

Source: Bureau of Justice Statistics. (2010a). *Prisoners in 2009*. Washington, DC: U.S. Department of Justice.

the way, America's love affair with prisons has claimed some hidden victims—economically marginalized women of color and their children.

TRENDS IN WOMEN'S CRIME: A REPRISE

Is the dramatic increase in women's imprisonment a response to a women's crime problem spiraling out of control? A look at the pattern of women's arrests provides little evidence of a dramatic change in the composition of women's crime. One crude measure will serve to make this point again. The number of arrests of adult women for serious violent crime has only marginally increased (3.4%) between 2000 and 2009 (Federal Bureau of Investigation, 2010, p. 239). However, the number of women incarcerated during the past decade has increased by 24% (Bureau of Justice Statistics, 2010a, 2010b).

WOMEN, VIOLENT CRIMES, AND THE WAR ON DRUGS

Another indication that the increase in women's imprisonment is not explained by a shift in the character of women's crime comes from information about the offenses for which women are being imprisoned (see Table 3.3). For the past decade and a half, roughly a third of women's incarceration is due to violent crimes. Indeed, the proportion of women in state prisons for violent offenses has declined since 1979: from 48.95% to 32% in 2001 to 34% in 2006 (Bureau of Justice Statistics, 1988, 2002a, 2010a). In states that have seen large increases in women's imprisonment, such as California, the decline is even sharper. In 2009, only 16% of the women admitted to the California prison system were being incarcerated for violent crimes, compared to 37.2% in 1982 (Bloom, Chesney-Lind, & Owen, 1994; California Department of Corrections and Rehabilitation [CDC&R], 2010, p. 44).

Other recent figures suggest that without any fanfare, the "war on drugs" has become a war on women and has contributed to the explosion in women's prison populations. More than one out of four women in U.S. prisons in 2006 was doing time for drug offenses (up from 1 in 10 in 1979), whereas less than one out of five men were imprisoned for drug convictions (Bureau of Justice Statistics, 2002a, p. 13, 2010; Snell & Morton, 1994, p. 3). Although the intent of get-tough policies was to rid society of drug dealers and so-called kingpins, over a third (35.9%) of the women serving time for drug offenses in the nation's prisons are serving time solely for "possession" (Bureau of Justice Statistics, 1988, p. 3). In California, over half (52%) of the women admitted to prison for drug crimes were convicted for possession only (CDC&R, 2010, p. 45).

The war on drugs, coupled with the development of new technologies for determining drug use (e.g., urinalysis), plays another, less obvious role in increasing women's imprisonment. Many women parolees are being returned to prison for technical parole violations because they fail to pass random drug tests. Of the 7,117 women incarcerated in California in 2009, approximately one in five were imprisoned

| Table 3.3 | Estimated Number of Sentenced Prisoners Under State Jurisdiction, by Offense and Sex Year-End 2006 | | |

	All Inmates	Male	Female
Total	1,331,100	1,238,900	92,200
Violent Offenses	693,400	661,600	31,800
Murder	168,600	158,200	10,200
Manslaughter	16,100	14,200	1,600
Rape	65,800	65,300	500
Other sexual assault	93,600	92,500	1,300
Robbery	178,900	171,600	7,500
Assault	133,900	125,500	7,800
Other violent	37,100	34,400	2,800
Property Offenses	258,200	230,700	27,500
Burglary	126,100	119,800	6,000
Larceny	49,500	41,900	7,800
Motor vehicle theft	22,700	21,000	1,600
Fraud	33,600	23,700	9,800
Other property	26,400	24,400	2,200
Drug Offenses	264,300	238,600	26,200
Public Order Offenses	101,300	95,700	5,500
Other/Unspecified	13,300	12,300	1,200

Source: Bureau of Justice Statistics. (2010). *Prisoners in 2009* (p. 13). Washington, DC: U.S. Department of Justice.

for parole violations (CDC&R, 2010, p. 30). In Oregon, during a one-year period (October 1992–September 1993), only 16% of female admissions to Oregon institutions were incarcerated for new convictions; the rest were probation and parole violators. This pattern was not nearly so clear in male imprisonment; 48% of the admissions to male prisons were for new offenses (Anderson, 1994). Finally, in Hawaii, other data underscore this point further: of individuals released during 1998 and tracked for two years on parole, nearly half (43%) were returned to prison. When examining the reasons for parole revocation, a gender difference emerges: 73% of the women were returned to prison for technical violations (as opposed to new crimes); this was true for a smaller, yet significant, percentage (64%) of male parolees (Chesney-Lind, 2002, p. 90).

Nowhere has the drug war taken a larger toll than on women sentenced in federal courts. In the federal system, the passage of harsh mandatory minimums for federal crimes, coupled with sentencing guidelines intended to "reduce race, class and other unwarranted disparities in sentencing males" (Raeder, 1993) have operated to the distinct disadvantage of women. They have also dramatically increased the number of women sentenced to federal institutions. From 2000 to 2009, approximately 2,700 women a year have been sentenced to imprisonment in federal court for drug trafficking (U.S. Sentencing Commission, 2010). Drugs that have come under amplified surveillance by the federal government within the last decade, such as methamphetamine and marijuana, have also greatly impacted women.[1] From 1995 through 2009, the number of women convicted of federal methamphetamine offenses increased by nearly 200% (from 239 offenders in 1996 to 700 in 2009), and female federal marijuana offenders were up by 51% (from 495 in 1996 to 751 in 2000; see Figure 3.1). Indeed, women now account for one out of every five arrests for methamphetamine in the federal system (Motivans, 2008). The number of women convicted of powder cocaine offenses and the number of female crack cocaine offenders also remained at a steady high of over 500 offenders in each drug category. In state prisons, women are 47% more likely to be doing time for a drug offense than are men (Bureau of Justice Statistics, 2010c).

Figure 3.1 Number of Female Drug Offenders Sentenced in Federal Court by Drug Type, 2009

Powder cocaine	589
Crack Cocaine	508
Heroin	240
Marijuana	751
Methamphetamine	700
Other	219

Source: United States Sentencing Commission, 2009 datafiles.

[1]Raeder (1993) notes, for example, that judges are constrained by these federal guidelines from considering family responsibilities, particularly pregnancy and motherhood, which in the past may have kept women out of prison. Yet the effect of these "neutral" guidelines is to eliminate from consideration the unique situation of mothers, especially single mothers, unless their situation can be established to be "extraordinary." Nearly 90% of male inmates report that their wives are taking care of their children; by contrast, only 22% of mothers in prison could count on the fathers of their children to care for the children during the mother's imprisonment (p. 69). This means that many women in prison, the majority of whom are mothers, face the potential, if not actual, loss of their children. This is not a penalty that men in prison experience. Additionally, although the *United States v. Booker* (2005) decision allowed for more judicial discretion and for judges to depart from the guidelines more easily, application of federal sentencing guidelines continued at a steady pace. Pre-Booker courts sentenced roughly 70% of offenders within the guidelines. In post-Booker years, about 60% are still sentenced within the guidelines (see U.S. Sentencing Commission, *2005–2009 Datafiles*).

Additionally, drugs such as methamphetamine and crack cocaine come attached with mandatory minimum prison sentences for relatively small amounts of drug trafficking. The consequence is that more and more women no longer receive probation for low-level offenses but, rather, receive prison. Thirty years ago, nearly two thirds of the women convicted of federal felonies were granted probation, but by 1991 only 28% of women were given straight probation (Raeder, 1993, pp. 31–32). According to the U.S. Sentencing Commission (2010), by 2009, less than one in ten female felons convicted in federal court received straight probation. The mean time to be served by women drug offenders increased from 27 months in July 1984 to a startling 67 months in June 1990 (p. 34). Taken together, these data explain why the number of women in federal institutions has skyrocketed since the 1980s. In 2008, women made up 6.7% of those in federal institutions, with 11,988 women behind bars (Motivans, 2010).

What about property offenses? Roughly 30% (29.8) of the women in state prisons were doing time for these offenses in 2009 (Bureau of Justice Statistics, 2010c). California, again, merits a closer look: Over a third (34.6%) of women in California state prisons in 2009 were incarcerated for property offenses (CDC&R, 2010, p. 15). These generally included low-level burglary, fraud, and petty theft with a prior record. Taken together, this means that nearly one woman in three (30.5%) is incarcerated in California for simple drug possession, petty theft with a prior, fraud, or low-level burglary (CDC&R, 2010, p. 15).

GETTING TOUGH ON WOMEN'S CRIME

Data on the offenses for which women are in prison and an examination of trends in women's arrests suggest that factors other than a shift in the nature of women's crime are involved in the dramatic increase in women's imprisonment. Simply put, the criminal justice system now seems more willing to incarcerate women.

What has happened in the last two decades? Although explanations are necessarily speculative, some reasonable suggestions can be advanced. First, it appears that mandatory sentencing for specific kinds of offenses—especially drug offenses—at both state and federal levels have affected women's incarceration. Legislators at the state and national level, perhaps responding to a huge increase in media coverage of crime but not necessarily the nation's actual crime rate, are escalating penalties for all offenses, particularly those associated with drugs (Mauer, 2006; Mauer & Huling, 1995).

Beyond this, sentencing reform, especially the development of sentencing guidelines and mandatory minimums resulting from "Three Strikes and You're Out" and "Truth in Sentencing" legislation, also has been a problem for women. In California, this has resulted in increasing the number of prison sentences for women who, due to such truth in sentencing policies, will be required to do at least 85% of their sentence behind bars (Blumstein, Cohen, Martin, & Tonry, 1983; CDC&R, 2010; Mauer, 2006). Sentencing reform has created some problems because the reforms address issues that have developed in the handling of male offenders and are now being applied to female offenders. Daly and Bordt's (1991) review of this problem notes, for example, that federal sentencing guidelines ordinarily do not permit a defendant's employment or family ties/familial responsibilities to be used as a factor in sentencing. She notes that these guidelines probably were intended to reduce class and race disparities in sentencing but their effect on women's sentencing was not considered. Bush-Baskette's (1999) analysis of the war on drugs resonates a similar theme: "Sentencing guidelines that disallow the use of drug addiction and family responsibilities as mitigating circumstances subject Black females to prison and long sentences under criminal justice supervision, as they do White females" (p. 222).

Finally, the criminal justice system has simply become tougher at every level of decision making. Langan (1991) notes that the chance of receiving a prison sentence following arrest has risen for all types of offenses, not simply those typically targeted by mandatory sentencing programs (p. 1569). This is specifically relevant to women because mandatory sentencing laws (with the exception of those regarding prostitution and drug offenses) typically have targeted predominantly male offenses, such as sexual assault, murder, and weapons offenses. Thus, Langan's research confirms that the whole system is now tougher on all offenses, including those that women traditionally have committed.

A careful review of the evidence on the current surge in women's incarceration suggests that this explosion may have little to do with a major change in women's behavior. This surge stands in stark contrast to the earlier growth in women's imprisonment, particularly to the other great growth of women's incarceration at the turn of the 20th century.

Perhaps the best way to place the current wave of women's imprisonment in perspective is to recall earlier approaches to women's incarceration. Historically, women prisoners have been few in number and were apparently an afterthought in a system devoted to the imprisonment of men. In fact, early women's facilities were often an outgrowth of men's prisons. In those early days, women inmates were seen as "more depraved" than their male counterparts because they were viewed as acting in contradiction to their whole "moral organization" (Rafter, 1990, p. 13).

The first large-scale, organized imprisonment of women occurred in the United States when many women's reformatories were established between 1870 and 1900. Women's imprisonment was justified not because the women posed a public safety risk, but because women were thought to need moral revision and protection. Important to note, however, is that the reformatory movement that resulted in the incarceration of large numbers of white, working-class girls and women for largely noncriminal or deportment offenses did not extend to women of color. Instead, as Rafter (1990) has carefully documented, African American women, particularly in the southern states, continued to be incarcerated in prisons where they were treated much like the male inmates. They frequently ended up on chain gangs and were not shielded from beatings if they did not keep up with the work (pp. 150–151). This racist legacy, the exclusion of Black women from the "chivalry" accorded White women, should be kept in mind when the current explosion of women's prison populations is considered.

The current trend in adult women's imprisonment seems to revisit the earliest approach to female offenders—women are once again an afterthought in a correctional process that is punitive rather than corrective. Women are also, however, no longer being accorded the benefits, however dubious, of the chivalry that had characterized the reformatory movement. Rather, they are increasingly likely to be incarcerated, not because society has decided to crack down on women's crime specifically, but because women are being swept up in a societal move to get tough on crime that is driven by images of violent criminals (almost always male and often members of minority groups) "getting away with murder."

A look at capital punishment demonstrates this point further. Although historically, women have received the death penalty far less frequently than men, the advent of get-tough approaches to crime ushered in a dramatic increase in the number of death sentences imposed on women (Morgan, 2000, p. 280; Streib, 2011; see Table 3.4). A total of 167 death sentences have been imposed upon female offenders from 1973 through late-2010 (Streib, 2011, p. 9). Five states (Texas, California, Florida, North Carolina, and Ohio) account for essentially half (83 of 167) of all such sentences, while the annual death-sentencing rate for female offenders during the last decade has averaged four per year (Streib, pp. 3–6). As of 2010, 55 women remained on death row in the United States, with the remaining 112 either executed, dead from natural causes, or received commuted life sentences. Despite the fact that domestic homicide is not a capital offense in most jurisdictions that utilize the death penalty, one quarter (14 of 55) of these fifty-five women received the death penalty for killing their husbands or boyfriends. Another one fifth killed their children or a child in their care (Streib, p. 10).

From 1990 to 2010, the total number of women executed exceeded the combined total of the previous four decades, despite declines in murder arrests for women. From 1984 to 2010, twelve women were executed in the United States (Streib, 2011). Table 3.4 summarizes the race, location, and victim of these 12 women.

This public mood, coupled with a legal system that now espouses equality for women with a vengeance when it comes to the punishment of crime, has resulted in this punitive attitude surrounding the death penalty and women and, in general, much greater use of imprisonment in response to women's crime. There also seems to be a return to the imagery of women's depravity for those women whose crimes (and race) put them outside of the ranks of *true women*. As evidence, consider the new hostility signaled by bringing child abuse charges against women who use drugs before the birth of their children (Chavkin, 1990; National Advocates for Pregnant Women [NAPW], 2011; Noble, 1988).

The fact that many of the women incarcerated in U.S. prisons are women of color who are doing time for drug offenses further distances them from images of womanhood that require protection from prison life. For this reason, when policymakers are confronted with the unanticipated consequences of the new get tough mood, their response is all too frequently to assail the character of the women they are jailing rather than to question the practice itself.

Table 3.4 Women Executed in the United States, 1984–2010

Year	Inmate	Race	State	Victim
11/02/1984	VELMA BARFIELD	White	NC	Boyfriend, by poison (also admitted to killing four others, including her mother and husband)
02/03/1998	KARLA FAYE TUCKER	White	TX	Acquaintance, by pickax
03/30/1998	JUDY BUENOANO	White	FL	Husband, by poison
02/24/2000	BETTY LOU BEETS	White	TX	Husband, by gunshot
05/02/2000	CHRISTINA RIGGS	White	AR	Two children, by poison (intended suicide but was revived)
01/11/2001	WANDA JEAN ALLEN	Black	OK	Girlfriend, by gunshot
05/01/01	MARILYN PLANTZ	White	OK	Husband, beaten and burned (hired boyfriend, who also received death)
12/04/01	LOIS NADEAN SMITH	White	OK	Son's ex-girlfriend, by gunshot
05/10/02	LYNDA LYON BLOCK	White	AL	Police officer, by gunshot (committed crime with husband, also executed)
10/09/02	AILEEN WUORNOS	White	FL	Stranger by gunshot (a *john*; 7 victims total)
09/15/05	FRANCES NEWTON	Black	TX	Husband, son, daughter by gunshot
09/23/10	TERESA LEWIS	White	VA	Husband, stepson by gunshot (hired boyfriend and accomplice)

Source: Streib (2010). Death Penalty for Female Offenders, January 1, 1973, to October 31, 2010.

BUILDING MORE WOMEN'S PRISONS

As a result of the surge in women's imprisonment, our country has gone on a building binge with regard to women's prisons. Prison historian Nicole Hahn Rafter (1990) observes that between 1930 and 1950, roughly two or three prisons were built or created for women each decade. In the 1960s, the pace of prison construction picked up slightly, with seven units opening, largely in southern and western states. During the 1970s, 17 prisons opened, including units in states such as Rhode Island and Vermont, which once relied on transferring women prisoners out of state. In the 1980s, 34 women's units or prisons were established; this figure is 10 times larger than the figures for earlier decades (Rafter, pp. 181–182).

To put this dramatic shift in another important historical context, consider the fact that only 30 years ago, the majority of states did not operate separate women's prisons. In 1973, only 26 states, Puerto Rico, and the District of Columbia, had separate institutions for women. Other states handled the problem differently; women were either housed in a portion of a male facility or, like Hawaii, Rhode Island, or Vermont, were imprisoned in other states (Singer, 1973). Looking backward, this pattern was very significant. The official response to women's crime during the 1970s was heavily influenced by the relative absence of women's prisons, despite the fact that some women were, during these years, committing serious crimes.

What has happened in the past few decades, then, signals a major and dramatic change in the way the country is responding to women's offenses. Without much fanfare and with little public discussion, the model of men's incarceration has been increasingly applied to women. Some of this punitive response to women's crime can be described as *equality with a vengeance*—the dark side of the equity or parity model of justice that emphasizes the need to treat women offenders as though they were equal to male offenders. As one correctional officer said at a national meeting, "An inmate is an inmate is an inmate."

But who are these inmates, and does it make sense to treat women in prison as though they were men? The next section examines what is known about the backgrounds of women currently doing time in state and federal prisons across the country.

PROFILE OF WOMEN IN U.S. PRISONS

Childhoods of Women in Prison

The most recent research on the characteristics of women doing time in state prisons across the country underscores the salience of themes identified early in this book—particularly the role of sexual and physical violence in the lives of women who come into the criminal justice system. This research also argues forcefully for a national discussion of the situation of women in our jails and prisons.

Snell and Morton (1994) surveyed a random sample of women and men (n = 13,986) in prisons around the country during 1991 for the Bureau of Justice Statistics. For the first time, a government study asked questions about women's and men's experiences of sexual and physical violence as children. They found, when they asked these questions, that women in prisons have experienced far higher rates of physical and sexual abuse than men. Forty-three percent of the women surveyed "reported they had been abused at least once" before their current admission to prison; the comparable figure for men was 12.2% (Snell & Morton, 1994, p. 5). A look at women in jail and prison in 1998 shows even higher estimates: 48% of women in jail and 57% in state prisons report prior histories of sexual or physical abuse (see Table 3.5).

For about a third of all women in prison (31.7%), the abuse started when they were girls and continued as they became adults. A key gender difference emerges

Table 3.5   Characteristics of Adult Women on Probation, in Jail, and in Prison

Probation	Jails	State Prisons	Race/Ethnicity
White	62%	36%	33%
Black	27	44	48
Hispanic	10	15	15
Other	1	5	4
Age			
24 and younger	20	21	
25–34	39	46	
35–44	30	27	
45–54	10	5	
55 and older	1	1	2
Median age	32 years	31 years	33 years
Marital Status			
Married	26	15	17
Widowed	2	4	6
Separated	10	13	10
Divorced	20	20	20
Never married	42	48	47
Education			
8th grade or less	5	12	7
Some high school	35	33	37
High school	39	39	39
Graduate/GED			
Some college or more	21	16	17
Report ever physically or sexually abused	41	48	57

Source: Bureau of Justice Statistics. (1999). *Women Offenders* (pp. 7–8). Washington, DC: U.S. Department of Justice.

here. A number of young men who are in prison (10.7%) also report abuse as boys, but it did not continue into adulthood. One in four women reported that their abuse started as adults, compared to only 3% of male offenders. Fully 33.5% of the women surveyed reported physical abuse, and a slightly higher number (33.9%) had been sexually abused either as girls or young women, compared to relatively small percentages of men (10% of boys and 5.3% of adult men in prison).

This survey also asked women about their relationships with those who abused them. Predictably, both women and men reported that parents and relatives contributed to the abuse they suffered as children, but female prisoners were far more likely than their male counterparts to say that domestic violence was a theme in their adult abuse; fully half of the women said they had been abused by a spouse or ex-spouse, compared to only 3% of male inmates.

The survey found ethnic differences in the role played by the juvenile and criminal justice system in the lives of women in prison. Overall, White women were slightly more likely to report having been in the foster care system or other institutions (21.1%) than African American or Hispanic women (14.1% and 14.4%, respectively). African American women and Hispanic women, by contrast, were far more likely than White women to report a family member (usually a brother) in prison (Snell & Morton, 1994).

Contrary to some stereotypes about drug use, more White and Hispanic women than African American women reported parental involvement with alcohol and drug abuse when they were girls. Over 4 out of 10 White women, and about a third of the Hispanic women, reported parental drug abuse, compared to only a quarter of the African American women. This underscores the need to focus on the specific interaction among culture, gender, and class in women's pathways to prison.

Current Offenses

A look at the offenses for which women are incarcerated quickly puts to rest the notion of hyperviolent, nontraditional women criminals. "Nearly half of all women in prison are currently serving a sentence for a nonviolent offense and have been convicted in the past of only nonviolent offenses" (Snell & Morton, 1994, p. 1). In fact, the number of women in prison for violent offenses, as a proportion of all female offenders, has fallen steadily over the past decades, whereas the number of women in prison has soared. In 1979, about half of the women in state prisons were incarcerated for violent crimes (Bureau of Justice Statistics, 1988). By 1986, the number had fallen to 40.7%, and in 2001 it was at 32.2% (Bureau of Justice Statistics, 2002a; Snell & Morton, p. 3). In 2009, one out of three women in U.S. prisons was there for a violent crime, compared to about 40% of male prisoners (Bureau of Justice Statistics, 2010a).

Snell and Morton (1994) also probed the gendered nature of the women's violence that resulted in their imprisonment. They noted that women prisoners were far more likely to kill an intimate or relative (50%, compared to 16.3%), whereas men were more likely to kill strangers (50.5%, compared to 35.1%). The last (1999) Bureau of Justice Statistics study that focused on women offenders showed similar findings. In 1998, over 93% of female homicide offenders killed an intimate, family member, or acquaintance. For men, only 76% killed someone they knew (see Table 3.6). Given the information already discussed in this book regarding the nature of women's violence and its relationship to their own histories and experiences of abuse, women's violent acts take on quite a different significance than men's violence.

Table 3.6   Relationship of Offender to Victim for Murder Offenses, 1998

Victim	Female	Male
Spouse	28.3%	6.8%
Ex-spouse	1.5	0.5
Child/stepchild	10.4	2.2
Other family member	6.7	6.9
Boyfriend/girlfriend	14.0	3.9
Acquaintance	31.9	54.6
Stranger	7.2	25.1
Number, 1976–1997	59,996	395,446

Source: Bureau of Justice Statistics. (1999). *Women Offenders* (p. 4). Washington, DC: U.S.Department of Justice.

Drugs and their role in women's violence are also apparent in these data; generally speaking, women doing time for crimes of violence were less likely to report a link between drugs and violence than women serving time for property or drug offenses. For example, only 11% of the women convicted of violent crimes used drugs at the time of their crime, compared to 25% of those serving time for property offenses, and 32% of those serving time for drug offenses (Bureau of Justice Statistics, 1999, p. 9). In Snell and Morton's (1994) study, the one exception to this generalization was found for women incarcerated for robbery. Not only did these women report that they were under the influence of the drug at the time of the robbery, but they were virtually the only women serving time for a violent offense who reported that they committed the offense "to get money for drugs" (p. 8). Women serving time for homicide were also slightly more likely to report greater use of drugs the month before the offense for which they were imprisoned and to report being under the influence of drugs at the time of the offense, but they rarely said that getting money to buy drugs was a motive for the crime.

Property Crimes

Many women in state prisons are serving time for larceny theft. Indeed, of the women serving time for property offenses (25.1% of all women in prison), about a third (30.2%) are doing time for larceny theft. This compares to only 18.2% of men who are doing time for property crimes. Fraud is another important commitment offense for women, accounting for 35% of women's but only 10.3% of men's, most serious property offenses. Men serving time for property offenses are more likely to be serving time for burglary (49.2%) (Bureau of Justice Statistics, 2010a).

Drug Use Among Women in Prison

Given the past history of the women in prison, it should come as no surprise that drug use, possession, and, increasingly, drug trafficking are themes in women's imprisonment. In 1979, only 10.5% of women in state prisons were serving time for drug offenses; by 1986, the proportion had increased to 12%; in 2006, 28.4% of all women in state prisons were doing time for drug offenses (Bureau of Justice Statistics, 1988, p. 3, 2010, p. 29; Snell & Morton, 1994, p. 3). Currently, over half of the women serving time for drug offenses are now serving time for drug trafficking. Although this offense sounds very serious, it must be placed in context. As we shall see later in this chapter, in a world where big drug deals are controlled almost exclusively by men (Green, 1996), women, many of whom are from desperately poor countries or from our own impoverished communities, are being cast or coerced into the role of serving as drug mules or couriers, only to be swept up in the escalating penalties that have characterized the past decade's war on drugs (Mauer & Huling, 1995).

National data on women in prison confirm that women prisoners have more problems with drugs than their male counterparts. Snell and Morton (1994) found that, contrary to the stereotype of the male drug addict committing crimes, "women in prison in 1991 used more drugs and used those drugs more frequently than men" (p. 7). For example, more female prisoners used drugs daily before imprisonment than male prisoners (41.5%, compared to 35.7%), and women were more likely than men to be under the influence of drugs when they committed the offense for which they were imprisoned (36.3%, compared to 30.6%). Finally, about a quarter of women in prison, but only a fifth of men, committed the offense for which they were imprisoned to buy drugs. Ominously, about a quarter of all women in prison had some form of drug treatment prior to imprisonment, and of those using drugs, 41.8% had treatment the month before their offense. These figures suggest that most interventions are not sufficient to help these women with their drug problems.

Cobbina's research (2009, 2010) also illustrates the strong role of drugs in women offenders' lives, criminal pathways, and their chances for successful reentry. In her interviews with 50 incarcerated or paroled women, 88 % of incarcerated and 79% of paroled women reported using drugs in their lifetimes (p. 38). "Of the women who used drugs, 74 percent of incarcerated women and 79 percent of paroled women had at least one member of their family who was drug addicted, indicating that women are more likely to use narcotic substances when members of their own family abuse drugs" (p. 38). A number of incarcerated (23%) and paroled (25%) women in the study stated that their initiation into the drug world began as a result of their exposure to illicit substances by their family during childhood or adolescence. Most stated that their desire for approval and acceptance by their peers and male intimate partner also influenced their decision. Finally, some stated they used drugs as a way to cope with negative life events (p. 37–38).

Women prisoners are also taking health risks by using drugs. Snell and Morton (1994) found that women prisoners were more likely than men to use needles to inject drugs (34%, compared to 24.3%) and to have shared needles with friends

(18%, compared to 11.5%). Again, contrary to many stereotypes, these rates were highest among White and Hispanic women, compared to African American women. For example, 41.6% of White women and 45.9% of Hispanic women had ever used a needle, compared to only 24% of African American women.

Perhaps as a result of these patterns, at the turn of the 21st century more women than men in prison were infected with HIV; in that year, 3.6% of all women in state prisons had the virus that causes AIDS, compared to 2.2% of male inmates. In New York, the state with the most HIV-positive female prisoners (600), the percentage of women inmates testing positive (18.2% of the female prison population) far outreached the percentage of male inmates testing positive for the virus (8%) (Maruschak, 2002). Although the number of inmates with HIV is decreasing overall, the rate is faster for men. Between 1999 and 2000, 7% fewer men in prison were known to be HIV positive; for women, the decrease was 2% (Maruschak, 2001, 2002).

Mothers Behind Bars

Nearly two thirds of women in prison have a child under the age of 18 (Glaze & Muraschak, 2008). Over the past two decades, the number of children who have a mother behind bars has increased 131% (Glaze & Muraschak, 2008). Many of these women will never see their children if this and other national studies (see Bloom & Steinhart, 1993) are accurate. Women in prison are five times more likely than men to have their children removed from immediate family members and placed into foster care or some other agency (Mumola, 2000).

Even those women who retain custody of their children are unlikely to see them. Snell and Morton (1994) found that 52.2% of the women with children under 18 had never been visited by their children. Most of the women who were able to be visited by their children saw them "less than once a month" or "once a month." More women were able to send mail to or phone their children, but even here, one in five never sent or received mail from their children, and one in four never talked on the phone with their children. This is despite the fact that many of these women, prior to their incarceration, were taking care of their children (unlike their male counterparts). More than 64% of mothers behind bars lived with their children prior to incarceration (Glaze & Muraschak, 2008). Moreover, because women's work is never done, it is more often the imprisoned woman's mother (the child's grandmother) who takes care of her children, whereas male inmates are more likely (89.7%) to be able to count on the children's mother to care of the child (Snell & Morton, p. 6).

These patterns are particularly pronounced among African American and Hispanic women. Black children are almost nine times more likely than White children to have a parent in prison and Hispanic children are three times more likely (Mumola, 2000; Sentencing Project, 2007). By age 14, among children born in 1990, the cumulative risk of parental imprisonment is 25.1–28.4% for African American children, while only 3.6–4.2% for White children (Foster & Hagan, 2009). Additionally, White female inmates more often report access to husbands as primary caretakers of their children, whereas African American women do not identify this as an option (Enos, 2001, p. 55). Although Black women and Hispanic women are more likely to share caretaking responsibilities with other family members and are less likely to rely upon foster care services, the ability of the family to effectively respond, both financially and emotionally, to the incarceration of a female family member with children is dependent upon social and economic status (Enos, 2001). This becomes highly problematic for women of color, because poverty and race are intertwined and families often have few resources to extend (Christian & Thomas, 2009).

Additionally, women of color are more likely to experience adverse parenting situations even before incarceration, as African American and Hispanic women more often live in communities that have intense exposure to dual modes of state intervention—the criminal justice system and child welfare services (Roberts, 2002). In Brown and Bloom's 2009 research on mothers on parole, nearly 24% ($n = 48$) of the women in this study had been involved with the state's Department of Human Services (DHS), Child Welfare Services Division for child maltreatment (p. 317). In addition, the state (or some other jurisdiction) had terminated the parental rights of 17% ($n = 34$) of the mothers in this study for one or more children. In the next chapter, a more in-depth discussion of mothering behind bars is developed.

RACE AND WOMEN'S IMPRISONMENT

Race as well as gender figures prominently in women's imprisonment. The numbers indicate that nearly half the women in the nation's prisons are women of color, notably 30% are African American and 16% are Hispanic (Sentencing Project, 2007). Moreover, the incarceration rate for African American women is nearly twice that of Hispanic women and 2.5 times that of White women: In 2009, one in 703 Black females was imprisoned, compared to about 1 in 1,987 White females and 1 in 1,356 Hispanic females (Bureau of Justice Statistics, 2010c).

Hidden in these data is the fact that the surge in women's imprisonment has disproportionately hit women of color in the United States. Further analysis of these survey data and other national data (Bureau of Justice Statistics, 2010c; Mauer, 2006; Mauer & Huling, 1995) has thoroughly documented the way in which the surge in women's imprisonment has been driven almost completely by a dramatic increase in the imprisonment of women of color. Although White women comprise 62% of women on probation, it is African American women who are most represented in jails and prisons.

Between 1986 and 1991, all women saw an increase in what Mauer and Huling (1995) call the "control rate" (the proportion of women under some form of correctional supervision—probation, jail, prison, or parole), but this rate jumped most dramatically for African American women. Although much of the nation's attention has been correctly focused on the horrific overcontrol of African American males whose control rate now approaches one out of every three young males between the ages of 20 and 29 (Mauer & Huling, 1995, p. 3), their sisters are also seeing increases in contact with the criminal justice system.

The control rate for African American women was 2.7% of all young women in 1989; by 1994, the rate had jumped 78% to 4.8% or 1 out of 20 young African American women) (Mauer & Huling, 1995, p. 5). The distance between the White and African American rates also widened so that well over three times as many young Black women have contact with the criminal justice system than do their White counterparts. Hispanic women have also seen their control rate increase by 18%, and their control rate is about double the rate for White women (2.2%).

Mauer and Huling (1995) present compelling evidence to support their contention that much of this increase can be laid at the door of the war on drugs, which many now believe has become a war on women, particularly on women of color. They also present a striking analysis of how the crackdown on drug use and trafficking has affected Black and Hispanic women. Specifically, although the number of women in state prisons for drug sales has increased by 433% between 1986 and 1991, this increase is far steeper for Hispanic women (328%) and for African American women (828%) than for White women (241%) (p. 20).

Huling (1995), in a subsequent paper, directly links these increases in women's incarceration to the fact that the war on drugs has been particularly harsh on those using and selling crack cocaine. This has a significant effect on African American women because "there are indications that women are more likely to use crack and are more likely to be involved in crack distribution sales relative to other drugs" (p. 8). Thus, she contends that, without much public fanfare, the war on drugs, and particularly the harsh penalties for the sale of crack cocaine (relative to powder cocaine and other drugs), has had a dramatic effect on the incarceration patterns of African American women. With the major focus of the drug war on low-level street users of crack cocaine, Black women, constructed by the media as *crack whores* and drug-addicted mothers, became "responsible" for crack's devastation in inner-city neighborhoods (see also Bush-Baskette, 1999, for similar argument). Consequently, Black women entered the criminal justice system at exacerbated rates.

Recall the research by English (1993) on women's and men's self-reported drug selling, wherein she found that female prisoners were much more likely than their male counterparts to report numerous small drug sales. This could mean that the patterns of women's drug selling, rather than the seriousness of their sales, expose them to more risk of arrest and incarceration.

The other hidden victims of the war on drugs are the women, many from foreign countries, who are serving time in U.S. prisons for being drug couriers. Huling (1996) notes that the lack of repatriation treaties between most "drug-demand countries" and "drug-supply countries" has meant that many drug couriers end up serving long prison terms in the country of their arrest. Initially, women from foreign countries entering the United States at airports, such as John F. Kennedy (JFK) in New York, were tried in federal court. As the federal prisons began to experience sharp increases in women's imprisonment, federal officials shifted the cases to state courts (Huling, 1996; see also English, 1993).

Reviewing the cases of women who were arrested at JFK airport during 1990 and 1991 for drug smuggling ($n = 59$), Huling (1996) found the following: Almost all (96%) had no history of involvement with the criminal justice system. Most

(95%) had not been convicted at trial but had instead plead guilty to a reduced charge. To avoid the New York laws that would have sentenced them to life terms, they plead guilty to a reduced charge that requires a "mandatory minimum" of 3 years to life in prison. Almost all of the women arrested were Hispanic (Huling, p. 53). Prosecutors, when asked about these patterns, argued that they had "no choice" but to pursue indictments for anyone found in possession of four ounces or more of an illegal drug.

Interviewing some of these women, Huling (1996) was able to document that many carried the drugs because of threats to their families, because they were trapped in abusive relationships with men involved in the drug trade, or because they had been duped or fooled. Despite this reality, Huling shows that New York politicians (including elected prosecutors) used the number of convictions of drug smugglers to document their "get tough on crime" stances, and despite a public outcry generated in part by Huling's work and the work of Sister Marion of Rikers Island, efforts to reform New York's harsh mandatory sentences failed.

DIFFERENT VERSUS EQUAL?

Given situations like those experienced by women charged with being drug smugglers, it should come as no surprise that the continuing debate over whether equality under the law is a good thing for women has special immediacy for those looking at the situation of women in the criminal justice system. To recap this debate (see Chesney-Lind & Pollock-Byrne, 1995, for a full discussion), some feminist legal scholars argue that the only way to eliminate the discriminatory treatment and oppression that women have experienced in the past is to push for continued equalization under the law; that is, to champion equal rights amendments and to oppose any legislation that treats men and women differently. They argue that although this may hurt in the short run, in the long run it is the only way that women will ever be treated as equal playing partners in economic and social spheres. For example, MacKinnon (1987) writes, "For women to affirm difference, when difference means dominance, as it does with gender, means to affirm the qualities and characteristics of powerlessness" (pp. 38–39). Even those who do not view the experience of women as one of oppression conclude that women will be victimized by laws created from "concern and affection" that are designed to protect them (Kirp, Yudof, & Franks, 1986).

The opposing argument is that women are not the same as men and because it is a male standard that equality is measured against, they will always lose. Therefore, one must consider differential needs (a sort of separate but equal argument). This would mean that women and men might receive differential treatment as long as it did not put women in a more negative position than the absence of such legislation. Conversely, the equalization proponents feel that, given legal and social realities, differential treatment for women will always be unequal treatment and by accepting different definitions and treatments, women run the risk of perpetuating the stereotype of women as different from and less than men.

One might reasonably ask how this legal debate, which has to date largely focused on the rights of women as workers, bears on women as prisoners. In fact, as the next section will demonstrate, the experience of women prisoners starkly illuminates some of the shortcomings of the conventional extremes of the different versus equal debate, because at different points in our nation's history, those who have imprisoned women have used each perspective to deal with the women they confined. This review of the history and current issues surrounding women's imprisonment will also highlight severe problems with the gender-blind approach to jailing women.

PRISONS AND PARITY

Initially, the differential needs approach was the dominant correctional policy. Almost from the outset, the correctional response to women offenders was to embrace the Victorian notion of "separate spheres" and to construct and manage women's facilities based around what were seen as immutable differences between men and women (Rafter, 1990). Women were housed in separate facilities and programs for women prisoners represented their perceived role in society. Thus, they were taught to be good mothers and housekeepers; vocational education was slighted in favor of domestic training. Women were hired to supervise female offenders in the belief that only they could provide for the special needs of female offenders and serve as role models for them. To some degree, this legacy still permeates women's prisons today. Typically, these prisons have sex-typed vocational programming and architectural differences (such as smaller living units and decentralized kitchens) in recognition of gender roles.

In sentencing, too, one could observe that the system treated women and men differently. Women were much less likely than men to be imprisoned unless the female offender did not fit the stereotypical female role, for example, if she was a "bad mother" who abused or abandoned her children, or if she did not have a family to care for (Chesney-Lind, 1987; Eaton, 1986). This resulted in one of the most dramatic disproportional ratios in criminal justice—women composed roughly only 4% of the total prison population for years. Of course, part of this was because most women committed far fewer serious crimes than men, but at least some part of the difference was due to sentencing practices (see Blumstein et al., 1983).

Certainly, the differential treatment of women in sentencing and prison programming is a thing of the past. Partially as a result of prisoner rights' litigation based on the parity model (see Pollock-Byrne, 1990), women offenders are being swept into a system that seems bent on treating women *equally*. Currently, the emphasis on women's prison construction and the architecture of women's prisons suggest that women get the worst of both worlds, correctionally. A couple of well-publicized scandals can serve to highlight the severe problems with a gender-blind approach to women's imprisonment.

In Alabama, the state reinstated male chain gangs with much fanfare in 1995, after they had been dropped in 1932 because of accounts of brutality and abuse.

The current practice involves men shackled in groups of five working along public highways, although some groups are assigned the job of breaking "large rocks into little ones" (Franklin, 1996, p. 8A). The country's current-get-tough-on-crime mood provided Alabama officials with the opening to reinstate these workgroups and even to involve some groups in grueling "busy work."

Alabama corrections officials were threatened with a lawsuit brought by male inmates suggesting that the practice of excluding women from the chain gangs was unconstitutional. The response from the Alabama Corrections Commissioner was to include women in the chain gangs (Franklin, 1996, p.3A). Ultimately, the governor forced the corrections chief to resign; the governor's spokesperson said simply, "It was just a philosophical difference. In his [the governor's] opinion, there is a difference in men and women (specifically) physically" (Hulen, 1996, p. A1

Although the issue of chain gangs for women is moot in Alabama, it has surfaced in other states. Proclaiming himself "an equal opportunity incarcerator," an Arizona sheriff has started one for women "now locked up with three or four others in dank, cramped disciplinary cells" (Kim, 1996, p. 1A). To escape these conditions, the women can *volunteer* for the 15-woman chain gang. Defending his controversial move, the sheriff commented, "If women can fight for their country, and bless them for that, if they can walk a beat, if they can protect the people and arrest violators of the law, then they should have no problem with picking up trash in 120 degrees" (p. 1A).

Other routine institutional practices, such as strip searches (sometimes involving body cavity searches), have also produced problems. In New York prisons, in response to complaints by male inmates that strip searches were often accompanied by beatings, video monitors (usually mounted on the wall) were installed in areas where searches occurred. When the women's prison, Albion Correctional Center, began to tape women's strip searches, though, fixed cameras were replaced by hand-held cameras (Craig, 1996, p. 1A). Fifteen women prisoners incarcerated at Albion filed complaints based on their experiences with strip searches. Specifically, they said that doors to the search area were occasionally kept open, that male guards were sometimes seen outside the doors watching the searches, and that, unlike the men's videos, which surveyed the whole room where the searches occurred, according to the women's lawyer, "these videotapes were solely focused on the woman. That amplified the pornographic effect of it" (Craig, 1996, p. 1A). Said one woman who was searched while men were "right outside a door and could see the whole incident, 'I knew they was watching . . . I was so humiliated . . . I felt like I was on display. I felt like a piece of meat'" (p. A6). Advocates for the women stressed the traumatic effect of such searches, given the histories of sexual abuse and assault that many women bring with them to prison.

Moreover, the women inmates suspected that prison officials were viewing the tapes and eventually filed complaints to stop routine videotaping of women prisoners. In addition to receiving over $60,000 in damages, the women were able to change the policy of routine videotaping of women's searches. As a result of their complaints, "a female inmate would be filmed only if officers believed she would resist the search" (Craig, 1996, p. A6). Presently, very few searches of women inmates are being videotaped in New York, but the possibility of abuse is present in almost all prisons.

Even without videotaping and other possible abuses, strip searches have quite different meanings for women and men. For example, a key point made by the Albion women was that, given the high levels of previous sexual abuse among women inmates, such searches had the possibility of being extremely traumatic. In fact, similar concerns have also surfaced in a Task Force Report to the Massachusetts Department of Health about the use of "restraint and seclusion" among psychiatric patients who have histories of sexual abuse (Carmen et al., 1996).

Finally, the most pervasive complaint that has accompanied women's imprisonment is the sexual abuse and harassment of women inmates by male guards. Owen's (1998) book, *In the Mix: Struggle and Survival in a Women's Prison,* includes the degrading experiences women encounter with male guards. Although the women in her study offered limited discussion about forced or consensual sexual relationships with staff, one woman illustrated the potential for harassment in day-to-day activities:

> If you are short, the officers, you can be seen from the (officer's) bubble. It is degrading. Sometimes you get a shower peeker. I told the other girls to block the shower. Then the officer got an attitude. You could tell. (p. 166)

As old as women's imprisonment (Beddoe, 1979), the sexual victimization of women in U.S. prisons is the subject of increasing news coverage and, more recently, international scrutiny. Scandals have erupted in California, Georgia, Hawaii, Ohio, Louisiana, Michigan, Tennessee, New York, and New Mexico (respectively, Stein, 1996; Meyer, 1992; Watson, 1992; Curriden, 1993; Sewenely, 1993; Craig, 1996; and Lopez, 1993), and the assumption has grown that prisons, here in the United States and elsewhere, are rife with this problem. So extensive is the concern that the issue has attracted the attention of Human Rights Watch (1993).

Details of these scandals yield the predictable charges and countercharges, but the storyline remains essentially unchanged; women in prisons, guarded by large numbers of men, are vulnerable. As one advocate for women in prison has noted, "We put [women] into an environment where they're controlled by men and men are willing to put their hands on them whenever they want to" (Craig, 1996, p. A1). The story that prompted this observation dealt with one of a series of sexual assaults reported by a young woman in a New York prison:

> Correctional officer Selbourne Reid, 27, came into the cell of a 21-year-old inmate at the maximum security prison in Westchester County. The inmate, at first asleep, was startled to find him in her cell. . . . On this night, Reid forced the woman to perform oral sex on him, according to the Westchester County district attorney's office. After he left, she spit the semen into a small bottle in her room. She told prison authorities about the attack, and gave them the semen for DNA analysis. (Craig, 1996, pp. 1A, 6A)

Similar accounts appear with distressing regularity, and even more disturbing is the fact that so few of the cases, unlike the one reported here, actually go to trial or result in the perpetrators being found guilty. Institutional subcultures in women's prisons that encourage correctional workers to cover for each other, coupled with inadequate protection accorded women who file complaints, make it unlikely that many women inmates will show the courage of the young woman in New York. Indeed, according to a memo filed by an attorney in the Civil Rights Division of the U.S. Department of Justice, the division found "a pattern of sexual abuse by both male and female guards" in Michigan women's prisons (Patrick, 1995).

Stein (1996 writes that a judge reviewing the situation of women in Washington D.C. jails noted that "the evidence revealed a level of sexual harassment which is so malicious that it violates contemporary standards of decency" (p. 24). If this is true, why do so few of these cases make it to court? Sadly, some of this involves the histories of women in prison, many of whom have engaged in prostitution, which allow the defendants to use the misogynist defense that it is impossible to rape a prostitute. Beyond this, the public stereotype of women in prison as *bad girls* means that any victim must first battle this perception before her case can be fairly heard. Finally, what little progress has been made is severely threatened by recent legislation that has drastically curtailed the ability of prisoners and advocates to sue over prison conditions (p. 24)—changes again likely to have been motivated by public perceptions of prisoners as violent men.

That women in prison are the recipients of "equity with a vengeance" does not necessarily mean that the abuses that used to exist in prisons that assumed gender difference have retreated completely. In fact, it appears that today's women in prison still receive some of the worst of the old separate spheres abuses, particularly in the area of social control. For example, McClellan (1994) examined disciplinary practices at men's and women's prisons in Texas. Using Texas Department of Corrections records, McClellan constructed two samples of inmates (271 men and 245 women) and followed them for a one-year period (1989). She documented that although most men in her sample (63.5%) had no citation or only one citation for a rule violation, only 17.1% of the women in her sample had such clear records. Women prisoners were much more likely to receive numerous citations and received them for different sorts of offenses than men. Most commonly, women were cited for "violating posted rules," whereas men were cited most frequently for "refusing to work" (p. 77). Finally, women were more likely than men to receive the most severe sanctions, including solitary confinement (p. 82).

McClellan's (1994) review of the details of women's infractions subsumed under the category "violation of posted rules" included such offenses as "excessive artwork ('too many family photographs on display'), failing to eat all the food on their plates, and for talking while waiting in the pill line" (p.85). Possession of contraband could include such things as an extra bra or pillowcase, peppermint sticks, or a properly borrowed comb or hat. Finally, "trafficking" and "trading" included instances of sharing shampoo in a shower and lighting another inmate's cigarette (p. 85).

McClellan (1994) concluded by observing that there exists "two distinct institutional forms of surveillance and control operating at the male and female facilities . . . this policy not only imposes extreme constraints on adult women but also costs the people of the State of Texas a great deal of money" (p. 87). Research like this provides clear evidence that women in prison are overpoliced and overcontrolled in institutional settings—a finding earlier researchers have noted, as well (see Burkhart, 1973; Mann, 1984). Whether this is an extension of historic interests in women's sexual behavior or whether, more prosaically, it is a function of the fact that, if men were controlled to the extent women were, they would probably riot, is unclear.

What is clear from all these accounts is that women in modern prisons may be subjected to the worst of both worlds. If McClellan's (1994) findings can be extended to other states, women in modern prisons continue to be overpoliced and overcontrolled (a feature of the separate-spheres legacy of women's imprisonment). At the same time, they are also the recipients of a form of equality that results in abuses that are probably unparalleled in male institutions (e.g., sexual exploitation by guards and degrading strip searches). Beyond this, correctional leaders are, in some cases, implementing grossly inappropriate and clearly male-modeled interventions, such as chain gangs and even boot camps, to deal with women's offenses (Elis, MacKenzie, & Simpson, 1992).

The enormous and rapid increase in women's imprisonment has clearly overwhelmed correctional officials who must scramble to come up with space, let alone programs, for the thousands of women coming through the doors (see Morash & Bynum, 1996). Yet prior to these huge population increases, things were not necessarily good for women inmates. Women inmates have never had the same range of programs as male offenders; this was often justified by their low numbers (see Pollock-Byrne, 1990). Because the current imprisonment boom has affected men's and women's facilities, even with larger numbers in women's prisons, women's special needs are unlikely to receive serious attention any time soon.

Some efforts have been made nationally, especially in improving the connection of children with their incarcerated mothers. For example, in California, some nonviolent female drug offenders are sentenced to Family Foundations, a community-based, residential drug treatment program, where they live with their children who are six and younger. The Women's Prison Association in New York assists women offenders in addressing the critical issues involved in women's pathways toward crime and in their successful return to the community after prison; these issues include substance abuse problems, victimization experiences, family disruption, housing needs, and vocational and employment issues (Conly, 1998). Lastly, the Children's Center in Bedford Hills, New York, allows women offenders to reside with their children until the children are one year of age. The women learn "to be good mothers," and the focus is on the women's mental health needs (National Institute of Justice, 1998, p. 8).

Despite programs such as these, there still exists a paucity of alternative and innovative approaches available to address women offenders' issues. A 1998 National Institute of Justice study demonstrates this point: in the study, state and prison-level administrators were asked to identify innovative programs for women in prison in their jurisdictions. Only three states reported high levels of innovative programming for women; 34 states identified none or limited availability (p. 6). On a more global level, given the differences between male and female prisoners, it seems extremely unlikely that women's experience of imprisonment will ever mirror men's experience—no matter how often the legal system insists on a gender-neutral stance. Nor, if the lessons are learned from these scandals, should women be treated as though they are men.

The abuses mentioned earlier force us to ask whether a gender-blind approach to imprisonment is fair or just. Is it the case that female prisoners are "disappearing" politically, in a country haunted by images of male drug kingpins and violent predators, because their convictions bolster those who are cynically manipulating the system and the public's fears to win an election? Finally, as the nation becomes increasingly aware of the surge in women's imprisonment from news accounts (LeBlanc, 1996), we need to question whether tax dollars spent on women's imprisonment could be better spent on programs for women in the community.

POLICY IMPLICATIONS AND WOMEN'S IMPRISONMENT

The United States now imprisons more people than at any time in its history and has the world's highest incarceration rate (Mauer, 1999, 2006). On any given day, over a million people are locked up, and an unprecedented number of prison cells are being planned. As a result, the fastest-growing sector of state and local economies, nationally, is correctional employment, which increased 108% during the 1990s, whereas total employment increased by just 13.5% (Center for the Study of the States, 1993, p. 2). Women in conflict with the law have become the hidden victims of the nation's imprisonment binge. Women's share of the nation's prison population, measured in either absolute or relative terms, has never been higher. Women were 4% of the nation's imprisoned population shortly after the turn of the 20th century. By 1970, the figure had dropped to 3%. By 2010, however, more than 7% of those incarcerated in state prisons in the country were women.

Is this increase in women's imprisonment being fueled by a similarly dramatic increase in serious crimes committed by women? The simple answer is *no*. As has been shown, the proportion of women in prison for violent crimes has dropped steadily, and the numbers of women incarcerated for petty drug and property offenses have soared. Large increases in women's imprisonment are due to changes in law-enforcement practices, judicial decision making, and legislative mandatory sentencing guidelines, rather than a shift in the nature of the crimes women commit.

As a nation, we face a choice. We can continue to spend our shrinking tax dollars on the pointless and costly incarceration of women guilty of petty drug and property crimes, or we can seek other solutions to the problems of drug-dependent women. Because so many of the women in prison in California are driven to drug use because of poverty and abuse, the real question before us is: detention or prevention?

The expansion of the female prison population has been fueled primarily by increased rates of incarceration for drug offenses, not by commitments for crimes of violence. The majority of women in America's prisons are sentenced for nonviolent crimes that are all too often a direct product of the economic marginalization of the women who find their way through the prison doors. As we have seen, changes in criminal justice policies and procedures over the past decade have contributed to the dramatic growth in the female prison population. Mandatory prison terms and sentencing guidelines are gender-blind and, in the crusade to get tough on crime, criminal justice policymakers have gotten tough on women, pushing them into jails and prisons in unprecedented numbers.

Most of these female offenders are poor, undereducated, unskilled, victims of past physical or sexual abuse, and single mothers of at least two children. They enter the criminal justice system with a host of unique medical, psychological, and financial problems.

The data summarized in this chapter suggest that women may be better served in the community because of the treatable antecedents and less serious nature of their crimes. A growing number of states are beginning to explore nonincarcerative strategies for women offenders, such as the ones aforementioned. Commissions and task forces charged with examining the effect of criminal justice policies on women are recommending sentencing alternatives and the expansion of community-based programs that address the diverse needs of women who come into conflict with the law.

In California, the Senate Concurrent Resolution (SCR) 33 Commission on Female Inmate and Parolee Issues examined the needs of women offenders. The commission's upcoming report is based on three central concepts:

1. Female inmates differ significantly from males in terms of their needs, and these gender-specific needs should be considered in planning for successful reintegration into the community.

2. Women are less violent in the community and in prison, and this fact provides opportunities to develop nonprison-based programs and intermediate sanctions without compromising public safety.

3. Communities need to share the responsibility of assisting in this reintegration by providing supervision, care, and treatment of women offenders (Bloom et al., 1994).

Although coming under some criticism in its effectiveness, California began a more gendered approach to corrections by developing nonprison institutions that housed incarcerated mothers with their children (see Haney, 2010).

Despite the growth of the female prison population, there has not been a commensurate increase in research devoted to the needs of these women, nor in designing prison treatment, discharge, and reentry programs specifically for female prisoners (Balis, 2007). One study (Morash, 2010) compared two sorts of philosophical approaches to supervision on probation and parole: one focused on compliance with rules and "equality" between male and females and the other focused on "gender responsive" issues in two Michigan counties. Reviewing probation and parole recidivism, Morash found that if attention is paid to women's unique-problems needs in a gender-responsive fashion (like focusing on domestic violence and the role of trauma in women's drug use), then building on women's strengths (e.g., the importance of relationships) produces better services and lower over-all recidivism. More importantly, she did not find that the gender-responsive approach backfired, sending more women back to jail or prison because of the more intensive supervision offered low-level female offenders, as some feared, because earlier studies of intensive supervision had produced just that outcome (pp. 147–148).

Overcrowding and overuse of women's prisons can be avoided by planning creatively for reduced reliance on imprisonment for women while reimagining and reinventing probation and parole to focus on gendered needs as well as cutting edge research on issues like drug addiction, trauma, and other challenges that plague women in the criminal justice system. Many advocate a moratorium on the construction of women's prisons and a serious commitment to the decarceration of women. They believe that every dollar spent locking up women could be better spent on services that would prevent women from resorting to crime. As one prisoner at the Central California Women's Facility commented,

> You can talk to them about community programs. I had asked my P.O. for help—but his supervisor turned him down. I told him that I was getting into a drinking problem, asked if he could place me in a place for alcoholics but he couldn't get permission. I was violated with a DUI—gave me eight months. I think people with psychological problems and with drug problems need to be in community programs. (Bloom et al., 1994, p. 8)

There are a range of effective residential and nonresidential community-based programs serving women offenders throughout the nation. Austin, Bloom, and Donahue (1992) reviewed limited program evaluation data and found the following common characteristics that appeared to influence successful program outcomes: continuum of care design, clearly stated program expectations, rules and sanctions, consistent supervision, diverse and representative staffing, coordination of community resources, and access to ongoing social and emotional support. They also suggested that promising approaches are multidimensional and deal specifically with women's issues.

As this chapter has indicated, we know what to do about crime, particularly crime committed by women. Any review of the backgrounds of women in prison immediately suggests better ways to address their needs. Whether it be more funding for drug treatment programs, more shelters for the victims of domestic violence, or more job training programs, the solutions to their problems are obvious. The question remains: Do we as a society have the courage to admit that the war on drugs (and indirectly on women) has been lost and at a great price (see Baum, 1996)? The hidden victims of that war have seen their petty offenses criminalized and their personal lives severely disrupted. *Is this our only choice?*

This chapter has suggested another choice. By focusing on strategies that directly address the problems of women on the economic and political margins rather than expensive and counterproductive penal policies, the pointless waste of the nation's scarce tax dollars could be stopped. To do this, there must be changes in public policy so that the response to women's offenses addresses human needs rather than the short-sighted objectives of lawmakers who often cannot see beyond the next sound bite or election. The greed of what might be called the *correctional industrial complex* must also be addressed. This term refers to those who benefit from prison construction (such as architectural and construction companies, unions representing prison guards, etc.), who might well seek to replace the mindless spending of the cold war with the equally mindless but profitable incarceration of the nation's poor and dispossessed.

Now that we have entered the new millennium, there are actually a few indications that some states are beginning to reexamine their incarceration practices. So, although the rate of women's imprisonment does stand at an historic high, the first decade of the new century saw several years in which the female rate of increase in imprisonment fell behind that of the male rate of increase. In 2009, fewer females (down 1%) were incarcerated than in 2008 (Bureau of Justice Statistics, 2010c).

Several states long associated with the women's imprisonment boom—notably California and New York—actually saw decreases in the number of women in their prisons. In California, the decrease that accelerated in 2001 was clearly tied to the passage of Proposition 36. This initiative, passed in 2000, diverted most people convicted of nonviolent drug possession to programs instead of prison. In the short time since its inception, it has caused the number of women sent to California prisons to drop by 10% (Martin, 2002, p. 1). The drop actually encouraged two Democratic lawmakers to propose closing one or two of California women's prisons in an attempt to address the state's budget deficit (p. 1).

California's experience provides a valuable lesson to the rest of the nation. Given the characteristics of the women in prison, it is clear that the decarceration of almost all of the women in United States prisons would not jeopardize public safety. Furthermore, the money saved could be reinvested in programs designed to meet women's needs, which would enrich not only their lives but the lives of many other women who are at risk for criminal involvement. Finally, by moving dollars from women's prisons to women's services, we will not only help women—we also help their children. In the process, we are also breaking the cycle of poverty, desperation, crime, and imprisonment, rather than perpetuating it.

DISCUSSION QUESTIONS

1. How has the war on drugs become a war against women, particularly African American women? Why do we have so many female drug offenders behind bars?

2. Compare and contrast the life histories of incarcerated women to incarcerated men. In what ways does gender matter in the lives of women who find themselves under the control of the criminal justice system?

3. This chapter has underscored several ways prison policies and supervision techniques in women's prisons are "male-modeled." How can we reshape these policies from being male-modeled to female-sensitive?

4. Imagine the United States implemented a nationwide policy to decarcerate women who are nonviolent offenders. What would be the positive and negative effects of such a policy?

SUGGESTED READINGS

Chesney-Lind, M., & Pasko, L. (2012). *The female offender: Girls, women, and crime* (3rd ed.). Thousand Oaks, CA: Sage.

Frost, N., Green, J., & Pranis, K. (2006). *Hard hit: The growth in women's imprisonment, 1977–2004*. New York, NY: Institute on Women and Criminal Justice.

Morash, M. (2010). *Women on probation & parole: A feminist critique of community programs and services*. Boston, MA: Northeastern University Press.

Owen, B. (1998). *In the mix: Struggle and survival in a women's prison*. New York: State University of New York.

WEBSITES

- Women's Prison Association
  http://www.wpaonline.org/institute/index.htm

- Women and Prison: A Site for Resistance
  http://womenandprison.org

- The Action Committee for Women in Prison
  http://www.acwip.net

- The Sentencing Project
  http://www.sentencingproject.org

REFERENCES

Anderson, S. (1994). *Comparison of male and female admissions one year prior to implementation of structured sanctions*. Salem: Oregon Department of Corrections.

Austin, J., Bloom, B., & Donahue, T. (1992). *Female offenders in the community: An analysis of innovative strategies and programs*. Washington, DC: National Institute of Corrections, National Council on Crime and Delinquency.

Balis, A. (2007). Female prisoners and the case for gender-specific treatment and reentry programs. In R. Greifinger (Ed.), *Public health behind bars: From prisons to communities*. New York, NY: Springer.

Baum, D. (1996). *Smoke and mirrors: The war on drugs and the politics of failure*. Boston, MA: Little, Brown.

Beddoe, D. (1979). *Welsh convict women.* Barry, Wales: Stewart Williams.

Bloom, B., Chesney-Lind, M., & Owen, B. (1994). *Women in prison in California: Hidden victims of the war on drugs.* San Francisco, CA: Center on Juvenile and Criminal Justice.

Bloom, B., & Steinhart, D. (1993). *Why punish the children?* San Francisco, CA: National Council on Crime and Delinquency.

Blumstein, A., Cohen, J., Martin, S. E., & Tonry, M. H. (Eds.). (1983). *Research on sentencing: The search for reform* (Vols. 1–2). Washington, DC: National Academy Press.

Brown, M., & Bloom, B. (2009). Reentry and renegotiating motherhood: maternal identity and success on parole. *Crime and Delinquency, 55*(2), 313–336.

Bureau of Justice Statistics. (1988). *Profile of state prison inmates, 1986.* Washington, DC: U.S. Department of Justice.

Bureau of Justice Statistics. (2002a). *Prisoners in 2001.* Washington, DC: U.S. Department of Justice.

Bureau of Justice Statistics. (2002b). *Probation and parole in 2001.* Washington, DC: U.S. Department of Justice.

Bureau of Justice Statistics. (2010a). *Prisoners in 2009.* Washington, DC: U.S. Department of Justice.

Bureau of Justice Statistics. (2010b). *Prison and jail inmates at midyear 2009.* Washington, DC: U.S. Department of Justice.

Bureau of Justice Statistics. (2010c). *Correctional populations in the United States, 2009.* Washington, DC: U.S. Department of Justice.

Burkhart, K. (1973). *Women in prison.* New York, NY: Doubleday.

Bush-Baskette, S. R. (1999). The war on drugs: A war against women? In S. Cook & S. Davies (Eds.), *Harsh punishment* (pp. 211–229). Boston, MA: Northeastern University Press.

California Department of Corrections and Rehabilitation. (2010). *California prisoners and parolees, 2009.* Sacramento, CA: Author.

Carmen, E., Crane, B., Dunnicliff, M., Holochuck, S., Prescott, L., Rieker, P., et al. (1996, January 25). *Massachusetts Department of Mental Health task force on the restraint and seclusion of persons who have been physically or sexually abused. Report and recommendations.* Boston: Massachusetts Department of Mental Health.

Center for the Study of the States. (1993, November). State-local employment continues to grow. Albany, NY: *Rockefeller Institute of Government, 15,* 2.

Chavkin, W. (1990). Drug addiction and pregnancy: Policy crossroads. *American Journal of Public Health, 80,* 483–487.

Chesney-Lind, M. (1987). Female offenders: Paternalism reexamined. In L. Crites & W. Hepperele (Eds.), *Women, the courts, and equality* (pp. 114–140). Newbury Park, CA: Sage.

Chesney-Lind, M. (2002). The unintended victims of mass incarceration. In M. Chesney-Lind & M. Mauer (Eds.), *Invisible punishment: The collateral consequences of mass imprisonment* (pp. 79–94). New York, NY: New Press.

Chesney-Lind, M., & Pollock-Byrne, J. (1995). Women's prisons: Equality with a vengeance. In J. Pollock-Byrne & A. Merlo (Eds.), *Women, law, and social control* (pp. 155–175). Boston, MA: Allyn & Bacon.

Christian, J., & Thomas, S. (2009). Examining the intersections of race, gender, and mass incarceration. *Journal of Ethnicity in Criminal Justice, 7*(1), 69–84.

Cobbina, J. E. (2009). *From prison to home: Women's pathways in and out of crime.* Unpublished PhD dissertation, University of Missouri, St. Louis.

Cobbina, J. E., Huebner, B. M., & Berg M. T. (2010). Men, women, and postrelease offending: An examination of the nature of the link between relational ties and recidivism.

Crime and Delinquency. (Published online before print October 18, 2010, doi: 10.1177/0011128710382348).

Conly, C. (1998). *The Women Prison's Association: Supporting women offenders and their families.* Washington, DC: National Institute of Justice.

Craig, G. (1996, March 23). Advocates say nude filming shows need for new laws. *Rochester Democrat and Chronicle,* pp. A1, A6.

Curriden, M. (1993, September 20). Prison scandal in Georgia: Guards traded favors for sex. *National Law Journal,* 8.

Daly, K., & Bordt, R. (1991). *Gender, race, and discrimination research: Disparate meanings of statistical "sex" and "race effects" in sentencing.* Department of Sociology: University of Michigan.

Eaton, M. (1986). *Justice for women?* Milton Keynes, England: Open University Press.

Elis, L., MacKenzie, D., & Simpson, S. (1992, October). *Women and shock incarceration.* Paper presented at the Focus group meeting, Department of Criminology, College Park, University of Maryland.

English, K. (1993). Self-reported crimes rates of women prisoners. *Journal of Quantitative Criminology, 9,* 357–382.

Enos, S. (2001). *Mothering from the inside: Parenting in a women's prison.* New York: State University of New York Press.

Federal Bureau of Investigation. (2010). *Crime in the United States—2009.* Washington, DC: U.S. Department of Justice.

Foster, H. &, Hagan, J. (2009). The mass incarceration of parents in America: Issues of race/ethnicity, collateral damage to children, and prisoner reentry. *The Annals of the American Academy of Political and Social Science, 623,* 179–194.

Franklin, R. (1996, April 26). Ala. to expand chain gangs—adding women. *USA Today,* p. 3A.

Glaze, L. E., & Bonczar, T. P. (2007). *Probation and parole in the United States, 2006.* Washington, DC: U.S. Department of Justice.

Glaze, L. E., & Bonczar, T. P. (2010). *Probation and parole in the United States, 2009.* Washington, DC: U.S. Department of Justice.

Glaze, L. E., & Maruschak, L. M. (2008, August). *Parents in prison and their minor children* (Special Report, rev. 2010). NCJ 222984. U.S. Department of Justice, Bureau of Justice Statistics.

Green, P. (Ed.). (1996). *Drug couriers: A new perspective.* London, England: Quartet.

Haney, L. (2010). *Offending women: Power, punishment, and the regulation of desire.* Berkeley, CA: University of California Press.

Hulen, T. (1996, April 28). *Governor's stand on women in chains: Insult or chivalry.* Birmingham News, pp. 1A, 2A.

Huling, T. (1995, November). *African American women and the war on drugs.* Paper presented at the annual meeting of the American Society of Criminology, Boston, MA.

Huling, T. (1996). Prisoners of war: Women drug couriers in the United States. In P. Green (Ed.), *Drug couriers: A new perspective* (pp. 46–60). London, England: Quartet.

Human Rights Watch. (1993). *The Human Rights Watch global report on prisons.* New York, NY: Human Rights Watch.

Kim, E. (1996, August 16). Sheriff says he'll have chain gangs for women. *Tuscaloosa News,* p. 1A.

Kirp, D., Yudof, M., & Franks, M. S. (1986). *Gender justice.* Chicago, IL: University of Chicago Press.

Langan, P. A. (1991, March 29). America's soaring prison population. *Science, 251,* 1569.

LeBlanc, A. (1996, June 2). A woman behind bars is not a dangerous man. *New York Times Magazine,* 34–40.

Lopez, S. (1993, July 8). Fifth guard arrested on sex charge. *Albuquerque Journal,* pp. A1, A2.

MacKinnon, C. (1987). *Feminism unmodified: Discourses on life and law.* London, England: Harvard University Press.

Mann, C. (1984). *Female crime and delinquency.* Tuscaloosa: University of Alabama Press.

Martin, M. (2002, April 21). Changing population behind bars: Major drop in women in state prisons. *San Francisco Chronicle.*

Maruschak, L. (2001). *HIV in prisons and jails, 1999.* Washington, DC: Bureau of Justice Statistics.

Maruschak, L. (2002). *HIV in prisons, 2000.* Washington, DC: Bureau of Justice Statistics.

Mauer, M. (1999). *The crisis of the young African American male and the criminal justice system.* Washington, DC: The Sentencing Project.

Mauer, M. (2006). *Race to incarcerate.* New York, NY: New Press.

Mauer, M., & Huling, T. (1995). *Young black Americans and the criminal justice system: Five years later.* Washington, DC: The Sentencing Project.

McClellan, D. S. (1994). Disparity in the discipline of male and female inmates in Texas prisons. *Women and Criminal Justice, 5*(2), 71–97.

Meyer, M. (1992, November 9). Coercing sex behind bars: Hawaii's prison scandal. *Newsweek,* 23–25.

Morash, M. (2010). *Women on probation & parole: A feminist critique of community programs and services.* Boston, MA: Northeastern University Press.

Morash, M., & Bynum, T. (1996). *Findings from the national study of innovative and promising programs for women offenders.* East Lansing: Michigan State University, School of Criminal Justice.

Morgan, E. (2000). Women on death row. In R. Muraskin (Ed.), *It's a crime: Women and justice* (pp. 269–283). Upper Saddle River, NJ: Prentice Hall.

Motivans, M. (2008). *Federal justice statistics, 2005.* Rockville, MD: Urban Institute.

Motivans, M. (2010). *Federal justice statistics, 2007.* Rockville, MD: Urban Institute.

Mumola, C. J. (2000, August). *Bureau of Justice Statistics special report: Incarcerated parents and their children.* NCJ 182335. Washington, DC: U.S. Department of Justice, Bureau of Justice Statistics.

National Advocates for Pregnant Women. (2011). *Medical and public health statements on the prosecution and punishment of pregnant women.* New York, NY: National Advocates for Pregnant Women.

National Institute of Justice. (1998). *Women offenders: Programming needs and promising approaches.* Washington, DC: Author.

Noble, A. (1988). *Criminalize or medicalize: Social and political definitions of the problem of substance use during pregnancy.* Sacramento, CA: Department of Health Services, Maternal and Child Health Branch.

Owen, B. (1998). *In the mix: Struggle and survival in a women's prison.* New York, NY: State University of New York.

Patrick, D. L. (1995, March 27). Letter to Gov. John Engler, Re: Crane and Scott Correctional Centers.

Pollock-Byrne, J. (1990). *Women, prison, and crime.* Pacific Grove, CA: Brooks/Cole.

Raeder, M. (1993, June). Gender and sentencing: Single moms, battered women and other sex-based anomalies in the gender free world of the federal sentencing guidelines. *20 Pepperdine Law Review 905.*

Rafter, N. H. (1990). *Partial justice: Women, prisons and social control.* New Brunswick, NJ: Transaction Books.

Roberts, D. (2002). *Shattered bonds: The color of child welfare.* New York, NY: Basic Civitas Books.

Sentencing Project. (2007). *Women in the criminal justice system.* Washington, DC: Author.

Sewenely, A. (1993, January 6). Sex abuse charges rock women's prison. *Detroit News,* pp. B1, B7.

Singer, L. R. (1973). Women and the correctional process. *American Criminal Law Review, 11,* 295–308.

Snell, T. L., & Morton, D. C. (1994). *Women in prison. (Special report).* Washington, DC: Bureau of Justice Statistics.

Stein, B. (1996, July). Life in prison: Sexual abuse. *The Progressive,* pp. 23–24.

Streib, V. (2011). *Death penalties for female offenders.* Retrieved from www.law.onu.edu/faculty/streib/femdeath.htm

U.S. Sentencing Commission. (2010). *2009 Datafiles.* Washington, DC: Author.

Watson, T. (1992, November 16). Ga. indictments charge abuse of female inmates. *USA Today,* p. A3.

West, H. C. (2010). *Prison inmates at mid-year—Statistical tables.* NCJ 230113. Bureau of Justice Statistics.

CHAPTER 4

Pregnancy and Motherhood Behind Bars

Zelma W. Henriques and Bridget P. Gladwin

INTRODUCTION

Of all the industrialized nations in the world the United States has the distinction of having the highest rate of incarceration. Recent studies have documented that our reliance on incarceration and our expanding prisons is going to accomplish less and cost more than it has in the past (Clear, 2007). The increasing rate of incarceration is not confined to men. The rapid growth of the female offender population is cause for concern. For example, between 1977 and 2007, there has been an increase of over *832%!* The male population grew 416% during the same period (West & Sabol, 2008). The majority of incarcerated women are mothers to at least one minor child, which makes the above increase in females incarceration rates even more worrisome. The story presented in Box 4.1 graphically highlights the problem of incarcerating mothers, and their experience with criminal justice agencies.

Box 4.1   Incarcerated Mothers and Child Experience

A child screams and cries out for her mother, "Mama, Mama, what's happening?" The mother is on her knees with her head lowered as handcuffs are firmly secured around her wrist. A young boy breaks away from the arms that held him and rushes to the police officer yelling, "Stop, don't hurt her. Leave my Mama alone. She ain't done nothing." The boy continues to thrash out, trying to rescue his mother amid a scene of confusion of blue and white rotating siren lights and dogs barking. (Bartlett, 2000)

STATISTICS ON INCARCERATION AND FAMILIES

- Nationally, more than 8.3 million children have parents under correctional supervision (either in prison, jail, on probation, or parole).
- More than 1.7 million children have a parent in state or federal prison.

- Nearly 62% of women in state prisons and 51% of men in state prisons are parents of children under 18.
- Women in state prisons are more likely than men in state prisons to have more than one child.
- Almost 68% of mothers in state prison report that their children live with a grandparent or other relative. The corresponding figure for incarcerated fathers is more than 17%.
- 62% of women incarcerated in state prisons are parents, and 84% of women incarcerated in federal prisons are mothers held in facilities that are over 100 miles from their last residence. In federal prisons, about 43% of parents are held over 500 miles from their last residence.
- Maintaining family ties can lessen the destructive aspects of parental incarceration by helping children process their mother's absence, easing family reunification after release, bolstering children's wellbeing and healthy development, and decreasing the likelihood that a mother will return to prison. (Correctional Association of New York, 2009)

While it is the intention of this chapter to discuss the subject of pregnancy and motherhood behind bars, a critical issue that must be examined is *why* there are so many women behind bars. Although this was discussed at length in the previous chapter by Pasko and Chesney-Lind (Chapter 3), it is important to reemphasize some of the causes as they are relevant to the discussion presented in this chapter.

This stunning growth of incarcerated women over the last twenty-five years has largely been fueled by several factors such as: (1) the war on drugs; (2) state mandatory minimum sentencing guidelines that largely dictate sentences based on the total quantity of drugs, resulting in judges having little discretion to consider the level or circumstances of women's involvement in an underlying drug offense, even though women very rarely play a central role in the drug trade; and (3) the equity or parity model of justice which emphasizes treating female offenders as though they were men, particularly when the outcome is punitive, in the name of equal justice. It would appear, therefore, that the three main factors related to the increased incarceration of women are: increase in criminal activity, particularly drug offending (war on drugs); policy changes; and applications of the male model of incarceration (Chesney-Lind, 1998).

An area of additional concern is that women of color have been disproportionately affected. In 2005, Black women were more than three times as likely as White women to be incarcerated, and Latina women were 60% more likely. African American and Latina women therefore, make up a disproportionate number of the women arrested, charged, and incarcerated for drug crimes (Brown, 2010). Bloom, Owen, and Covington's 2003 National Institute of Corrections report on "Gender-Responsive Strategies," notes that the majority of women (approximately 85%), in the criminal justice system are on either probation or parole supervision (i.e., community corrections). Two thirds of these women are White. In contrast, women in prisons and jails (institutions) are more likely to be women of color (see Table 4.1).

| Table 4.1 | Characteristics of Women Under Correctional Supervision | | | |

Characteristic	Percentage Under Community Supervision	Percentage in Jail	In State Prison	Percentage in Federal Prison
Race/ethnicity				
White	62	48	33	29
African American	27	44	48	35
Hispanic	10	15	15	32
Median age	32	31	33	36
High School	60	55	56	73
Diploma/GED	42	48	47	34
Single	Unknown	60	62	Unknown
Unemployed	72	70	65	59
Mother of Minor Children				

Source: B. Bloom, B. Owen, & S. Covington (2003). *Gender Responsive Strategies.* National Institute of Corrections.

PROFILE OF FEMALE OFFENDERS

- Minorities overrepresented in their early to mid-30s
- History of substance abuse problems
- History of physical and sexual abuse
- Mental and emotional disorders
- From fragmented families that include other family members who have also been involved with the criminal justice system
- Mothers of minor children
- Single mothers
- Majority have never been married
- Majority did not complete high school
- Poor economic conditions
- Limited or no work experience
- Low self-esteem
- Usually accomplices to males
- Criminal acts motivated by concerns about relationships
- Most likely to have been convicted of a drug offense or other nonviolent offenses

Since 75%–80% of female offenders are mothers, what to do with young children has become a more pressing concern for correctional systems. In 2007, 1.7 million children had a parent incarcerated in a state or federal prison in the United States, representing an increase of 80% since 1991 (Glaze & Maruschak, 2008). Racial differences are seen as one examines the racial description of parents within the general prison population. In 2007, approximately 48% of the mothers behind bars were White, with Black and Hispanic mothers representing 28% and 17% respectively (Glaze & Maruschak, 2008). Table 4.2 illustrates the actual numbers, by race of mothers behind bars for the year 2007.

Table 4.2   Estimated Number of Mothers in State and Federal Prisons by Race, 2007

Race/Ethnicity	Number of Mothers	Number of Children
White	29,000	60,000
Black	16,100	39,600
Hispanic	8,800	22,900
Total*	58,200	131,000

Source: L. E. Glaze & L. M. Maraschak. (2008). *Parents in prison and their minor children* (Special report). U.S. Department of Justice, Bureau of Justice Statistics.

*Includes other races such as American Indians, Alaska Natives, Asians, Native Hawaiians, other Pacific Islanders and persons identifying 2 or more races.

Note: The overrepresentation of Blacks and Hispanics is relative to the general population.

THE PROBLEM FOR THE CORRECTIONAL SYSTEM

Incarcerated women who are pregnant or have recently given birth present a particular challenge to correctional systems. Researchers such as Boudouris (1996) and Goshin and Byrne (2009) noted that when dealing with pregnant inmates the following issues must be addressed:

- Should these women be treated any differently than other incarcerated women?
- Who should provide for their children?
- Should infants live in correctional institutions with their incarcerated mothers?
- Does mother-child bonding in prisons, play a role in the rehabilitation of women who are mothers?
- What can correctional institutions realistically provide for inmates and their families?

Some of these questions are not new. A national survey in 1948 indicated that state correctional facilities in the United States generally chose to return pregnant inmates to local jails or transfer them to a community co-residence alternative site. This was done for the duration of their pregnancy and for a period of time following delivery of a child, in lieu of incarcerating newly delivered women without their infants (Shepard & Zemans, 1950). At the time of the 1948 survey, 13 states had statutory provisions allowing incarcerated mothers to keep their children in prison with them (e.g., prison nurseries). However, certain concerns led to the closure of many of the nursery programs by the 1970s. These concerns centered around the following: (a) security, (b) program management, (c) civil liability and the potential adverse effects of the prison environment on child health and development, and (d) the difficulty of eventual separation of mother and child for women with long sentences (Brodie, 1982; Radosh, 1988).

Ten years later, by the 1980s, prison nurseries were again considered the best theoretical solution to the problem of incarcerating women with infants but not necessarily practical for financially-burdened systems (Baunach, 1986). Therefore, the issues of female incarceration and what to do with young children remain and have become more pressing as we rely increasingly on prisons to punish.

Some contend that prison is not an ideal atmosphere for children (Women's Prison Association [WPA], 2009; Goshin & Byrne, 2009). Others have expressed concerns that children who spend their early years in prison will grow to accept this as a normative setting (Drummond, 2000). Despite these concerns, it is important to acknowledge the fact that keeping mothers and children together maybe far less harmful than separating the mother and child during a period of incarceration. To this end, state correctional systems, are continuously searching for gender-responsive programs for female inmates which are aimed at maintaining the mother-child relationship. Nursery programs have seen resurgence in spite of their costs. In a 1998, survey of parenting programs in 40 women's prisons in three states—New York, Nebraska, and South Dakota—reported functioning nursery programs (Pollack, 2002). By 2001, a survey by the National Institute of Corrections (NIC) revealed that an additional four states had implemented nursery programs—Massachusetts, Montana, Ohio, and Washington. As of August 2008, seven states provided nursery programs in at least one of their women's facilities: Illinois, Indiana, Massachusetts, Nebraska, New York, South Dakota, and Washington State. By 2010, five additional states have implemented nursery programs—Idaho, Ohio, Tennessee, Texas, and West Virginia. A total of 12 states now have nursery programs (The Rebecca Project, 2010).

Before examining in detail, the issues connected with the bonding between mother and child when the mother is incarcerated, issues of pregnant women who become incarcerated must be addressed. It is therefore important to look at federal and state policies on prenatal care and the shackling of pregnant inmates. While there is no systematic documentation at the state or at the federal level of how many women give birth while incarcerated, the 2007 Bureau of Justice Statistics (BJS) stated that, on average, 5% of women who enter into state prisons are pregnant and 6% of women in jails are pregnant. The issue of women being pregnant and giving birth while incarcerated presents many problems for correctional administrators. These problems focus on prenatal care, shackling, pregnancy, and birth programs.

Prenatal Care

Thirty-eight states have failed to institute adequate policies requiring that incarcerated pregnant women receive adequate prenatal care, despite the fact that many women in prison have high-risk pregnancies (The Rebecca Project, 2010). High-risk pregnancies are due to certain economic and social problems experienced by women that led them to be incarcerated. These problems include poverty, lack of education, physical and sexual abuse, and inadequate health care. These high-risk pregnancies are often complicated by drug and alcohol abuse, smoking, and sexually transmitted infections (Hotelling, 2008).

Shackling

Shackling is any combination of handcuffs, leg irons, chains over the shoulders, and belly chains used to confine or restrict the movements of an inmate. It used to be customary for jails and prisons to use restraints on pregnant women whenever they leave the institution and even in labor and delivery. This was done as a matter of course regardless of whether the woman has a history of violence, history of abscondence/escape, or her state of consciousness. This practice is based on using the male model of incarceration (The Rebecca Project, 2010). Such practice considered to be barbaric and meant that women were often shackled to their hospital beds, and correctional officers maintained control of the keys. In one case, a woman reported that when the delivery began, the officer could not be found to unlock her shackles. Thus she could not part her legs (Amnesty International, 1999).

The American College of Obstetricians and Gynecologists (ACOG) released a statement in June 2007, supporting an end to the practice of shackling mothers in labor and delivery. The ACOG argued that the physical restraints have interfered with the ability of physicians to safely practice medicine by reducing their ability to assess and evaluate the physical condition of the mother and fetus. Such practice has made the labor and delivery process more difficult than it needs to be and consequently puts both mother and unborn life at risk. Accordingly, many states began to adopt laws against the harmful practice of shackling, supporting the departure from such practice (The Rebecca Project, 2010).

In 2008, the Federal Bureau of Prisons ended the routine use of restraints for women in labor and limited shackling to cases in which a woman presents a danger to herself, the baby, or the staff. Five states have similar policies. New York State became the sixth, when Governor Patterson signed the "Anti-Shackling Bill" (S.1290-A/A.3373-A). The New York State Senate and Assembly passed this legislation on May 20, 2009. This historic legislation prohibits the inhumane practice of shackling pregnant inmates who are in labor. This bill also prohibits state and local correctional authorities from using restraints on a pregnant female inmate who is being transported for childbirth, during labor and delivery, and in postnatal recovery. An exception to this rule is made under extraordinary circumstances where restraints are determined to be necessary to prevent the woman from injuring herself, medical, or correctional personnel. In these instances, a pregnant woman may be cuffed by one wrist.

Currently 10 states have implemented policies on prohibiting or limiting shackling. These states are: California, Colorado, Illinois, New Mexico, New York, Pennsylvania, Texas, Vermont, Washington, and West Virginia. Of the states without laws to address shackling, 22 states either have no policy at all addressing when restraints can be used on pregnant women or have a policy which allows for the use of dangerous leg irons or waist chains (The Rebecca Project, 2010).

Pregnancy and Birth Programs

Recognizing that there is a need for effective birth education and support for incarcerated women, some states have doula birth support programs. Schroeder and Bell (2005) provide an ongoing multiagency doula program which provides emotional and physical support for pregnant women in urban jails located in King's County, Washington. In Cook County, Chicago, Illinois, the Bureau of Health Services began the doula program for incarcerated women in 2001. The target population is women who are likely to give birth while incarcerated in the Cook County jail. Doulas are trained to provide physical, emotional, and informational support to these women during pregnancy, birth, and postpartum. The doulas then proceed to provide incarcerated women with prenatal education, continuous support throughout the entire labor and birth, and daily postpartum hospital visits (Hotelling, 2009).

Motherhood Behind Bars

In 2003, the National Institute of Corrections (NIC) published a report on gender-responsive interventions for incarcerated women. The report acknowledged that the majority of incarcerated women are mothers, that these mothers desire above all else to maintain ties with their children (Bloom, Owen, & Covington, 2003; Goshin & Byrne, 2009; Henriques 1982). Morash and Schram (2002) wrote, "Even though some incarcerated mothers may endure feelings of failure and loss and have little or no contact with their children, their identification as mothers is central" (pp. 74–75). The NIC report emphasized the effect that poverty, trauma, and substance abuse have on incarcerated women. A number of disorders are known to be related to traumatic experience. Posttraumatic stress disorder (PTSD) is the most obvious and well recognized. There is also a high level of comorbidity between PTSD and depression, anxiety, substance abuse, and many physical disorders. The connection between addiction and the trauma for women is intricate and not easily disentangled. When you consider these factors for women who are or become mothers while incarcerated, the scope and complexity of the problem become evident.

While conventional society views prisons as places of punishment and terror, there is a mounting body of evidence that, for some, prisons are, in fact, viewed as safe havens—places of relative comfort and stability (Henriques & Jones-Brown, 2000). Pregnant women are assured of shelter they might not have had outside of imprisonment. In jail or prison, they are protected from homelessness, malnutrition, and substance abuse; they are housed, fed, and clothed. Many women are also separated from their abusive partners and their access to alcohol, cigarettes, and recreational drugs. In fact, some women have reported they actually violated their terms of probation when they found out they were pregnant so that they would be incarcerated, and thus be able to protect their babies (Spryas cited in Hotelling, 2008).

Children of prison inmates appear to be the hidden victims of their parents' crime. They often show signs of distress caused by the lack of a stable home life and parental separation. Studies have shown that children of incarcerated persons are more likely to experience: (1) anxiety, depression, aggression, (2) decline in school performance, attention disorders, and truancy, and (3) teen pregnancy and symptoms of posttraumatic stress. These are not the only problems. Evidence indicates that many of these children follow their parents into the criminal justice system (Gabel & Johnston, 1995; Simmons, 2000). It is noteworthy that the basic premise of the intergenerational cycle of incarceration suggests that children who experience traumatic childhood events like abuse, neglect, and parental addiction in addition to parental incarceration, are more likely than other children to be imprisoned themselves (Dalley & Michels, 2009). Understanding the impact of parental incarceration on children is complicated because negative outcomes may be related to any number of variables—parent-child separation, the crime and arrest that preceded incarceration, or general instability, poverty, and inadequate care at home. The degree to which a child is affected by a parent's separation may be due to other factors such as the age at which the child is separated from the parent, the length of the separation, the level of disruption and the availability of family or community support (Parke & Clark-Stewart, 2003).

Whatever the reasons for the negative outcomes on the children of incarcerated mothers, it is clear that intervention is needed to change these outcomes. What should these interventions be? Correctional systems have initiated a variety of programs aimed at addressing the problems resulting from the incarceration of mothers. The programs include prison nurseries, community-based residential facilities, parenting education programs, parent visitation programs, and telephone and correspondence programs.

Prison Nurseries

The primary goal of most prison nurseries is to promote bonding between mothers and children while giving mothers tools to become better parents. A secondary goal is to reduce recidivism among incarcerated mothers by encouraging them to make lifestyle changes following release.

State departments of corrections are funded by taxpayers. While there is limited information on what it costs to operate prison nurseries, we know that the costs vary from state to state. Washington State provides a model on how to operate a nursery program in a cost-effective way. In Washington State, in order to underwrite the costs of their prison nursery, money from social services budgets is used to supplement the cost. Rowland & Watts (as cited in Goshin & Byrne, 2009) write that Washington State additionally partners with community-based organizations to obtain support.

When children are placed in prison nurseries, it enables them to bond with their mothers and facilitates positive early childhood development. In these settings, both mothers and their infant children receive professional support which they would not otherwise receive in the community. This is beneficial to their overall wellbeing. Whatever prison nurseries cost the correctional systems, the overall benefits to society far outweigh these costs. When a mother is incarcerated, young children are frequently placed in foster care. The psychological and mental health care and other related costs which are a consequence of separating mothers from their children are well documented (WPA, 2009). Programs such as foster care, welfare, special education programs, and future incarceration are decidedly more costly than funding programs that might help to reduce the negative outcomes which are evident in the children of incarcerated mothers. Failure to provide these programs for incarcerated mothers may cost the society more in the long run. In addition, such programs may also facilitate drug rehabilitation and reduce overall recidivism among this population.

Much has been said about the importance of prison nurseries. During this century, New York State has led the movement to provide long-term nursery care for children born to incarcerated women. While other states have had nursery programs at some point, only New York has provided long-term nursery care continuously for 111 years. New York established its first long-term care nursery in 1901, in what is now known as the Bedford Hills Correctional Facility. In 1930, Governor Franklin D. Roosevelt signed a New York State correction law bill: Section 611 (see Appendix 4.5). This bill allowed women in New York State prisons and jails to keep their babies with them for 12 months. Under current program guidelines, women in New York State prisons may keep their babies 12 to 18 months.

In 1990, New York established a second nursery program at Taconic Correctional Facility, a medium security facility for women, near the Bedford Hills Correctional facility. The Taconic nursery was started under a federal grant and supported by New York State funds. Unlike the nursery at Bedford Hills, the Taconic nursery is specifically for women with substance abuse problems. In addition to parent education, substance abuse treatment is a mandatory part of the nursery program.

Box 4.2   **The New York Experience**

In 1995, a not-for-profit, nonsectarian organization called Hour Children was established with a mission to support families in the criminal justice system in New York State. As Hour Children grew and became a strong presence in New York State prisons, they received a family services contract from the New York State Department of Correctional Services to manage the Taconic nursery, and among other services, to manage an enhanced

(Continued)

(Continued)

mother-child visitation program in the prison's visiting room. Because of the need for supportive services for women coming out of prison, Hour Children provides transitional housing for mothers and their babies coming out of New York State prisons or for women reuniting with children who have been living either in foster care or with family members. Of three residences dedicated to mothers coming out of prison, one residence is the only official New York State work release site for a woman to live with her infant. The other two residences provide affordable, permanent, supportive housing for 12 families. In February 2010, Hour Children, launched a new mentoring program. This innovative program will mentor adult female offenders' prerelease and postrelease, provide training to the mentors, and provide transitional services to assist women with reintegration back to their communities. This program is one of 36 awarded across the nation by the U.S. Department of Justice's Bureau of Justice Assistance with funding from the Second Chance Act. The driving force behind Hour Children is Sister Theresa Fitzgerald whose passion for helping female offenders has led her to establish much needed programs to help women in and out of New York State prisons (for information on these programs go to: www.hourchildren.org).

Besides the Hour Children program, New York State is fortunate to have the Women's Prison Association and Home Inc. (WPA). This is a not-for-profit agency which has been in existence over 150 years. Among their many programs, WPA works to create opportunities for change in the lives of women prisoners, ex-prisoners, and their families (for more information on WPA programs go to www.wpaonline.org).

Descriptions of other nursery programs which are in operation in prisons in other states as of 2008 are described in Appendix 4.1 (At the time the chapter was written, the state of California had to abandon its nursery program due to budgetary constraints). Only one jail has a functioning nursery program—Rikers Island (see Appendix 4.3) (WPA 2009).

| Box 4.3 | **The Effectiveness of Nursery Programs** |

Like many other inmates at the Ohio Reformatory for Women, Amanda Burns didn't learn her lesson the first time she was incarcerated. After being released in 2000, she was arrested again a year later for trying to cash stolen checks and was sentenced to 11 more months in prison.

But her latest stint in Marysville has been different. For the past four months she's shared a room in the prison's 16-month-old nursery with her infant daughter Rhianna, who was born earlier this year while Burns was serving her sentence.

Burns said becoming a mother and spending time with her daughter has changed her. "Honestly, if I didn't have Rhianna, I probably would still be going," said Burns, 22, during an interview at the nursery earlier this month.

Source: Ghose (2002). Stateline.org is a nonpartisan, nonprofit news service of the Pew Center on the States that reports and analyzes trends in state policy.

Empirical data on mothers who have participated in prison nursery programs indicates that the primary goal of nursery programs appears to have been met in the decreased rates of recidivism. For example, all states with nursery programs report significant reductions in the recidivism rate of women who participated in a nursery program as compared with those who did not. On March 29, 2011, the Illinois Department of Corrections reported a 0% recidivism rate during the four years of operation of their nursery program "Moms and Babies" (Illinois Department of Correction News). The Ohio Reformatory for Women reports an 11% recidivism rate for women who participated in the nursery program as compared with 30% for nonparticipants. In Nebraska, the recidivism rate for women who participated in the nursery program was 9% as opposed to 33% for those who had not (WPA, 2009). Washington State reports a 10% recidivism rate for their nursery participants. New York reports similar statistics.

Attachment is directly linked to child development (Azar, 1995). Therefore, prison nurseries create environments that support age-appropriate development. Children are not simply housed while the mothers serve their sentences. The oldest U.S. nursery, Bedford Hills Correctional Facility in New York State, has a day care center and emphasizes developmentally stimulating materials in the infant sleeping and recreation areas. Three of the newer nurseries grew from existing parent education programs, and the majority mandate prenatal and infant care education for woman participants (Goshin & Byrne, 2009).

Goshin and Byrne's 2009 research clearly demonstrates that children in a prison nursery program exhibit measurable rates of secure attachment consistent or exceeding population norms. This is in stark contrast to children raised in the community during maternal incarceration.

Community-Based Residential Parenting Programs

Community-based residential parenting (CBRP) programs divert women, and in some cases, mothers of young children, from prison. They offer women an opportunity to serve out court imposed sentences in the community. Many of the programs are designed for women who have histories of substance abuse and provide treatment alongside parenting support. These programs are utilized at various stages of the criminal justice system, from pretrial through incarceration, as a condition of parole, or as a requirement for probation.

CBRP programs are different from prison nurseries.

- They are often operated by not-for-profit organizations that partner, or have contracts, with local departments of corrections to provide supervision, housing, and social services in a community setting.
- The women are usually allowed to gain approval to leave the facilities to attend doctor's appointments, social services appointments, or other programs in the community.
- The facility settings are often home-like, with mother and child sharing a private bedroom.

Community-based residential parenting programs share one of the same goals as nursery programs—to promote bonding between mother and child. However, unlike prison nurseries, the children who participate in CBRP programs are not necessarily born in custody. Mothers are often allowed to bring their small children with them into the program. Most CBRP programs allow children to stay with their mothers until they reach school-age. The duration of the child's stay is often tied to the length of the mother's sentence (WPA, 2009). Community-based residential parenting programs for states and the Federal Bureau of Prisons are described in Appendix 4.2, and 4.4 (WPA, 2009).

Prison nurseries and community-based residential facilities are the more desirable intervention strategies currently in use for women under criminal justice supervision, and their infant children (Goshin & Byrne, 2009). The rationale for investing in these programs rests upon the evidence that early mother-child bonding results in positive future outcomes for both mother and child (Azar, 1995). Other programs currently utilized are parent education programs and specialized visitation programs. Mail and telephone calls are used to increase mother-child contacts.

Parent Education Programs: Alternatives to Prison Nurseries and Community-Based Residential Programs

If nurseries and community-based residential programs are not possible, the more cost-effective and practical programs to assist incarcerated women are parent education programs. These programs are aimed at helping women to overcome barriers to successful parenting and are now considered a critical, gender-responsive strategy in correctional institutions housing female offenders (Loper & Tuerk, 2006; Pollock, 2002)

Prior to imprisonment, many women replicate the parenting styles of their own families. As the data have demonstrated thus far, the women have significant personal issues that have influenced their lives and the lives of their children. Most notably, prior to their current imprisonment, the women were often single mothers who were experiencing significant emotional and substance abuse problems, while attempting to parent their often troubled children. In addition, it was not uncommon for these women to be involved in volatile relationships (Dalley & Michels, 2009).

Shortcomings in parenting begin in the community. Some of the barriers to effective parenting are related to mental health and substance abuse problems. The level of mental health problems obviously impacts the women's personal and social functioning. Their significant addiction and mental health problems (women with dual diagnoses) are likely to greatly impact their relationship with their children and their ability to parent. Despite these issues, it is not unusual to find that children love and protect their mothers (Henriques, 2002). For example, a mother who had abused her kids becomes incarcerated. The kids were placed in foster care. The kids would not eat and cried endlessly. A special visit had to be arranged between mother and children. The need for parent education programs is therefore evident.

While the focus of this chapter is on incarcerated mothers and their children, this in no way diminishes the important role that fathers play in the lives of their children. It should be noted that New York State has had a parenting program for fathers since 1986, when the Osborne Association implemented the first comprehensive parenting program for incarcerated fathers in New York State prisons (For more information on Osborne Association Programs go www.osborneny.org). This program was one of the first in the nation and continues today, 25 years later, in Sing Sing Correctional Facility in Ossining, New York. Box 4.4 presents and discusses parenting programs for incarcerated fathers.

Box 4.4   Parenting Programs: Fathers in Prison

By Anna Curtis,
University of Massachusetts, Amherst

The research on fathers in prison is still developing. Some researchers have focused on the negative impact of parental incarceration on children (Wildeman, 2009), the impact on communities as incarcerated men move from prison back to home (Clear, 2007; Travis & Waul, 2003), and the ways that the penal system systematically denies men their role as fathers (Lanier, 2003). Still other analyses have considered how incarceration affects men's connectedness with their children (Edin, Nelson, & Paranal, 2004) and the struggles of juvenile fathers to negotiate incarceration and fatherhood (Nurse, 2002). Hairston (2001a, 2001b) reports that many incarcerated fathers have had difficulty maintaining contact with their children.

Drawing on the Survey of Inmates in State and Federal Correctional Facilities, Glaze and Maruschak (2009) report that an "estimated 1,559,200 children had a father in prison at midyear 2007; nearly half (46%) were children of black fathers" (p. 2). Of those incarcerated fathers, 35.5% reported that they lived with at least one of their children in the month before their incarceration (p. 5). Wildeman (2009) argues that parental incarceration is more likely to affect Black children and the children of those without high school diplomas, and he states that by, "age 14, 50.5% of black children born in 1990 to high school dropouts had a father imprisoned" (p. 265). In other words, the consequences for parental incarceration are concentrated among the most disadvantaged children.

A recent set of articles on incarcerated fathers has explored the various ways prison can affect men's identities as fathers. Arditti, Smock, and Parkman (2005), for example, argued that incarceration diminishes men's belief that they are good fathers and increases their feelings of helplessness. Roy and Dyson (2005) examined the ways that prison intensified conflicts between men and their children's mothers. This last article is particularly important when considering whether or not men in prison remain in contact with their children. Unlike mothers in prison, the majority of incarcerated fathers (88%) report that the other parent is the current caregiver (Glaze & Maruschak, 2009). As a result, incarcerated fathers' relationships with their children's mothers significantly impacts whether or not they will receive contact visits from their children.

Until recently, incarcerated men's parental roles was largely ignored; however, over the past decade a number of programs emerged aimed at providing men in prison with training and resources to father from prison (Jeffries, Menghraj, & Hairston, 2001). Even with the recent increase in programs aimed at helping men remain connected to, and positively involved with, their families, most incarcerated fathers do not have access to fatherhood programs.

(Continued)

(Continued)

References

Arditti, J. A., Smock, S. A., & Parkman, T. S. (2005). It's been hard to be a father: A qualitative exploration of incarcerated fatherhood. *Fathering: A Journal of Theory, Research, & Practice about Men as Fathers, 3*(3), 267–288.

Clear, T. (2007). *Imprisoning communities: How mass incarceration makes disadvantaged neighborhoods worse.* New York, NY: Oxford University Press.

Edin, K., Nelson, T. J., & Paranal, R. (2004). Returning to strangers: Newly paroled young fathers and their children. In M. E. Patillo, D. F. Weiman, & B. Western (Eds.), *Imprisoning America: The social effects of mass incarceration.* New York, NY: Russell Sage Foundation.

Glaze, L. E., & Maruschak, L. M. 2008. *Parents in prison and their minor children.* Special report. NCJ 222984. Washington, DC: U.S. Department of Justice, Bureau of Justice Statistics.

Hairston, C. F. (2001a). The forgotten parent: Understanding the forces that influence incarcerated fathers' relationships with their children. In C. Seymour & C. F. Hairston (Eds.), *Children with parents in prison* (pp. 149–171). New Brunswick, NJ: Transaction.

Hairston, C. F. (2001b). Fathers in prison: Responsible fatherhood and responsible public policies. *Marriage & Family Review, 32*(3/4), 111–135.

Jeffries, J., Menghraj, S., & Hairston, C. F. (2001). *Serving incarcerated and ex-offender fathers and their families: A review of the field.* New York, NY: Vera Institute of Justice.

Lanier, C. (2003). Who's doing the time here, me or my children? Addressing the issues implicated by mounting numbers of fathers in prison. In J. I. Ross & S. C. Richards (Eds.), *Convict criminology.* Belmont, CA: Wadsworth.

Nurse, A. M. (2002). *Fatherhood arrested: Parenting from within the juvenile justice system.* Nashville, TN: Vanderbilt University Press.

Roy, K. M., & Dyson, O. L. (2005). Gatekeeping in context: Babymama drama and the involvement of incarcerated fathers. *Fathering: A Journal of Theory, Research, & Practice about Men as Fathers, 3*(3), 289–310.

Travis, J., & Waul, M. (Eds.). (2003). *Prisoners once removed: The impact of incarceration on children, families, and communities.* Washington, DC: Urban Institute Press.

Wildeman, C. (2009). Parental imprisonment, the prison boom, and the concentration of childhood disadvantage. *Demography, 46*(2), 265–280.

PRISON VISITATION PROGRAMS

Prison visitation programs can potentially benefit the incarcerated parent and provide emotional and psychological continuity for family members (Arditti, 2008). Prison policies directly and indirectly impose significant challenges to maintaining family connections. Prison assignments are made on the basis of bed space not family proximity. Prisons are often in remote areas of the state, hundreds of miles from major urban areas where family are usually located, making visits time consuming and expensive (Travis & Visher, 2005)

Studies show that visits to a parent in prison or jail are usually helpful in keeping children connected to their parents and serve to strengthen family bonds. Most children manage the crisis of parental incarceration better when they visit their parents. Extended contact is needed in order to enhance secure attachment (Robertson, 2007). However, maintaining contact with children during incarceration, through visitation, can be challenging. Arditti (2008) has listed some of the common problems associated with visitation:

- Transportation—particularly when the inmate is housed far from home
- Expenses—gas, airfare, hotel, meals, snacks in the visiting room
- Parenting stress—due to interaction with correctional staff
- Boredom—restriction for children in the visiting room
- Emotional and cognitive reactions precipitated by visit
- Accompaniment—many children, caregivers, and prison authorities are unhappy about allowing children to visit imprisoned parents by themselves.
- Child-unfriendly visiting areas—lack of eating or play areas for children (Goshin & Byrne, 2009; WPA, 2009; Robertson, 2007; Correctional Association, 2006)

Some of the above mentioned challenges have been overcome by specialized visitation programs such as Girl Scouts Behind Bars (GSBB) and Mothers and Their Children (MATCH) (Morash & Schram, 2002). GSBB now operates in several states. In systems which cannot implement these kinds of programs, current technology can be used to implement visits via video conferencing. In addition to visitation programs, correctional institutions encourage mothers to maintain contact through telephone calls and correspondence.

RETAINING PARENT-CHILD RELATIONSHIPS: INTERNATIONAL PERSPECTIVE

The importance of maintaining mother-child relationships when a mother is incarcerated within the United States was described in detail. Nevertheless, it is of great interest and importance to examine how different countries address the issue of incarcerating women who are mothers, as this may help in educating policy makers and future policies.

In countries where telephones are commonplace, phoning (as compared to writing letters) appears to be a more popular means of enabling mothers to stay in contact with their children.

An Irish study found that over half of prisoners interviewed (using a small sample of 26), reported having spoken to their children on an almost daily basis. Only 15% exchanged cards and letters every week or longer (King, n.d.). Similar trends emerge from research in other countries. This contact has positive impacts: parents who talk to their children seem to adjust better to the prison environment, while children appear to cope better with the separation if they have more contact with their imprisoned parent (Murray, 2005).

Where phone calls are limited or are not possible, written communication is the more widely used method for incarcerated mothers maintaining contact with their children. In addition to letters, mothers sometimes send their children photos or objects they have bought or made: for example, a workshop at San Vittore prison in Italy allows imprisoned mothers to "make relational objects" for their children, thus helping to maintain mother-child relationship. This is particularly important for foreign national women and their children who live in a different country (Quaker Council for European Affairs, 2007): also, in Chapter 14, Weiss and Vasquez, discuss the challenges of illegal immigrants who end up behind bars and are not able to connect with family and children.

It should be noted that phone calls and letters are only used depending on the child's age and level of literacy. In these situations, alternative means of maintaining contact must be used. For example, there are programs which allow imprisoned parents to produce an audio recording of a book for their children to listen to. These programs have been credited with strengthening the parent-child relationship, raising self-esteem of prisoners, and improving literacy among both children and prisoners (more information can be found at www.storybook.co.uk, as cited in Robertson, 2007).

A review of the literature has found that many prisons run programs, events, and courses designed to sustain and strengthen children's relationships with their imprisoned parent:

Australia: A project in Victoria State, Australia, offers fathers the opportunity to develop their parenting skills (Robertson, 2007).

Spain: In October 2008, Spain opened an External Mother Unit (Unidad Externa de Madres) in Palma, Majorca. The development of such unit by department of prison services represents Spain's effort to break the cycle of social marginalization and incarceration for female offenders and their young children. These units aim to provide children with a harmonious environment while simultaneously preparing the mothers to integrate into a community and care for their children (Fintuch, 2010).

Denmark: Children are allowed to go to their parent's room and have their visit there. (Robertson, 2007).

Afghanistan: Mother and child accommodation is provided and some prisons have crèches or (as in Policharki prison in Afghanistan) schools for the children of detainees (Bunton, as cited in Robertson, 2007).

India: Prisons in Karnataka State, India, have set up crèches and nursery schools attended by children imprisoned with their parents, children of prison officials, and children living close to the prison (Rajendran, as cited in Robertson, 2007)

Kenya: Thika Women's Prison in Kenya began holding "Remote Parenting Days" in 2007. A similar program exists in China (Opiyo, as cited in Robertson, 2007)

Canada: Children with mothers imprisoned in the Maison Tanguay facility in Montreal, Canada, can live with them for two days a week in a trailer on the facility grounds (Cunningham & Baker, as cited in Robertson, 2007).

United Kingdom: The United Kingdom had a nursery program which was evaluated by Lisa Catan in the middle 1980's. This program appeared to have had many shortcomings. Catan described an environment where children's movements were severely restricted, and infants were left strapped in prams or chairs for hours. Catan made recommendations which advised greater attention to creating a child-friendly and stimulating environment. There is evidence that these recommendations have been implemented in the UK, but no further evaluation research has been reported (Goshin & Byrne, 2009)

It should be noted that in the last multinational survey published, the Alliance of Non-Governmental Organizations on Crime Prevention and Criminal Justice queried 70 nations in 1987 to find that only Suriname, Liberia, the Bahamas, and the United States routinely separated imprisoned mothers from their children (Kauffman, 2006).

POLICY IMPLICATIONS

It is clear that motherhood and parenting are important issues to women behind bars. Further, these issues should be important to society as whole. Parental neglect affects not just children of incarcerated individuals but entire communities (Clear, 1994). For this reason it is important that whenever possible mothers and children will not be separated. Specifically, we recommend that whenever possible, women with nonviolent offenses, who are pregnant, or are custodial parents, should be given community-based sanctions. This will allow them to live in community-based residential programs which will prevent mother-child separation while allowing them to address the issues that contributed to their criminal activity. Additionally, all facilities that house women offenders should implement gender-responsive programs that recognize this important truism: "When men go to prison, potential role models are lost. When women go to prison, families fall apart" (Understanding Prison Health Care, 2002).

When prison nursery programs are not an available option, other programs such as parent education and visitation should be encouraged to maintain contact between mothers and their children. Barriers to effective visitation should be eliminated. Utilization of new technologies such as video conferencing and Skype can facilitate face to face contact. All of the programs detailed should be supplemented by telephone calls and correspondence programs.

In state correctional systems, there is no uniform or adequate attention given to mothers' needs and concerns. The impact of incarceration on children is not viewed as a responsibility of the correctional system. It appears that many women are not screened to determine whether they have responsibilities, concerns, or pressures related to their children. In state prisons with 500 or more women, only 40% of administrators indicated all women had routine screening which related to mothering. In state prisons with populations under 100, this kind of screening was not done. Not only do prison administrators lack systematic knowledge of women prisoners' involvement with their children, but concerns about women and their children are overshadowed by administrators' belief that substance abuse and mental health issues are greater and more pressing (Morash & Schram, 2002). This situation must be addressed by prison administrators in order to adequately provide for the needs of inmate mothers.

The important thing to remember is that mother-child contact should be encouraged and maintained especially when the incarcerated mother indicates that she intends to reunite with her child or children upon release and reintegration. Policies and programs should attempt to facilitate this very important need. For example, the Adoption and Safe Families Act of 1997 required social services agencies to file a termination of parental rights petition when a child has been in care 15 of the last 22 months, unless there is a compelling or other reason for not filing such a petition. This act was very destructive in its application. Fortunately, the destructive aspects of this act were removed in 2010. Chapter 113 of the laws of 2010 amended the Social Services Law to explicitly include parental incarceration or participation in a residential substance abuse treatment program as a possible basis NOT to file a petition to terminate parental rights. This is indeed a step in the right direction as far as governmental policies go.

Additionally, in order to better prepare incarcerated women for reentry, and to face life's daily challenges and reduce recidivism, correctional systems must develop two basic types of programming:

- Viable in-prison prerelease programs—The level of abuse and trauma that most women have experienced prior to incarceration mandate that both intensive mental health and addiction treatment be provided in prison (Dalley & Michels, 2009), along with parenting programs and educational, vocational, life skills programs.
- Postrelease, supportive aftercare programs similar to the Hour Children programs in New York State and Women Prison Association programs—These programs must be sensitive to the issue of race, class, and culture because women's ideas about motherhood and family are influenced by these factors. In addition, these programs must recognize that children have varying needs depending on the age of the child, and that caregivers are an important factor in facilitating parent-child contact.

The interconnected nature of criminal justice involvement, family disintegration, and child abuse/neglect means that the criminal justice system and child welfare systems must work together to meet the needs of incarcerated mothers (WPA, 2009).

The below story, presented in Box 4.5, illustrates the need for viable reentry programs with supportive services in the community. Accordingly, Table 4.3 presents a summary of basic life skills that need to be addressed through a reentry and reintegration program for incarcerated mothers.

Box 4.5	Scenario That Illustrates the Need for Reentry Programs for Incarcerated Mother

D. H. was arrested and convicted for a drug offense in the 1980s. She was given a sentence of 20 years to life under the Rockefeller Drug Laws. She was the mother of five, ages 2 to 12, who were left in the care of an elderly aunt who died during D. H.'s incarceration. D. H. served 16 years of her sentence and was released to go home to a family that was broken, bitter, and confused as to what role their mother could now play in their adult lives.

During D. H.'s incarceration, she had visits from her children in the visiting room as well as overnight visits through the family reunion program. D. H. was under the impression that even though she was in prison, she was still parenting her children from the inside.

Upon her release, D. H. attempted to deal with her children if they were still minors, although they were now young adults. She felt that they should respect her and adhere to her rules as they had done prior to her incarceration. This led to an internal and open family battle which resulted in a painful and traumatic reentry. (An anecdotal story from Women's Advocate Ministry, a not-for-profit organization that works with female offenders in New York)

Table 4.3   A Model for Successful Community Reintegration

Reentry Phase	Basic Life Areas*				
	Subsistence/ Livelihood	Residence	Family	Health and Sobriety	Criminal Justice Compliance
SURVIVAL	Gate money Public assistance Soup kitchens Pantries Maintain basic hygiene	Family or friend Shelter Street	Find children Make contact	Continue with previous medication regimens Avoid Relapse Emergency room care	Report to parole regularly
STABILIZATION	Public assistance Workfare Training/ education Low wage or subsidized job	Transitional residence Family or friend	Supervised visitation Get refamiliarized	Drug treatment Treatment of urgent physical and mental health issues Counseling	Comply with requirement

(Continued)

Table 4.3   (Continued)

Reentry Phase	Basic Life Areas*				
	Subsistence/ Livelihood	Residence	Family	Health and Sobriety	Criminal Justice Compliance
SELF-SUFFICIENCY	Job that pays a living wage and provides benefits	Permanent housing (with public subsidy, if necessary)	Reunify with family Receive family counseling Caring for others	Regular health visits paid by health insurance Ongoing support Structured-12 step therapy Community activities	Earn reduced supervision or complete parole

Source: L. Jacobs. (2005). *Improving the odds: Women in community corrections.* WPA.

*The other basic need is for encouragement, support, and orientation to new things.

** Subsistence includes transportation, food, clothing, and all out of pocket expenses.

CONCLUSION

The profile of female offenders provided earlier in this chapter, clearly illustrates their multifaceted and complex array of needs related to poverty, family disintegration, trauma, substance abuse, and mental health problems. Many of the inmates are also mothers. Any parent knows that raising children is not an easy undertaking. The mother's involvement in the criminal justice system and her separation from her children further complicates the task.

The responsibility placed on the criminal justice system, to handle these myriad of problems presented by inmate mothers and effectuate positive changes, is enormous. However, in spite of the obvious negativity of the prison environment, the prison experience provides the inmates with teachable moments. For many of them such experience gives them pause in their lives and the opportunity to be sober and free from the trauma of their lives in the community. If they are willing, and with the help of effective gender-responsive programs, they can retreat, regroup, and begin their path back to a positive, fulfilling life.

There has been no scarcity of research aimed at identifying the pathways which have led female offenders to the criminal justice system. Research has also identified the variety of problems which must be addressed if women are to lead productive lives and care for their children. Public attitudes and the high cost of providing services and programs to women in prison have been cited as the reason why the problems presented by female inmate mothers have not been addressed in a robust way.

Despite these costs, we suggest that the criminal justice system and taxpayers, cannot afford *not* to provide meaningful programs for female offenders that recognize the needs of their children and the consequences of inaction.

The price of incarcerating women is not limited to the cost of a prison cell, food, and clothing. Locking up woman can also mean paying the costs for putting and supporting the child or children in foster care, treating health and mental health conditions that have worsened during incarceration, and providing public assistance and shelter for those who are homeless and destitute following release (Frost, Greene, & Pranis, 2006).

Through the pages of this chapter, different program options were presented and discussed, both in the United States and internationally, which correctional systems can utilize to begin to address the issues and problems of this very vulnerable population. The options range from pregnancy and birth programs and prison nurseries to community-based residential parenting programs and visitation programs, to name a few. A description of the most expensive programs and the least expensive programs was presented. What is now needed is the understanding by the administrators of criminal justice systems, that if too little or nothing is done, we will continue to inflict pain on the innocent victims of a mother's incarceration—the children. We will be contributing to the next cycle of bad outcomes—the growing cycle of crime in our society. Can we afford that cost?!!!.

As Life magazine writer Claudia Dowling so eloquently states. "A mother may be guilty, but a child is always innocent" (Dowling as cited in Morton, 2004).

DISCUSSION QUESTIONS

1. What are some of the negative effects of incarceration on mothers? What are some of the effects on children?

2. How can prisons address these issues? Why is it important to address these issues?

3. Why is contact between women prisoners and their children important? What are some of the obstacles to maintaining contact?

4. What program components do you think are important in prison programs for incarcerated mothers?

5. How are risk factors such as previous lifestyle, homelessness, poverty, substance abuse, domestic abuse histories, health problems, and mental health interrelated in the lives of women prisoners?

6. How may the conditions mentioned in Question 5 affect pregnancy outcomes for incarcerated women?

7. Incarceration may both increase and decrease the risks of pregnant inmates. What does this mean?

8. What types of social support would be beneficial to pregnant prisoners? How could these be provided to women who are incarcerated?

9. What are some of the problems faced by pregnant women in jail or prison? What are some of the solutions or alternatives to issues surrounding medical care for pregnant prisoners?

10. What types of health and mental health programs are needed in women's prisons?

SUGGESTED WEBSITES

- Bedford Hills Correctional Facility in New York:
  http://www.correctionalassociation.org/publications/download/wipp/facility_reports/bedford_2005.pdf

- Hour Children Services to children of incarcerated and formerly incarcerated women:
  http://hourchildren.org

- New York Correction—Article 22—§ 611 Births to Inmates of Correctional Institutions and Care of Children of Inmates of Correctional Institutions:
  http://law.onecle.com/new-york/correction/COR0611_611.html

- Osborne Association Programs:
  http://www.osborneny.org

- The Rebecca Project for Human Rights:
  http://www.rebeccaproject.org

- Women's Prison Association:
  http://www.wpaonline.org

REFERENCES

Amnesty International. 1999. United States of America: "Not part of my sentence": Violations of the human rights of women in custody. Available at http://www.amnesty.org

Arditti, A. J. (2008). Parental imprisonment and family visitation: A brief overview and recommendations for family friendly practice. *CW360*: Spring 2008. University of Minnesota, Center for Advanced Studies in Child Welfare.

Azar, B. (1995, September) The bond between mother and child. *Monitor on Psychology, 28*. Available at http://www.apaonline.org

Bartlett, R. (2000, December). Helping inmate moms keep in touch-Prison programs encourage ties with children. *Corrections Today 62*(7), 102–104.

Baunach, P. J. (1986). *Mothers in prison*. New Brunswick, NJ: Transition.

Bloom, B., Owen, B., & Covington, S. (2003). *Gender-responsive strategies: Research practice and guiding principles for women offenders*. Washington, DC: National Institute of Corrections.

Boudouris, J. (1996). *Parents in prison: Addressing the needs of families*. Lanham, MD: American Correctional Association.

Brodie, D. L. (1982). Babies behind bars: Should incarcerated mothers allowed to keep their newborns with them in prison? *University of Richmond Law Review, 16*: 677–692.

Brown, G. (2010). *The intersectionality of race, gender, and reentry: Challenges for African-American Women*. Washington, DC: American Constitution Society.

Bunton, B. (2007). 22 to a cell: Life in a notorious Afghan prison. In O. Robertson, *The impact of parental imprisonment on children*. Retrieved from http://www.quno.org/geneva/pdf/humanrights/women-in-prison/ImpactParentalImprisonment-200704-English.pdf

Chesney-Lind, M. (1998). Women in prison: From partial justice to vengeful equity. *Corrections Today, 60*, 66–73.

Clear, T. R. (1994). *Harm in American penology: Offenders, victims, and their communities.* Albany: State University of New York.

Clear, T. R. (2007). *Imprisoning communities: How mass incarceration makes disadvantaged neighborhoods worse.* New York, NY: Oxford University Press.

Correctional Association of New York. (2006). *Women in prison project.* New York, NY: Author.

Correctional Association of New York. (2009). *Women in prison fact sheet.* New York, NY: Author.

Dalley, L. P., & Michels, V. (2008) Women destined to failure: Policy implications of the lack of proper mental health and addiction treatment for female offenders. In R. L. Gido & L. Dalley (Eds.), *Women's mental health issues: Across the criminal justice system.* (pp.160–176). Upper Saddle River, NJ: Prentice Hall.

Drummond, T. (2000, November 6). Mothers in prison. *Time Magazine,* 105–107.

Fintuch, S. (2010). New Spanish practice aims to break the cycle among mothers and children. *Correction Today, 72*(6), 38–48.

Frost, N. A., Greene, J., & Pranis, K. (2006). The Punitiveness Report- *HARD HIT: The growth in the imprisonment of women, 1977–2004.* Retrieved February 29, 2012, from http://www.wpaonline.org/institute/hardhit/HardHitReport4.pdf

Gabel, K., & Johnston, D. (1995). *Children of incarcerated parents.* New York, NY: Lexington Press.

Ghose, D. (2002). *Nursery program aids jailed moms in four states.* Retrieved February 29, 2012, from http://www.stateline.org/live/printable/story

Glaze, L. E., & Maruschak, L. M. (2008, August). *Parents in prison and their minor children.* (Special Report. NCJ 222984). Washington, DC: U.S. Department of Justice, Bureau of Justice Statistics.

Goshin, S., & Bryne, L. (2009). Converging streams of opportunity for prison nursery programs in the United States. *Journal of Offender Rehabilitation, 48*(4), 271–295. doi:10.1080/10509670902848972

Goshin, L. S., & Byrne, M. W. (2009). Converting streams of opportunity for prison nursery programs in the United States. *Journal of Offender Rehabilitation, 48*(4), 271-295.

Henriques, Z. W. (1982). *Imprisoned mothers and their children: A descriptive and analytical study.* Washington, DC: University Press of America.

Henriques, Z. W. (2002). Diversion programming: Integrating treatment with criminal justice sanctions for women with co-occurring disorders. In S. Davidson & H. Hills (Eds.), *Series on justice-involved women with mental illness and co-occurring disorders.* Delmar, NY: National GAINS Center.

Henriques, Z. W., & Jones-Brown, D. (2000). Prison as a safe haven for African American women. In D. Jones-Brown & M. W. Markowitz (Eds.), *The system in black and white: Exploring the connections between race, crime, and justice* (pp. 267–273). Westport, CT: Praeger.

Hotelling, B. A. (2008). Perinatal needs of pregnant, incarcerated women. *The Journal of Perinatal Education, 17*(2), 37–44.

Illinois Department of Corrections News. (2011, March 29). Retrieved February 29, 2012, from http://www.idoc.state.il.us/subscriptions/news/default.shtml

Kaufman, K. (2006). Prison nurseries: New beginnings and second chances. In R. Immarigeon (Ed.), *Women and girls in the criminal justice system: Policy issues and practice strategies.* Kingston, NJ: Civic Research Institute.

King, D. (n.d.). Parents, children & prison: Effects of parental imprisonment on children. Center for Social and Educational Research, Dublin Institute of Technology. In O. Robertson (2007), *The impact of parental imprisonment on children.* Available at: http://www.quno.org/geneva/pdf/humanrights/women-in-prison/ImpactParentalImprisonment-200704-English.pdf

Lopez Loper, A. B., & Tuerk, E. H. (2006). Parenting programs incarcerated parents: Current research and future directions. *Criminal Justice Policy Review 17,* 407–427.

Morash, M., & Schram, P. J. (2002). *Prison experience: Special issues of women in prison.* Prospect Heights, IL: Waveland Press.

Morton, J. B. (2004). *Working with women offenders in correctional institutions.* East Peoria, IL: Versa Press.

Murray, J. (2005). The effects of imprisonment on families and children of prisoners. In A. Liebling & S. Maruna (Eds.), *The effects of imprisonment.* Cullompton, England: Willan.

Opiyo, P. (2007). Joy amid despair: Women's prisons host families of inmates. In O. Robertson, *The impact of parental imprisonment on children.* Retrieved from http://www.quno.org/geneva/pdf/humanrights/women-in-prison/ImpactParentalImprisonment-200704-English.pdf

Parke, R. D., & Clarke-Stewart, K. (2003). The effects of parental incarceration on children: Perspectives, promises, and policies. In J. Travis & M. Waul (Eds.), *Prisoners once removed.* Washington, DC: Urban Institute.

Pollock, J. M. (2002). Parenting programs in women's prisons. *Women & Criminal Justice, 14*(1), 131–154. doi:10.1300/J012v14n01_04

Quaker Council for European Affairs. (2007). *Women in Prison: A Review of Conditions in Member States of the Council of Europe.* Available at http://www.qcea.org

Radosh, P. (1988). Inmate mothers: Legislative solutions to a difficult problem. *Crime and Justice, 11,* 61–77.

Rajendran, S. (2007). Nursery schools set up in jails in the State. In O. Robertson, *The impact of parental imprisonment on children.* Retrieved from http://www.quno.org/geneva/pdf/humanrights/women-in-prison/ImpactParentalImprisonment-200704-English.pdf

Robertson, O. (2007). *The impact of parental imprisonment on children.* Retrieved from http://www.quno.org/geneva/pdf/humanrights/women-in-prison/ImpactParental Imprisonment-200704-English.pdf

Schroeder, C., & Bell, J. (2005). Doula birth support for incarcerated pregnant women. *Public Health Nursing, 22*(1), 53–58.

Sharp, S. F. (2003). *The incarcerated woman.* Englewood Cliffs, NJ: Prentice Hall.

Shepard, D., & Zemans, E. S. (1950). *Prison babies: A study of some aspects of the care and treatment of pregnant inmates and their infants in training school, reformatories, and prisons.* Chicago, IL: John Howard Association.

Simmons, C. W. (2002). Children of incarcerated parents. *CRB Note, 7*(2), 1–11. Retrieved from http://www.library.ca.gov/crb/CRBSearch.aspx

The Rebecca Project. (2010). *Mothers behind bars: A state-by-state report card and analysis of federal policies on conditions of confinement for pregnant and parenting women and the effect on their children.* Washington, DC: National Women's Law Center.

Travis, J., & Visher, C. A. (2005). Prison reentry and the pathways to adulthood: Policy perspectives. In D. W. Osgood (Ed.), *On your own without a net.* (p.161). Chicago, IL: Chicago University Press.

Understanding prison health care: Women's health. (2002). Funded by Stanford University School of Medicine, Arts and Humanities Medical Scholars Program.

West, H. C., & Sabol, W. J. (2009). *National prisoner statistical data series: Prison inmates at midyear 2008.* Washington, DC: U.S. Department of Justice, Bureau of Justice Statistics.

Women's Prison Association. (2009, May). *Mothers, infants and imprisonment: A national look at prison nurseries and community-based alternatives.* Retrieved from http://www.wpaonline.org

APPENDIX 4.1

Prison Nursery Programs

California				
Facility	Started	Capacity	Duration of Child's Stay	Policy for Participation
California Institution for Women, Corona	Scheduled to open September 2009	16 women– 10 with infants and 6 who are pregnant	Up to 18 months	The California Institute for Women is the only female facility in the state that has **a Mother-Child Reunification Program.** The final policies for participation in the nursery are still being drafted. After women spend up to 18 months in the nursery they will be transitioned onto parole or into a community-based program such as the Community Prison Mothers Program. In addition to the planned nursery, the facility runs a child-visiting program and mother-father mediation program. All pregnant women are placed in this institution and other women can request to sentenced or transferred there.
Additional Information: http://www.cdcr.ca.gov/Visitors/Facilities/CIW.html				

Illinois				
Facility	Started	Capacity	Duration of Child's Stay	Policy for Participation
Decatur Correctional Center, Decatur	2007	5 mother/ infant pairs	Up to 24 months	To qualify for the **Moms & Babies Program** a woman must have committed a non violent offense and be within two years of release after giving birth.
Additional Information: http://www.idoc.state.il.us/subsections/facilities/information.asp?instchoice=dct				

Indiana				
Facility	Started	Capacity	Duration of Child's Stay	Policy for Participation
Indiana Women's Prison, Indianapolis	2008	10 mother/ infant pairs and 4 nannies	Up to 18 months	To participate in the **Wee Ones Nursery Program,** the child must be born in custody and the mother must be eligible for release by the time the child is 18 months old. Mothers and nannies who have been convicted of child abuse or a violent crime are not eligible to participate in the nursery.
Additional Information: http://www.in.gov/indcorrection/facility/iwp/general.htm				

(Continued)

(Continued)

Ohio				
Facility	Started	Capacity	Duration of Child's Stay	Policy for Participation
Ohio Reformatory for Women, Marysville	2001	20 mothers and up to 21 infants	Up to 18 months	To qualify for the **Achieving Baby Care Success Program** women must give birth while in state custody and can not have a violent criminal record. Women must attend family training courses, adhere to rules and be in good mental and physical condition. Only women who are serving a sentence of 18 months or less at the time of delivery are eligible.

Additional Information: http://www.drc.state.oh.us/Public/orw.htm

Nebraska				
Facility	Started	Capacity	Duration of Child's Stay	Policy for Participation
Nebraska Correctional Center for Women, York	1994	15 mother/ infant pairs	18 months; can be extended at staff discretion	To participate in the nursery the mother must give birth while in state custody and not have a violent criminal record. She also should not have any serious mental health concerns. A screening committee reviews each case before women are placed in the nursery. The mother must be able to complete her sentence by the time the child is 18 months old to be eligible.

Additional Information: http://www.corrections.state.ne.us/institutions/nocw.html

New York				
Facility	Started	Capacity	Duration of Child's Stay	Policy for Participation
Bedford Hills Correctional Facility, Bedford Hills	1901	29 mother/ infant pairs	The child can stay for up to 18 months if the mother will be paroled by then, otherwise the child must leave the facility at 12 months of age.	Several aspects of a woman's past are examined before she can participate in the nursery. This includes determining who is going to have custody of the child, if the mother has a history of involvement with the child welfare system, the length of her sentence, past episodes of incarceration, and the nature of her crime. Women who have committed arson or who have a history of child abuse are not eligible for the nursery. A woman must give birth while in custody to qualify for the program.
Taconic Correctional Facility, Bedford Hills	1990	15 mother/ infant pairs	12-18 months depending on the mothers program.	

Additional Information: http://www.docs.state.nv.us/docs.html

South Dakota				
Facility	Started	Capacity	Duration of Child's Stay	Policy for Participation
South Dakota Women's Prison, Pierre	1998	No limit	30 Days	Women who give birth while in custody are allowed to participate in the program as long as the mother's crime was nonviolent in nature. AH ll (All) expenses related to the baby's care are the responsibility of the mother, including health care expenses. Mothers keep their infants in their cells. Other women at the facility are able to take classes to become babysitters and thé mothers are able to choose who they would like to act as their babysitter.
Additional Information: http://www.state.sd.us/oorrections/womens.htm				

Washington				
Facility	Started	Capacity	Duration of Child's Stay	Policy for Participation
Washington Correctional Center for Women, Gig Harbor	1999	20 mother/ infant pairs	Up to 36 months	To qualify for the **Residential Parenting Program*** the mother's sentence must be completed within three years of giving birth. The women must also be classified as minimum custody and be convicted of a nonviolent offense.
Additional Information: http://www.residentialparentina.com/index.htm				

*The Washington State Correctional Center for Women refers to their program as a Residential Parenting Program – for the purpose of this brief it is considered a Prison Nursery Program

West Virginia				
Facility	Started	Capacity	Duration of Child's Stay	Policy for Participation
Lakin Correctional Center for Women*, West Columbia	Opening July 1, 2009	5 mother/ infant pairs	Up to 18 months	The **KIDS (Keeping Infant Development Successful)** Unit will be available to pregnant women who are within 18 months of release or parole. The nursery is made up of modular homes located outside the prison's perimeter fence. To participate in the nursery the mother must not have been convicted of a sex crime or a crime against a child and must be free of disciplinary write-ups.
Additional Information: http://www.wvdoc.com/wvdoc/PrisonsandFacilities/LakinCorrectional Center/tabid/50/Default.aspx				

Source: Women Prison Association.

*This program is still in the planning stages. The timeline for implementation may change as well as other program elements.

APPENDIX 4.2

Community-Based Residential Parenting Programs

Alabama				
Facility/ Location	Started	Capacity	Duration of Child's Stay	Policy for Participation
Lovelady Center, Birmingham	Originally started in 1997 and expanded greatly in 2005	Currently 300 women and 100 children in the residential program	No limit on the child's age; women participate in a 6–12 month program	The **Lovelady Center** is a community-based program that serves as an alternative to incarceration, as a residence for those on parole or probation and **as a prerelease program**. The policies for participation vary based on **each** woman's circumstance.
Additional Information: www.loveladycenter.org				

California				
Facility/ Location	Started	Capacity	Duration of Child's Stay	Policy for Participation
Community Prison Mother Program				A woman must first be housed in a state prison, from which she is able to apply for the program. Women must be pregnant or parenting a child under age six, convicted of a nonviolent drug offense and have at least 90 days left on her sentence. Each woman is allowed to have up to two children reside with her.
Project Pride, Oakland	Program started in 1980	24 total beds	Up to 6 years of age	
Turning Point, Bakersfield		24 total beds		
Pomona Los Angeles		23 total beds		
Family Foundations Program				The Family Foundations Program is an alternative sentencing program administered by California Department of Corrections for women who are convicted of nonviolent offenses and who have histories of drug abuse. Women must be pregnant or parenting a child under the age of six and be sentenced no longer than 36 months. As an alternative to incarceration, the women must be sentenced directly to **a** Family Foundation Program; they can not transfer from a state prison. The mother spends 12 months in this highly structured residential treatment program followed by a 12-month aftercare/ transition period to help her successfully reenter society.
Santa Fe Springs	1999	35 women and 40 children	Up to 6 years of age	
San Diego	2000			
Fresno	2007			
Additional Information: http://www.leginfo.ca.gov/cgi-bin/waisgate?WAISdocID=98397927644+1+0+0&WAISaction=retrieve				

Mothers, Infants and Imprisonment–www.wpaonline.org

Connecticut				
Facility/ Location	Started	Capacity	Duration of Child's Stay	Policy for Participation
NEON* Women's and Children's Halfway House, Waterbury	1988	19 women and up to 12 children	Up to 10 years of age	Women who have served part of their sentence in prison and are interested in reunifying with their children, and women who are pregnant and meet other program requirements are transferred from the York Correctional Institution to this program. Women are allowed to leave the facility to attend parenting programs and work. Some women are allowed to stay at the house past their sentences if they are not ready to reenter the community.
Additional Information: www.neoncaa.org				

*Norwalk Economic Opportunity Now

Illinois				
Facility/ Location	Started	Capacity	Duration of Child's Stay	Policy for Participation
MOM's Program, Chicago	1999	16 beds	Up to pre-school age	The Sheriffs **MOM's Program** is a therapeutic community drug treatment program for pregnant female pre-trial substance abuse/mental health detainees. Women can either be sentenced to the program by a judge or admitted if they meet criteria such as being convicted of a nonviolent offense, having no history of absconding from previous programs and having a bond that is not over $300,000.
Additional Information: www.cookcountysheriff.org/womensjustice/moms.html				

North Carolina				
Facility/ Location	Started	Capacity	Duration of Child's Stay	Policy for Participation
Our Children's Place*, Chapel Hill	Will open in mid-2010	Start with 10 women and up to 20 children; then increase capacity to 20 women and up to 40 children	The child can stay until he/ she is ready to start kindergarten	To participate in this residential program the mothers must be classified as minimum security and be convicted of a nonviolent offense. The woman's sentence must also end by the time the child is ready to start kindergarten. The mother must have custody of her child; the child does not have to be born while in custody.
Additional Information: http://ourchildrensplace.com/ * This program is still in the planning stages. The timeline for implementation may change.				

(Continued)

(Continued)

North Carolina, cont.				
Summit House Greensboro, Charlotte, Raleigh	1987	26 Families through their 3 facilities	Up to 7 years of age	Summit House is an alternative to an incarceration program to which pregnant women or women with small children may be sentenced to instead of as an alternative to prison. To qualify for Summit House a woman must be 17 years of age or older, convicted of a nonviolent offense and be pregnant or have custody of her children. Women are usually sentenced to this program for 12–24 months.
Additional information: www.summithouse.org				

Massachusetts				
Facility/ Location	Started	Capacity	Duration of Child's Stay	Policy for Participation
Spectrum Women and Children Program, Westborough	1989	13 women and up to 11 or 12 children	Up to 2 years of age	Formerly the Neil J. Houston House, this residential substance abuse program is open to women who are either on parole, probation or are incarcerated. To qualify, a woman must have a substance abuse problem, have not been convicted of a violent offense and not have any serious mental health issues. The child does not have to be born in custody to participate in this program. Based on a community corrections model, women are able to leave the facility only with approval from the Department of Corrections.
Additional Information: www.spectrumhealthsystems.org				

Vermont				
Facility/ Location	Started	Capacity	Duration of Child's Stay	Policy for Participation
Lund Family Center, Burlington	The Lund Family Center started about 115 years ago but their relationship with the DOC is only six to seven years old.	21 mother/ child pairs	Up to 5 years of age	The Lund Family Center's residential program is open to pregnant or parenting women in need of residential drug or mental health services who are between the ages of 12 and 28 and who have children under five years of age. Although the program does not focus entirely on women with criminal justice involvement, some women are sentenced to this program as an alternative to incarceration. Women from the criminal justice system can be accepted to participate if they were convicted of nonviolent offenses, are pregnant or have custody of their child/ren. A woman's sentence should be completed by the time the child turns five years old.
Additional Information: www.lundfamilycenter.org/treatment/residentlal services.shtml				

APPENDIX 4.3

Jails With Nursery Programs

New York				
Facility	Started	Capacity	Duration of Child's Stay	Policy for Participation
Rikers Island – Rose M Singer Center, New York City	1989	15 mothers/16 infants	Up to 12 months	Women sentenced to Rikers Island and women who are awaiting transfer to Bedford Hills or Taconic state facilities may apply for the nursery six months into their pregnancies. A medical and mental health evaluation is conducted as well as an Administration for Children Services investigation. The nature of the mother's crime is taken into consideration when she is evaluated for the nursery program.
Additional Information: http://www.nyc.gov/html/doc/html/home/home.shtml				

Source: Women Prison Association.

APPENDIX 4.4

Federal Bureau of Prisons Residential Parenting Programs

MINT Facilities*				
Facility/ Location	Started	Capacity	Duration of Child's Stay	Policy for Participation
Hartford House Hartford, CT	Unknown	5 mother/ infant pairs	3 months	Women are moved to this facility from the federal prison FCI Danbury in CT. Most women admitted to this site have two years or less remaining on their sentence.
Tallahassee MINT Program Tallahassee, FL	1998	10 mother/ infant pairs	12 months	Women can be moved to this facility from any federal prison in the country. No restriction on the length of the women's sentence for participation was reported.
Triangle Center MINT Program Springfield, IL	Mid-Late 1990s	4 mother/ infant pairs	3 months	Women arrive at this program from any federal facility in the country. The mothers receive three months prenatal care and then three months of mother-child bonding. The Triangle Center has relationships with several community-based services and the women are allowed to leave the facility with an escort to take advantage of these services.
Volunteers of America Fort Worth, TX	early 1980s	20 mother/ infant pairs	3 months	Women may be transferred from any federal facility in the country towards the end of their pregnancy, however most come from FMC Carswell. There is no restriction on the length of the women's sentence for participation. This is the original MINT program location.
Greenbrier Birthing Center Hillsboro, WV	1994	20 mother/ infant pairs	18 months	Women are transferred to this facility from any federal facility in the country. The mother's sentence cannot be longer than 15 years to participate. This site offers the most extensive programming and has the longest time allotment.
Additional Information: www.bop.gov/inmate_programs/female.jsp				

Source: Women Prison Association.

*Unable to contact BSSW-CSC (Pregnant Offender) in Phoenix, AZ and CCI Mother with Infant Program in San Francisco, CA for interviews.

Mothers, Infants and Imprisonment–www.wpaonline.org

APPENDIX 4.5

New York Correction—Article 22—§ 611 Births to Inmates of Correctional Institutions and Care of Children of Inmates of Correctional Institutions

1. If a woman confined in any institution as defined in paragraph c of subdivision four of section two of the correction law or local correctional facility as defined in paragraph (a) of subdivision sixteen of section two of the correction law, be pregnant and about to give birth to a child, the superintendent as defined in subdivision twelve of section two of the correction law or sheriff as defined in paragraph c of subdivision sixteen of section two of the correction law in charge of such institution or facility, a reasonable time before the anticipated birth of such child, shall cause such woman to be removed from such institution or facility and provided with comfortable accommodations, maintenance and medical care elsewhere, under such supervision and safeguards to prevent her escape from custody as the superintendent or sheriff or his or her designee may determine. No restraints of any kind shall be used during transport to or from the hospital, institution or clinic where such woman receives care; provided, however, in extraordinary circumstances, where restraints are necessary to prevent such woman from injuring herself or medical or correctional personnel, such woman may be cuffed by one wrist. In cases where restraints are used, the superintendent or sheriff shall make and maintain written findings as to the reasons for such use. No restraints of any kind shall be used when such woman is in labor, admitted to a hospital, institution or clinic for delivery, or recovering after giving birth. Any such personnel as may be necessary to supervise the woman during transport to and from and during her stay at the hospital, institution or clinic shall be provided to ensure adequate care, custody and control of the woman. The superintendent or sheriff or his or her designee shall cause such woman to be subject to return to such institution or local correctional facility as soon after the birth of her child as the state of her health will permit as determined by the medical professional responsible for the care of such woman. If such woman is confined in a local correctional facility, the expense of such accommodation, maintenance and medical care shall be paid by such woman or her relatives or from any available funds of the local correctional facility and if not available from such sources, shall be a charge upon the county, city or town in which is located the court from which such inmate was committed to such local correctional facility. If such woman is confined in any institution under the control of the department, the expense of such accommodation, maintenance and medical care shall be paid by such woman or her relatives and if not available from such sources, such maintenance and medical care shall be paid by the state. In cases where payment of such accommodations, maintenance and medical care is assumed by the county, city or town from which such inmate was committed the payor shall make payment by issuing payment instrument in favor of the agency or individual that provided such accommodations and services, after certification has been made by the head of the institution to which the inmate was legally

confined, that the charges for such accommodations, maintenance and medical care were necessary and are just, and that the institution has no available funds for such purpose.

2. A child so born may be returned with its mother to the correctional institution in which the mother is confined unless the chief medical officer of the correctional institution shall certify that the mother is physically unfit to care for the child, in which case the statement of the said medical officer shall be final. A child may remain in the correctional institution with its mother for such period as seems desirable for the welfare of such child, but not after it is one year of age, provided, however, if the mother is in a state reformatory and is to be paroled shortly after the child becomes one year of age, such child may remain at the state reformatory until its mother is paroled, but in no case after the child is eighteen months old. The officer in charge of such institution may cause a child cared for therein with its mother to be removed from the institution at any time before the child is one year of age. He shall make provision for a child removed from the institution without its mother or a child born to a woman inmate who is not returned to the institution with its mother as hereinafter provided. He may, upon proof being furnished by the father or other relatives of their ability to properly care for and maintain such child, give the child into the care and custody of such father or other relatives, who shall thereafter maintain the same at their own expense. If it shall appear that such father or other relatives are unable to properly care for and maintain such child, such officer shall place the child in the care of the commissioner of public welfare or other officer or board exercising in relation to children the power of a commissioner of public welfare of the county from which such inmate was committed as a charge upon such county. The officer in charge of the correctional institution shall send to such commissioner, officer or board a report of all information available in regard to the mother and the child. Such commissioner of public welfare or other officer or board shall care for or place out such child as provided by law in the case of a child becoming dependent upon the county.

3. If any woman, committed to any such correctional institution at the time of such commitment is the mother of a nursing child in her care under one year of age, such child may accompany her to such institution if she is physically fit to have the care of such child, subject to the provisions of subdivision two of this section. If any woman committed to any such institution at the time of such commitment is the mother of and has under her exclusive care a child more than one year of age the justice or magistrate committing such woman shall refer such child to the commissioner of public welfare or other officer or board exercising in relation to children the power of a commissioner of public welfare of the county from which the woman is committed to be cared for as provided by law in the case of a child becoming dependent upon the county.

Source: New York State Correctional Law, free access available at: http://law.onecle.com/new-york/correction/COR0611_611.html

CHAPTER 5

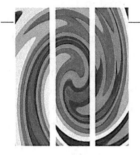

Chronically Ill Inmates

Elizabeth C. Dretsch

HISTORY OF MEDICAL CARE IN U.S. PRISONS

Until the 1970s there was an absence of national data concerning the number of correctional institutions that provided medical facilities, treatment or services to their inmates. It was assumed most did not provide such services. What little we do know about the type and amount of health care services that existed during this time period is limited to state studies or evidence presented in court cases (National Commission on Correctional Health Care [NCCHC], 2001). Until the 1970s there were also no formal intake procedures used to assess the health status of incoming prisoners. It was merely assumed, based on theoretical correlations between criminal activity, poverty, and poor health overall, that those individuals coming to prison were in poorer health than their free world counterparts (Clark, 1971). Correctional facilities were believed to have the "worst health care system in the United States" (Shervington, 1974) but these claims were rarely substantiated with empirical evidence. The literature at this time period merely provided assumptions about the overall status of health care and focused on specific conditions that contributed to poor health of persons within the correctional facilities (McMullan, 2011).

In 1975, The Office of Health and Medical Affairs (1975) provided a list of living conditions deemed unacceptable that were believed to contribute to the poor health of inmates incarcerated during this time period. These unacceptable living conditions included overcrowding, lack of sanitary conditions, poor dietary provisions, and absence of exercise or recreational outlets (NCCHC, 2001). The physical infrastructure of correctional facilities during this time period were often outdated, dilapidated, or in major states of disrepair. Once these conditions were officially documented, recommendations were made for correcting them.

The American Public Health Association provided the first national standards for health care specifically written for correctional institutions in 1976 (NCCHC, 2001). Although standards were finally in place, they lacked any legal mechanism for making the facilities comply. Furthermore, accreditation was the only tangible reward for adherence to these standards. The Georgia State Prison in Reidsville, Georgia, was the first correctional institution in the United States to receive accreditation for their health system (NCCHC, 2001) and this occurred in 1982.

Today most correctional institutions, jails and prisons, require some form of screening for preexisting mental or medical conditions at the point of intake. The purpose of these screenings is to determine whether or not the individual may require specialized care or additional testing. These screening techniques may be as simple as having the inmate or detainee answer questions about their medical needs on a specified intake form or may consist of an actual medical evaluation by a health care professional. Once preexisting medical conditions are identified a treatment plan is designed by health care professionals. Every institution adopts its own operating procedures that specify how an inmate must seek mental health or medical attention after intake. In some institutions this consists of completing a request form that specifies their complaints and results in an appointment with a medical professional. The manner in which medical emergencies are handled will also vary greatly depending on what type of treatment is needed and what is available at the institution. Some prisons have their own hospitals and medical professionals on site while others contract with local hospitals and provide transportation and security in the event of medical emergencies (McMullan, 2011).

CHRONIC ILLNESSES

In 2008, the Centers for Disease Control (CDC) reported that in the general population, hypertension and diabetes are the two most common chronic illnesses among adults. Both of these conditions are major risk factors associated with other serious and potentially deadly health conditions like coronary heart disease and renal kidney failure (Tomlinson & Schechter, 2003). In addition to diabetes and hypertension, some of the most common chronic illnesses affecting individuals residing in correctional facilities nationwide that will be discussed in this chapter include: asthma, heart disease, obesity, and other communicable diseases.

FACTS AND FIGURES

The number of individuals residing in correctional facilities in the United States has quadrupled over the past 25 years and continues to climb (Wilper et al., 2009). In 2009, over 7.2 million people were either on probation, parole, or incarcerated in jails or prisons, representing approximately 3.1% of the U.S. adult population (Glaze, 2010).

According to Rest Ministries.org (2009), approximately 20.6 % (100 million) of the general population suffers from at least one chronic illness[1]. Research indicates

[1]Rest Ministries.org hosts the National Invisible Chronic Illness Awareness Week website.

that individuals entering jails and prisons are more likely to suffer from chronic medical conditions, substance abuse issues and mental illness (Freudenberg, 2001; NCCHC, 2002) than members of the unincarcerated general population. The health status of prison inmates seems to be lower because of both the inmates' risky behavior and the prison environment (Kanato, 2008). In a recent study published in the American Journal of Public Health, it was reported that 38.5% of all federal inmates (49,702), 38.7% of local jail inmates (244,336) and 42.8% of all state inmates (524,116) have at least one chronic illness (Wilper et al., 2009). Since inmates have a constitutional right to receive adequate healthcare while they are incarcerated, states must ensure they allocate enough funding for healthcare costs within their budgets[2]. It is estimated that the average state prison will allocate at least 10% of their annual budget for inmate healthcare expenses (Kaplan, 1999). Approximately $3 billion is spent each year on inmate healthcare nationwide (Kaplan, 1999).

Researchers have identified three areas that have contributed to the increase in inmate health care costs: the rising number of inmates aging behind bars due to tougher legislation mandating life sentences or mandatory minimums; "inflation in the medical services industry; and an increase in the number of inmates with drug-related conditions such as HIV/AIDS, tuberculosis, and kidney disease" (Scott, 2004).

Table 5.1   Percentage of Individuals With at Least One Chronic Illness

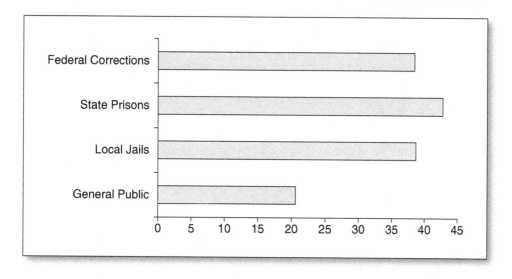

---

[2]*Estelle v. Gamble* 1976 held that a state must provide for the basic needs of any individual they deprive of liberty. *Ruiz v. Estelle* 1980 established the state's legal obligation to provide medical care to individuals that are incarcerated. This requirement to provide medical care also includes mental health care. These cases are described in more detail later in this chapter.

CHRONICALLY ILL INMATES

The term **chronic illness** refers to any illness that may result in death or requires a long-term medical or psychiatric treatment approach to maintain an acceptable quality of life. This treatment plan may include but is not limited to the use of prescription drugs, surgical procedures, or other therapeutic techniques that impose higher costs on the correctional institution where the inmate resides. The most prevalent and costly chronic illnesses are discussed in this chapter.

Asthma is a lung condition that causes one's airways to become constricted or blocked, making it difficult and sometimes impossible to breathe. There is no cure for asthma but there are treatments available that will help keep the symptoms under control and prevent a serious asthma attack from occurring. A serious asthma attack without intervention to open the airways can result in death. According to the Mayo Clinic (2011), there are four general categories of asthma:

(1) *Mild intermittent*—mild symptoms up to two days a week and up to two nights a month

(2) *Mild persistent*—symptoms more than twice a week but no more than once a day

(3) *Moderate persistent*—symptoms once a day and more than one night a week

(4) *Severe persistent*—symptoms throughout the day on most days and frequently at night

According to the American Diabetes Association (2011), *diabetes* is defined as:

A condition characterized by hyperglycemia resulting from the body's inability to use blood glucose for energy. In Type 1 diabetes, the pancreas no longer makes insulin and therefore blood glucose cannot enter the cells to be used for energy. In Type 2 diabetes, either the pancreas does not make enough insulin or the body is unable to use insulin correctly.

Diabetes is the most common cause of blindness in adults and leads to painful neuropathy and amputation of limbs (Tomlinson & Schechter, 2003). Individuals diagnosed with diabetes must carefully monitor their blood sugar and may also have to be administered daily insulin injections.

Between 60% and 70% of all Americans are either overweight or obese. A person's body mass index is used to determine their ideal weight and is also used to determine whether someone is either overweight or obese. Body mass index (BMI) is calculated by multiplying a person's weight in pounds by 703, then dividing that answer by his or her height in inches and finally, dividing that answer by height in inches again. An adult who's BMI is between 25 and 29 is considered to be overweight while a person with a BMI over 30 is diagnosed as obese. According to the American Heart Association (2011), obesity increases the risks of other health problems such as heart disease, stroke, high blood pressure, and diabetes.

Hypertension is the medical term used to describe high blood pressure. Normal blood pressure is typically at or below 120 (systolic)/80 (diastolic). When the systolic pressure is above 140 or the diastolic pressure measures above 90, it is considered high. Hypertension is typically treated with one of the following medicines: alpha blockers, angiotensin-converting enzyme (ACE) inhibitors, angiotensin receptor blockers (ARBs), beta blockers, calcium channel blockers, central alpha agonists, diuretics, rennin inhibitors (including Tekturna), or vasodilators[3].

Coronary heart disease, also called heart disease, is the leading cause of death in the United States for men and women[4]. Heart disease is usually the result of fatty material and other substances forming a plaque build-up on the walls of the arteries, causing them to narrow. The narrowing of these arteries results in a slowing down of the blood flow to the heart or can prevent blood flow, altogether, resulting in death. Symptoms of heart disease can range from chest pains to shortness of breath following activity, leading to a sudden heart attack. According to the CDC (2011), costs associated with cardiovascular disease were estimated at over $350 billion in 2010.

Communicable diseases include the human immunodeficiency virus (HIV), acquired immunodeficiency syndrome (AIDS), syphilis, gonorrhea, chlamydia, tuberculosis (TB), and hepatitis C (HCV). Sexually transmitted diseases (STDs) such as syphilis, chlamydia and gonorrhea are all easily treated with medication if diagnosed properly. They may result in additional health consequences if left undiagnosed or not properly treated. All of these STDs make the transmission of HIV more likely.

The hepatitis C virus (HCV) is a serious health concern due to the over representation of this disease in correctional facilities and the devastating health consequences when left untreated. HCV is a disease typically acquired through the exposure of contaminated blood, for example, sharing a needle with an infected person. HCV is currently the leading cause of end-stage liver disease which often results in death without a liver transplant and long-term immunosuppressive therapy (Murray, Pulvino, Baillargeon, Paar, & Raimer, 2007). It is also noted that HCV is the top reason for liver transplants in the United States (NIH, 2002). It is estimated that somewhere between 15 and 40% of individuals incarcerated in U.S. jails and prisons are infected with the HCV, despite the fact that the rate of infection among the general population is only 1.6% (Murray et al., 2007).

Another communicable disease that negatively impacts correctional facilities nationwide is the human immunodeficiency virus (HIV) and acquired immune deficiency syndrome (AIDS). HIV/AIDS is a virus that is transmitted through either sexual relations and/or exposure to blood (e.g., sharing unclean needles with an infected person). The incidence of AIDS in correctional facilities is noted to be five times higher than the rate of infection in the general population (Ruby, 2002). Despite the belief that prisons are "breeding grounds" for the spread of HIV/AIDS, most inmates were infected in the community prior to their incarceration (Hammett, 2006).

---

[3]This information was retrieved from the following website, http://www.medicinenet.com/kidney_disease_hypertension-related/page3.htm.

[4]Coronary heart disease: MedlinePlus Medical Encyclopedia. (n.d.). Retrieved from http://www.nlm.nih.gov/medlineplus/ency/article/007115.htm.

Those most likely to contract HIV during incarceration are "younger, non-white males serving time for sex crimes" (Krebs, 2006).

HIV attacks the body's immune system which eventually results in the development of AIDS, leaving the infected person highly susceptible to a range of infections, cancers, and other illnesses. This virus also attacks the central nervous system (CNS) resulting in progressive dementia and potentially leading to a serious wasting syndrome. According to a report published by the Bureau of Justice Statistics (BJS), there were 21,897 (1.5% of the prison population) inmates residing in either state or federal prisons with confirmed cases of HIV or AIDS infections at the end of 2008 (Maruschak & Beavers, 2009). The life expectancy of individuals with this disease has significantly increased due to the availability of new medications and better treatment methods.

In the general population, sexually active persons are strongly encouraged to use condoms to prevent the spread of HIV. However, most prisons consider condoms to be contraband, and as such, they are strictly prohibited. Furthermore, anyone caught possessing contraband is subject to administrative sanctions. There are a few correctional facilities that believe providing condoms to sexually active inmates or to those that request them, is a wise move and helps to prevent the spread of this deadly disease. State prison systems in Mississippi and Vermont, along with jails in Los Angeles, New York, Philadelphia, San Francisco, and the District of Columbia, currently provide condoms to inmates (Hammett & Harmon, 1999).

Tuberculosis (TB) disease is caused by a bacterium called *Mycobacterium tuberculosis* (CDC). The bacteria usually attack the lungs, but TB bacteria can attack any part of the body such as the kidney, spine, and brain (CDC). If not treated properly, the disease can be fatal (CDC). TB is five to ten times more prevalent in prisons than in the general population according to the World Health Organization (1998). Individuals can have TB and not become sick or contagious. There is a latent version of the disease that is diagnosed during a tuberculosis skin test or blood test, but is otherwise asymptomatic. The other form of TB is highly contagious and may not manifest itself until at least three weeks after the initial infection. The infected person may not be aware that he or she has it, absent a skin test or blood test, for several years. Treatment for TB is available and is usually remedied with 6 to 12 months of treatment.

SCREENING FOR MEDICAL AND MENTAL ILLNESSES

According to the NCCHC, most prisons and jails fail to conform to national health care guidelines for mental health screening and treatment (2002). Furthermore, in 2002, NCCHC reported that "17 percent of jails and prisons do not provide recommended intake screening for mental illness, and 40 percent of jails and 17 percent of prisons do not provide recommended mental health evaluations."

Detection of medical or mental health problems usually follows a three-prong process. This process includes screening for all inmates, assessment for those flagged during the screening process, and an additional evaluation of those in need by a trained professional. These procedures should occur within both a jail and prison setting immediately following the inmate's arrival.

Most jails do not have the time or financial resources to administer lengthy psychological assessments or evaluations to all incoming inmates, but still need to ensure they are able to provide mental health treatment to individuals who need it. This is where screening instruments are useful. An ideal screening tool should consist of 6–24 items, take no longer than 10–15 minutes to complete, and should be available for free or relatively no cost (McMullan, 2011; Sacks, 2008). It is important to note that a screening tool does not necessarily determine the type or severity of a disorder, only the probability that this person might have a disorder and whether or not additional assessment is required. The primary purpose of screening is to identify persons who require further evaluation.

The NCCHC has set forth nationally recognized standards for medical and mental health screening of incarcerated populations. These standards are required for accreditation purposes, but they are completely voluntary to those agencies not seeking accreditation. Some facilities choose not to go through accreditation due to costs associated with participation. However, the few thousands of dollars spent on this process could result in significant, long-term savings by preventing unnecessary and costly lawsuits. Inadequate health care is the second biggest reason for lawsuits in prison and jails in the United States (NCCHC, 2011).

Despite constitutional requirements for standard medical and mental health treatment for inmates[5], a nationally standardized screening instrument currently does not exist (Steadman, Scott, Osher, Agnese, & Robins, 2005). Ideally, jails and prisons will conduct an initial medical and mental health assessment of all incoming inmates during the intake process[6]. Most jails currently administer some form of mental health screening for inmates during their initial booking process (Steadman & Veysey, 1997; Veysey & Bichler-Robertson, 2002), but the content of these screening instruments vary greatly from facility to facility and have questionable validity (Teplin, 1990). Many criminal justice agencies create their own screening tools that are not standardized or tested for reliability and validity (Swartz & Lurigio, 2006). To date, there is not a standardized screening tool used in correctional facilities to test inmates for mental illness (Steadman et al., 2005; McMullan, 2011).

The first mental health screening tool, the Referral Decision Scale (RDS), was developed by Teplin and Swartz (1989) as a way to quickly screen for schizophrenia and major mood disorders in jail populations. This instrument consisted of 14 items and was initially used as a means of identifying those individuals who might need additional mental health assessments. The most commonly used screening instruments include the Brief Jail Mental Health Survey (BJMHS)[7], the Symptom Checklist-90, the Brief Symptom Inventory (Steadman et al., 2005), and the Correctional Mental Health Screen for Women (CMHS-W); (Goldberg & Higgins, 2006). Research indicates that the BJMHS is the most appropriate screening tool for use in male correctional populations. It can be administered on average within 2.5 minutes and correctly classified 73.5% of the male inmate population during the study.

[5]*Estelle v. Gamble*, 1976, and *Ruiz v. Estelle*, 1980.

[6]The Federal Bureau of Prisons provides a copy of their intake screening form on their website and this form is provided for illustration purposes in Figure 5.1.

[7]A copy of the BJMHS is presented in Figure 5.2.

Unfortunately, the same study also revealed that the BJMHS resulted in a high false-negative rate for female inmates (Steadman et al., 2005). The CMHS-W[8] yielded better results than the BJMHS for screening within female populations and is therefore recommended for screening females. The development and validation of these tools were made possible by grant funding through the National Institute of Justice (NIJ). Both tools are subsequently made available in the public domain and are included in this textbook to provide an illustration[9].

Screening for co-occurring mental and substance use disorders is becoming more prevalent in criminal justice setting today. Although the BJMHS and CMHS-W have been identified as valid tools for mental health screening in jail and prison populations, these tools are not intended to identify individuals with dual diagnosis. The Criminal Justice Co-Occurring Disorders Screening Instrument (CJ-CODSI) was developed to provide professionals with a brief yet standardized screening instrument (Coen, Sacks, & Melnick, 2006). Co-occurring mental and drug dependency disorders complicate treatment goals by interfering with adherence to specific treatment plans and often contribute to patient relapse (Fletcher & Wexler, 2003).

An initial screening should be provided during booking by a correctional officer to identify persons who potentially require more medical and/or psychological attention. Screening tools for mental health should include at a minimum, indicators for schizophrenia, bipolar disorder, and major depressive disorders (Lurigio & Swartz, 2006).

Medical screenings should at a minimum include questions concerning the existence of serious medical conditions that require treatment. Most correctional facilities do not allow inmates to retain their own medications so it is essential to provide them with facility-issued replacements as quickly as possible. Correctional staff members are in a unique position to provide useful information to the mental health professionals based upon their constant contact and observation of these individuals. Training for correctional staff members should provide them with some basic warning signs and tips for making appropriate and inappropriate observations. Often times, our observations are heavily influenced by our own personal frame of reference. Our perceptions of events vary based upon our own personal experiences, also known as our frame of reference. When reporting observations it is extremely important to remain objective when reporting behaviors of individuals. Reporting an observation that "Jimmy was talking to himself and swaying back and forth in his cell today" is much more useful than reporting that "Jimmy was acting crazy" (Van Voorhis, Braswell, & Lester, 2009). When in doubt it is better to provide too much detail and information than not enough.

The costs of screening all incoming inmates for chronic illnesses like diabetes and hypertension significantly reduces the costs incurred when such illnesses remain undiagnosed and subsequently untreated (Tomlinson & Schechter, 2003). The effects of screening would enable more aggressive treatment earlier on, subsequently

[8]A copy of the CMHS-W is presented in Figure 5.3.

[9]For copies of the instruments and the full grant reports, visit www.ncjrs.org/pdffiles1/nij/grants/210829.pdf and www.ncjrs.org/pdffiles1/nij/grants/213805.pdf. Retrieved March 1, 2012.

Figure 5.1	Screening Form Used by the Federal Bureau of Prisons[10]

---

[10]Located on the Federal Bureau of Prisons' website at http://www.bop.gov/policy/forms/BP_A0360.pdf.

Figure 5.1   (Continued)

Alcohol History: Please complete the following:

Type used: (beer, wine, vodka, etc.)	How often:(daily, weekly)	Usual Amount	Date of last drink

Have you ever had, or are you now having, any withdrawal symptoms when you have stopped using drugs or alcohol:
□ No   □ Yes
If yes, please describe: _____

Do you use:

Tobacco: □ Yes   □ No   How much? _____Pack/Day   How long? _____Years

7.   PAIN ASSESSMENT:

Do you currently suffer from any painful condition?   □ No   □ Yes - Location: _____

8.   DENTAL: Do you currently have any of the following:

□ Pain in teeth or mouth	□ Swelling in mouth, jaws, or neck	□ Dental emergency which you feel must be addressed immediately

9.   HISTORY OF ABUSE: Please complete the following: if applicable: □ Not applicable

TYPE OF ABUSE	WHAT AGE(s) OR WHEN
□ Physical	
□ Emotional	
□ Sexual	

10.   FEMALE HEALTH: Women please complete the following:

Date of last menstrual period:_____   # of Pregnancies: _____   Are you pregnant now?: □ Yes □ No □ Don't know

Date of last pap smear:_____
Results: □ Normal   □ Abnormal   □ Don't know

Date of last mammogram: _____
Results: □ Normal   □ Abnormal   □ Don't know

Type of Birth Control:
□ Birth Control Pills   □ IUD   □ Diaphragm   □ None   □ Other: _____

Are you taking hormones for menopause or after hysterectomy?   □ Yes   □ No   Check vaccinations you have had: □ Measles □ Mumps □ Rubella

Have you ever had any of the following? (If yes, what year?)
□ Abnormal Pap

□ Breast Biopsy

□ Hysterectomy

11.   ALL INMATES - Please describe any other medical or mental health concerns you have:

12.   DIET:

□ Diabetic	□ Low salt	□ Low fat	□ Vegetarian	□ Other _____
Current weight:		Usual weight:		

13. IMMUNIZATIONS: Have you received any of the following vaccinations:

□ Tetanus (when):_____	□ Hepatitis A	□ Hepatitis B	□ Pneumonia ["Pneumovax"] (when):_____

I have answered all questions truthfully and to the best of my ability.

Inmate Signature:	Date:

PDF   Prescribed by P6031   This form replaces BP-S360 of FEB 05

BP-A360.060   **HEALTH INTAKE ASSESSMENT/HISTORY** CDFRM   **PART 2**

HEALTH CARE PROVIDER: Please complete the following:

Inmate Name:	Register No:	Institution:

A. **INMATE NEEDS FOLLOW-UP FOR THE FOLLOWING:** (Provider will review inmate responses and comment where necessary)

ISSUE OR CONDITION	COMMENTS (Indicate if urgent treatment is necessary)
Infectious disease: ☐ Yes ☐ No Draining skin lesions: ☐ Yes ☐ No Signs of lice? ☐ Yes ☐ No Signs of scabies? ☐ Yes ☐ No	
☐ Skin condition: include trauma markings, bruises, jaundice, recent tattoos, needle marks, or other indications of drug use	
☐ Drug/alcohol withdrawal	
☐ Mental Health Issues	
☐ Pain Management	
☐ Physical disabilities/deformities	
☐ Cardiovascular disease	
☐ Diabetes	
☐ Asthma	
☐ Cancer	
☐ Dental problems	
☐ OB/Gyn	
☐ Other: _____	

B. **OTHER COMMENTS OR PHYSICAL FINDINGS:** (Record vital signs if indicated)

C. ☐ **MEDICATION AND OTHER ORDERS WRITTEN ON SF-600 FORM**

D. ☐ **MEDICATION CONSENT FORMS SIGNED**

E. ☐ **INSTRUCTED INMATE HOW TO OBTAIN MEDICAL, DENTAL, AND MENTAL HEALTH SERVICES**

Provider Signature:	Printed Name/Credentials:
Date:	Time:

PDF   Prescribed by P6031   This form replaces BP-S360 of FEB 05

(Continued)

Figure 5.1   (Continued)

BP-A360.060   **EVALUACIÓN DE SALUD INICIAL E HISTORIAL MÉDICO   PARTE 1**
FEB 05
DEPARTAMENTO DE JUSTICIA DE EE.UU.   AGENCIA FEDERAL DE PRISIONES

This is a translation of an English-language document provided as a courtesy to those not fluent in English.   If differences or any misunderstandings occur, the document of record shall be the related English-language document.

Esta es una traducción de un documento escrito en inglés, distribuido como una cortesía a las personas que no pueden leer inglés.   Si resulta alguna diferencia o algún malentendido con esta traducción, el único documento reconocido será la versión en inglés.

Nombre: Número: Institución:
Reo Recibido de: ▪ Tribunal   ▪ Cárcel   ▪ Rendimiento Volunatrio   ▪ Otros

<u>REO</u>: POR FAVOR COMPLETE DEL 1 AL 14.

1. **MEDICAMENTOS**:   Por favor haga una lista de todo medicamento actual, la cantidad, fecha y hora de la última dosis.

2. **ALERGIAS**: Por favor marque y explique cualquier alergia que haya tenido.
   ▪ Medicinas:
   ▪ Comidas: ▪ Otras:

3. **ENFERMEDADES**:   Marque cualquier condición actual o que haya tenido en el pasado.
   ▪ Ataque/enfermedad del corazón ▪ Cuágulos de sangre ▪ Angina   ▪ Diabetes   ▪ Anemia crónica
   ▪ Enfermedades pulmonares   ▪ Asma   ▪ Derrame Cerebral ▪ Presión alta ▪ Convulsión/Epilepsia
   ▪ Cáncer   Tipo: Cuando?:   ▪ Otras:

4. **ENFERMEDADES INFECCIOSAS**: Marque cualquier condición actual o que haya tenido en el pasado.
   ▪ Prueba de TB positiva   ▪ Tuberculosis ▪ Escupir sangre ▪ Tos persistente- ¿cuanto tiempo? ▪ Sudor de noche
   ▪ Varicela or culebrilla   ▪ Gonorréa   ▪ Clamidia   ▪ ¿Tiene sarpullido, llagas o heridas
                                                                      abiertas? ¿Dónde?
   ▪ SIDA (desde cuando)   ▪ Hepatitis (Typo):   ▪ Herpes
   ▪ ¿Ha viajado recientemente ▪ Sifilis   ▪ Transfución de sangre
   afuera de EE.UU.?   ▪ ¿Recibió Tratamiento?   ¿Cuándo?
   ¿Cuándo?   ¿Cuando?   ¿Por qué?
   ¿Dónde?   ¿Donde?
   ¿Esta en riesgo de contratar HIV o Hepatitis porque comparte agujas, tiene sexo de alto riesgo o tatuajes?
      ▪ Sí   ▪ No   ▪ No sé
   (Si no lo sabe, por favor hable con un médico sobre cualquier inquietud que tenga y solicite un examen, si es apropiado.)

5. **CONDICIÓN NERVIOSA**: Marque cualquier condición actual o que haya tenido en el pasado
   ¿Ha tenido problemas mentales?   ▪ No   ▪ Sí   Explique:
   ▪ Ideas de Suicidio   ▪ Trauma de la cabeza   ▪ Pérdida del conocimiento
     ¿Cuándo?   ¿Cuándo?   ¿Cuándo?
                                         ¿Cómo?   ¿Cómo?
   ▪ Intento de Suicidio   ¿Cuándo?   ¿Cómo?

6. **DROGAS Y ALCOHOL**:   ¿Esta usando o ha usado alguna de las siguientes sustancias?

SUSTANCIA	¿CÓMO? (Agujas, Fumado, Inhalado, Pildoras)	ULTIMA FECHA DE USO
▪ Tranquilizantes (Valium, Xanax, etc)		
▪ Opiatos (Heroina, Metadona, Oxycodona, Vicodin, otros)		
▪ Barbitúricos (Fenobarbital, Seconal, otros)		
▪ LSD/Alucinógenos/PCP		
▪ Marihuana		
▪ Otros		

Historial de Alcohol: Por favor complete lo siguiente:

Tipo usado:(cerveza, vino, vodka, etc)	Frecuencia (a diario, semanal)	Cantidad Normal	Fecha de su último trago

Ha tenido o tiene actualmente algun síndrome de abstinencia después de parar su uso de drogas o alcohol?
- No   • Sí
Si marcó si, explíquelo

¿Usa usted:

Tabaco?:   • Sí   • No   ¿Cuanto?   Cajas al dia   ¿Cuanto tiempo?   Años

7. EVALUACIÓN DE DOLOR:

¿Sufre de algún dolor?   • No   • Sí   ¿Donde?

8. PROBLEMAS DENTALES: ¿Tiene alguno de los siguientes? :

• Dolor de boca o de dientes	• Inflamación en la boca, la mandíbula o el cuello	• Emergencia dental que necesita atención inmediata

9. HISTORIAL DE ABUSO: Por favor complete lo siguiente, si es aplicable   • No es aplicable

TIPO DE ABUSO	¿A QUE EDAD O CUANDO?
• Físico	
• Emocional	
• Sexual	

10. INFORMACIÓN DE SALUD FEMENINA: Mujeres, por favor completen lo siguiente:

Fecha de su última menstruación: Embarazos:	¿Está embarazada ahora? • Sí • No • No sé
Fecha de su último exámen Papanicolao Resultado: • Normal • Anormal • No sé	¿Ha tenido algunos de los siguientes? (Si contesta "SÍ" indique el año)
Fecha de su último mamograma Resultado: • Normal • Anormal • No sé	• Papanicolao anormal
Método de control de embarazo: • Píldoras anticonceptivas • DIU • Diafragma • Ninguno • Otro	• Biopsia del seno
¿Esta tomando hormonas para la menopausia o después de una histerectomia? • Sí • No	Marque las vacunas que ha tenido: • Sarampión • Paperas • Rubeola	• Histerectomia

11. TODOS LOS REOS - Por favor describa cualquier inquietud médica o mental adicional que usted tenga:

12. DIETA:

• de Diabetico	• Baja en sal	• Baja en grasa	• Vegetariana	• Otra
Peso actual:		Peso normal:		

13. INMUNIZACIONES: ¿Ha recibido algunas de las siguientes vacunas?

• Contra el Tétano (¿Cuando?)	• Hepatitis A	• Hepatitis B	• Neumonía (Pneumovax) (¿Cuando?)

He contestado todas las preguntas sinceramente y con la mejor habilidad.

Firma del Reo: Fecha:

increasing survival rates, lower morbidity rates, and reduce costs associated with complications.

Voluntary serologic screening for HCV would be a more affordable approach toward screening since HCV testing is relatively expensive. Screening for common risk factors associated with those infected with HCV would also help correctional facilities better target those in need of additional testing. The primary risk factors associated with HCV infection include a history of injection drug use, known HIV infection, or high-risk sexual activity.

LEGAL REQUIREMENTS ASSOCIATED WITH THE PROVISION OF MEDICAL CARE AND TREATMENT

When an individual becomes a prisoner of the government (federal, state, or local) their incarceration by its very nature prevents them from freely seeking medical care and treatment within the community. This deprivation of liberty subsequently makes the incarcerating authority responsible for their care and safety (Cripe & Pearlman, 2005). Denial of medical care is not prescribed by law as part of a person's sentence. Furthermore, the infliction of unnecessary suffering on a prisoner stemming from a failure to treat his or her medical needs is inconsistent with contemporary standards of decency and violates the Eighth Amendment.

Prior to 1962, inmates were subjected to civil death upon incarceration, stripping them of their constitutional rights. Up until this point, the U.S. Supreme Court adopted a hands-off approach toward inmate affairs, believing the correctional administrators were more capable of determining what was appropriate and in the best interest of the inmates. Another concern that kept courts from intervening was the fear that interfering in state and local matters would be seen as a violation of federalism or would undermine the authority of the correctional administrators. It wasn't until *Robinson v. California* (1962) that the federal courts were given the green light to review state court decisions without fear of violating federalism. One of the greatest contributions of this case was ensuring all citizens, even those serving time for the commission of a criminal act, are entitled to the protection of their constitutional and civil rights. Although the courts recognized that the interest of the states may prevent such rights from being applied exactly as they would in the outside world, in the name of public safety and security, they do at least eliminate the notion that incarceration was tantamount to civil death.

There are three additional significant cases that helped pave the way for inmate rights concerning the provision of medical care. These cases include: *Newman v. Alabama* (1972); *Estelle v. Gamble* (1976), and *Farmer v. Brennan* (1994). Collectively these cases ensured inmates of three basic rights concerning their medical care: (1) the right to basic access to care; (2) a right to the care that is ordered for them; and (3) a right to a professional, medical judgment (NCCHC, 2001). Each of these cases and their individual contributions are specified below.

Newman v. Alabama (1972) involved a class action suit on behalf of state prisoners alleging that they were deprived of proper and adequate medical treatment. They asserted this deprivation violated their Eighth and Fourteenth Amendment rights,

Figure 5.2   Brief Jail Mental Health Screen

Section 1

| Name: _____ | Detainee #: _____ | Date: __/__/__ | Time: _____   AM |
| First   Middle   Last | | | PM |

Section 2

Questions	No	Yes	General Comments
1. Do you *currently* believe that someone can control your mind by putting thoughts into your head or taking thoughts out of your head?			
2. Do you *currently* feel that other people know your thoughts and can read your mind?			
3. Have you *currently* lost or gained as much as two pounds a week for several weeks without even trying?			
4. Have you or your family or friends noticed that you are *currently* much more active than you usually are?			
5. Do you *currently* feel like you have to talk or move more slowly than you usually do?			
6. Have there *currently* been a few weeks when you felt like you were useless or sinful?			
7. Are you *currently* taking any medication prescribed for you by a physician for any emotional or mental health problems?			
8. Have you *ever* been in a hospital for emotional or mental health problems?			

Section 3 (Optional)

Officer's Comments/Impressions (check *all* that apply):

☐   Language barrier   ☐   Under the influence   ☐   Non-cooperative
                                          of drugs/alcohol

☐   Difficulty understanding questions   ☐   Other, specify:

Referral Instructions: This detainee should be referred for further mental health evaluation if he/she answered:

- **YES to item 7; OR**
- **YES to item 8; OR**
- **YES to at least 2 of items 1 through 6; OR**
- **If you feel it is necessary for any other reason**

☐   Not Referred
☐   Referred on ____/____/_____ to _____
Person completing screen _____

Source: Located on the Federal Bureau of Prisons' website at http://www.bop.gov/policy/forms/BP_A0360.pdf.

Figure 5.3   Correctional Mental Health Screen for Women (CMHS-W)

Name: _____ Last, First, MI	Detainee #: _____	Date: __/___/__ mm/dd/year	Time: _____:_____

Questions	No	Yes	General Comments
1. Do you get annoyed when friends and family complain about their problems? Or do people complain you are not sympathetic to their problems?			
2. Have you ever tried to avoid reminders of, or to not think about, something terrible that you experienced or witnessed?			
3. Some people find their mood changes frequently as if they spend everyday on an emotional rollercoaster. For example, switching from feeling angry to depressed to anxious many times a day. Does this sound like you?			
4. Have there ever been a few weeks when you felt you were useless, sinful, or guilty?			
5. Has there ever been a time when you felt depressed most of the day for at least 2 weeks?			
6. Do you find that most people will take advantage of you if you let them know too much about you?			
7. Have you been troubled by repeated thoughts, feelings, or nightmares about something terrible that you experienced or witnessed?			
8. Have you ever been in the hospital for non-medical reasons, such as a psychiatric hospital? (Do NOT include going to an emergency room if you were not hospitalized.)			

TOTAL # YES:	General
	Comments:

Refer for further Mental Health Evaluation if the Detainee answered

Yes to **5** or more items *OR* if you are concerned for any other reason

o   URGENT Referral   on _ _ / _ _ / _ _ _ _ to _____

o   ROUTINE Referral   on _ _ / _ _ / _ _ _ _ to _____

o   Not Referred

Person Completing Screen: _____

Source: Located on the Federal Bureau of Prisons' website at http://www.bop.gov/policy/forms/BP_A0360.pdf.

leading them to seek declaratory and injunctive relief. The district court held that it was failure on the part of the Board of Corrections to provide sufficient medical facilities and staff to ensure inmates the basic elements of adequate medical care. This in turn constituted willful and intentional violation of inmate rights. The denial of access to medical personnel, failure to provide prescribed medicines and other medical treatment constitute cruel and unusual punishment. The court further held the entire Alabama prison system was in violation of the Eighth and Fourteenth Amendments of the U.S. Constitution.

The U.S. Supreme Court case *Estelle v. Gamble* (1976) paved the way by setting specific standards for the provision of medical care of inmates. In 1976, the U.S. Supreme Court heard the case of *Estelle v. Gamble* concerning an inmate who was injured performing prison labor and denied adequate medical care and treatment. This inmate was furthermore penalized for his medical condition through the use of solitary confinement since he was no longer capable of performing the labor required of the other inmates. The U.S. Supreme Court ruled that the

> deliberate indifference to serious medical needs of prisoners constitutes unnecessary and wanton infliction of pain proscribed by Eighth Amendment whether the indifference is manifested by prison doctors in response to prison needs or by prison guards in intentionally denying or delaying access to medical care or intentionally interfering with treatment once prescribed; regardless of how evidenced deliberate indifference to prisoner's serious illness or injuries states cause of action under civil rights statute.[11]

It should also be noted though, that physician error in and of itself does not constitute a violation of one's Eighth Amendment right to be free from cruel and unusual punishment since members of the general population are also subjected to the same risks. However, if the state knowingly hires a physician that does not meet "minimum standards of competence" or this physician is unable to provide adequate medical care and attention due to an "excessive caseload" or "inadequate facilities," then the state may be in violation of the Eighth Amendment.[12]

The "deliberate indifference" criteria applies to all forms of medical treatment or aspects of care that may result in "unnecessary and wanton infliction of pain," which is prevented by the Eighth Amendment of the U.S. Constitution, if left untreated. Cases brought before the courts involved not just allegations of outright denial of medical care, but also involved allegations of inadequate care, improper medical care, and the conduct of prison officials prohibiting medical care (Palmer, 2010, p. 226). Most cases involving medical care are addressed using the due process clause of the Fifth and Fourteenth Amendments or the cruel and unusual clause of the Eighth Amendment. The Eighth Amendment also prohibits the state from punishing individuals for having a medical condition or physical ailment, and the

---

[11]*Estelle v. Gamble*, 1976.

[12]*Estelle v. Gamble*, 1976.

equal protection clause is used to prevent prison authorities from treating a group of inmates differently based on their medical condition.

Farmer v. Brennan (1994) was a case involving a man incarcerated prior to completing a sex change to female. Despite his obvious vulnerability (i.e., feminine appearance and mannerisms) he was placed in general population with other male inmates and was subsequently subjected to repeated beatings and rapes, ultimately resulting in his contraction of HIV. The courts ruled in this case, a prison official's "deliberate indifference" to a substantial risk of serious harm to an inmate violates the cruel and unusual punishment clause of the Eighth Amendment. Although the prison was not required to provide the inmate with a sex change operation, they should have known that placing this inmate in general population would result in a substantial risk of serious harm.

Inmates are now guaranteed access to proper medical care under Section 1983 of the U.S. Code and denial of these rights is remedied by litigation. This section of the U.S. Code permits prisoners to sue correctional officials in federal court when the conditions of confinement fail to meet constitutional standards. A physician who contracts with the state to provide medical care to inmates acts under the color of state law and is also liable for civil violations under 42 USC 1983.[13] This not only pertains to the provision of basic health care, but also includes mental health care.

Under the Americans with Disabilities Act (ADA), inmates are also entitled to receive adequate accommodations for disabilities during incarceration. This includes access to buildings, adequate transportation accommodations, and communication devices (i.e., hearings aids, glasses, etc.). This also includes providing inmates with wheelchairs or prosthetic devices if they are unable to walk. Although states are immune to monetary damages under the sovereign immunity clause of the Eleventh Amendment, they may be forced to comply through the use of an injunction if they are found not to be in compliance of the ADA standards (NCCHC, 2001). The U.S. Supreme Court 1998 decision in *Bragdon v. Abbott* (Bingswanger, 2010) established protection for people infected with HIV/AIDS under the auspices of the ADA.[14] The U.S. Supreme Court held that services could not be denied to individuals simply because the practitioner was afraid of contracting HIV. The justices maintained that under the ADA, policies and procedures must rely on objective, scientific evidence regarding the "statistical likelihood" of transmission. The dentist who denied services to patients with HIV was in direct violation of this ruling because there was a lack of empirical evidence supporting the statistical likelihood that treating patients with HIV would result in transmission of the virus.

In summation prison officials must provide inmates with reasonable medical care and treatment; this includes, but is not limited to, the provision of dental care, medical care, and psychiatric care.

---

[13]*West v. Atkins*, 487 U.S. 42 (1988) and *Ort v. Pinchback*, 786 F.2d 1105 (11th Cir. 1986) were two federal court cases that set forth this precedence.

[14]Protection begins from the moment of infection.

TELEMEDICINE

Telemedicine is a relatively new approach to correctional health care that makes use of modern technology to provide inmates with an interactive healthcare experience. Telemedicine provides an alternative medical experience that allows patients and physicians to communicate in real time using video equipment. This approach is helpful in correctional settings because it eliminates the barriers once imposed by physical distance from one another. Telemedicine office visits are similar to the experience of using a web camera to communicate with others on the Internet; although, the equipment used for telemedicine is much more powerful than any standard webcam, and the visual images projected are much clearer. Patients are also able to submit a list of their symptoms along with video recordings or digital photographs of their afflictions to a physician for documentation, diagnosis, and treatment purposes. Telemedicine can also be used in conjunction with on-site medical personnel in situations where a specialist's opinion is warranted.

The Federal Bureau of Prisons (FBP) began looking more closely into the telemedicine system as a means of reducing the risks associated with transporting inmates for medical care and treatment purposes. This danger was made abundantly clear in October of 1987 when a Lewisburg Federal Penitentiary guard was murdered while attempting to escort a prisoner back from a visit to the Geisinger Medical Center in Pennsylvania. The unarmed prison guard was killed in an escape attempt. The inmate being escorted was Paul Iasiello. He was a convicted kidnapper serving time in the Lewisburg Federal Prison at the time of the incident. Iasiello was in the process of being transported back to the prison following a medical visit when two gunmen came out from the emergency room and began firing at the unarmed escorts (Philadelphia Inquirer, 1987). Although Iasiello was initially able to escape with the two gunmen, all three were captured shortly after the incident when their getaway vehicle crashed at an intersection (Chicago Tribune, 1987). This incident sparked the FBP to inquire into alternative methods for providing inmates with medical care and diagnosis.

The first federal prison telemedicine suite was located at the U.S. Penitentiary at Allenwood, Pennsylvania, and was operational in September of 1996. This suite was linked with the Department of Veterans Affairs Medical Center (VAMC) in Lexington, Kentucky. The U.S. Penitentiary at Lewisburg, Pennsylvania, began utilizing a telemedicine suite in January of 1997. This pilot program had three major goals: (1) to reduce the safety risks associated with the transportation of inmates outside of the prison to visit healthcare professionals for the purposes of medical treatment and diagnosis; (2) to increase the inmate's access to specialists that otherwise would not be available to them due to their location; and (3) to reduce the amount of time inmates traditionally had to wait before being able to see a specialist (Nacci, 1999).

A telemedicine approach is perhaps best suited for larger correctional facilities that require large numbers of consultations with specialists or facilities that would incur significant travel expenses by bringing specialists to their facility on a regular basis. While the costs of the telemedicine program may be high initially, the use of this technology in jails and prisons reduces the need to transfer inmates to other facilities for specialist care, thereby reducing the safety risks posed to medical professionals working with inmates. The costs required in the start-up phase may be too costly for smaller facilities. Correctional facilities adopting a telemedicine program must incur costs associated with the equipment itself and technological installation fees, in addition to other basic operational expenses. The equipment alone is estimated to cost facilities somewhere between $80,000 and $100,000 (Gailiun, 1997). The benefits, however, go far beyond financial savings and include such benefits as reducing security risks by eliminating the need for transportation of inmates to specialty care provider offices, decreasing the waiting periods for prisoners needing specialty care, and increasing the access for inmates to specialty-care providers who otherwise may not have been available to them (NIJ, 1999). The Federal Bureau of Prisons was able to reduce specialty-care costs by $100 per consultation by using telemedicine (NIJ, 1999).

COSTS ASSOCIATED WITH THE TREATMENT OF CHRONICALLY ILL INMATES

At least 30 states now require inmates to pay a copayment for the medical care they receive (Kaplan, 1999). The copayment amounts range from $2 to $10 and the copayment is obviously waived for those deemed indigent (Kaplan, 1999).

Treatment for the Hepatitis C Virus

The antiviral therapy used to treat HCV infections costs anywhere between $7,000 and $20,000. Individuals that do not receive proper care and treatment for HCV are at risk of developing end-stage liver disease and will require a liver transplant with long term immunosuppressive therapy in order to stay alive. According to the United Network for Organ Sharing (UNOS, n.d.) a liver transplant may cost more than $523,400.

It is estimated that liver transplant recipients will also incur additional follow-up charges around $21,900. Following all liver transplants, patients will need to endure immunosuppressive therapy which involves the use of medications that range anywhere from $5.00 a month to over $2,000 a month. In addition to the immunosuppressive medications, recipients are also typically required to make use of antirejection drugs and other medications that can easily exceed $10,000 a year and can sometimes be required for the rest of the person's life (UNOS, n.d.).

Asthma Treatment

The most common treatment for asthma involves the use of inhaled corticosteroids. Some of the most commonly used medications under this category include fluticasone, budesonide, mometasone, flunisolide, and beclomethasone. Asthma can be a very costly disease since people diagnosed with moderate to severe asthma

Table 5.2	Estimated Costs Associated With Diabetes Complications
Congestive heart failure	$2,188.40
Amputation	$4,808.46
Heart disease	$15,952.00
Blindness	$16,207.00
End-stage renal disease	$46,207.00
Stroke	$50,000.00

Source: Tomlinson & Schechter, 2003.[15]

typically need to take three different medications (Griffin, 2011). It is estimated that the annual treatment costs for asthma could exceed $4,900 per person (Cisternas et al., 2003) depending on the severity of the condition.

Diabetes, Hypertension and Heart Disease Treatment

Among adults aged 20–74, diabetes continues to be the leading cause of kidney failure, nontraumatic lower-extremity amputations, and blindness (CDC, 2008). The costs associated with aggressive diabetic treatments can be as high as $1,983 a year (Eastman et al., 1997). Hypertension typically requires medications and at least five checkups a year to monitor the patient's progress. When using the least expensive generic medications, the costs can be as little as $388.40 a year (Pearce, Furberg, Psaty, & Kirk, 1998). Failure to properly treat these disorders could result in complications such as congestive heart failure, foot or leg amputation, blindness, heart disease, end-stage renal disease, and stroke (Tomlinson & Schechter, 2003).

Treatment for HIV

The increased availability of treatment options for HIV/AIDS patients have significantly contributed to the increased life expectancy of those infected with the virus. Not only have the medications used to treat this virus been advanced, but the cost of treatment is far more affordable as well. While initial antiretroviral drugs ran anywhere from $10,000 to $15,000 per person per year, now this has been significantly reduced. Advances in the pharmaceutical realm coupled with the invention of generic alternative treatment makes treatment available today for as low as $88 per person per year.[16]

Most HIV patients are now prescribed a Highly Active Antiretroviral Therapy (HAART) treatment approach consisting of three different medications

---

[15]The information presented in this table came from the Tomlinson & Schechter (2003) source.

[16]This is possible when using the d4T, 3TC & NVP drug combination.

(AVERT.org, 2011). This approach allows the body to keep the HIV infection in the body relatively low and stops the weakening of the immune system to allow it to recover from any damage caused by HIV pretreatment. The most commonly used drug combination for this approach involves d4T (stavudine a.k.a. Zerit), 3TC (lamivudine a.k.a. Epivir) and NVP (nevirapine a.k.a. Viramune).

FEMALE INMATES

The incarceration of a pregnant woman presents unique dilemmas for correctional institutions. According to the Bureau of Justice Statistics, approximately 25% of women residing in correctional institutions are either pregnant or postpartum. The literature indicates that pregnant women in correctional facilities are most likely to experience complications during pregnancy due to an increased likelihood they are suffering from a whole host of other health issues and risk factors such as being HIV positive; having another sexually transmitted disease; being obese; being malnourishment; being in poor physical health overall; and suffering from some form of emotional distress such as anxiety and/or depression (Fogel, 1995; Goldkuhle, 1999; Hufft, Fawkes, & Lawson, 1993). According to McMullan (2011), most pregnant women entering a correctional facility are considered to be a high-risk pregnancy based on their lifestyle prior to admissions (p. 256).

Failure to seek prenatal care during this period of gestation could result in a serious medical emergency. The potential complications associated with pregnancy make this a serious health care need, and lack of the provision of care during this time period could constitute a violation of the Eighth Amendment.[17] Correctional institutions must provide the option for an incarcerated woman to terminate an unwanted pregnancy even if she is unable to pay for the procedure herself.[18] Although female inmates are not entitled to retain custody of their children immediately following birth, they do have the right to breastfeed them during subsequent visitations if they so choose.[19] Further detailed discussion on motherhood behind bars was presented in the previous chapter, Chapter 4.

According to the CDC (2009), the most commonly reported infectious disease in the United States in 2008 was chlamydia trachomatis (CT). However, many more cases go undiagnosed and unreported because they are often times asymptomatic in women (CDC, 2011b). Untreated CT infections can translate into additional health issues for women like pelvic inflammatory disease, ectopic pregnancies, and infertility (Eng & Butler, 1997). Furthermore, another serious concern for both males and females with untreated infections is the fact that such an infection increases the likelihood of HIV infection and transmission (CDC, 2009).

There is a disproportionate CT infection rate of 8.5% among females entering jails compared to the 6% rate of CT infection found in the general population

---

[17]*Boswell v. Sherburne County*, 1988.

[18]*Monmouth County Correctional Institution Inmates v. Lanzaro*, 1987.

[19]*Berrious-Berrios v. Thornburg*, 1989.

(CDC, 2011b). As with many of the other health issues discussed in this chapter, there is a higher prevalence of CT infections in adult jails overall and a high rate of gonococcal infections as well (CDC, 2009; Mertz, Voigt, Hutchins, Levine, & the Jail STD Prevalence Monitoring Group, 2002; Skolnick, 1998).

Cervical cancer and breast cancer are two additional serious health concerns for female inmates. Annual health exams are essential to ensure early detection and successful treatment for cervical dysplasia. Early detection of cervical abnormalities can ensure treatment before the dysplasia reaches a cancer stage. A recent study indicates that 6.3% of female inmates have cervical cancer (Bingswanger, 2010). Although most annual exams included a basic breast exam, it is further recommended that every woman between the ages of 35 to 40 have a mammogram screening annually to help ensure the early detection of breast cancer. Next to nonmelanoma skin cancer, breast cancer is the second most common form of cancer among women and is the leading cause of cancer-related deaths for women across all racial and ethnic populations in the United States (CDC, 2011a). In 2007, there were 202,964 women diagnosed with breast cancer and 40,598 reported deaths resulting from it (CDC, 2011a).

ELDERLY INMATES

In the year 2000, 42,300 inmates 55 years of age or older were incarcerated in federal or state prisons, representing 3.4% of the total number of inmates (Beck, Karberg, & Harrison, 2001) incarcerated nationwide. These numbers are expected to continue to rise. In fact, every four years the number of older inmates doubles (Clear & Cole, 1997, p. 262). Some researchers predict that by 2030 one third of the U.S. prison population will be comprised of inmates 50 or older (Enders, Paterniti, & Meyers, 2005).

It is estimated that the average prisoner under the age of 55 who is not HIV positive will require approximately $20,000 per year for care and custody. On the other hand, an elderly inmate averages between $60,000 and $70,000 a year for care and custody (Ornduff, 1996; Williams et al., 2006). Chronic illnesses are most prevalent among elder inmates and consume a huge chunk of the budget set aside for health care expenses each year (Smyer & Burbank, 2009).

In the general population, healthcare professionals often rely on one of the Activities of Daily Living (ADL) scales to assess a person's ability to care for themselves. This is helpful in determining if and when additional assistance and care are needed. Typically, they are concerned with the person's ability to accomplish the five most common ADL's: bathing, eating, using the toilet, dressing, and transferring. In prison, there are additional physical requirements inmates must be able to do in order to avoid getting into trouble. These activities include being able to drop to the floor for drills, stand for inmate counts, walking to and from the dining hall for meals, climbing up and down the bunk beds, and being able to hear the orders given by correctional staff members (Smyer & Burbank, 2009; Williams et al., 2006). As the inmate's capacity to successfully complete these tasks unassisted diminishes their life in prison becomes more complicated. Chronic illnesses such as arthritis may reduce a person's ability to perform these daily tasks as well. Arthritis is the most common cause of disability for Americans reporting activity limitations (CDC, 2006). For further discussion and information on elderly inmates and related health challenges see Chapter 7.

ALTERNATIVES FOR TREATING THE CHRONICALLY ILL AND ELDERLY

According to the American Correctional Association (2001) about half of all states now offer geriatric facilities or other programs designed for elderly inmates. These range from designating the entire correctional facility as a geriatric prison (or infirmary) to the designation of special housing units within larger prison facilities to ensure these vulnerable inmates are housed together and separated as much as possible from the general population. Other states are experimenting with the concept of correctional nursing homes in an attempt to increase the amount of care and assistance required for this unique population of elderly inmates (Aday, 1999; Flynn, 1992; Marquart, Merrianos, & Doucet, 2000).

Another alternative idea geared toward caring for the unique needs of the elderly and terminally ill inmate involves providing them with hospice care and making arrangements for appropriate aftercare if they are released before dying (Aday, 2006, p. 236). The Louisiana State Penitentiary (LSP), in Angola is a maximum security prison that currently houses a little over 5,000. Most of these inmates have been sentenced to life without parole which means that approximately 85% of them will die behind bars (Tillman, 2000). The LSP Hospice Program began in January of 1998 to provide dying inmates with palliative care upon their request. This program is unique in that it involves a team of experts including, physicians, nurses, social workers, chaplains, bereavement specialists, dietary, and ancillary personnel (Tillman, 2000). Perhaps the most unusual aspect of this program is their use of fellow prisoners, who volunteer and have been specially trained, to provide dying inmates with emotional support, companionship, and assistance with typical activities of daily living. These inmates have a vested interest in seeing this program succeed since many of them will one day rely on this program as they themselves prepare for the end of life.

COMPASSIONATE RELEASE

Compassionate release is another alternative for terminally ill inmates. Compassionate release refers to the practice of releasing inmates that have been diagnosed with a terminal illness to allow them to die outside of the prison. This option allows the correctional facility to avoid the expenses associated with providing medical care and treatment to dying inmates. Other terms used to describe this practice are medical release, medical parole, medical furlough, and humanitarian parole. One of the most controversial cases of compassionate release occurred in Britain when they released the Lockerbie Bomber. This option is currently available under various names for inmates in the Federal Bureau of Prisons and 36 of the 50 state prisons (Roney, 2008).

The practice of releasing an individual from prison based on medical grounds is known as compassionate release, medical release, medical furlough, medical parole, and humanitarian parole. Releasing an inmate based on medical illness can be a very controversial practice. This type of policy is often adopted by correctional facilities in an attempt to help reduce the medical costs associated with caring for a permanently incapacitated or terminally ill inmate. Inmates are not eligible for federal healthcare programs like Medicaid or Medicare while they are incarcerated. This means the states that incarcerate them are responsible for covering all medical costs associated with their treatment while they are behind bars. Since the courts have ruled that inmates have a guaranteed constitutional right to medical and mental health care during their incarceration, this financial burden is mandatory.[20]

Congress enacted a federal statute[21] to allow for the early release of inmates based on "extraordinary and compelling reasons." In 2008, there were 36 states in addition to the federal government that allowed for the release of inmates who are diagnosed with a terminal illness or deemed permanently incapacitated (Roney, 2008). Compassionate release is not unique to the United States. Other countries that also have a mechanism in place to release terminally ill inmates prior to the completion of their sentence include Scotland, England, Wales, China, France, and New Zealand.

The controversy surrounding compassionate release usually involves the balancing act between saving taxpayers' money and ensuring public safety. Unlike typical early release programs that are designed to carefully examine an inmate's progress toward rehabilitation before releasing them, compassionate release is granted solely on the inmate's health status and the amount of money required to care for them.

One of the most controversial cases of compassionate release began in 2009 when the British government elected to release the man known as the "Lockerbie Bomber." Abdelbaset al-Megrahi of Libya was convicted of one of the worst terrorist attacks Britain had ever seen. In 1988, Pan Am Flight 103 exploded over Scotland resulting in the death of 270 people. Megrahi was convicted of planting the bomb that was responsible for this explosion. On January 31, 2001, he was convicted of murder and sentenced to serve life imprisonment in a Scottish prison. In 2009, Megrahi appealed to the Scottish government for compassionate release based on his recent diagnosis of terminal prostate cancer. The doctor that diagnosed him gave him less than six months to live and the devolved Scottish government granted his request based largely on this diagnosis. Megrahi was released on August 20, 2009. The controversy surrounding his release still lives on today.[22]

---

[20]*Estelle v. Gamble*, 1976; *Ruiz v. Estelle*, 1980.

[21]Federal Statute 18 USC 3582 (c) (1) (A) (i).

[22]Megrahi died in Tripoli on May 20, 2012.

MENTALLY ILL INMATES

There are very few jails nationwide that are able to provide inmates with a comprehensive range of mental health services (Steadman & Veysey, 1997; NCCHC, 2002).

The *DSM-IV-TR*[23] is considered the *bible* of mental health diagnostics and consists of 16 major diagnostic classes that allow mental health professionals to use labels when trying to categorize people suffering from mental illness and can assist them as they develop treatment plans. Therefore, the *DSM-IV-TR* was consulted in defining the mental disorders presented in this section. This section will only describe the most common and most important categories of mental disorders that exist in correctional settings. The following chapter, Chapter 6, by Nicholas and Bryant presents a thorough discussion on the various challenges of dealing with mentally ill inmates. Please note that it is not uncommon for individuals to have more than one diagnosis and the criteria in the *DSM-IV-TR* is intended to provide guidelines for diagnosis, but ultimately the mental health professionals are expected to properly diagnose a patient based on their specialized training.

The most common mental disorders that exist in the prison setting and general population are mood disorders. The primary symptom in this category is a disturbance in mood, but this disturbance is expressed in an extreme manner (e.g., crying all the time, constantly feeling depressed, frequently feeling suicidal, or having excessive energy, severe sleep deprivation marked with significantly diminished decision making capabilities) for an extended period of time. Major depressive disorder is lumped into this category along with bipolar disorder, cyclothymia and dysthmic disorder. Depression is commonly found in the correctional setting and can be attributed partially to the series of losses an inmate experiences upon incarceration (Van Voorhis et al., 2009).

Another factor to be considered is suicidal tendency. Suicide prevention is important due to the legal consequences and costs associated with wrongful death suits in the event an inmate does kill himself in custody. One quarter of all suicide deaths occur within the first two days following intake. Forty-eight percent of inmates who commit suicide did so within the first week of custody (Mumola, 2005). *Balla v. Idaho Board of Corrections* (1984) ruled that prisons and jails are legally obligated to provide a mental health screening at intake in order to identify potentially serious problems (i.e., suicidal tendencies). Most lawsuits following suicides are based on one of three issues: (1) failure to properly identify suicidal inmates; (2) failure to protect and properly monitor inmates once identified; and (3) not properly responding to suicide attempts (McMullan, 2011). Simple screening procedures may help reduce the number of lawsuits and legal liability associated with suicides that occur in custody each year. One commonly used screening tool within correctional facilities is the Beck Hopelessness Scale. Most lawsuits focus on the lack of or complete absence of adequate screening for suicidal tendencies. Appropriate screening and

---

[23]A revision of the *DSM* is currently underway and publication of the fifth edition is expected to occur in May of 2013.

training for staff members who come into regular contact with inmates may further reduce the suicide rates within correctional institutions. Prevention is the key for potential cases of suicide.

Another important category of mental disorders, because they have the potential to pose a threat to correctional security and safety if undiagnosed or improperly treated, are psychotic disorders. "Psychotic disorders are almost always preexisting but can be exacerbated by the conditions of incarceration" (Van Voorhis et al., 2009). Medications are often used to help control the symptoms associated with this type of disorder, but the individual may not reveal they are on these medications during the initial intake or classification process or they may have stopped taking their medications prior to being arrested and incarcerated. The major symptom of psychotic disorders is psychosis. *Psychosis* is typically defined as having delusions and/or hallucinations that are visual, auditory, olfactory or tactile in nature and sometimes taste. The most widely known psychotic disorder is schizophrenia but others include brief psychotic disorder, delusional disorder, schizoaffective disorder, schizophreniform, and shared psychotic disorder. All of these disorders aside from the brief psychotic disorder will require long-term monitoring and medical treatment. These individuals pose a threat to the safety and security within a correctional facility, especially when improperly treated or undiagnosed, because their behavior and actions are often unpredictable.

Mental retardation is defined by the American Psychiatric Association (2000) as an individual that has an intelligence quotient (IQ) score about 70 or below (although it can be higher if the second criteria is met) coupled with deficits in adaptive behavior and usually requires that this condition of retardation was clear during their developmental years. It is important to note that just as a person with an IQ of 70 may not fit the criteria of mentally retarded if they are able to demonstrate their adaptive functioning is good, a person with an IQ of 72 may be considered mentally retarded if their adaptive functioning is poor. The adaptive functioning criteria addresses the individual's ability to effectively cope with the normal demands of life in an independent manner in the same way that other individuals of that age are able to do (American Psychiatric Association, 2000). These individuals may have difficulties adapting to the expectations and demands within a correctional setting and may become an administrative problem by resorting to violence when they are unable to master normal social and cognitive skills (Conley, Luckasson, & Bouthilet, 1992). Studies estimate the prevalence of mental retardation among inmates to be somewhere between 2% and 10% of the inmate population (Smith, Algozzine, Schmid, & Hennly, 1990; Van Voorhis et al., 2009).

New York State Association for Retarded Children Incorporated vs. Carey (1975) established that prisoners of state mental facilities have a constitutional right to receive treatment regardless of the nature of their residency (i.e., voluntary or involuntary). If a state engages in the legally permissible practice of involuntary civil commitment of sexual offenders for an indefinite period of time, they must provide these individuals with reasonable mental health care or a treatment program tailored to meet their recovery needs (Palmer, 2010, p. 225). Often times these civil commitment practices are employed without a criminal conviction or prior to a prisoner being released back into the community immediately following the completion of their prison term. The California Supreme Court ruled in *People v. Feagley* (1975) that such individuals are entitled to care when their commitment is involuntary, and their release is dependent on either becoming cured from their mental disorder or being able to show significant improvement to where they would no longer pose a serious threat to themselves or society. Since the practice of involuntary civil commitment of sexual offenders is based on the rationale that this person is "mentally disordered" and thus poses a serious threat to society, and since their release is based on their ability to be cured or to significantly improve their mental condition, such treatment opportunities must be made available to them. Failure to provide adequate individual treatment options that would allow them to work toward being released constitutes a violation of their constitutional right to due process under the Fifth and Fourteen Amendments and a violation of the cruel and unusual punishment clause of the Eighth Amendment[24] (Palmer, 2010, p. 225). For an in-depth discussion on mentally ill offenders behind bars refer to the next chapter, Chapter 6.

ADMINISTRATION OF MEDICATION PRACTICES

Inmates have a constitutional right to adequate medical care and this includes access to treatment and medications prescribed by their doctors. Medications must be dispensed every day of the year up to four times a day (McMullan, 2011). While the correctional facilities must provide access to treatment, it is important to note that inmates have a constitutional right to refuse medical care or treatment[25] unless the correctional administration can demonstrate a compelling reason to force the inmate to comply, and this is typically done in the name of safety.[26] This includes refusal to take their prescribed medications. Due to the high costs associated with medications and in an attempt to cut down on excess cost, some correctional facilities have established committees to oversee the amount and types of medications prescribed.

The manner in which a correctional facility decides to handle the delivery of prescription and over-the-counter medications (OTC) to its inmate population widely varies. The most common approaches adopted include a keep-on-person program, a centralized distribution program, a delivery program, or a combination approach.

Some correctional facilities opt for a keep-on-person (KOP) approach which allows the inmates to maintain possession of their medication(s) and take them as prescribed without the hassle of distribution lines or an additional burden on staff to deliver the medications and ensure they are taken. While this type of approach works well with OTC drugs such as aspirin and lower risk prescriptions medications used to treat chronic illnesses[27] it is not recommended for psychotropic drugs

---

[24]*Ohlinger v. Watson*, 1980.

[25]*Cruzan v. Director, Missouri Department of Health*, 1990.

[26]*North Dakota ex rel. Timothy Schuetzle v. Vogel*, 1995.

[27]Examples of medications suitable for KOP programs would be asthma inhalers and glucophage for diabetes patients.

or other medications that have the potential to be abused. KOP programs are also not reliable for the purposes of auditing medication compliance.

An alternative approach to medication administration in a correctional facility is a program that ensures the medications are delivered to the inmates that need them on a daily basis and several times a day if need be. One type of delivery program is a directly-observed therapy program. This involves the delivery of medications by a nurse or alternative authorized medical professional with medical training (i.e., licensed or registered nurse) who delivers the medication to the inmate and not only watches to ensure it has been properly taken but additionally asks the inmate to submit to an oral examination afterwards to make certain the medications were indeed ingested. These programs allow for the careful documentation of medication distribution and provide meaningful documentation for the purposes of compliance auditing.

Other institutions opt for a centralized distribution center where all inmates requiring medicines must arrive and physically pick up their medications as needed. This can be problematic for inmates that are required to show up several times a day to receive their medications, because most inmates are not granted the freedom to come and go as they please and may be prevented from receiving their medications for a variety of reasons based on these movement restrictions. Their inability to access their medications freely is problematic because it denies them their prescribed medications, but also because when they do not show up, they are recorded as being medically noncompliant. Another problematic situation involves individuals placed in segregation who require medicines. Clearly these inmates will need to have their medications delivered to them.

Another issue surrounding the administration of medications within correctional settings involves the manner in which prescriptions are refilled. Some facilities rely on inmates to request refills when needed. It is important that this request process is timely and readily available to those who need it. If correctional facilities do not have an automated system for refilling prescriptions, then they must rely on the manual signature of a medical doctor prior to every refill. In these situations, it is imperative the inmate be granted an appointment on a regular basis prior to the refill being necessary. If the prescription is automatically refilled, then the correctional facility must merely ensure that the refills take place in a timely manner. Some correctional facilities house their own pharmacies while others rely on outside pharmacies and either pick up the prescriptions on a regular basis or have them delivered.

POLICY IMPLICATIONS

The U.S. Supreme Court refused to hear cases involving the segregation and mandatory testing of inmates for HIV. The court's decision to deny *certiorari* for these cases without comment indicates they are not yet ready to rule on the controversial subject matter. This lack of action provides correctional facilities with the legal discretion they need to continue their segregation practices.

The U.S. Supreme Court held in *Bragdon v. Abbott* (1998) individuals infected with HIV/AIDS are protected from discrimination under the auspices of the Americans with Disabilities Act (ADA).[28] However, the U.S. Supreme Court denied *certiorari* to hear a case in 2000 involving the segregation of HIV positive inmates from other inmates residentially, in the classrooms and workplaces, and essentially all other programs.[29] The 11th Circuit Court of Appeals held that the segregation of prisoners with HIV from other inmates did not violate the ADA. Absent a Supreme Court ruling, correctional facilities can continue to segregate inmates who are HIV positive from the general population without legal consequences. These segregation practices have resulted in inmates being denied access to educational and religious programs solely based on the fact they are HIV positive.

Although the ruling of the 11th Circuit Court of Appeals was upheld by the denial of *certiorari*, there are many opponents to this practice. Individuals in the free world are granted confidentiality when they are diagnosed with HIV and would never be subjected to segregation. The practice of segregating inmates with HIV from the general prison population has been condemned by the National Commission on AIDS, the National Commission on Correctional Health Care, and the Federal Bureau of Prisons as having absolutely no legitimate basis in the interest of maintaining public health. It is also noted that inmates with other similar diseases such as Hepatitis C are not subjected to such segregation practices. Is there a compelling argument based on security that justifies the segregation of HIV positive inmates?

Another controversial issue surrounding the treatment of inmates with HIV involves the practice of mandatory HIV testing within the correctional facility. Individuals in the general population are not subjected to mandatory HIV testing. Absent further clarification or guidance from the U.S. Supreme Court, some correctional facilities require testing of all inmates upon arrival for HIV while others refuse to test inmates at all. As of 2006, only 21 states required mandatory testing of all inmates for HIV upon their admission or at some point during their incarceration (Maruschak, 2006). Forty-seven states provide testing upon the inmates' request or if they show signs and symptoms of the disease while incarcerated. These states also test inmates exposed to the virus during incarceration. Five states test inmates before they are released, three state correctional systems test all inmates at some point during custody and four states, in addition to the federal prison system, test inmates periodically at random.

The World Health Organization and the Centers for Disease Control and Prevention encourage individuals to use condoms in order to prevent the spread of HIV during sexual activity. While this prevention technique is available to members of the general population, it is not always the case for those serving time in a correctional facility. The incidence of HIV and AIDS infections within correctional facilities is noted to be five times higher than the rate of infection in the general population (Ruby, 2002). The top three states with the most HIV positive or confirmed AIDS cases were New York, Florida, and Texas (Maruschak, 2006).

Some state prisons have opted to provide inmates with condoms in an effort to reduce the spread of HIV and other STDs. The state prison systems in Mississippi and Vermont, along with jails in Los Angeles, New York, Philadelphia, San Francisco,

---

[28]Protection begins from the moment of infection.

[29]*Davis v. Hopper* (1984).

and the District of Columbia currently provide condoms to some of their inmates (Hammett & Harmon, 1999). However, most correctional facilities throughout the United States do not. In fact, condoms are considered contraband and anyone caught in possession of them will face the prospect of administrative sanctions. Some view the provision of condoms to inmates inside prison as a means of encouraging forbidden sexual activity and violence. Others believe it is a necessary step in preventing the continued spread of HIV.

DISCUSSION QUESTIONS

1. What are the benefits of adopting a mandatory chronic illness screening policy for all incoming inmates? What would the potential drawbacks be for a mandatory screening policy in a correctional facility? Which medical or mental illnesses should be screened for?

2. What are some of the advantages of having a keep-on-person medication policy within a correctional setting? Which medications would be best suited for a keep-on-person medication policy? What are some of the potential administrative issues associated with a keep-on-person medication policy within a correctional setting?

3. How should correctional facilities handle elderly inmates? Do you believe they should be housed in separate prisons? Why or why not? Do you believe correctional facilities should provide hospice care for inmates that are terminally ill or dying? Why or why not?

4. Should HIV positive inmates (or those infected with AIDS) be housed separately from the other inmates in the general population? Why do you feel this way? As a correctional administrator, would you recommend that all inmates be mandatorily tested for HIV while they are incarcerated? Why or why not? If so, when would this take place (i.e., during admission, sometime during incarceration, prior to release)?

5. Do you believe inmates should be eligible for compassionate release if they are diagnosed with a terminal illness? Why or why not? Do you believe the financial burden of caring for a dying inmate should be considered when determining whether or not to release them early?

SUGGESTED READINGS

Aday, R. H. (2003). *Aging prisoners: Crisis in American corrections.* Westport, CT: Praeger.

Dvoskin, J. A., & Steadman, H. J. (1998). Chronically mentally ill inmates: The wrong concept for the right services. *International Journal of Law and Psychiatry, 12(2/3).*

Greifinger, R. B. (2007). *Public health behind bars: From prisons to communities.* New York, NY: Springer.

Nacci, Peter L. (1999). *Telemedicine can reduce correctional health care costs: An Evaluation of a prison telemedicine network.* NCJ175040. Washington, DC: U.S. Department of Justice, National Institute of Justice.

Nacci, P. L., Turner, C. A., Waldron, R. J., & Broyles, E. (2002, May). *Implementing telemedicine in correctional facilities.* NCJ 190310. Washington, DC: U.S. Department of Justice, National Institute of Justice. Retrieved from http://www.ncjrs.gov/pdffiles1/nij/190310.pdf

Puisis, M. (2006). *Clinical practice in correctional medicine* (2nd ed.). Philadelphia, PA: Mosby Elseiver.

Wilson, J., & Barboza, S. (2010). The looming challenge of dementia in corrections. *CorrectCare,* Spring 2010. Retrieved from http://ncchc.org/pubs/CC/dementia.html

WEBSITES OF INTEREST

- Academy of Correctional Healthcare Professionals
  http://www.correctionalhealth.org/index.asp

- CDC resource cost calculator for treating chronic illnesses at
  http://www.cdc.gov/chronicdisease/resources/calculator/index.htm

- The National Commission on Correctional Healthcare
  http://www.ncchc.org/index.html

- The National Institute of Corrections
  http://nicic.gov

- The Centers for Disease Control (report on inmates with HIV)
  http://www.cdc.gov/mmwr/preview/mmwrhtml/mm5515a1.htm

REFERENCES

Aday, R. H. (2003). *Aging prisoners: Crisis in American corrections.* Westport, CT: Praeger.

American Diabetes Association. (2011). *Common terms.* Retrieved from http://www.diabetes.org/diabetes-basics/common-terms/

American Heart Association. (2011). Obesity Information. Retrieved from http://www.heart.org/HEARTORG/GettingHealthy/WeightManagement/Obesity/Obesity-Information_UCM_307908_Article.jsp#.TvC2lTU7WAg

American Psychiatric Association. (2000). *Diagnostic and statistical manual of mental disorders* (4th ed., Text Revision). Washington, DC: Author.

AVERT.org. (2011). Aids & HIV information. Retrieved from http://www.avert.org/

Balla v. Idaho Board of Corrections. 1984 Nov 1; 595:1558–1583.

Beck, A. J., Karberg, J. C., & Harrison, P. M. (2001). *Prison and jail inmates at midyear 2001.* NCJ 191702. Washington, DC: U.S. Department of Justice, Bureau of Justice Statistics. Retrieved from http://www.bluelineradio.com/DOJPRISON JAIL.pdf

Bingswanger, I. A. (2010). Chronic medical diseases among jail and prison inmates. *CorrDocs* (Winter 2010). Available at corrections.com

Bragdon v. Abbott, 524 U.S. 624 (1998).

Bureau of Justice Statistics. (2011). *Key facts at a glance.* Retrieved from http://bjs.ojp.usdoj.gov/content/glance/corr2.cfm

California Pacific Medical Center. (2011). *Financial matters: Liver transplant costs.* Retrieved from www.cpmc.org/advanced/liver/patients/topics/finance.html#Transplantation Costs on March 28, 2011

Centers for Disease Control and Prevention. (2006). *Prevalence of doctor-diagnosed arthritis and arthritis-attributable activity limitation—United States, 2003–2005.* MMWR 2006; 55:1089–1092. Retrieved from http://www.cdc.gov/mmwr/preview/mmwrhtml/mm5540a2 .htm

Centers for Disease Control and Prevention. (2008). *National diabetes fact sheet, 2007.* Atlanta, GA: Author. Retrieved from http://www.cdc.gov/Diabetes/pubs/factsheet07.htm

Centers for Disease Control and Prevention. (2009, November). *Sexually transmitted disease surveillance, 2008.* Atlanta, GA: Author.

Centers for Disease Control and Prevention. (2010). *National chronic kidney disease fact sheet: general information and national estimates on chronic kidney disease in the United States, 2010.* Atlanta, GA: Author.

Centers for Disease Control and Prevention. (2011a). Breast cancer statistics. Retrieved from http://www.cdc.gov/cancer/breast/statistics

Centers for Disease Control and Prevention. (2011b). *Evaluation of large jail STD screening programs, 2008–2009.* Retrieved from http://www.cdc.gov/std/publications/JailScreening 2011.pdf

Centers for Disease Control and Prevention. (n.d.). *United States Cancer Statistics: 1999–2007.* Retrieved fromhttp://apps.nccd.cdc.gov/uscs/

Centers for Disease Control. (n.d.). Tuberculosis (TB). Retrieved from http://www.cdc.gov/tb/ topics/basics/default.htm

Chicago Tribune (October 14, 1987). *Guard killed, 3 seized as prison escape fails.* Retrieved March 1, 2012, from http://articles.chicagotribune.com/1987–10–14/news/8703170298_ 1_two-gunmen-prison-van-penitentiary

Cisternas, M. G., Blanc, P. D., Yen, I. H., Katz, P. P., Earnest, G., Eisner, M. D., Shiboski, S., & Yelin, E. H. (2003). A comprehensive study of the direct and indirect costs of adult asthma. *Journal of Allergy and Clinical Immunology, 111*(6), 1212–1218.

Clark, R. (1971). *Crime in America.* New York, NY: Pocket Books.

Clear, T. R., & Cole, G. F. (1997). *American Corrections.* Wadsworth.

Coen, C., Sacks, S., & Melnick, G. (2006, November 1). Screening for co-occurring mental and substance use disorders in the criminal justice system. Paper presented at the annual meeting of the American Society of Criminology (ASC), Los Angeles, CA.

Conley, R., Luckasson, R., & Bouthilet, G. (1992). *The criminal justice system and mental retardation: Defendants and victims.* Baltimore, MD: P. H. Brookes.

Cripe, C. A., & Pearlman, M. E. (2005). *Legal aspects of corrections management* (2nd ed.). Sudbury, MA: Jones and Bartlett.

Eastman, R. C., Javitt, J. C., Herman, W. H., Dasbach, E. J., Copley-Merriman, C., Maier, W., Dong, F., Manninen, D., Zbrozek, A. S., Kotsanos, J., Garfield, S. A., & Harris, M. (1997). Model of complications of NIDDM II: Analysis of the health benefits and cost-effectiveness of treating NIDDM with the goal of normoglycemia. *Diabetes Care, 20*(5), 735–744.

Enders, S. R., Paterniti, D. A., Meyers, F. J. (2005). An approach to stimulate effective decision-making in medical treatment, advance care planning, and end-of-life care for women in prison. *Journal of Palliative Medicine 8*(2), 432–439.

Eng, T. R., & Butler, W. T. (Eds.). (1997). *The hidden epidemic: Confronting sexually trans-mitted diseases.* Washington, DC: National Academy Press.

Estelle v. Gamble (1976), 429 U.S. 97

Farmer v. Brennan (1994), 511 U.S. 825.

Federal Bureau of Prisons. (2010). *Health Intake Assessment/History Form*. Retrieved from http://www.bop.gov/policy/forms/BP_A0360.pdf

Fletcher, B. W., & Wexler, H. K. (2005). National criminal justice drug abuse treatment studies (CJ-DATS): Update and progress. *Justice Research and Statistics Association: The Forum, 23*(5), 1, 6–7.

Flynn, E. E. (1992). The graying of America's prison population. *The Prison Journal, 72*(1/2), 77–98.

Fogel, C. I. (1995). Pregnant prisoners: Impact of incarceration on health and health care. *Journal of Correctional Health Care, 2*, 169–190.

Freudenberg, N. (2001). Jails, prisons, and the health of urban populations: A review of the impact of the correctional system on community health. *Journal of Urban Health, 78*(2), 214–235.

Gailiun, M. (1997). Telemedicine takes off. *Corrections Today, 4*, 68–70.

Glaze, L. E. (2010). Correctional populations in the United States, 2009. *Bureau of Justice Statistics Bulletin*. Retrieved from http://bjs.ojp.usdoj.gov/content/pub/pdf/cpus09.pdf

Goldberg, A. L., & Higgins, B. R. (2006). *Brief mental health screening for corrections intake*. Rockville, MD: National Institute of Justice.

Goldkuhle, U. (1999). Health service utilization by women in prison: Health needs indicators and response effects. *Journal of Correctional Health Care, 1*, 63–83.

Griffin, R. M. (2011). Lowering the costs of asthma treatment. Retrieved from http://www.webmd.com/asthma/features/lowering-costs-asthma-treatment

Hammett, T. M. (2006). HIV in prisons. *Criminology & Public Policy, 5*, 109–112.

Hammett, T. M., & Harmon, P. (1999). *Issues and practices in criminal justice, 1996–1997. Update: HIV/AIDS, STDs, and TB in correctional facilities*. Washington, DC: National Institute of Justice. Available at http://www.ncjrs.gov

Hufft, A. G., Fawkes, L. S., & Lawson, W. T. (1993). Care of the pregnant offender. In *Female offenders: Meeting needs of a neglected population*. Lanham, MD: American Correctional Association.

Kaplan, S. (1999). Healthcare costs rising as prisoner population grows and ages. *Stateline. org*. Retrieved from http://www.stateline.org/live/ViewPage.action?siteNodeId=136&languageId=1&contentId=13721

Kanato, M. (2008). Drug use and health among prison inmates. *Current Opinion in Psychiatry, 21*(3), 252–254.

Krebs, C. P. (2006). Inmate factors associated with HIV transmission in prison. *Criminology & Public Policy, 5*(1), 113–135.

Lundstrom, S. (1994). Dying to get out: A study on the necessity, importance, and effectiveness of prison early release programs for elderly inmates suffering from HIV disease and other terminal-centered illnesses. *BYU Journal of Public Law, 8*(1). Retrieved from Academic Search Complete.

Lurigio, A. J., & Swartz, J. A. (2006). Mental illness in correctional populations: The use of standardized screening tools for further evaluation or treatment. *Federal Probation, 70*(2), 29–35.

Marquart, J., Merrianos, D., & Doucet, G. (2000). The health-related concerns of older prisoners: Implications for policy. *Ageing and Society, 20*(1), 79–96.

Maruschak, L. M. (2006). *Bureau of Justice Statistics special report: Medical problems of jail inmates*. NCJ 210696. Washington, DC: U.S. Department of Justice, Bureau of Justice. Retrieved from http://bjs.ojp.usdoj.gov/content/pub/pdf/mpji.pdf

Maruschak, L. M., & Beavers, R. (2009). HIV in prisons 2007–08. *Bureau of Justice Statistics Bulletin,* NCJ 228307. Washington, DC: U.S. Bureau of Justice. Retrieved from http://bjs.ojp.usdoj.gov/content/pub/pdf/hivp08.pdf

Mayo Clinic. (2011). *Asthma.* Retrieved from http://www.mayoclinic.com/health/asthma/DS00021/DSECTION=treatments-and-drugs

McMullan, E. C. (2011). Seeking medical and psychiatric attention. In L. Gideon & H. Sung (Eds.), *Rethinking corrections: Rehabilitation, reentry, and reintegration* (pp. 253–277). Thousand Oaks, CA: Sage.

MedicineNet.com. (n. d.). *High blood pressure and kidney disease.* Retrieved from http://www.medicinenet.com/kidney_disease_hypertension-related/page3.htm

MedlinePlus Medical Encyclopedia. (n.d.). *Coronary heart disease.* Retrieved from http://www.nlm.nih.gov/medlineplus/ency/article/007115.htm

Mertz, K. J., Voigt, R. A., Hutchins, K., Levine, W. C., & Jail STD Monitoring Group (2002). Findings from STD screening of adolescents and adults entering corrections facilities: implications for STD control strategies. *Sexually Transmitted Diseases, 29*(12), 834–839.

Monmouth County Correctional Institution Inmates v. Lanzaro (1987), 834 F.2d 326.

Mumola, C. J. (2005). Suicide and homicide in state prisons and local jails. Special report. NCJ 210036. Washington, DC: U.S. Department of Justice, Bureau of Justice Statistics Special Report.

Murray, O. J., Pulvino, J., Baillargeon, J., Paar, D., & Raimer, B. G. (2007). Managing hepatitis C in our prisons: Promises and challenges. *CorrectCare.* Retrieved from http://www.ncchc.org/pubs/CC/managing_hcv.html

Nacci, Peter L. (1999). *Telemedicine can reduce correctional health care costs: An evaluation of a prison telemedicine network.* NCJ175040. Washington, DC: U.S. Department of Justice, National Institute of Justice. Retrieved from http://www.nij.gov/pubs-sum/175040.htm

National Commission on Correctional Health Care. (2001). *Correctional health care: Guidelines for the management of an adequate delivery system.* Chicago, IL: National Commission on Healthcare.

National Commission on Correctional Health Care. *The health status of soon-to-be-released inmates, 1.* Retrieved from http://www.ncchc.org/pubs/pubs_stbr.vol1.html

National Commission on Correctional Health Care (2011). *Standards for health services in juvenile detention and confinement facilities.* Retrieved from http://www.ncchc.org/pubs/catalog.html#standards

National Institute of Health. (2002). *Management of Hepatitis C: 2002.* National Institutes of Health Consensus Conference Statement of June 10–12, 2002. Retrieved from http://consensus.nih.gov/2002/2002HepatitisC2002116html.htm

National Institute of Justice. (n.d.). *Correctional mental health screen for women.* Retrieved from http://www.asca.net/system/assets/attachments/2640/MHScreen-Women082806.pdf?1300974694

National Institute of Justice. (1999). *Telemedicine can reduce correctional health care costs: An evaluation of a prison telemedicine network.* Washington, DC: Author. Retrieved from https://www.ncjrs.gov/pdffiles1/175040.pdf

New York State Association for Retarded Children Incorporated vs. Carey, 393 F. Supp. 715.

Newman v. Alabama (1972), 349 F. Supp. 278 (E.D.N.Y. 1975).

Office of Health and Medical Affairs. (1975). *Key to health for a padlocked society.* Lansing: Michigan Department of Corrections.

Ohlinger v. Watson, 652 F.2d. 775 (9th Circuit 1980).

Ornduff, J. S. (1996). Releasing the elderly inmate: A solution to prison overcrowding. *Elder Law Journal, 4,* 173–200.

Palmer, J. W. (2010). Right to rehabilitation programs, right to medical aid, and right to life. In *Constitutional rights of prisoners* (9th ed., pp. 221–257). New Providence, NJ: Mathew Bender.

Pearce, K. A., Furberg, C., Psaty, B. M., & Kirk, J. (1988). Cost minimization and the number needed to treat in uncomplicated hypertension. *American Journal of Hypertension, 11*, 618–629.

People v. Feagley, 14 Cal.3rd 388 (1975).

Philadelphia Inquirer. (October 14, 1987). Lewisburg guard dies in shootout with two trying to free inmate. Retrieved March 1, 2012, from http://nl.newsbank.com/nl-search/we/ Archives?p_product=PI&s_site=philly&p_multi=PI&p_theme=realcities&p_action=search&p_ maxdocs=200&p_topdoc=1&p_text_direct-0=0EB29D98393248D0&p_field_direct-0=document_id&p_perpage=10&p_sort=YMD_date:D&s_trackval=GooglePM

Rector, F. L. (1929). *Health and medical service in American prisons and reformatories*. New York, NY: National Society of Penal Information.

Rest Ministries.org. (2009). The National Invisible Chronic Illness Awareness Week. Retrieved from http://www.restministries.org/invisibleillness/statistics.htm

Robinson v. California, 370 U.S. 660 (1962).

Roney, M. (2008, August 14,). *Thirty-six states release ill or dying inmates*. Retrieved March 1, 2012, from http://www.usatoday.com/news/nation/2008-08-13-furloughs_N.htm#

Ruby, W. H. (2002). Treatment of HIV in prison populations: Issues and strategies. *Advanced Studies in Medicine, 2*(6), pp. 184–188. Retrieved from http://www.jhasim.com/files/ articlefiles/pdf/Treating%20HIV%20Infection%20in%20Prison%20Populations-%20 Issues%20and%20Strategies.pdf

Ruiz v. Estelle, 503 F. Supp. 1265 (S. D. Tex., 1980).

Sacks, S. (2008). Brief overview of screening and assessment for co-occurring disorders. *International Journal of Mental Health and Addiction, 6*(1), 7–19.

Scott, M. (2004). Inmate healthcare. *Law and Order, 52*(8), 116–118. Retrieved from http:// www.ncjrs.gov/App/Publications/abstract.aspx?ID=206927

Shervington, W. (1974). Prison, psychiatry and mental health. *Psychiatric Annals, 3*, 43–60.

Skolnick, A. A. (1998). Look behind bars for key to control of STDs. *Journal of the American Medical Association, 279*(2), 97–98.

Smith, C., Algozzine, B., Schmid, R., & Hennly, T. (1990). Prison adjustment of youthful inmates with mental retardation. *Mental Retardation, 28*, 177–181.

Smyer, T., & Burbank, P. M. (2009). The U.S. correctional system and the older prisoner. *Journal of Gerontological Nursing, 35*(12), 32–37.

Steadman, H. J., Scott, J. E., Osher, F., Agnese, T. K., & Robins, P. C. (2005). Validation of the brief jail mental health screen. *Psychiatric Services, 56*, 816–822.

Steadman, H. J., & Veysey, B. M. (1997, January). *Providing services for jail inmates with mental disorders*. NCJ 162207. Washington, DC: U.S. Department of Justice, National Institute of Justice.

Substance Abuse and Mental Health Administration (SAMHSA). (2005, July). *Brief jail mental health screening*. Retrieved March 1, 2012, from http://www.gainscenter.samhsa.gov/ pdfs/disorders/bjmhsform.pdf

Swartz, J., & Lurigio, A. J. (2006). Screening for serious mental illness in populations with co-occurring substance use disorders: Performance of the K6 scale. *Journal of Substance Abuse Treatment, 31*(3), 287–296.

Teplin, L. A., & Swartz, J. (1989). Screening for severe mental disorders in jail: The development of the referral decision scale. *Law and Human Behavior, 13*(1), 1–18.

Teplin, L. A. (1990). Detecting disorder: The treatment of mental illness among jail detainees. *Journal of Consulting and Clinical Psychology, 58*, 233–236.

Tillman, T. (2000). Hospice in prison: The Louisiana state penitentiary hospice program. *Innovations in End-of-Life Care, 2*(3) Retrieved from http:// www.edc.org/lastacts

Tomlinson, D. M., & Schechter, C. B. (2003). Cost-effectiveness analysis of annual screening and intensive treatment for hypertension and diabetes mellitus among prisoners in the United States. National Commission on Correctional Health Care. Retrieved from http://www.ncchc.org/stbr/Volume2/Report9_Tomlinson.pdf

United Network for Organ Sharing. (n.d.). *Financing a transplant.* Retrieved from http://www.transplantliving.org/beforethetransplant/finance/costs.aspx

Van Voorhis, P., Braswell, M., & Lester, D. (2009). Diagnosis and assessment of criminal offenders. *Correctional counseling & rehabilitation* (7th ed.). New Providence, NJ: Matthew Bender.

Veysey, B. M., & Bichler-Robertson, G. (2002). Providing psychiatric services in correctional settings. In *The health status of soon-to-be-released inmates: A report to Congress,* (2), 157–165. Chicago, IL: National Commission on Correctional Health Care.

Williams, B. A., Linquist, K., Sudore, R. L., Strupp, H. M., Willmott, D. J., & Walter, L. C. (2006). Being old and doing time: Functional impairment and adverse experiences of geriatric female prisoners. *Journal of the American Geriatrics Society, 54*, 702–707.

Wilper, A. P., Woolhandler, S., Boyd, J. W., Lasser, K. E., McCormick, D., Bor, D. H., & Himmelstein, D. U. (2009). The health and health care of US prisoners: Results of a nationwide survey. *American Journal of Public Health, 99*, 666–672.

Wilson, J., & Barboza, S. (2010). The looming challenge of dementia in corrections. *CorrectCare,* Spring 2010. Retrieved from http://ncchc.org/pubs/CC/dementia.html

World Health Organization. (1998). *Guidelines for the control of tuberculosis in prisons.* Geneva, Switzerland: Author.

CHAPTER 6

Mentally Ill Inmates: Jails and Prisons as the New Asylum

Lorie A. L. Nicholas and Gerard Bryant

INTRODUCTION

Mentally Ill Man Held After Sneaking Past Security at JFK, Boarding Flights Without a Ticket

A Maryland man with a history of mental illness was ordered held without bail Wednesday on charges that he snuck aboard a jetliner at Kennedy Airport without a ticket. Ronald Youchen Wong, 30, stole a boarding pass then bypassed the Transportation Security Administration checkpoint. Brooklyn Magistrate Cheryl Pollack noted that Wong has a rap sheet for petty crimes all over the country when he was supposed to be receiving psychiatric treatment. "His own mother says he disappears for two weeks at a time and she doesn't know where he goes," Pollack said.

John Marzulli, *New York Daily News* (March 17, 2011)

Long Island Man Stabs Child Playing Video Games at Dave & Buster's

The wild eyed Long Island man who stabbed an 8-year-old boy playing video games has a history of mental illness and had planned the attack. Evan Sachs, 23 was allegedly carrying a note saying he was committed to hurting a child when he walked into a Dave & Buster's Friday night and plunged a knife into the boys back five times. Sachs' lawyer, Charles Rosenblum said his client is under psychiatric care, and takes five different medications.

Lukas Alpert, *New York Daily News* (October 10, 2010)

Texas Mother Kills Son, Eats Brain

Reports have surfaced of a Texas mother named Otty Sanchez, 33, who gruesomely murdered her only child. Sanchez had spent years in and out of psychiatric care. . . . What stunned the police into silence was the scene they walked into on Sunday, where they found Sanchez suffering from self-inflicted wounds to her chest and her throat, screaming 'I killed my baby! I killed my baby!' The baby boy just three and a half weeks old was dismembered, with three of his toes chewed off, his head severed and his brains ripped out. Apparently Sanchez ate some of the child's brains; telling police that the devil made her do it. . . . Doctors are now wondering whether or not post-partum depression came into play, which would make this the most recent in a string of cases in which mothers have killed their children after giving birth in Texas.

Article by Mariela Rosario at www.latina.com/lifestyle/
news-politics/texas-mother-kills-son-eats-brain (July 2009)

The above news stories are unfortunately just a handful of events which have occurred illustrating cases with the combination of mental illness and crime. In all instances, because a crime was committed, law enforcement (the police) become immediately and directly involved.

However, the question at hand is where should the person with a history of mental illness be placed? Should this person be confined to a jail cell or some alternative type of treatment facility that will address his or her mental illness? In the first case, Ronald Youchen Wong was placed in jail and held without bail (Marzulli, 2011)). In the second case, Evan Sachs, who had no criminal record, was charged with second degree attempted murder, first degree assault, and possession of a dangerous weapon (Carrega & Goldstein, 2010; Alpert, 2010). In the case of Otty Sanchez, she is being charged with capital murder. After the crime was committed, she was sent for treatment at a hospital and held on a $1 million dollar bail.

HISTORY OF MENTAL HEALTH CARE IN CORRECTIONS

According to the Citizens Commission on Human Rights (Adi, Pagel, Urbanek, & Whitaker, 2003), "mental illness has become an epidemic striking one out of every four people in the world today" (p. 3). Historically, people with mental illness were confined in prisons. Benjamin Rush, America's first psychiatrist (Mason, 2007) sought to have the mentally ill removed from prisons and placed in asylums. Dorothea Dix is also known for her crusade to appeal the transfer of the mentally ill from prisons to asylums. Many of the mentally ill at the time were imprisoned, not because they had committed a crime, but because society deemed their behavior appalling.

Pennsylvania Hospital was the first site to open America's first ward for the mentally ill. Since at that time society was still attempting to understand mental illness and the behaviors of the mentally ill, "patients were chained by the wrist, ankle, or waist . . . and were bled and purged, and their scalps were shaved and blistered" (Mason, 2007, pp. 1–4). The medical treatments of bloodletting, purging, and blistering were eventually stopped, and more humane care was implemented. For example, patients received exercise and experiential therapy to help them gain self-control. A majority of mental patients have continued to be involuntarily detained in mental institutions (Adi et al., 2003). The psychiatric institutions established since the 1600s were seen as a solution to maintain public safety and social order (Adi et al., 2003). The perception at the time was that the mentally ill could not be cured, but only subdued and confined (Adi et al., 2003) Amid the 1960s, when institutions encountered problems "curing" mentally ill patients, drug dependent patients were discharged into the streets by psychiatric hospitals (Adi et al., 2003). The intent was that these patients would be serviced at community mental health centers, provided with psychotropic medication, and rehabilitated back into the community. This plan resulted in a widespread release of patients who became homeless and were for the most part, unmedicated.

This plan, which was a major initiative to foster the prevention of mental illness under the community mental health, was termed *deinstitutionalization* and was labeled as a failure. *Deinstitutionalization* which began in the 1950s and 1960s sought to close down beds for mental health patients in state hospitals and treat seriously mentally ill patients with antipsychotic medication as they were released back into the communities for follow-up care. President John F. Kennedy signed for government support of the mental health centers to receive funding through the Mental Retardation Facilities and Community Mental Health Centers Construction Act of 1963 (referred to as the Mental Health Act of 1963). This act was to provide funding of mental health treatment for severe mentally ill populations released to the community (McMullan, 2011).

With the Mental Health Act of 1963, mentally ill patients unable to function in the community were committed to hospitals "often for the rest of their lives, with no hope of reintegration into the community" (Fagan & Ax, 2011, p. 38). With the increased numbers of homeless people, Fagan & Ax (2011) noted the strain this population created on "mental health, social services and law enforcement agencies." This population went from being homeless to being incarcerated. Charges included "vagrancy, disorderly conduct, and theft" (p. 11). Of interest to note, the mentally ill were historically incarcerated. Through the advocacy work of Dr. Rush and Dorothea Dix, the mentally ill were moved to hospitals. We have now returned to the conditions of the 1840s in which large numbers of mentally ill people are being placed back into the prisons (Torrey, Kennard, Eslinger, Lamb, & Pavle, 2010). Many have argued that the prison system has become the new asylum, providing mental health services to seriously mentally ill populations (Fagan & Ax, 2011; Wynn, 2001). This shift of individuals with serious mental illness from the state mental hospitals into correctional facilities has been referred to as *transinstitution- alization* (Fagan & Ax, 2011; Arngo, 2002).

Jails and Prisons as the New Asylums

As of June 30, 2008, there were over 2.3 million people incarcerated in the United States (Bureau of Justice Statistics, 2009). It is estimated that more than half of all inmates in the U.S. are believed to have a serious mental illness (Clear, Cole, Reisig, & Petrosino, 2012; James & Glaze, 2006). The prison system is believed to house three times as many mentally ill people than the psychiatric institutions (Abramsky & Fellner, 2003). According to Insel (2003), the three largest psychiatric institutions in the United States are the Los Angeles County Jail, the Chicago Cook County Jail, and New York City's Rikers Island Jail.

So, how do the mentally ill arrive in prison?

The police officer is the first responder to the scene of a crime or crisis event. When the police arrive on the scene, they assess the situation and determine what should happen. Police officers are given the power of arrest authority. Depending on the scenario at hand, the police officer may decide to dismiss someone with a warning or arrest the person(s). The situation becomes challenging when a mentally ill person is involved (This area will be discussed further later on in the chapter).

HISTORY OF PSYCHOLOGY

During World War II, treatment programs that utilized the knowledge of psychiatrists, psychologists, and social workers were used to help treat trauma in men and women veterans. Newly appointed wardens of prison facilities, many of whom were military veterans, suggested the use of these treatment programs for trauma would also benefit inmates throughout correctional facilities (federal, state, and local) (Carlson, Roth, & Travisono, 2008). The implementation of these treatment programs led to the medical model which highlighted three primary components: diagnosis, evaluation, and treatment. In *diagnosis,* a decision is made about one's mental health condition. The *evaluation* determines the diagnosis of one's physical or mental health condition. The *treatment* is the medical care given to the patient to address the physical or mental health condition. These three components aided in the classification of the inmate (Clear & Cole, 1997), to meet their placement and treatment needs. Some conflicts which psychologists and social workers faced at the time was that programs providing individual and group therapy were viewed by prison personnel as being "soft on crime toward a society focused on punishment"(Carlson et al., 2008).

In the 1930s, Congress created the Federal Bureau of Prisons (BOP). Through this agency, innovative programs were introduced to corrections and later adopted by state and local facilities. The BOP innovative programs focused on more humane treatment of prisoners and utilized professional staff such as psychiatrists and psychologists. On October 30, 2008, President George W. Bush signed into law The Mentally Ill Offender Treatment and Crime Reduction Act of 2004. This was an act that sought to focus on psychological treatment interventions for mentally ill offenders (Jeglic, Maile, & Calkins-Mercado, 2011). This act provided mentally ill offenders with increased access to mental health treatment both while incarcerated and upon reentry into society, and funding to train mental health and correctional staff (American Psychological Association, 2004). As the prison system was refining its approach to the management and treatment of inmates, several court cases were instrumental in helping to formulate the prisons approach.

*Court Cases Instrumental in the Treatment
of Mentally Ill Offenders*

Through the outcome of several legal court cases, mental health staff in correctional facilities are required to provide treatment for mental illness. Some of the legal court cases have included:

- *Estelle v. Gamble* (1976) held that the state must provide for basic human needs after depriving a person of his or her liberty (i.e., incarceration).
- *Ruiz v. Estelle* (1980) established a state's obligation to provide medical care for those whom it is punishing by incarceration. This includes mental health care.
- *Balla v. Idaho Board of Corrections* (1984) obligated prisons and jails to provide a mental health screening at intake in order to identify potentially serious problems (e.g. suicidal tendencies).
- *Washington v. Harper* (1990) granted inmates the same rights to refuse treatment as citizens not incarcerated, but the due process clause permits a state to treat an incarcerated inmate having a serious mental disorder with antipsychotic medication against his will, under the condition that he is dangerous to himself or others and the medication prescribed is in his best medical interest.
- *Casey v. Lewis* (1993) stated that the rights of inmates under the Eighth Amendment are violated when correctional facilities fail to provide them with psychiatric and psychological treatment.

Researchers indicate that following the cases of *Estelle v. Gamble* and *Ruiz v. Estelle*, the courts determined that adequate correctional mental health care should meet, at a minimum, the following criteria (Chaiken & Shull, 2007; Dlugacz & Low, 2007; Mason, 2007):

- Screen and evaluate incoming inmates for mental disorders
- Provide meaningful treatment to inmates who are in segregation or special housing units (SHU)
- Train mental health staff in sufficient numbers to identify and provide treatment in an individualized manner to inmates with treatable serious disorders
- Maintain complete, accurate, and confidential mental health records
- Have qualified staff prescribe and administer medications in a manner consistent with professional standards
- Implement a suicide prevention program which includes methods for identifying, treating and supervising inmates with suicidal tendencies

MENTAL HEALTH COURTS

Although the primary focus of this chapter is to address mentally ill inmates inside the prison system, there is an alternative to incarceration for mentally ill inmates who meet the required criteria. This alternative to incarceration is referred to as the mental health courts. Mental health courts were designed to address the concern of incarcerating mentally ill offenders. Through the use of mental health courts, the goal is to reduce the number of mentally ill inmates in prison and provide them with treatment. In terms of the criteria to be considered for participation in the mental health courts, McMullan (2011) states that the person must "be identified as having a mental illness or co-occurring disorder before participation" (p. 265), demonstrated by a history of documented mental illness. Through the mental health court, the mentally ill offenders are monitored and must maintain compliance with their treatment plan. Studies reviewed by Sarteschi, Vaughn, and Kim (2011), evaluating the effectiveness of mental health courts, have found that mentally ill offenders who completed the court program were less likely to recidivate in comparison to those who did not participate in the court program. The following scenario on Bennie Anthony demonstrated the use of the mental health courts program.

The Case of Benny Anthony

When Bennie Anthony is on parole, he's a personable fellow with an easy laugh, a taste for top hats and a ready greeting. When off parole, his wayfaring spirit leads him to the bus station, followed by a homeless shelter, a jail cell, and, if he's lucky, mental health treatment.

Anthony, 61, was diagnosed with schizophrenia in 1974. Like many schizophrenics, he doesn't believe he needs medication. He's spent decades cycling in and out and between mental hospitals and correctional institutions.

"FRONTLINE" met Bennie Anthony in 2004 while he was in prison on two counts of aggravated arson, for which he served 17 years. When he was released in 2005, Anthony voluntarily joined the Assertive Community Treatment (ACT) program in Cleveland, Ohio, which found him housing, required him to stay on medication, and supplied him with community-based support and mental health treatment. He did well until his parole ended in 2006.

He took a Greyhound to Pittsburgh and within a few months was living in a park. Homeless and not on medication, Anthony was arrested 10 times in a year. His last arrest in that series, for assault, led him in April 2008 to Mental Health Court, Pittsburgh's jail diversion program. Mental Health Court found him housing, and when "FRONTLINE" met Anthony again in the summer of 2008, he was doing very well. He was on medication and receiving regular mental health treatment in the community—both conditions of his parole.

Then, in January 2009—shortly before Anthony could have completed his parole through Mental Health Court—for reasons unclear, he stopped taking his medication and boarded a bus to Akron, Ohio. There, he was arrested. And when he returned to Pittsburgh in mid-February, he was arrested for having left town, a parole violation. Anthony was placed in the mental health unit of the Allegheny County Jail, where he received medication and stabilized.

UPDATE: On April 17, 2009, Anthony was released from jail and returned to the personal care home where he had been living. He was readmitted back into the Mental Health Court program and successfully completed the terms of his Mental Health Court probation on Oct. 9, 2009. He is now living on his own.

Source: Adapted from "Benny Anthony," FRONTLINE online, April 2009 (updated December 2010), WGBH Educational Foundation. http://www.pbs.org/wgbh/pages/frontline/released/stories/anthony. html#ixzz1izbtUL7T

In the case of Bennie Anthony, the mental health court program was instrumental in eventually helping him to successfully transition to living on his own. However, not all cases are as successful as we will see in the next scenario with Jerry Tharp.

The Case of Jerry Tharp

"FRONTLINE" first met Jerry Tharp as he was nearing his November 2004 prison release. He had served nine years for robbing a pharmacy. Four months after being paroled, Tharp committed the same type of crime in Middletown, Ohio. He told the arresting officers that he robbed a pharmacy because he wanted to go back to prison. In October 2005, he did.

While in prison, Tharp, 34, is often transferred to the psychiatric hospital unit. He suffers from religious preoccupations and has a long history of mutilating his body. He has said he cuts and burns himself "to let the demon out" and that the acts relieve his pain. Tharp has also eaten inanimate objects, including pencils, nail clippers, toothbrushes, a radio antenna, razor blades, and an entire Sony Walkman. Tharp admits that, at times, his behaviors are an effort to get attention, but he has made at least one serious attempt at suicide by swallowing packets of hair removal gel, along with 10 pens and a paper clip.

UPDATE: Tharp is scheduled for release from prison in November 2009. He says that when he was released in 2004 he was unprepared to care for himself and had difficulty adjusting to the ways the world had changed while he was in prison.

When he's in a positive mood, Tharp talks of the community services that will be in place for him when he's released. He says that he plans to live with his stepmother and work at a factory with his brother. When he's feeling negative, Tharp says he just can't make it outside of prison and that when he's released, he will commit a crime that will ensure his imprisonment for life.

UPDATE (Dec. 6, 2010): Jerry Tharp was released on Nov. 12, 2009. He was out for less than two weeks before being charged with rape and sexual imposition. He is expected to be released again on Sept. 12, 2020. Posted April 28, 2009; updated December 6, 2010.

Source: Adapted from "Jerry Tharp," FRONTLINE online, April 2009 (updated December 2010), WGBH Educational Foundation. http://www.pbs.org/wgbh/pages/frontline/released/stories/tharp. html#ixzz1izcdXQqM

In the case of Jerry Tharp, some inmates become institutionalized and become fearful of living on the outside and will do whatever it takes to jeopardize their freedom or upon release, commit a crime to return to prison. Overall, mental health court programs are perceived as cost effective. At this present time, they will continue to be utilized to help reduce the incarceration of the mentally ill and to get them the treatment they need. As mentioned earlier, not all mentally ill inmates are placed in mental health court programs. Many are still incarcerated and must be screened, monitored, and treated inside the prison walls. For these inmates, they often come into contact with the mental health professionals in the correctional setting.

THE ROLE OF MENTAL HEALTH
PROFESSIONALS IN CORRECTIONS

Psychiatrists, psychologists, and other mental health professionals working in prison settings must often maintain dual roles. On the one hand, they are responsible for the mental health care and treatment of inmates at the facility. At the same time, mental health professionals are responsible for following the security and safety procedures of the correctional facility. At times, this dual role may present with some conflict. For example, psychiatrists performing under the professional guidelines of care for a patient may encounter security issues. At some prison facilities, medications approved at community mental health centers or hospitals, may not be allowed in a prison setting. In addition, confidentiality may also present as problematic. For instance, in some facilities, and depending on the security level of the inmate, an officer may be required to be in the room while a psychologist is counseling an inmate. In this respect, the psychologist would not have any control over the officer maintaining privacy. The tasks of psychologists and other mental health professionals may include, but is not limited to, the following (refer to Table 6.1):

Table 6.1	Duties and Responsibilities of Psychologists/Correctional Mental Health Professionals

- Screen and evaluate incoming inmates for mental illness or current suicidal ideation
- Provide crisis and suicide prevention and intervention services
- Participate on Crisis Support Teams for institutional emergencies
- Conduct forensic evaluations and assessments for the courts
- Administer, interpret, and evaluate psychological assessments (intellectual, personality, vocational)
- Develop individual treatment and follow-up care plans
- Provide individual, group psychotherapy, or psychoeducational groups
- Monitor inmates on antipsychotic medications
- Conduct 30-day reviews of inmates housed in segregated/special housing units (SHU)
- Help inmates reintegrate into society
- Provide substance abuse counseling
- Provide pregnancy counseling
- Write reports and documentation (i.e., intake screenings, suicide risk assessments)
- Provide consultative services to health services, administration (warden, associate warden, captain), custody staff (lieutenants, correctional officers), and the legal department
- Participate in professional development activities
- Provide staff training on suicide prevention, sexual abuse/assault, and employee assistance program
- Counsel correctional staff, as requested
- Supervise volunteers and student interns
- Serve on institutional committees (i.e., affirmative action, employees club, Correctional Workers Week)
- Conduct research on various correctional and criminal justice related topics

Source: Lorie A. L. Nicholas and Gerard Bryant.

In meeting the needs of the inmate population in general, and in particular, the needs of the mentally ill inmates, psychologists/mental health professionals may be called upon to provide recommendations. These recommendations may assist in the housing placement (i.e., SHU, medical center, general population of incarcerated inmates, or outside treatment needs of inmates being released). Inmates in solitary confinement or Special Housing Units (SHU) also need close screening and monitoring. In solitary confinement/SHU, an inmate is placed in isolation due to presenting with disruptive behavior (i.e., assault on staff, creating a shank/weapon), or signing themself into protective custody (PC) due to being afraid to be in the general population with other inmates. In this setting of solitary confinement/SHU, an inmate may be isolated from human contact (with the exception of staff) or placed with a cellmate under twenty-three hour lockdown, with one hour of recreation. Research has shown that approximately 70% of isolated inmates feel that they are on the "verge of an emotional breakdown (Haney, 2006 p. 53)." Here is one inmate's thought on being "In the Hole"—SHU isolation:

In the Hole

In the hole, where C.O.'s would love to see you hang yourself

And your only dream is to find the means to get out of this cell

Cause it seems like Hell when you can't even tell whether it's night

Or it's day.

No razors to shave, no way to get paid, no place for the made

One must be brave and face each day, expecting the worst

You gotta prepare cause inside here, insanity lurks

so when it hurts you're feeling like you can't go on

You stay strong cause that pain will not last long.

In the hole, where the C.O.'s would love to see you cut your throat,

And your only goal is to keep a hold of what's left of your soul.

Cause they mess with your hopes and step on your toes trying to see

If you'll break,

It's a game to be played, a fight too stay sane, a place for the crazed,

One must maintain and busy his brain, or all will be lost

If you don't change but come out the same, then DAUG you the boss,

So when the cost seems like too much and tomorrow is hopeless,

You continue to cope push aside your sorrows and keep your focus.

—Anonymous

Psychologists need to work closely with correctional staff to ensure that inmates in solitary confinement or SHU settings are adequately screened. Psychological reactions developed during SHU confinement may persist long after a prisoner has been released into general population or released from prison. With this in mind, aftercare or follow-up services should incorporate counseling. In review of screening the general population of inmates, there may be some inmates who deny any mental health concerns, not wanting to be labeled as "mentally ill." This group of inmates may view the label of being "mentally ill" as a sign of weakness which may present as an obstacle to protecting themselves in jail. An inmate may also deny mental health concerns because they lack insight about their mental illness and may feel that there is nothing wrong with them. A psychologist wants to be sensitive to the survival tactics inmates employ at the expense of their mental health. Once the psychologist understands why the inmate may be refusing or denying treatment or medication, counseling can be directed at addressing these concerns.

MENTAL HEALTH SERVICES IN CORRECTIONS

Screening Assessment

Once a person is arrested and is brought to a correctional facility, the role of the psychologist begins. The screening assessment of an inmate should ideally take place upon entry into the facility. Three other occasions in which inmates should be screened for high-risk behaviors are: (a) while detained, throughout the duration of their placement; if counseling is requested by inmate, upon receiving a referral from a staff person, or if a crisis situation arises; (b) upon transfer to another correctional facility; or (c) release back into the community. During the screening process, inmates should be assessed for co-occurring mental and substance use disorders so that they may be treated accordingly. The Psychology Intake Screening Assessment Questionnaire should be completed by all inmates entering the prison facility. This instrument will provide psychologists with a brief snapshot of the inmate. Some of the information gathered on this questionnaire include: past mental health treatment, current medication use, past and current suicidal history, history of sexual abuse, and presence of visual or auditory hallucinations (refer to Chapter 5 for an example of the Psychology Services Intake Screening Assessment Questionnaire).

One limitation of the Psychology Services Intake Screening form is that the information is gathered through self-report. With this in mind, if you have a severely psychotic inmate in denial of his or her psychiatric health, the inmate may not endorse past or current mental health treatment, use of psychotropic medications, or past or recent suicidal attempts. If this should occur, many mental health service departments in prison settings have other checks and balances in place that will eventually bring this inmate to the attention of mental health staff. Although it will be discussed later, staff are trained to observe behavior and make referrals. All inmates arriving to prison are also medically screened. During this evaluation, this may bring to light mentally ill inmates. In addition, an inmate acting erratically on the unit will draw the attention of other inmates who will also bring this inmate to the attention of staff.

Forensic Evaluations

Some psychologists conduct forensic evaluations within the prison to determine competency to stand trial, while others may seek to determine the existence of insanity at time of offense. These evaluations are conducted to determine whether an inmate is incompetent to stand trial, not guilty by reason of insanity, and guilty but mentally ill. An inmate found incompetent to stand trial may be required to be restored to competency so the trial process may proceed. "If restoration is highly unlikely, the state must decide whether to drop the criminal charges and, if necessary, initiate involuntary civil commitment proceedings" (Bartol & Bartol, 2008 p. 161). During involuntary civil commitment, a person is admitted to a mental health facility against their will. The goal is to continue treatment to restore competency. If there is no likelihood that an inmate could be restored and criminal proceedings resumed, under the civil law, this individual can be committed to a mental institution (Bartol & Bartol, 2008).

Cultural Beliefs and Malingering Behavior

Cultural Beliefs

Psychologists and mental health professionals must be able to differentiate cultural factors and malingering behaviors from an inmate with actual mental illness. In light of cultural issues, there may be times when a person's culture or beliefs may be misinterpreted as a mental disorder. In some cultures, hearing the voices or seeing visions of a deceased loved one may be the norm (Ortega, 2011), yet if a psychologist is unfamiliar with that culture, the person may be diagnosed with manifestations of a psychotic disorder such as auditory and visual hallucinations.

Malingering

When an inmate is malingering, he is attempting to fake illness or symptoms in order to avoid a duty or task or to obtain some type of gain. For example, an inmate may fake illness or symptoms in order to obtain medication or some type of financial compensation in a lawsuit. If an inmate knows the symptoms to fake, malingering can present as a challenge, making it difficult to distinguish from legitimate clinical (Axis I) or personality disorders (Axis II).

Professional Operational Standards and Guidelines

Psychologists and mental health professionals working in prison settings are required to follow the rules, laws, and regulations of that particular facility. In addition, psychologists working in correctional settings may follow the professional operational standards and guidelines developed by professionally related organizations. For instance, the American Association for Correctional and Forensic Psychology (AACFP, 2000) provides guidelines for the delivery of mental health services to criminal offenders, both adults and juveniles, held in local, state, or federal facilities as well as in the community. Other areas this organization covers include "research on the etiology, assessment, and treatment of criminal behavior, confidentiality issues, staffing requirements, duty to warn, segregation, and other topics along the lines of correctional and forensic work. Although a nationally standardized screening instrument currently does not exist (Steadman, Scott, Osher, Agnese, & Robins (2005), standards and guidelines of the national organizations (i.e., Joint Commission on Accreditation of Health Care, National Commission on Correctional Mental Health Care, etc.) require that all inmates be thoroughly assessed for mental health needs and suicidal history and ideation upon arrival. Therefore, many correctional facilities conduct the screening assessments with instruments developed by their agency that meet the guideline criteria.

In 1946, the American Prison Association published guidelines for state correctional systems. These guidelines focused on helping administrators to maintain order in the prison, combat prison overcrowding, and reduce rioting and other prison disturbances. The American Association of Correctional and Forensic Psychology (AACFP) formerly known as the American Association For Correctional Psychology, currently has 66 standards to guide the work of mental health staff in the prison. In addition to these standards, psychologists must conform to the ethical guidelines of the American Psychological Association (APA). There are several correctional and health care organizations that set the guidelines for the standards of medical and mental health care within the correctional environment and for continuity of care. Therefore, inmate's medical and mental health care needs are addressed whether an inmate is transferred to another corrections setting or released back in the community. These organizations include:

- American Psychiatric Association
- National Commission on Correctional Health Care (NCCHC)
- Joint Commission on Accreditation of Health Care (JCAHO)
- American Correctional Association (ACA)
- American Medical Association (AMA)
- American Public Health Association (APHA)
- National Institute of Corrections (NIC)
- *World Health Organizations International Classification of Diseases* (ICD)
- *Diagnostic and Statistical Manual of Mental Disorders* (DSM)

Upon review of the standards of the American Correctional Association (ACA, 2004), the ACA has cited twelve basic elements of correctional mental health care that should be in place at all correctional facilities for the identification and treatment of mentally ill inmates (Table 6.2).

Table 6.2	ACA Twelve Basic Elements of a Correctional Facility

1. Screening and comprehensive assessments, including the evaluation of co-occurring disorders, when indicated, to determine risk and level of impairment

2. Crisis stabilization services for offenders suffering from acute episodes

3. Policies on the prescription, distribution, and administration of psychotropic medication

4. Continued access to mental health services while housed in disciplinary or administrative segregation

5. Coordination and collaboration among treatment service providers

6. Establishment of a multidisciplinary treatment team in correctional facilities that includes correctional officers, and mental health, and other treatment professionals to develop and monitor treatment plans, including medication monitoring; a mental health professional should have a lead role on the treatment team

7. Suicide prevention strategies, including a policy on recognition, prevention, and treatment methods

8. Policies on restraint and seclusion, and on involuntary psychotropic medication use

9. Development of medical and legal guidelines that address informed consent, confidentiality, treatment refusal, mental health commitments, right to treatment, guardianship issues, requirements of the Health Information Portability and Accountability Act (HIPAA), and special needs housing

10. A holistic approach that emphasizes cognitive, social and coping skills development, relapse prevention, and repayment and restoration to victims

11. Specialized training on mental health issues on at least an annual basis, including training of mental health professionals on security issues

12. Transition treatment planning in cooperation with parole and community mental health agencies and other service providers prior to release to ensure continuity of care

Source: Thienhaus & Piasekci (2007), *Correctional Psychiatry*, pp. 118–123.

Classification and Diagnosis of Mental Health Disorders

In addition to the general standards and guidelines for correctional facilities in the medical and mental health treatment of inmates, more specific guidelines were directed at the labeling and diagnosis of mentally ill inmates. In 1948, the sixth edition of the *World Health Organization's International* **Classification of Diseases** (ICD) was developed. For the first time in this publication, psychiatric disorders were viewed as diseases (Adi et al., 2003). In 1952, the American Psychiatric Association published the *Diagnostic and Statistical Manual of Mental Disorders* (DSM) in the United States. This manual was psychiatry's early steps toward creating a system of diagnosis (Adi et al., 2003). At the time of this publication in 1952, the manual included 112 mental disorders (which included brain, psychotic, and personality disorders, and sexual deviation, including pedophilia and homosexuality (Adi et al., 2003). With the *DSM-IV* (printed in 1994) mental disorders increased to 374 from the original 112 documented in 1952. Today, the current *Diagnostic and Statistical Manual of Mental Disorders* (*DSM IV-TR*, 2000), a fourth edition with revised text, is used as the standard for mental health diagnosis. There are five different levels (Axes) of classification in the *DSM IV-TR*.

Axis I—The first level describes clinical disorders. Some common examples found in a prison setting include: depressive disorder, anxiety disorder, attention deficit disorder, hyperactivity disorder, bipolar disorder, phobias, and schizophrenia.

Axis II—The second level describes personality disorders and mental retardation. Among the most common Axis II disorders found in a prison setting are: antisocial personality disorder, borderline personality disorder, dependent personality disorder, paranoid personality disorder, paranoid personality disorder, schizoid personality disorder, narcissistic personality disorder, obsessive compulsive personality disorder, and mental retardation. Primary attention is given to the first two axes during the assessment process. Axis I and Axis II disorders may be found alone or in combination with each other.

Axis III—The third level describes general medical conditions which become important to understand a patient's physical condition. This section would include brain injuries, hypothyroidism, HIV/AIDS, respiratory or digestive problems, and so forth. Some of these physical conditions can aggravate existing illnesses, and in turn may cause the patient to present with symptoms similar to those under the clinical or personality disorders. "Medical studies show that 'mental problems' can be actually caused by an undiagnosed physical illness or condition" (Adi et al., 2003). The *DSM–IV-TR* gives the example that the notation of a personality change may in fact be due to a substance abuse problem or the medical condition of a brain tumor.

Axis IV—This level includes the psychosocial and environmental problems that may impact the diagnosis, treatment and prognosis of the Axis I and Axis II disorders (i.e. stressful negative life events, death of a family member, sexual/physical abuse, academic problems, loss of job, economic, health care or legal problems).

Axis V—This level provides the Global Assessment of Functioning (GAF). This is based on the clinician's judgment of how a patient is functioning overall, taking into consideration the previous factors.

The mental health conditions of inmates are based on the following care level factors:

Mental Health Care Level:

Care Level 1: Healthy inmate, with limited need for psychological services

Care Level 2: Inmate is stable, mentally ill inmate with a need for periodic, but not intensive psychological services

Care Level 3: Inmate requires weekly contact with psychology services staff

Care Level 4: Inmate is acutely mentally ill, in need of psychiatric hospitalization

THE INTERACTION BETWEEN PSYCHOLOGISTS AND CORRECTIONAL STAFF

Correctional staff includes the administration (wardens, associate wardens, captains), correctional officers, noncustodial staff (unit managers, unit counselors, receptionist), and all other department personnel (religious, education/recreation, psychology, legal, food services, facilities, etc.). The psychology department participates in the basic training for new employees and in the annual refresher training courses for all staff. Staff members are thoroughly trained in terms of inmate behaviors and various mental health issues or concerns (i.e., suicide) that they need to pay attention to. The training of all correctional staff members that have general contact with inmates is critical, because often, reports about an inmate's behavior come to the attention of psychology services, as a result of the observations from correctional staff. Dr. Haddad (Gater, 2011) points out:

> Security staff is with inmates 24 hours a day and can provide valuable input from their perspective, and they should also be educated about mental illness in order to interact with and understand these inmates better. (p. 20)

In handling inmates with serious mental illness, it is important that psychologists inform correctional staff of challenges they may encounter working with this population and with specific individuals. For instance, an inmate who is paranoid and believes people are poisoning his or her food would be handled differently than an inmate who is not paranoid. All staff working in corrections are also trained in the recognition of high-risk behaviors and signs of suicide risk. As McMullan (2011) points out, correctional staff need to be trained to provide the mental health professional with a description of the inmate's behavior (see Chapter 5). "Reporting an observation that 'Jimmy was talking to himself and swaying back and forth in his cell' is much more useful than reporting that 'Jimmy was acting crazy.'" (McMullan, 2011, p. 268) As stated earlier, it is usually through the observations of correctional staff that an inmate comes to the attention of psychology services. Psychology services staff should also communicate with correctional staff so they are aware of any special needs or behaviors of the mentally ill inmate on their unit. In this manner, a correctional officer observing a mentally ill inmate disheveled, talking and laughing to himself would have been made aware by mental health staff that this behavior is the "norm" for this particular inmate and not to be alarmed by the behavior.

Despite their beliefs or values about a particular inmate (i.e., a sex offender or severely mentally ill inmate), a correctional officer must remain "firm but fair" in their interactions with all inmates. According to Knoll (2007), mental health staff who work in corrections "will find that achieving an appropriate balance between mental health and security concerns is both a skill and a daily priority" (pp. 2–18). Applebaum (2005) adds respecting and acknowledging the expertise of the correctional officer can aid the mental health professional in achieving this balance. With this in mind, developing a positive rapport and a respectful collaboration with correctional staff is paramount to addressing the treatment needs of mentally ill inmates.

In working corrections, reciprocal communication between mental health staff (psychiatrists, psychologists, social workers, and other mental health staff) as well as with correctional staff is just as imperative—especially when it comes to addressing the housing placement needs or treatment of a mentally ill inmate. Mental health staff should work together to ensure appropriate treatment (i.e., medication) for the mentally ill inmate.

Basic Services for Inmate Populations

In the community, the police officer is often the first responder to the scene of a crime or crisis event. Police officers are responsible for maintaining order in the community. When the police arrive on the scene, they assess the situation, and determine what should happen. Police officers are given the power of authority. Depending on the scenario at hand, the police officer may decide to make an arrest or dismiss the individual with a warning. If arrested, upon entry into the prison system, inmates are faced with the challenge of adapting to the cultural norms and expectations of that particular prison system. Along with the loss of their freedom in society, inmates must get used to a structured, monotonous routine, obeying staff orders, pat and strip searches, memorizing an inmate number, and wearing a standard uniform. In general, inmates arriving into a correctional setting must learn to develop survival skills and adapt to that particular social environment of the prison. Each prison setting will most likely be different due to the level of the prison (minimum, medium, maximum, supermax, local, state, federal), location of the prison (state, city, rural), set-up of the prison (low-rise, high-rise) as well as other structural factors. So, every time an inmate relocates to a different prison, he must develop the survival skills and adapt to each particular prison environment. In addition to conforming to the prison routine, inmates must also acclimate to the underground prison rules of the other inmates.

As more and more inmates are staying in prison for longer periods of time, prison conditions may have a greater impact on the psychological distress of the inmates (Haney, 2002). As Knoll (2007) notes, the mental and emotional dullness of repetition leads to "trivial circumstances to take on critical importance in the eyes of inmates" (pp. 2–22). For example, fights may break out over who has the largest piece of chicken or who was next in the shower. An inmate's ability to cope within the prison environment has led to some psychologists investigating the psychosocial factors that affect one's psychological adjustment in prison (MacKenzie & Goodstein, 1986; Porporino & Zamble, 1984; Toch, 1977; Wright, 1993).The effects of these changes on the psychological well-being of inmates over the past two decades are still unclear, and we must rely primarily on studies conducted between 1970 and the early 1990s. Although this list may not be comprehensive, Table 6.3 outlines some of the problems long-term inmates may be distressed over.

Table 6.3	Problems of Long-Term Inmates

- Fear of permanent loss of outside relationships
- Health problems associated with aging
- Finding companions with similar interests
- Friendships with short-term inmates ending prematurely
- Dealing with younger impulsive/aggressive inmates
- Increased concern over relationships with staff
- Negotiating the prison bureaucracy
- Increased dependence on prison staff
- Gradual loss of interest in the outside world
- Increased degree of introversion
- Increased risk of suicide

Services for Special Needs Populations

Police

As stated earlier, the police officer has the power of arrest authority. The police officer can make the decision to arrest someone or dismiss the person with a warning. However, the situation becomes challenging when a person with a mental disorder is involved. The *DSM-IV-TR* (American Psychiatric Association, 2000) defines a mental disorder as a "clinically significant behavioral or psychological syndrome or pattern that occurs in an individual and that is associated with present distress or disability." Munetz, Fitzgerald, and Woody (2006) reported that in 2003, 52 mentally ill individuals were killed by law enforcement officers and seven officers were killed by mentally ill individuals during these encounters. Due to the role of police officers as first responders to situations in which mentally ill individuals may be involved, many police departments have collaborated with mental health professionals to provide mandated training on dealing with mentally ill populations. According to Psychologist Linda Teplin (2000), police officers have three basic choices in dealing with a mentally ill person:

1. Transport the person to a psychiatric facility

2. Arrest the person

3. Resolve the matter on the spot

Despite these three basic choices, Teplin (2000) is clear that other problems can still arise. If a police officer decides to transport the person to a psychiatric facility, there is a possibility that the psychiatric facility will not accept the mentally ill person. If the person is labeled as dangerous to others or has an active substance abuse problem, the psychiatric facility may deny accepting them. In this case, the police officer may have no other choice but to arrest the person. On the other hand, arresting the mentally ill has encountered criticism. There are those who contend that the individual is being penalized because of their mentally disordered behavior. Once a mentally ill individual is arrested, and depending on the legislation of that state, the mental health courts may be an avenue to address the needs of the mentally ill.

Psychologist

With a severely mentally ill inmate, when a psychologist is experiencing difficulty communicating with him, or it is determined that an inmate is not a reliable historian about his mental health, a psychologist may need to request the assistance of the inmate's lawyer for any additional mental health records available. The psychologist can also reach out to the inmate's family or the other prisons or hospital cites where the inmate may have been detained in the past, or to gather as much accurate information as possible about the inmate's mental health status and treatment.

Medication

Mentally ill inmates should be educated about their mental illness and medication prescriptions. Johnson (2008) believes by educating inmates they will be more prone to being compliant with their medication treatment. Inmates should also be educated about their psychotropic medications, their uses, and side effects. Psychotropic medications are the most widely used treatment for mental illness. The U.S. Bureau of Justice Statistics reported that in 2000, an estimated 114,400 inmates nationwide received psychotropic drugs while incarcerated (Beck & Maruschak, 2001). While psychotropic medication is widely used to treat mental illness, psychotropic medication is also widely misused by the inmates. Inmates may malinger to obtain medication with the intent of getting high since they may not have access to drugs used out on the street (marijuana, cocaine, LSD, etc.) or obtain medication to sell or barter for other goods or services from other inmates. With this in mind, whenever an inmate is given psychotropic medication, the nurse or physician assistant distributing the medication must make sure that the inmate has swallowed the medication. This task is done by mouth checks and having the inmate move their tongue around to make sure they did not "cheek" their medication (hide medication on side of their mouth or under their tongue).

Correctional Staff

Correctional staff often view mentally ill inmates as more difficult and challenging to manage due to their disruptive behavior. Offenders with mental illnesses obtain more disciplinary problems per year than nonmentally ill offenders (O'Keefe & Schnell, 2008; James & Glaze, 2006; Feder, 1991). When these behaviors occur, both psychologists and correctional staff must determine whether these disruptive behaviors are the result of mental illness or an inmate intentionally being disruptive and manipulative. Fagan & Ax (2011), describe some of the behaviors of disruptive inmates:

> Cell flooding, fire setting, refusing to exit cells, perhaps with the intention of provoking a forced cell extraction and/or scuffle with staff; self-harm, such as threatening to or actually mutilating themselves via cutting or insertion of objects into their bodies; physically assaulting others; throwing feces or urine; or spitting at others. (p. 309)

Mentally Ill Offender

As Sawyer and Moffitt (2011) point out, mentally ill inmates are incarcerated because they were unable to adhere to societal norms and expectations. Therefore, in the correctional facility, mentally ill inmates may continue to encounter difficulty adhering to prison rules and regulations.

Despite their legitimate mental health needs, the correctional facility and mental health staff must work together to determine appropriate disciplinary action. As mentioned earlier, inmates arriving into a correctional setting must learn to develop survival skills and adapt to the social environment of that particular setting. At times, a mentally ill inmate may encounter problems adjusting in the prison environment. There may also be times when their behaviors may be misinterpreted as signs of resistance to treatment (Fagan & Ax, 2011). An inmate not following a direct order from a correctional officer to make their bed or stand up for the count may often be written up for disobedience.

As Helfand (2011) stated, in order to treat the person, one must understand the *function of the behavior*. In other words, what is that particular behavior accomplishing for the inmate? Is the inmate trying to kill herself, get released from SHU, or get a particular staff person's attention? In treating the inmate, the behavioral goals outlined must be able to be accomplished within the confines of the prison facility. For some behaviors, a baseline can be established with the goal to reduce the frequency and eventually eliminate the behavior. For example, for an inmate who engages in daily self-injury and mutilation, the goal would be replacing that desire to cut with a much more positive option. At times, treatment may require a combination of treatment modalities such as cognitive skills, behavioral skills, and medication—working on impulse control to avoid cutting, and overcoming skill deficits with positive reinforcements.

Punishments for disruptive behaviors may reinforce attention, create a power struggle between inmates and "the system," and cause the inmates to escalate their disruptive behaviors as their way of feeling in control of the situation and in their mind "win." With this in mind, punishments need to be designed to control the disruptive inmate's behavior, while at the same time, teaching the inmates that their behaviors will warrant further disciplinary action, rather than them getting what they want. When it is determined that a mentally ill inmate has violated the rules of the institution and has received an incident report (a document that writes up the inmate's behavior which will result in time in segregation (SHU) or loss of privileges (visits, phone calls, commissary), the question becomes: *Should the mentally ill inmate be placed in SHU like a nonmentally ill inmates?*

Psychologists are often called upon to determine whether a mentally ill inmate who was placed in SHU should be disciplined for their disruptive behavior or activities. While assessing and treating mentally ill inmates is of high importance for those who have control of their behavior and actions, their mental illness does not excuse them of disciplinary action, and they can be held accountable. While there are some who believe that segregation in SHU can in itself be extremely stressful and may exacerbate a preexisting illness or the inmate's behavioral and emotional problems (Fagan & Ax, 2011; Haney, 2003), what must be taken into consideration in making this decision is the well-being of each mentally ill individual. In other words, address each incident on a case by case basis.

In time, most inmates adapt to the incarceration experience. Eventually, they find ways to stay busy and productive. For those inmates who continue to struggle with being incarcerated, they may present with other problems. For example, some younger inmates with pent-up energy may become disruptive out of boredom or not knowing how to handle their frustrations and anger.

At times, an inmate may seek immediate gratification in having their concerns addressed. If based on their perception, the concern is not addressed in a timely manner, the inmate may become frustrated and angry. This frustration and anger may be wrongfully misdirected toward staff or other inmates, inciting fights or other types of conflict. Others may begin to feel helpless and hopeless concerning their present circumstances. For some, this sense of hopelessness, combined with depressive mood can lead to feelings of imminent danger—acting impulsively to hurt someone else or even themselves. When suicide becomes the motive, the psychology services department plays a critical role in helping that individual work through the current circumstances or assist with basic adaptation to the prison environment.

Suicide and Self-Inflicted Injury Behaviors

"It's a Battle We Have to Fight EVERYDAY"

By Jamie in Tennessee

I'm not sure when it all started, but I think I've always dealt with depression. I just didn't always understand it. The first memory I have of it was when I was six and my grandfather died. I remember trying to hide my feelings because I thought I felt different than everyone else. I wouldn't even cry. Everyone thought I was too young for it to bother me, so I didn't let them know it did.... When I was seven, my oldest sister (who is ten years older than me) started to molest me. I'm not sure why, I guess now I think it was just a normal sexual curiosity she had. When I was 13, a guy I was talking to raped me. It was the turning point of my mental health. I knew it was wrong, but I didn't say anything, partly because I was scared he would hurt me again and partly because I was so embarrassed and ashamed. It ate away at me, until I couldn't take it anymore. I started telling my teachers that I didn't want to live anymore, but my parents just ignored it, even when I cut my wrist.

(Continued)

(Continued)

   I got married to a guy that I only knew for three months so I could get out the house, I did okay at handling things until after my first 2 boys were born. I had two miscarriages before my third son. That's when I began to notice a change . . . I started cutting all the time. It became an addiction and I couldn't stop. It got so bad that I went to my primary care doctor and he admitted me in a mental hospital . . . I had three suicidal attempts, one by cutting my wrist, and two by trying to overdose . . . "

Souce: Adapted from Mental Health America "It's a battle we have to fight EVERDAY," realLIVES program, Mental Health America website, Jan. 2009. http://www.mentalhealthamerica.net/reallives/index.cfm/2009/1/10/Its-a-battle-we-have-to-fight-EVERDAY

Jamie's story incorporates the components of mental health, suicide attempts, and self-inflicted injury behaviors. In addition, the reader gains insight into Jamie's earliest recollection of her depression and how her life transpired from the point of her grandfather's death.

This next section will further explore the components of suicide and self-inflicted injury behaviors.

Suicide

The prison suicide rate by the late 1990s was cited as 15 per 100,000 compared to the suicide rate in the society at large in the United States as 12 per 100,000 (Hayes, 2005; National Center for Health Statistics, 2005). Dlugacz and Low (2007) cite that the suicide rate in the prison system is much higher than in society. Some reasons for this increase of suicide in prison may include poor adjustment to the prison setting, isolation and loss of family contact and social supports, and stressors of dealing with various prison components (other inmates) combined with current court case. Mumola (2005) provides the following statistics related to suicide:

25% of all suicide deaths occur within two days

48% of inmates who commit suicide do so within the first week of custody

80% of suicides in prison occur in the victim's cell

The number of suicide attempts, suicide risk assessments, and suicide watches has steadily increased over the past decade within the Federal Bureau of Prisons. In fact, in nearly all cases the numbers in these areas have either nearly doubled or tripled over the course of the past ten years. This may be attributed to the fact that prisons have been receiving more mentally ill offenders and correctional staff are receiving more frequent and advanced training on how to recognize signs of depression and thus making more referrals of inmates to mental health personnel. High security prisons followed by pretrial facilities are the most likely places where suicides occur. This may be attributed to the fact that high security institutions house a greater number of mentally ill offenders, when compared to medium, low, and minimum security facilities. Inmates in pretrial facilities, facing perhaps their first incarceration and uncertain futures, and who may experience anxiety and depression, are more at risk for suicides than sentenced inmates.

In terms of location, the largest numbers of suicides in the FBOP tend to occur in the Special Housing Unit (SHU). This is not surprising given the fact SHUs are more isolated than any other areas in a correctional setting, and mentally ill inmates are often placed in this setting as a consequence of violating prison rules. Hanging is the most common method used in suicides. This is directly related to notion that materials used in suicides, for example, bed sheets, are more accessible to the inmate population. Other common methods employed include overdosing on medication (from Tylenol purchased in commissary to prescribed medication); cutting wrist, neck, or other body areas with shaving razors; jumping off the top tier of the housing unit.

A relatively new phenomenon in prison has been an increase in the number of inmates convicted of sex offenses, to include child pornography and molestation, who have committed suicide. Beyond the speculation that some of these inmates may have committed suicide out of fear of being in prison and possibly being targeted for violence by other inmates, this phenomenon warrants further investigation.

A psychologist must be able to tease out suicidal behavior of a high-risk inmate versus a manipulative inmate. In Thienhaus (2007), for instance, "an inmate who ties a piece of clothing around his neck may intend only to secure transfer to a single cell. But inmates end up dead as a result of clumsily staged suicidal acts" (pp. 1–15). In screening inmates, a psychologist needs to do a thorough assessment and must document various key factors: the foreseeability of imminent suicide based on current factors, suicide risk factors, absence of risk factors, past suicidal behavior, and last suicidal thoughts. A thoroughly documented screening assessment of an inmate is crucial when evaluating a potentially suicidal inmate. Written documentation to assess current suicidal status should be made after interviewing the inmate. As Dlugacz and Low (2007), note, "Any delay in documentation may raise doubts about the credibility and motives of the physician" (pp. 3–18), if that inmate were to in fact kill himself. Written documentation should include direct quotes from the inmate about current suicidal status (both active thoughts and absence of thoughts) and protective factors. Along with an inmate's verbal statements, observations should be noted about an inmate's behavior (i.e., are verbal statements consistent with nonverbal behaviors).

Self-Inflicted Injury Behavior

In addition to suicidal behaviors, staff must also be cognizant to inmates who may deny suicidal behavior, but yet engage in self-inflicted injury behaviors (SIBs). When inmates repeatedly engage in self-injury behavior, this can often leave staff feeling helpless and frustrated.

Correctional staff members are helpless because inmates can injure themselves with any items around the unit and frustrated because the SIBs may engage in these behaviors repeatedly, which at times can lead to accidental death. Individuals engaged in self-injurious behavior often seek opportunities to hurt themselves. This may include cutting themselves with sharp objects that they may easily obtain from things around the unit (i.e., razor, broken plastic spoon, sharpened toothbrush handle), scratching or burning themselves, or asphyxiation. Also, these cuts, scratches, or burns may be done anywhere on their body (stomach, legs, arms) which are often covered by clothing. Many believe that SIB occur more frequently while incarcerated because the inmates are unable to access their "normal" stress relief activities (i.e., substance abuse) that they utilized on the outside (Fagan & Ax, 2011; Trestman, 2000). With SIBs, it is always important to take them seriously and identify adaptive resources inmates can utilize to tolerate distress. In working with SIBs, psychologists may need to identify replacement behaviors that fit for the inmate and role play successful use of the replacement behaviors. Inmates should be positively acknowledged for use of appropriate coping resources. The inmate should be made aware of consequences that he or she will receive if they engage in SIBs.

According to the American Psychiatric Association guidelines (2000), an adequate suicide prevention program must include the following items listed in Table 6.4. A thorough suicide screening should contain the checklist of items similar to what has been documented in Table 6.5. These guidelines should be adjusted to include self-injurious behavior as well.

No matter how many years of experience a psychologist or mental health professional may have, no expert can state whether an inmate will ever commit suicide or not. This is why thorough, written documentation is important to prepare, along with direct quotes from the inmate, or any other supportive documentation indicating that at the time of interview, the inmate was not suicidal and also denied a desire for self-inflicted behavior. This is also why all suicidal threats should be taken seriously.

Table 6.4   Guidelines for Suicidal Prevention Programs

American Psychiatric Association Guidelines (pp. 6–8)

- Staff training
- Screening and identification of high-risk inmates
- Policies to insure adequate monitoring
- A clear and effective referral system to mental health
- Timely evaluation by mental health staff
- Appropriate housing options for monitoring and safety
- Communication among mental health, correctional, and other staff
- Timely provision of mental health services
- Clear and adequate documentation of suicidal risk and behaviors
- Quality improvement review of suicide incidents
- Critical incident debriefing

Table 6.5   Suicide Risk Assessment Checklist

Sex Offender

    History of violence
    History substance abuse
    Suicidal ideation/threat in the past (Dates: _____)
    Previous suicide attempts (Where, when, why, and how [methods] ____)
    Family history of suicide
    History of mental illness (Axis I diagnosis ___/Axis II diagnosis___)
    First prison term
    Sentence status
    History of poor impulse control or coping skills
    Chronic, serious, or terminal illness
    Recent suicidal ideation, attempt, or self-injury (acute or chronic)
    Recent release from a psychiatric hospital
    Anxious, agitated, or fearful
    Disturbance of mood (depression or mania)
    Lack of perceived support system
    Hopelessness
    Helplessness
    Feelings of guilt or worthlessness
    Fearful for safety
    Anniversary of important loss
    Recent rejection or loss
    Single-cell placement
    Well planned or highly lethal suicide attempt or ideation in past or present
    Hoarding or cheeking medication
    Recent trauma or threat to self-esteem
    Recent assaultive or violent behavior
    Predeath behaviors (e.g., suicide note, giving things away)

Protective Factors

    Family support/children at home
    Religious support
    Supportive friends
    Insight into problem
    Realistic life plan
    Exercises regularly
    Group activities
    Job assignment
    Other _____

Source: Adapted from the California Department of Corrections—February 2003, in O. J. Thienhaus, 2007, pp. 6–8)

WOMEN IN PRISON

Another special needs population detained in prison that should receive special attention is women. Although a broader discussion on female offenders behind bars is available in Chapter 3 and Chapter 4, the status of women in prison is briefly addressed below. Although the area of mentally ill juveniles in the criminal justice system will not be addressed in this chapter, it is important to note that mental illness is also a major area of concern for the juvenile population. Many youth entering correctional facilities may have histories of mental illness, psychiatric hospitalizations, substance abuse, physical, sexual, or emotional trauma or abuse, self-inflicted or suicidal behavior and may be on psychiatric medications. In addition, some youth may arrive in a correctional setting as a result of a behavioral outburst due to an undiagnosed mental disorder. Since juveniles, both males and females, present with a wider array of concerns, this population should be addressed separately. For further discussion on juveniles behind bars, refer to Chapter 2.

The Case of Ms. A

"Ms. A is a 43-year-old woman who was admitted to the jail infirmary after tearful and angry outbursts in the intake screening area. Well known to the medical staff, Ms. A has been in this jail ten times in the last three years, each time for prostitution charges. She has three children but the court terminated her parental rights years ago. She reports that she has been living on the streets ever since her fiancé beat her and kicked her out of the motel where they had been living. She reports daily heroin use and has a painful upper extremity abscess. She is edentulous. Her current symptoms are 'depressed, sick can't sleep' and she requests the medications that she received two years ago from an outside physician: Trazadone, Paroxetine, and Valproic Acid 'for my bipolar-schizophrenia, they really leveled me out,' Ms. A also asks for any medication that will 'make it so I don't think or feel anything.'" (Piasecki, 2007, p. 15-2)

"The brief case set out above illustrates some of the problems of women in jails and prisons. Ms. A. has a substance use disorder, she has been in an abusive relationship, she is separated from her children, she lacks housing, and she lacks income" (Piasecki, 2007, p. 15-2). West & Sabol (2009) and Greenfeld & Snell (1999) note that from their review of incarceration rates throughout the U.S. history, there are more women in prison today. Between 2000 and 2008, there was an increase in female offenders of 25%. Several researchers have attributed the increase in women's incarcerations to drug addictions and changes in the drug laws. Piasecki (2007) cites the increase number of women in prison reflects the 51.4% increase in drug arrests for women from 1992 to 2001.

It is believed that more than 60% of women in prison require mental health and substance abuse services (Owen, 2000). Women in prison are believed to be at a heightened level of mental distress in comparison to men. James and Glaze (2006) report that "Relative to men, proportionately more female offenders suffered from a serious mental illness (9.6% vs. 17.4%), had previously received inpatient psychiatric care (8.8% vs. 15%), and had previously used psychotropic medications (11.4% vs. 24.3%)." In a study by Messina, Grella, Burdon, and Prendergast (2007), it is noted that both men and women experience early childhood trauma. In addition, these authors stress that both groups need mental health and substance abuse treatment. However, the difference between men and women is the degree and intensity of these treatment needs and how they should be addressed in the criminal justice system.

In order to understand mental illness among female offenders, Loper & Levitt (2011) suggest that this requires knowledge of the "troubled histories of women who offend as well as the particular stressors of incarceration" (p. 215). It is believed by some authors that mental illness and substance abuse among female offenders are directly or indirectly the outcome of high levels of victimization and trauma. Based on a review of the literature, these researchers found that a large portion of female offenders have experienced traumatic histories: physical, psychological, and sexual abuse; victimization; mental illness; substance abuse; and financial and social problems (Allen, Latessa, Ponder, & Simonsen, 2007; Loper & Levitt, 2011).

According to Moloney, van den Bergh, and Moller (2009), "Women who have been victimized can be re-traumatized by prison experiences such as pat searches, internal physical searches, privacy violations, and verbal belittlement" (p. 217). How a woman responds to these experiences may strongly influence her coping ability in the prison setting. Female offenders may also be dealing with severe financial stressors, especially if they are the head of a single-parent household. Financial instability has been found to be a major risk factor in the prediction of female offending. Treatment for mentally ill female offenders needs to be comprehensive. Based on research by Loper and Levitt (2011), women relate to the world in the context of relationships. Therefore, these authors suggest that treatment occur within a relational framework that emphasizes social support. Loper and Levitt (2011) add that the interventions should directly target histories of trauma and victimization. In addition, Bartol & Bartol (2008) emphasize that female offenders require treatments that enhance their self-confidence, acknowledge the effect of physical, psychological, and sexual abuse on their lives, and help women to obtain control of their lives and teach them life skills.

The psychology services departments throughout the BOP provide basic mental health care to all interested inmates. There are also programs geared to special needs populations. As mentioned earlier, the psychology department services includes screening, assessment, treatment, individual counseling, group counseling, mental health and drug abuse counseling, self-help groups, and psychoeducational classes. Based on the mental health care level (Levels 1 through 4) or services that would be beneficial to the inmates, programs offered at various sites throughout the BOP include:

1. Drug Abuse Programs

NONRESIDENTIAL DRUGE ABUSE TREATMENT—available in every Federal Bureau of Prison institution and meets each individual's treatment needs.

RESIDENTIAL DRUG ABUSE TREATMENT—provides intensive drug abuse treatment to inmates diagnosed with a drug disorder. Inmates are housed together on a treatment unit, apart from the general population. If inmate is a nonviolent offender, he or she may receive up to a year off their sentence once they successfully complete the residential drug treatment program.

2. Abuse and Trauma Programs

RESOLVE PROGRAM (Women's prisons only)—a nonresidential program for female inmates with a history of physical or sexual abuse. There is also a Resolve Counseling component for women with a history of trauma and mental health issues, and Trauma Life Workshops which include psychoeducational components. These address challenges of dealing with exposure to traumatic life events.
Purpose of program:

- Decrease the incidence of trauma-related psychological disorders and improve inmates' level of functioning
- Increase the effectiveness of other treatment such as RDAP and health services interventions
- Manage inmates more effectively by reducing recidivism and enhancing the ability of inmates to function as productive citizens

Drug Abuse/Dual Diagnosis Program.

CHALLENGE (High-security institutions only)—an intensive, residential program for inmates with drug abuse and/or mental health problems. Inmates are housed together separated from the general population.
Core Curriculum—includes cognitive skills, problem solving, criminal lifestyles, relapse prevention; may also include additional curriculum resources to address anger, Axis II, trauma, and stress management.

3. Specialized Mental Health Programs

Federal Bureau of Prison offers several residential mental health programs for inmates with severe emotional, cognitive, and behavioral problems.

BRAVE PROGRAM—the Bureau Rehabilitation and Values Enhancement (BRAVE) Program is a residential treatment program that facilitates the adjustment of young, medium security, first-time male inmates into the bureau; for inmates identified as having difficulty conforming to prison rules. Along with the goal of improving adjustment in prison, program works to reduce the number of incidents of misconduct and identify and treat the psychological disorders that may contribute to criminal activity and poor adjustment.
The BRAVE Program serves three important roles:

- facilitates the adjustment of medium security inmates entering bureau custody for the first time
- improves institution security and reduces incidents of all misconduct, serious and minor
- enhances early identification and appropriate clinical intervention of psychological disorders which may contribute to criminal activity and poor institution adjustment

SKILLS PROGRAM—treatment for inmates with learning or achievement deficits; specialized treatment unit for inmates with significant, intellectual impairment (e.g., education) coupled with significant deficits in personality/adaptive behaviors (e.g., communication/social skills problems/poor institutional adjustment). Program is designed to improve the institutional adjustment of inmates who have intellectual and social deficiencies. Inmates with lower IQs, neurological deficits from acquired brain damage, fetal alcohol syndrome, and remarkable social-skills deficits often become victimized or manipulated by more sophisticated inmates.

Components include communication skills, social-skills training, values development, anger management, assertiveness training, problem solving, criminal thinking elimination, career counseling, functional literacy, arithmetic, language arts, personal hygiene, and lifestyle balance (fitness, exercise, and nutrition).

AXIS II PROGRAM—a residential program for severe Axis II personality disordered inmates. The goal is to identify, treat, and improve the adjustment and management in prison and reduce incidents of misconduct.

EVIDENCE BASED THERAPEUTIC INTERVENTION RESCOURCES—Basic Cognitive Skills is an rational behavior therapy program for inmates; teaches offenders about rational self-counseling, the rules of rational thinking, and the use of a Rational Self-Analysis (RSAs) to better manage their lives.

4. Sex Offender Programs

SEX OFFENDER MANAGEMENT PROGRAM (SOMP) (male institutions only)—this program is for the management and monitoring of sex offenders. It imposes correctional management plans on sex offenders who engage in risk-relevant behaviors. Risk-relevant behavior refers to conduct related to a sexual offender's history that indicates of risk of future sexual offending upon release (e.g., collecting sexual pictures of children, attempting to contact potential child victims).

SEX OFFENDER TREATMENT PROGRAMS (SOTPs)—Commitment and Treatment Program—The Adam Walsh Child Protection and Safety Act requires the bureau to review releasing sex offenders for possible certification as sexually dangerous persons. Postsentenced persons and civilly-committed sex offenders receive treatment in the *SEX OFFENDER TREATMENT PROGRAM* (SOTP).

Sex Offender Treatment Program-Residential (SOTP-R)—intensive program for high risk sexual offenders.

Sex Offender Treatment Program-Nonresidential (SOTP-NR)—moderate intensity program for low to moderate risk sexual offenders. Many of the inmates in the SOTP-NR are first time offenders with internet sex charges.

CHALLENGES TO TREATMENT—psychologists working within the confines of the correctional facility often face obstacles and challenges to their work. Most times the obstacles faced are due to safety and security of the correctional facility. At times, psychologists may encounter obstacles to completing their work.

This may include:

1. Being unable to adequately implement mental health services due to level of institutional security (minimum, medium, maximum, supermax)

2. Interruption of clinical services due to lockdowns, mandatory counts, controlled movements, conflict of scheduling (medical appointments, law library, legal visits)

3. Limitations on confidentiality due to required treatment records being placed in an inmate's file which several staff may have access to viewing

4. The administration not supporting the psychologist's recommendations for a mentally ill inmate due to security concerns taking priority

5. An inmate being transferred to another prison in the middle of treatment

6. Lack of adequate treatment resources

7. Conflict of interest (security vs. mental health needs)

8. Lack of disclosure by inmate due to viewing psychologist as the prison establishment/multiple relationships

9. Conflict in collaborating treatment needs and services with other departments

10. Inmates in need of Care Level 4 (setting may not transfer immediately due to paperwork and legal factors that need to be resolved before an inmate can be moved)

11. Medication management

12. Manipulative/malingering inmates

Limitations of Confidentiality

In addressing Point 3, limits of confidentiality, there are ethical guidelines that a psychologist should follow regarding confidentiality with a client. However, in a prison setting, maintaining confidentiality can become problematic. The American Association for Correctional and Forensic Psychology's (AACFP) 2000 standards suggest that non-mental health staff should have access to confidential information on a *need to know* basis. The AACFP indicate that mental health staff should be responsible for interpreting the client's psychological information. Even though the psychology department maintains client files under lock and key, when the psychology notes on an inmate are required for the inmate's primary file, the documentation may very well become public to other staff members as the paperwork transfers from hand to hand in the inmates file.

Multiple Relationships

In the Federal Bureau of Prisons, all staff members function as correctional officers first, and their profession is secondary to the institution needs. Conflicts may arise when a psychologist plays the role (multiple relationships, Point 8) of a correctional officer shaking down an inmate, taking all unauthorized items. The inmate then indicates he or she is stressed out after losing these personal unauthorized belongings and requests to see a psychologist. That correctional officer then switches hats indicating that they are in fact a psychologist as well, and the inmate can talk to them.

Under the American Psychological Association's Ethical Principles, psychologists are supposed to avoid engaging in multiple relationships. However, in the prison setting, the psychologist's role may at times present with a conflict of interest, because of the dual role as a psychologist and a correctional officer.

Conflict in Collaboration of Treatment Needs

In addressing Point 9 there are times when an inmate's problem may be questionable in terms of which department is most suitable to address the inmate's concern. For example, the health services department may feel that an inmate expressing sleep problems is best handled by psychology services. But after an assessment, the psychology services department may feel that the inmates sleep problem is a medical concern.

Inmates in Need of Care Level 4

Regarding Point 10, when it has been determined that an inmate is in need of Care Level 4 (inmate is acutely mentally ill and in need of psychiatric hospitalization), there may be times when an inmate may not transfer immediately. While paperwork and legal components are being resolved, the inmate is left in the care of the current facility that is not fully equipped to address those special needs. Usually, forced medication cannot be provided at the present site so correctional and mental health staff must care for this inmate as best as possible until the inmate is able to be transferred to the hospital setting. In the cases when mentally ill inmates are released from prison, they often do not get the follow-up care they need. As a result, they often return to jail. It is generally more expensive to treat mentally ill inmates in a prison setting. Mentally ill inmates tend to stay in jail longer. At times, they can be a management problem, or they may be abused, bullied, or sexually victimized by more aggressive inmates. They are also more likely to commit suicide. Therefore, as they await transfer, it is of utmost importance that the psychologist maintains close monitoring on the mental health and well-being of these inmates.

Manipulative/Malingering Inmates

With Point 12, manipulative/malingering inmates often prove challenging and taxing the resources and services of the correctional staff. Malingering behaviors are usually motivated by such factors as attempts to avoid work, obtain medication, obtain financial compensation, or obtain reduction in sentence by presenting with mental health issues. At times, when dealing with a manipulative/malingering inmate, the use of a *behavioral management plan* may need to be implemented. A behavior management plan is utilized for managing disruptive behavior that is primarily focused on the disruptive behavior. These disruptive behaviors are intentional and voluntary and not due to a severe mental illness. The inmate has control of their behaviors and can stop the disruption at any point. A sample outline of a behavior management plan can be found in Appendix 6.1. The primary goals of a behavior management plan are the following:

- Prevent inmate from harming himself or others
- Prevent manipulative inmate from abusing situations such as remaining on suicide watch for extended periods of time, when they are not suicidal, but choosing to avoid other settings such as Special Housing Unit (SHU) or being placed in general population
- Discourage inmate from escalating disruptive behaviors while encouraging and rewarding adaptive behaviors

The behavioral management plan includes the application of restraints appropriate to the level of the inmate's disruptive behavior directed at harming self or others. Inmate may present with deliberate, self-injurious behavior not indicative of suicidal intent, allowing a variety of interventions to be applied other than placement on suicide watch (which would be the inmate's goal, to be placed back on suicide watch). The behavior management plan works to ensure inmate safety and to manage manipulative suicidal threats and gestures. An inmate under the behavior management plan may present with disruptive behaviors such as being impatient, demanding, breaking food trays, and making superficial cuts on body, covering the window, flooding the cell, smearing feces, expressing auditory hallucinations, overdosing on pills stored up, aggression toward staff, throwing feces and urine, throwing food around cell, banging head on wall, and sleeping under bed so staff cannot see them. As can be expected, the behavior management plan has stirred up some controversy given the premise that in the case of an inmate who was on suicide watch, they are placed under SHU conditions.

Challenges to treatment also require that a psychologist be able to act fast and think on his feet during crisis and emergency situations. During these incidents, the psychologist and other correctional staff do not have time to plan, but must respond or act immediately. In the case of a suicide taking place, there is no time to plan. Staff members need to be able to think and respond quickly.

Some scenarios that a psychologist may encounter can include:

- Inmate attempting to drown him or herself in the toilet while on suicide watch
- Inmate jumping on top of sink, and breaking sink while on suicide watch
- Inmate reported a few minutes ago that he was at peace with GOD, walks to back of cell and as fast as he can, runs into glass door, cracking open his forehead
- A SHU inmate breaks sprinkler head flooding cell, then stuffs toilet with uniform and keeps flushing toilet, adding to flood of cell
- Inmate on suicide watch in four points continues to try to bite the flesh off their skin
- Female inmate found sitting on floor of TV room in a pool of blood and continues to slice both wrists
- An inmate locked in SHU a few hours ago, reported to staff that he needs to speak with his wife

He added that he speaks to his wife every day. He knew while in SHU he would only get a phone call every 30 days. When the officer returns to the cell after trying to find out for inmate if the lieutenant would be able to come speak with him, the officer found the inmate hanging from a noose attached to the top bunk of bed.

As psychologists continue to work and refine their position in correctional settings, these challenges must be addressed. As new challenges arise, they need to be dealt with as well. In light of a correctional setting that is always evolving, there will be some issues that may not be resolved easily and may remain ongoing as psychologists continue to refine their position in the prison system.

POLICY IMPLICATIONS

Police/Law Enforcement Training

Deinstitutionalization was created to move mentally ill populations out of psychiatric hospitals and back into the community. Instead, jails and prisons, the new asylums housing mentally ill inmates, have come full circle. Historically, the mentally ill housed in the prison system were moved to psychiatric hospitals then deinstitutionalized out to the community, and now have migrated back into the prison system. As stated earlier, police are the first responders to critical and crisis incidents in the community. The police officer has arrest authority to determine whether to let the person go with a warning or arrest them. In the case of someone who is mentally ill and has committed a crime, the police officer must make a judgment call in terms of whether this person can go to jail or requires psychiatric hospitalization. Since the police are the first ones to arrive at the scene of a crisis or crime, it is highly recommended that police officers and law enforcement staff in general receive ongoing training in handling and defusing situations in which a mentally ill person may be involved. The training should include role playing and debriefing of cases which involved the mentally ill to determine whether the situation was handled appropriately, and feedback and constructive criticism in terms of how the case could have been improved. Similar to police officers, correctional staff are also in need of ongoing training in managing mentally ill populations within the prison system.

Prison systems need to be responsive to the diverse prison population. Mental health staff must provide services to ethnic minority groups whom are overrepresented in the prison facility. In addition, Mental health staff, as well as correctional staff will need training on cultural factors relevant to that particular culture/ethnic group so that the inmate's behaviors are not misunderstood or misdiagnosed. Mental health staff must continuously keep their knowledge, abilities, and skills upgraded. This can be done through attending annual psychological and other professional and career-related conferences and events (for a listing of various organizations, go to the list of suggested websites). These conferences can help correctional mental health staff stay up-to-date on the latest trends in mental health. Staff can also stay abreast through current book publications and research being conducted in the field of mental health.

Treatment and Continuity of Care

Correctional mental health staff must work as a team to ensure that mentally ill inmates are receiving appropriate and adequate treatment, and that they are taking psychotropic medication as prescribed. In the event that a severely psychotic mentally ill inmate arrives to a correctional setting without a mental health file, there need to be components put in place that allows for the ability of the correctional facilities legal department, or mental health staff to communicate with this inmate's lawyer, family members, or both, to understand the mental health needs of this inmate. This will enable the psychologist to gather background information on the inmate which would include hospitalizations, past or recent suicide attempts, family history of mental illness, and so on. If for any reason, there is treatment disruption due to an inmate being moved to another housing unit within the facility, or transferred to another correctional facility, it would be very important for mental health staff to ensure that the treatment and medication regimen follows that inmate to the next housing unit. If the inmate is in fact transferred to another correctional facility, mental health staff should reach out to the mental health staff of the other correctional facility to update them on the current mental health treatment that the inmate had been receiving. This will help to ensure continuity of care. Also, along this same line, an inmate's file should be updated. Therefore, written documentation concerning an inmate's care, mental health history, and current psychotropic medications can be reviewed. The implementation of storing files via computer through the use of electronic health records can allow access to files across jurisdictions, including federal, state, city, and local jails. Severely mentally ill inmates released from prison need to have in place a treatment plan that lays out step by step, the type of aftercare treatment they need. This should include whether the inmate is required to receive mental health counseling, where, and how often, the type of psychotropic medication(s) that the inmate is currently prescribed, how often the inmate is supposed to take the medication each day, and the duration of the time frame that inmate is required to take that medication (i.e., three to six months, one year). Any other mental health treatment needs required for the inmate should be specified in this plan as well.

Funding

As with any type of program or services, how well a program is able to operate depends on the funding provided. In order for mental health services to adequately be implemented in correctional facilities for both the staff and the inmates, the prison must have an adequate budget. It would be ideal for mentally ill inmates to have access to services and resources upon arrival to a correctional facility, during their incarceration, and post incarceration. The deinstitutionalization process already demonstrated what happened when the funding was not provided adequately and placed in to the community centers. The result was a large number of mentally ill patients being released back into the community, unmedicated, homeless, and left to struggle in their attempts to fit back into society. As a result of criminal charges, mentally ill individuals are transitioned back into the prison system (transinstitutionalization). As the National Commission on Correctional Health Care (2003) points out, in order for mental ill individuals and clients with substance abuse problems to be successful in reintegrating back into society, there must be a discharge plan in place and collaboration with health care providers in the community.

Policymakers need to continuously advocate on ensuring that funds are allocated for the treatment and rehabilitation of mentally ill inmates, while incarcerated and once aftercare procedures are implemented. Any barriers or obstacles encountered in the rehabilitation or reintegration process needs to be addressed immediately. Any delays can make the difference in having an unmedicated mentally ill inmate released to the streets with the high probability of recommitting a crime.

Collaboration and Integration of Services

Integration of services should include the criminal justice system (legal), mental health professionals, healthcare department, and community care systems. Together these departments can work on behalf of ensuring the most appropriate plan for the mentally ill inmate while incarcerated, as well as upon release from prison. Communication throughout these systems would be critical so that each department takes responsibility for meeting the treatment needs of the inmate. Some situations may present with a role conflict as to which department is most appropriate to service a particular inmate. In an example provided earlier, an inmate may present with a sleeping problem. In this case, it may be advantageous for both the psychology department and health services department to collaborate and determine what would be the most appropriate course of action to treat this inmate's presenting problem. At times, the mission and philosophy of the psychologist or mental health professionals, and that of the correctional administration may differ—for instance a rehabilitative approach versus punitive measures. In this respect, communication becomes very important and coming to an agreement in terms of the most suitable approach is very important. At times, a mentally ill inmate may be instrumental taking an active role in the planning of their treatment and reintegration plans. This may help to ensure compliance and reduce resistance. The inmate should be provided with clear communication regarding the expectations and responsibility's they are required to maintain while incarcerated and once released from prison back in the community.

DISCUSSION QUESTIONS

1. What types of things would you suggest as an alternative to incarceration for mentally ill populations?

2. Should psychologists be required to perform all correctional officer duties or based on their code of ethics have some restrictions to avoid a dual relationship?

3. What types of treatment do you feel would be helpful to female offenders?

4. What types of policies and procedures would you implement for self-injury behaviors (SIBs)?

5. What might be some possible ways to ensure compliancy of mentally ill inmates continuing treatment upon release?

6. What are some ways a correctional facility can reduce or avoid malingering behaviors?

7. What future work do you feel needs to be done in the area of mental health services in correctional settings?

SUGGESTED READINGS

American Association for Correctional and Forensic Psychology. (2000). Standards for psychology services in jails, prisons, correctional facilities, and agencies. *Criminal Justice and Behavior, 27*, 433–525.

American Correctional Association. (2003). *Standards for adult correctional institutions* (4th ed.). Alexandria, VA: Author.

American Psychiatric Association. (2000). *Guidelines for psychiatric services in jails and prisons* (2nd ed.). Washington, DC: Author.

Arditti, J., & Few, A. (2008). Maternal distress and women's re-entry into family and community life. *Family Process, 47*, 303–321.

Brabender, V. A., Fallon, A. E., & Smolar, A. I. (2004). *Essentials of group therapy.* Hoboken, NJ: Wiley.

Charles, D. R., Abram, K. M., McCelland, G. M., & Teplin, L. A. (2003). Suicidal ideation and behavior among women in jail. *Journal of Contemporary Criminal Justice, 19,* 65–81.

Clear, T. R., Clear, V. B., & Burrell, W. D. (1989). *Offender Assessment and Evaluation.* Cincinnati, OH: Anderson.

Covington, S., & Bloom, B. (2006). Gender responsive treatment and services in correctional settings. *Women and Therapy, 29,* 9–33.

Fagan, T. J., Cox, J., Helfand, S. J., & Aufderheide, D. (2010). Self-injurious behavior in correctional settings. *Journal of Correctional Health Care, 16*(1), 48–66.

Feder, L. (1991). A comparison of the community adjustment of mentally ill offenders with those from the general prison population. *Law & Human Behavior, 15,* 477–493.

Fellner, J. (2006). A corrections quandary: Mental illness and prison rules. *Harvard Civil Rights-Civil Liberties Law Review, 41,* 391–412.

Gideon, L., & Sung, H. (2010). *Rethinking corrections: Rehabilitation, reentry and reintegration.* Thousand Oaks, CA: Sage.

Haney, C. (2006). *Reforming punishment: Psychological limits to the pains of imprisonment.* Washington, DC: American Psychological Association.

Herndon, J. S. (2001). Law enforcement suicide: Psychological autopsies and psychometric traces. In D. C. Sheehan & J. I. Warren (Eds.), *Suicide and law enforcement.* Washington, DC: FBI Academy.

International Association for Correctional and Forensic Psychology. (2010, July). Standards for psychology services in jails, prisons, correctional facilities, and agencies. *Criminal Justice and Behavior 37*(7), 749–808.

James, D. J., & Glaze, L. E. (2006). *Mental health problems of prison and jail inmates.* Special report. NCJ 213600. Washington, DC: U.S. Department of Justice, Bureau of Justice Statistics.

Jeglic, E. L., Vanderhoof, H. A., & Donovick, P. J. (2005). The function of self-harm behaviors in a forensic population. *International Journal of Offender Therapy and Comparative Criminology, 49,* 131–142.

Kupers, T. (1999). *Prison madness: The mental health crisis behind bars and what we must do about it.* San Francisco, CA: Jossey-Bass.

Lord, E. A. (2008). The challenges of mentally ill female offenders in prison. *Criminal Justice and Behavior, 35*(8), 928–942.

National Commission on Correctional Health Care. (2008). *Standards for mental health service in correctional facilities.* Chicago, IL: Author.

Rogers, R. (2008). *Clinical assessment of malingering and deception.* New York, NY: Guilford Press.

Ruiz, A., Dvoskin, J., Scott, C., & Metzner, J. (Eds.). (2010). *Manual of forms and guidelines for correctional mental health.* Arlington, VA: American Psychiatric Association.

Scott, C. L., & Gerbasi, J. B. (2005). *Handbook of correctional mental health treatment.* Washington, DC: American Psychiatric Publishing.

Travis, J. (2005). *But they all come back: Facing the challenges of prisoner reentry.* Washington, DC: Urban Institute Press.

World Health Organization (WHO). (2003). International classification of diseases (ICD-10) (10th Ed.). Albany, NY: WHO Publications Center.

World Health Organization (WHO). (2002). Preventing suicide: A resource for prison officers on mental and behavioral disorders. Geneva, Switzerland: Author.

SUGGESTED WEBSITES

- American Correctional Association
  http:// www.aca.org
- American Foundation for Suicide Prevention
  http:// www.afsp.org
- American Psychiatric Association
  http:// www.psych.org
- American Psychological Association
  http:// www.apa.org
- Asian American Psychological Association
  https://aapaonline.org/
- The Association for Women in Psychology
  http:// www.awpsych.org
- Association of Black Psychologists
  http:// www.abpsi.org
- Bureau of Justice Statistics
  http:// www.ojp.gov/bjs
- Federal Bureau of Prisons
  http:// www.bop.gov
- Human Rights Watch
  http:// www.hrw.org
- National Commission on Correctional Health Care
  http:// www.ncchcon.org
- National Institute of Corrections
  http:// www.nicic.org
- National Institute of Mental Health
  http:// www.nimh.nih.gov
- National Latina/o Psychological Association
  http:// www.nlpa.ws
- Native American Resources
  http:// www.nativeamericanresources.blogspot.com
- The Sentencing Project
  http:// www.sentencingproject.org
- Substance Abuse and Mental Health Services Administration
  http:// www.samhsa.gov

REFERENCES

Abramsky, S., & Fellner, J. (2003). *Ill-equipped: U.S. Prisons and offenders with mental illness*. New York, NY: Human Rights Watch.

Abt Associates Inc. (2000). *Addressing correctional officer stress: Programs and strategies*. Washington, DC: U. S. Department of Justice, National Institute of Justice.

Adams, K. (1992). Adjusting to prison life. In M. Tonry (Ed.), *Crime and justice: A review of research* (Vol. 16, 275–359). Chicago, IL: University of Chicago Press.

Adi, R., Pagel, M. J., Urbanek, A. P., & Whitaker, J. (2003). *The real crisis in mental health- A report, conclusions and recommendations*. Available at Citizens Commission on Human Rights, http://www.cchr.org.

Allen, H. E., Latessa, E. J., Ponder, B. S., & Simonsen, C. E. (2007). *Corrections in America*. Upper Saddle River, NJ: Prentice Hall.

Alpert, L. I. (2010, October 10). Sicko who stabbed 8-year-old boy planned to attack a child at Dave & Buster's. New York, NY: *Daily News*.

American Association for Correctional Psychology (AACP; now known as American Association for Correctional and Forensic Psychology). (2000). Standards for psychology services in jails, prisons, correctional facilities, and agencies: 2nd edition. *Criminal Justice and Behavior, 27*, 433–494.

American Correctional Association. (2004). Policy statement. Retrieved from www.aca.org

American Psychiatric Association. (2000). *Diagnostic and Statistical Manual of Mental Disorders*. (4th ed., Text Revision). Washington, DC: Author.

American Psychological Association. (2004, October 6). *The American Psychological Association applauds passage of the Mentally Ill Offender Treatment and Crime Reduction Act of 2004*. Washington, DC: Author. Available at http://www.apa.org

Applebaum, K. (2005). Practicing psychiatry in a correctional culture. In C. Scott & J. Gerbasi (Eds.), *Handbook of correctional mental health*. Washington, DC: American Psychiatric Press.

Arngo, B. (2002). Transcarceration: A constructive ethnology of mentally ill offenders. *The Prison Journal, 81*(2) 162–186.

Bartol, C. R., & Bartol, A. M. (2008). *Introduction to Forensic Psychology*. Thousand Oaks, CA: Sage.

Beck, A. J., & Maruschak, L. M. (2001). *Mental health treatment in state prisons, 2000*. Washington, DC : U.S. Department of Justice, Office of Justice Programs, Bureau of Justice Statistics.

Bureau of Justice Statistics. (2009). *Re-entry trends in the United States*. Retrieved March 4, 2012, from http://www.ojp.usdoj.gov/bjs/reentry.htm

Carlson, P. M., Roth, T., & Travisono, A. P. (2008). History of Corrections. In P. M. Carlson & J. S. Garrett (Eds.), *Prison and jail administration* (2nd Ed.). Boston, MA: Jones & Bartlett.

Carrega, C., & Goldstein, J. (2010, October 10). Stabber out to kill. New York, NY: *New York Post*.

Chaiken, S., & Shull, J. (2007). Mental health treatment of inmates in segregated housing. In O. J. Thienhaus & M. Piasecki (Eds.), *Correctional Psychiatry*. Kingston, NJ: Civic Research

Clear, T. R., & Cole, G. F. (1997). *History of corrections in America*. Belmont, CA: Wadsworth.

Clear, T. R., Cole, G. F., Reisig, M. D., & Petrosino, C. (2012). *American corrections brief.* Belmont, CA: Wadsworth Cenage.

Dlugacz, H. A., & Low, J. Y. (2007). Key considerations in liability management and the correctional psychiatrist. In O. J. Thienhaus & M. Piasecki (Eds.), *Correctional psychiatry*, Kingston, NJ: Civic Research Institute.

Fagan, T. J., & Ax, R. K. (Eds.). (2011). *Correctional mental health handbook.* Thousand Oaks, CA: Sage.

Feder, L. (1991). A comparison of the community adjustment of mentally ill offenders with those from the general prison population. *Law & Human Behavior, 15,* 477–493.

Frontline. *The story of Bennie Anthony.* (2010, April 28, updated 2010, December 6). Available at http://www.pbs.org/wgbh/pages/frontline/released/stories/anthony.html

Frontline. *The story of Jerry Tharp.* (2009, April 28, updated 2010, December 6). Available at http://www.pbs.org/wgbh/pages/frontline/released/stories/tharp.html

Gater, L. (2011, Jan/Feb). Prison mental health treatment: Trying to keep up with the outside world. *Corrections Forum 20*(1).

Greenfeld, L., & Snell, T. L. (1999). *Women offenders. Bureau of Justice Statistics special report.* NCJ 175688. Washington, DC: U.S. Department of Justice, Bureau of Justice, National Criminal Justice Available at http://www.ncjrs.gov.

Haney, C. (2002, January 30). *The psychological impact of incarceration: Implication for post-prison adjustment.* Paper presented at the "From Prisons to Home" conference at the NIH, Bethesda, MD. The Urban Institute, U.S. Department of Health and Human Services, Washington, DC.

Haney, C. (2003). Mental health issues in long term and supermax confinement. *Crime & Delinquency, 49,* 124–156.

Haney, C. (2006). Mental health issues in long term solitary and "supermax" confinement. In R. Tewksbury (Ed.), *Behind bars: Readings on prison culture.* Upper Saddle River, NJ: Pearson Education.

Hayes, L. (2005). Suicide prevention in correctional facilities. In C. L. Scott & J. B. Gerbasi (Eds.), *Handbook of correctional mental health.* Washington, DC: American Psychiatric Association Press.

Helfand, S. J. (2011) Managing Disruptive Offenders. In T. J. Fagan & R. K. Ax (Eds.), *Correctional mental health.* Thousand Oaks, CA: Sage.

Insel, T. R. (2003). *Beyond the clinic walls: Expanding mental health, drug, and alcohol services research outside the specialty care system.* Presented at NIMH Mental Health Services Conference, Washington, DC.

James, D. J., & Glaze, L. E. (2006, September 6). *Mental health problems of prison and jail inmates.* NCJ213600. Washington, DC: U.S. Department of Justice, Bureau of Justice Statistics.

Jeglic, E. L., Maile, C., & Calkins-Mercado, C. (2011). Treatment of offender populations. In L. Gideon & H. Sung (Eds.), *Rethinking corrections: Rehabilitation, reentry, and reintegration* (pp. 37–70). Thousand Oaks, CA: Sage.

Johnson, S. C. (2008). Mental Health. In P. M. Carlson & J. S. Garrett (Eds.), *Prison and jail administration.* Boston, MA: Jones and Bartlett.

Knoll IV, J. L. (2007). Impact of the structure and function of corrections on inmates' mental health. In O. J. Thienhaus & M. Piasecki (Eds.), *Correctional psychiatry* (Ch.2, pp. 1–34). Kingston, NJ: Civic Research Institute.

Knoll IV, J. L. (2010, May). Suicide in correctional settings: Assessment, prevention and professional liability. *Journal of Correctional Health Care, 16*(3) 188–204.

Loper, A. B., & Levitt, L. (2011). Mental health needs of female offenders. In T. J. Fagan & R. K. Ax (Eds.), *Correctional mental health handbook*. Thousand Oaks, CA: Sage.

MacKenzie, D., & Goodstein, L. (1986). Stress and the control beliefs of prisoners: Inmate adjustment and indigenous correctional personnel. *Criminal Justice and Behavior, 12,* 17–27.

Marzulli, J. (2011, March 17). Mentally ill man held after sneaking past security at JFK, boarding flights without a ticket. *New York Daily News.*

Mason, M. N. (2007). Setting the stage: A brief history of detention centers and mental illness in the United States. In O. J. Thienhaus & M. Piasecki (Eds.), *Correctional psychiatry* (Ch. 1, pp.1–14). Kingston, NJ: Civic Research Institute.

McMullan, E. C. (2011). Seeking medical and psychiatric attention. In L. Gideon & H. Sung (Eds.), *Rethinking corrections: Rehabilitation, reentry, and reintegration*. Thousand Oaks, CA: Sage.

Mental Health in America (2009, January 10). *It's a battle we have to fight EVERYDAY.* Available at www.mentalhealthamerica.net/reallives

Messina, N., Grella, C., Burdon, W., & Prendergast, M. (2007). Childhood adverse events and current traumatic distress: A comparison of men and women drug-dependent prisoners. *Criminal Justice and Behavior, 34,* 1385–1401.

Moloney, K. P., van den Bergh, B. J., & Moller, L. F. (2009). Women in prison: The central issues of gender characteristics and trauma history. *Public Health, 123,* 426–430.

Mumola, C. J. (2005). *Suicides and homicides in state prisons and local jails.* NCJ 210036. Washington, DC: U.S. Department of Justice, Bureau of Justice Statistics.

Munetz, M. R., Fitzgerald, A., & Woody, M. (2006). Police use of the taser with people with mental illness in crisis. *Psychiatric Services, 57,* 883.

National Center for Health Statistics. (2005). Retrieved March 4, 2012, from www.cdc.gov/nchs/faststats/suicide.htm

National Commission on Correctional Health Care. (2002, March) *The health status of soon-to-be-released inmates: A report to Congress, 1,* p.22. Chicago, IL: Author

O'Keefe, M. L., & Schnell, M. J. (2008). Offenders with mental illness in the correctional system. *Journal of Offender Rehabilitation, 45,* 81–104.

Ortega, C. N. (2011). Issues in multicultural correctional assessment and treatment. In T. J. Fagan and R. K. Ax (Eds.), *Correctional mental health handbook* (pp. 125–143). Thousand Oaks, CA: Sage.

Owen, B. (2000). Prison security. In N. H. Rafter (Ed.), *Encyclopedia of women and crime.* Phoenix, AZ: Oryx.

Piasecki, M. (2007). Psychiatric care of incarcerated women. In O. J. Thienhaus & M. Piasecki (Eds.), *Correctional psychiatry* (Ch. 15, pp. 1–23). Kingston, NJ: Civic Research Institute.

Porporino, F., & Zamble, E. (1984). Coping with imprisonment. *Canadian Journal of Criminology, 26,* 403–421.

Rosario, M. (2009, July 29). *Texas mother kills son, eats brain.* Available at http://www.latina.com/lifestyle/News-politics/texas-mother-kills-son-eats-brain

Sarteschi, C. M., Vaughn, M. G., & Kim, K. (2011). Assessing the effectiveness of mental health courts: A quantitative review. *Journal of Criminal Justice, 39,* pp.12–20.

Sawyer, D. A., & Moffitt, C. (2011). Correctional Treatment. In T. J. Fagan & R. K. Ax (Eds.), *Correctional mental health handbook*. Thousand Oaks, CA: Sage.

Stacy, M., & Lush, T. (2011, January 28). *Police: Army officer's wife kills her 2 'mouthy' teens.* Associated Press.

Steadman, H. J., Scott, J. E., Osher, F., Agnese, T. K., & Robbins, P. C. (2005). Validation of the Brief Jail Mental Health Screen. *Psychiatric Services, 56*(7), 816–822.

Sullivan, L. (2006, July 28). *Working the isolation unit: A prison officer's tale.* Retrieved March 4, 2012, from http://mentallyillinprison.blogspot

Teplin, L. A. (2000, July). Police discretion and mentally ill persons. *National Institute of Justice Journal,* 8–15.

Thienhaus, O. J. (2007). Suicide risk management in the correctional setting. In O. J. Thienhaus & M. Piasecki (Eds.), *Correctional psychiatry* (Ch. 6, pp.1–15). Kingston, NJ: Civic Research Institute.

Toch, H. (1977). *Living in prison: The ecology of survival.* New York, NY: Free Press.

Torrey, E. F., Kennard, A. D., Eslinger, D., Lamb, R., & Pavle, J. (2010, May). More mentally ill persons are in jails and prisons than hospitals: A survey of the states. Arlington, VA: National Sheriffs Association. Available at http://treatmentadvocacycenter.org

Trestman, R. L. (2000). Behind bars: personality disorders. *Journal of American Academy of Psychiatry and Law, 28,* 232–235.

West, H. C., & Sabol, W. J. (2009). *Prison inmates at midyear 2008—Statistical tables.* Bureau of Justice Statistics special report. NCJ 225619. Washington, DC: U.S. Department of Justice, Bureau of Justice Statistics. Available at http://bjs.ojp.usdoj.gov

Wright, K. (1993). Prison environment and behavioral outcomes. *Journal of Offender Rehabilitation, 20,* 93–113.

Wynn, J. (2001). *Inside Rikers: Stories from the world's largest penal colony.* New York, NY: St. Martin's Griffin.

APPENDIX 6.1

Behavior Management Plan

PURPOSE

A behavioral management plan is for managing disruptive behaviors, not mental health treatment. It is intended for inmates who are not mentally ill, however their disruptive behaviors (e.g., conditional suicidal threats, self-harming behaviors, etc.) are considered to be intentional voluntary and for secondary gain, and *not* due to mental illness.

A behavioral management plan is developed to ensure the safety of staff, inmates, and institutional security. The behavioral management plan is designed to be the least restrictive means necessary to safely manage an inmate and will include specific criteria for the discontinuation of interventions.

Psychologists play an important role in their institutions' effort to effectively control disruptive inmate behavior. The goal of the behavioral management plan is the elimination or reduction of problem behavior and the development of behavior patterns consistent with favorable institution adjustment. Used appropriately, and effectively, behavioral management plans are nonpunitive and therapeutic; and they are not used as disciplinary measures.

APPLICATION TO SUICIDE PREVENTION

In the event of a deliberate self-injurious behavior not reflecting suicidal ideation or intent, several interventions, aside from suicide watch may be implemented. Once an inmate has been evaluated by a Psychologist, and the Psychologist determines that the suicidal behaviors (i.e. statements, self-injurious behaviors, and/or other disruptive behaviors) do not reflect suicidal intent, and suicide watch is not deemed as appropriate, a behavioral management plan can be used instead to ensure inmate safety and to manage manipulative suicide threats and/or gestures.

BACKGROUND

This section provides background information on inmate such as age, race, length of incarceration, whether inmate is a holdover or sentenced, any disciplinary record, and any other pertinent information:

Inmate X is a 21 year old, African American male, who is a holdover inmate from (name other facility) currently being detained in prison on charges of attempted murder and possession of a firearm. He was placed in Special

Housing Unit (SHU) upon his arrival on (date of arrival) due to an extensive disciplinary record.

Reason for Current Placement on Suicide Watch

This section gives background information as to why inmate initially was placed on suicide watch:

On Wednesday evening, at approximately 10:00 pm, the SHU Lieutenant contacted psychology and indicated that Inmate X had stated intent to kill himself after a use of force was required to extract inmate X from the cell. Inmate X blocked the cell window and door with his mattress and refused to remove the mattress, cuff up and be rotated to another cell. After reiterating to the psychologist an intent to kill himself, inmate X was placed on suicide watch.

History of Disruptive Behaviors

This section provides history of disruptive behaviors prior to and while detained at current facility:

Inmate X has 20 incidents of extremely disruptive and aggressive behaviors, since being detained at (name of facility). He also has a history of making suicidal threats in order to be removed from SHU and placed on suicide watch. [Remainder of information in this section would include actual dates and times of events].

Mental Health History

This section provides any mental health history regarding this inmate:

Aside from a history of making suicidal threats, inmate X does not have any mental health history, and upon arrival to this facility, and during several interviews, denied any mental health history or use of psychotropic medication.

Psychiatric Medication and Compliance (if applicable)

Recent Adjustment

This section provides information on inmate's adjustment:

Upon placement in the suicide watch cell, inmate X was smiling and immediately began laughing and joking with staff. Inmate acknowledged he was never suicidal; he just wanted to get out of SHU.

Since his placement on suicide watch inmate X presentation has continued to inform the psychologist that he is feeling suicidal. However, his behavior and actions are not consistent with an inmate who is suicidal. He continues to joke and laugh with staff, indicating he needed a break from SHU where he could be in a single cell.

BEHAVIORAL MANAGEMENT PLAN GOALS

There are two key goals of this plan. The first, in light of his suicidal statements, is preventing inmate X from harming himself while he is housed at (name of facility). The second is preventing the inmate from abusing suicide watch policies in order to avoid being housed in SHU.

DISRUPTIVE BEHAVIORS DURING SUICIDE WATCH AND REASONS FOR INITIATING BEHAVIOR MANAGEMENT PLAN

This section provides information concerning an inmate's disruptive behavior.

Examples of Disruptive Behavior

- Assaultive behavior
- Breaking sprinkler head
- Fecal misuse
- Sexual acting out
- Holding a food slot
- Refusing to relinquish restraints
- Self-injurious behavior—cutting, making nooses, inserting objects into one's body
- Refusing a cellmate

In terms of managing the disruptive behavior, during the interview, the psychologist might explore with the inmate the reasons for the behavior to successfully influence it. Based on the interview, the psychologist can assess What is driving the behavior—fear, mental illness/personality disorder, skill deficits ?

Observation of inmate X's behaviors since being placed on watch have found him to be alert, fully oriented, and without signs or symptoms consistent with an individual who is experiencing emotional distress, a mood disorder (i.e., depression, anxiety) or a psychotic disorder (i.e., delusions, hallucinations). His speech and thought processes are consistently organized, coherent, and goal-directed. He has not displayed symptoms or behaviors consistent with an individual who is suicidal, mentally ill, or severely emotionally distressed.

INITIAL CONTROLS

This section provides information on the placement of the SHU inmate and the contents that will be authorized in the cell.

SHU Cell Assignment

Prior to moving, the SHU cell will be thoroughly searched for any items that may be used for self-harm. The cell should have no blind spots and must be free of any structural damage (e.g., broken windows).

Items Allowed in Cell

An Authorized Cell Property list will be posted on the cell door and a psychologist's signature will confirm each authorized item. Initial strict restrictions on the items allowed for inmate X are aimed at reducing his ability to interfere with safe operations of SHU, including his blocking visibility inside his cell, and his using items for self-harm.

ONGOING CONTROLS

This section will indicate the controls to be implemented while inmate X is on the Behavioral Management Plan:

The following controls have been established to minimize the occurrence of disruptive behaviors and self-harm:

If the inmate X is removed from his cell for any reason, he should have a visual search upon leaving and returning to his cell. His cell should be thoroughly searched prior to his return to the cell. Any significant findings during visual searches and shake downs should be communicated to the captain and chief psychologist and documented in the SHU log.

DETERRING DISRUPTIVE BEHAVIORS

Inmate discipline procedures will be used to deter disruptive behaviors. Staff will submit incident reports for prohibited behavior. Prohibited behaviors include, but are not limited to, disruptive behaviors such as: cursing and using abusive language against staff, verbal threats against staff, threatening to flood the cell, throwing urine and other substances from underneath his cell door, covering the door window to block visibility, possession of any unauthorized items in the cell (razor, underwear, magazines). Inmate X will also receive incident reports for acts of self-injury.

Use of Progressive Restraints

The application of restraints will be considered as a method of controlling his ability to harm himself or others. The Warden must approve the application of ambulatory or 4-point restraints on the inmate. The use of progressive restraints is to prevent self-harm and not for punishment.

Ambulatory Restraints

The following behaviors that may lead to placement on ambulatory restraints:
Inmate creates items that could be used to harm himself or others (i.e. attempting to tear his blanket or use any other cloth items for unauthorized purposes, prevents visual monitoring of himself by hiding (i.e., hiding in the shower) and/or attempts to conceal his behavior from others by covering his door.

Four Point Restraints

The following behaviors may lead to placement on four point restraints:
Inmate attempts to harm himself while in ambulatory restraints (e.g., banging his head against the wall; or attempting to cut himself by rubbing against metal edges).

REINFORCING APPROPRIATE BEHAVIOR

Provides information as to the amount of contact by Psychology Services, and reinforcement of appropriate behaviors:

Frequent initial monitoring will be scheduled in order to facilitate adjustment to Special Housing. For one week following his return to Special Housing, inmate X will be seen daily on weekdays by a psychologist. Weekend and holiday monitoring will occur only if a psychologist has come in to provide policy-mandated monitoring of inmates in suicide watch.

In order to reinforce appropriate behavior, additional property and privileges as noted in the reinforcement table, will be authorized if no self-injury or disruptive behavior has occurred. Property authorizations may be rescinded if items are damaged or misused. All property authorizations will be documented on the Authorized Cell Property list on the cell door.

Contingent upon the inmate maintaining behavioral control, he may receive the following reinforcements:

Routine Procedures

Recreation

Inmate X may be permitted outdoor recreation as dictated by the Reinforcement schedule. However, he will attend recreation alone until he is authorized a standard SHU Uniform.

Response to Self-Injury

If inmate X engages in any type of self-injury, a medical assessment will be conducted and appropriate medical treatment will be provided. An incident report will also be submitted and the Operations Lieutenant will notify the duty psychologist or the on-call psychologist.

Progressive restraints may be used to prevent further self-injury. The Operations Lieutenant will ensure that restraint procedures are followed, including any required notifications and authorizations.

Preventing Staff Manipulation

In most cases, property restrictions, progressive restraints, and medical intervention if indicated, will be sufficient to manage inmate X suicidal threats and gestures. All reasonable efforts will be made to avoid placing him on suicide watch (i.e., calling duty psychologist during regular hours, consulting with the on-call psychologist outside of regular hours).

Review and Implementation

Provides information on the administrative staff involved in reviewing the Behavioral Management Plan. The Health Services Administrator will also be consulted and will also receive a copy of the behavior management plan.

Amendments to Plan

In order to ensure rapid staff response to changing behavior management needs, procedural adjustments may be made by verbal consultation with Psychology, the Captain and the Associate Warden of Operations. However, no adjustments may be made prior to such consultation.

CHAPTER 7

Older and Geriatric Offenders: Critical Issues for the 21st Century

Ronald H. Aday & Jennifer J. Krabill

Over the past several decades, the level of attention directed toward managing aging prisoners has risen substantially. Internationally, research from the United Kingdom (Howse, 2003; Wahidin & Cain, 2006); Sweden (Fazel & Grann, 2002); France (Steiner, 2003); Canada (Gal, 2002); Australia (Grant, 1999; Dawes, 2009); and Japan (Johnson, 2000) indicate these countries, along with the United States, are all grappling with nearly identical issues associated with an aging prison population. Without timely attention to the experiences of geriatric offenders, officials globally will undeniably be presented with a crisis that, in return, would negatively impact all aspects of the correctional system. Despite the fact that nations around the globe are confronted with the dilemma of managing increasingly large numbers of older offenders, prisons have been slow to respond to the social, physical, and mental health needs of this special subgroup of inmates. Although a number of countries have commissioned studies to examine and make policy recommendations, the body of knowledge available on forecasting future policies for aging prisoners remains limited (Sterns, Lax, Sed, Keohane, & Sterns, 2008.)

Correctional officials are now realizing the enormity of their responsibilities for addressing age-related needs in the areas of health, safety, protection, recreation, and socialization (Aday, 2003). The primary aim of this chapter will provide a voice to aging prisoners' experiences and highlight approaches for addressing these concerns. In the process, we will identify characteristics officials use in defining older offenders, distinguish among types of elderly offenders, and discuss how various medical and mental health problems, left unaddressed, negatively affect institutional adjustment. Looking to the future, we will shed light on concerns such as major advantages of age—segregated housing, the growing need for assisted living, nursing home or hospice units—as well as the demand for compassionate release, medical parole, and community-based alternatives to incarceration. Finally, consideration will be given to examining the impact the challenges associated with managing the geriatric prison population today will have on sentencing practices in the 21st century.

GRAYING OF AMERICAN PRISONS

During the past several decades, there has been significant interest given to the prevalence of criminal activity among older adults. During the 1980s, the notion that the country was experiencing a "geriatric crime wave" received considerable media attention (Flynn, 2000). Although offenders age 50 and older continue to maintain the lowest overall crime rate of all adult age groups, Table 7.1 indicates the number of arrests among individuals in this age category are rapidly increasing. For example, the number of age 50 and over arrests increased from 473,162 in 1998 to 895,419 in 2009. As Table 7.1 clearly shows, the near doubling of older citizen arrests actually has occurred during the past five years. Significant increases in criminal activity are obvious for both males and females and approximately 15% of older adult crimes are serious felonies leading to incarceration. Table 7.2 supports the notion that older adults are involving themselves more frequently in drug and often related property crimes.

The majority of older males, however, are incarcerated in state prisons either for murder, sexual crimes, or drugs while females are more likely to be serving time for murder or drug-related crimes (Aday, 2003; Aday & Krabill, 2011). As the baby boom population continues to swell the ranks of older adulthood, the number of

Table 7.1 Gender Differences in Number and Percentage of Arrests for All Crimes Age 50 and Over (1998–2009)

| | Number of Arrests (1998–2009) | | | |
	1998	2004	2009	Percentage Change
Males				
50–54	194,912	266,395	377,048	+93.4
55–59	98,742	127,852	190,341	+92.7
60–64	51,319	59,614	85,009	+65.6
65+	53,325	49,672	64,082	+20.1
Total	398,298	503,533	716,480	+44.4
Females				
50–54	38,805	62,340	99,500	+156.4
55–59	17,457	26,702	42,964	+146.1
60–64	8,300	11,597	18,592	+124.0
65+	10,302	10,638	17,883	+73.5
Total	74,864	92,639	178,939	+139.0
Grand Total	473,162	533,969	895,419	+89.2

Source: U.S. Department of Justice, Bureau of Justice Statistics (1998, 2004, 2009). *Sourcebook of Criminal Justice Statistics.*

Table 7.2	Gender Differences in Number of Arrests for Crime Index for Persons Age 50 and Over (1998–2009)

	Number of Arrests (1998–2009)							
	1998		2004		2009		Percentage Change	
	M	F	M	F	M	F	M	F
Violent Crimes								
Murder	477	85	498	88	614	82	+28	−03
Rape	1,135	10	1,160	7	1,306	10	+15	NC
Robbery	885	102	1,490	169	2,234	299	+152	+193
Agg. Assault	16,115	2,456	17,454	3,225	24,007	5,133	+49	+109
Property Crimes								
Burglary	2,800	590	4,254	883	7,286	1,432	+160	+159
Larceny-Theft	23,372	13,167	30,321	16,809	43,801	27,420	+87	+108
Auto Theft	1,167	163	1,627	238	1,796	316	+53	+93
Arson	345	99	409	118	505	132	+46	+33
Selected Crimes								
Drugs	23,676	3,855	42,184	8,186	63,809	13,725	+169	+256
Other Assaults	41,955	6,519	44,182	9,580	64,992	15,366	+54	+135

Source: U.S. Department of Justice, Bureau of Justice Statistics (1998, 2004, 2009). *Sourcebook of Criminal Justice Statistics*.

arrests and certain incarceration will no doubt continue in the foreseeable future creating any number of end-of-life challenges for correctional officials.

With the graying of America, the increased use of punitive sentencing policies leading to selective incapacitation, and greater numbers of older adults committing violent offenses, all have contributed to the unprecedented growth of aging prisoners (Aday & Krabill, 2011; Auerhahn, 2002). With a massive construction in prison beds, correctional administrations nationwide have been pressed with increased responsibilities for receiving and responding to older adult populations. In 1990, the Corrections Yearbook indicated there were 33,499 inmates who were age 50 and over residing in state and federal institutions. This number tripled to 113, 358 by 2000 comprising 8.2% of the total prison population at that time (Aday, 2003). This growth trend continued and in 2010 that number had risen to over 200,000 or about 13% of the total prison population. This number includes over 7,000 incarcerated females age 50 years and older representing about 6% of the older adult population. Of those grouped in the older prisoner category, over 112,000 are 55 years of age and older with 16,405 being over 65 (American Correctional Association (ACA), 2010; Sabol, West, & Cooper, 2009). Assuming sentencing trends remain constant, it has been predicted that offenders 50 and older will account for one third of the inmate population by 2030 (Rikard & Rosenberg, 2007; Williams et al., 2006).

While prison administrators have primarily been interested in the management of older male offenders, officials also have begun to devote increasingly more attention to the experiences of women aging in prison. Even though women over 50 account for only 6% of all offenders (Sterns et al., 2008), the graying of our nation's prisons cannot be understood apart without regard for gender-specific issues older women present to management (Aday & Krabill, 2011; Williams et al., 2006). In addition to addressing concerns common to other geriatric offenders (educational deficits, histories of unemployment), response to this population includes assistance in over-coming stressors associated with extensive histories of abuse and prior involvement in prostitution or work in the sex industry. With older women, administration must also recognize the impact that the onset of menopause has on offenders' qualities of life. While the small number makes it more challenging to offer the range of services available in men's facilities, states are recognizing the impact a failure to act will have on the aging women now and after postrelease. Thus, many are developing instructional activities with consideration to the need for an intersection between age and gender sensitivity (Aday & Krabill, 2011).

DEFINING THE OLDER OFFENDER

Defining *old* as it applies to the prison setting is an extraordinarily challenging task for correctional administrators due to biological, psychological, and social positions of offender populations. Working with geriatric offenders, for example, entails treating those whose lives have been fraught with excess alcohol consumption, smoking, sexual promiscuity, and heavy manual labor that, taken together, have impacted healthy aging. Following the entrance into the prison setting, any preexist-ing symptoms are vulnerable to further deterioration as medical services tend to lag behind mainstream medicine in terms of offering necessary treatment (Deaton, Aday, & Wahidin, 2009; Vaughn & Collins, 2004; Watson, Stimpson, & Hostick, 2004). Concerns such as psychiatric, neurological, dermatological, gastrointestinal, respiratory, musculoskeletal, and cardiovascular conditions, for example, have been reported to remain untreated in older adult offenders (Fazel, Hope, O'Donnell, & Jacoby, 2004). Coupled with environmental hazards associated with residence in this institutional setting, elders may discover it nearly impossible to avoid the early aging process that has been discussed extensively throughout the extant literature.

The inability to agree on what constitutes an elderly offender is one of the more troublesome aspects of comparing research outcomes. A review of the literature reveals that care must be taken to account for the fact that background socioeconomic statuses, lifestyle choices, access to preventive health care, and now, institutional stressors make offenders 10 to 15 years older physiologically than their chronological age (Aday, 2003; Wahidin & Aday, 2010; Wick & Zanni, 2009; Williams et al., 2010). The National Institute of Corrections defines older inmates as those 50 years of age or older and the American Correctional Association recommends that prisoners should be classified by level of physical impairment, regardless of age (Wick & Zanni, 2009). Although states may use various criteria to classify this subset of the inmate population, the ages 50 and 55 are the two most widely recognized ages utilized for early intervention (Sterns et al, 2008). However, caution should be used when using chronological age exclusively to define the onset of old age. As in the general population, some individuals are considered old at 50 or 60 because of excessive chronic conditions while other may be comparatively young from a health standpoint at age 70 or 80. With some individuals thriving in this environment, sensitivity must be granted to inmate diversity and care taken to ensure the climate is one conducive to supporting all offenders into their later adulthood years.

OLDER OFFENDER TYPES

Correctional management must recognize that aging prisoners are truly a diverse group, with varying background demographics, experiences with the criminal justice system, health problems, or service needs. Sentence histories and lengths, for example, may often be key determinants of stressors faced while incarcerated, engagement in health-seeking behaviors, and coping mechanisms adopted for adjustment purposes (Loeb, Steffensmeier, Kassab, 2011; Reed, Alenazi, Potterton, 2009). In creating a climate most responsive to their concerns, care should be taken to distinguish among the needs of new, chronic, or aging offenders (Aday, 2003, Smyer & Gragert, 2006). The chronic offender or multiple recidivists may spend a significant amount of his or her life revolving in and out of prison. Typically the crimes committed would more likely mirror those of a younger offender.

However, today much attention is being directed toward the management of the new elderly offenders or those who have entered prison relatively late in life. It has been noted that this group of inmates entering prison after the age of 50 collectively comprise slightly less than half of the total geriatric prison population (Wahidin & Aday, 2010). As a whole, this group is more likely to commit violent crimes (murder or sexual offenses) against another person compared to the vast number of chronic offenders. In working with these offenders, sensitivity must be communicated to problems inherent to the nature of their crimes. The following provides some of the unique characteristics of first-time offenders that typically provide challenges for prison staff:

- Frequently suffer from prison shock/difficulties in coping with late-life imprisonment
- May be estranged from families due to violent crimes committed against family members
- May have grief issues related to loss of family, friends, and life on the outside in general
- May have guilt issues due to sexual offenses/homicides against family members
- May experience fear associated with late-life incarceration, especially for frail vulnerable inmates

- May isolate themselves from the larger social milieu, spending much time in their cells
- May experience suicide ideation, common among inmates entering prison with mental health issues
- May have unrealistic expectations about prison health care often comparing with outside experiences

Given the problems new elders have coping with incarceration, assistance must be given to ensure they receive sufficient stimulation, nourishment, and rest until they become acclimated with the subculture and adopt strategies for adaptation.

Another group of elder offenders for whom administration must provide supportive services, long-term offenders, are identified as having arrived at prison prior to age 50 and having served twenty or more years behind bars. Typically, these elders face complex problems in the areas of preserving external relations, establishing and maintaining internal relationships, physiological deterioration, prison environments, and indeterminate sentencing practices (Aday, 2003; Flanagan, 1995, Leigey, 2010). Inmates soon realize that family and friends on the outside cannot place their lives on hold for the duration of the inmates' sentences, and thus, neither wish nor request their loved ones make personal sacrifices or to be burdened by them (Aday, 2003).

In terms of the environment, long-term offenders and lifers hold numerous concerns about issues centered around aspects of institutional living as the dining hall, commissary, opportunities for personal hygiene (showers, laundry, haircuts), security, medical care—with such reservations being documented in both men's (Paluch, 2004) and women's (George, 2010) facilities. It has been argued, due to the sentence length, these inmates have begun to view these prison facilities as their "permanent home," and thus, desire and request officials to afford them basic amenities that would make the time occupied in this setting more tolerable (Aday & Krabill, 2011). In managing these offenders, consideration must be given to addressing the following:

- Many have outlived family members or have slowly disengaged from them
- The strain of knowing that separation from outside contacts may be permanent
- The lack of social skills, training, and resources to make successful community transition
- The realization that dying in prison is likely and the fears associated with the process
- Lack of prison work roles to enhance self-esteem and promote purpose of life
- Locating family/community members who will accept aging inmates eligible for parole
- Loss of ability to make own decisions due to dementia or other mental health disorders
- Gradual decline in functional health conditions restricting prison movement

Understanding these and other special needs of the older prison population is important as inmates attempt to construct an orderly "life" behind bars. In order for this process to occur, the environment must be responsive to inmates as they *age in place*.

ASSESSING OLDER INMATES' HEALTH

Today the level of attention invested in improving the quality of life that each of the above mentioned groups experience as they travel along the life course is truly phenomenal—with many advocating in support of a bio-psycho-social approach to understanding the concerns touching the lives of the geriatric offender (Kerbs, 2000). Specific to the prison setting, this approach recognizes the link between health or well-being and variables such as the geriatric offenders' imported demographic histories, patterns of substance abuse, housing assignments, cellmate and/or peer interactions, victimization, staff support, available coping mechanisms, sentence length, quality of health care, community support, and plans for reentry back into the communities at large. While Chapter 5 discusses the various issues of chronically ill inmates in the general population context, the following subtopics address important health and social indicators that offer considerable influence in the successful adjustment to prison life among older and geriatric inmates.

Physical Health Indicators

When examining the health status of older inmates, it is important to include prior life experiences in combination with current health changes during incarceration (Marquart, Merianos, Herbert, & Carroll, 1997). Older inmates are usually in worse health than their counterparts outside prison because they develop health issues much earlier due to their previous lifestyle, socioeconomic factors, and the prison environment (Glamser & Cabana, 2003). This rapid decline or accelerated biological aging has been attributed to the following factors (Aday, 2003; Fabelo, 1999; Fattah & Sacco, 1989):

- Tendency to engage in high-risk behaviors (smoking, drugs, alcohol, unhealthy diets) prior to incarceration
- Lack of preventive health care prior to incarceration due to lack of access and not practicing healthy aging behaviors
- Unhealthy lifestyles fostered in prison, including poor diets and general lack of exercise
- Greater rate of infectious disease than persons of the same age on the outside
- Harshness and stressors of prison life, especially those housed in maximum security prisons
- Stressors associated with an abusive past, alienation, and sleep disturbances.

Unarguably, creating a system within which medial needs can be accommodated must begin with identifying the physical and functional impairments most likely to affect this special needs population. Recently, large-scale, nationwide surveys conducted on health-related concerns experienced by a graying inmate population have directed our attention to the specific medical needs that geriatric offenders present officials. Sterns and colleagues (2008) projected an estimated 45% of offenders ages 50 and older and 82% of those 65 and older have chronic health problems. In general, aging prisoners rate their health as fair to poor, having deteriorated since incarceration and with a high degree of comorbidity. On average, older male samples report several chronic conditions—including arthritis, hypertension, heart diseases, emphysema, diabetes, and intestinal problems—as leading problems (Aday, 2003; Smyer & Gragert, 2006). In fact, 46% of inmates over the age of 50 reported having health problems at the time of their arrival into prison (Beckett, Peterneli-Taylor, & Johnson, 2003). As a result, older inmates generally need more medical and mental health services than younger people (Cohn, 1999).

In particular, the issue of penal health care is of primary importance for aging female inmates, who as a general rule, place a greater demand on prison medical and psychiatric services than males (Caldwell, Jarvis, & Rosefield, 2001; Gibbons & Katzenbach, 2006). Research has found that women seek health care two and one half times the rate of males, but frequently prisons fail to adjust staffing ratios in female institutions (Ammar & Erez, 2000). Exposed to high rates of violence and victimization, many female inmates enter prison already highly marginalized in the wider society. With backgrounds of poverty and unemployment and a history of prior drug abuse, most have suffered from personal stress, trauma associated with sexual and physical abuse, and fear in many stages of their lives (Morash, Bynum, & Koons, 1998). A large five-state study of 327 older females (Aday & Krabill, 2011) concluded that females had similar health problems as men with the addition of menopausal problems. However, the older women did report, on average, slightly over four (4.2) chronic health conditions.

Functional Health Status

As a microcosm of larger society, correctional institutions also hold a growing number of elders who are disabled and unable to negotiate environmental demands. Similar to other older adult populations, aging prisoners may experience complications performing various Activities of Daily Living (ADL) (i.e., bathing, eating, dressing) or Instrumental Activities of Daily Living (IADL) (i.e., taking medications, managing personal finances). Others, however, may be unable to engage in various tasks specific to survival in the given setting. Prison Activities of Daily Living (PADLs) may be challenging for individuals of advanced age to complete include standing in line for counts, dropping for alarms, and hearing staff orders. In recent years, the prevalence of functional impairments among aging prisoners has been projected to be approximately 10% for older men and slightly higher (16%) for geriatric female offenders (Colsher, Wallace, Loeffelholz, & Sales, 1992; Fazel, Hope, O'Donnell, Piper, & Jacoby, 2001). It is important to note, however, that when specific prison issues are considered, the percentage may rise as high as two thirds of older offenders (Williams et al., 2006). Since these concerns may elevate the offenders' risk of fall or injury, lower their morale, cause them to fear for their personal safety, and dissuade them from participating in the larger prison routine, staff must be encouraged to remain sensitive to potential signals of concern prior to needed interventions.

The activities that older people can engage in are important indicators of both how healthy they are and what services and environmental accommodations they need in order to cope with chronic conditions. Table 7.3 provides an interesting

| Table 7.3 | Gender Comparisons for Functional Health Status | |

Characteristic	Males = 302	Females = 327
Vision problems	39.3	87.6
Hearing problems	72.9	32.4
Difficulty walking long distances	48.6	57.2
Difficulty standing up to 15 minutes	37.5	59.3
Incapable of ascending/descending stairs	51.4	33.1
Require ground level housing	60.2	49.7
Require a flat, even terrain for walking	52.5	38.6
Require a lower bunk	68.9	84.1

Source: Aday (2001). *A comprehensive health care assessment of aging and infirm inmates.* Tennessee Department of Corrections; Aday (2009). *Health indicators for women aging in prison.* National Commission for Correctional Health Care Annual Conference.

Note: Mean age for males is 65; mean age for females 56.

comparison of the gender differences in the functional health status of two large samples of older inmates housed in southern states. Although the functional health status of the male sample was assessed by nursing staff and their counterpart's assessment based on self-reports, it is still apparent that both groups are limited in their abilities to negotiate a prison's physical environment. Obviously, the more frail and infirm the elder is, the greater challenges administration will face in encouraging involvement with the outdoor pursuits. Taken together, concerns such as the need to walk distances between buildings (particularly in inclement weather) or take periodic breaks while engaged in the activities themselves, can place the older adults involved in positions where they feel pressed to decline opportunities for involvement (Aday, 2003; Aday & Krabill, 2011; Harrison, 2006).

MENTAL HEALTH NEEDS

In addition to the vast number of chronic illnesses found in this subgroup of offenders, research has also shown that mental health issues are much more prevalent in prison than in the community (Haugebrook et al., 2010; Maschi, Morgen, Zgoba, Courtney, & Ristow, 2011; also refer to Chapter 6). Given their backgrounds, lifestyles, environment, and abuse histories, aging prisoners can present officials with a variety of mental health conditions requiring care. Following the deinstitutionalization movement of the 1970s, administrations have been fraught with the ever-increasing responsibilities for providing care to offenders who would have once received treatment in other contexts (Baillargeon, Bingswanger, Penn, Williams, & Owen, 2009). In fact, large-scale, nationwide surveys have projected the number of geriatric offenders with mental illness to be in the range of 40% (James & Glaze, 2006).

Other research based on small convenience samples report that, in select institutions, the prevalence of specific mental conditions may be much higher, occasionally exceeding half of the older prison population (Barak, Perry, & Elizur, 1995; Fazel et al., 2001; Taylor & Parrott, 1988).

Middle-aged offenders have been reported to require treatment for issues including depression, anxiety, substance abuse, personality disorders, and schizophrenia whereas those of advanced age may need support for Alzheimer's and other dementias (Caverly, 2006; Cox & Lawrence, 2010; Meeks, Sublett, Kostiwa, Rodgers, & Haddix, 2008; Regan, Alderson, & Regan, 2002).

Female inmates typically have higher rates of mental health problems than males (James & Glaze, 2006). Aday & Krabill (2011) reported that in a group of 327 older women (mean age = 56) only 23% scored within a normal depression range. One third of this sample was diagnosed with moderate depressive symptoms while one fourth scored in the high range and one in five reported severe levels of depression. Although there were no racial differences found, the authors did find that older incarcerated women with abuse histories were far more likely to suffer from depression and other mental disorders. These findings support other research that have found a significant link with childhood and adult traumatic experiences and life-event stressors as predictors of comorbid psychiatric conditions including anxiety, depression, PTSD, drug and alcohol abuse, and associated health problems (Haugebrook et al., 2010; Messina & Grella, 2006). For those entering prison with a low sense of self-esteem and fractured external support group, the prison environment can also serve as a source of stress leading to a further decline in mental well-being (Aday & Krabill, 2011).

Older inmates with multiple health conditions and who are mentally fragile frequently find themselves engaging in frequent thoughts about dying in prison (Aday, 2005–2006; Deaton, Aday, & Wahidin, 2009). To many inmates, dying in prison is one of the most dreadful things they can encounter (Byock, 2002) and one of the biggest regrets (Bolger, 2004). The notion of dying in a foreign place, in a dependent and undignified state is a very distressing thought. Contributing to the death anxiety of older inmates are the thoughts often associated with getting sick in prison or having to rely on prison health care in a time of crisis. Based on past experiences where medical staff have been found to humiliate inmates, to deny giving care such as withholding or delaying essential medications (Vaughn & Collins, 2004), inmates remain anxious about end-of-life issues such as dying in prison. Stoller (2003) reports that in many cases, health care access is "continually thwarted by rules, custodial priorities, poor healthcare management, incompetence, and indifference" (p. 2263). Inmates also frequently report negative experiences associated with watching other inmates die in prison and the lack of respect they received (Deaton, Aday, & Azrini, 2009).

As an increasing number of inmates continue to *age in place*, the onset of dementia is becoming a more common occurrence. It has been noted that Alzheimer's effect 15 to 25% of individuals who are 65 years and older (Sterns et al., 2008). Wilson and Barboza (2010) estimate that currently over 3,500 inmates currently possess symptoms of dementia. However, due to the frequency of comorbidity found among aging inmates and the regimented lifestyle of prison, this figure is expected to be much higher since few health care systems screen for cognitive impairments (Aday, 2003, Sterns, et al., 2008). While in the modern correctional environment, elders are expected, and required to maintain some general abilities for problem solving (Roof, 2010; Sottile, 2009; Williams et al. 2009). In any given day, surviving and thriving in the larger prison subculture requires elders to perform tasks such as familiarizing themselves with, identifying and adhering to staff commands, presenting themselves for structured activities, avoiding potentially conflict-ridden situations, and following medical's prescribed instructions. As dementia progresses, inmates may have difficulty performing Activities of Daily Living or being mentally oriented to their surroundings to the degree that they can remember to take medications, handle their personal possessions such as managing their financial account. In some cases, it has been noted that some cognitively impaired inmates may not even recall why they are incarcerated (Sottile, 2009; Wilson & Barboza, 2010).

Unfortunately, though, geriatric mental health experiences are not easily diagnosed or treated from within this setting. As a collective, older adults have very low utilization rates for available services (Hooyman & Kiyak, 2011). In the prison setting, many discover, clientele are highly unlikely to disclose their problems or symptoms when treatments are available (Yorston & Taylor, 2006). Instead, elders desire to preserve their image among prison peers—denying or suppressing their true emotions in favor of a more socially desirable appearance (Vega & Silvermann, 1988). Any problems with conditions such as depression, for example, are more likely to be of a somatic nature—with few elders explicitly identifying or calling attention to mood or affective concerns. Older adults who suffer from depression may simply reduce their activity level, withdraw, and become invisible (Sterns et al., 2008).

Isolation and Social Needs

Understanding the social world experienced by older inmates is an important component for responding to their special needs (Aday, 2006b). Sykes (1958) in his classical work, *The Society of Captives: A Study of a Maximum Security Prison*, observes that prisoners have to endure a variety of structural deprivations termed as the *pains of imprisonment*. Generally, these deprivations include losses of liberty, autonomy, security, products and services, and heterosexual relations. Prison offers a new subculture, a foreign set of rules, and language that can be overwhelming for mentally-fragile inmates. Goffman (1961) has referred to the entry into the total institution as a "civil death" (p. 16) which results in inmates being exposed to a series of social and psychological attacks that negatively undermine the sense of self. In particular, for geriatric inmates to adapt to prison life can be a challenging task where stark living environments evoke a wide range of human emotions including "frustration, anger, fear, sadness, and resentment" (Haney, 2006, p. 169). Older more frail inmates may devote a substantial portion of their day-to-day existence trying to minimize the dangers of imprisonment. Creating an effective social milieu is one of the most crucial, yet most challenging tasks that prison administrators will likely be presented with when preparing to manage a growing geriatric prison population.

Despite more liberal visiting and correspondence policies in recent times, inmates still must relinquish substantial contact with family and friends of the outside. For example, the Bureau of Justice Statistics reports that in 1999 only 43% of inmates housed in state prisons had received a personal visit from at least one child since incarceration (Mumola, 2000). Although Aday and Krabill (2011) reported that one third of a large sample of older females never receive face-to-face family visits and another 25% only do so once or twice a year, about 80% do remain in contact with family either by visits, letters, or by phone. The literature reports a number of barriers exist that currently that serve to reduce inmate-family interactions. Prior research has reported that inmates are less likely to receive personal visits when families live greater distances from the prison (Arditti & Few, 2006; Christian, 2005). Inmate families can incur enormous expenses when traveling long distances that also require lodging and other related expenses. Institutional barriers also exist which include restrictive visitation times and rules (Hoffmann, Dickinson, & Dunn, 2007) and lack of access to phones or excessive financial charges associated with long-distance calls (Wahidin, 2004).

Overall, geriatric offenders have much smaller social networks than other segments of the inmate population (Bond, Thompson, & Malloy, 2005). Although the presence of a cohesive network is a significant positive predictor of institutional adjustment (Sabath & Cowles, 1988), incarceration is considered to be a time when bonds tend to deteriorate. A significant number, for example, spend their later adulthood years in this environment single, separated, or divorced (Aday, 2003; Aday & Krabill, 2011; Kratcoski & Babb, 1990). Due to circumstances not always within the offenders' immediate range of personal control, other relationships as well are highly fragile, volatile, and vulnerable to deterioration or dissolution without formal intervention and assistance. While these individuals advance in age in correctional settings, loved ones (parents and siblings) are growing older in community settings. With this transition, many may be experiencing their own declines in health, strength/stamina, or desires to exert the energy necessary to sustain meaningful connections over extended periods of time.

Being separated from family members can prove to be difficult especially for many older female inmates. Not being able to fulfill the role of parent or grandparent everyday can be frustrating. Some older female inmates serving life sentences have been unable to interact with their children or grandchildren in the "free world." This can be a tremendous strain for a grandmother, who knows she cannot provide her grandchild the emotional support she formerly did, and for the grandchild who continually inquires as to when grandma will be returning home. For some older inmates serving long sentences, visitation from family or friends on the outside can cause a continuous grief reaction with each visit. For these inmates, it becomes easier to do the time by requesting their families and members of the free world not visit. This technique of compartmentalization is one way some older females tend to cope with long-term incarceration and family separation (Aday & Krabill, 2011; George, 2010; Williams et al., 2006).

There has been an ongoing debate about whether to house older offenders in the prison mainstream or in special needs facilities (Aday, 2003; Kerbs & Jolley, 2009). The mere physical condition and architectural structure of the institution create significant problems for the elderly inmate with functional limitations. In the past, prison systems were basically designed to house primarily young, active inmates. Now, older more frail offenders often find the prison environment to be unfriendly due the prison design which may challenge an inmate's mobility capabilities as well as a living environment with age-appropriate lighting, climate controls and noise levels. As we move forward, states will have great difficulty providing specialized, assisted living facilities for all the older and disabled offenders who might otherwise qualify (Sterns et al., 2008). With overcrowding and skyrocketing health care costs coupled with severe budget crises in any number of states, dedicating enough beds to this high-risk population will, no doubt, be problematic.

Studies have found that older inmates report feeling unsafe and vulnerable to attack by younger inmates, and expressed a preference for rooming with people their own age (Marquart, Merianos, & Doucet, 2000; Walsh, 1990). When they are housed in mainstream facilities, the presence of psychological, financial, physical, and albeit infrequently, sexual abuse is a continual fear to be fought (Kerbs & Jolley, 2009).This can be particularly true for the new elderly offender coming into unknown environment late in life and ripe for potential victimization. Vega and Silverman (1988) reported that abrasive relations with other inmates were the most disturbing incidents elderly prisoners had to cope with while incarcerated. Fifty-five percent of their respondents indicated that abrasive situations occurred on a daily basis. These factors, among others, often result in fear and increasing stress for the older inmate. An inmate's perception of the danger of possible abuse may be intensified as the inmate ages. The simple "fear of victimization" by younger inmates is also extremely prevalent among elderly inmates. Wilson and Vito (1986) found that inmates housed in a geriatric unit felt vulnerable simply because the most dangerous and unpredictable inmates were held in close proximity.

AGING PROGRAMS AND SERVICES

Housing Accommodations

Prisons have not been traditionally geared to the needs and vulnerabilities of older people (Abner, 2006). However, over the past 20 years, numerous states have had no choice but to build special needs facilities or secure nursing homes to accommodate the increasing number of geriatric inmates. A little over half of the states now provide geriatric accommodations, ranging from selected clustering, dedicated units, free-standing prisons, or dedicated secure nursing home facilities (Abner, 2006; Aday, 1999; ACA, 2001; Sterns et al., 2008). Some states have converted old tuberculosis or mental health hospitals into special facilities for aged and infirm inmates (Aday, 2003) while others have relied on new construction. Grouping inmates with similar health care needs is considered a more efficient way for correctional personal to respond effectively to the unmet needs of elderly prisoners.

Special geriatric accommodations provide aging inmates with a quieter living environment and are considered safer than living in the general prison population

(Marquart et al., 2000). Handrails, lower bunks on main-floor tiers, elevated toilets, and wheelchair accessibility are provided in most specialized units (Aday, 2006a). When prisons have low security risks, the facilities often permit the older offender increased privacy by designing rooms with doors. Additional amenities in newer facilities include prison-controlled thermostats, fluorescent lighting, strobe lighted fire alarms, and non-slippery flooring services (Falter, 1999). In the Oregon Department of Correction's geriatric unit (Anno, Graham, Lawrence, & Shansky, 2004), inmates are provided hospital-style beds equipped with extra padding, toilets, sinks, and showers that are handicapped accessible and inmates use a therapeutic gym equipped with a pool table configured at a lower height to accommodate wheelchairs. Closed-captioned television and specially equipped phones are available for the hearing impaired.

While the majority of elder inmates indicate they would prefer to live in age-segregated housing (Aday, 2006a), this option is not always possible. The prisoner's medical condition and security level are factors that must be taken into consideration before he or she is placed into an aged-infirm unit. Distance to living relatives is also a consideration when thinking about living in a special needs facility. Also, beds in special needs facilities are limited, with some units having long waiting lists (Aday, 2003; Sterns et al., 2008). Others may actually wish to remain in mainstream housing where they can remain more engaged, mentor younger peers, and to feel younger themselves (Aday & Krabill, 2011; Gallagher, 2001).

Although states differ markedly in terms of the breadth and range of activities being occupied specifically to accommodate this special needs group (Lemieux, Dyeson, & Castiglone, 2002), research has estimated that approximately 15 states currently provide at least some form of structured recreational program to target geriatric inmates (Anno et al., 2004). Several having psychologists, social workers, or other similar professionals on staff with specializations in geriatrics has made significant advancements in terms of designing programming to accommodate the various biological, psychological, and social changes that accompany the aging process. Popular activities that administration are being encouraged to adopt for use with the geriatric offender, for example, include age-appropriate work and educational opportunities, religion, assorted leisure pursuits (arts, crafts, gardening, woodworking), group work activities, and individual psychotherapy.

Florida, Ohio, Pennsylvania, Alabama, Georgia, Virginia, and Louisiana are a handful of states that have offered more ambitious programming for older offenders. However, the most comprehensive best practice model worthy of recognition in illustrating how programming can be designed and implemented to accommodate the special needs of the geriatric offender is the Structured Senior Living Program (SSLP) at the Northern Nevada Correctional Center (Harrison, 2006). The men are housed together in a separate unit and given a set of physical, social, and mental activities to perform on a regular basis. One of the most critical components responsible for the success of the True Grit program is the highly-structured eligibility requirements, which have been revised as necessary throughout the program's history (Harrison & Benedetti, 2009). Box 7.1 provides a summary of the program rules and diverse activities targeted at both cognitively and physically impaired inmates. The significance of SSLP can't be overstated given the fact that it was built on sheer creativity and community partnerships.

Box 7.1 True Grit: Structured Senior Living Program (SSLP)

By Ronald H. Aday

Northern Nevada Correctional Center

The Structured Senior Living Program (SSLP) was established in 2004 as a response to the unique needs of an increasing number of vulnerable elderly inmates. Primary goals of SSLP are to make available daily activities that include the encouragement of "personal, mental, emotional, and spiritual growth" among its 130 participants. The program also requires for each inmate to participate in educational activities which directly confronts their reason for incarceration (i.e., drug or sex offenses). Since its inception, the program has served 265 men including 38 who died while in prison and another 92 who were successfully paroled. The program uses no state tax dollars and relies on a cadre of inmate and community volunteers.

Participants: The age limit is 60 years and inmates must be referred by a caseworker, have a positive history of prison adjustment, and be willing to abide by strict rules.

Program Rules: Each True Grit participant must sign a contract when entering the program and each participant is required to complete the following activities:

- Initialing the daily program sign-in sheet, and reading the activity board for a listing of the daily program activities
- Maintaining personal hygiene: grooming, showering, and wearing clean clothing
- Maintaining personal living area including making the bed, ensuring food items are properly stored, cleaning the inmate's personal living area, and adhering to all housing unit and personal living area rules
- Initialing the daily work assignment sheet and completing the assigned SSLP daily tasks, which normally include cleaning hallways, activity rooms, bathrooms, showers, and other general living areas
- Maintaining personal SSLP and state-issued clothing ensuring that all clothing items are clean and in good repair

Program Diversity: Diversion therapy activities that are considered to be highly effective in enhancing the participants' overall qualities of life include the following:

Life skills training. Through guest speakers and the use of current periodicals, the Community Involvement Program helps participants increase interpersonal and social skills that are important whether they remain in prison or reintegrate into the free world. Such activities and skills include: meal planning on a budget, nutrition, microwave cooking, decision making, time management, goal setting, victimization (elder abuse, identify theft, and telephone and Internet scams), financial planning, and acquiring or reacquiring necessary identification documents.

Music appreciation. With a comprehensive collection of cassette tapes and compact discs (CDs), participants enjoy jazz, big bands, 60s, 70s, and 80s rock & roll, country & western, contemporary, and classical music. Each day a different type of music is featured in the SSLP activity rooms.

(Continued)

(Continued)

Music groups. Several music groups provide a variety of activities and opportunities for social engagement. The SSLP Choir—a 20-man ensemble—performs weekly, the SSLP Doo-Wop group, along with rock, country and spiritual groups frequently practice and entertain fellow inmates.

Art appreciation. Many SSLP members are talented artists and a successful drawing and painting program is an active component of True Grit. Led by a talented, retired art teacher from a nearby college, the program emphasizes drawing with pencils, charcoal, and pastels, and paining with acrylics and oils.

Beading. Beading provides enhanced cognitive function and improved manual dexterity and is a regular activity that provides participants with the opportunity to learn how to create beaded jewelry, wrist or headbands, decorative beaded art objects, and other unique items.

Puzzles and games. Active participation in puzzles and games provides cognitive therapy, problem solving, and coping skills training. Many of these activities are designed to stimulate areas of the brain damaged by dementia and Alzheimer's disease while offering an opportunity for socialization and fun.

Crafts program. As a means of enhancing and maintaining physical dexterity for those with arthritis, the program provides materials for latch-hooking rugs, crocheting afghans, and creating needlepoint art. Several dozen men work regularly on individual projects in this voluntary diversion therapy activity.

Physical fitness activities. The SSLP's physical fitness program includes an assortment of weekly aerobic exercise opportunities, game, and activities. These include the use of exercise equipment, weight training, stretching, volleyball, tennis, softball, horseshoes, Ping-Pong, basketball, billiards, and walking.

Pet therapy. With the assistance of the local area Delta Society, every month, two or three dogs make visits to the program, providing the men (many of whom are serving life sentences) companionship and the opportunity to bond with therapy dogs.

Writing groups. This program assists men who will be serving, in effect, life sentences, the opportunity to prepare themselves physically, mentally, spiritually, and emotionally for end-of-life issues.

Physical fitness: True Grit offers an impressive selection of sporting activities designed with the needs of geriatric offenders in mind. For those confined to wheelchairs, wheelchair softball, basketball, and bowling, provide attractive opportunities for involvement.

References

Harrison, M. T. (2006). True grit: An innovative program for elder inmates. *Corrections Today*, December, 46–49.
Harrison, M. T. (2009). *The Structured Senior Living Program: Program Update*. Northern Nevada Correctional Center, Carson City, NV.

Harrison & Benedetti (2009) have documented a number of program successes for the True Grit program. For example, according to the nursing staff, the number of infirmary visits by elderly inmates has decreased and the amount of psychotropic and psychoactive medications has also declined. The general feeling of well-being of the men in the program has increased markedly. One inmate serving a life sentence communicated the importance of the program when he stated, "Before True Grit, I spent 23 hours a day in my rack. Now I am in the program, writing and performing songs." Another 87-year-old participant who enjoys wheelchair basketball games mentioned, "I haven't had this much fun in years" (Harrison, 2006, p. 48). Due to the successful nature of the men's program, a similar program has been established for 38 women housed at the Women's Unit. Although a more elaborate evaluation of the program will help document more formally the program's outcomes, True Grit does show significant promise as a best-practice model.

PROGRAMS FOR HEALTHY AGING

Because of the high prevalence of physical and mental health care needs among older inmates, this group of offenders requires more frequent, complex, and costly medical services.

In meeting this challenge, several promising approaches are being explored and adopted for use in enhancing the quality of life for men and women who are advancing in age within correctional settings. Despite the accelerated aging process, many aging prisoners earnestly desire to engage in health-seeking behaviors and report positive outcomes. In fact, many define their health in remarkably favorable terms—noting their conditions have remained the same, improved slightly, or even greatly while they have been incarcerated (Loeb, Steffensmeier, & Myco, 2007). Similar to their mainstream counterparts, these individuals highly commend the system for affording them opportunities to become involved in pursuits that not only leave them feeling healthier, but also assist them in improving their self-esteem, alertness, energy, motivation to engage in pleasurable activities, coping mechanisms, and sleeping habits (Loeb, Steffensmeier, & Lawrence, 2008). Older lifers, in particular, speak in remarkably favorable terms about viewing prison as prime locations where they have, over time, learned to maximize any opportunities presented before them (Leigey, 2010).

In recent years, the use of chronic care clinics has been identified as a highly effective and cost-efficient approach to disease management for this population (Anno et al. 2004; Mitka, 2004). Numerous states such as Florida, for example, have established clinics well-regarded for responding to geriatric oncology, endocrine, gastrointestinal, cardiovascular, and renal problems (Florida Corrections Commission, 2008–2009). For patients utilizing these services, clinics provide a wealth of much needed information and assistance in overcoming barriers that traditionally interfere with recovery and management of the conditions. Chronic care clinics, for example, provide highly welcomed forums through which time and space is granted toward discussion of issues such as diagnoses, treatments, side effects, or even the effects that delays in treatment would most likely have on their overall well-being (Linder & Meyers, 2007). In establishing clinics to serve the intended purpose, though, care must be taken to protect against potential problems (i.e., poly-pharmacy, violations to inmate privacy) that can originate from addressing and responding to each condition on an independent basis.

Since factors such as education are considered to be essential to shaping the geriatric offenders' health (Bishop & Merten, 2011; Loeb et al., 2011), administrations have begun to examine their roles or responsibilities in teaching geriatric offenders practical skills they can adopt and integrate into their daily routines to maximize positive outcomes. With the growth of the geriatric population, institutions have developed structured programming with the needs of older adult audiences in mind. Among these include age-appropriate nutrition and exercise programming as well as various seminars oriented toward providing elders guidance in examining health attitudes. Ohio Department of Rehabilitation and Correction (1999), for example, reports offering the following health-related programs for geriatric participants:

- Age-specific stress reduction, anger management, AA and NA programs
- Courses on memory improvement, with emphases on providing strategies and practical tips on immediate, short-term, and long-term recall
- Medication education and management, with lecture and activities oriented toward familiarizing them with issues such as drug classification, benefits to adherence, side effects of commonly dispersed drugs
- Programming, in conjunction with the Central Ohio Area on Aging/OSU Health Services Center, to teach them to recognize and respond to specific health–related changes—including sensory/mobility impairments, osteoporosis, depression, and dementia
- Seminars oriented toward providing education on enrollment in Medicare, Medicaid programs, as well as other topics highly recommended and effective for use with those will be returning to the communities

Without question, activities of this nature must be accompanied by changes within the larger operations to best promote healthier lifestyles. Unarguably, two of the most widely recognized and cited areas focus on the need for improving the elders' diets and exercise. Today, for example, much emphases is now being placed on encouraging administration to reconsider the nutritional content of available meals and offer individuals greater varieties in terms of fruits, vegetables, and foods lower in starch and sugar content (Aday & Krabill, 2011). In the process, challenges that must be overcome include the limited resources with which food services have to operate and the intense pressure to serve large crowds within relatively brief periods of time (Wick & Zanni, 2009). Enhanced sensitivity, for example, must be directed to the fact that individuals with conditions such as dysguesia, dysphasia, or dental problems receive more time to eat or that those requiring light snacks between the evening meal and breakfast the next morning receive them.

Although much less is known about the long-term benefits that geriatric offenders may receive from early intervention, evidence suggests that these offenders do have an orientation to the future in mind and think about health maintenance in terms of continuity of established routines. Given the number of health conditions related to lifestyle choices, most involve some form of educational component that encourage personal responsibility. Since aging prisoners may not always be aware that opportunities for self-improvement exist (Formby & Abel, 1997; Loeb & Steffensmeier, 2006; Loeb et al., 2011), education encourages self-confidence (Loeb et al., 2011), and that practices engaged in today affect their maintenance of health-seeking behaviors following release (Loeb et al., 2007), encouraging preventative care, early detection, and intervention will undeniably remain a major priority of policymakers and officials in the 21st century. Ideally, lessons learned during incarceration would be reinforced by community networks and family support to ensure healthy lifestyle changes are long lasting (Higgins & Severson, 2009).

OTHER END-OF-LIFE PROGRAMMING

Over the last several years, our nation has witnessed a remarkable rise in the number of programs oriented toward delivering quality end-of-life care to inmate populations. Although research has not maintained records of the specific number of facilities with formal hospice services, some have estimated the number of states with hospices to be in the vicinity of 25—with several including California, Texas, and New York having multiple hospices throughout the state (Anno et al., 2004; Linder & Meyers, 2009)—and growth projected to continue well into the 21st century (Hoffman & Dickenson, 2011). In the process, heightened attention is being placed on examining issues such as admission standards, need for interdisciplinary care, narcotics, special privileges, family support, and discharge procedures (Linder & Enders, 2011; Linder, Enders, Craig, Richardson, & Meyers, 2002). It is now well accepted, for example, that administration follow a mixed-model approach to care—pushing for curative treatment and transitioning over to a palliative-based focus only after no improvement to medical statuses can be achieved (Dubler, 1998).

Without question, the key to establishing and maintaining effective prison hospice programming and services must begin with support from a wide range of parties. Correctional administration, other facilities, and community agencies must all be in agreement and willing to offer assistance and guidance as the need arises. Additionally, connections to the National Prison Hospice Association can be considered an enormous asset and advantage to those in the formative stages of development. In locations where there may only be one facility in the state that has (or plans to have) to operate a hospice, connections to other prisons in the region can be a much needed and welcomed approach to identifying patients who may have otherwise remained overlooked, and thus, uninvited to obtain the benefits that the program may have to offer (Bronstein & Wright, 2006). Prior to their involvement in patient-centered care, staff members receive orientation and instruction in infusing hospice concepts or principles into the prison environment with specialized training modules prepared and delivered in accordance with their particular responsibilities in mind (Boyle, 2002; Linder & Enders, 2011; Linder et al., 2002).

Most importantly, prison hospices are structured in a manner that recognizes the entire prison community—the patients, family, staff, peers, and volunteers—as being touched and deeply affected by the dying experience. Nationwide, development of hospice programming is considered to be most effective when there are bereavement-oriented services in place to respond to complex emotions that all represented parties have throughout the entire ordeal. Supportive outreach services, for example, must be planned to specific problems likely to be encountered, goals each may want to have in mind for involvement in support services, materials that would prove useful for those supporting offenders through their final days of life to have in their possession, as well as tools for evaluating client satisfaction or outcomes (National Palliative Care and Hospice Organization, 2009). In terms of correctional officers, for example, it may be strongly recommended to have resources available (complementing training in hospice) to assist them in remaining focused on the responsibilities at hand in the midst of inmate death (Taylor, 2002).

Understandably, many of the fears that correctional officers must respond to in their work with terminally ill offenders are unique to the given atmosphere and culture. Prison deaths, for example, differ markedly from those occurring in other environments in terms of concerns such as pain management, autonomy, and opportunities for exchanging social support (Bick, 2002; Mezey, Dubler, Mitty, & Brody, 2002; Tillmam, 2000). Given the nature of the crimes, most do not have freedom to either express their need for powerful narcotics or to have brokers advocating on their behalf. Although facilities may permit inmate use of morphine or patient-controlled analgesia pumps, policies remain restrictive in comparison to mainstream settings. Instead, care is still largely dependent upon staff on call, sick call hours, and the offender's willingness to disclose symptoms to the provider (Linder & Meyers, 2007). In most facilities, records of criminal histories may prevent optimum care in that such care dissuades physicians, nurses, and other providers from engaging in the open communication patterns needed to establish treatment regimen and execute them to completion (Smyer, Gragert, & Martins, 2006). Of course, in prisons, other inmates may have their own insecurities (such as fears of deserving punishment, relapse, or violating religious convictions) that cause reservations about accepting certain medications whenever they may be available (Linder & Meyers, 2009).

Other structured programming is also now available to cognitively impaired inmates who are considered terminal. For example, the recently established Dementia Unit at Fishkill Regional Medical Unit in New York, offers specialized care for patients with dementia-related conditions like Alzheimer's, Parkinson's, or Huntington's disease, and other assorted psychiatric or medical disorders (Sottile, 2009). All workers at the dementia unit—nurses, corrections officers, housekeepers—go through a 40-hour training course focusing on working with the cognitively impaired. Housed on the third floor of the prison's medical center, this 30-bed unit offers a wide range of fitness-related programming including bowling, miniature golf, stretch/exercise games, as well as a wide range of other outdoor and indoor options aimed at encouraging movement and physical activity. Moreover, administration recognizes the influence that addictions and interpersonal activity have had on shaping their patterns of conduct—offering ASAT (substance abuse), ART (anger management), and individual or group counseling to assist in promoting well-being. Additionally, leisure activities such as classical music or movie hours, bingo games and puppies behind bars are readily available to keep those cognitively-impaired elders who would otherwise be vulnerable to vegetation in other prison settings. Other facilities, such as the Deerfield Special Needs Unit in Virginia, who also cater to offenders suffering from the dementias, report comparable programming activities/services to ensure this segment of the population is fully integrated into programming with a purpose (Badgett, 2006).

POLICY IMPLICATIONS

As the aging prison population continues to increase, managing the special needs of this population poses a number of dilemmas that deserves special recognition among policy makers. While it is apparent that correctional officials and politicians are becoming more sensitive to the unique challenges created by the graying of our American prison system, barriers will continue to interfere with the ability for states to respond effectively. States continue to be faced with rising health care costs associated with caring for inmates who are older and sicker than ever before (Wahidin & Aday, 2010). While sentiment continues for establishing special needs facilities, the economic feasibility to provide special housing and treatment for such an emerging group of geriatric inmates is probably not realistic. With many states in dire economic duress and faced with federal mandates for providing medical care to all those incarcerated, this crisis in corrections will continue into the foreseeable future. In fact, age will be considered one of the biggest issues facing the criminal justice system in the foreseeable future.

A major barrier in responding fully to the special needs of the aging inmate is the lack of adequately trained prison staff (Cox & Lawrence, 2010; Knapp & Elder, 1997–1998). To meet this challenge responsibility, a professionally trained prison staff that can work comfortably with geriatric inmates will be essential. Prison staff needs to be specifically trained to understand the social and emotional needs of the older adult population, dynamics of death and dying, procedures for identifying depression, and a system for referring older inmates to experts in the community. Functional assessment providing early and accurate identification of the complex needs of older inmates will be critical for case management. Maintaining good communication between custody staff and health care providers will play an important role in the management process. Researchers should also continue to examine current prison conditions and programs to recommend policies and procedures to standardize the management approach to the crisis.

Considering the number of geriatric and terminally ill inmates, discussion must also focus on identifying more promising alternatives. One of the most commonly cited solutions to issues raised in this chapter focuses on the notion of compassionate release. Currently, an estimated 43 states have formal policies in place permitting terminally ill offenders to return home and occupy the final days of life peacefully, restfully, and contentedly with family and friends (Anno et al., 2004). Although each state uses slightly different criteria for determining eligibility, most consider characteristics such as prior criminal histories, security threats, remaining sentence lengths, and projected life expectancies in the process. In addition, most take into close consideration the fact that geriatric offenders have remained largely removed from mainstream society for extended periods of time, and thus, require from them evidence of a place of future residence before considering their applications. Without family, friends, or nursing homes willing to accept the individuals back into the community and offer supportive services while they make the needed adjustments, release can be even more unsettling or terrifying than institutionalization itself. Provisions, for example, must be taken to protect against homelessness (Williams et al., 2010). Perhaps the most critical issue to be addressed in preparation for the release of the older offender focuses on issue of how and by whom the population would be managed following reintegration into mainstream society. Given the number of citizens who continue to harbor reservations about this population and hold rigid views that persons released could enter nursing homes, cause injury to other residents, or continue to need more structured discipline than could ever be afforded outside the context of corrections, early release remains undersupported (Boothby & Overduin, 2007; Chiu, 2010). In order to facilitate a smooth, effective transition, policymakers must address whether decisions to release these individuals merely redirects or deflects the burdens of responsibility for their care onto other parties (Rikard & Rosenberg, 2007; Chiu, 2010). Very frequently, record-keeping making comparisons among the expense associated with care by each of the available alternatives can be a highly effective approach for boosting public confidence.

The Project for Older Prisoners (POPS) has been advocating the early release of elder prisoners since 1989 (Aday, 2003). Although early release is clearly out of the question for some, many of the older and geriatric inmates are considered to have an exceptionally low risk of reoffending. In fact, the POPS program has been directly responsible for the release of approximately 500 older prisoners with not a single one returning to prison. As a whole, less than 3% of older inmates released back to society are found guilty of reoffending (Aday, 2003). By using a careful screening and placement process, there is little doubt that early release of aging inmates should be given more consideration by policy makers. In particular, a large number of older female inmates would be prime candidates for early release, many of whom were severely battered before turning to criminal activity (Aday & Krabill, 2011).

In concluding our discussion of the special needs of the geriatric offender, some degree of attention must be placed on sentencing concerns. It has long been argued that sentences have a differential impact on elders in comparison to their younger counterparts (Muelher-Johnson & Dhami, 2010). For older adults, even the presence of five to ten year terms can often become the equivalent of life sentences. Due to the stressors discussed throughout this chapter, reform is necessary—with policymakers reevaluating statuses that promote lengthy, mandatory minimums. Punitive three-strikes policies, for example, must be restructured to ensure that men and women are not detained unnecessarily into their later adult years (Auerhann, 2002; Kerbs, 2000; Mauer, King, & Young, 2004). In looking to the future, it may appear more humane to determine sentence lengths for older adults only after carefully weighing issues such as the percentage of the individuals' lives that are likely to be remaining and related health problems. Regardless, any number of strategies will have to be implemented to manage the aging prison population and its impact on the correctional system.

DISCUSSION QUESTIONS

1. Discuss the various factors that have contributed to the graying of our nation's prisons over the last several decades.

2. Attention has often been placed on the distinctions between new, chronic/repeat, and long-term offenders. In working with aging prisoners, why would knowledge of these various subgroups be important in responding to their special needs?

3. Discuss why many states use the age of 50 as a marker for treating older offenders as a special needs category.

4. Mental illness is considered a major problem when designing programs to address the special needs of older offenders. What specific challenges do correctional face in responding to inmates with dementia and other related disorders?

5. What are some of the major advantages to housing geriatric offenders with their similarly aged counterparts raised in the literature in discussing mainstream versus segregation options?

6. How does the True Grit model program presented in the chapter address the most commonly cited problems with housing and treating the age-specific needs of geriatric programs?

SUGGESTED READINGS

Aday, R. H. (1994). Golden years behind bars: Special programs and facilities for elderly inmates. *Federal Probation, 23,* 162–172

Aday, R. H., & Krabill, J. J. (2011). *Women aging in prison: A neglected population in the criminal justice system.* Boulder, CO: Lynne Rienner.

Cox, J. F., & Lawrence, J. E. (2010). Planning services for elderly inmates with mental illness. *Corrections Today, 74*(3), 74–78.

Deaton, D., Aday, R., & Wahidin, A. (2009). The effect of health and penal harm on aging female prisoners views of dying in prison. *Omega: Journal of Death and Dying, 60*(1), 51–70.

Kerbs, J. J., & Jolley, J. (2009). A commentary on age segregation for older prisoners: Philosophical and pragmatic considerations for correctional systems. *Criminal Justice Review, 34,* 119–139.

Loeb, S. B., Steffensmeier, D., & Kassab, C. (2011). Predictors of self-efficacy and self-rated health for older male inmates. *Journal of Advanced Nursing, 67*(4), 811–820.

McGrath, C. (2008). Oral health behind bars. A study of oral disease and its impact on the life quality of an older prison population. *Gerodontology, 19*(2), 109–114.

Shantz, L & Frignon, S. (2009). Aging, women and health: From the pains of imprisonment to the pains of reintegration. *International Journal of Prisoner Health, 5*(1) 3–15.

Taylor, M. (2010). Prison receivership proposals pose significant financial risks. Retrieved from http://www.Lao.ca.gov./analysis/2010/crim_justice/receiver/receiver_031610.pdf

Vaughn, M. S., & Smith, L. G. (1999). Practicing penal harm medicine in the United States: Prisoners' voices from jail. *Justice Quarterly, 16*(1), 175–231.

Waring, S. C., Doody, R. S., Pavlik, V. N., Massman, P. J., & Chan, W. (2005). Survival among patients with dementia form a large multi-ethnic population. *Alzheimer's Disease and Associated Disorders 19*, 178–183.

Williams, B. A., & Abradales, R. (2007). Growing older: challenges of prison and reentry for the aging population. In R. Greifinger (Ed.), *Public health behind bars: From prisons to communities* (pp. 56–72). New York, NY: Springer

Williams, B., Lindquist, K., Sudore, R., Strupp, H., Wilmott, D., & Walter, L. (2006). Being old and doing time: Functional impairment and the adverse experiences of geriatric female offenders. *Journal of the American Geriatrics Society, 54*(4), 702–707.

Williams, M. E., & Rikard, R.V. (2004). Marginality or neglect: An exploratory study of policy and programs for aging female inmates. *Women and Criminal Justice, 15*(3), 121–141.

WEB RESOURCES

- Summary of research findings and policy implications for the state of Florida:

  http://www.schmalleger.com/schmalleger/corrections/aginginmates.pdf

- Jonathan Turley, director of the Project on Older Prisons, discusses the options available to prison systems in dealing with thousands of inmates growing old behind bars. NPR. 30 minutes:

  http://www.npr.org/templates/story/story.php?storyId=130837434&ft=1&f=1070

- A National Survey of Older Prisoner Health, Mental Health and Programming is presented here:

  http://law-journals-books.vlex.com/vid/survey-older-prisoner-mental-programming-56047532

- This Vera Institute website provides several reports on geriatric inmates including

  It's About Time: Aging prisoners, increasing costs, and geriatric release.

  http://www.vera.org/search/node/geriatric+inmates

- YouTube provides several short documentaries on issues associated with aging in prison.

  http://www.youtube.com/watch?v=SnsB92HegIg

REFERENCES

Abner, C. (2006, November/December). Graying prisons: States face challenges of an aging inmate population. *State News, 49*(10), 8–12.

Aday, R. H. (1999). Golden years behind bars: A 20-year follow-up. Paper presented at the annual meeting of the Academy of Criminal Justices Sciences, Orlando, FL.

Aday, R. H. (2003). *Aging prisoners: Crisis in American corrections.* Westport, CT: Praeger.

Aday, R. H. (2005–2006). Aging prisoners' concerns toward dying in prison. *Omega: Journal of Death and Dying, 52*(3), 199–216.

Aday, R. H. (2006a). Managing aging prisoners in the United States. In A. Wahidin and M. Cain (Eds.), *Ageing, crime and society* (pp. 210–229). London, U.K.: Willan.

Aday, R. H. (2006b). Aging prisoners. In B. Berkman (Ed.), *Handbook on social work in health and aging* (pp. 231–244). New York, NY: Oxford University Press.

Aday, R. H., & Krabill, J. J. (2011). *Women aging in prison: A neglected population in the criminal justice system.* Boulder, CO: Lynne Rienner.

American Correctional Association. (2010). *Adult and juvenile directory.* Lanham, MD: Author

American Correctional Association. (2001). Elderly inmates: Survey summary. *Corrections Compendium, 26*(5), 7–21.

Ammar, N. H., & Erez, E. (2000). Health delivery systems in women's prisons: The case of Ohio. *Federal Probation, 64*(2), 19–27.

Anno, J., Graham, C., Lawrence, J. E., & Shansky, R. (2004). *Correctional health care: Addressing the needs of elderly, chronically ill and terminally ill inmates.* Retrieved from http://nicic.org

Arditti, J. A., & Few, A. L. (2006). Mother's reentry into family life following incarceration. *Criminal Justice Policy Review, 17*(1), 103–123.

Auerhahn, K. (2002). Selective incapacitation, three strikes, and the problem of aging prison populations: Using simulation modeling to see the future. *Criminology & Public Policy, 1,* 353–388.

Badgett, B. (2006). Deerfield correctional center programs that address the needs of an aging and ill population. Presented at the Central Plains Geriatric Education Center Conference on Aging and End-of-Life Issues in Prison, Kansas City, MO.

Baillargeon, J., Bingswanger, I. A., Penn, J. V., Williams, B. A., & Owen, J. M. (2009). Psychiatric disorders and repeat incarcerations: The revolving prison door. *American Journal of Psychiatry, 166,* 103–109.

Barak, Y., Perry, T., & Elizur, A. (1995). Elderly criminals: A study of the first criminal offense in old age. *International Journal of Geriatric Psychiatry, 10*(6), 511–516.

Beckett, J., Peterneli-Taylor, C. P., & Johnson, R. (2003). Aging matters: Growing old in the correctional system. *Journal of Psychosocial Nursing and Mental Health Services, 41,* 12–18.

Bick, J. A. (2002). Managing pain and end-of- life care for prison inmates: The California medical facility experience. *Journal of Correctional Health Care, 9*(2), 131–147.

Bishop, A. J., & Merten, M. J. (2011). Risk of comorbid health impairment among older male inmates. *Journal of Correctional Health Care, 17*(1), 34–45.

Bolger, M. (2004). Offenders. In D. Oliviere & B. Monroe (Eds.), *Death, dying and social differences* (pp. 133–148). New York, NY: Oxford University Press.

Bond, G. D., Thompson, L. A., & Malloy, D. M. (2005). Lifespan differences in the social networks of prison inmates. *International Journal of Aging and Human Development, 61,* 161–178.

Boyle, B. A. (2002.). The Maryland Division of Correction Hospice Program. *Journal of Palliative Medicine, 5*(5), 671–675.

Bronstein, L. R., & Wright, K. (2006). The impact of prison hospice: Collaboration among social workers and other professionals in a criminal justice setting that promotes care for the dying. *Journal of Social Work in End of Life and Palliative Care, 2*(4), 85–102.

Byock, I. R. (2002). Dying well in corrections: Why should we care? *Journal of Correctional Health Care, 9*(2), 107–117.

Caldwell, C., Jarvis, M., & Rosefield, H. (2001). Issues impacting today's geriatric female offenders. *Corrections Today, 63*(5), 110–113.

Caverly, S. J. (2006). Older mentally ill inmates: A descriptive study. *Journal of Correctional Health Care, 12*(4), 262–268.

Chiu, T. (2010). *It's about time: Aging prisoners, increasing costs, and geriatric release.* Vera Institute of Justice. Available at http://www.vera.org/search/node/geriatric+inmates

Christian, J. (2005). Riding the bus: Barriers to prison visitation and family management strategies. *Journal of Contemporary Criminal Justice, 21*(1), 31–48.

Cohn, F. (1999). The ethics of end-of-life care for prison inmates. *Journal of Law, Medicine, and Ethics. 27*(3), 252–259.

Colsher, P. L., Wallace, R. B., Loeffelholz, P. L., & Sales, M. (1992). Health status of older male prisoners: A comprehensive survey. *American Journal of Public Health, 82*(6), 881–884.

Cox, J. F., & Lawrence, J. E. (2010). Planning services for elderly inmates with mental illness. *Corrections Today, 74*(3), 74–78.

Dawes, J. (2009). Ageing prisoners: Issues for social work. *Australian Issues for Social Work, 62*(2), 258–271.

Deaton, D., Aday, R., & Wahidin, A. (2009). The effect of health and penal harm on aging female prisoners' views of dying in prison. *Omega: Journal of Death and Dying, 60*(1), 51–70.

Dubler, N. N. (1998). The collusion of confinement and care: End of life care in prisons and jails. *The Journal of Law, Medicine, and Ethics, 26*(2), 149–156.

Fabelo, T. (1999). Elderly offenders in Texas prisons. Criminal Justice Policy Council. Austin, TX.

Falter, R. G. (1999). Selected predictors of health services needs of inmates over 50. *Journal of Correctional Health Care, 6*, 149–175.

Fattah, E. A., & Sacco, V. F. (1989). *Crime and victimization of the elderly.* New York, NY: Springer.

Fazel, S., & Grann, M. (2002). Older criminals: A descriptive study of psychiatrically examined offenders in Sweden. *International Journal of Geriatric Psychiatry, 17*, 907–913.

Fazel, S., Hope, T., O'Donnell, I., & Jacoby, R. (2004). Unmet treatment needs of older prisoners: A primary care survey. *Age and Ageing, 33*, 396–398.

Fazel, S., Hope, T., O'Donnell, I., Piper, M., & Jacoby, R. (2001). Health of elderly male prisoners: Worse than the general population, worse than younger prisoners. *Age and Ageing, 30*, 403–407.

Flanagan, T. J. (1995). *Long-term imprisonment: Policy, science, and correctional practice.* Thousand Oaks, CA: Sage.

Florida Corrections Commission (2008–2009). *State of Florida Correctional Medical Authority. Annual Report.* Available at www.doh.state.fl.us

Flynn, E. E. (2000). Elders as perpetrators. In M.B. Rothman, B. D. Dunlop, & P. Entzel (Eds.), *Elders crime and the criminal justice system: Myths, perceptions and reality in the 21st century* (pp. 43–86). New York, NY: Springer.

Formby, W. A., & Abel, C. F. (1997). Elderly men in prison. In J. I. Kosburg & L. W. Kaye (Eds.), *Elderly men: Special problems and professional* challenges (pp. 98–112). New York, NY: Springer.

Gal, M. (2002). The physical and mental health of older offenders. *FORUM on Corrections Research, 14*(2), 1–6.

Gallagher, E. M. (2001). Elders in prison: Health and well-being of older inmates. *International Journal of Law and Psychiatry, 24*, 325–333.

George, E. (2010). *A woman doing life: Notes from a prison for women.* New York, NY: Oxford University Press.

Gibbons, J., & Katzenbach, N. B. (2006). *Confronting confinement.* Retrieved from http://www.prisoncommission.org.uk

Glamser, F. D., & Cabana, D. A. (2003). Death in a total institution: The case of a prison death. In C. Bryant (Ed.), *Handbook of death and dying* (pp. 495–501). Thousand Oaks, CA: Sage.

Goffman, E. (1961) *Asylums: Essays on the social situation of mental patients and other inmates.* Garden City, NY: Doubleday.

Grant, A. (1999). Elderly inmates: Issues for Australia: Trends and issues in crime and criminal justice. Australia Institute of Corrections. Retrieved from http://aic.gov.au

Haney, C. (2006). *Reforming punishment: Psychological limits to the pains of imprisonment.* Washington DC: American Psychological Association.

Harrison, M. T. (2006). True Grit: An innovative program for elderly inmates. *Corrections Today, 68*(7), 46–49.

Harrison, M. T. (2009). *The Structured Senior Living Program: Program update.* Carson City, NV: Northern Nevada Correctional Center.

Harrison, M. T., & Benedetti, J. (2009). Comprehensive geriatric programs in a time of shrinking resources: "True Grit" revisited. *Corrections Today, 71*(5), 44–47.

Haugebrook, S., Maschi, T., Zgoba, K., Kimaschi, T., Morgen, K., & Brown, D. (2010). Trauma, stress, health, and mental health issues among ethnically diverse older adult prisoners. *Journal of Correctional Health Care. 16*(3), 220–229.

Higgins, D., & Severson, M. E. (2009). Community reentry and older adult offenders: Redefining social work roles. *Journal of Gerontological Social Work, 52*(8), 784–802.

Hoffman, H. C., & Dickenson, G. E. (2011). Characteristics of prison hospice programs in the United States. *American Journal of Hospice and Palliative Medicine, 28*, 245–252.

Hoffman, H. C., Dickinson, G. E., & Dunn, C. L. (2007). Communication policy changes in state correctional facilities from 1971 to 2005. *Criminal Justice Review, 32*, p. 47-64.

Hooyman, N. R., & Kiyak, H. (2011). *Social gerontology: A multidisciplinary perspective.* Boston, MA: Addison-Wesley.

Howse, J. (2003). *Growing old in prison: A coping study on older prisoners.* London, England: Centre for Policy on Ageing and Prison Reform Trust.

James, D., & Glaze, L. (2006). *Mental health problems of prisons and jail inmates.* NCJ 213600. Washington, DC: U.S. Department of Justice, Bureau of Justice Statistics.

Johnson, E. H. (2000). Elders and Japanese corrections. In M. B. Rothman, B. D. Dunlop, & P. Entzen (Eds.), *Elders, crime, and the criminal justice system* (pp. 222–235). New York, NY: Springer.

Kerbs, J. J. (2000). The older prisoner: Social, psychological, and medical considerations. In M. B. Rothman, B.D. Dunlop, & P. Entzen (Eds.), *Elders, crime and the criminal justice system* (pp. 229–252). New York, NY: Springer.

Kerbs, J. J., & Jolley, J. (2009). A commentary on age segregation for older prisoners: Philosophical and pragmatic considerations for correctional systems. *Criminal Justice Review, 34*, 119–139.

Knapp, J. L., & Elder, K. B. (1997–1998). Assessing prison personnel's knowledge of the aging process. *Journal of the Oklahoma Criminal Justice Research Consortium 4*: 50–54.

Kratcoski, P. C., & Babb, S. (1990). Adjustment of older inmates: An analysis of institutional structure and gender. *Journal of Contemporary Criminal Justice, 6*, 264–281.

Leigey, M. (2010). For the longest time: The adjustment of inmates to a sentence of life without parole. *The Prison Journal, 90*, 247–268.

Lemieux, C. M., Dyeson, T. B., & Castiglone, B. (2002). Reviewing the literature on prisoners who are older: Are we wiser? *The Prison Journal 82*(4), 440–458.

Linder, J. F., & Enders, S. R. (2011). Key roles for palliative social work in correctional settings. In T. Antilio & S. Otis-Green (Eds.), *Oxford textbook of palliative social work* (pp. 153–168), New York, NY: Oxford University Press.

Linder, J. F., Enders, S. R., Craig, E., Richardson, J., & Meyers, F. J. (2002). Hospice care for the incarcerated in the United States: An introduction. *Journal of Palliative Medicine, 5*(4), 549–552.

Linder, J. F., & Meyers, F. J. (2007). Palliative care for prison inmates: "Don't let me die in prison." *Journal of the American Medical Association, 298*, 894–901.

Linder, J. F., & Meyers, F. J. (2009). Palliative and end-of-life care in correctional settings. *Journal of Social Work and End of Life Care 5*(1/2) 7–33.

Loeb, S. J., & Steffensmeier, D. (2006). Health status, self-efficacy beliefs, and health-promoting behaviors of older male prisoners. *Journal of Correctional Health Care, 12*(4), 269-278.

Loeb, S. J., & Steffensmeier, D. (2010). Older inmate's pursuit of good health: A focus group study. *Research in Gerontological Nursing, 2*, 214–224.

Loeb, S. J., Steffensmeier, D., & Kassab, C. (2011). Predictors of self-efficacy and self-rated health for older male inmates. *Journal of Advanced Nursing, 67*, 811–820.

Loeb, S. J., Steffensmeier, D., & Lawrence, F. (2008). Comparing incarcerated and community-dwelling older men's health. *Western Journal of Nursing Research, 30*, 234–249.

Loeb, S. J., Steffensmeier, D., & Myco, P. M. (2007). In their own words: older male prisoners' health beliefs and concerns for the future. *Geriatric Nursing, 28*, 319–329.

Marquart, J. W., Merianos, D. E., & Doucet, G. (2000). The health-related concerns of older prisoners: Implications for policy. *Ageing and Society, 20*, 79–96.

Marquart, J. W., Merianos, D. E., Hebert, J. L., & Carroll, L. (1997). Health conditions and prisoners: A review of research and emerging areas of inquiry. *Prison Journal, 77*(2) 184–208.

Maschi, T., Morgen, K., Zgoba, K., Courtney, D., & Ristow, J. (2011). Age, cumulative trauma and stressful life events, and post-traumatic stress symptoms among older adults in prison: Do subjective impressions matter? *The Gerontologist, 51*, 675–686.

Mauer, M., King, R. S., & Young, M. C. (2004). *The meaning of life: Long prison sentences in context.* Washington, DC: The Sentencing Project.

Meeks, S., Sublett, R., Kostiwa, I., Rodgers, J. R., & Haddix, D. (2008). Treating depression in the prison nursing home: Demonstrating research to practice transitions. *Clinical Case Studies, 7*(6), 555–574.

Messina, N., & Grella, C. (2006). Childhood trauma and women's health outcomes in a California prison population. *Journal of Public Health, 96*, 1942–1848.

Mezey, M., Dubler, N., Mitty, E., & Brody, A. (2002) What impact do setting and transitions have on the quality of life at the end of life and the quality of the dying process? *The Gerontologist, 42*, 54–67.

Mitka, M. (2004). Aging prisoners stressing health care system. *Journal of the American Medical Association, 292*, 423–424.

Morash, M., Bynum, T., & Koons, B. A. (1998). *Women offenders: Programming needs and promising approaches*. NCJ 171668. Washington DC: US Department of Justice, National Institute of Justice.

Mueller-Johnson, K. U., & Dhami, M. K. (2010). Effects of offenders' age and health on sentencing decisions. *The Journal of Social Psychology, 150*(1), 77–97.

Mumola, C. J. (2000). *Incarcerated parents and their children*. Bureau of Justice Statistics special report. NCJ 182335. Washington DC: US Department of Justice, Bureau of Justice Statistics.

Ohio Department of Rehabilitation and Correction. (1999). *Older offenders: The Ohio initiative.*, Columbus, OH: Author.

Paluch, J. (2004). *A life for a life: Life imprisonment, America's other death penalty*. Los Angeles, CA. Roxbury.

National Hospice and Palliative Care Organization. (2009). *Quality guidelines for hospice and end of life care in correctional settings* Retrieved from http://www.nhpco.org/files/public/access/corrections/CorrectionsQualityGuidelines.pdf

Regan, J. J., Alderson, A., & Regan, W. M. (2002). Psychiatric disorders in aging prisoners. *Clinical Gerontologist, 26* (1/2), 117–124.

Reed, P., Alenazi, Y., & Potterton, F. (2009). Effect of time in prison on prisoners' use of coping strategies. *International Journal of Prisoner Health, 5*(1), 16–24.

Rikard, R.V., & Rosenberg, E. (2007). Aging inmates: A convergence of trends in the American criminal justice system. *Journal of Correctional Health Care, 13*, 150–162.

Roof, J. G. (2010). Geriatric offenders. In C. L. Scott (Ed.), *Handbook of correctional mental health* (2nd ed.) (pp. 373–594). Arlington, VA: American Psychiatric Publishing.

Sabath, M. J., & Cowles, E. L. (1988). Factors affecting the adjustment of elderly inmates to prison. In B. McCarthy & R. Langworthy (Eds.), *Older offenders: Perspectives in criminality and criminal justice* (pp. 178–196). New York, NY: Praeger.

Sabol, W., West, H., & Cooper, M. (2009). *Prisoners in 2008*. NCJ 228417. Washington, DC: U.S. Department of Justice, Bureau of Justice Statistics.

Sottile, E. (2009). Managing the cognitively impaired: From concept to implementation. Presented at the National Commission on Correctional Health Care Annual Conference, Las Vegas, NV.

Smyer, T., & Gragert, M. (2006). Health issues of aging prisoners. In P. Burbank (Ed.), *Vulnerable older adults: Health care needs and interventions* (pp. 57–74). New York, NY: Springer.

Smyer, T., Gragert, M., & Martins, D. C. (2006). Aging prisoners: Strategies for health care. In P. Burbank (Ed.), *Vulnerable older adults: Health care needs and intervention* (pp. 75–97). New York, NY: Springer.

Steiner, E. (2003). Early release for seriously ill and elderly prisoners: Should French practice be followed? *Probation Journal, 50*(3), 267–273.

Sterns, A. A., Lax, G., Sed, S., Keohane, P., & Sterns, R. S. (2008). Growing wave of older prisoners: A national survey of older prisoner's health, mental health, and programming. *Corrections Today, 70*(4), 70–72, 74–76.

Stoller, N. (2003). Space, place, and movement as aspects of health care in three women's prisons. *Social Science and Medicine, 5*, 2263–2275.

Sykes, G. M. (1958). *The society of captives: A study of a maximum security prison.* Princeton, NJ: Princeton University Press.

Taylor, P. B. (2002). End-of-life care behind bars. *Illness, Crisis and Loss. 10*(3), 233–241.

Taylor, P. J., & Parrott, J. M. (1988). Elderly offenders: A study of age-related factors among custodially remanded prisoners. *British Journal of Psychiatry, 152,* 340–346.

Tillman, T. (2000). Hospice program in prison: the Louisiana State Penitentiary Hospice Program. *Journal of Palliative Medicine, 3*(4), 513–524.

Vaughn, M. S., & Collins, S. C. (2004). Medical malpractice in correctional facilities: State tort remedies for inappropriate and inadequate health care administered to prisoners. *The Prison Journal, 84* (4), 505–534.

Vega, W. M., & Silverman, M. (1988). Stress and the elderly convict. *International Journal of Offender Therapy and Comparative Criminology, 32*(2), 153–162.

Wahidin, A. (2004). *Older women in the criminal justice system: Running out of time.* London, England: Jessica Kingsley.

Wahidin, A., & Aday, R. H. (2010). Later life and imprisonment. In D. Dannefer & C. Phillipson (Eds.), *The SAGE handbook of social gerontology* (pp. 587–596). Thousand Oaks, CA: Sage.

Wahidin, A., & Cain, M. (2006). *Aging, crime and society.* London, England: Willan.

Walsh, C. E. (1990). Needs of older inmates in varying security settings. Unpublished doctoral dissertation. Rutgers University, NJ.

Watson, R., Stimpson, A., & Hostick, T. (2004). Prison health care: A review of the literature. *International Journal of Nursing Studies, 41*(2), 119–128.

Wick, J. Y., & Zanni, R. (2009). Challenges in caring for aging inmates. *Consultant Pharmacist, 24*(6), 424–436.

Williams, B. A., Lindquist, K., Hill, T., Baillargeon, J., Mellow, J., Griefinger, R., & Walter, L. C. (2009). Caregiving behind bars: Correctional officer reports of disability in geriatric prisoners. *Journal of the American Geriatrics Society, 57*(7), 1286–1292.

Williams, B., Lindquist, K., Sudore, R., Strupp, H., Wilmott, D., & Walter, L. (2006). Being old and doing time: Functional impairment and adverse experiences of geriatric female prisoners. *Journal of the American Geriatrics Society, 54*(4), 702–707.

Williams, B. A., Baillargeon, J. G., Lindquist, K., Walter, L. C., Covinsky, K. E., Whitson, H. E., Steinman, M. A. (2010). Medication prescribing practices for older prisoners in the Texas prison system. *American Journal of Public Health, 100*(4), 756-761.

Wilson, J., & Barboza, S. (2010). Addressing the rising prevalence of dementia in corrections: Updates in correctional health care. Nashville, TN

Wilson, D. G., & Vito, G. F. (1986). Imprisoned elders: The experience of one institution. *Criminal Justice Policy Review, 1*(4), 399–421.

Wright, K. N., & Bronstein, L. (2007). Creating decent prisons: Serendipitous findings about prison hospice. *Journal of Offender Rehabilitation, 44*(4), 1–16.

Yorston, G. A., & Taylor, P. G. (2006). Commentary: Older offenders—No place to go? *Journal of American Academy of Psychiatry and Law, 34*(3), 333–337.

CHAPTER 8

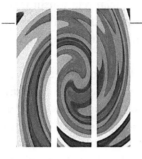

Gay and Lesbian Inmates: Sexuality and Sexual Coercion Behind Bars

Christopher Hensley, Helen Eigenberg, and Lauren Gibson

INTRODUCTION

Early prison literature sought to explain the development of prison culture. The conceptual models that were developed to explain inmate-on-inmate sexual activity in prison also were grounded in broader theoretical paradigms. The deprivation model emphasizes how the pains of imprisonment affect prison adjustment (Sykes, 1958). Inmates suffer from many forms of deprivation, including the deprivation of liberty, goods and services, autonomy, security, and heterosexual activity. In other words, the deprivation model holds that much of inmate behavior can be explained because of the nature of the prison environment itself. In contrast, the importation model focuses on behaviors prior to prison and argues inmate behavior is less the result of the effects of the prison experience and more about the socialization of inmates prior to prison, especially given their propensity for deviant behavior (Irwin, 1980; Irwin & Cressey, 1962). In other words, inmates "bring" their behavior into the prison with them. The situational model emphasizes the unique characteristics of the prison and the effect these circumstantial factors have on inmate behavior behind bars. These three approaches have been applied to a myriad of inmate behavior and are concepts that have a long historical tradition in prison research.

Social constructionism, however, is a newer theoretical approach which has not been used in research with a great deal of frequency on prison sexuality. Social constructionism examines how societies, individuals, and groups create or "construct" their perceived social reality. For example, it assumes that concepts, including things like sexual identity and gender (and the behavior that is often associated with them) are not inherent. We create these concepts, in part, because of socialization, but also because of the ways we interact, think, and reproduce social relationships. Individuals participate in an ongoing process whereby people create social relationships on an ongoing basis, often without thinking about the process itself. Each of these theoretical orientations has been applied to sexuality in prison in some form or fashion, as is illustrated below.

Fishman (1934) was one of the first authors to talk about sexual activity in prison. His observations were based solely on his extensive experience working in prisons. He argued that sexual deprivation in prison led to homosexuality in male prisons and first employed the concept of situational homosexuality. He identified "true" homosexuals as men who were stereotypically effeminate and prone to victimization by predators. He also categorized men who were "driven" to engage in same sex behavior, including nonconsensual behavior (as evidenced by his naming these men as "wolves"), because they were denied opportunities for "normal" heterosexual activities due to the unique nature of the prison.

These concepts continued to be expressed in prison sexuality research for decades. Most researchers built on these ideas developing a variety of typologies and classifications schemes that purported to define homosexuality in male institutions; however, often the research failed to clearly distinguish between consensual sex and rape (Eigenberg, 1989, 1994, 2000a, 2000b, 2002). Most of these typologies tended to classify men as true or situational homosexuals. True homosexuals were men who had a homosexual orientation prior to incarceration (Buffum, 1972; Clemmer, 1940; Kirkham, 1971; Sagarin, 1976; Sykes, 1958), and who imported this behavior. These men, however, were portrayed stereotypically as effeminate, passive sexual partners, but sometimes they also were described as victims who were "turned out" (pressured into sexual activities). The more general literature on homosexuality at the time (and most individuals) viewed homosexuality and heterosexuality according to a dichotomous classification scheme; people were either *gay* or *straight*. Sexual orientation was viewed as a static, fixed characteristic of individuals (see Eigenberg, 1992). This approach did not recognize bisexuality or the notion of a changing sexual orientation. It also portrayed homosexuality as pathological and in need of a "cure," and associated homosexuality with inappropriate gender socialization. Thus, true homosexuals were described in a manner consistent with more general social beliefs about sexuality. This approach, however, also presented a theoretical challenge because scholars studying sexuality in prison had to account for the fact that seemingly "normal" (e.g., heterosexual) men also engaged in same-sex behavior.

This group of men provided a challenge to most theoretical paradigms of the time that were used to understand homosexuality (Eigenberg, 1992). Scholars dealing with prison sexuality used the concepts of situational homosexuality and sexual deprivation to explain this apparent contradiction. This deprivation was a pain of imprisonment (Sykes, 1958) as men dealt with "sex starvation" (Clemmer, 1940, p. 261) by men who "craved sex" (Lee, 1965, p. 57) in the "giant faggot factory" (Lee, 1965, p. 57). Inmates lost their "self-control" because of the sight and smell of naked bodies (Karpman, 1948, p. 479), making men "anxious" because of pent-up tension that needed release (Chonco, 1989, p. 79). An unstated assumption was that men *had* to have sex and that they sometimes lacked control, leading to situational rape. Thus, much of the literature that purported to discuss situational homosexuality, in fact, dealt with coercive sexuality, including rape. For example, some men who supposedly engaged in situational homosexuality were described as punks (Kirkham, 1971; Sykes, 1958), and made homosexuals (Buffum, 1972) involuntary recruits (Sagarin, 1976) and jailhouse turnouts (Sagarin, 1976). These men were deemed to be made homosexuals as opposed to born homosexuals.

A social constructionist approach also was useful to explain the notion of situational homosexuality, though few studies used this conceptual approach. It contends that sexual identity is a social construct and that sexual orientation may better be understood as fluid concept rather than a static trait (Eigenberg, 1992). For example, social constructionists define sexual identity on a continuum ranging from exclusive heterosexuality to exclusive homosexuality, rather than a dichotomous category. Homosexuality, and what it means to be a homosexual, has a social, historical, political, and cultural context which affects both how society views it and how individuals classify themselves (see Eigenberg, 1992). Thus, the situational nature of incarceration *and* the ability of people to shift sexual orientations and behaviors allow individuals to engage in same-sex behavior in prison while retaining their definition of themselves as heterosexuals (Eigenberg, 1992). It also helps explain why early studies of prison sexuality tended to portray male homosexuality as abnormal while also describing female same-sex behavior in prison as supporting and a replication of traditional family structures (Ward & Kassebaum, 1964, 1965) because society generally has viewed male and female homosexuality differently in some regards.

The sexuality of an inmate continues to bring a set of unique challenges to managing a prison. In fact, gay and lesbian inmates comprise a particularly vulnerable group in prison. They are more likely to engage in consensual same-sex sexual activity and are at a much higher risk of being sexually victimized. Some studies have found that sex in prison leads to more violence in prison, including more sexual violence (Nacci & Kane, 1983, 1984a, 1984b).

The effects of sexual victimization are complex and far reaching. They include physical injury (Beck & Harrison, 2007); the spread of HIV/AIDS and other sexually transmitted diseases (Dumond & Dumond, 2002; Maruschak, 2007); psychological damage, including depression, suicidal thoughts, anxiety, and posttraumatic stress disorder (Dumond & Dumond, 2002); and increases in other types of nonsexual violence in prison (Fagan, Winnerstrom, & Miller, 1996). Furthermore, "if inmates have fears, whether real or imagined, of being sexually assaulted during the completion of their prison sentences, it is not conducive to their rehabilitation" (Worley, Worley, & Mullins, 2010, p. 82). All of these issues have an impact upon prisons, but since most inmates are ultimately released, the effects of prison rape also, ultimately, affect society at large.

INMATE ARGOT AND THE SEXUAL HIERARCHY

Researchers who have examined prison life have found that inmates use a special type of language within the prison subculture that often reflects the "distorted norms, values, and mores of the offenders" (Dumond, 1992, p. 138). Einat and Einat (2000) write that as such, this language, or prison argot, is largely distinct from those outside of prison and serves six distinct functions:

> The need to be different and unique; alleviation of feelings or rejection and refusal; facilitation of social interactions and relationships; declaration of belonging to a subculture or social status; a tool of social identification leading to a sense of belonging to a group; and secrecy. (pp. 310–311)

One critical component of correctional institution culture which builds upon argot roles is the prison sexual hierarchy. Within this structure the roles, activities, and actors involved in sexual activities are assigned unique, institutionally specific labels. According to Dumond (1992), "while the terms may have changed somewhat over the decades, prison slang defines sexual habits and inmates' status simultaneously, using homosexuality as a means of placing individuals within the inmate caste system" (p. 138). These sexual scripts define an inmate's position within the prison society.

The Male Sexual Hierarchy and Argot Roles

In 1934, Fishman conducted one of the first ethnographies on sex in male prisons. The penitentiary at Welfare Island in New York was a prison where men were commonly sent for offenses such as soliciting members of the same-sex for money, indecent exposure, and attempting to corrupt a minor. Fishman noted that men who came into this prison for such offenses were often passive and were known by other inmates as *punks*, *girls*, *fags*, *pansies*, or *fairies*. These men had feminine characteristics and often wore makeup in prison. Other men, known as *top men* or *wolves*, took advantage of these inmates. In other words, such sexual argot roles marked the feminine prisoner as an appropriate target for sexual assault.

Several other early studies found that inmates engaging in homosexual activity were divided into three categories based on the sexual hierarchy (Donaldson, 1993; Kirkham, 1971; Sykes, 1958; Wooden & Parker, 1982). The first category contained those inmates who played an active, aggressive role (masculine) in homosexual relations. Inmates referred to these men as *wolves*, *voluntary aggressors*, *jockers*, *studs*, or *daddies*. The second and third categories of inmates played more passive and submissive roles. These men were known as *punks* and *fags*.

The stress on "masculinity" in prison contributed to inmates adopting the role of wolf. Wolves adopted an aggressive role and often preyed on inmates through coercion. Although wolves engaged in homosexual behavior with fags, the goal for wolves in these relationships was nothing more than physical release. However, raping punks reinforced the wolves' masculinity and maintained their high position in the status hierarchy. Through aggressive behavior, wolves also managed to escape the stigma of being labeled a homosexual.

Fags engaged in homosexuality because they were born that way. In other words, a fag adopted the same role in prison as he would have in the free community. The fag was known by his exaggerated feminine mannerisms, often wearing makeup and dressing in women's clothing. The fag fulfilled the stereotype of the homosexual in the free community and was viewed by inmates as playing a "natural" role. They were considered gender nonconformists and posed little threat to the masculinity of other inmates. Fags were defined as having "pussies," not "assholes," and wore "blouses," not "shirts" (Donaldson, 1993). Fags, *effeminates*, or *queens* held more status than punks in the hierarchical division of homosexual roles.

Punks or jailhouse turnouts, on the other hand, initially engaged in homosexual behavior through coercion. Inmates viewed punks as cowards who were morally weak and unable to defend themselves in prison. Thus, they were also often targets of sexual attacks. Donaldson (1993) argued that punks had some common characteristics, including being younger, inexperienced first-time offenders, middle class, White, and physically smaller in size. They were viewed as having lost their masculinity as a result of submitting to a more aggressive inmate. Punks often chose to engage in homosexual behavior in prison for protection or for goods and services. Kirkham (1971) and Sykes (1958) discovered that punks were on the lowest rung of the hierarchical division. Punks were considered slaves and wolves used them as commodities.

Fleisher (1989) found many of these same terms at the United States Penitentiary at Lompoc, California, with a few notable differences. Fags and fuck-boys were the female sex-role players in the institution. Both groups claimed homosexuality and were described as homosexual by other inmates. However, fags were effeminate homosexuals who were often distinguishable by their gait, dress, hair, and speech. Fuck-boys, on the other hand, were not distinguishable by these traits. Straights and turnouts were the male sex-role players in the institution. They did not consider themselves homosexual, nor did the other inmates define them as homosexual. Straights used fags for sexual gratification. However, some straights developed long-term sexual relationships with other straights and these relationships were guarded by privacy. Turnouts took a passive strategy by seducing inmates with commissary privileges or other items.

Hensley, Wright, Tewksbury, and Castle (2003c) noted that inmates continued to discuss the three traditional sexual roles found in male prisons (i.e., wolves, fags, and punks). However, inmates at the facilities did make two new revelations about the roles that inmates assumed while incarcerated and the structure of the hierarchy itself. Inmates discussed that there were two subcategories within both the wolf and fag roles.

Inmates portrayed the wolf role as containing two distinct subcategories that they labeled the *aggressive wolf* and the *nonaggressive* wolf. The aggressive wolf was depicted as someone of African American descent who was both physically and verbally "tough." These inmates entered prison with a heterosexual orientation and maintained their masculinity by sexually assaulting younger, weaker inmates (punks).

Raping a punk had more to do with power than sex. They maintained their masculine identification by participating in active roles during sex. When asked about their current sexual orientation, all of the self-described aggressive wolves maintained their heterosexual identity (Hensley et al., 2003c).

Nonaggressive wolves or *teddy bears*, on the other hand, typically did not sexually assault their sex partners. Rather, they sought sexual relationships with other inmates (*fish* or *closet gays*) who were willing to engage in consensual homosexual activity while in prison. They tended to be Caucasian men who entered prison with a heterosexual identity and maintained their masculine role by participating in active roles during sex. However, when asked about their current sexual orientation, over half of the nonaggressive wolves answered that they were now bisexual. Thus, many of these inmates—because of the lack of heterosexual sex in prison—had changed their self-concepts regarding their sexual orientation (Hensley et al., 2003c).

The two subcategories of fags included the fish and the closet gays. Fish (although previously thought to be newly entering inmates) were typically African American men who took on a feminine role and appearance. Although it violated institutional rules and regulations, they wore makeup, displayed female mannerisms, and took on female nicknames. Fish entered into prison life homosexual and maintained their homosexual identity by assuming the passive role during sexual activity. Some fish sold themselves for canteen goods and cigarettes, while others developed relationships with nonaggressive wolves (Hensley et al., 2003c).

Closet gays were typically Caucasian males who entered prison with a hidden homosexuality identity. Closet gays had the ability to take on both the active and passive role during sexual activity. They did, however, try to maintain masculine appearances and mannerisms. They typically sought other closet gays in hopes of forming a "true love" relationship (Hensley et al., 2003c).

According to the inmates in the study, the status fags received had progressed upwardly to now equal that of the wolves. Fish and aggressive wolves were the most respected and feared groups within the prison sexual hierarchy. Many inmates feared fish because they were known for their aggressive and jealous behavior. Closet gays and nonaggressive wolves typically maintained equal status with each other. However, they were slightly beneath the fish and aggressive wolves on the pecking order. Punks continued to remain at the bottom of the prison sexual hierarchy. Inmates continued to view punks as cowards who were physically and morally weak (Hensley et al., 2003c).

THE FEMALE SEXUAL HIERARCHY AND ARGOT ROLES

Ward and Kassebaum (1964) and Giallombardo (1966) were early researchers who studied homosexual behavior in female prisons. Their study uncovered two major distinctions among homosexual roles at the Frontera Correctional Institution in California and the Alderson Federal Penitentiary in West Virginia. The inmates defined these argot labels as the *true homosexual* or *lesbian* and the *jailhouse turnout* or *penitentiary turnout*.

The inmates defined the true homosexual as a woman who was a homosexual before being incarcerated. These women typically participated in homosexual activity in prison and remained homosexual upon their release. The jailhouse turnout was introduced to homosexual behavior while in prison. Estimates by staff and inmates suggested that the majority of homosexual activities in female prisons involved the jailhouse turnout (Ward & Kassebaum, 1964).

Whether a female represented a true homosexual or a jailhouse turnout, other distinctions in argot roles existed as well. One such role was known as the *butch*, *stud*, *stud broad*, or *drag butch*. The butch maintained the dominant role in the homosexual relationship by being the aggressive sexual partner. The butch manifested many masculine characteristics including short hair, a lack of makeup, and a masculine gait. Ward and Kassebaum (1964) also established a variation in the butch role in which the female did not manifest masculine characteristics. However, the female did maintain the dominant role in the homosexual relationship. Females who were seemingly unattractive or who were already inclined toward masculine habits were more likely to designate themselves butch.

The complementary role to the butch was known as the *femme*. The femme maintained her feminine characteristics while taking a passive and submissive role in the homosexual relationship. The butch/femme couples in prison mirrored patriarchal, heterosexual relationships which existed in the free community. The butch provided protection and economic stability while the femme provided passive sexual relations and housekeeping services (Ward & Kassebaum, 1964).

Giallombardo (1966) also discovered two further distinctions in inmate sexual argot. The *trick* was a woman who allowed herself to be exploited for a variety of reasons. Rather than establishing a sincere relationship, the trick was typically involved in several, unstable relationships. The trick was usually exploited economically, especially as a source of labor. Inmates frowned upon these weak women. The inmates had a name for the women who exploited the tricks. These women were known as *commissary hustlers*. The commissary hustler maintained a traditional homosexual relationship with one female, while establishing sexual relationships with other females for economic reasons. Therefore, any woman involved with the commissary hustler other than the main female was labeled a trick. The commissary hustler provided the trick with a list of items needed from the commissary. The trick often complied because she anticipated that the hustler would leave her "wife" and become involved in a serious relationship with her instead.

A *chippie* was a woman who exploited each situation for material or sexual gratification (Giallombardo, 1966). Unlike the commissary hustler, the chippie did not establish one sincere relationship. Therefore, the chippie was often labeled the prison prostitute. The chippie was promiscuous and the inmates often scorned this type of behavior. Contrary to the chippie role, there were women who were promiscuous solely for sexual gratification. These women were known as *kick partners*. The inmates reported that some women chose to enter into this role for a variety of reasons. One reason given was that some women preferred to become kick partners rather than assume the responsibilities of a permanent relationship. Kick partners also included a group of women who exchanged partners and maintained friendly relations. The inmates at Alderson did not look down upon the kick partners because they usually were very discrete.

Giallombardo (1966) also learned of three other distinctions at the Alderson Penitentiary. Inmates distinguished between the punk, fag, and turnabout. The punk in the female prison was someone who manifested feminine characteristics while assuming the stud role. Women who played the stud role in prison were expected to exhibit male characteristics. In Alderson, punks were despised and ridiculed by inmates for playing a false part.

On the other hand, fags in female prisons were considered sincere by the inmates because they were true lesbians. The fag was justified because the inmates rationalized that they were born that way or something happened to them in their life that made them become a lesbian. Since it resembled their true identity in the free community, the inmates viewed the stud role as natural for the fag to adopt in prison (Giallombardo, 1966).

The turnabout in Alderson was so labeled due to the inmates claimed expertise at assuming either role in prison. Based upon the benefits associated with the role, the turnabout could play either the male or female role. Thus, the inmates held the turnabout in low esteem. Inmates reported that they preferred a woman to choose her role and remain in that role. Inmates valued the structured setting and deviation from that structure was frowned upon (Giallombardo, 1966).

Greer (2000) conducted the most recent study addressing argot roles in women's prisons. She found that the nature of interpersonal relationships in female facilities had changed. Intimate sexual relationships were formed on the basis of "playing games" and economic manipulation. The study also noted less use of labels and specifically defined argot roles, showing the changing nature of female prisons. Contrary to previous research, inmates did not seem to portray specific feminine or masculine characteristics when involved in a homosexual relationship. Inmates also suggested that women often engaged in sexual relationships for economic gain. The inmates with the highest status in the facility were the ones who had the most money in their accounts. The women who sought sexual relationships for this reason were consistently referred to as canteen whores or commissary whores. The label of *lesbian* still applied to those women who identified themselves as such before incarceration. Women who only engaged in homosexual behavior while in prison were referred to as turnouts or bisexuals. Inmates reported that lesbians often formed the most stable relationships, if they chose to participate in them while in prison. Most other sexual relationships were marked by mistrust and manipulation.

CONSENSUAL SEXUAL BEHAVIOR

Within the realm of research on the sexual activities of incarcerated men and women, one of the less discussed topics is that of consensual sex between inmates. Given that consensual activities would imply that inmates are engaging in willing homosexual behavior, which has seldom been discussed by researchers and society until the last 40 years, it is unsurprising that research on consensual sexual behavior in prisons is rare. The research on consensual homosexual behavior has evolved in different ways for both males and females in prison. Early research on consensual activity between females tended to believe that girls and women were trying to develop a family model with each other because of such a deprivation from normative society (Ford, 1929; Halleck & Hersko, 1962; Otis, 1913; Selling, 1931; also see Sykes, 1958). Even some contemporary research examines same-sex relationships in female prisons as a result of forming make-believe families (Greer, 2000; Huggins, Capeheart, & Newman, 2006), while others have viewed it as a part of sexuality or the changing interpersonal relationships within female prisons (Hensley, Tewksbury, & Koscheski, 2002). By contrast, consensual activity in male prisons has long been ignored and even denied, as early researchers defined sexual activities between male inmates solely as sexual coercion (Fishman, 1934; Nacci & Kane, 1983, 1984a, 1984b). Contemporary research on male consensual sex, at least, has evolved to accept consensual homosexual activities as not a perversion, but rather another aspect of sexuality (Hensley, 2001; Tewksbury, 1989; Wooden & Parker, 1982).

Consensual Sex in Male Prisons

Early researchers largely examined consensual sex in male prisons as an extension of coercive sex, or discussed homosexuality as a situational act (Fishman, 1934). To date, the earliest empirical study on consensual sexual activity between male inmates was published in 1982. Wooden and Parker (1982) examined male sexual behavior among 200 inmates in a California prison and found that 65% of those men had engaged in homosexual activities during their incarceration; however, 78% of the sample identified as heterosexual. Bisexuals comprised 11% of the sample and only 10.5% of the respondents identified as homosexual. According to Wooden and Parker (1982), the sample was overrepresented by "effeminate homosexuals" and "vulnerable heterosexual youngsters" (p. 9). Apparently, California used this prison as a place to house many known homosexuals in the department of corrections, a common practice of the 1980s.

Following a violent outbreak at the U.S. Penitentiary at Lewisburg, Pennsylvania, in the early 1980s, Nacci and Kane (1983, 1984a, 1984b) launched a two-part research project investigating homosexual activity and sexual aggression behind bars. Lewisburg, a predominantly nonviolent institution, encountered eight inmate murders and numerous inmate-on-inmate assaults over a 26-month period. Five of the eight murders were determined to be sexually motivated. In response to this unexplained increase in violence, 330 face-to-face interviews were conducted and surveys were distributed to a random sample of male inmates in 17 federal prison facilities. The findings revealed that 12% of the inmates in lower security institutions had participated in homosexual activity while incarcerated in their current institution. In penitentiaries that housed more dangerous offenders who were serving longer sentences, the percentages were much higher (30%). As a method of receiving more detail about the nature of the homosexual acts, inmates who admitted to same-sex activity were asked to specify their role in the activity. The majority of inmates were "inserters," not "insertees." As one would expect, the masculine role (inserter) was identified with being heterosexual, while the feminine role (insertee) was associated with being a homosexual or bisexual.

Similarly, Tewksbury (1989) surveyed 150 Ohio inmates in order to examine their sexual activities and sexual orientations. He discovered that over three fourths of the inmates viewed themselves to be exclusively heterosexual. Of the entire sample, 18% had engaged in consensual sex during their incarceration. In 1995, Saum, Surratt, Inciardi, and Bennett undertook a study to investigate homosexual behavior in male prisons. Using data gathered from 101 inmates in a medium-security prison in Delaware, the researchers found that 2% of the sample had engaged in sexual activity with another inmate the previous year.

Hensley (2001) examined consensual homosexual activities among male inmates by interviewing 174 Oklahoma inmates in multiple-security prisons. Of the sample, 78.7% self-identified as heterosexual, 13.2% as bisexual, and 8% as homosexual. In terms of sexual activities, 18.4% had engaged in kissing, 23.6% in rubbing, 24.1% in touching, 23.6% in oral sex, and 20.1% in anal sex during their incarceration.

Hensley, Tewksbury, and Wright (2001) administered questionnaires to 142 male inmates in a southern maximum-security correctional facility. The questionnaires were designed to gain information regarding inmates' homosexual behavior while incarcerated, as well as their sexual orientation prior to and during incarceration. When asked to identify their sexual orientation before prison, 79% considered themselves heterosexual, 6% homosexual, and 15% bisexual. When asked to identify their sexual orientation since incarceration, 69% considered themselves to be heterosexual, 7% homosexual, and 23% bisexual. As a method of identifying predictor variables of homosexual behavior, a set of logistic regression analyses were performed. Religion and race were found to be the most salient variables in predicting homosexual behavior among incarcerated males. Protestants were less likely than non-Protestants to engage in homosexual behavior while in prison. Non-White inmates were less likely than White inmates to engage in homosexual behavior while incarcerated. Factors, including age, education, amount of time served, and type of offense, had no statistically significant effect on inmates' sexual activity in prison.

Consensual Sex in Female Prisons

Early studies in female prisons focused not on sexual activities, but on pseudo-families and same-sex relationships that females created while incarcerated. The first notable article on these relationships was by Otis (1913) who discussed same-sex relationships between girls of different races in reform institutions. While not a formal study, Otis examined colloquial expressions and the behaviors of girls as they entered the institution and subsequently the institutional society that created and maintained these relationships. When girls entered the institution, they would receive love notes and tokens from other girls, asking for their "love" to be accepted (Otis, 1913, p. 113). If accepted, the girls would enter a relationship that sometimes was sexual.

In 1929, Ford published a study that examined consensual sexual behaviors among incarcerated adolescent females, beginning the research that focused on pseudofamilies and expanding upon Otis' article. Ford (1929) found that homosexuality could range from simple friendship that had a fantasized romantic relationship to sexual relationships, which included mutual masturbation and cunnilingus. Upon entering the institution, girls were approached and asked to choose between the girls and the matrons, which would decide her social life for the rest of her incarceration. If she chose not to join the girls, she would be left alone, but by choosing to side with the girls, the new arrival would become available for a *friendship*, which was the term for a homosexual relationship (p. 443). Ford also found that girls of different races (White and Black) chose to have friendships with each other over girls of the same race. Oftentimes, when a girl was caught engaging in another friendship, rivalries formed and relationships became convoluted and confusing. Ford (1929) noted that after incarceration, the girls usually did not engage in homosexual behavior again.

Selling (1931) identified several different types of same-sex relationships, which included individual homosexuality, group family relationships, secondary families, and single families. He also identified two primary categories for females, that of *mother* and *grandmother*. In individual homosexuality, girls became couples with each other, colloquially known as "honies" (Selling, 1931, p. 248). Physical behavior consisted of holding each other, kissing, and fondling, while the relationship was continued through notes and presents sent to each other. Just as Ford (1929) found, girls in these relationships adopted gender roles conforming to regular society, that of "husband" and "wife" (p. 248).

In group family relationships, secondary families, and individual families, large extended families formed because of the individual relationships between girls. Girls could simultaneously be mother, daughter, sister, aunt, and father, because of the many relationships that existed (Selling, 1931). Girls adopting masculine roles were usually called by masculine versions of their names or by masculine family names. Despite the gender roles, there was no evidence that those who adopted male roles were considered the dominant in the couple (Selling, 1931). Primarily, the mother and grandmother roles held the most power within families. Finally, Selling (1931) found that out of 500 inmates, 10 of the girls were engaged in actual homosexual relationships.

Together, these three pioneering studies established the basis for most literature on consensual sex in female institutions. Unfortunately, these authors neither used any sort of statistical analysis in their studies nor gave definitions of sexual acts, homosexual behaviors, or anything deeper than naming relationships. Researchers did not touch the topic again until 1962, when Halleck and Hersko finally brought a clear methodological study into the subject. Using biographical details and a questionnaire, the authors examined sociological and psychological reasons behind homosexual behavior in 57 incarcerated girls. They found that 69% of girls had been involved in homosexual behaviors, which included dating (through sending notes and presents), holding hands, dancing, kissing on the facial area, breast fondling (rare), genital stimulation (rare), and other activities (Halleck & Hersko, 1962).

Like in the pioneer studies, some girls in relationships attempted to adopt gender roles mirroring those in heterosexual relationship. Given that most of the relationships were superficial and the girls did not appear to be "sexually perverted," the authors argued that homosexual behaviors were a result of the environment of the institution, not deprivation of heterosexual relationships (Halleck & Hersko, 1962, p. 913).

Research in this area continued to focus on the pseudofamily, though slowly researchers began to examine homosexual behavior more closely, focusing more on the psychological side instead of the behavioral side (see Giallombardo, 1966; Heffernan, 1972; Ward & Kassebaum, 1965). Many researchers began to abandon the deprivation theoretical model to adopt a more social constructionist model, arguing that the environments and social forces of female prisons affected homosexuality (see Propper, 1978, 1981, 1982).

In 1978, Propper examined homosexual behaviors in the first exhaustive study on incarcerated females. She collected self-reported data from 396 respondents in juvenile institutions, finding that 14% of inmates were engaged in a superficial homosexual relationship with another girl. Most homosexual behavior included writing letters, holding hands, hugging, kissing, passionate kissing, and sexual activities. Using this data on homosexual behavior, Propper (1981) developed a model close to social constructionism, called the sociopsychological model. She argued that homosexual behavior in prison institutions was affected by different social and psychological variables such as culture, personality, biology, and mentality. She expanded this argument concerning pseudofamilies, arguing that involvement in make-believe families was not a result of a need for sexual gratification, but for an intense and subconscious desire for security, companionship, normality, attention, and acceptance.

Research on female consensual sex in prison stalled for almost two decades, until 1998 when Owen examined homosexual behavior, make-believe families, and same-sex friendships within an all-female facility. Owen (1998) found that the complexity of interpersonal relationships relied on an even more complex system of needs that existed between inmates that were emotional, practical, material, sexual, and familial in nature. Friendships were nonsexual, equal, and reciprocal between inmates. Make-believe families mirrored those found in the pioneer studies, with an older or more mature woman assuming a motherly role and taking care of other inmates (Owen, 1998). Finally, homosexual behavior within the institution was believed to be widespread by inmates and wardens (e.g., almost everyone doing it), but the actual percentage of the inmate population who engaged in homosexual behavior ranged between 30% and 60% (Owen, 1998).

Greer (2000) found that, in agreement with previous studies, same-sex relationships and consensual homosexual behavior continued to exist in female prisons at similar rates, but that in some cases, the make-believe family did not exist. Instead, women sought out female partners for sexual relationships out of loneliness, but chose not to seek out friendships out of mistrust, unease with their peers, and the frequently changing inmate population (Greer, 2000). Owen's (1998) and Greer's (2000) rates of at least a third of inmates being involved in same-sex, nonplatonic relationships were mirrored by Hensley, Tewksbury, and Koscheski (2002). The purpose of their study was to address not only same-sex sexual behavior within a female correctional facility, but to ascertain which demographic and incarcerated-related variables affected female inmates' participation in five same-sex sexual behaviors (kissing, touching, receiving oral sex, and performing oral sex, and a fifth variable constructed as a composite of the first four to measure the rate of homo-sexual behavior) during incarceration. The sample was drawn from 245 female inmates in a southern correctional facility.

Age and length of time served were found to be the most salient variables that predicted female consensual same-sex sexual activity (Hensley et al., 2002). A series of logistic regression analyses were performed to test if the predictor variables had an effect on the dependent variables. The most salient variables in the models that predicted consensual same-sex sexual activity while incarcerated were age and amount of time served. Both variables were statistically significant predictors of all five dependent variables. Age showed the greatest influence on female inmates' same-sex sexual behavior. Women under the age of 34 were more likely to have engaged in all five types of behavior. The length of time that a woman had served in prison was also a statistically significant predictor of all five dependent variables. Women who had served longer periods of time incarcerated were more likely than women who had served shorter periods of time to have engaged in same-sex sexual activities with another inmate. Race, however, was a statistically significant predic-tor of only two forms of same-sex sexual behavior (touching another inmate in a sexual way and receiving oral sex). Non-White women were more likely to admit to touching another woman in a sexual manner and to receive oral sex from another female inmate. The only other statistically significant variable in the equation was religion. Women who reported a non-Protestant religious affiliation were more likely to have performed oral sex on another inmate than those who reported a Protestant religious affiliation. Factors, including education, type of offense, and security level, had no statistically significant effect on female inmates' sexual activity in prison (Hensley et al., 2002).

Most recently, Huggins et al. (2006) took a fresh look at pseudofamilies and dyads in female prisons by examining responses from 214 questionnaires from two Texas female prisons. Some of those within pseudofamilies reported that wardens treated them differently, even negatively, because of their association with the pseudofamily. They believed that inmates and wardens thought of them as engaging in homosexual relationships, and that to avoid any differential treat-ment, they would have to avoid any relationships not considered normal by society. Like previous studies, Huggins et al. (2006) found that 32.2% of non-pseudofamily members had engaged in same-sex relationships of either a roman-tic or sexual nature, and of pseudofamily members, the rate rose to over 50%. The most common reason for entering into these relationships was the desire for affection, love, and companionship; other reasons were power, sexual pleasure, protection, food, and material objects. In nonplatonic relationships, sexual con-tact was occasional and usually only amounted to kissing, hugging, and emotional intimacy.

STUDIES OF SEXUAL COERCION

There are two types of sexual victimization in prisons: inmate-on-inmate and staff-on-inmate. Historically, most research has concentrated on coercive acts involving inmates and generally has been confined to male prisons. Early literature on women's prisons concentrated more on consensual sexual behavior between inmates and sexual behavior involving staff and inmates. More recently, attention has shifted to a more comprehensive analysis of both types of assaults in both male and female facilities due to the influence of the Prison Rape Elimination Act (PREA) of 2003. This type of research is important because it allows for a more complex understanding of patterns of behavior and also helps contextualize the gendered nature of these behaviors. Unfortunately, many of these studies fail to clearly separate their data and analyses so that it is impossible to precisely evaluate the differences in rates committed by inmates versus staff members. The following sections, however, will focus only on inmate-on-inmate sexual assaults in male and female prisons.

Box 8.1   The Prison Rape Elimination Act of 2003

The Prison Rape Elimination Act (PREA) of 2003 required the Bureau of Justice Statistics (BJS) to annually gather data and provide analysis about the incidence and effects of prison rape as part of the National Prison Rape Statistics Program. It charged the National Institute of Corrections (NIC) to establish a national clearinghouse to provide educational materials and training programs to all types of correctional administrators nationwide. PREA also established a national commission charged with developing standards with regard to detection, prevention, and response. It is based on a zero-tolerance approach toward prison rape and, therefore, has the power legislatively to withhold federal funds to states that fail to comply with national standards PREA is designed to address inmate-on-inmate assaults, as well as staff-on-inmate sexual contact. Staff conduct includes rape and so-called consensual acts; although, by policy and law, there is no such thing as a consensual act between a staff member and inmate in the context of correctional institutions. PREA, however, is not concerned with consensual sexual activity between inmates. P. L. 108–79 is available at http://www.ojjdp.gov/about/PubLNo108-79.txt

---

Inmate-on-Inmate Sexual Assault in Male Prisons

Around the 1970s, research tended to shift the attention from homosexuality in female prisons to violent sexual aggression in male prisons. Davis (1968) was one of the first researchers to do so. He interviewed 3,304 inmates in the Philadelphia jail system and analyzed institutional records. His methodology is not clear, but he concluded that slightly less than 3% of inmates were raped at any time during incarceration. He labeled it as an "epidemic" (p. 5).

Lockwood (1980) conducted interviews and examined background information from inmate files in the New York prison system to study 107 men who had been targets of sexual aggression at any time in prison. Based on interviews, he found that 8% of the men were sexually assaulted and 7% were touched or grabbed. Wooden and Parker (1982) found that 9% of heterosexual inmates in the general population reported they were the victim of a sexual assault at any time in that particular prison. This study was one of the first to note that sexual orientation affected victimization. Homosexual men reported experiencing higher rates of victimization.

A study conducted in the federal prison system produced some of the earliest, systematic data on male rape in prison (Nacci & Kane, 1983, 1984a, 1984b). The authors found that 11% of the inmates were targets of attempted sexual assaults. However, less than 1% of the sample reported that they had been forced to perform sexual acts sometime during their incarceration.

Several subsequent studies have found the rape rates also to be about 1%. Tewksbury (1989) found that no inmates reported a rape in their current facility, but 4.5% of the inmates indicated that another inmate had tried to have sex through force or threats. Saum et al. (1995) discovered that only one inmate reported being raped, although five reported attempted rapes at some time while in prison. Hensley, Tewksbury, and Castle (2003b) interviewed 174 Oklahoma inmates and discovered that a sizeable minority reported they had been sexually threatened (13.8%); however, few inmates reported rape (1.2%) at any time during incarceration. Similarly, Maitland and Sluder (1998) surveyed 111 inmates in a Midwestern prison and found that less than 1% of the inmates reported they had been forced to participate in sexual activity.

More recent studies have found higher victimization rates. Struckman-Johnson, Struckman-Johnson, Rucker, Bumby, and Donaldson (1996) surveyed 474 men about sexual assaults in three Nebraska prisons. The authors found 21% of male inmates had experienced either attempted or completed acts of forced sexual contact while incarcerated. Other researchers analyzing these data estimated, on average, that 16% of the men in the Nebraska study were sexually victimized by inmates sometime during their incarceration (Gaes & Goldberg, 2004). Struckman-Johnson and Struckman-Johnson (2000) replicated their previous study in seven men's prisons in Midwestern states. Of the 1,788 inmates, 21% had been pressured or forced to participate in a sexual act while incarcerated. Gaes and Goldberg (2004) noted that the data indicated that, on average, about 7% of inmates in the Midwestern states study had been victimized by another inmate at some time during incarceration.

In another comprehensive study, Wolff, Blitz, Shi, Bachman, and Siegel (2006) used computer-assisted technology to survey 6,964 New Jersey incarcerated men. They found that about 4% of male inmates reported some type of sexual victimization committed by another inmate in the past six months.

Jenness, Maxson, Sumner, and Matsuda (2007) conducted a study of 370 male inmates housed in California. They found that 4.4% of the inmates reported experiencing a sexual assault while incarcerated at any time. Warren, Jackson, Booker, Loper, and Burnette (2010) interviewed 288 men in Ohio and Texas prisons about sexual victimization. The authors found that about 6% of the inmates reported other inmates had engaged in sexual contact with them against their will (of a broad based nature, including rapes and unwanted touching and kissing).

Finally, national survey data from inmates provide information about sexual victimization. Two of these surveys have been conducted by the Bureau of Justice Statistics (BJS) as part of the legislative mandate dictated by PREA. In the most recent version, computer-assisted surveys were administered to 30,029 male and female inmates in state and federal prisons. Beck and Harrison (2010) found that approximately 2% of male inmates reported an incident of sexual victimization, including forced anal sex, oral sex, and unwanted touching of a sexual nature that was perpetuated by another inmate in the 12 months prior to the survey.

Inmate-on-Inmate Sexual Assaults in Female Prisons

Struckman-Johnson et al. (1996) reported that 3 of 42 women (7%) were either groped or fondled in one Nebraska prison as part of their larger study that concentrated on male victimization. Two of these assaults involved inmates. Struckman-Johnson and Struckman-Johnson (2006) surveyed 468 women in three Midwestern prisoners and found there was variation in victimization rates for women by facility. In one prison, 27% of the women indicated they had been pressured or forced to have sexual contact against their will (including touching) sometime during incarceration, but the figures were much lower in the other two prisons (8% and 9%). In the first prison, 5% of women were raped, but none reported rapes in the other two institutions. Staff accounted for a large percentage of these acts, ranging from 20% to 50%. Data were not thoroughly disaggregated to distinguish between staff and inmate perpetrators.

Hensley, Castle, and Tewksbury (2003a) studied female inmate-on-inmate assaults in a southern female correctional facility. Of the 245 respondents, over 4% of the inmates reported that they had been sexually coerced by other female inmates. Only 2% admitted to having sexually coerced another inmate.

In the comprehensive study of New Jersey inmates previously discussed, Wolff et al. (2006) used computer-assisted technology (which allows respondents to self-report on a computer screen their own sensitive information about prison rape) to survey 564 female inmates about sexual victimization. They found that about 21% of the sample reported some type of sexual victimization committed by another inmate in the past six months. Only 4% of the inmates reported a nonconsensual sexual act (including rape and oral assault) which was committed by another inmate.

Blackburn, Mullins, and Marquart (2008) administered surveys to 436 women incarcerated in a southern prison. The authors found that 17% of the female inmates reported sexual victimization in prison. Only 3% of the women experienced a completed sexual assault some time during incarceration. Unfortunately, the study failed to distinguish between staff and inmate perpetrated assault, making it difficult to determine the nature and context of these incidents.

Warren et al. (2010) also examined victimization rates for women in Ohio and Texas prisons. Based on face-to-face interviews with 183 women, the authors found that about 7% of the women reported sexual victimization by other inmates involving physical contact (including kissing or touching) at some point while incarcerated. Similarly low rates of female victimization rates were reported nationally. The most recent survey data gathered by BJS as part of the PREA mandate indicated that about 3% of female inmates reported an incident of sexual victimization perpetrated by another inmate in the 12 months prior to the survey (Beck & Harrison, 2010).

Box 8.2   Staff-on-Inmate Sexual Assaults

National survey data from incarcerated inmates provide information about sexual victimization that has not been reported to officials. Two of these surveys have been conducted by staff from the Bureau of Justice Statistics as part of the legislative mandate dictated by PREA. In both surveys, about 3% of inmates reported an incident of staff misconduct in the past 12 months (Beck & Harrison, 2007, 2010). While these rates are relatively low, it is important to remember they are incident rates that examine victimization in the year prior to administering the survey. When used to calculate population estimates based on the most recent survey, Beck and Harrison (2010) report that this victimization rate would amount to approximately 41,200 inmates (both male and female) annually experiencing staff sexual misconduct in prisons. Male inmates more often reported experiencing staff misconduct (about 3%) compared to females (about 2%). Similar to official reports, many self-reported acts involved "willing" inmates. About two thirds (64%) of acts involving staff misconduct with male inmates were willing compared to only about one third (30%) of acts involving female inmates. In prisons, the majority of female inmates (72%) were victimized only by male staff and most male inmates (69%) were victimized by female staff.

POLICY IMPLICATIONS

Prior to PREA, there was very little information about administrative responses to sexuality in prison (Zweig & Blackmore, 2008). The situation has improved somewhat since then. There are three general categories of risk associated with prison sexuality that suggest different responses to address the issue: individual, group, and systemic (Sisco & Becker, 2007).

Individual Risk Factors

Some individual risk factors include social needs, impressing peers, building reputation, and avoiding exploitation (Beck & Harrison, 2006; Beck, Harrison, & Adams, 2007; Guerino & Beck, 2011). Many of these factors are associated with coercive sexuality more so than consensual acts. It will be difficult for correctional administrators to address these factors, in part, because it will require inmates to make individual change. These aspects of incarceration also are not limited to sexual acts, and these factors are part of the very core of inmate culture. Administrators, however, might be able to help inmates avoid exploitation.

In the past few years, inmate orientation programs have become more common (Thompson, Nored, & Dial, 2008; Zewig & Blackmore, 2008). These programs attempt to inform inmates about their risk of victimization and provide information about policies, reporting, and administrative responses; although, few have taken on the more difficult task of changing the inmate culture. There is a need for more comprehensive training that addresses "the constellation of related beliefs" that makes up the inmate culture, including attitudes that blame and trivializes victimization, while also affecting how victimization is defined (Fowler, Blackburn, Marquart, & Mullings, 2010, p. 194). Furthermore, this type of change is more desperately needed in jails, given that most inmates spend a fair amount of time in local and county facilities prior to conviction and transfer to prisons. More attention needs to be given to programming at this level, though resources are often limited, making this type of work unlikely.

Another individual risk factor may be sexual deprivation. As stated previously, there is some argument that it motivates both consensual and coercive sexual behavior. As a result, some researchers have argued that conjugal visits are ways to address the issue. The few studies that have been conducted on conjugal visits have shown that they maintain family stability and decrease violent behavior (Hensley, Rutland, & Gray-Ray, 2000). Conjugal and family visitation programs are easy to implement within correctional facilities especially if correctional administrators make the effort to address the positive consequences to the general public.

Group Factors

There has been almost no research on perpetrators of sexual violence in prison. Instead the focus has been on victim characteristics (Sisco & Becker, 2007). Some victimization trends appear to suggest that sexual orientation may be one of the characteristics associated with victimization. The overwhelming majority of studies find that homosexual, bisexual, transsexual, and transgendered inmates are at higher risk for sexual assaults in institutions than are heterosexuals in both male and female institutions (Austin, Fabelo, Gunter, & McGinnis, 2006; Beck & Harrison, 2010; Dumond, 2006; Hensley, Koscheski, & Tewksbury, 2005; Hensley et al., 2003b; Jenness, Maxson, Sumner, & Matsuda, 2007; Nacci & Kane, 1984a, 1984b; Struckman-Johnson & Struckman-Johnson, 2006; Tewksbury & Potter, 2005; Warren et al., 2010; Wolff et al., 2006; Wooden & Parker, 1982). Apparently nonheterosexuals are more likely to be seen as fair game because they already engage in same sex behavior, ignoring the profound difference between consensual and coercive sexual activity.

Despite the fact that research has concentrated on the identification of victim characteristics, this information may be the least effective in terms of identifying effective administrative responses. The only significant policy response to this information is related to housing units and the possibility of segregated assignments. For example, if homosexual, bisexual, transsexual, and transgendered inmates self-identified their sexual orientation, they could be placed in separate units. Historically, segregation has been one of the most common responses to coercive sexuality. Victims or inmates who are being targeted for victimization have been isolated in protective custody units for their own safety. This practice continues to be common (see Beck & Harrison, 2010; Guerino & Beck, 2011). This action effectively punishes victims while perpetrators often are free to find other victims. Protective custody usually is not very different than disciplinary segregation. Inmates are locked down in their cell (often 23 hours a day), have limited movement (in terms of work and recreation), and suffer a general decline in lifestyle. In addition, once inmates are identified as protective custody cases, they often cannot escape this label, which can, in turn, make them vulnerable to further assaults, simply because of this status.

The problem with focusing on victim characteristics is not a new one or unique to prisons; however, as victimologists have long noted, victims are not in control of their victimization. A more effective strategy would be to spend more time and energy (both in terms of research and in terms of policy and practice) on identifying and isolating predators. Prosecution also would send a strong message that this behavior will not be tolerated.

Systemic Factors

Systemic factors include organizational and structural issues that the administration may have more control over. They include poor programming, inadequate supervision, and untrained staff (Sisco & Becker, 2007). At its most basic level, there is a need for better programs to address inmate sexuality. Inmates who are victims of sexually coercive behavior need medical attention, but that appears to be lacking. For example, analyses of official reports nationally indicate that about one fourth to one third of inmates in substantiated incidents received no medical treatment (Beck & Harrison, 2006; Beck et al., 2007). Inmates who participate in consensual acts also need medical attention such as screening for sexually transmitted diseases; however, they are not likely to come forward, as that would require admitting to prohibited behavior and could result in disciplinary action. Victims also need counseling services to help them cope with their experience. Unfortunately, there is a problem securing sufficient and quality counseling in most prisons, regardless of the reason for the service. To receive either service, victims must be identified. They must report their victimization or correctional staff must identify it if there is any chance for treatment to occur.

Officers may increase the risk for sexual victimization of inmates if they fail to provide adequate supervision. For example, if officers fail to be diligent in terms of walking around their posts or keeping an eye on particularly risky areas, inmates may be more vulnerable to victimization. A great deal of research finds cells and housing units are particularly dangerous areas for sexual victimization (Jenness et al., 2007; Struckman-Johnson & Struckman-Johnson, 2000; Warren et al., 2010). Two thirds to three fourths of assaults in both men and women's facilities occur in these areas. Housing units should be particularly amenable to adequate supervision, if staffing levels are appropriate for the facility and officers are conscientiously patrolling their assigned areas.

Inadequate supervision also may be impacted by the attitudes of staff. Some research has concentrated on both correctional officers and wardens perceptions of sexuality. In prisons, both consensual and coercive homosexual activities which involve two inmates are against the rules and inmates who engage in either act may be exposed to disciplinary sanctions. Correctional officers, responsible for policing the prison, most often are the first responders in this process; however, it is not clear how discretion impacts their decisions (see Eigenberg, 1989, 2000a, 2000b, 2002). Officers may provide inadequate supervision by failing to enforce the rules. For example, some officers may choose to ignore acts because they are embarrassed to confront inmates about sexual activity. Officers also might be reluctant to enforce the rules if they perceive sexual acts to be consensual. Officers may be reactive, enforcing the rules only when they are brought to their attention in an overt manner (e.g., an inmate reports a rape), or they might be more proactive and recognize the symptoms of inmates who are being threatened with rape or who exhibit signs of victimization. Officers also might prevent some sexual activity by vigilant supervision of their assigned areas and/or of locations where sexual activity might occur.

At the other end of the continuum, however, officers may contribute to the problem. They may use derogatory language for known victims or gay/lesbian offenders. They may use housing assignments to intimidate inmates, threatening inmates to assignments in cells with known sexual predators or allowing inmates who are engaging in consensual sexual activity to be assigned together. Thus, some officers may be proactive in their attempts to deter and prevent sexual activity and others may, indirectly or directly, facilitate victimization in a variety of ways.

Staff must be trained on how to appropriately identify and respond to sexual activity (Dumond 2000, 2003; Dumond & Dumond, 2002; Eigenberg, 1989, 1994, 2000a, 2000b, 2002; Nacci & Kane, 1984a, 1984b). Post-PREA, prison officials are engaging in more training, especially for correctional officers (Thompson et al., 2008; Zweig & Blackmore, 2008); however, there is a need for more in-depth research on the content and quality of the training. There also is a need for research to determine whether trained officers affect the safety of facilities, by preventing acts or ensuring better reporting and more effective correctional response.

In general, then, several specific actions seem warranted. With regard to inmate-on-inmate assault, increased supervision of housing units seems to be an obvious place to start. Single cells might also help inhibit sexuality in institutions, but they are unlikely given current overcrowding and governmental budget constraints. Organizations would benefit from better screening and classification procedures to allow staff to identify and segregate potential aggressors and victims. Better inmate orientation programs also seem to be in order. To better respond to staff-on-inmate misconduct, administrators need to adequately train and supervise staff and inmates, minimize role ambiguity (by clarifying boundaries), protect staff who come forward and report, and allow for anonymous reporting of incidents (Smith & Yarussi, 2007). Many of these recommendations have recently been incorporated since the passage of PREA, but research is needed to evaluate their efficacy.

DISCUSSION QUESTIONS

1. What other policies could lawmakers use to manage sexual misconduct in prison?

2. How should prison wardens define sexual assault, rape, and consensual sex for the purpose of restricting sex between inmates?

3. What are alternative methods that correctional staff could use to handle inmates that are likely to be targets of sexual assaults, or conversely, likely to prey on other inmates?

4. How can sexual roles of inmates change during incarceration? (e.g., can a wolf become a punk, or can a fag become a wolf?) What could such changes imply about the prison subculture?

5. Are there any positive influences that come from sexual activities between inmates?

SUGGESTED READINGS

Alarid, L. (2000). Sexual orientation perspectives of incarcerated bisexual and gay men: The county jail protective custody experience. *The Prison Journal, 80*(1), 80–95.

Bowker, L. (1982). *Prison victimization.* New York, NY: Elsevier North Holland.

Fishman, J. (1951). *Sex in prison.* London, England: John Lane, Bodley Head.

Fleisher, M., & Krienert, J. (2008). *The myth of prison rape: Sexual culture in American prisons.* Lanham, MD: Rowman and Littlefield.

Groth, A. (1979). *Men who rape: The psychology of the offender.* New York, NY: Plenum.

Ibrahim, A. (1974). Deviant sexual behavior in men's prisons. *Crime & Delinquency, 20*(1), 38–44.

Propper, A. (1989). Love, marriage, and father-son relationships among male prisoners. *The Prison Journal, 69*(2), 57–63.

Struckman-Johnson, C., & Struckman-Johnson, D. (2002). Sexual coercion reported by women in three Midwestern prisons. *The Journal of Sex Research, 39*(3), 217–227.

Tewksbury, R., & West, A. (2000). Research on sex in prison during the late 1980s and early 1990s. *The Prison Journal, 80*(4), 368–378.

Wolff, N., & Shi, J. (2009). Contextualization of physical and sexual assault in male prisons: Incidents and their aftermath. *Journal of Correctional Health Care, 15,* 58–69.

REFERENCES

Austin, J., Fabelo, T., Gunter, A., & McGinnis, K. (2006). *Sexual violence in the Texas prison system.* NCJ 215774. Washington, DC: U.S. Department of Justice, National Institute of Justice.

Beck, A., & Harrison, P. (2006). *Sexual violence reported by correctional authorities, 2005.* NCJ 214646. Washington, DC: U.S. Department of Justice, Bureau of Justice Statistics.

Beck, A., & Harrison, P. (2007). *Sexual victimization in state and federal prisons reported by inmates, 2007.* NCJ 219414. Washington, DC: U.S. Department of Justice, Bureau of Justice Statistics.

Beck, A., & Harrison, P. (2010). *Sexual victimization in state and federal prisons reported by inmates, 2008–2009.* Washington, DC: U.S. Department of Justice, Bureau of Justice Statistics.

Beck, A., Harrison, P., & Adams, D. (2007). *Sexual violence reported by correctional authorities, 2006*. NCJ 218914. Washington, DC: U.S. Department of Justice, Bureau of Justice Statistics.

Blackburn, A., Mullins, J., & Marquart, J. (2008). Sexual assault in prison and beyond: Toward an understanding of lifetime sexual assault among incarcerated women. *The Prison Journal, 88*(3), 351–377.

Buffum, P. (1972). *Homosexuality in prisons*. Washington, DC: U.S. Department of Justice, Law Enforcement Assistance Administration.

Chonco, N. (1989). Sexual assaults among male inmates: A descriptive study. *The Prison Journal, 69*(1), 72–82.

Clemmer, D. (1940). *The prison community*. Boston, MA: Christopher Publishing House.

Davis, A. (1968). Sexual assaults in the Philadelphia prison system. In D. Peterson & C. Thomas (Eds.), *Corrections: Problems and prospects* (2nd ed., pp. 102–113). Englewood Cliffs, NJ: Prentice Hall.

Donaldson, S. (1993). *A million jockers, punks, and queens: Sex among male prisoners and its implications for concepts of sexual orientation*. Retrieved from http://spr.igc.org/en/stephendonaldson/doc_01_lecture.html

Dumond, R. (1992). The sexual assault of male inmates in incarcerated settings. *International Journal of the Sociology of Law, 20*(2), 135–157.

Dumond, R. (2000). Inmate sexual assault: The plague which persists. *The Prison Journal, 80*(4), 407–414.

Dumond, R. (2003). Confronting America's most ignored crime problem: The Prison Rape Elimination Act of 2003. *The Journal of the American Academy of Psychiatry and the Law, 31*, 354–360.

Dumond, R. (2006). The impact of prisoner sexual violence: Challenges of implementing Public Law 108–79 the Prison Rape Elimination Act of 2003. *Journal of Legislation, 32*, 142–164.

Dumond, R., & Dumond, D. (2002). Training staff on inmate sexual assault. In C. Hensley (Ed.), *Prison sex: Practice and policy* (pp. 89–100). Boulder, CO: Lynne Rienner.

Eigenberg, H. (1989). Male rape: An empirical examination of correctional officers' attitudes toward male rape in prison. *The Prison Journal, 68*(2), 39–56.

Eigenberg, H. (1992). Homosexuality in male prisons: Demonstrating the need for a social constructionist approach. *Criminal Justice Review, 17*, 219–234.

Eigenberg, H. (1994). Rape in male prisons: Examining the relationship between correctional officers' attitudes toward male rape and their willingness to respond to acts of rape. In M. Braswell, R. Montgomery, & L. Lombardo (Eds.), *Prison violence* (2nd ed., pp. 145–166). New York, NY: Anderson.

Eigenberg, H. (2000a). Correctional officers and their perceptions of homosexuality, rape, and prostitution in male prisons. *The Prison Journal, 80*(4), 415–433.

Eigenberg, H. (2000b). Correctional officers' definitions of rape in prison. *Journal of Criminal Justice, 28*(5), 435–449.

Eigenberg, H. (2002). Prison staff and male rape. In C. Hensley (Ed.), *Prison sex: Practice and policy* (pp. 49–66). Boulder, CO: Lynne Rienner.

Einat, T., & Einat, H. (2000). Inmate argot as an expression of prison subculture: The Israeli case. *The Prison Journal, 80*(3), 309–325.

Fagan, T., Winnerstrom, D., & Miller, J. (1996). Sexual assault of male inmates: Prevention, identification and intervention. *Journal of Correctional Health Care, 3*(1), 49–65.

Fishman, J. (1934). *Sex in prison: Revealing sex conditions in America's prisons*. New York, NY: National Library Press.

Fleisher, M. (1989). *Warehousing violence*. Newbury Park, CA: Sage.

Ford, C. (1929). Homosexual practices of institutionalized females. *Journal of Abnormal and Social Psychology, 23,* 442–449.

Fowler, S., Blackburn, A., Marquart, J., & Mullings, J. (2010). Would they officially report an in-prison sexual assault? An examination of inmate perceptions. *The Prison Journal, 90*(2), 220–243.

Gaes, G., & Goldberg, A. (2004). *Prison rape: A critical review of the literature*. Retrieved from: http://www.ncjrs.gov/App/Publications/abstract.aspx?ID=234861

Giallombardo, R. (1966). *Society of women: A study of a woman's prison*. New York, NY: Wiley.

Greer, K. (2000). The changing nature of interpersonal relationships in a women's prison. *The Prison Journal, 80*(4), 442–468.

Guerino, P., & Beck, A. (2011). *Sexual victimization reported by adult correctional authorities, 2007–2008*. NCJ 231172. Washington, DC: Department of Justice, Bureau of Justice Statistics.

Halleck, S. L., & Hersko, M. (1962). Homosexual behavior in a correctional institution for adolescent girls. *American Journal of Orthopsychiatry, 32,* 911–917.

Heffernan, E. (1972). *Making it in prison: The square, the cool, and the life*. New York, NY: Wiley.

Hensley, C. (2001). Consensual homosexuality activity in male prisons. *Corrections Compendium, 26*(1), 1–4.

Hensley, C., Castle, T., & Tewksbury, R. (2003a). Inmate-to-inmate sexual coercion in a prison for women. *Journal of Offender Rehabilitation, 37*(2), 77–87.

Hensley, C., Koscheski, M., & Tewksbury, R. (2005). Examining the characteristics of male sexual assault targets in a southern maximum-security prison. *Journal of Interpersonal Violence, 20*(6), 667–679.

Hensley, C., Rutland, S., & Gray-Ray, P. (2000). Inmate attitudes toward the conjugal visitation program in Mississippi prisons: An exploratory study. *American Journal of Criminal Justice, 25*(1), 137–145.

Hensley, C., Tewksbury, R., & Castle, T. (2003b). Characteristics of prison sexual assault targets in male Oklahoma correctional facilities. *Journal of Interpersonal Violence, 18,* 595–607.

Hensley, C., Tewksbury, R., & Koscheski, M. (2002). The characteristics and motivations behind female prison sex. *Women & Criminal Justice, 13*(2), 125–140.

Hensley, C., Tewksbury, R., & Wright, J. (2001). Exploring the dynamics of masturbation and consensual same-sex activity within a male maximum-security prison. *Journal of Men's Studies, 10*(1), 59–71.

Hensley, C., Wright, J., Tewksbury, R., & Castle, T. (2003c). The evolving nature of prison argot and sexual hierarchies. *The Prison Journal, 83*(3), 289–300.

Huggins, D., Capeheart, L., & Newman, E. (2006). Deviants or scapegoats: An examination of pseudofamily groups and dyads in two Texas prisons. *The Prison Journal, 86,* 114–139.

Irwin, J. (1980). *Prisons in turmoil*. Boston, MA: Little, Brown.

Irwin, J., & Cressey, D. (1962). Thieves, convicts, and the inmate culture. *Social Problems 10*(2), 142–155.

Jenness, V., Maxson, C., Sumner, J., & Matsuda, K. (2007). Violence in California correctional facilities: An empirical examination of sexual assault. *The Bulletin of the Center for Evidence-Based Corrections, 2*(2). Retrieved from http://ucicorrections.seweb.uci.edu/pubs#bulletins

Karpman, B. (1948). Sex life in prison. *Journal of Criminal Law and Criminology, 38,* 475–486.

Kirkham, G. (1971). Homosexuality in prison. In J. Henslin (Ed.), *Studies in the sociology of sex* (pp. 325–344). New York, NY: Appleton-Century-Crofts.

Lee, D. (1965, November). Seduction of the guilty: Homosexuality in American prisons. *Fact Magazine,* 57–61.

Lockwood, D. (1980). *Sexual aggression in prison.* New York, NY: Elsevier.

Maitland, A., & Sluder, R. (1998). Victimization and youthful prison inmates: An empirical analysis. *The Prison Journal, 78,* 55–73.

Maruschak, L. (2007). *HIV in prisons, 2005.* NCJ 218915. Washington, DC: U.S. Department of Justice, Bureau of Justice Statistics.

Nacci, P., & Kane, T. (1983). The incidence of sex and sexual aggression in federal prisons. *Federal Probation, 7,* 31–36.

Nacci, P., & Kane, T. (1984a). Inmate sexual aggression: Some evolving propositions and empirical findings, and mitigating counter-forces. *Journal of Offender Counseling, Services, and Rehabilitation, 9,* 1–20.

Nacci, P., & Kane, T. (1984b). Sex and sexual aggression in federal prisons: Inmate involvement and employee impact. *Federal Probation, 8,* 46–53.

Otis, M. (1913). A perversion not commonly noted. *Journal of Abnormal Psychology, 8,* 113–116.

Owen, B. (1998). *In the mix: Struggle and survival in a women's prison.* Albany: SUNY Press.

Prison Rape Elimination Act of 2003, P. L. 108–79. (2003). Retrieved from http://www.ojjdp.gov/about/PubLNo108–79.txt

Propper, A. (1978). Lesbianism in female and coed correctional institutions. *Journal of Homosexuality, 3*(3), 265–274.

Propper, A. (1981). *Prison homosexuality: Myth and reality.* Lexington, MA: Lexington Books.

Propper, A. (1982). Make-believe families and homosexuality among imprisoned girls. *Criminology, 20*(1), 127–138.

Sagarin, E. (1976). Prison homosexuality and its effect on post-prison sexual behavior. *Psychiatry, 39,* 245–257.

Saum, C., Surratt, H., Inciardi, J., & Bennett, R. (1995). Sex in prison: Exploring the myths and realities. *The Prison Journal, 75*(4), 413–430.

Selling, L. (1931). The pseudo family. *American Journal of Sociology, 37,* 247–253.

Sisco, M., & Becker, J. (2007). Beyond predicting the risk of sexual victimization in prison: Considering inmate options and reporting avenues for addressing an inherent problem. *Criminology and Public Policy, 6*(3), 573–584.

Smith, B., & Yarussi, J. (2007). *Breaking the code of silence: Correctional officers' handbook on identifying and addressing sexual misconduct.* Washington, DC: National Institute of Corrections.

Struckman-Johnson, C., & Struckman-Johnson, D. (2000). Sexual coercion rates in seven Midwestern prison facilities for men. *The Prison Journal, 80*(4), 379–390.

Struckman-Johnson, C., & Struckman-Johnson, D. (2006). A comparison of sexual coercion experiences reported by men and women in prison. *Journal of Interpersonal Violence, 21,* 1591–1615.

Struckman-Johnson, C., Struckman-Johnson, D., Rucker, L., Bumby, K., & Donaldson, S. (1996). Sexual coercion reported by men and women in prison. *Journal of Sex Research, 33*(1), 67–76.

Sykes, G. (1958). *The society of captives: A study of a maximum security prison.* Princeton, NJ: Princeton University Press.

Tewksbury, R. (1989). Measures of sexual behavior in an Ohio prison. *Sociology and Social Research, 74*(1), 34–39.

Tewksbury, R., & Potter, R. (2005). Transgendered prisoners: A forgotten group. In S. Stojkovic (Ed.), *Managing special population in jails and prisons* (pp. 1–16). Kingston, NJ: Civic Research Institute.

Thompson, R., Nored, L., & Dial, K. (2008). The Prison Rape Elimination Act (PREA): An evaluation of policy compliance with illustrative excerpts. *Criminal Justice Policy Review, 19,* 414–437.

Ward, D., & Kassebaum, G. (1964). Homosexuality: A mode of adaption in a prison for women. *Social Problems, 12*(2), 159–177.

Ward, D., & Kassebaum, G. (1965). *Women's prison: Sex and social structure.* Chicago, IL: Aldine.

Warren, J., Jackson, S., Booker, A., Loper, M., & Burnette, M. (2010). *Risk markers for sexual predation and victimization in prison.* NCJ 230522. Washington, DC: U.S. Department of Justice, National Institute of Justice.

Wolff, N., Blitz, C., Shi, J., Bachman, R., & Siegel, J. (2006). Sexual violence inside prisons: Rates of victimization. *Journal of Urban Health, 83,* 835–848.

Wooden, W., & Parker, J. (1982). *Men behind bars: Sexual exploitation in prison.* New York, NY: Plenum Press.

Worley, V., Worley, R., & Mullins, J. (2010). Rape lore in correctional settings: Assessing inmates' awareness of sexual coercion in prisons, *Southwest Journal of Criminal Justice, 7*(1), 65–86.

Zweig, J., & Blackmore, J. (2008). *Strategies to prevent prison rape by changing the correctional culture.* Washington, DC: U.S. Department of Justice, National Institute of Justice.

CHAPTER 9

Special Needs Offenders in Correctional Institutions: Inmates Under Protective Custody

Holly A. Miller and Leah McCoy

INTRODUCTION

Since the inception of prisons, there has been a need to further segregate some inmates from the general prison population. The type of segregation within a prison is determined by the inmate's need for protection or the institution's need for protecting the orderly running of the institution. For example, the segregation may be disciplinary detention for punitive reasons or protective custody to protect an inmate from some sort of threat within the general prison population. The use of segregation to discipline and protect inmates is common practice in both federal and state prisons. Practitioners and researchers often disagree about the management and use of protective custody. Researchers and prison theorists opine that most inmates who claim that they need protection should receive it. Prison officials, on the other hand, assert that it should only be prison officials who determine which inmates are separated from the general population and placed in protective custody. As the population of protective custody inmates has grown exponentially over the last several decades, the courts have guided protective custody procedures and conditions in attempt to reduce possible negative effects and protect inmate rights.

This chapter will provide the current statistics of protective custody utilization, information on the most common types of inmates who are placed in protective custody, legal considerations, consequences of the segregation, and explain common practices and policies for inmates under protective custody. The chapter will conclude with research and policy implications from what we know now about the segregation of protective custody inmates.

DEFINING PROTECTIVE CUSTODY

Special housing segregation within both state and federal prisons is the separation of an inmate from the general prison population. There are typically three forms of segregation including administrative segregation, disciplinary detention, and protective custody. Administrative segregation is the separation of an inmate for investigative or other prison administrative purposes. It is a form of separation from the general population administered by prison staff when continued presence of an offender in the general population would pose a serious threat to life, property, self, staff or other offenders or to the orderly operation or security of the facility. Offenders pending investigation for disciplinary or criminal proceedings, detainees, and presentence holds may be included in this status designation. For example, if an inmate is being investigated for an institution infraction or has come forward to the prison officials to report ongoing criminal activity within the prison, the inmate will be placed in segregation while prison officials explore the allegations. Administrative segregation is considered a nonpunitive status with the restrictions imposed to ensure safety and the orderly running of the institution.

Disciplinary detention is considered a punitive separation of an inmate from the general prison population for those inmates who have been found guilty of an institutional infraction. Disciplinary detention is typically a specified number of days of confinement in a cell determined by the infraction committed. It is often referred to as a prison within a prison. These inmates have violated prison policy (e.g., refused work, threatened another inmate or staff, found to be in possession of contraband such as alcohol or weapons) and are therefore being punished. Since these inmates are already being punished for their crimes and separated from the community, prison officials remove more rights and utilize disciplinary detention. Generally, this form of segregation is the most restrictive with fewer privileges than inmates housed in administrative segregation or protective custody.

Protective custody (PC) is used to provide protection for inmates who are being threatened in some way by other inmates. The American Correctional Association (ACA) defines protective custody as "a form of separation from inmates in the general population for inmates requesting or requiring protection from other inmates for reasons of health or safety" (2009). In most circumstances, inmates under protective custody have requested their placement there and have a desire to be separated from the general prison population because they fear that they will be harmed if they remain in the general population. However, prison officials can, and sometimes do, place an inmate into PC against his or her request if they believe that inmate is in danger in the general prison population. Formal definitions of PC and conditions therein, are applied by prison authorities, and many jurisdictions include a specific definition in policy and statute documents. Inmates have the legal right to request protective custody if they feel that their lives may be in danger from other inmates in the general population. Protective custody requests will be granted if prison officials find that the inmate is truly at risk. In some situations, the inmate may be transferred to a protective custody unit or another prison, but under most prison protective custody procedures, inmates are placed in a more restricted environment often times in similar circumstances as inmates held for administrative purposes or for disciplinary reasons.

A review of the empirical literature related to penology fails to demonstrate a consistent mention of PC until the 1960s (Henderson, 1990). Historically, however, there have been philosophical debates revolving around the issue of congregation versus segregation. The debate in America focused on the principles of the Auburn and Pennsylvania systems of discipline. There was strong support from penological reformers, particularly those of the Auburn system, for isolating the offender by placing the inmate into an environment where he or she was forced to rethink criminal and deviant inclinations. During the period of the industrial prison in the first part of the 20th century, segregation was used by prison wardens to house undisciplined and unindustrious individuals. A study which analyzed the use of punitive isolation, administrative segregation, and PC in Washington State Penitentiary during the 1960s and 1970s indicated that there was a decline in the use of punitive segregation and isolation, and increases in the use of PC, suspended segregation, and administrative segregation (Barak-Glantz, 1982). It was during this period when prisons began to keep statistics on the PC population.

Estimating the prevalence of inmates under PC is difficult because jurisdictions differ in their definition. However, it has been projected that approximately between 3.2% and 6.5% of all prison or jail populations are under PC at any given time (Robertson, 1987). In the last couple of decades the number of inmates placed in PC housing has increased dramatically. Although there is much speculation surrounding the reasons why PC numbers have increased (see Box 9.1), three major themes can be identified. The first theme accounts for PC placement increases by overall prison system changes. For example, system changes have influenced overcrowding conditions of many prisons (e.g., sending more individuals to prison for longer time periods), the classifying of inmates in such a way that more violent offenders are placed in the same unit, and the deinstitutionalization of the mentally ill are examples given to explain why more offenders are requesting placement in PC. Researchers report that the primary reason for the burgeoning size of the PC population is the acute fear of violence with the prison system (Anderson, 1980; Robertson, 1987). Indeed the murder and sexual assault rates in prison are significantly higher than in the free world (Beck & Hughes, 2005; U.S. Department of Justice, 2011).

Box 9.1   Cited Reasons for the Increase in PC Utilization

System Changes

- Prison overcrowding
- Lessened warden authority
- Increase in prison violence
- Increased contact between inmates
- Amount of drugs available in prison
- Prison classification systems that place more violent offenders together
- Mental health deinstitutionalization

(Continued)

(Continued)

- Public humanitarian concern for inmates
- Judicial incursion into prison management

Offender Characteristics

- Increased gang involvement
- More "first timers"
- More sexual offenders
- Higher rates of drug and violence related inmates
- Higher rates of informers
- More inmates who are psychologically vulnerable

Protective Custody Living Conditions

- Quieter conditions
- Single cell
- Continued access to prison programming
- Judicial requirements of equal programming access

As prisons have moved away from the solitary confinement-type incarceration (Pennsylvania System), inmates have much more freedom to move around the prison allowing for more inmate-to-inmate interaction increasing the likelihood of violence and assaults. Thus, inmates may have more fear of being assaulted or killed in the current correctional atmosphere compared to previous decades where inmates were more closely watched and restricted in their movements. Additionally, there has been an increase in public (and prison culture) stigma associated with some crimes and some human conditions. For example, individuals who have been found guilty of a sexual crime carry extra stigma, fear, and hatred among both the general population in the free world and within prison. Individuals who have mental illnesses or are homosexual or bisexual also are subjected to increased stigma, fear, and assault. These societal fears and bias make it much more likely that an inmate who fits one of these criteria will be assaulted or even killed. See Box 9.2 for a recent example.

Box 9.2   John J. Geoghan

John J. Geoghan, 68, former Catholic priest and convicted child molester, died after being strangled by an inmate serving a life sentence for killing a man he believed was gay; in a maximum security facility in Shirley, Massachusetts. Geoghan was accused of sexually abusing up to 150 boys during his 30 years as a priest, and last year was convicted of fondling a 10-year-old boy in Boston in 1991. After his sentencing, Geoghan was sent to the protective custody facility in Shirley because authorities worried he would be attacked by fellow inmates. Joseph L. Druce, 37, who has been charged with the murder, reportedly planned the killing for more than a month, according to another prisoner.

A single guard was on duty, in charge of 22 prisoners in Geoghan's cell block, according to the Worcester district attorney.

Source: Based on "Milestones" article, Jarrett Banks, Sept.2003. TIME.com. http://www.time.com/time/magazine/article/0,9171,480334,00.html#ixzz1KjKC1FFK

Other influences of increased PC placement include prison overcrowding and mandated sentencing. Inmates are often housed in dormitory-like units where there is much more access to other inmates. Dormitory-style housing has been found to have higher rates of assault and other prison rule violations (Gaes, 1985; Wooldredge, 1996). Additionally, mandatory sentencing has left fewer incentives for inmates to control their behavior inside prison walls. If an inmate is not receiving any relief on his or her sentence for good behavior, there is less incentive to behave well.

The second theme is offender characteristics. Over the last several decades, there has been an increase in the amount of gang membership in prison, there are more first-timers or naïve inmates in prison, and significantly more sexual offenders begin incarcerated. More inmates are arriving to prison with the PC status due to their serving as informers against other criminal defendants (Angelone, 1999; Boucouvalas & Pearse, 1985; Jacobs, 1982). Additionally, since the deinstitutionalization of individuals with mental illness, more inmates with psychological disorders have ended up in the criminal justice system.

The third theme that is evident from the literature is that the increase in PC placement is due to the inmate's belief that their time will be easier under PC conditions than in the general population. For example, inmates may see the PC conditions such as living in a quieter, single-person cell while still having access to programs, as more desirable than living in the general population (Angelone, 1999; Wormith, Tellier, & Gendreau, 1988).

Enormous variations in the conditions of PC exist across jurisdictions and criminal justice agencies. Similar to other prison policies there is much leeway provided in the definition and procedure for PC by the American Correctional Association. Although current policies and laws indicate that PC inmates should not be restricted from programs and privileges similar to general population inmates, often times they are housed under similar circumstances as inmates in administrative segregation and disciplinary detention. In fact, research has indicated that PC inmates commonly live under conditions that are much more restrictive and depriving than the general population inmate (e.g., Angelone, 1999).

COMMON INMATE TYPES PLACED IN PC

Although the prison authorities decide which inmates are placed in PC, the prison subculture influences PC assignments by instigating aggressive and other types of negative behaviors toward certain types of inmates (see Box 9.3 for a list of inmate types placed in PC). The most common types of inmates placed in PC are gang members under threat, witnesses to the state or federal law enforcement or prison officials, sexual offenders, criminal justice personnel, homosexuals, and the mentally ill. Anderson (1980) reported that PC staff estimated that 16% of the PC population were housed there over sexual assault concerns, 32% because they were thought to be informers, 29% in avoidance of retaliation, 5% for mental disturbances, 7% to avoid their work detail, and 10% for "other reasons." Additionally, Toch (2001) has reported that PC is comprised of the following types of offenders: sex offenders, informers, mentally ill, and inmates facing retaliation for unpaid debts.

Box 9.3   Types of Inmates Placed in Protective Custody

- Witnesses (informers)
- Gang members under threat
- Gang members attempting to leave gang
- Sexual offenders
- Previous criminal justice personnel: previous judges, police officers, correctional officers
- Some mentally ill
- Inmates who are afraid of assaults because of their build, age, or sexuality
- Inmates attempting to manipulate the system
- Inmates whose lives may be in danger from another inmate that they have preyed upon
- Inmates who are unable to pay off gambling or other debts to inmates
- Inmates nearing the end of their sentence and are trying to avoid disciplinary infractions
- Inmates with notorious criminal cases

Protective custody was first utilized by inmates who provided witness testimony against other defendants in criminal proceedings. Federal and state prosecution of organized crime offered protective custody status to offenders who agreed to testify against other defendants. PC is also utilized by prison officials for inmates who serve as institutional informers. Although witness or informer protection now comprises a smaller amount of PC inmates, it remains a powerful stigma of PC, inmates in PC, and even staff that work in PC. In fact, inmates who are rumored or believed to be informants, but are not, within the general population often will request PC placement in order to protect themselves from inmate threats.

Gang members are another group of inmates who may be placed in protective custody. Even though they may be perceived as dangerous, disruptive, or posing a problem for management (Shalev, 2008), there are instances where gang members may be placed in protective custody. For example, gang members may become informants by snitching on fellow gang members or by reporting to officials about gang activity, renouncing the informant's membership in the gang as a result.

Witnesses to gang activity may be placed in protective custody, although many are opposed to it because such a classification may give the impression that the witness is a snitch. Correctional staff may protect witnesses from defendants by keeping the witness and defendant separate while in jail and on the way to and from court, keeping open communication with the witness or the witness's attorney (if represented) regarding potential intimidation, and by ensuring that the defendant's friends or family members are not visiting the witness (Anderson, 2007). Gang members may fear entry into protective custody because they may perceive themselves as cowardly, or they may fear being viewed as cowardly by fellow inmates. However, for some gang members, it becomes a matter of life or death; in that case, they may choose to enter protective custody to protect themselves (Blatchford, 2008; Reiter, 2010).

Research indicates that a large percentage of inmates placed in protective custody request placement because they are either afraid of sexual assault due to already experiencing an assault, being younger or having a smaller build, or are homosexual or bisexual (Alarid, 2000; Angelone, 1999; Robertson, 1987). Research also indicates that sexual assault in prison is a valid fear (Blackburn, Mullings, & Marquart, 2008; Dumond, 1992, 2000; Wolff & Shi, 2009). The U.S. Department of Justice (2011) estimated that 200,000 incarcerated adults and juveniles experienced some form of sexual assault in 2008 (see Beck & Hughes, 2005; Thomson, Nored, & Dial, 2008). In fact, recognizing the problem of sexual assault in prison, Congress passed the first federal law addressing the sexual assault of prisoners in 2003: the Prison Rape Elimination Act (PREA). The main purpose of the law was to establish a zero-tolerance policy for prison rape among correctional facilities, to require prisons to prioritize and institutionalize policies aimed at detecting, preventing, reducing, and punishing prison rape, and to "increase available data and information on the incidence of prison rape" (Thomson et al., 2008, p. 416). Thus, the knowledge of prison sexual assault problems, officials behind PREA call for the creation of national standards to govern the prevention and detection of sexual abuse and sexual violence in prison facilities, as was discussed in Chapter 8 by Hensley, Eigenberg, and Gibson, in regard to sexuality and sexual coercion behind bars.

One of the most cited and well-known studies examining the experience of gay men in prison is the Wooden and Parker's (1982) study of over 200 general population inmates in a medium security institution in California. Among the inmates included in their study were 80 gay men and 14 heterosexual men who reported that they had been raped or coerced into sexual activity while serving their criminal sentence. Their findings indicated that homosexual and bisexual inmates were significantly more likely to be harassed (and assaulted) by other inmates as well as prison staff. In attempt to extend the finding of Wooden and Parker's 1982 study and to obtain a more contemporaneous sample of gay and bisexual inmates, Alarid (2000) examined the experience of gay and bisexual men in PC in a county jail. She assessed 56 men who requested PC because of their sexual orientation and compared their demographics, characteristics, and answers on questionnaires to a random sample of male offenders in the jail general population ($n = 447$). The majority of the PC men reported that they were disrespected and threatened by both fellow inmates and staff members in the jail, were pressured less for sex in PC than the general population, and were more likely to report fear if they displayed more feminine characteristics than the gay/bisexual men who identified with more traditional masculine characteristics.

Transgender inmates have also experienced disproportionate levels of vulnerability. They are likely to experience high levels of physical and sexual violence as a result of their increased vulnerability (Edney, 2009). Transgender inmates are marginalized in ways which are not comparable to other groups of inmates. Overall, they fare much worse in terms of health, homelessness, participation in sex work, and sexual victimization history (Sexton, Jenness, & Sumner, 2010). Arkles (2009) argues that involuntary placement in protective custody is one of the greatest threats to transgendered inmates. They are more likely to be attacked in protective custody because it is easier for abusive staff to access such inmates alone while out of sight of other prisoners and video surveillance. When transgender inmates speak up about mistreatment, correctional staff retaliates by setting them up for trouble or writing false disciplinary reports. Transgender inmates are often deprived of necessary healthcare, including hormones and surgery, forcing them to live as a gender with which they do not identify. They are often targeted for extreme violence and unending verbal harassment, potentially leading to self-harm or suicide attempts.

Mentally ill inmates make up another large percentage of segregated and PC placements (O'Keefe, 2008; O'Keefe, Klebe, Stucker, Sturm, & Leggett, 2010). The National Institute of Mental Health (2010) reports a 5% rate of serious mental illness in the community. Among the population of general inmates, the rate is higher at about 18% (Ditton, 1999; O'Keefe & Schnell, 2008). Additionally, a similar phenomenon is evident among those inmates that are further segregated, with rates as high as 50% of inmates having a severe mental illness (O'Keefe, 2008). Inmates with mental illness may ask to be placed in PC, but often are placed there by prison officials who believe that they may be vulnerable to other inmates because of their mental illness symptoms. In one of the few studies examining PC inmates specifically, Wormith, Tellier, and Gendreau (1988) sought to assess whether PC inmates had characteristics that differentiated them from the general population inmates. They interviewed and assessed 80 inmates either serving time in PC or in the general population at an institution in Ontario, Canada. The inmates were matched on sentence length and time served. Results indicated that 46% of the PC inmates requested PC because of prison problems and threats, 16% because of their offense (e.g., sex offense), 16% from problems they experienced in the community, and 24% were due to the personal characteristics of the inmate. Although the authors found no physical characteristic differences between the PC and general population inmates, there were significant differences in mental health problems. Seventy percent of inmates under PC placement were found to have histories of mental disorders and current reported symptoms compared to 42% of the general population. Additionally, almost

67% of the inmates in PC reported begin physically or sexually assaulted in the general population compared to 15% of the inmates serving their time only in the general population.

LEGAL CONSIDERATIONS

Like many changes in law and policy, change in the procedures, process, and conditions of PC have been brought about by inmates who have filed suit against correctional institutions, wardens, and correctional officers. From the 1970s to the present, a series of court rulings have contributed to the policies and procedures for PC. Protective custody suits have been primarily in the legal domains of prison, warden, officer liability, due process, and prisoner rights. The courts have consistently found that prison officials have a duty to take reasonable precautions to protect inmates under their care. For example, when prison officials become aware of serious risk of potential harm to inmates and fail to provide secure housing, they have been found liable (e.g., *Roland v. Johnson*, 1988; *Young v. Quinlan*, 1991). In one of the first court cases, *Landman v. Royster* (1971), the ruling required the state of Virginia Department of Corrections to create procedures to ensure inmate protection. The Supreme Court has ruled that prison officials must investigate an inmate's vulnerability and if an inmate is vulnerable the officials have a duty to protect that individual from harm. This has taken two forms for PC inmates. First, the prison officials have a duty to assess the possibility of threats for vulnerable inmates. Second, if the prison officials become aware of vulnerability through the inmate informing them of the threat, prison officials must take action. This does not guarantee that an inmate will be placed in PC, but law requires an investigation by prison officials to render a determination if a true threat exists. If a true threat exists, prison officials have a duty to protect that inmate. In *Woodhouse v. Virginia* (1973), the Fourth Circuit Court of Appeals ruled that an inmate can be awarded damages if he or she proves a pervasive risk of harm from other inmates to which prison officials failed to reasonably respond. The courts have ruled that prison officials are not civilly liable for actions that they take or do not take in regards to protective custody as long as they did not ignore a clearly established right held by the inmate. Court cases have indicated that the most significant prison official liability occurs when an inmate requests PC placement, prison officials deny that placement, and the inmate in subsequently harmed. To prove liability, an inmate must establish that the injury was a result of deliberate indifference. The deliberate indifference standard, set by *Estelle v. Gamble* (1976), is that an inmate should be protected from unnecessary harm, and that reasonable care should be exercised in the maintenance of the inmate's life and health.

The last two domains in court rulings involve the constitutional rights of the PC inmate. While some specific rights have been addressed by the law, there is no standard for PC, thus, there is no clear consensus about PC inmate-specific rights. The majority of litigation in this area has included examination of whether prison officials have violated inmate federal rights. In most circumstances litigation has addressed due process rights and conditions of confinement. The courts have ruled that there are differences in due process for inmates who request PC from inmates who are placed in PC involuntarily. Inmates who request PC are not entitled to the same due process protections such as hearings or periodic reviews of their status, although periodic reviews are not uncommon for all PC inmates. Inmates who are involuntarily placed in PC are automatically entitled to the basic due process rights that require notice and an opportunity to be heard before a possibly adverse action is taken against them. The second most common constitutional right that PC inmates have brought to litigation is the Eighth Amendment prohibiting cruel and unusual punishment. Most of the cases brought before courts have involved claims of confinement conditions that constitute cruel and unusual punishment. These claims usually involve either the physical conditions of the PC units or cells or the lack of program availability. The courts have ruled that PC inmates should be provided with similar services and facilities as are available for inmates in the general population. Common constitutional rights addressed in court rulings include the practice of religion, the ability to recreate, and the right to receive educational and mental health services. The courts have also found that prison officials may be held liable for Eighth Amendment violations if "deliberate indifference" is evident. Deliberate indifference exists when prison officials are aware of the risk of harm to an inmate, but fail to take reasonable precautions to protect that inmate. There remains a lack of consensus regarding the rights of PC inmates, but no liability has been found when prison officials have taken reasonable care in the protection of vulnerable inmates. However, when deliberate indifference exists, prison officials have been held liable.

ISSUES OF CONFINEMENT AND ISOLATION

Over the last several decades there has been a rapid increase in the number of inmates who are segregated from the remainder of the prison population. While isolation may have positive effects—protection from victimization, greater feelings of safety, and decreased stress and environmental stimulation (Minor, Wallace, & Parson, 2008)—the negative effects can be more serious and long-lasting. Research on the effects of segregation over the years has ranged from complete sensory deprivation (e.g., no light, sound) to the effects of prison programming deprivation. The following section provides an overview of segregation conditions and subsequent effects of such confinement over the decades.

Effects of Segregation and Isolation

Early prison inmate segregation was often referred to as "the hole" because it consisted of sensory deprivation—a cold, dark, isolated cell within the prison. Thus, several older studies measuring the effects of segregation focused on the effects of being deprived from most sensory stimulation. As segregation conditions in prison started to evolve, prison conditions began to center around isolation and solitary confinement rather than complete sensory deprivation.

Much of the research that has measured the effects of segregation has done so while inmates were in isolation or in sensory deprivation conditions. Although inmates may still be segregated for various reasons, these conditions have become more humane in recent years. A more humane form of inmate segregation that has emerged in jails and prisons is PC. Inmates who are threatened or attacked or have an increased likelihood of being threatened or attacked may either request placement or become involuntarily placed there for enhanced safety. There have been very few studies which have sought to determine if the harm that an inmate faces while in PC is greater than the harm that the inmate would face if housed in the general population. This section will discuss studies that have measured the effects of sensory deprivation, solitary confinement, protective custody, and other forms of inmate isolation, and how these effects have changed over time as a result of the changes which have occurred within the inmate segregation environment.

Early studies measuring the effects of sensory deprivation (SD) often did so in an experimental setting, where subjects were deprived for short terms, usually around eight hours or less. SD effects may vary depending on the time frame of the experiment, the experimental situation, and the nature of the subjects involved (Jackson & Pollard, 1962). While many studies have used only male subjects in their SD experiments, some studies have measured the effects of SD in both males and females. For example, one study sought to measure confinement, social isolation/restriction, prior knowledge of SD effects, and sensation-seeking personality characteristics in a group of 36 males and 36 females. One third of subjects from each group were assigned to one of three experimental conditions: SD, social isolation, and social confinement. The researchers found that in the SD condition, females had significantly higher scores than males on measures of loss of reality, worry, time orientation, and somatic symptoms.

On the other hand, males scored higher on measures of sexual thoughts and positive feelings (Zuckerman, Persky, Link, & Basu, 1968). Another study placed a group of 72 boys and girls into one of three deprivation conditions: social and sensory, social, and nondeprivation. It was indicated that the results of boys who were placed in the social deprivation condition were similar to boys who were placed in the nondeprivation condition. Girls placed in the social deprivation condition scored more similarly to girls placed in sensory and social deprivation (Hill & Stevenson, 1964). In both studies, females were more likely to experience negative effects from SD.

The psychological effects of SD have also been analyzed. Zubek, Hughes, and Shephard (1971) compared the effects of SD and perceptual deprivation (PD) in 61 males. Subjects were placed in one of three groups for four days. Compared to the control group, those who were placed in the SD and PD groups reported significantly higher occurrences of persistent and vivid dreams, visual hallucinations, inefficient thought processes, subjective restlessness, and temporal disorientation. There were no significant differences between the SD and PD groups. The PD group showed a significantly better attitude than the SD and control groups toward the experimenters. Tetlock and Suedfeld (1976) analyzed the effects of SD and attitude centrality upon belief instability. It was found that subjects placed in SD for 24 hours demonstrated greater belief instability related to central and peripheral attitudes. Intelligence and conceptual complexity measures did not have a significant correlation with instability. The psychological effects from SD are generally found to be negative.

Findings related to the cognitive effects of SD appear to be inconsistent. Studies have generally indicated the presence of one of the three following patterns: SD causes intellectual impairment, SD causes intellectual improvement, or SD has no impact on intellectual performance (Suedfeld, 1968). It has been indicated that low presensory deprivation scores on a cognitive test are predictive of sensory deprivation intolerance (Fuerst & Zubek, 1968). Another study found an interaction between task complexity and drive arousal, which is linked to differential performance on complex tasks (Suedfeld, 1968). Rossi, Nathan, Harrison, and Solomon (1969) presented slide series, differing in levels of meaning, to student nurses in SD and control conditions. It was found that rates of responding were higher for more meaningful slides in both conditions, but for less meaningful slides, response rates were higher for those in the deprivation condition. MacNeil and Rule (1970) sought to determine if people who vary in conceptual structure differed in their preference for simple or complex messages while placed in SD. Those who were classified as concrete subjects were more likely to request the simple message over the complex message, while those who classified as abstract were more likely to request the complex message. These findings have demonstrated inconsistencies in the findings of the effects of SD on cognitive functioning.

Experimental studies of solitary confinement have been conducted in actual isolation cells within prisons. Walters, Callagan, and Newman (1963) analyzed a group of long-term prisoners who volunteered to serve four days in an isolation cell. Compared to nonisolated prisoners, isolated prisoners reported increased anxiety levels following the posttest period.

Isolated prisoners were also found to rate the concepts of "solitary" more positively, while "society" was rated more negatively. They were also found to have reduced levels of verbal productivity. In another study, Grassian (1983) interviewed 14 inmates who were placed in solitary confinement to determine the presence of psychological effects. It was found that inmates demonstrated various defense mechanisms to minimize their reactions to isolation, including rationalization, denial, avoidance, repression, and distortion. Other symptoms which were experienced among the inmates included hypersensitivity to external stimuli, hallucinations, massive free-floating anxiety, impulse control problems, and difficulties with thinking, concentration, and memory.

More recent studies have further examined the effects of solitary confinement on inmates. In their review of the literature, Bonta and Gendreau (1990) found inconclusive evidence to demonstrate the *pains of imprisonment*. They suggested that future research should focus on individual differences of such effects. Smith (2006) analyzed previous studies of individual effects of solitary confinement that have found a wide range of serious psychological and physiological effects on inmates, including insomnia, confusion, hallucinations, anger, and impaired memory. The conditions of solitary confinement may vary and can have an impact on the effects which are experienced. A recent study which analyzed historical findings in a group of Danish prisoners from 1870 through 1920 found that psychiatrists believed that mental disorders were caused by biological traits instead of situational factors. Prison conditions were downplayed and biological degeneration was used as an alternative explanation to describe the effects of solitary confinement (Smith, 2008). Although solitary confinement is generally found to have negative effects, this may vary from individual to individual.

Two studies analyzed groups of Canadian inmates. In one study, solitary confinement inmates scored lower on the California Psychological Inventory, particularly on scales measuring socialization and conformity, but no consistent significant differences were found between inmates in the general population and those placed in solitary confinement (Suedfeld, Ramirez, Deaton, & Baker-Brown, 1982). Most inmates placed in solitary confinement did not report extreme stress levels or unpleasantness, but what unpleasantness was experienced centered on complaints of mistreatment or limited amenities rather than sensory or social deprivation. Inmates with higher measured levels of intelligence were found to adapt to solitary confinement differently, but the groups did not differ on how tolerable they reported conditions to be (Suedfeld et al., 1982). Another study included 60 inmates who were either voluntarily or involuntarily placed in solitary confinement, or were selected from the general inmate population over a 60-day time period. Inmates in the segregated (96%) and nonsegregated (87%) groups had previously experienced solitary confinement, indicating a prior negative impact on mental health. When given the NEO Five-Factor Personality Inventory (Costa and McCrae, 1992), segregated inmates were found to score higher than nonsegregated inmates on levels of Neuroticism, indicating that they are more likely to experience negative effects such as sadness, fear, and the inability to cope with stress. However, inmates who scored highly in this domain appeared to adapt and cope with placement in solitary confinement. Segregated inmates scored lower than nonsegregated inmates on the Extraversion, Openness, Agreeableness, and Conscientiousness scales (Zinger, Wichmann, & Andrews, 2001). The psychological functioning of segregated inmates did not reveal any deterioration over the 60-day time period.

Some studies have questioned the effects of segregation on mental health by suggesting that some people are less resilient to change due to their personality or because of a preexisting mental illness. Glancy and Murray (2006) reviewed the literature on the effects of the placement of inmates in solitary confinement. Overall, the research reviewed in this study did not indicate the presence of negative mental health effects from solitary confinement. There was very little evidence to conclude that most inmates kept in solitary confinement for various reasons would experience mental health effects as a result. However, some inmates may be vulnerable to mental health effects due to their preexisting personality organization, mental disorders, or individual circumstances.

Placement in segregation may result in increased levels of psychological distress and decreased contact with mental health professionals. Miller (1994) analyzed 30 male inmates who were placed in one of three levels of housing in a federal correctional facility: general population, administrative detention, and disciplinary segregation. It was found that the level of psychological distress that inmates experience varies depending on the level of restriction, with increased restrictions leading to increased levels of psychological distress and symptomology. A later study by Miller and Young (1997) once again compared these three groups of inmates.

Compared to inmates in the general population, inmates placed in disciplinary segregation were found to experience more feelings and thoughts of inadequacy, withdrawal, inferiority, and isolation. They were also more likely to report feelings and thoughts of anger, aggression, and resentment than inmates in the general population as well as those housed in administrative detention (Miller and Young, 1997). However, it could not be determined if these characteristics existed prior to their placement or as an effect of segregation placement.

Suicide is a very serious effect which may result from segregation. Suicide is a relatively infrequent occurrence in prisons, with suicide rates in state prisons at approximately 14 per 100,000 as of 2002 (Mumola, 2005). Hayes (1997) summarized nine suicides that occurred over a two-year period in a large municipal jail which had a suicide rate that was above average. Five of the victims were found to have a past history of suicidal behavior or psychiatric treatment resulting in placement in a forensic unit. A significant finding was that eight of these cases involved placement in protective custody. He, Felthous, Holzer, Nathan, and Veasey (2001) analyzed the characteristics of suicide victims and the presence of mental disorders. Between June 1996 and June 1997, 25 suicides occurred within the Texas Department of Criminal Justice (TDCJ) Prison System. It was found that 15 (60%) of the victims were diagnosed with a psychiatric illness prior to incarceration. The percentage of inmates in this sample who suffered from a psychiatric disorder while incarcerated increased to 76%. The most common psychiatric disorders occurring among the suicide victims were mood disorders (64%), personality disorders (56%), and psychotic disorders (44%). High rates of drug and alcohol abuse (68% each) were also found to increase the risk of suicide.

Common acute and chronic stressors experienced which may have contributed to suicide include disrupted relationship, sentence hearings, undesired placement, and conflicts with other inmates (He, Felthous, Holzer, Nathan, & Veasey, 2001). Two studies (Way, Miraglia, Sawyer, Beer, & Eddy, 2005; Way, Sawyer, Barboza, & Nash, 2007) focused on suicide victims from New York prisons. Way and colleagues (2005) analyzed mental health records of 76 suicide victims who had committed suicide in prison between 1993 and 2001 and found that risk factors which contributed to suicide included agitation, prison stressors, substance abuse, mental illness, being in a single cell, and a history of violent offenses. Way and colleagues (2007) found that most suicides occurred within eight weeks of placement in special disciplinary housing units. Slow deterioration of mental health did not appear to have an impact on the occurrence of suicide for inmates housed in these units. The researchers suggest that other triggers for these inmates should be explored in future studies.

Inmates who are placed in segregation are not only separated from the remainder of the prison population, but they are generally excluded from much of the normal programming, routines, and activities available to inmates who are housed in the mainstream institution (Haney, 2003a). Exercise, dining, religious activities, and access to personal belongings are all extremely limited. Furthermore, segregated inmates usually have very few opportunities for employment and participation in educational and therapeutic programming (Arrigo & Bullock, 2008). The level of activity and program participation that is allowed for segregated inmates varies from one jurisdiction to another. In some prisons, such programming is available to inmates in order to improve their behavior, skills, and knowledge, while some prisons do not provide any type of programming for segregated inmates. Those which provide educational programs do so in one of several ways. Some prisons allow televisions in cells which provide education and programming through closed circuit television. This is sometimes supplemented with instructors who provide assistance through cell-front visits. There are other prisons which permit classes in rooms that are in close proximity to housing units. Work activities are generally not allowed; however, opportunities for employment are available for inmates preparing for release from the segregated environment. Exercise in most prisons is limited to three to seven times per week for one-hour intervals for protective custody inmates. Inmates are escorted to and from the exercise area by two or more correctional officers, which involves considerable number of staff per week. During this time, inmates are more likely to demonstrate combative or resistive behavior or the exchange of contraband (Riveland, 1999).

The effects of program deprivation are summarized by Pizarro and Stenius (2004). They found that when inmates were placed in restrictive environments for extended periods of time, they tended to develop significant psychological problems or experience an exacerbation of symptoms from existing problems, but the extent of such problems was unclear. It is suggested that segregated inmates who are housed in such facilities for long periods of time and do not have access to social activities or programming should experience the most significant effects from segregation, but this may also depend on the inmate's characteristics. Because the findings from these studies may vary due to small sample sizes, differing conditions of segregation, and differences in the length of confinement, it can be difficult to generalize their results to segregated inmates in other facilities.

Lovell, Johnson, and Cain (2007) compared a sample of supermax inmates to a matched sample of general population inmates on recidivism rates upon release. Results indicated that offenders who were released right from segregation (supermax) had higher recidivism rates and recidivated significantly quicker than general population inmates who were matched on mental health and criminal history variables. Additionally, the segregated inmates released directly into the community from supermax recidivated higher and at a more rapid rate than their colleagues in supermax who were provided a release from segregation (step down) three months prior to their prison release. The authors hypothesized that this effect may be due to segregation-inducing paranoia and social anxiety to the extent that it made the inmates being released right from segregation more likely to experience trouble adjusting to the free world and social society.

In one of the few longitudinal studies on the effects of segregation, O'Keefe, Klebe, Stucker, Sturm, and Leggett (2010) followed a sample of administrative segregation inmates for one year. The authors stated three goals for their study: (1) to determine which, if any, psychological domains were affected, and in which direction, by the prison conditions of administrative segregation and general population; (2) to assess whether inmates with mental illness deteriorate differentially from those without mental illness in the various prison conditions; and (3) to compare the impact of long-term segregation against the general prison setting and psychiatric care prison. Similar to previous research, the inmates housed in segregation were found to have more psychological and cognitive problems than inmates in the general population. However, the segregated inmates had these symptoms upon their placement. Additionally, these symptoms initially were lowered after being placed in segregation and remained fairly stable throughout the year. Thus, this study indicated that segregated conditions did not produce negative symptoms, nor did segregation make existing symptoms worsen.

Very little research has specifically addressed the effects of PC. One of the first studies focusing on PC inmates was conducted by Pierson (1987), who found that PC inmates tend to have more physical, psychological, and intellectual difficulties than inmates in the general population, which may increase their risk of experiencing harm. Another study was conducted by Brodsky and Scogin (1988), who conducted systematic psychological interviews with 69 male inmates housed in PC at three large, maximum-security institutions. They found psychopathological effects in approximately two thirds of inmates in PC at two of these institutions. In these institutions, inmates were not allowed to participate in vocational or educational programming and they were largely confined to their cells. Some of the effects which inmates reported included anxiety, depression, hallucinations and delusions, anger, physical symptoms, and sleep disturbances. In the third institution analyzed, there was sufficient cell space, inmates were allowed to participate in programming, and inmates were more mobile.

No adverse effects were found in inmates who were housed in PC at this institution (Brodsky & Scogin, 1988). These results indicated that PC itself is not necessarily damaging, but the impact of isolation and a restrictive environment has potential for negative effects.

Overall, segregation research has indicated that the effects of confinement may vary depending on the segregation environment and individual. For example, "the hole" is found to have effects akin to sensory deprivation, which has consistently demonstrated negative effects. Psychological, physical, and emotional effects of segregation which have been found in more recent studies include feelings of personal inadequacy, psychosocial adjustment problems, withdrawal, anxiety, depression, and suicide (Hayes, 1997; Miller & Young, 1997; Zinger et al., 2001). While many studies have found these effects in segregated inmates, other studies have found mixed results or did not indicate any effects which have resulted from segregation (Bonta & Gendreau, 1990; Glancy & Murray, 2006; O'Keefe et al., 2010; Suedfeld et al., 1982). Although the specific research on the effects of PC is sparse, it seems reasonable to conclude that the consequences of being placed in PC may be determined by specific segregation conditions and the previous psychological functioning of offenders placed there. Please see Box 9.4.

| Box 9.4 | **Crime and Punishment** |

Social scientist Craig Haney exposes the psychologically devastating conditions inside our nation's 'supermax' prisons.

By Jennifer McNulty

Craig Haney remembers the first time he saw William Wagner. It was during a tour of Pelican Bay, California's state-of-the-art high-security prison on the desolate north coast.

"I remember him because he was so dramatically psychotic," recalls Haney, a professor of psychology at University of California, Santa Cruz, who was gathering evidence for a lawsuit on conditions of solitary confinement inside Pelican Bay. "He was lying in the fetal position, disturbed and incoherent."

A longtime heroin addict whose criminal history consisted of drug-related theft, Wagner deteriorated in Pelican Bay. Along with nearly half the prison's population, he was held in solitary confinement, or so-called "supermax" conditions. "He was transferred to solitary for fighting, and after that he just unraveled and became catatonic," says Haney, an expert on the psychological effects of incarceration. Despite his obvious suffering, Wagner was never hospitalized or given proper treatment while he was incarcerated.

The next time Haney encountered Wagner, it was too late. Just five months after he was released from Pelican Bay, Wagner was facing capital murder charges for a slaying committed during a robbery in Sacramento. "Here was a man who had previously committed only nonviolent offenses stemming from his drug addiction, and within a few months on the streets, he was accused of committing capital murder," says Haney, whose testimony contributed to a judge's landmark ruling that conditions at Pelican Bay "may press the bounds of what most humans can psychologically tolerate."

We may never know for sure if the despair Wagner experienced while incarcerated contributed to the slaying, but the warehousing of unprecedented numbers of people has dramatically increased prison overcrowding and brutality while exhausting prison resources for medical and mental health services. Haney, whose research has documented the long-term psychological damage inmates are experiencing, warns that surging prison populations and deteriorating conditions are a dangerous combination.

Haney is quoted here saying:

A comprehensive assessment of the extensive clinical data collected on this issue, including the nature and extent of the psychic indices of stress employed, the unique and consistent psychopathological reactions that have been found, and the harmful secondary effects that have been documented in virtually every study on the question, point to the damaging psychological effects of punitive, isolated prison housing itself.....Direct studies of the effects of prison isolation have documented a wide range of harmful psychological effects, including increases in negative attitudes and affect, insomnia, anxiety, panic, withdrawal, hypersensitivity,

(Continued)

(Continued)

ruminations, cognitive dysfunction, hallucinations, loss of control, aggression, rage, paranoia, hopelessness, lethargy, depression, emotional breakdowns, self-mutilation, and suicidal impulses. ***There is not a single study of solitary confinement wherein non-voluntary confinement that lasted for longer than 10 days failed to result in negative psychological effects.***

Source: Based on "Crime & Punishment," Jennifer McNulty, *UC Santa Cruz Review* online. Summer 2000 issue. http://review.ucsc.edu/summer.00/crime_and_punishment.html

POLICY IMPLICATIONS

As the definition of segregation in general, and protective custody specifically, is different in each state, replication of existing research is warranted with detailed descriptions of segregation/protective custody details. Research is needed that explores how the different components and conditions of protective custody may impact inmates differently. The existing research is inconsistent (at best) on the effects of segregation, supermax, and protective custody conditions. Existing research is also quite sparse compared to many other aspects of the correctional experience. Much future research is warranted to truly understand the effects (both negative and positive) of protective custody. Research that incorporates both qualitative and quantitative data, including interviews, mental health records, and longitudinal analyses would provide additional knowledge on how inmates are impacted by confinement conditions.

Future research should also focus on the prison segregation environment. Inmates at certain levels of segregation may have an increased likelihood for acting out or experiencing psychological problems. If inmates demonstrate psychological problems, the use of less restrictive environments for punishment, protection, or administrative purposes could potentially reduce the number of problems within segregation units and decrease inmate problems after release from segregation. It has been indicated that there may be a level of segregation that, rather than solving mental health problems, becomes a mental health issue and a problem for prison officials (Miller & Young, 1997). Changing the segregation environment may reduce the number of problems faced by both inmates and prison administration.

The research on segregation, similar to the majority of correctional data overall, includes only male inmates. Similar research is needed with female inmates in protective custody as their pathways and effects of segregation may be very different than their male counterparts. Research has already indicated that female offenders have higher rates of mental illness and trauma-related backgrounds than male offenders (Green, Miranda, Daroowalla, & Siddique, 2005; McClellan, Farabee, & Couch, 1997; Zlotnik & Pearlstein, 1997). Additionally, research has indicated that female offenders are more likely than male offenders to utilize socialization and the development of "families" with their fellow female inmates (Colica, 2010; Owen, 1998; Severance, 2005) and this development of pseudo-family is helpful in their adjustment and functioning within prison. Given their higher rates of mental illness, histories of trauma, and need for social involvement, it may be that female inmates experience more deleterious effects of segregation or protective custody than male inmates. Future research is warranted to examine this hypothesis.

Although research indicates that the staff working in protective custody holds similar stigmatizing views toward protective custody inmates as the general population inmates, little research has examined the specific effects of staff interaction. Of the research that has included inmate staff interaction in segregation, authors have suggested that the adverse psychological effects of segregation are significantly related to the way inmates are treated by correctional staff (Bonta & Gendreau, 1995; Rogers, 1993; Suedfeld et al., 1982). Protective custody inmates have the most interaction with the correctional staff working in that unit, and as a result, that staff may have tremendous influence on the effects of this type of segregation on those inmates. Additionally, evaluation of protective custody staff training and intervention programs would greatly add to our understanding of the effects of staff interaction and long-term effects of protective custody. Segregation and PC-specific correctional staff must be appropriately trained and supervised. Staff could greatly benefit from training in conflict management, mental illness, and the effects of abusive treatment. The staff should also be held accountable for their interactions with PC inmates.

As correctional institutions are moving toward evidence-based models and practices to improve the rehabilitation opportunities for offenders, they have had to rely on more subjective and court decisions on how to handle protective custody. Future research in all the areas mentioned of PC would serve not only our scientific knowledge on the effects of segregation, but serve to provide evidence for correctional personnel to utilize in their PC policy and procedure decisions.

Research is both lacking, dated, and inconsistent in result for PC and segregation in general. Additionally, PC conditions vary across states and prison and jail systems. Thus, it is difficult to make specific policy recommendations for the procedures of protective custody. It is impossible to conclude whether protective custody serves its purpose without causing undue pain and punishment to the inmates housed under those segregated conditions. Research, does however inform that the least restrictive placement with access to programming and mental health resources has the best impact on protective custody inmates (e.g., Brodsky & Scogin, 1988; Pizarro & Stenius, 2004). Inmates who are placed in protective custody, solitary confinement, or other forms of segregation while in prison may experience negative effects. Some of these effects may be temporary, while others may be considered permanent if they are not properly addressed. In an attempt to alleviate these short-term and long-term effects, some policy implications should be taken into consideration. Time limits should be placed on the use of segregation (Haney, 2003a) as well as avoiding keeping inmates in isolation for 22 to 24 hours per day (Smith, 2006). Reducing the amount of time that the inmate is placed in segregation increases the likelihood of meaningful social contact and decreases the effects of segregation.

One result that is consistent across segregation research, whether it is administrative segregation, disciplinary detention, supermax, or protective custody, is the fact that there is a significantly higher level of inmates with mental health issues than in the general population of inmates (e.g., Lovell, 2008; Metzner & Fellner, 2010; O'Keefe, 2008). Additionally, research has indicated that conditions of segregation/protective custody can exacerbate the symptoms of mental illness (Kurki & Morris, 2001). Thus, an important policy recommendation is the inclusion of some sort of mental health assessment and intervention for inmates held in protective custody. To treat and possibly improve mental health services for protective custody inmates is an important reality facing corrections agencies. Research informs that it is important to screen and assess inmates prior to their PC placement in order to determine their vulnerability to harm that may occur as a result of their segregation as well as to serve as a baseline for continued or exacerbated mental health issues while housed in PC. While in PC, it is important to continue to assess mental health functioning on an ongoing basis and provide some sort of services to those inmates who are experiencing deleterious effects of segregation. Zinger, Wichmann, and Andrews (2001) suggest that psychologists should conduct more elaborate assessments which could detect minor or less obvious forms of deterioration that would not be as easily detected when a standard form is utilized, one that only highlights general mental health issues.

Besides general mental health services for PC inmates, there is a large majority of sexual offenders housed in PC. It is recommended that treatment services be also offered to these offenders as research has indicated that it can reduce the likelihood of recidivism (e.g., Hanson, Bourgon, Helmus, & Hodgson, 2009). In many states there are specific treatment program units for sexual offenders. For example, in the Texas Department of Criminal Justice, there are two units that serve as treatment programs for male sexual offenders and one for female sexual offenders. If it is possible, sexual offenders should be transferred out of PC to these types of units where they will receive treatment, not have to be housed in a segregated status, and will not have the threat of nonsexual offending inmates harming them because of their offense. If this type of unit is not available, it is recommended that the sexual offenders housed in PC have access to sexual offender treatment services.

Research has also reported the positive effects of programming participation for inmates in general (Colvin, 1992; McCorkle, Miethe, & Drass, 1995; Shoferr, 1999). To reduce the possibility of negative effects of segregation, increased inmate participation in rehabilitation, education, and work training programs would promote a more tolerable atmosphere for both inmates and correctional staff. Participation in such programs can provide inmates with relevant skills along with a sense of meaning, which can be beneficial for successful reintegration into society (Huey & McNulty, 2005). Institutions with a variety of programs should be established which give inmates an opportunity to engage in meaningful activities (Haney, 2003b). Inmates who participate in these programs would most likely have a decreased likelihood of negative effects from their segregated experience as well as an increased likelihood of succeeding in the free-world upon release from prison.

DISCUSSION QUESTIONS

1. How does protective custody differ from other forms of inmate segregation?

2. What are the major types of inmates placed in protective custody and why?

3. What have been the leading legal arguments that have directed the procedure and conditions of protective custody?

4. What were some of the psychological and cognitive effects that were found in early experimental studies of sensory deprivation?

5. One of the most serious effects resulting from segregation in prisons is suicide. What are some of the risk factors that may increase an inmate's likelihood of committing suicide?

6. From what we know now about protective custody effects and policy, what are the next research steps?

SUGGESTED READINGS

Angelone, R. (1999). Protective custody inmates. In P. Carlson & J. Garrett (Eds), *Prison and jail administration: Practice and theory.* Gaithersburg, MD: Aspen.

Barak-Glantz, I. L. (1983). Who's in the hole? *Criminal Justice Review, 8,* 29–37.

Brodsky, S. T., & Scogin, F. R. (1988). Inmates in protective custody: First data on emotional effects. *Forensic Reports, 1,* 267–280.

Grassian, S. (2006). Psychiatric effects of solitary confinement. *Washington University Journal of Law and Policy, 22,* 325–383.

Miller, K. L. (2010). The darkest figure of crime: Perceptions of reasons for male inmates to not report sexual assault. *Justice Quarterly, 27*(5), 692–712.

O'Keefe, M. L., Klebe, K. J., Stucker, A., Sturm, K., & Leggett, W. (2011). *One year longitudinal study of the psychological effects of administrative segregation.* NCJ 232973. Retrieved from http://www.ncjrs.gov/pdffiles1/nij/grants/232973.pdf

Robertson, J. E. (1987). The constitution in protective custody: An analysis of the rights of protective custody inmates. *University of Cincinnati Law Review, 56,* 91–143.

Robertson, J. E. (1999). Cruel and unusual punishment in United States prisons: Sexual harassment among male inmates. *The American Criminal Law Review, 36,* 1–51.

Smith, P. S. (2006). The effects of solitary confinement on prison inmates: A brief history and review of the literature. *Crime and Justice, 34,* 441–528.

Wormith, J. S., Tellier, M., & Gendreau, P. (1988). Characteristics of protective custody offenders in a Provincial correctional centre. *Canadian Journal of Criminology, 30*(1), 39–58.

Zinger, I., Wichmann, C., & Andrews, D. A. (2001). The psychological effects of 60 days in administrative segregation. *Canadian Journal of Criminology and Criminal Justice, 43*(1), 47–83.

REFERENCES

Alarid, L. F. (2000). Sexual orientation perspectives of incarcerated bisexual and gay men: The county jail protective custody experience. *The Prison Journal, 80*(1), 80–95. American Correctional Association.

American Correctional Association. Standards and accreditation: Seeking accreditation: *Glossary of terms.* Available at http://www.aca.org

Anderson, D. C. (1980, August). Price of Safety—'I Can't Go Back Out There'. *Corrections Magazine, 6*(4), 6–15.

Anderson, J. (2007). Gang-related witness intimidation. *National Gang Center Bulletin, 1.* Retrieved from www.nationalgangcenter.gov/documents/NGCbulletin_ 207.pdf

Angelone, R. (1999). Protective custody inmates. In P. Carlson & J. Garrett (Eds), *Prison and jail administration: Practice and theory.* Gaithersburg, MD: Aspen.

Arkles, G. (2009). Safety and solidarity across gender lines: Rethinking segregation of transgender people in detention. *Temple Political & Civil Rights Law Review, 18,* 515–560.

Arrigo, B. A., & Bullock, J. L. (2008). The psychological effects of solitary confinement on prisoners in supermax units: Reviewing what we know and recommending what we should change. *International Journal of Offender Therapy and Comparative Criminology, 52*(6), 622–640.

Barak-Glantz, I. L. (1982). A decade of disciplinary, administrative, and protective control of inmates in the Washington State Penitentiary: A research note. *Journal of Criminal Justice, 10,* 481–492.

Beck, A. J., & Hughes, T. (2005). *Sexual violence reported by correctional authorities, 2004.* NCJ 210333. Washington, DC: U.S. Department of Justice, Bureau of Justice Statistics.

Blackburn, A., Mullings, J., & Marquart, J. (2008). Sexual assault in prison and beyond: Toward an understanding of lifetime sexual assault among incarcerated women. *The Prison Journal, 88,* 351–377.

Blatchford, C. (2008). *The black hand: The story of Rene "Boxer" Enriquez and his life in the Mexican Mafia.* New York, NY: HarperCollins.

Bonta, J., & Gendreau, P. (1990). Reexamining the cruel and unusual punishment of prison life. *Law and Human Behavior, 14*(4), 347–372.

Bonta, J., & Gendreau, P. (1995). Reexamining the cruel and unusual punishment of prison life. In T. J. Flanagan (Ed.), *Long-term imprisonment: Policy, science, and correctional practice* (pp. 75–94). Thousand Oaks, CA: Sage.

Boucouvalas, M., & Pearse, P. R. (1985). Educating the protective custody inmate for self-directness: An adult learning contract approach. *Journal of Correctional Education, 36*(3), 98–105.

Brodsky, S. T., & Scogin, F. R. (1988). Inmates in protective custody: First data on emotional effects. *Forensic Reports, 1,* 267–280.

Carlson, P. M., & Garrett, J. S. (2008). *Prison and jail administration: Practice and theory* (2nd ed.). Sudbury, MA: Jones and Bartlett.

Colica, K. (2010). Surviving incarceration: Two prison-based peer programs build communities of support for female offenders. *Deviant Behavior, 31*(4), 314–347.

Colvin, M. (1992). *The penitentiary in crisis.* Albany: State University of New York Press.

Costa, P. T., & McCrae, R. R. (1992). *Revised NEO personality inventory and NEO five-factor inventory professional manual.* Odessa, FL: Psychological Assessment Resources.

Ditton, P. M. (1999). *Mental health and treatment of inmates and probationers.* Washington DC: U.S. Department of Justice, Bureau of Justice Statistics.

Dumond, R. (1992). The sexual assault of male inmates in incarcerated settings. *International Journal of the Sociology of Law, 20,* 135–157.

Dumond, R. (2000). Inmate sexual assault: The plague that persists. *Prison Journal, 80,* 407–414.

Edney, R. (2009). To keep me safe from harm? Transgender prisoners and the experience of imprisonment. *Deakin Law Review, 9*(2), 327–338.

Estelle v. Gamble, 429 U.S. 97 (1976).

Fuerst, K., & Zubek, J. P. (1968). Effects of sensory and perceptual deprivation on a battery of open-ended cognitive tasks. *Canadian Journal of Psychology, 22*(2), 122–130.

Gaes, G. G. (1985). The effects of overcrowding in prisons. *Crime and Delinquency, 6,* 95–146.

Glancy, G. D., & Murray, E. L. (2006). The psychiatric aspects of solitary confinement. *Victims and Offenders, 1*(4), 361–368.

Grassian, S. (1983). Psychopathological effects of solitary confinement. *American Journal of Psychiatry, 140*(11), 1450–1454.

Green, B. L., Miranda, J., Daroowalla, A., & Siddique, J. (2005). Trauma exposure, mental health functioning and program needs of women in jail. *Crime and Delinquency, 51,* 133–151.

Haney, C. (2003a). Mental health issues in long-term solitary and "supermax" confinement. *Crime & Delinquency, 49*(1), 124–156.

Haney, C. (2003b). The psychological impact of incarceration: Implications for post-prison adjustment. In J. Travis & M. Waul (Eds.), *Prisoners once removed: The impact of incarceration and reentry on children, families, and communities* (pp. 33–66). Washington DC: Urban Institute Press.

Hanson, K. R., Bourgon, G., Helmus, L., & Hodgson, S. (2009). The principles of effective correctional treatment also apply to sexual offenders: A meta-analysis. *Criminal Justice and Behavior, 39*(9), 865–891.

Hayes, L. (1997). From chaos to calm: One jail system's struggle with suicide prevention. *Behavioral Sciences and the Law, 15*(4), 399–413.

He, X. Y., Felthous, A. R., Holzer, C. E., Nathan, P., & Veasey, S. (2001). Factors in prison suicide: One year study in Texas. *Journal of Forensic Science, 46*(4), 896–901.

Henderson, J. (1990). *Protective custody management in adult correctional facilities: A discussion of causes, conditions, attitudes, and alternatives.* Washington, DC: National Institute of Corrections.

Hill, K. T., & Stevenson, H. W. (1964). Effectiveness of social reinforcement following social and sensory deprivation. *Journal of Abnormal and Social Psychology, 68*(6), 579–584.

Huey, M. P., & McNulty, T. L. (2005). Institutional conditions and prison suicide: Conditional effects of deprivation and overcrowding. *The Prison Journal, 85*(4), 490–514.

Jackson, C. W., & Pollard, J. C. (1962). Sensory deprivation and suggestion: A theoretical approach. *Behavioral Science, 7*(3), 332–342.

Jacobs, J. B. (1982, March/April). Limits of racial integration in prison. *Criminal Law Bulletin 18*(2), 117–153.

Kurki, L., & Morris, N. (2001). The purposed, practices, and problems of supermax prisons. *Crime and Justice: A Review of Research, 28,* 385–424.

Landman v. Royster, 333 F. Supp (E.D. Va. 1971).

Lovell, D. (2008). Patterns of disturbed behavior in a supermax population. *Criminal Justice and Behavior, 35*(8), 985–1004.

Lovell, D., Johnson, L. C., & Cain, K. C. (2007). Recidivism of supermax prisoners in Washington State. *Crime and Delinquency, 53,* 633–656.

MacNeil, L. W., & Rule, B. G. (1970). Effects of conceptual structure on information preference under sensory-deprivation conditions. *Journal of Personality and Social Psychology, 16*(3), 530–535.

McClellan, D. S., Farabee, D., & Crouch, B. M. (1997). Early victimization, drug use, and criminality: A comparison of male and female prisoners. *Criminal Justice and Behavior, 24,* 455–476.

McCorkle, R., Miethe, T., & Drass, K. (1995). The roots of prison violence: A test of the deprivation, management, and not-so-total institution models. *Crime & Delinquency, 41,* 317–331.

Metzner, J. L., & Fellner, J. (2010). Solitary confinement and mental illness in U.S. prisons: A challenge for medical ethics. *Journal of the American Academy of Psychiatry and Law, 38*(1), 104–108.

Miller, H. A. (1994). Reexamining psychological distress in the current conditions of segregation. *Journal of Correctional Health Care, 1*(2), 39–53.

Miller, H. A., & Young, G. R. (1997). Prison segregation: Administrative detention remedy or mental health problem? *Criminal Behaviour and Mental Health, 7*(1), 85–94.

Mumola, C. (2005). *Suicide and homicide in state prisons and local jails.* NCJ 210036. Washington, DC: U.S. Department of Justice, Bureau of Justice Statistics.

O'Keefe, M. L. (2008). Administrative segregation from within: A corrections perspective. *The Prison Journal, 88*(1), 123–143.

O'Keefe, M. L., Klebe, K. J., Stucker, A., Sturm, K., & Leggett, W. (2010). *One year longitudinal study of the psychological effects of administrative segregation.* Washington, DC: U.S. Department of Justice, Office of Justice Programs.

O'Keefe, M. L., & Schnell, M. (2008). Offenders with mental illness in the correctional system. *Journal of Offender Rehabilitation, 45,* 81–104.

Owen, B. (1998). *In the mix: Struggle and survival in a women's prison.* Albany: State University of New York Press.

Pierson, T. A. (1987). Protective custody: The Missouri experience with comparative state analysis. NCJ 111314. Jefferson City: Missouri Department of Corrections and Human Resources.

Pizarro, J., & Stenius, V. M. K. (2004). Supermax prisons: Their rise, current practices, and effect on inmates. *The Prison Journal, 84*(2), 248–264.

Reiter, K. (2010). *Parole, snitch, or die: California's supermax prisons & prisoners, 1987–2007.* University of California, Berkeley: Institute for the Study of Social Change. Retrieved from: http://escholarship.org/uc/item/04w6556f

Riveland, C. (1999). *Supermax prisons: Overview and general considerations.* Washington, DC: U.S. Department of Justice, National Institute of Corrections.

Robertson, J. E. (1987). The Constitution in protective custody: An analysis of the rights of protective custody inmates. *University of Cincinnati Law Review, 56,* 91–143.

Rogers, R. (1993). Solitary confinement. *International Journal of Offender Therapy and Comparative Criminology, 37*(4), 339–349.

Roland v. Johnson, 856 F.2d 764 (6th Cir. 1988).

Rossi, A. M., Nathan, P. E., Harrison, R. H., & Solomon, P. (1969). Operant responding for visual stimuli during sensory deprivation: Effect of meaningfulness. *Journal of Abnormal Psychology, 74*(2), 188–192.

Severance, T. A. 2005. "You know who you can go to": Cooperation and exchange between incarcerated women. *Prison Journal, 85*(3), 343–367. Thousand Oaks, CA: Sage.

Sexton, L., Jenness, V., & Sumner, J. M. (2010). Where the margins meet: A demographic assessment of transgender inmates in men's prisons. *Justice Quarterly, 27*(6), 835–866.

Shalev, S. (2008). *A sourcebook on solitary confinement.* London, England: Mannheim Centre for Criminology.

Shoferr, S. (1999). The freedom from violence program: An untraditional approach to violence management. *International Journal of Offender Therapy and Comparative Criminology, 43*, 49–60.

Smith, P. S. (2006). The effects of solitary confinement on prison inmates: A brief history and review of the literature. *Crime and Justice, 34*, 441–528.

Smith, P. S. (2008). Degenerate criminals: Mental health and psychiatric studies of Danish prisoners in solitary confinement, 1870–1920. *Criminal Justice and Behavior, 35*(8), 1048–1064.

Suedfeld, P. (1968). The cognitive effects of sensory deprivation: The role of task complexity. *Canadian Journal of Psychology, 22*(4), 302–307.

Suedfeld, P., Ramirez, C., Deaton, J., & Baker-Brown, G. (1982). Reactions and attributes of prisoners in solitary confinement. *Criminal Justice and Behavior, 9*(3), 303–340.

Tetlock, P. E., & Suedfeld, P. (1976). Inducing belief instability without a persuasive message: The roles of attitude centrality, individual cognitive differences, and sensory deprivation. *Canadian Journal of Behavioral Science, 8*(4), 324–333.

Thomson, R., Nored, L., & Dial, K. (2008). The prison rape elimination act (PREA): An evaluation of policy compliance with illustrative excerpts. *Criminal Justice Policy Review, 19*, 414–437.

Toch, H. (2001). The future of supermax confinement. *Prison Journal, 81*(3), 376–388.

U.S. Department of Justice. (2011). National standards to prevent, detect, and respond to prison rape (28 CFR Part 115), *Federal Register, 76*, 6248–6302.

Walters, R. H., Callagan, J. E., & Newman, A. F. (1963). Effect of solitary confinement on prisoners. *American Journal of Psychiatry, 119*, 771–773.

Way, B. B., Miraglia, R., Sawyer, D. A., Beer, R., & Eddy, J. (2005). Factors related to suicide in New York state prisons. *International Journal of Law and Psychiatry, 28*(3), 207–221.

Way, B. B., Sawyer, D. A., Barboza, S., & Nash, R. (2007). Inmate suicide and time spent in special disciplinary housing in New York state prison. *Psychiatric Services, 58*(4), 558–560.

Wolff, N., & Shi, J. (2009). Victimization and feelings of safety among male and female inmates with behavioral problems. *The Journal of Forensic Psychiatry & Psychology, 20*(S1), 56–77.

Wooden, W. S., & Parker, J. (1982). *Men behind bars: Sexual exploitation in prison.* New York, NY: Plenum.

Woodhouse v. Virginia, 478 F.2d 889 (4th Cir. 1973).

Wooldredge, J. (1996). Research note: A state-level analysis of sentencing policies and inmate crowding in state prisons. *Crime & Delinquency, 42*, 456–466.

Wormith, J. S., Tellier, M., & Gendreau, P. (1988). Characteristics of protective custody offenders in a Provincial correctional centre. *Canadian Journal of Criminology, 30*(1), 39–58.

Young v. Quinlan, 960 F.2d 351 (1991).

Zinger, I., Wichmann, C., & Andrews, D. A. (2001). The psychological effects of 60 days in administrative segregation. *Canadian Journal of Criminology and Criminal Justice, 43*(1), 47–83.

Zlotnik, C., & Pearlstein, T. (1997). Posttraumatic stress disorder (PTSD) comorbidity, and childhood abuse among incarcerated women. *Journal of Nervous and Mental Disease, 185*, 761–763.

Zubek, J. P., Hughes, G. R., & Shephard, J. M. (1971). A comparison of the effects of prolonged sensory deprivation and perceptual deprivation. *Canadian Journal of Behavioral Science, 3*(3), 282–290.

Zuckerman, M., Persky, H., Link, K. E., & Basu, G. K. (1968). Experimental and subject factors determining responses to sensory deprivation, social isolation, and confinement. *Journal of Abnormal Psychology, 73*(3), 183–194.

CHAPTER 10

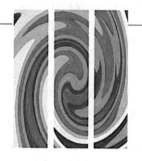

Sex Offenders Behind Bars: Considerations for Assessment and Treatment

Christian Maile, Cynthia Calkins-Mercado, and Elizabeth Jeglic

INTRODUCTION

Recent estimates suggest there are over 600,000 sex offenders registered in the United States (National Center for Missing and Exploited Children, 2007). The impact of these offenders' crimes has affected a significant proportion of the population. According to one recent national epidemiological study, 32.3% of women and 14.2% of men reported experiencing some form of childhood sexual abuse (Briere & Elliott, 2003). Furthermore, research indicates that approximately 12.7% of adult women will be raped at some point in their lives (Resnick, Acierno, Holmes, Kilpatrick, & Jager, 1999). As a result of sexual assault and abuse, many victims experience negative psychological sequelae such as depression, substance abuse/dependence, and posttraumatic stress disorder (PTSD) (Chapman, Dube, & Anda, 2007; Letourneau, Resnick, Kilpatrick, Saunders, & Best, 1996; Resnick et al., 1999). It is clear that sexual assault and abuse represent a serious social problem.

A considerable amount of research has been conducted in an attempt to better understand the nature of sex offending. Our understanding of the characteristics and etiology of sex offending has grown enormously over the last two decades. Similarly, over the last 15–20 years, substantial advancements have been made in our ability to predict reoffending among sex offenders and promising treatments have been developed that have been found to be effective in reducing reoffending (Lindsay, Hogue, Taylor, Steptoe, Mooney, O'Brien, et al., 2008; Ward, Mann, & Gannon, 2007). Despite advances in assessment and treatment technologies for sex offenders, there has been a growing realization that current assessment, treatment, and risk management models may not be generalizable to all sex offenders. Research has demonstrated that sex offenders are a heterogeneous group (Nezu, Greenberg, & Nezu, 2006). Consequently, there is limited research detailing the special assessment, treatment, and risk management needs of understudied subgroups of sex offenders such as adolescent, female, intellectually disabled, and internet sex offenders, and sexually violent predators (SVPs).

Adolescents are responsible for a significant proportion of sexual assaults (Pastore & Maguire, 2007; U.S. Department of Justice, 2008) and the number of treatment programs specifically designated for treating this subgroup of offenders has proliferated over the last 20 years (Smallbone, Crissman, & Rayment-McHugh, 2009). This subgroup of sex offenders has unique developmental needs that are not met by traditional adult-oriented sex offender assessment and treatment programs; accordingly, adult-oriented programs have been adapted for use with adolescent sex offenders.

Female sex offenders, although representing only a small proportion of the sex offender population (Cortoni, 2009), have been receiving increasing clinical and empirical attention. Although there is scant literature available regarding female sex offenders, it has been acknowledged that current assessment, treatment, and risk management paradigms, developed and validated for male sex offenders, may not be appropriate for use with this subgroup of offenders (Vandiver & Walker, 2002).

Some research indicates that intellectual disability (ID) is more common among sex offenders than among general population members (Hayes, 2002). Revised approaches to the assessment, treatment, and risk management of sex offenders with ID have been developed to accommodate their cognitive limitations, and preliminary research on these approaches appears promising (Lindsay, Marshall, Neilson, Quinn, & Smith, 1998; Lindsay, Ollie, Baillie, & Smith, 1999; O'Connor, 1996; Rose, Jenkins, O'Connor, Jones, & Felce, 2002).

Recent research indicates that that although internet sex offenders may share some characteristics with prototypical sex offenders, they may have unique etiological determinants and behavior patterns that may have important implications for their management and treatment (Seto, Hanson, & Babchishin, 2011; Wolak, Finkelhor, Mitchell, & Ybarra, 2010).

Finally, sexually violent predators (SVPs), sex offenders deemed to be at the highest risk for reoffense and requiring civil commitment, constitute a small, but growing subgroup of offenders warranting special treatment and management consideration.

The purpose of this chapter is to provide a brief overview of research investigating the limitations of current assessment, treatment, and risk management approaches with these specific subgroups of offenders. A brief overview of the unique challenges faced by sex offenders in navigating the correctional system and how this relates to the effective assessment and treatment of this offender population is presented. Current approaches to assessment, treatment, and risk management of prototypical sex offenders will then be reviewed, followed by discussion of special considerations regarding the treatment and management issues specific to each of these subgroups of sex offenders.

SEX OFFENDERS AND THE PRISON ENVIRONMENT

Before presenting current sex offender assessment and treatment techniques, a brief discussion regarding the unique challenges faced by sex offenders within the prison system and how these challenges may impact evaluation and treatment engagement is warranted.

It is well known that sex offenders—criminals who offend against the most vulnerable members of society (i.e., women and children)—are among the most vilified of criminals; even among other offenders, they are viewed with disdain and disgust (Schwaebe, 2005). As a result, while incarcerated, sex offenders are often subject to considerable ridicule, harassment, and even physical and sexual violence at the hands of other non-sex offenders (Palermo, 2005; Palermo & Farkas, 2001). Research and anecdotal evidence suggest that many sex offenders, in an effort to avoid the harassment and abuse that would result being identified as a sex offender, may go to great lengths to the hide the nature of their offenses from other inmates (Schwaebe, 2005).

Of particular relevance, sex offenders may refuse to participate in sex offender-specific treatment to prevent their identity as sex offenders from being revealed to other inmates (Schwaebe, 2005). Even when sex offenders do agree to participate in treatment programs, they may be reluctant to disclose details relevant to their treatment (e.g., deviant sexual preferences, additional prior sex offenses, etc.) for fear these details may be divulged to other inmates by fellow group members. Sex offenders, by virtue of their identity, are placed in a difficult situation. On the one hand they are encouraged, and often required, to provide complete disclosure in order to participate meaningfully in treatment, while on the other, they are aware that disclosing certain details or even attending sex offender treatment, despite institutional effort to ensure confidentiality, may result in their sex offender status being revealed.

Although it may be difficult to help sex offenders overcome these challenges, separating sex offenders from the prison general population may reduce stigmatization of a sex offender identity and may help to circumvent some of these issues. Even when this is not feasible, it is important for mental health professionals involved in providing services to sex offenders to be aware of how the prison environment may influence engagement in evaluation and rehabilitation efforts (Palermo, 2005; Schwaebe, 2005).

Sex Offender Assessment and Treatment Overview

Research and application of sex offender assessment and treatment has evolved substantially over the last few decades (Ward et al., 2007). Particular growth has taken place in the area of risk assessment, with the field progressing from reliance on subjective clinical judgment to the development and utilization of sophisticated actuarial risk assessment instruments that incorporate both static and dynamic risk factors for recidivism (Lindsay et al., 2008). There have also been advancements in the development and implementation of sex offender treatment programs, with idiosyncratic treatment approaches being gradually replaced with more standardized treatment programs grounded in cognitive-behavioral and social learning theory.

Assessment for Treatment

An evaluation of recidivism risk is an important aspect of assessment for treatment placement. In fact, one of the principles of the Risk-Need-Responsivity model (Andrews & Bonta, 1998, 2007), a prominent offender treatment paradigm, described in more detail in the following section, stipulates that treatment intensity should match an offender's risk level. Numerous standardized risk assessment instruments have been developed to assist in the evaluation of recidivism risk among sex offenders and are routinely used to help make treatment decisions. Some of these tests require evaluators to combine weighted risk factor items to obtain total risk scores and probabilistic estimates of recidivism:

- The Sex Offender Risk Appraisal Guide—SORAG (Quinsey, Harris, Rice, & Cormier, 1998, 2006)
- The Rapid Risk Assessment for Sex Offense Recidivism—RRASOR (Hanson, 1997)
- The Minnesota Sex Offender Screening Tool-Revised—MnSOST-R (Epperson, Kaul, Huot, Hesselton, Alexander, & Goldman, 2000)
- The Static-99 (Hanson & Thornton, 2000)

Other instruments provide evaluators with a list of empirically validated factors associated with recidivism; structured clinical judgment is then used to determine a general level of recidivism risk:

- The Sexual Violence Risk-20—SVR-20 (Boer, Hart, Kropp, & Webster, 1997)
- The Risk for Sexual Violence Protocol—RSVP (Hart, Kropp, Laws, Klaver, Logan, & Watt, 2003)

In addition to evaluations of risk, comprehensive assessments for treatment may entail assessments of personality such as the MMPI-II (Butcher, Graham, Ben-Porath, Tellegen, Dahlstrom, & Kaemmer, 2001) and cognitive functioning like the WAIS-IV (Wechsler, 2008). The data obtained from such assessments can provide valuable insight into an offender's personality structure, interpersonal style, and cognitive abilities which can help in the creation of individualized treatment plans. In particular, cognitive impairment may have important implications for treatment (as outlined later in the Intellectually Disabled Sex Offender section).

The assessment of deviant sexual arousal/preference is also an important component of accurate assessment for treatment, as offenders with deviant sexual preferences may require additional intervention in order to reduce recidivism. Specific instruments and methods have been developed for the assessment of deviant sexual arousal/preference. Self-report inventories such as Nichols and Molinder's (1984, 2000)

Multiphasic Sex Inventory-II (MSI-II) can be useful aids in assessing for deviant sexual history, as well as cognitive styles and behavioral/emotional traits associated with deviant sexual interest. Assessment tools that provide more direct measures of deviant sexual arousal and/or interest have also been used extensively with sex offenders, and may be particularly useful when the validity of self-reported information may be questionable. Two such measures are penile plethysmography (PPG) and the Abel Assessment for Sexual Interest (Abel, Huffman, Warberg, & Holland, 1998). PPG is a physical measure of deviant sexual arousal and measures growth in penile circumference in response to visual or aural sexual stimuli. The Abel Assessment for Sexual Interest is a computer-based program measuring deviant sexual interest. The program presents sexual images of children, juveniles, and adults of varying ages, measuring viewing time across stimulus images; comparison against normative viewing times is used to assess for deviant sexual interests, with longer viewing times suggesting greater sexual interest.

The assessment of offense-supportive beliefs and attitudes (also referred to as cognitive distortions) is another important domain to be assessed as part of a comprehensive evaluation. Several measures have been developed for this purpose. The Abel-Becker Cognition Scale or ABCS (Abel, Becker, & Cunningham-Rathner, 1984) and the Bumby MOLEST and RAPE scales (Bumby, 1996) are two examples of well-researched and commonly used measures for assessing offense-supportive cognitive distortions.

Treatment Models

Over the last three decades, several major cognitive-behavioral therapy-based (CBT-based) models of treatment have been specifically developed or adapted for use with sex offenders. These are the three most well-established models of treatment:

- The relapse prevention—RP model (Pithers, Marques, Gibat, & Marlatt, 1983; Marques & Nelson, 1989)
- The Risk-Need-Responsivity—RNR (Andrews & Bonta, 1998, 2007)
- The Good Lives Model—GLM (Ward & Stewart, 2003)

Relapse Prevention (RP) Model. The relapse prevention (RP) model was originally developed for use with substance abusers (Chaney, O'Leary, & Marlatt, 1978; Marlatt & Gordon, 1980, 1985), but has since been adapted for use with sex offenders (Pithers et al., 1983; Marques & Nelson, 1989). The primary objective in relapse prevention is to teach offenders about, and to help develop insight, into the offense chain or cycle. Offenders are taught to identify factors that led to their offense(s) and are provided with self-monitoring strategies so that they may proactively intervene to disrupt the offense cycle, preventing recidivism.

Although the RP model has served to advance the field of sex offender theory, treatment, and management (Keeling & Rose, 2005), there have been some serious criticisms leveled against it. Some critics have argued that the RP model provides an overly simplistic etiological theory of sex offending, specifying only one offense pathway for all offenders (Hanson, 2000; Laws, 2003; Ward & Hudson, 2000). Other researchers have criticized the lack of empirical support regarding its effectiveness in reducing recidivism among sex offenders (Marshall & Anderson, 1996). Finally, the RP model has been faulted for exclusively targeting criminogenic risk factors for change, ignoring other factors that may help sex offenders reintegrate more successfully into their communities and lead more meaningful, productive, and prosocial lives.

Risk-Need-Responsivity (RNR) Model. As the name of the treatment suggests, there are three core principles that make up the RNR model. The first principle, *risk,* asserts that the level or intensity of intervention should be commensurate with the offenders' assessed level of risk. That is, offenders deemed to be higher risk should receive more intense intervention services than sex offenders deemed to be lower risk. The second principle, *need,* asserts that interventions should target the unique dynamic risk factors, or criminogenic needs, that contributed to the sexual offense. The third principle, *responsivity,* stipulates that treatment should be tailored to meet the unique characteristics—that is, motivation level, cognitive abilities, interpersonal skills—of each offender (Andrews & Bonta, 1998, 2007). Furthermore, the greater the adherence to the RNR model, the greater the reduction in sexual recidivism rates. Andrews and Bonta (2007) report that residential and community-based treatment programs that adhered to all three principles showed greater (17% and 35%, respectively) reductions in recidivism than programs that did not adhere to all three principles.

Good Lives Model. In response to the growing dissatisfaction with the RP and RNR models, the Good Lives Model (GLM) has recently been developed as an alternative model of sex offending behavior and treatment (Ward, 2002; Ward & Stewart, 2003; Lindsay, Ward, Morgan, & Wilson, 2007; Whitehead, Ward, & Collie, 2007). This model regards offenders as individuals who, like all humans, seek to fulfill basic human needs and goals such as developing a sense of autonomy and productivity, as well as intimate relationships with other people (Ward, 2002; Ward & Stewart, 2003). Unfortunately, sex offenders often attempt to fulfill these needs in antisocial ways (e.g., seeking to fulfill intimacy needs with children), bringing them into conflict with the criminal justice system. According to this model, the goal of treatment should not be to change these needs, but to help sex offenders find more prosocial ways of fulfilling them. To this end, treatment should incorporate identification of overarching life goals as well as identify criminogenic risk factors (as in RP and RNR models), and help sex offenders develop the strategies and skills necessary to both achieve these life goals and prevent recidivism (Yates & Ward, 2008).

It should be noted that the three treatment models described above are not incompatible with one another. In fact, current views favor integrating components of RP and RNR with the Good Lives model to achieve optimal treatment outcomes (Ward & Stewart, 2003; Wilson & Yates, 2009).

Treatment Efficacy and Effectiveness

In 1974, Martinson published a controversial article concluding that offender treatment simply did not work. A decade later, Furby, Weinrott and Blackshaw (1989) published a review of 42 studies and likewise concluded that sex offender treatment was ineffective in reducing recidivism rates. Although these studies refuted the effectiveness of sex offender treatment, they also served as the catalyst for the development of new and more sophisticated CBT-based treatment paradigms, including the relapse prevention, risk-need-responsivity (RNR), and Good Lives model described earlier. Since the development and implementation of these new treatment models, research revisiting the topic of treatment efficacy and effectiveness has demonstrated significant positive treatment effects in reducing general and sexual recidivism among sex offenders (Hall, 2005; Hanson et al., 2002; Looman, Dickie, & Abracen, 2005; Losel & Schmucker, 2005; Scalora & Garbin, 2003).

Two recent meta-analytic reviews of the sex offender treatment efficacy/effectiveness literature have found that current treatment approaches, particularly those based in CBT, are effective in reducing recidivism rates among sex offenders (Hanson et al., 2002; Losel & Schmucker, 2005). Hanson and colleagues (2002) reported an overall positive effect for modern treatment programs on sexual recidivism rates of sex offenders, with 12.3% of treatment completers and 16.8% of nontreatment completers reoffending. Furthermore, modern treatment approaches demonstrated superior treatment effects than more outdated treatment approaches, with a 9.9% recidivism rate reported for offenders who received modern forms of treatment versus a 17.4% recidivism rate reported for offenders who received the outdated forms of treatment. Numerous other studies have also supported the effectiveness of modern treatment approaches in reducing general and sexual recidivism among sex offenders (Barbaree & Seto, 1997; Gallagher, Wilson, Hirschfield, Coggeshall, & MacKenzie, 1999; Hanson, 2000; Looman, Abracen, & Nicholaichuk, 2000; Marshall, Barbaree, & Eccles, 1991; McGrath, Cumming, Livingston, & Hoke, 2003; McGrath, Hoke, & Vojtisek, 1998; Nicholaichuk, Gordon, Gu, & Wong, 2000; Scalora & Garbin, 2003). In sum, recent studies revisiting the topic of sex offender treatment efficacy/effectiveness suggest that CBT-based sex offender treatment programs offer substantial promise, significantly reducing both general and sexual recidivism among sex offenders.

Community Reintegration/Risk Management

The ultimate goal of treatment and rehabilitation efforts is to successfully reintegrate sex offenders into the community and prevent recidivism. Among the most important risk management strategies is the evaluation of recidivism risk. A significant amount of research has been undertaken in an effort to identify offender (e.g., age, deviant sexual preference) and offense-related characteristics (e.g., victim gender) that are most strongly related to recidivism (e.g., Hanson & Bussière, 1998; Hanson

& Morton-Bourgon, 2005; Harris, Rice, & Quinsey, 1993). Based on this empirical data, researchers have created numerous, well-validated risk assessment instruments:

- Sex Offender Risk Appraisal Guide—SORAG (Quinsey et al., 1998; 2006)
- Rapid Risk Assessment for Sex Offense Recidivism—RRASOR (Hanson, 1997), Minnesota Sex Offender Screening Tool-Revised—MnSOST-R (Epperson, Kaul, Huot, Hesselton, Alexander, & Goldman, 2000)
- Static-99 (Hanson & Thornton, 2000)
- Sexual Violence Risk-20—SVR-20 (Boer, Hart, Kropp, & Webster, 1997)
- Risk for Sexual Violence Protocol—RSVP (Hart, Kropp, Laws, Klaver, Logan, & Watt, 2003)

Such instruments are vital for both effective assessment of treatment needs and post-treatment risk management planning.

Extensive analyses have been conducted comparing the ability of these various risk assessment instruments in predicting sexual recidivism, and are reviewed elsewhere (see Barbaree, Seto, Langton, & Peacock, 2001; Bartosh, Garby, Lewis, & Gray, 2003; Harris, Rice, Quinsey, Lalumiere, Boer, & Lang, 2003; Sjostedt & Langstrom, 2002). Results consistently demonstrate that actuarial risk assessment instruments consistently outperform clinical judgment alone (see Grove et al., 2000). The accuracy of these instruments will no doubt increase as they are further researched and refined. In addition, in the interest of maintaining the principle of best practice, the use of actuarial risk assessment instruments provide the most accurate prediction of recidivism available and provide a much-needed level of objectivity, reliability, and accountability in evaluations of recidivism (Janus & Prentky, 2003).

ADOLESCENT SEXUAL OFFENDERS

Adolescent offenders are responsible for a considerable proportion of sexual offenses, accounting for approximately 20% of forcible rape and other sexual crimes in the United States (Pastore & Maguire, 2007; U.S. Department of Justice, 2008). Furthermore, minors account for 43% of sexual offenses against very young children (ages 6 and younger) (National Center for Juvenile Justice, 1999). Despite evidence that adolescents who commit sexual offenses constitute a serious social dilemma, research into the assessment and treatment of this group of sexual offenders has only recently emerged.

Assessment for Treatment

Assessment for risk of recidivism is an important factor in treatment planning for adolescent sex offenders, often determining whether they will be placed in residential or community-based treatment. However, progress in the development and validation of risk assessment instruments for use with adolescent sex offenders has been hampered by several factors. First, there is a general lack of research investigating the predictive utility of such instruments with adolescent sex offenders (Miner, 2002; Worling & Curwen, 2001). Second, the rapid developmental changes that occur during adolescence make the identification of stable risk factors for recidivism in this group difficult (Price, 2003). Finally, as with adult sex offenders, low base rates of sexual recidivism and the heterogeneity of adolescent sex offenders present obstacles to the development of risk assessment instruments (Caldwell, 2002; Prentky & Righthand, 2003; Price, 2003; Smith & Monastersky, 1986). Despite these obstacles, several instruments have been recently developed and received some validation for use with adolescent sex offending populations (Prentky et al., 2010)

Among the most well-studied and commonly used adolescent sex offender-specific risk assessment instruments are Prentky and Righthand's (2003) Juvenile Sex Offender Assessment Protocol-II (J-SOAP-II) and Worling and Curwen's (2001) Estimate of Risk of Adolescent Sexual Offense Recidivism (ERASOR). The evidence regarding the predictive utility of these instruments is mixed, with some studies supporting their validity (Martinez, Flores, & Rosenfeld, 2007; Prentky et al., 2010; Skowron, 2004), some refuting their validity (Caldwell, Ziemke, & Vitacco, 2008; McCoy, 2007; Viljoen, Elkovitch, Scalora, & Ullman, 2009; Viljoen et al., 2008), and others supporting their utility only with specific subsets of adolescent sex offenders, for example, high-risk adolescent sex offenders (Rajlic & Gretton, 2010). Despite these mixed findings, these instruments are recommended as a useful objective guide and adjunct to a comprehensive clinical assessment (Parks & Bard, 2006; Prentky et al., 2010).

Treatment Techniques

Early models of adolescent sex offender treatment were largely based on CBT-models of adult sex offender treatment (Hunter, Gilbertson, Vedros, & Morton, 2004; Smallbone, Crissman, & Rayment-McHugh, 2009). However, recent criticism regarding the efficacy or effectiveness of adult-based models of treatment with adolescent sex offenders (Chaffin & Bonner, 1998; Letourneau & Miner, 2005; Parks & Bard, 2006) has resulted in the development and preliminary validation of treatments better suited to meet the unique social and developmental needs of adolescent sex offenders. Although cognitive-behavioral approaches to treatment are the generally accepted and empirically-supported treatment of choice for adolescent sex offenders (Efta-Breitbach & Freeman, 2004; Reitzel & Carbonell, 2006; Walker, McGovern, Poey, & Otis, 2004), there is growing evidence that more systemic treatment approaches such as multisystemic treatment (MST) may provide a more comprehensive treatment option when dealing with this group of offenders (Henggeler, Schoenwald, Borduin, Rowland, & Cunningham, 1998).

MST was designed to address a number of issues believed to be related to the juvenile offense cycle such as maladaptive cognitive styles and attitudes, social and relational difficulties (at multiple levels, including peer, family, and school), and symptoms of mental illness (e.g., depression) when appropriate. MST utilizes numerous empirically supported treatment techniques based in cognitive-behavior therapy, social learning, strategic and structural family therapy, as well as behavioral training for the juvenile's parents or primary caregivers. Preliminary results suggest MST's more holistic approach may effect a wider variety of positive treatment changes, including reduced sexual recidivism, among adolescent sexual offenders (Borduin, Henggeler, Blaske, & Stein, 1990; Borduin, Schaeffer, & Heiblum, 2009; Letourneau et al., 2009) than more traditional individual-level treatment approaches.

Treatment Efficacy and Effectiveness

Two recent meta-analyses investigating the effectiveness of adolescent sex offender-specific treatment (Reitzel & Carbonell, 2006; Walker et al., 2004) found CBT-based treatment programs produced statistically significant decreases in sexual recidivism. In their 10-study meta-analysis ($N = 644$), Walker and colleagues (2004) reported that established treatments for male adolescent sexual offenders fared well—with cognitive-behavioral treatments faring the best—in reducing recidivism rates. Reitzel and Carbonell (2006) reported similarly encouraging results based on their meta-analysis of nine studies comparing a range of treatment modalities (CBT-based, psycho-educational, humanistic, psychodynamic, MST, etc.). With a total sample of approximately 3,000 male adolescent sex offenders and an average follow-up period of 59 months, the authors reported an average weighted effect size of 0.43, demonstrating a significant effect of treatment on reducing sexual recidivism.

Although there are too few studies examining the efficacy/effectiveness of MST approaches in the treatment of adolescent sexual offenders to allow for meta-analysis, the three randomized MST efficacy studies conducted to date have supported the use of this approach (Borduin et al., 1990; Borduin et al., 2009; Letourneau et al., 2009). In the earliest study examining the efficacy of MST as a treatment for adolescent sexual offenders, Borduin and colleagues (1990) randomly assigned 16 adolescent sex offenders to either MST or individual therapy (blending psycho-dynamic, humanistic, and behavioral approaches). After a 3-year follow-up period, results showed that adolescents assigned to the MST condition recidivated at a significantly lower rate than adolescents assigned to the individual therapy condition—12.5% versus 75% for sexual recidivism and 25% versus 50% for general recidivism, respectively. In a more recent randomized clinical trial comparing the effectiveness of MST to community services, Borduin et al. (2009) found adolescent sex offenders assigned to the MST condition demonstrated lower general and sexual recidivism rates, as well as superior overall adjustment, than adolescent offenders assigned to the community services condition. Finally, in a second recent randomized clinical trial, Letourneau and colleagues (2009) found that adolescent sex offenders assigned to MST displayed significantly greater reductions in sexual behavior problems, substance use, out-of-home placements, delinquency, and externalizing symptoms than adolescent offenders assigned to treatment-as-usual.

Community Reintegration/Risk Management

Strategies recommended for the risk management of adolescent sex offenders involve a posttreatment evaluation of recidivism risk, development and implementation of "safety plans," involvement of family members in recidivism prevention, and establishment of community support. Accurate assessment of recidivism risk is an important component of risk management planning and can help determine the level of support services and monitoring required (Christodoulides, Richardson, Graham, Kennedy, & Kelly, 2005). A safety plan—a set of strategies and skills used by the adolescent to help prevent recidivism—should be developed prior to completion of treatment and provided to the adolescent as a self-management aid (Calley, 2007). Ideally, family members should be involved in addressing relevant family issues and help the adolescent offender maintain treatment gains and follow safety plans (Christensen, Margolin, & Sullaway, 1992). Finally, an aftercare plan, which may include follow-up drug or alcohol treatment services, should be developed and implemented, if clinically indicated.

Given the rapid developmental changes that occur during adolescence, risk management planning for adolescent sex offenders may require consistent reevaluation and refinement. Fortunately, research suggests that current treatment approaches and risk management strategies that take this into account are effective in reducing recidivism among adolescent sex offenders (Bourduin et al., 2009; Letourneau et al., 2009).

FEMALE SEX OFFENDERS

In 1997, Mary Kay Letourneau, a 34-year-old teacher from Des Moines, Washington, was arrested and charged with the statutory rape of one of her students, 17-year-old Vili Fualaau, with whom she had been having sexual relations for the past four or five years. After serving approximately seven years in prison, she was released and required to register as a sex offender in Washington State. In April of 2000, Heather Ingram, a 30-year-old high school teacher from Sechelt, British Columbia, Canada, was charged with the sexual exploitation of one of her 17-year-old male students. She received a conditional sentence of 10 months, followed by one year of probation for the offense. With increasing media attention drawing attention to cases like this, involving women perpetrating sexual abuse upon children, there has been a recent increase in interest in examining this specific subtype of sex offender.

Unfortunately, relatively little is known about female sex offenders as compared to their male counterparts. Sex offending has generally been considered a male phenomenon and it has long been believed that females were not capable of engaging in such behavior (Wijman, Bijleveld & Hendriks, 2010). While it is true that women comprise only about 5% of all convicted sex offenders (Cortoni, 2009), this doesn't mean that they are not worthy of study, or that their crimes are any less harmful to their victims. Further, there is some evidence that many sexual offenses perpetrated by female sex offenders go unreported and that up to 63% of female victims and 23% of male victims report being sexually victimized by a female (Schwartz & Cellini, 1995).

The few studies that have examined characteristics female sex offenders have found that they are a heterogeneous group that offends for different reasons and in different circumstances than male sex offenders (Vandiver & Walker, 2002). Based upon clinical observations of 16 female sex offenders, Matthews, Matthews, and Speltz (1989) proposed three subtypes of females who perpetrate sex crimes: (1) *male-coerced*—women who were typically passive and dependent and who were pressured by their male partner to engage in the abuse; (2) *predisposed*—women with histories of sexual abuse and mental illness who offended alone and usually against their own children or young relatives; and (3) *teacher/lover*—women who struggle with issues of self-esteem and view themselves as engaging in relationships with their young adolescent victims and thus do not view their actions as criminal. These subtypes were recently supported using a statistical approach in large sample of 450 female sex offenders (Vandiver & Kercher, 2004).

Assessment for Treatment

As with any sex offender, a comprehensive assessment for treatment with female sex offenders should take into account multiple factors. These include the type and extent of the sexual offending behavior, psychological functioning, medical issues, psychosocial functioning, family and environmental history, as well as any individual factors that may have contributed to or sustained the sexual offending behavior (Center for Sex Offender Management [CSOM], 2007). While there are several tools that have been designed to assess the various factors associated with sex offending such as cognitive distortions, these scales have all been developed for, and normed on, male sex offenders and thus cannot be reliably applied to female sex offenders.

Actuarial measures of recidivism risk are important tools for assessing risk among male sex offenders. Scales like the Static-99 (Hanson & Thornton, 2000) and MnSOST-R (Epperson et al., 2000) are used extensively with male sex offenders to make placement and release decisions. To date, no such tools have been developed for use with female sex offenders (CSOM, 2007). However, researchers have suggested that females who have engaged in sexual crimes share many of the same risk factors of other females involved in the criminal justice system such as a history of victimization and trauma, and mental health and substance abuse issues (Chesney-Lind & Sheldon, 2004; Denov & Cortoni, 2006). One of the few scales that has been validated for use with female offenders is the Level of Services Inventory—Revised (Andrews & Bonta, 1995; Hoge, Andrews, & Lescheid, 2002; Schmidt, Hoge, & Gomes, 2005). While the scale was developed for use with male offenders and does not address sexual recidivism specifically, it can be used in guiding assessment and treatment decisions among female sex offenders (CSOM, 2007).

Physiological measures of deviant sexual arousal and interest such as the penile plethysmograph and viewing time are often considered to part of a comprehensive risk assessment battery for male sex offenders as deviant interest and arousal have been linked to an increased recidivism risk (Hanson & Bussiere, 1998). The relationship between deviant arousal and interest and sexual offending is less clear among female sex offenders. Further, the measures available to measure deviant arousal and interest (such as the vaginal photoplethysmograph and viewing time) have not been well researched and thus they are not currently recommended for use with female sex offenders (Underwood, Robinson, Mosholder, & Warren, 2006).

Treatment Techniques

Traditionally, treatment programs for female sex offenders have been the same or similar to those offered for men. However, more recently, researchers and clinicians have acknowledged that women may have unique needs, thus requiring gender-responsive treatment services (Denov & Cortoni, 2006; Koons, Burrow, Morash, & Bynum, 1997; Morash, Bynum, & Koons, 1998). This falls in line with the responsivity principle of the *risk-need-responsivity* (RNR) model of treatment (Andrews, Bonta, & Hoge, 1990), which suggests that treatment should be targeted to meet the offender's specific needs. Recommended targets for treatment of female sex offenders include: developing and maintaining healthy intimate relationships; developing self-reliance; adopting a positive self image; enhancing emotion management; reducing self-destructive behaviors; increasing assertiveness and social skills; and developing healthy sexual expression and boundaries (CSOM, 2007). Additionally, it has been found that many women who engage in sexually abusive behaviors have been victims of sexual abuse or other types of trauma themselves. Thus, it is recommended that sex offender treatment for women include victimization issues for those women for whom this is applicable; however, caution should be taken not to use victimization to justify or minimize the sexually abusive behavior.

Treatment Efficacy and Effectiveness

Relatively little research has specifically examined the effectiveness of treatment for female offender populations in general and female sex offenders specifically. In 1999, Dowden and Andrews performed a meta-analysis of 26 studies that investigated the effectiveness of corrections-based treatment for female offenders and found support for the RNR model of treatment. According to the principles of RNR, they found larger treatment effects for programs targeting higher risk (rather than lower risk) female offenders as well as those that focused on criminogenic (versus noncriminogenic) needs. More specifically, those programs that focused on the interpersonal criminogenic needs of the female offenders such as family process or antisocial associates were most strongly associated with decreases in reoffending. Additionally, treatment programs that addressed antisocial cognitions and self-control deficits were also related to decreased recidivism (Dowden & Andrews, 1999). However, Dowden and Andrews did not find that programs that focused on substance abuse or basic education to be associated with treatment outcome in female offenders. Therefore, the limited research that exists suggests that effective treatment for female offenders may be similar to that of males. However, it is unclear how much of this applies specifically for a female sex-offending population.

Community Reintegration/Risk Management

Very little research has been done examining which practices and strategies are most effective for successful community reintegration and risk management among female sex offenders. As was initially the case with treatment, community integration for female sex offenders generally follows the same model as that for males. For example, Cumming and McGrath (2005) have suggested that practices used with men such as restricting employment such that the offender will not be able to gain access to potential victims (e.g. teacher, daycare provider), and limiting pornographic or sexually explicit materials, may also decrease the risk for reoffending among female sex offenders.

While reintegration practices are important in preventing future recidivism, a recent study of 1,466 female sex offenders in New York State found lower recidivism rates for women as compared to those of male sex offenders after 5 years (Sandler & Freeman, 2009). Only 1.8% ($n = 32$) of the sample reoffended sexually. However, those who did reoffend were more likely to have a criminal history including misdemeanors, felonies, or drug charges as compared to those who did not reoffend, suggesting that more criminalized female sex offenders should perhaps be monitored more closely following release.

A recent trend in sex offender management is a move toward the Good Lives Model (GLM) of sex offender treatment. The GLM is centered on the perspective that each individual has basic needs such as relatedness, competence, autonomy, happiness, and health (Deci & Ryan, 2000; Thakkar, Ward, & Tidmarsh, 2006; Ward & Stewart, 2003), and (sexual) offending represents a maladaptive but effective way to meet these needs. Based upon this model, offending may be decreased if the offender's individual needs are understood and if more adaptive means of meeting these needs are found (Ward & Stewart, 2003). While intuitively the GLM seems to be a good match to meet the needs of female sex offenders, to date there has been very little written documentation about how the GLM model would apply to female sex offenders specifically. Furthermore, there is currently no known data examining the efficacy of this model when applied to the management of female sex offenders.

INTELLECTUALLY DISABLED SEXUAL OFFENDERS

Research indicates that intellectual disabilities (ID) occur in the sex offender population at higher rates than in the general population (Hayes, 2002), with between 10–15% of convicted sex offenders diagnosable with an intellectual disability—generally IQ scores of 80 or less as measured by standardized intellectual ability instruments (Murphy, Coleman, & Haynes, 1983; Nezu et al., 2006; O'Connor, 1997). Researchers have begun to explore the relationship between intellectual disability and sex offending in more detail over the last several years, recognizing that current mainstream assessment and treatment models may not be appropriate for use with this unique subset of sex offenders (Courtney, Rose, & Mason, 2006; Craig & Hutchinson, 2005; Keeling & Rose, 2005; Lambrick & Glaser, 2004; Lindsay, Elliot, & Astell, 2004; Nezu et al., 2006; Rice, Harris, Lang, & Chaplin, 2008).

Assessment for Treatment

As with all sex offenders, accurate assessment for treatment requires assessment across several domains. A formal assessment of intellectual ability, using the WAIS-IV or another well-validated measure, as well as literacy and reading comprehension, such as Wilkinson and Robertson's (2006) Wide Range Achievement Test-4 (WRAT-4), should be conducted to ensure treatment is tailored to the offender's capabilities (Keeling, Beech, & Rose, 2007). Keeling and colleagues (2007) also recommend that evaluators assess adaptive functioning, for example, communication, self-care, social and life skills, as this can greatly aid in appropriate treatment placement. Instruments such as the Vineland Adaptive Behavior Scales, Second Edition (Vineland-II) by Sparrow, Cicchetti, and Barra (2005) or the American Association on Mental Retardation Adaptive Behavior Scale—Residential and Community (AAMR ABS 2nd Edition) by Nihira, Leland, & Lambert, 1993) are suggested for this purpose (Keeling, Beech, & Rose, 2007)

As with all sex offenders, sex offenders with ID should be carefully assessed for the presence of deviant sexual preferences (Keeling, Beech, & Rose, 2007). Penile plethysmography (Haaven & Schlank, 2001; Lambrick & Glaser, 2004), as well as self-report measures, such as the Multiphasic Sex Inventory (Nichols & Molinder, 1984, 2000), and the Wilson Sex Fantasy Questionnaire (Wilson, 1988) can be useful for this purpose. The updated MSI may be particularly useful with sex offenders with ID as it requires only a seventh-grade reading ability and is also available on audiotape for offenders with reading comprehension difficulties. In some cases, administration of self-report instruments in an interview format may enhance comprehension and increase the reliability of information obtained (Clare, 1993). However, as these instruments are not normed on sex offenders with ID, determinations of deviant sexual preferences should be made with caution. Additionally, assessment of cognitive distortions and pro-offending beliefs should be assessed using a number of established instruments such as the Abel-Becker Cognition Scale (Abel, Becker, & Cunningham-Rathner, 1984) or the Bumby MOLEST and RAPE scales (Bumby, 1996).

Finally, a risk assessment should be conducted to help inform treatment planning. Research on the risk assessment of sex offenders has proliferated over the last two decades; however, research investigating the predictive utility of existing risk assessment tools with sex offenders with ID has been relatively limited (Harris & Tough, 2004; Keeling, Rose, & Beech, 2007; Lambrick & Glaser, 2004; Lindsay & Beail, 2004). Despite this lack of research, it has been suggested that risk assessment instruments normed on general sex offenders may be appropriate for use with sex offenders with ID (Harris & Tough, 2004; Wilcox, 2004). Two studies have supported the use of Hanson's Rapid Assessment of Sexual Offense Recidivism (1997) with sex offenders with ID (Boer, Tough, & Haaven, 2004; Tough, 2001). The Static-99 (Hanson & Thornton, 2000) has also received some support for use with this population (Blacker, Beech, Wilcox, & Boer, 2011; Lindsay et al., 2008).

Treatment Techniques

The development of treatment programs specifically for sex offenders with ID has been relatively slow (Nezu, Nezu, & Dudek, 1998; Wilcox, 2004). For sex offenders with ID, treatment must be carefully customized to match their level of intellectual functioning, emphasizing the importance of a thorough pretreatment assessment. For lower functioning sex offenders with ID (i.e., those with severe intellectual disability), more traditional behavioral treatment approaches—such as using token economies and other operant conditioning techniques—are recommended and still commonly used (Wilcox, 2004).

For higher functioning sex offenders with ID, those with borderline to mild intellectual disability, treatment approaches incorporating and emphasizing cognitive components (O'Connor, 1997), are finding increasing support. Most such programs have been adapted from mainstream CBT-based sex offender treatments programs (Lambrick & Glaser, 2004; Nezu, Nezu, & Dudek, 1998; Nezu, Nezu, & Gill-Weiss, 1992). As such, treatment programs for sex offenders with ID typically follow the CBT/social learning model and address many of the same treatment targets as traditional sex offender treatment programs such as: assertiveness and social skills training, emotion regulation, sexual education, drug and alcohol education, functional analysis, behavior modification. Relatively minor modifications to traditional sex offender treatment protocols may help to improve therapeutic engagement (Lambrick & Glaser, 2004). For instance, important treatment concepts should be presented in an easy-to-follow manner, using simplified terminology and visual imagery when possible and appropriate. Failure to present treatment material in a simplified way may lead sex offenders with ID to feeling overwhelmed and to disengage from treatment (Lambrick & Glaser, 2004).

Treatment Efficacy and Effectiveness

Fortunately, there is growing evidence suggesting that treatments adapted from mainstream CBT-based sex offender treatment programs are also effective with sex offenders with ID. Treatment outcome studies have generally been positive, reporting treatment gains when CBT-based treatment programs are implemented (Lindsay et al., 1998, 1999; O'Connor, 1996; Rose et al., 2002). However, one recent studying examining the effectiveness of treatment adapted for use with sex offenders with ID did not report such promising results. Keeling, Beech, and Rose (2007) report that both ID and non-ID offenders—matched on risk category, sex of victim, type of offense and age—failed to show significant posttreatment gains on a number of outcome variables (e.g., self-reported loneliness, development of positive relationships skills, victim empathy). These results should be interpreted with caution, as noted by the authors, due to several methodological limitations of their study, including small sample size and poor population definitions which may have led to overlap between ID and non-ID groups.

Community Reintegration/Risk Management

Although there is some evidence that existing treatment programs may be effective in reducing recidivism rates among sex offenders with ID, there may be important factors that need to be considered when developing risk management strategies for this group (Nezu et al., 2006). For instance, more extensive community and social support services may be required to achieve satisfactory community reintegration in these offenders. Extra contingency management systems may need to be implemented and carefully monitored in order to ensure that sex offenders with ID utilize these support services and maintain therapeutic gains (Nezu et al., 2006). As with other sex offenders, relapse prevention plans should be created for sex offenders with ID, providing offenders with skills and strategies to help them avoid situations that would increase likelihood of recidivism. Despite these potential additional challenges in managing sex offenders with ID, research indicates that current treatment approaches—while in need of refinement and further validation—seem to be producing significant positive clinical change in this subset of sex offenders.

INTERNET OFFENDERS

Still little is understood about management and treatment strategies for offenders known to have committed an Internet-related sexual offense (accessing, downloading, distributing child pornography and/or using the Internet to gain access to potential victims), as Babchishin, Hanson, and Hermann (2011) report. Indeed, whether the term *Internet offenders* can itself be used to describe this subgroup of offenders is worthy of discussion. The findings of Seto et al. (2011), who in recent meta-analyses examined the extent to which offenders with an online sexual offense commit offline offenses, indicated that Internet offenders may not limit their offending to online offenses and may, in some ways, appear more like prototypical sex offenders. Indeed, Seto and colleagues (2011) found that approximately one in every eight offenders had been arrested, charged, or convicted of a contact sexual offense, though the prevalence was even higher (more than one in every two) when self-report data was used. In regard to recidivism, considerably more offline offenders (approximately 13%) go on to commit contact offenses; (Hanson & Bussière, 1998; Hanson & Morton-Bourgon, 2004) than do online offenders; Seto et al. (2011) found only 2.0% of online offenders to have recidivated with a new contact sexual offense. Although these findings suggest a certain degree of overlap between online and offline offenders, empirical research is necessary to adequately answer the question of whether online offenders should be considered a distinct subgroup.

Assessment for Treatment

Presently, there is evidence to suggest that individuals who use the Internet in some manner to perpetrate sexual offenses may differ in important ways from more traditional groups of sexual offenders with regard to the etiological determinants, motivations, and patterns of their behavior, thus implying that prevention, risk management, and treatment goals may necessarily differ. Even within groups of offenders who commit Internet-based offenses, there may be wide variation with regard to degree of dangerousness and sexual deviation as well as range of overall criminality (Wolak et al., 2010). Indeed, those who use the Internet to view child pornography may differ in important ways from those whose primary goal is to chat with underage youth solely for the purpose of fantasy and also from those who use the Internet to facilitate an offline meeting. A thorough assessment should seek to establish not only the developmental antecedents to the crime and unique motivational factors, but should also establish prior offense history, as online offenders with a contact sex offense history are among those most likely to recidivate (Seto & Eke, 2005) and, as such, may warrant the most intensive treatment or management services under the risk-need-responsivity (RNR) model (Andrews, Bonta, & Hoge, 1990). Indeed, issues of risk level, the unique treatment needs of the offender, and the offender's responsivity to treatment are important assessment considerations for this population, as with others (Andrews et al., 1990).

Treatment Techniques and Efficacy/Effectiveness

Despite this need for detailed assessment considerations, as yet, there is no well-established model unique to the treatment needs of men who engage in online sexual offenses. Cognitive behavioral and relapse prevention approaches, which have demonstrated treatment efficacy with more general sex offender populations may be appropriate for those with Internet-related sexual offenses (Nicholaichuk, Gordon, Gu, & Wong, 2000; Yates, 2003). Cognitive behavioral strategies that specifically target attitudes and beliefs that support online offending (e.g., minimization of harm or victim blaming) are likely to be the most efficacious. The findings of Babchishin and colleagues (2011) suggest that online offenders may avoid emotional closeness, and as such, cognitive behavior strategies that target the affective components and beliefs related to the avoidance of close interpersonal relationships might have particular value. As noted, Andrews and colleagues argue that treatment services should be targeted to those offenders who are deemed to be at highest risk to recidivate, and such programs must target the offender's crimenogenic needs and be based upon a cognitive behavioral (CBT) model (Andrews et al., 1990; Andrews & Bonta, 1998; Ward, Vess, Collie, & Gannon, 2006). Additionally, evidence from a meta-analysis of outcome studies on samples of prototypical offenders shows that treatment programs that adhered to risk-need-responsivity (RNR) principles showed the largest reductions in both general and sexual recidivism (Hanson, Bourgon, Helmus, & Hodgson, 2009).

Community Reintegration/Risk Management

Although existing treatment models may be appropriate for use with this population, the use of existing risk management techniques may be challenging, perhaps requiring calibration of actuarial risk tools so as to account for risk factors unique to online offenders. Initial research suggests, however, that although the base rate of reoffending is considerably lower for online offenders, the risk factors for reoffense (criminal history, substance abuse problems, sexually deviant interests) are similar to those of offline offenders (Seto et al., 2011; Seto & Eke, 2005). As with any offender population, ensuring that offenders have the necessary supports to desist from engaging in future crime is of paramount importance. Thus, ensuring that offenders have access to supportive social networks, treatment services, and other community supports to manage their individual risk factors is essential. Babchishin and colleagues (2011) found that although online offenders showed no differences from normative community samples in terms of education, they were twice as likely to be unemployed. Employment, a critical factor in crime desistance, has been shown to promote positive community adjustment and lower recidivism (Kruttschnitt, Uggen, & Shelton, 2000; Laub & Sampson, 2001). Although research is still developing with this population, present knowledge suggests that factors critical to the community reentry for general offender populations (e.g., employment), and risk factors relevant to sexual offender populations specifically, are relevant to identifying and managing the risk of those with internet-based offenses.

SEXUALLY VIOLENT PREDATORS

Sexually Violent Predator (SVP) legislation, now in its second decade of existence, allows for the postsentence civil commitment of a certain subclass of offenders deemed to have (a) a history of sexual offense, (b) a current mental abnormality or personality disorder, (c) a risk of engaging in future sexual offenses, and (d) some connection or link between the mental abnormality and future harm (*Kansas v. Hendricks*, 1997). Currently, 20 states have SVP legislation, with most recent estimates indicating that there are 5200 individuals held under SVP laws (Associated Press, 2010).

Assessment for Commitment

Because the statute dictates that civil commitment under SVP legislation be narrowly applied to certain offenders, evaluators routinely attempt to ascertain whether an offender has a mental abnormality or personality disorder, whether the offender is at risk of future sexual offense, and whether the offender has the requisite history of sexual crime. Research has found that those selected for commitment have a greater number of prior sexual and nonsexual arrests than those not selected for commitment (Levenson, 2004; New York State Office of Mental Health, 2009). Actuarial risk tools, which estimate probability of future offending by comparing an offender against group data on individuals known to have recidivated, are routinely used in the evaluation of offenders being considered for SVP commitment. Empirical findings demonstrate that offenders selected for commitment have higher actuarial risk scores than noncommitted offenders. Indeed, offenders recommended for commitment have been found to have higher scores on the Static-99 (Hanson & Thornton, 2000), the Minnesota Sex Offender Screening Tool-Revised (Epperson, Kaul, Huot, Hesselton, Alexander, & Goldman, 2000), and the Rapid Risk Assessment of Sexual Offense Recidivism (Hanson, 1997) than those not recommended for civil management (New York State Office of Mental Health, 2009; Levenson, 2004). Evaluation for psychopathy, or characterological deficits in affect and tendency toward antisocial conduct as typically measured by Hare's (2003) Psychopathy Checklist-Revised (PCL-R), is also sometimes considered in the evaluation of offenders under SVP statutes given its association with violence and sexual violence (Hanson & Bussière, 1998; Hanson & Morton-Bourgon, 2004; Quinsey et al., 1998). Assessment of psychopathy occurs in approximately half of commitment evaluations (Jackson & Hess, 2007; Levenson & Morin, 2006), though most consider it critical to SVP evaluations (Jackson & Hess, 2007). Indeed, findings from Florida and Washington State reveal that offenders selected for SVP commitment have elevated scores on the PCL-R (Levenson, 2004; Jackson & Richards, 2007).

Due to the fact that SVP statutes also require finding of a mental abnormality or personality disorder that is causally linked to sexual offending, most mental health professionals use the American Psychiatric Association's *Diagnostic and Statistical Manual of Mental Disorders (DSM-IV-TR)* (2000) to communicate symptom patterns. Sexual deviance disorders such as pedophilia or other paraphilia, have been found to be the most prevalent psychiatric disorders among those committed as SVPs (Becker, Stinson, Tromp, & Messer, 2003; Elwood, Doren, & Thornton, 2010; Jackson & Richards, 2007), though comorbid substance use (Ellwood et al., 2010; Jackson & Richards, 2007) and antisocial personality disorder (Becker et al., 2003; Ellwood et al., 2010; Jackson & Richards, 2007) are common. More severe forms of mental illness are, however, much less common, particularly in comparison to rates of ordinary (non-SVP) civil commitment statutes. For example, Vess, Murphy, and Arkowitz (2004) observed that just over 10% of SVPs were diagnosed with a psychotic or severe mood disorder, while over 90% of those committed under other mentally disordered offender statutes were diagnosed with schizophrenia, schizoaffective disorder, bipolar disorder, or major depression.

Treatment Techniques and Efficacy/Effectiveness

The constitutionality of SVP laws rests, in part, on their basis in providing treatment services to offenders (Prentky, Janus, Barbaree, Schwartz, & Kafka, 2006). And currently all states provide treatment services to committed SVPs (Prentky et al., 2006), though offenders may opt not to participate in treatment. Although cognitive behavioral interventions show the greatest treatment effect with sex offender populations (Nicholaichuk et al., 2000; Yates, 2003), the efficacy of treatment interventions with SVP populations is difficult, if not impossible, to assess given that so few offenders are released from commitment facilities (Prentky et al., 2006). Indeed, in a national survey of SVP practices, Gookin (2007) reported that just over 10% of those committed as SVPs were eventually discharged or released. Aside from concerns over treatment efficacy, Prentky and colleagues (2006) note that treatment with those committed as SVPs may be especially challenging given ongoing litigation, issues of voluntariness with regard to treatment participation, the conflicted role of treatment providers who may be requested to document and testify about treatment participation, and the attitude of committed offenders, who may show elevated rates of hopelessness and anger (Robilotta, Jeglic, & Mercado, 2009).

As noted, risk assessment is routinely employed in the evaluation of offenders for civil commitment. Given the costly nature of SVP commitment and the statutory reliance on identification of those most at risk of reoffending, use of actuarial risk assessment in the commitment hearings ensures that the most dangerous offenders are those selected for commitment. Community reintegration for SVPs, though important, has received less attention, which results from the fact that a relatively small percentage of those committed as SVPs are eventually released back into the community. In Minnesota, for example, not one offender has been released since passage of the commitment law in 1994 (Associated Press, 2010). It is likely, however, that the risk of some offenders can be effectively managed in the community. Given the burden that growing numbers of committed offenders place on state budgets (Associated Press, 2010) as well as the severe liberty deprivation inherent in this policy measure, there is growing need to identify those who can be expected to live safely in the community given effective management interventions.

POLICY IMPLICATIONS

Currently, the prevention of recidivism is largely limited to use of sanctions and monitoring of offenders by the criminal justice system. Modern treatment programs offer promising alternative or adjunctive approaches to reducing recidivism, by providing offenders with the skills to prevent reoffending and to improve the quality of their lives (Levenson, 2003; Beck & Klein-Saffran, 1990). Unfortunately, at present, treatment is not mandated as part of incarceration, meaning many offenders may complete their sentences without receiving treatment. Of those offenders who do receive treatment, many do not receive empirically-supported treatments despite evidence that such treatments are effective in reducing recidivism (e.g., Andrews et al., 1990; Andrews & Bonta, 1998, 2007). Further complicating matters, even when empirically-supported treatments are available and offered an antagonistic prison environment may dissuade many sex offenders from participating meaningfully or altogether in treatment (Palermo, 2005; Schwaebe, 2005).

Current treatment and management paradigms have also been adapted for use with a variety of specific sex offender populations, including adolescent, female, intellectually disabled, and internet sex offenders; preliminary evidence suggests that these adapted treatments are effective in reducing recidivism and aiding sex offenders in successfully reintegrating into the community. Reducing sexual recidivism will also alleviate the enormous costs associated with treating victims of sexual abuse and assault (Chapman et al., 2007; Letourneau et al., 1996; Resnick et al., 1999) and incarcerating sex offenders who reoffend (Post, Mezey, Maxwell, & Wibert, 2002). Therefore, it is incumbent upon researchers and clinicians to educate stakeholders and policy-makers regarding the importance of empirically-supported sex offender treatments in reducing recidivism. It is hoped that such education will encourage the adoption of treatment and management strategies designed to address the unique needs of subgroups of sex offender not met through traditional approaches.

DISCUSSION QUESTIONS

1. What are the strengths and weaknesses of each of the treatment models presented in this chapter (i.e., Relapse Prevention, RNR, Good Lives Model)?

2. Specialized treatment approaches have been developed for use with special sub-types of sex offenders; however, often more general sex offender treatment approaches are used. Why do you think this is?

3. What components of treatment do you think are most important in reducing recidivism?

4. Do you think current sex offender community reintegration strategies are effective? If not, how do you think they could be improved?

SUGGESTED READINGS

Andrade, J. T., Vincent, G. M., & Saleh, F. M. (2006). Juvenile sex offenders: A complex population. *Journal of Forensic Science, 51*, 163–167. doi:10.1111/j.1556–4029.2005.00010.x

Andrews, D. A, & Bonta, J. (2007). *The psychology of criminal conduct* (4th ed.). Cincinnati, OH: Anderson.

Babchishin, K. M., Hanson, K. R., & Hermann, C. A. (2011). The characteristics of online sex offenders: A meta-analysis. *Sexual Abuse: A Journal of Research and Treatment, 23*, 92–123. doi:10.1177/1079063210370708

Borduin, C. M., Henggeler, S. W., Blaske, D. M., & Stein, R. (1990). Multisystemic treatment of adolescent sexual offenders. *International Journal of Offender Therapy and Comparative Criminology, 35*, 105–114. doi:10.1177/0306624X9003400204

Courtney, J., & Rose, J. (2004). The effectiveness of treatment for male sex offenders with learning disabilities: A review of the literature. *Journal of Sexual Aggression, 10*, 215–236. doi:10.1080/13552600412331286558

Dowden, C., & Andrews, D. A. (1999). What works for female offenders: A meta-analytic review. *Crime & Delinquency, 45*, 438–452. doi:10.1177/0011128799045004002

Federal Bureau of Investigation. (2001). *Age-specific arrest rates and race specific arrest rates for selected offenses, 1993–2001*. Retrieved March 9, 2012, from http://www.fbi.gov/ucr/adducr/age_race_specific.pdf

Furby, L., Weinrott, M. R., & Blackshaw, L. (1989). Sex offender recidivism: A review. *Psychological Bulletin, 105*, 3–30.

Gookin, K. (2007). *Comparison of state laws authorizing involuntary commitment of sexually violent predators: 2006 update, revised* [Electronic version]. (No. 07–08–1101). Olympia: Washington Institute for Public Policy.

Hanson, R. K., Gordon, A., Harris, A. J. R., Marques, J. K., Murphy, W., Quinsey, V. L., & Seto, M. C. (2002). First report of the Collaborative Outcome Project on the effectiveness of psychological treatment for sex offenders. *Sexual Abuse: A Journal of Research and Treatment, 14,* 159–194. doi:10.1177/107906320201400207

Henggeler, S. W., Schoenwald, S. K., Borduin, C. M., Rowland, M. D., & Cunningham, P. B. (1998). *Multisystemic treatment of antisocial behavior in children and adolescents.* New York, NY: Guilford.

Jackson, R. L., Rogers, R., & Shuman, D. W. (2004). The adequacy and accuracy of sexually violent predator evaluations: Contextualized risk assessment in clinical practice. *International Journal of Forensic Mental Health, 3,* 115–129.

Keeling, J., Beech, A. R., & Rose, J. L. (2007). Assessment of sexual offenders with an intellectual disability: The current position. *Aggression and Violent Behavior, 12,* 229–241. doi:10.1016/j.avb.2006.08.001

Lindsay, W. R., Murphy, L., Smith, G., Murphy, D., Edwards, Z., Chittock, C., et al. (2004). The Dynamic Risk Assessment and Management System: An assessment of immediate risk of violence for individuals with offending and challenging behavior. *Journal of Applied Research in Intellectual Disabilities, 17,* 267–274. doi:10.1111/j.1468–3148 .2004.00215.x

Martinson, R. (1974). What works? Questions and answers about prison reform. *The Public Interest, 35,* 22–54.

Matthews, R., Matthews, J., & Speltz, K. (1989). *Female sexual offenders: An exploratory study.* Brandon, VT: Safer Society Press.

Pithers, W. D., Marques, J. K., Gibat, C. C., & Marlatt, G. A. (1983). Relapse prevention with sexual aggressives: A self-control model of treatment and maintenance change. In J. G. Greer & I. R. Stuart (Eds.), *The sexual aggressor: Current perspectives on treatment* (pp. 214–239). New York, NY: Van Nostrand Reinhold.

Jackson, R. L., Rogers, R., & Shuman, D. W. (2004). The adequacy and accuracy of sexually violent predator evaluations: Contextualized risk assessment in clinical practice. *International Journal of Forensic Mental Health, 3,* 115–129.

Prentky, R. A., Janus, E., Barbaree, H., Schwartz, B. K., & Kafka, M. P. (2006). Sexually violent predators in the courtroom: Science on trial. *Psychology, Public Policy, and Law, 12,* 357–393. doi:10.1037/1076–8971.12.4.357

Quinsey V. L. (2004). Risk assessment. In W. R. Lindsay, J. L. Taylor, & P. Sturmey (Eds.), *Offenders with developmental disabilities.* Chichester, England: Wiley.

Seto, M. C., & Hanson, K. R. (2011). Introduction to special issue on internet-facilitated sexual offending. *Sexual Abuse: A Journal of Research & Treatment, 23,* 3–6. doi:10.1177/ 1079063211399295

Seto, M. C., Hanson, R. K., & Babchishin, K. M. (2011). Contact sexual offending by men with online sexual offenses. *Sexual Abuse: A Journal of Research & Treatment, 23,* 124–145. doi:10.1177/107906063210369013

Tough S., & Hingsburger, D. (1999). Counseling sex offenders with intellectual disabilities who deny. *Mental Health Aspects of Intellectual Disabilities, 2,* 1–5.

Vandiver, D. M., & Walker, J. T. (2002). Female sex offenders: An overview and analysis of 40 cases. *Criminal Justice Reviews, 27,* 284–300. doi:10.1177/073401680202700205

Ward, T., & Stewart, C. A. (2003). Criminogenic needs and human needs: A theoretical model. *Psychology, Crimes, and Law, 9,* 125–153. doi:10.1080/1068316031000116247

Wilcox, D. T. (2004). Treatment of intellectually disabled individuals who have committed sexual offences: A review of the literature. *Journal of Sexual Aggression, 10,* 85–100. doi: 10.1080/13552600410001670955

Wilcox, D. T., Beech, A., Markall, H. F., & Blacker, J. (2009). Actuarial risk assessment and recidivism in a sample of UK intellectually disabled sex offenders. *Journal of Sexual Aggression, 15,* 97–106. doi:10.1080/13552600802578577

REFERENCES

Abel, G. G., Becker, J. V., & Cunningham-Rathner, J. (1984). Complications, consent and cognitions in sex between children and adults. *International Journal of Law and Psychiatry, 7,* 89–103.

Abel, G. G., Huffman, J., Warberg, B., & Holland, C. L. (1998). Visual reaction time and plethysmography as measures of sexual interest in child molesters. *Sexual Abuse: A Journal of Research and Treatment, 10,* 81–95. doi:10.1177/107906329801000202

American Psychiatric Association. (2000). *Diagnostic and statistical manual of mental disorders* (4th ed. text rev.). Washington, DC: Author.

Andrews, D. A., & Bonta, J. (1995). *The levels of service inventory-revised.* Toronto, ON, Canada: Multi-Health Systems.

Andrews, D. A, & Bonta, J. (1998). *The psychology of criminal conduct* (2nd ed.). Cincinnati, OH: Anderson.

Andrews, D. A, & Bonta, J. (2007). *The psychology of criminal conduct* (4th ed.). Cincinnati, OH: Anderson.

Andrews, D. A., Bonta, J., & Hoge, R. D. (1990). Classification for effective rehabilitation: Rediscovering psychology. *Criminal Justice and Behavior, 17,* 19–52. doi:10.1177/0093854890017001004

Associated Press. (2010, June 22). Sex offender confinement costing states too much. *CBS News.* Retrieved from http://www.cbsnews.com/stories/2010/06/22/national/main6605890.shtml

Babchishin, K. M., Hanson, K. R., & Hermann, C. A. (2011). The characteristics of online sex offenders: A meta-analysis. *Sexual Abuse: A Journal of Research and Treatment, 23,* 92–123. doi:10.1177/1079063210370708

Barbaree, H. E., & Seto, M. C. (1997). Pedophilia: Assessment and treatment. In D. R. Laws & W. T. O'Donoghue (Eds.), *Sexual deviance: Theory, assessment, and treatment* (pp. 175–193). New York, NY: Guilford Press.

Barbaree, H. E., Seto, M. C., Langton, C. M., & Peacock, E. J. (2001). Evaluating the predictive accuracy of six risk assessment instruments for adult sex offenders. *Criminal Justice and Behavior, 28,* 490–521. doi:10.1177/009385480102800406

Bartosh, D. L., Garby, T., Lewis, D., & Gray, S. (2003). Differences in the predictive validity of actuarial risk assessments in relation to sex offender type. *International Journal of Offender Therapy and Comparative Criminology, 47,* 422–438. doi:10.1177/0306624X03253850

Beck, J. L., & Klein-Saffran, J. (1990). Home confinement and the use of electronic monitoring with federal parolees. *Federal Probation, 54,* 23–24.

Becker, J. V., Stinson, J., Tromp, S., & Messer, G. (2003). Characteristics of individuals petitioned for civil commitment. *International Journal of Offender Therapy and Comparative Criminology, 47,* 185–195. doi:10.1177/0306624X03251114

Blacker, J., Beech, A. R., Wilcox, D. T., & Boer, D. P. (2011). The assessment of dynamic risk and recidivism in a sample of special needs sexual offenders. *Psychology, Crime, & Law,* 75–92. doi: 10.1080/10683160903392376

Boer, D. P., Hart, S. D., Kropp, P. R., & Webster, C. D. (1997). *Manual for the Sexual Violence Risk–20: Professional guidelines for assessing risk of sexual violence.* Vancouver, BC, Canada: British Columbia Institute Against Family Violence.

Boer, D. P., Tough, S., & Haaven, J. (2004). Assessment of risk manageability of intellectually disabled sex offenders. *Journal of Applied Research in Intellectual Disabilities, 17,* 275–283. doi:10.1111/j.1468–3148.2004.00212.x

Borduin, C. M., Henggeler, S. W., Blaske, D. M., & Stein, R. (1990). Multisystemic treatment of adolescent sexual offenders. *International Journal of Offender Therapy and Comparative Criminology, 35,* 105–114. doi:10.1177/0306624X9003400204

Borduin, C. M., Schaeffer, C. M., & Heiblum, N. (2009). A randomized clinical trial of multisystemic therapy with juvenile sexual offenders: Effects on youth social ecology and criminal activity. *Journal of Consulting and Clinical Psychology, 77,* 26–37. doi:10.1037/a0013035

Briere, J., & Elliott, D. M. (2003). Prevalence and symptomatic sequelae of self-reported childhood physical and sexual abuse in a general population sample of men and women. *Child Abuse & Neglect: The International Journal, 27,* 1205–1222.

Bumby, K. M. (1996). Assessing the cognitive distortions of child molesters and rapists: Development and validation of the MOLEST and RAPE scales. *Sexual Abuse: A Journal of Research and Treatment, 8,* 37–54.

Butcher, J. N., Graham, J. R., Ben-Porath, Y. S., Tellegen, A., Dahlstrom, W. G., & Kaemmer, B. (2001). *MMPI–2: Minnesota Multiphasic PersonalityInventory-2: Manual for administration, scoring, and interpretation* (Rev. ed.). Minneapolis: University of Minnesota Press.

Caldwell, M. F. (2002). What we do not know about juvenile sexual reoffense risk. *Child Maltreatment, 7,* 291–302.

Caldwell, M., Ziemke, M., & Vitacco, M. (2008). An examination of the sex offender registration and notification act as applied to juveniles: Evaluating the ability to predict sexual recidivism. *Psychology, Public Policy, and Law, 14,* 89–114. doi: 10.1037/a0013241

Calley, N. G. (2007). Integrating theory and research: The development of a research-based treatment program for juvenile male sex offenders. *Journal of Counseling & Development,* 85(2), 131–142.

Center for Sex Offender Management. (2007). *Female sex offenders.* Silver Spring, MD: Author.

Chaffin, M., & Bonner, B. (1998). Don't shoot, we're your children: Have we gone too far in our response to adolescent sexual abusers and children with sexual behavior problems? *Child Maltreatment, 3,* 314–316. doi: 10.1177/1077559598003004003

Chaney, E. F., O'Leary, M. F., & Marlatt, G. A. (1978). Skill training with alcoholics. *Journal of Consulting and Clinical Psychology, 46,* 1092–1104.

Chapman, D. P., Dube, S. R., & Anda, R. F. (2007). Adverse childhood events as risk factors for negative mental health outcomes. *Psychiatric Annals, 37*(5), 359–364.

Chesney-Lind, M., & Sheldon, R. G. (2004). Girls, delinquency and juvenile justice (3rd ed.). Belmont, CA: Wadsworth.

Christensen, A., Margolin, G., & Sullaway, M.M. (1992). Interparental agreement on child behavior problems. *Psychological Assessment,* 4(4), 419–425

Christodoulides, T. E., Richardson, G., Graham, F., Kennedy, P. J., & Kelly, T. P. (2005). Risk assessment with adolescent sex offenders. *Journal of Sexual Aggression: An international, interdisciplinary forum for research, theory and practice, 11*(1), 37–48.

Cortoni, F. (2009, November). *Recidivism rates of female sex offenders: A meta-analytic review.* Paper presented at the annual meeting of the American Society of Criminology, Philadelphia, PA.

Courtney, J., Rose, J., & Mason, O. (2006). The offense process of sex offenders with intellectual disabilities: a qualitative study. *Sexual Abuse: A Journal of Research and Treatment, 18,* 169–191. doi:10.1007/s11194–006–9010–7

Craig, L., & Hutchinson, R. B. (2005). Sexual offenders with learning disabilities: Risk recidivism, and treatment. *Journal of Sexual Aggression, 11,* 289–304. doi:10.1080/13552600500273919

Cumming, G. F., & McGrath, R. J. (2005). Supervision of the sex offender: Community management, risk assessment, and treatment. Brandon, VT: Safer Society Press.

Deci, E. L., & Ryan, R. M. (2000). The "what" and "why" of goal pursuits: Human needs and the self-determination of behavior. *Psychological Inquiry, 11,* 227–268.

Denov, M., & Cortoni, F. (2006). Women who sexually abuse children. In C. Hilarski & J. S. Wodarski (Eds.), *Comprehensive mental health practice with sex offenders and their families* (pp. 71–99). Binghamton, NY: Haworth Press.

Dowden, C., & Andrews, D. A. (1999). What works for female offenders: A meta-analytic review. *Crime & Delinquency, 45,* 438–452. doi:10.1177/0011128799045004002

Efta-Breitbach, J., & Freeman, K. A. (2005). Treatment of juveniles who sexually offend: An overview. *Journal of Child Sexual Abuse, 13,* 125–138. doi:10.1300/J070v13n03_07

Elwood, R. W., Doren, D. M., & Thornton, D. (2010). Diagnostic and risk profiles of men detained under Wisconsin's sexually violent person law. *International Journal of Offender Therapy and Comparative Criminology, 54,* 187–196. doi:10.1177/0306624X08327305

Epperson, D. L., Kaul, J. D., Huot, S. J., Hesselton, D., Alexander, W., & Goldman, R. (2000). *Minnesota Sex Offender Screening Tool-Revised (MnSOST-R) Technical paper: Development, validation, and recommended risk level cut scores.* Retrieved March 9, 2012, from http://www.psychology.iastate.edu/faculty/epperson/TechUpdatePaper12–03.pdf

Furby, L., Weinrott, M. R., & Blackshaw, L. (1989). Sex offender recidivism: A review. *Psychological Bulletin, 105,* 3–30.

Gallagher, C. A., Wilson, D. B., Hirschfield, P., Coggeshall, M. B., & MacKenzie, D. L. (1999). A quantitative review of the effects of sex offender treatment on sexual reoffending. *Corrections Management Quarterly, 3*(4), 19–29.

Gookin, K. (2007). *Comparison of state laws authorizing involuntary commitment of sexually violent predators: 2006 update, revised.* Document No. 07–08–1101. [Electronic version]. Olympia: Washington Institute for Public Policy.

Grove, W. M., Zald, D. H., Hallberg, A. M., Lebow, B., Snitz, E., & Nelson, C. (2000). Clinical versus mechanical prediction: A meta-analysis. *Psychological Assessment, 12,* 19–30. doi:10.1037//1040–3590.12.1.19

Haaven, J., & Schlank, A. (2001). The challenge of treating the sex offender with developmental disabilities. In A. Schlank (Ed.), The sexual predator: Vol.2: Legal issues, clinical issues, and special populations (pp. 13.1–13.19). Kingston, NJ: Civic Research Institute.

Hall, G. C. (1995). Sex offender recidivism revisited: A meta-analysis of recent treatment studies. *Journal of Consulting and Clinical Psychology, 63,* 802–809.

Hanson R. K. (1997). The development of a brief actuarial risk scale for sexual offense recidivism. User Report No. 1997–04. Ottawa, ON; Department of the Solicitor General of Canada.

Hanson, R. K. (2000). What is so special about relapse prevention? In D. R. Laws, S. M. Hudson, & T. Ward (Eds.), *Remaking relapse prevention: A sourcebook* (pp. 27–38). Thousand Oaks, CA: Sage.

Hanson, R. K., Bourgon, G., Helmus, L., & Hodgson, S. (2009). *A meta-analysis of the effectiveness of treatment for sexual offenders: Risk, need, and responsivity.* [User Report 2009–01]. Ottawa, ON: Public Safety Canada.

Hanson, R. K., & Bussière, M. T. (1998). Predicting relapse: A meta-analysis of sexual offender recidivism studies. *Journal of Consulting and Clinical Psychology, 66,* 348–362. doi:10.1037/0022–006X.66.2.348

Hanson, R. K., Gordon, A., Harris, A. J. R., Marques, J. K., Murphy, W., & Quinsey, V. L., & Seto, M. C. (2002). First report of the Collaborative Outcome Project on the effectiveness of psychological treatment for sex offenders. *Sexual Abuse: A Journal of Research and Treatment, 14,* 159–194. doi:10.1177/107906320201400207

Hanson, R. K., & Morton-Bourgon, K. E. (2004). *Predictors of sexual recidivism: An updated meta-analysis.* [User Report 2004–02]. Ottawa, ON: Public Safety Canada.

Hanson, R. K., & Morton-Bourgon, K. E. (2005). The characteristics of persistent sexual offenders: A meta-analysis of recidivism studies. *Journal of Consulting and Clinical Psychology, 73,* 1154–1163. doi:10.1037/0022–006X.73.6.1154

Hanson, R. K., & Thornton, D. (2000). Improving risk assessment for sex offenders: A comparison of three actuarial scales. *Law and Human Behavior, 24,* 119–136.

Hare, R. D. (2003). *Manual for the Psychopathy Checklist-Revised* (2nd ed.). Toronto, ON, Canada: Multi-Health Systems.

Harris, G. T., Rice, M. E., & Quinsey, V. L. (1993). Violent recidivism of mentally disordered offenders: The development of a statistical prediction instrument. *Criminal Justice and Behavior, 20,* 315–335. doi:10.1177/0093854893020004001

Harris, G. T., Rice, M. E., Quinsey, V. L., Lalumiere, M. L., Boer, D., & Lang, C. (2003). A multisite comparison of actuarial risk instruments for sex offenders. *Psychological Assessment, 15,* 413–425. doi:10.1037/1040–3590.15.3.413

Harris, A. J. R., & Tough, S. (2004). Should actuarial risk assessments be used with sex offenders who are intellectually disabled? *Journal of Applied Research in Intellectual Disabilities, 17,* 235–241. doi:10.1111/j.1468–3148.2004.00211.x

Hart, S. D., Kropp, P. R., Laws, D. R., Klaver, J., Logan, C., & Watt, K. A. (2003). *The Risk for Sexual Violence Protocol* (RSVP). Burnaby, BC, Canada: Mental Health Law & Policy Institute, Simon Fraser University.

Hayes, S. (2002). Adaptive behavior and background characteristics of sex offenders with intellectual disabilities. Paper presented at the International Association for the Scientific Study of Intellectual Disabilities, Inaugural Conference of IASSID Europe, University College Dublin, Ireland.

Henggeler, S. W., Schoenwald, S. K., Borduin, C. M., Rowland, M. D., & Cunningham, P. B. (1998). *Multisystemic treatment of antisocial behavior in children and adolescents.* New York, NY: Guilford.

Hoge, R. D., Andrews, D. A., & Lescheid, A.W. (2002). *The youth level of service/case management inventory.* Toronto, ON, Canada: Multi-Health Systems.

Hunter, J. A., Gilbertson, S. A., Vedros, D., & Morton, M. (2004). Strengthening community-based programming for juvenile sexual offenders: Key concepts and paradigm shifts. *Child Maltreatment, 9*(2), 177–189

Jackson, R. L., & Hess, D. T. (2007). Evaluation for civil commitment of sex offenders: A survey of experts. *Sexual Abuse: A Journal of Research & Treatment, 19,* 425–448. doi:10.1007/s11194–007–9062–3

Jackson, R. L., & Richards, H. J. (2007). Diagnostic and risk profiles among civilly committed sex offenders in Washington State. *International Journal of Offender Therapy and Comparative Criminology, 51,* 313–323. doi:10.1177/0306624X06292874

Janus, E. S., & Prentky, R. A. (2003). The forensic use of actuarial risk assessment with sex offenders: Accuracy, admissibility and accountability. *American Criminal Law Review, 40,* 1443–1449.

Kansas v. Hendricks, 521 U.S. 346 (1997).

Keeling, J. A., & Rose, J. L. (2005). Relapse prevention with intellectually disabled sexual offenders. *Sexual Abuse: A Journal of Research and Treatment, 17,* 407–423. doi:10.1007/s11194-005-8052-6

Keeling, J., Beech, A. R., & Rose, J. L. (2007). Assessment of sexual offenders with an intellectual disability: The current position. *Aggression and Violent Behavior, 12(2),* 229–241. doi:10.1016/j.avb.2006.08.001

Keeling, J. A., Rose, J. L., & Beech, A. R. (2007). Comparing sexual offender treatment efficacy: Mainstream sex offenders and sexual offenders with special needs. *Journal of Intellectual and Developmental Disability, 32,* 117–124. doi:10.1080/13668250701402767

Koons, B. A., Burrow, J. D., Morash, M., & Bynum, T. (1997). Expert and offender perceptions of program elements linked to successful outcomes for incarcerated women. *Crime & Delinquency, 43,* 512–532. doi:10.1177/0011128797043004007

Kruttschnitt, C., Uggen, C., & Shelton, K. (2000). Predictors of desistance among sex offenders: The interaction of formal and informal social controls. *Justice Quarterly, 17,* 61–88.

Lambrick, F., & Glaser, W. (2004). Sex offenders with an intellectual disability. *Sexual Abuse: A Journal of Research and Treatment, 16,* 381–392. doi:10.1177/107906320401600409

Laub, J. H., & Sampson, R. F. (2001). Understanding desistance from crime. *Crime and Justice, 28,* 1–69.

Laws, R. D. (2003). The rise and fall of relapse prevention. *Australian Psychologist, 38(1),* 22–30.

Letourneau, E., & Miner, M. (2005). Juvenile sex offenders: A case against the legal and clinical status quo. *Sexual Abuse: A Journal of Research and Treatment, 17,* 293–311. doi: 10.1177/107906320501700304

Letourneau, E. J., Henggeler, S. W., Borduin, C. M., Schewe, P. A., McCart, M. R., Chapman, J. E., & Saldana, L. (2009). Multisystemic therapy for juvenile sexual offenders: 1-year results from a randomized effectiveness trial. *Journal of Family Psychology, 23,* 89–102. doi: 10.1037/a0014352

Letourneau, E. J., Resnick, H. S., Kilpatrick, D. G., Saunders, B. E., & Best, C. L. (1996). Comorbidity of sexual problems and posttraumatic stress disorder in female crime victims. *Behavior Therapy, 27(3),* 321–336.

Levenson, J. S. (2003). Policy interventions designed to combat sexual violence: Community notification and civil commitment. *Journal of Child Sexual Abuse, 12,* 17–52.

Levenson, J. S. (2004). Sexual predator civil commitment: A comparison of selected and released groups. *International Journal of Offender Therapy and Comparative Criminology, 48,* 638–648. doi:10.1177/0306624X04265089

Levenson, J. S., & Morin, J. W. (2006). Factors predicting selection of sexually violent predators for civil commitment. *International Journal of Offender Therapy and Comparative Criminology, 50,* 609–629. doi:10.1177/0306624X06287644

Lindsay, W. R. (2002). Research and literature on sex offenders with intellectual and developmental disabilities. *Journal of Intellectual Disability Research, 46,* 74–85. doi:10.1046/j.1365-2788.2002.00006.x

Lindsay, W. R., & Beail, N. (2004). Risk assessment: Actuarial prediction and clinical judgement of offending incidents and behaviour for intellectual disability services. *Journal of Applied Research in Intellectual Disabilities, 17,* 229–234. doi:10.1111/j.1468–3148.2004.00212.x

Lindsay, W. R., Elliot, S. F., & Astell, A. (2004). Predictors of sexual offence recidivism in offenders with intellectual disabilities. *Journal of Applied Research in Intellectual Disabilities, 17,* 299–305. doi:10.1111/j.1468–3148.2004.00217.x

Lindsay, W. R., Hogue, T. E., Taylor, J. L., Steptoe, L., Mooney, P., O'Brien, G., et al. (2008). Risk assessment in offenders with intellectual disability. *International Journal of Offender Therapy and Comparative Criminology, 52,* 90–111. doi:10.1177/0306624X07308111

Lindsay, W. R., Marshall, I., Neilson, C., Quinn, K., & Smith, A. H. W. (1998). The treatment of men with a learning disability convicted of exhibitionism. *Research in Developmental Disabilities, 19,* 295–316.

Lindsay, W. R., Ollie, S., Baillie, N., & Smith, A. H. W. (1999). Treatment of adolescent sex offenders with intellectual disabilities. *Mental Retardation, 37,* 201–211.

Lindsay, W. R., Ward, T., Morgan, T., & Wilson, I. (2007). Self-regulation of sex offending, future pathways and the good lives model: Applications and problems. *Journal of Sexual Aggression, 13,* 37–50. doi:10.1080/13552600701365613

Looman, J., Abracen, J., & Nicholaichuk, T. P. (2000). Recidivism among treated sexual offenders and matched controls: Data from the Regional Treatment Centre (Ontario). *Journal of Interpersonal Violence, 15,* 279–290. doi:10.1177/088626000015003004

Looman, J., Dickie, I., Abracen, J. (2005). Responsivity issues in the treatment of sexual offenders. *Trauma, Violence, & Abuse, 6,* 330–353. doi:10.1177/1524838005280857

Losel, F., & Schmucker, M. (2005). The effectiveness of treatment for sexual offenders: A comprehensive meta-analysis. *Journal of Experimental Criminology, 1*(1), 117–146.

Marlatt, G. A., & Gordon, J. R. (1980). Determinants of relapse: Implications for the maintenance of behavior change. In P. O. Davidson & S. M. Davidson (Eds.), *Behavioral medicine: Changing health lifestyles* (pp. 410–452). New York, NY: Brunner/Mazel.

Marlatt, G. A., & Gordon, J. R. (1985). Relapse prevention: Theoretical rationale and overview of the model. In G. A. Marlatt & J. R. Gordon (Eds.), *Relapse prevention: maintenance strategies in the treatment of addictive behaviours* (pp. 3–71). London, England: Guilford Press.

Marques, J. K., & Nelson, C. (1989). Understanding and preventing relapse in sex offenders. In M. Gossop (Ed.), *Relapse and addictive behaviour* (pp. 96–106). New York, NY: Tavistock/Routledge.

Marshall, W. L., & Anderson, D. (1996). An evaluation of the benefits of relapse prevention programs with sexual offenders. *Sexual Abuse: A Journal of Research and Treatment, 8*(3), 209–221. doi:10.1177/107906329600800305

Marshall, W. L., Barbaree, H. E., & Eccles, A. (1991). Early onset and deviant sexuality in child molesters. *Journal of Interpersonal Violence, 6,* 323–336. doi:10.1177/088626091006003005

Martinez, R., Flores, J., & Rosenfeld, B. (2007). Validity of the Juvenile Sex Offender Assessment Protocol–II (J-SOAP-II) in a sample of urban minority youth. *Criminal Justice and Behavior, 34,* 1284–1295. doi:10.1177/0093854807301791

Martinson, R. (1974). What works? Questions and answers about prison reform. *The Public Interest, 35,* 22–54.

Matthews, R., Matthews, J., & Speltz, K. (1989). *Female sexual offenders: An exploratory study.* Brandon, VT: Safer Society Press.

McCoy, W. K. (2007). *Predicting treatment outcome and recidivism among juvenile sex offenders: The utility of the J-SOAP-II and ERASOR in an outpatient treatment program* (Unpublished doctoral dissertation). Sam Houston State University, Huntsville, TX.

McGrath, R. J., Cumming, G., Livingston, J. A., & Hoke, S. E. (2003). Outcome of a treatment program for adult sex offenders: From prison to community. *Journal of Interpersonal Violence, 18*(1), 3–17. doi:10.1177/0886260502238537

McGrath, R. J., Hoke, S. E., & Vojtisek, J. E. (1998). Cognitive-behavioral treatment of sex offenders: A treatment comparison and long-term follow-up study. *Criminal Justice and Behavior, 25,* 203–225. doi:10.1177/0093854898025002004

Miner, M. H. (2002). Factors associated with recidivism in juveniles: An analysis of serious juvenile sex offenders. *Journal of Research in Crime and Delinquency, 39,* 421–436.

Morash, M., Bynum, T. S., & Koons, B. A. (1998). *Women offenders: Programming, needs and promising approaches.* Washington, DC: U.S. Department of Justice, National Institute of Justice, Research in Brief.

Murphy, W. D., Coleman, E. M., & Haynes, M. A. (1983). Treatment evaluation issues with the mentally retarded sex offender. In J. G. Greer & I. R. Stuart (Eds.), *The sexual aggressor: Current perspectives on treatment* (pp. 22–41). New York, NY: Van Nostrand Reinhold.

National Center for Juvenile Justice. (1999). *Juvenile offenders and victims: 1999 national report.* Washington, DC: U.S. Department of Justice, Office of Juvenile Justice and Delinquency Prevention.

National Center for Missing and Exploited Children. (2007). *Map of registered sex offenders in the United States.* Retrieved from http://www.missingkids.com/en_US/documents/sex-offender-map.pdf

New York State Office of Mental Health. (2009). *2008 annual report on the implementation of Mental Hygiene Law Article 10.* New York: New York State Office of Mental Health.

Nezu, C. M., Nezu, A. M., & Dudek, J. A. (1998). A cognitive behavioral model of assessment and treatment for intellectually disabled sexual offenders. *Cognitive and Behavioral Practice, 5,* 25–64.

Nezu, C. M., Nezu, A. M., & Gill-Weiss, M. J. (1992). *Psychopathology in persons with mental retardation: Clinical guidelines for assessment and treatment.* Champaign, IL: Research Press.

Nezu, C. M., Greenberg, J., & Nezu, A. M. (2006). Project STOP: Cognitive behavioral assessment and treatment for sex offenders with intellectual disability. *Journal of Forensic Psychology Practice, 6,* 87–103. doi:10.1300/J158v06n03_06

Nicholaichuk, T., Gordon, A., Gu, D., & Wong, S. (2000). Outcome of an institutional sexual offender treatment program: A comparison between treated and matched untreated offenders. *Sexual Abuse: A Journal of Research and Treatment, 12,* 139–154. doi:10.1177/107906320001200205

Nichols, H. R., & Molinder, I. (1984). *Multiphasic Sex Inventory manual.* Available from Nichols & Molinder, 437 Bowes Drive, Tacoma, WA, or at http://www.nicholsandmolinder.com

Nichols, H. R., & Molinder, I. (2000). *Multiphasic Sex Inventory-II manual.* Available from Nichols & Molinder, 437 Bowes Drive, Tacoma, WA, or at http://www.nicholsandmolinder.com

Nihira, K., Leland, H., & Lambert, N. (1993). Adaptive Behavior Scale- Residential and Community. Austin, TX: Pro-ed.

O'Connor, W. (1996). A problem-solving intervention for sex offenders with an intellectual disability. *Journal of Intellectual and Developmental Disability, 21,* 219–235.

O'Connor, W. (1997). Towards and environmental perspective on intervention for problem sexual behaviour in people with an intellectual disability. *Journal of Applied Research in Intellectual Disabilities, 10,* 159–175. doi:10.1111/j.1468–3148.1997.tb00015.x

Palermo, G. B. (2005). Prisonization and sexual offenders: A compounded problem. *International Journal of Offender Therapy and Comparative Criminology, 49,* 611–613. doi:10.1177/0306624X05281331

Palermo, G. B., & Farkas, M. A. (2001). *The dilemma of the sexual offender.* Springfield, IL: C.C. Thomas.

Parks, G. A., & Bard, D. E. (2006). Risk factors for adolescent sex offender recidivism: Evaluation of predictive factors and comparison of three groups based upon victim type. *Sexual Abuse: A Journal of Research and Treatment, 18,* 319–342. doi: 10.1177/107906320601800402

Pastore, A. L., & Maguire, K. (Eds.). (2007). *Sourcebook of criminal justice statistics: 31st Edition* [Electronic version]. Available: http://www.albany.edu/sourcebook

Pithers, W. D., Marques, J. K., Gibat, C. C., & Marlatt, G. A. (1983). Relapse prevention with sexual aggressives: A self-control model of treatment and maintenance change. In J. G. Greer & I. R. Stuart (Eds.), *The sexual aggressor: Current perspectives on treatment* (pp. 214–239). New York, NY: Van Nostrand Reinhold.

Post, L. A., Mezey, N. J., Maxwell, C., & Wibert, W. N. (2002). The rape tax: Tangible and intangible costs of sexual violence. *Journal of Interpersonal Violence, 17,* 773–782. doi:10.1177/0886260502017007005

Prentky, R. A., Janus, E., Barbaree, H., Schwartz, B. K., & Kafka, M. P. (2006). Sexually violent predators in the courtroom: Science on trial. *Psychology, Public Policy, and Law, 12,* 357–393. doi:10.1037/1076–8971.12.4.357

Prentky, R. A., Nien-Chen, L., Righthand, S., Schuler, A., Cavanaugh, D., & Lee, A. F. (2010). Assessing risk of sexually abusive behavior among youth in a child welfare sample. *Behavioral Sciences and the Law, 28,* 24–45. doi:10.1002/bsl.920

Prentky, R. A., & Righthand, S. (2003). *Juvenile Sex Offender Assessment Protocol-II (J-SOAP-II) manual.* Bridgewater, MA: Justice Resource Institute.

Price, D. (2003). A developmental perspective of treatment for sexually vulnerable youth. *Sexual Addiction & Compulsivity, 10,* 225–245.

Quinsey, V. L., Harris, G. T., Rice, M. R., & Cormier, C. A. (1998). *Violent offenders: Appraising and managing risk.* Washington, DC: American Psychological Association.

Quinsey, V. L., Harris, G. T., Rice, M. E., & Cormier, C. A. (2006). In V. L. Quinsey et al., *Violent offenders: Appraising and managing risk* (2nd ed.). Washington, DC: American Psychological Association. doi: 10.1037/11367-000 http://www.apa.org/pubs/books/4316068.aspx

Rajlic, G., & Gretton, H. M. (2010). An examination of two sexual recidivism risk measures in adolescent offenders: The moderating effect of offender type. *Criminal Justice and Behavior, 37,* 1066–1085. doi:10.1177/0093854810376354

Reitzel, L. R., & Carbonell, J. L. (2006). The effectiveness of sexual offender treatment for juveniles as measured by recidivism: A meta-analysis. *Sexual Abuse: A Journal of Research and Treatment, 18*(4), 401–421.

Resnick, H., Acierno, R., Holmes, M., Kilpatrick, D. G., & Jager, N. (1998). *Prevention of post-rape psychopathology: Preliminary findings of a controlled acute rape treatment study.* Charleston: Medical University of South Carolina, National Crime Victims Research and Treatment Center.

Rice, M. E., Harris, G. T., Lang, C., & Chaplin, T. C. (2008). Sexual preferences and recidivism of sex offenders with mental retardation. *Sexual Abuse: A Journal of Research and Treatment, 20*(4), 409–425

Robilotta, S., Jeglic, E., & Mercado, C. C. (2009, November). Sex offenders' emotional reactions to civil commitment: A qualitative analysis. Paper presented at the annual meeting of the American Society of Criminology (ASC), Philadelphia, PA.

Rose, J., Jenkins, R., O'Connor, C., Jones, C., & Felce, D. (2002). A group treatment for men with intellectual disabilities who sexually offend or abuse. *Journal of Applied Research in Intellectual Disabilities, 15,* 138–150. doi:10.1046/j.1468–3148.2002.00110.x

Sandler, J. C., & Freeman, N. J (2009). Female sex offender recidivism: A large-scale empirical analysis. *Sexual Abuse: A Journal of Research and Treatment, 21*(4), 455–473. doi:10.1177/1079063209347898

Scalora, M. J., & Garbin, C. (2003). A multivariate analysis of sex offender recidivism. *International Journal of Offender Therapy and Comparative Criminology, 47*(3), 309–323. doi:10.1177/0306624X03047003005

Schmidt, F., Hoge, R. D., & Gomes, L. (2005). Reliability and validity analysis of the Youth Level of Services/Case Management Inventory. *Criminal Justice and Behavior, 32,* 329–344. doi:10.1177/0093854804274373

Schwaebe, C. (2005). Learning to pass: Sex offenders' strategies for establishing a viable identity in the prison general population. *International Journal of Offender Therapy and Comparative Criminology, 49,* 614–625. doi:10.1177/0306624X05275829

Schwartz, B., & Cellini, H. (1995). Female sex offenders. In B. Schwartz & H. Cellini (Eds.). *The sex offender: Corrections, treatment and legal practice* (pp. 5-1–5-22). Kingston, NJ: Civic Research Institute.

Seto, M. C., & Eke, A. W. (2005). The criminal histories and later offending of child pornography offenders. *Sexual Abuse: A Journal of Research & Treatment, 17,* 201–210. doi:10.1007/s11194–005–4605-y

Seto, M. C., Hanson, R. K., & Babchishin, K. M. (2011). Contact sexual offending by men with online sexual offenses. *Sexual abuse: A Journal of Research & Treatment, 23,* 124–145. doi:10.1177/107906063210369013

Sjostedt, G., & Langstrom, N. (2002). Assessment of risk for criminal recidivism among rapists: A comparison of four different measures. *Psychology, Crime & Law, 8,* 25–40. doi:10.1080/10683160208401807

Skowron, C. (2004). *Differentiation and predictive factors in adolescent sexual offending* (Unpublished doctoral dissertation). Carleton University, Ottawa, ON, Canada.

Smallbone, S., Crissman, B., & Rayment-McHugh, S. (2009). Improving therapeutic engagement with adolescent sex offenders. *Behavioral Sciences and the Law, 27,* 862–877. doi:10.1002/bsl.905

Smith, W. R., & Monastersky, C. (1986). Assessing juvenile sexual offenders' risk for reoffending. *Criminal Justice and Behavior, 13,* 115–140.

Sparrow, S. S., Cicchetti, D. V., & Barra, D. A. (2005). *Vineland Adaptive Behavior Scales, Second Edition (Vineland-II).* San Antonio, TX: Pearson.

Thakkar, J., Ward, T., & Tidmarsh, P. (2006). A reevaluation of relapse prevention with adolescents who sexually offend: A good lives model. In H. E. Barbaree & W. L. Marshall (Eds.), *The juvenile sex offender* (2nd ed.) (pp. 313–335). New York, NY: Guilford.

Tough, S. E. (2001). *The evaluation of two standard risk assessments (RRASOR, 1997; STATIC-99, 1999) on a sample of adult males who are developmentally disabled with significant cognitive deficits.* (Master's thesis). Retrieved from http://www.collections canada.gc.ca/obj/s4/f2/dsk3/ftp04/MQ58817.pdf

Underwood, L. A., Robinson, S. B., Mosholder, E., & Warren, K. M. (2008). Sex offender care for adolescents in secure care: Critical factors and counseling strategies. *Clinical Psychology Review, 28*(6), 917–932.

U.S. Department of Justice. (2008). *Crime in the United States, Table 39, Personal crimes of violence, 2007* [Data file]. Retrieved from http://bjs.ojp.usdoj.gov/content/pub/pdf/cvus07.pdf

Vandiver, D. M., & Kercher, G. (2004). Offender and victim characteristics of registered female sexual offenders in Texas: A proposed typology of female sexual offenders. *Sexual Abuse: A Journal of Research and Treatment, 16,* 121–137. doi:10.1177/1079063204 01600203

Vandiver, D. M., & Walker, J. T. (2002). Female sex offenders: An overview and analysis of 40 cases. *Criminal Justice Reviews, 27,* 284–300. doi:10.1177/073401680202700205

Vess, J., Murphy, C., & Arkowitz, S. (2004). Clinical and demographic differences between sexually violent predators and other commitment types in a state forensic hospital. *The Journal of Forensic Psychiatry & Psychology, 15,* 669–681. doi:10.1080/14789940410 001731795

Viljoen, J. L., Elkovitch, N., Scalora, M. J., & Ullman, D. (2009). Assessment of reoffense risk in adolescents who have committed sexual offenses: Predictive validity of the ERASOR, PCL: YV, YLS/CMI, and Static-99. *Criminal Justice and Behavior, 36,* 981–1000. doi:10.1177/0093854809340991

Viljoen, J. L., Scalora, M., Cuadra, L., Bader, S., Chavez, V., Ullman, D., & Lawrence, L. (2008). Assessing risk for violence in adolescents who have sexually offended: A comparison of the J-SOAP-II, SAVRY, and J-SORRAT-II. *Criminal Justice and Behavior, 35,* 5–23. doi:10.1177/0093854807307521

Walker, D. F., McGovern, S. K., Poey, E. L., & Otis, K. E. (2004). Treatment effectiveness for male adolescent sexual offenders: A meta-analysis and review. *Journal of Child Sexual Abuse, 13,* 281–293. doi:10.1300/J070v13n03_14

Ward, T. (2002). Good lives and the rehabilitation of offenders: Promises and problems. *Aggression and Violent Behavior, 7*(5), 513–528.

Ward, T., & Hudson, S. M. (2000). A self-regulation model of relapse prevention. In D. R. Laws, S. M. Hudson, & T. Ward (Eds.), *Remaking relapse prevention with sex offenders* (pp. 79–101). Thousand Oaks, CA: Sage.

Ward, T., Mann, R. E., & Gannon, T. A. (2007). The good lives model of offender rehabilitation: Clinical implications. *Aggression and Violent Behavior, 12,* 87–107. doi:10.1016/j .avb.2006.03.004

Ward, T., & Stewart, C. A. (2003). Criminogenic needs and human needs: A theoretical model. *Psychology, Crimes, and Law, 9,* 125–153. doi:10.1080/1068316031000116247

Ward, T., Vess, J., Collie, R. M., & Gannon, T. A. (2006). Risk management or goods promotion: The relationship between approach and avoidance goals in treatment of sex offenders. *Aggression & Violent Behavior, 11,* 378–393. doi:10.1016/j.avb.2006.01.001

Wechsler, D. (2008). *Wechsler adult intelligence scale: Fourth edition.* San Antonio, TX: The Psychological Corporation and Harcourt Brace.

Whitehead, P. R., Ward, T., & Collie, R. M. (2007). Applying the good lives model of rehabilitation to a high-risk violent offender. *International Journal of Offender Therapy and Comparative Criminology, 51,* 578–598. doi:10.1177/0306624X06296236

Wijman, M., Bijleveld, C., & Hendriks, J. (2010). Women don't do such things! Characteristics of female sex offenders and offender types. *Sexual Abuse: A Journal of Research and Treatment, 22*(2), 135–156. doi:10.1177/1079063210363826

Wilcox, D. T. (2004). Treatment of intellectually disabled individuals who have committed sexual offences: A review of the literature. *Journal of Sexual Aggression, 10,* 85–100. doi:10.1080/13552600410001670955

Wilson, G. D. (1988). Measurement of sex fantasy. *Sex and Marital Therapy, 3,* 45–55.

Wilson, R. J., & Yates, P. M. (2009). Effective interventions and the Good Lives Model: Maximizing treatment gains for sexual offenders. *Aggression and Violent Behavior. 14*(3), 157–161.

Wilkinson, G. S., & Robertson, G. J. (2006). *Wide Range Achievement Test 4 professional manual.* Lutz, FL: Psychological Assessment Resources.

Wolak, J., Finkelhor, D., Mitchell, K. J., & Ybarra, M. L. (2010). Online "predators" and their victims: Myths, realities, and implications for prevention and treatment. *Psychology of Violence, 1*(S), 13–35. doi:10.1037/2152–0828.1.S.13

Worling, J. R., & Curwen, T. (2001). The "ERASOR:" Estimate of Risk of Adolescent Sexual Recidivism (Version 2.0). Toronto, ON, Canada: Safe-T Program, Thistletown Regional Centre.

Yates, P. M. (2003). Treatment of adult sexual offenders: A therapeutic cognitive-behavioural model of intervention. *Journal of Child Sexual Abuse, 12,* 195–232. doi:10.1300/J070v12n03_08

Yates, P. M., & Ward, T. (2008). Good lives, self-regulation, and risk management: An integrated model of sexual offender assessment and treatment. *Sexual Abuse in Australia and New Zealand: An Interdisciplinary Journal, 1,* 3–20.

CHAPTER 11

Redemption From the Inside-Out: The Power of Faith-Based Programming

Barbara H. Zaitzow and Richard S. Jones

INTRODUCTION

In the United States, where more than 1.6 million people are imprisoned in state and federal prisons and more than 400,000 work at them, prisons are big business (Bureau of Justice Statistics, 2009). As an abstract term, prison is quite simple: it's a place where a person's freedom, movements, and access to basically everything is restricted, usually as punishment for committing a crime. But for anyone who has ever done hard time, a prison is so much more: it's a place where dignity, privacy, and control are given up to guards and prison administrators, where isolation and boredom can drive someone insane, and where the simplest of necessities seem like luxuries. Life in prison has changed drastically in the past 25 years. As a result of changes in legislative responses to the war on drugs and judicial decision making, America outstrips every other nation in the world in the number of people it puts in its prisons. According to a study by the Pew Research Center (2008), one out of every 100 adults in the United States is in prison or jail. Prisons are more crowded, and as a result, availability of educational and vocational programs is being reduced because of financial crises, and inmate-on-inmate violence is increasing.

When most people hear about unpleasant conditions in U.S. prisons, they don't feel particularly bad for the convicts. However, there has been a prison reform movement since, at least, the 1700s, when religious groups such as the Quakers objected to prison conditions. Reformers lobby for better treatment by guards, better equipped medical facilities, well-funded education programs, and more humane treatment. These people aren't criminal sympathizers—they simply have strong beliefs, for ethical or religious reasons, that even convicted criminals should be granted basic human rights. And, quite simply, the foundation upon which American prisons were created rested on the belief in the "perfectibility of people." There's

319

another reason people want to reform prisons. More than 90% of all prisoners are eventually released (Petersilia, 2003). When they are released, often the only skills they acquired in prison were those that allowed them to survive. They may be paranoid or bitter. They may have learned that the only proper response to a problem is violence. Their social skills have atrophied. Getting a decent job as a convicted criminal is hard enough—add in these factors and it can become very difficult for formerly incarcerated individuals to reassimilate themselves into the outside world.

In looking for answers to the numerous challenges facing people who live or work in prison settings, the role of religion and spirituality continues to be a topic of great interest and controversy and is the focus of this chapter.

HISTORICAL OVERVIEW

The history of the United States corrections system is one filled with irony and a never-ending attempt to reduce crime through deterrence, incapacitation, and rehabilitation. While founded upon the humanitarian and religious ideals of redemption, reform, and reintegration, the U.S. correctional system has evolved into a mechanism by which society controls particular segments of the population it deems a risk to the public safety of communities. With 2.3 million people incarcerated in our nation's prisons and jails today as well as an additional 6 million persons on probation and parole, programming is critical.

Historically, religion in the United States has played a significant role in the reform efforts to rehabilitate criminals, largely because the deeply embedded Judeo-Christian concepts of repentance and redemption suggest that people are capable of moral regeneration. Indeed, the link between penology and religion in the United States can be traced to the 18th century when religious groups such as the Quakers began to enter prisons and presumably helped rehabilitate inmates by preaching their gospel. Under Quaker philosophy, a major goal of confinement was penance through required Bible study and reflection on one's sins (Sumter & Clear, 2005). In fact, the two earliest U.S. prisons, Auburn in New York State and Eastern State Penitentiary in Philadelphia, Pennsylvania, were grounded on redemptive principles when they opened in the 1820s. Auburn, stressing redemptive discipline and hard labor, reflected what some see as the spirit of the *Protestant ethic*. Eastern State Penitentiary, although later adopting the labor-discipline model, began as a Quaker experiment to create a system in which prisoners would be confined to their cells to study and receive religious instruction so that they might reflect on their offenses. Both systems were guided by an implicit notion of the malleability of human nature: Auburn, through changing behavior by instilling discipline, and Eastern State Penitentiary, by changing character through religious instruction (Johnston, 1994).

The influence of religion in prisons continued through the 19th century and into the 20th century, as prisons began including chapels in their design. By the mid-20th century, religion was recognized as an accepted program in virtually all U.S. prisons, and most prisons employed prison chaplains and allowed volunteer lay persons to tend to prisoners' religious needs. However, with limited exceptions, religious rights extended primarily to the two Christian doctrines of Catholics and Protestants. The growth of the Black Muslim religion in prisons set the stage for litigation demanding that non-Christians receive the same rights and privileges as people of other faiths (special diets, access to clergy and religious publications, opportunities for group worship). For example, in *Fulwood v. Clemmer* (1962),[1] the U.S. District Court of the District of Columbia ruled that Black Muslims have the same right to practice their religion and hold worship services as do inmates of other faiths. In 1963, the Warren Court handed down its landmark decision in *Cooper v. Pate* (1964),[2] which resurrected 19th-century civil rights legislation and provided the legislative justification for redressing state civil rights complaints in federal courts. This opened the door for litigation challenging restrictions on prisoners' right to practice religion. In *Cruz v. Beto* (1971),[3] the court further expanded protected groups in ruling that a Buddhist prisoner must be given a "reasonable opportunity of pursuing his faith comparable to the opportunity afforded fellow prisoners who adhere to conventional religious precepts."

The rights of some religious groups were curtailed by prison administrators' fears that prisoners were using religion as a ploy for political action, as a shield for gang activity, or as a means to obtain illicit resources. For example, up to the 1970s, many prison administrators continued to believe that Black Muslims were primarily a radical political group posing as a religion, and they did not grant them the benefits accorded to persons who practiced conventional religions. Other prisoners creatively attempted to establish idiosyncratic religions with esoteric needs as a means of acquiring resources, such as "ritualistic" wine, steak, and less restricted access to sex. Although litigation on such trivial grounds were often dramatized by the media and prison officials hostile both to prisoners and their litigation, such cases were relatively infrequent and quickly dismissed by the courts.

Litigation to expand the religious rights and privileges of prisoners led some critics to argue that the judiciary, not prison administrators, had gone too far and that prisoners could easily circumvent prison rules simply by invoking a religious premise. However, case law applies the reasonableness test to inmates' right to practice their religion with regard to the special security needs of prisons. The U.S. Supreme Court has found such restrictions appropriate as long as they are necessary to further legitimate penological objectives.[4]

In the past 20 years, Muslims, Orthodox Jews, Native Americans, Sikhs, Rastafarians, Wiccans, and other groups have gained some of the rights considered necessary for the practice of their religions and have broken new legal ground in First Amendment issues. Court decisions have upheld prisoners' rights to be served meals consistent with religious dietary laws, to correspond with religious leaders and possess religious literature, to wear a beard if one's religious belief requires it, and to assemble

---

[1]See *Fulwood v. Clemmer*, 206 F.Supp 370 (1962).

[2]See *Cooper v. Pate*, 378 U.S. 546 (1964).

[3]See *Cruz v. Beto*, 405 U.S. 319, 322 (1971).

[4]See *O'Lone v. Shabazz*, 107 S.Ct. 2400 (1987) and *Turner v. Safley*, 482 U.S. 78 (1987).

for religious services. Federal and state governments have contributed to the expansion of legitimate religious groups and practices in prisons by enacting legislation that, although intended primarily to protect the religious rights of free individuals, have also expanded those of prisoners.

Today, a variety of groups are actively involved with prisoners in an attempt to address their offending behavior as well as offering support. Furthermore, such ministry is not confined to Christianity, though this religious orientation dominates in prisons with aggressive and well-organized proselytizing and promoting Christian values in the integrated content of programs. For example, Florida's faith-based prisons have been criticized for building prison programming and control around denominational precepts (Besen, 2004). Prison Fellowship Ministries, the largest and best known organization, has developed partnerships with at least four states to implement Christian-based programs intended to provide a model for other prisons (Nolan, 2002). Brazil's Humaita Prison was designed to turn the prison into a Christian community, reportedly with some success (Johnson, 2002). The Baptist Experiencing God program in Angola prison is given credit for reducing violence, escapes, and providing stability to the inmate culture (Frink, 2004).

CONTEMPORARY ROLE OF PRISON RELIGION

The fact that religion is now on the national criminological agenda resulted from a complex set of factors: (1) the growth of the Restorative Justice movement which often draws on biblical notions of justice (Johnston & Van Ness (2006); (2) the widespread appeal of Native American, Christian, Islamic, and other religious practices such as Transcendental and Buddhist meditation among prisoners (O'Connor & Pallone, 2002); (3) a call from the U.S. Catholic Bishops for an end to the death penalty (U.S. Conference of Catholic Bishops, 2000); (4) the passing in 2001 and upholding by the Supreme Court in 2006 of the Religious Land Use and Institutionalized Persons Act (RLUIPA) that substantially strengthened the constitutional right of people to practice their religion in prison; (5) President George W. Bush's faith-based initiative; (6) and the growth of faith-based prisons or prison units around the country, including Alaska, Iowa, Louisiana, New Mexico, Texas, Florida, Ohio, Kansas, and the Federal Bureau of Prisons as well as in other countries such as Brazil and England (Burnside, Loucks, Adler, & Rose, 2005).

Prison Ministry

A. Chaplains

Religion has always played a vital role in corrections. Throughout history, Catholic priests, Protestant pastors, and an occasional Jewish rabbi were available to inmates. Faith and religion have often been important sources of strength for those caught in the criminal justice system. Most of the direct influence of religion in corrections has been accomplished through the work of correctional chaplains.

Early prison chaplains in the United States held positions of relative importance which is not surprising considering they were part of a system created by religious groups. They were responsible for visiting inmates, providing services and sermons, and also served as teachers, librarians, and record keepers. At times, the chaplain might also act as an ombudsman for the inmates when issues of maltreatment would arise. Chaplains were not always welcome in correctional facilities as they were viewed as being naive and susceptible to inmate manipulation. In fact, during the development of the reformatory, many prison administrators considered chaplains to be a hindrance to running a prison. However, the Clinical Pastoral Education Movement of the 1920s and 1930s resulted in the reemergence of prison chaplaincy in a positive light. The professionalization of prison chaplaincy work was evident in the organized methods of study and dissemination of the gospel by competent professional chaplains who were able to meld their work as yet another form of applied rehabilitation. Today, it is common that the prison chaplain is an educated and multiskilled person who is generally accepted as helpful by the diverse groups of individuals who live and work in the prison setting.

By the laws of the Religious Freedom Restoration Act instated in 1993, states are obligated to the best of their abilities to accommodate the spiritual needs of its incarcerated population. Muslims, Christians, Jews, Buddhists, Wiccans, Native Americans, and a wide variety of other religious groups practice their rituals under one roof, often within inches of each other. Most of the groups are led by state-employed chaplains and sometimes by civilian volunteers who have overcome fears, stereotypes, and prejudices, to pray and heal with individuals and groups of inmates. Prison chaplaincy services may provide a benefit in lowering facility infractions and reducing recidivism (Rioux, 2007). There is growing evidence to support the efficacy of cognitive-behavioral programs in the correctional environment; however, few formal studies have been conducted on faith-based cognitive programs (Hall, 2003).

Currently, the widespread financial crisis affecting so many state governments has created a situation of uncertainty for the future of prison chaplaincy. As states have been forced to cut overall spending, some of them have also eliminated state-paid prison chaplains from their organizational charts. The rationale given by some legislators in these states is that religious services can be provided by volunteers at no cost. This reasoning reflects a limited understanding of the chaplain's role as one who only provides worship services and sacramental rites, but it overlooks important issues such as facilitating the constitutional rights of all offenders to practice their religion and providing skilled pastoral care. In the long run, these roles and others may save the state more money in terms of fewer lawsuits and providing effective treatment programs.

Potential Bumps in the Religious Road to Redemption

State budget crises are forcing states to search for ways to cut prison costs. Their choices include allowing privately-sponsored evangelical prison ministries to replace chaplains at lower costs or for free, dropping below the national standard of one chaplain per 500 prisoners, or replacing the paid chaplains with volunteers. Colorado recently replaced all the chaplains in its state prisons with an evangelical Christian prison ministry that offered services for free. In Texas, lawmakers cut 62 state prison chaplain positions in 2003, a 40% reduction. In Georgia, legislators are considering a proposal to replace state-funded chaplains with volunteers.

Evangelical Christians are moving into cash-strapped state prisons to supplement and, in some cases, replace existing chaplain services. Their mission is answering Jesus' call to visit the imprisoned and recognizing the power of faith to transform troubled inmates into productive citizens. Their work is supported by private donations and encouraged by the government's emphasis on faith-based social services. Correctional officials say they are grateful for the free or low-cost help. But many people challenge the fairness and legality of giving one religious group unusual access to prisoners.

Critics say evangelicals have a conflict: their faith tells them to win converts, but the law requires prisons—and those who work there—to respect and even encourage the inmates' own religious beliefs, whatever they are. Some inmates, professional chaplains, and non-Christian religious leaders accuse evangelical Christians of barring prisoner access to nonevangelical ministers and of forcing inmates to endure evangelizing. Some prison programs grant special privileges for those who profess Christian beliefs. A federal judge in Iowa has ruled that the Bible-based prison program, InnerChange Freedom Initiative (an organization with ties to Charles Colson's Prison Fellowship Ministries), violated the First Amendment's freedom-of-religion clause by using state funds to promote Christianity to inmates (Hughes, 2006). The decision has set the stage for an appeals process that is expected to explore more broadly the constitutionality of the Bush administration's religion-based initiative programs.

People of faith care about the inmates, and evangelical Christians have been particularly attentive to their needs and those of their families. Nearly everyone agrees that religion can bring discipline, focus, and purpose to prisoners' lives. Yet religion isn't accepted as a cure-all, and many see dangers in what they perceive as either the underuse or overuse of it in prison. Experts are divided over whether there is solid evidence that religious programs do a better job rehabilitating prisoners than do secular ones (Mears, 2007). Many worry that chaplaincy cuts may deprive inmates of spiritual support, while others worry that faith will be illegally foisted on this captive audience.

B. Prison Ministry Work

The purpose of incarceration is to attempt to reform people and not to punish them vindictively. The word *penitentiary* derives from the notion of prison as a place where the imprisoned may reflect on their misdeeds and repent of them (i.e., be penitent). This dovetails neatly with the religious concept of changing one's life through conversion. The conversion experience is stressed most emphatically in evangelical Christianity. Prisoners who are Jewish or Islamic, or who adhere to other non-Christian religions, face the problem of unfamiliarity. Special needs related to their religious observances—such as holidays and dietary laws—may or may not be accommodated gladly. Therefore, it is not surprising that in recent years, prison ministry has become primarily the domain of evangelical Christians. Today's prison ministries tend to seek reform of individual prisoners, not the criminal justice system.

Christian involvement to those men and women behind bars falls into five general areas of ministry: evangelism, on-going discipleship (to include counseling), follow-up to ex-prisoners, providing full and part-time chaplains, and ministry to the families. All prison ministries rely heavily upon the local religious community to provide volunteers to energize the outreaches they offer. The vast majority of these ministries exhort, equip, and assist the volunteer in their ministry to the prisoner. Of the five areas, by far the most emphasis is placed on evangelism. A variety of faith-based programs have been offered in the prison setting as well as in the community. Box 11.1 provides a sampling of programs that have gained nationwide attention.

Box 11.1 **Sample of Faith-Based Programs in Correctional Setting**

- Aleph Institute (http://aleph-institute.org)—The mission and purpose of Project H.E.L.P. is the rehabilitation of inmates and improved family, social, and work ethic accomplished by behavior modification modalities that integrate principles of Jewish law and tradition with psychological principles. The program will integrate religious/ spiritual, educational/vocational, therapeutic, and case management services to create a comprehensive approach to helping the inmate and his or her family. They provide assistance to Jewish and non-Jewish prisoners who request their assistance.
- Kairos Prison Ministry International (http://kairosprisonministry.org/)—This group has three programs that address the spiritual needs of incarcerated men, women, and children, and to their families and to those who work inside prisons. The interdenominational team of volunteers—both clergy and laypersons—works in cooperation with the prison chaplain to select participants. Kairos "Inside," "Outside," and "Torch" programs currently operate in hundreds of prisons and communities throughout the U. S. and abroad. More than 170,000 incarcerated men and women have been introduced to Kairos since its inception, and over 20,000 volunteers donate their time and resources for this effort.
- Prison Fellowship (http://www.prisonfellowship.org)—The organization partners with churches across the United States—and around the world—to share the love of Christ and serve the special needs of prisoners, ex-prisoners, and their families, including the children. The organization provides several programs for inmates and their family members including "Angel Tree" that serves the children of prisoners in various capacities and includes programs like Angel Tree Christmas, Angel Tree Camping, and Angel Tree Mentoring; the "Pen Pal Program" matches prisoners with someone on the outside to write to them regularly and offers encouragement and emotional/spiritual support, but cannot help with financial or legal needs; "Inside Journal" is Prison Fellowship's newspaper that is produced for incarcerated women and men in state and federal prisons in the United States and includes encouraging articles on ex-prisoners who are now succeeding in life, profiles on celebrities who have a vibrant faith in Christ, helpful Bible studies, guidance on

(Continued)

(Continued)

    making the most of prison time, information on preparing for release from prison,
    current news that relates to prisoners and the criminal justice system, and some
    humorous pieces just for fun.

*   Prisoner & Family Ministry—(http://www.lssi.org/Service/PrisonerAndFamily-
    MinistryOverview.aspx) Lutheran Social Services of Illinois (LSSI) provides sev-
    eral programs to incarcerated women including "Visits to Mom" that transports
    children to every department of corrections facility housing women, through
    their corps of volunteer drivers and monthly bus trips; "Relatives as Parents Pro-
    gram" that is a support group for grandmothers and other caregivers; "Re-Con-
    nections" provides a place where newly-released women are given encouragement
    and referrals to community resources and services that address their needs; the
    "Storybook Project" provides books and tape recorders to inmate mothers so
    they can record and mail stories to their children on tape; LSSI's "Building
    Homes: Rebuilding Lives" program where homes are built for economically dis-
    advantaged families using walls built by prisoners at the Hardin County Work
    Camp who participate in this program.

What all of these faith groups would appear to have in common is a fervent belief that people can change. The normative prescriptions for restoration of the human spirit are taught routinely in churches and synagogues. It is no wonder, then, that religious institutions have come to acquire a certain ownership of the problem of deviance and its moral remedy. Concerted rehabilitation efforts have been funneled into a wide variety of prison ministries. There are literally thousands of small, inde- pendent churches and religious organizations that operate prison ministries today. Services provided by prison ministries range from the distribution of Bibles and other religious materials to more comprehensive programs such as family counsel- ing, legal aid, and victim-offender reconciliation/mediation. In spite of these efforts there are concerns regarding the role of religion within prison. For some, these concerns focus upon the economics of overcrowded prisons; with resources stretched to breaking point, it is feared that the government is allowing charitable organizations to take over its role. Others fear that prisoners' inherent vulnerability leaves them liable to be swayed by the tangible benefits religious groups are able to offer, leaving little real choice for the individual.

THE SEPARATION OF CHURCH AND STATE DEBATE

Faith and religion play a complex and controversial role in the criminal justice sys- tem. From the growing number of Christian ministries and Bible-study groups in prison to church-based inner city programs for ex-prisoners to the recent contro- versy over the role of posting the Ten Commandments in public spaces, the influence of faith and religion, especially Christianity, is visible in all aspects of the legal and criminal justice systems. And while faith and religion have often been important sources of strength for those caught in the criminal justice system, critiquing the role of faith becomes tricky. When is faith empowering and when is it being used to oppress? Should we fight for increased religious access or a ban on the practice of religion in the criminal justice system? The positive role faith and religion may play in an individual's life must be balanced with the reality that some spiritual conversions occur in the name of improved living conditions (e.g., faith-based pods) as compared to true individual change(s) and that some religious programming may occur as the manipulation of faith to push a conservative cultural and policy agenda which must be exposed and resisted.

The rise of the religious, or faith-based, prison at the turn of the 21st century bears witness to the remarkable resilience of religion in shaping the philosophy of punishment. It seems that most of the attention over the past two to three decades has focused on Prison Fellowship Ministries, started by former Watergate figure, Chuck Colson. In the beginning, it sought no outside funds from government, instead focusing on grass roots organizing through churches and lay ministries. Early efforts focused on volunteers visiting prisons to spread the word. It evolved into prison ministry, with training for volunteers who would serve as mentors to the incarcerated and eventually assist former prisoners with their reentry. Critical shortages in prison funding for programming assisted the growth in acceptance for prison fellowship among criminal justice professionals. The program continued to evolve to the point of proposals to run entire wings of some prisons. In the last decade, prisons that incorporate religion in various ways have sprouted around the country—in Florida, Iowa, Kansas, Minnesota, and Texas—and there are some indications, though preliminary, inconclusive, and hotly contested, that inmates who participate in religious instruction and "programming" recidivate at significantly lower rates than those who do not. The early success of these programs (and, some say, the preferential treatment accorded to participants in them) has resulted in high demand and long waiting lists. Florida has recently opened its second faith-based prison, this one for women, and more such programs are presently being planned and implemented. Religious prisons raise very serious questions of constitutionality and effectiveness, and most of the critical commentary to date has focused either on the various complicated Establishment Clause concerns or the programs' inconclusive recidivism results.

Criminologists, scholars, and civil liberties groups have warned against expanding faith-based prison programs, citing questions about their constitutionality and the effect on prisoners' behavior. Some experts dispute claims that faith-based rehabilitation leads to fewer future arrests. Others have questioned whether such programs amount to special treatment for religious prisoners or proselytizing. One major concern expressed by critics of expanded religious programming focuses on the additional benefits provided to participants by the religious programs. For example, volunteer inmate participants in the InnerChange Freedom Initiative receive Bible and computer classes, mentors from local congregations, and the promise of postrelease jobs (Nolan, 2002). While participation in InnerChange does not require participants to be Christians, they must participate in all of the programs, which centers on the transforming power of Jesus. Because of these additional benefits, critics are justifiably concerned that in order for inmates to receive these benefits, program participants are exposed to only one religious philosophy, thereby endorsing a Christian religion over the other religious faiths. Other critics wonder why an inmate must embrace religion in order to receive benefits—such as vocational/educational training, mentorship, family counseling, and job placement—that have been shown to reduce recidivism. If programs such as InnerChange due show positive results in reducing recidivism, there still remain questions whether the outcome is the result of religious conversion, the result of educational/vocational programming, mentorship or other forms of social support, or some combination thereof.

DOING PRISON TIME

Inmates in today's prisons do not serve their terms in isolation. Rather, prisoners form a society with traditions, norms, and a leadership structure. Some members of this society may choose to associate with only a few close friends (Jones & Schmid, 2000); others form cliques along racial or "professional" lines (Carroll, 1974). Still others may be the politicians of the convict society; they attempt to represent convict interests and distribute valued goods in return for support. Just as there is a social culture in the free world, there is a prisoner subculture on the inside. Membership in a group provides mutual protection from theft and physical assault, the basis of wheeling and dealing activities, and a source of cultural identity (Irwin, 1980). The inmate subculture helps inmates cope with the challenges, frustrations, deprivations, and pains of imprisonment that are part of the prison experience (Sykes, 1958). These deprivations are somewhat alleviated or neutralized through a collective response, which is in clear-cut opposition to the desires of prison officials.

Various factors affect the extent of an inmate's assimilation into the prison culture. These include personal characteristics such as age, race, marital status, socioeconomic status, educational attainment, and extent of criminal involvement (Drowns & Hess, 1995). Clemmer (1958) found that inmates incarcerated for short periods, as a year or so, were neither assimilated into the prison culture nor had they become prisonized. Most people can endure deprivations for short periods of time because they can see an end to their torment. For those facing long sentences, prison becomes home. For many, faced with years behind walls, life becomes a strategy for survival. To make it in this environment, inmates must adapt to its more unpleasant features (Zaitzow, 1999).

Most prisoners hope to adapt quickly to prison culture, do their time, and leave. For them, the short prison stay may be insufficient to motivate any significant personal transformation. Prisoners who serve longer sentences have different adaptation mechanisms and, for them, adaptation is a longer, more complex process. For some, adaptation entails reinforcing behavior patterns that are counterproductive and debilitating. For others, adaptation entails withdrawal. However, for a small but significant group, a personal transformation occurs in which they admit their offenses and attempt to redirect the focus of their life by transforming themselves and helping others through the study and practice of religious precepts.

Doing "Religious/Spiritual" Time

Prisons have real consequences for the people who enter them. When prison environments lack effective programming and treatment, allow for the persistence of dangerous and deprived conditions of confinement, and continue to use forceful or potentially damaging techniques of institutional controls, the people who reside in those environments are impacted by the harmful and destructive effects or consequences of such exposure. For short-term and long-term prisoners, the incarceration experience takes a unique toll.

People often turn to religion or (re)discover a spiritual identity in times of crisis, like while lying in a hospital bed with a critical illness or while holding on for dear life during an earthquake. These moments can instantly illuminate the frailty and brevity of life, causing a sudden realization of our dependence on some type of spiritual core. One might question the authenticity of a faith conversion made in such dire circumstances—Is the decision genuine or is it spurred only by fear in a last ditch effort to "make it into heaven?" As one can imagine, a similar phenomenon happens behind prisons walls, to such an extent that it's been coined *jailhouse religion*. Such life-changing events may be short-lived or such spiritual awakenings may, indeed, last a lifetime. But, it is important to understand the level of spiritual commitment in order to minister to men and women in prison.

Religion can serve, at least, four roles in prison. First, it provides answers to the prisoner's questions about life. Second, it provides rules to adhere to, which makes inmate management easier. Third, it is experiential. In other words, something intrinsic takes place (salvation or conversion) which is evident to the inmate and later to those around him or her. Finally, religion plays a social role bringing together like-minded inmates for worship, Bible study and other faith-related activities. This togetherness gives the inmate a sense of belonging and positively impacts the prison's culture.

There is evidence that religion helps make prisons more manageable. In one study, the researcher found that prisoners often seek God to cope with inmate life, which is marked by depression, guilt, and self-contempt. Here, highly religious inmates evidence lower rates of depression and commit fewer disciplinary infractions than other inmates (Clear et al., 1992). In another study, correctional officials from three states credited Prison Fellowship's religious programming with improved morale, lower rates of depression, and fewer disciplinary infractions. Administrators generally agree that programs are important in dealing with the problem of time on the prisoners' hands. They know that the more programs prisons offer, the less likely inmate idleness turns into hostility. Prisoner religious organizations present a unique opportunity to channel inmates' energies and use their talents in meaningful and beneficial ways (Fox, 1982).

Conning or Conversion: Does It Really Matter?

While some inmates, staff, and members of society share the belief that inmates practice religion to manipulate or con others into early release decisions or to influence wardens or chaplains to improve prison living conditions, prisoner religious organizations present a unique opportunity to channel inmate energies and use their talents in meaningful and beneficial ways (Thomas & Zaitzow, 2006).

A. Psychological-Emotional Benefits

It is difficult to determine the motivations for prisoners' involvement with religious programs while incarcerated. This difficulty is caused by the fact that religious belief and practice is an individual matter and exacerbated by the psychological complexities of living in prison. In some cases, the person may simply be practicing their faith. Here, they may have grown up practicing a religion, joined a religion later in life, or developed the interest during incarceration. Their faith can provide them with a direction that is better than their present psychological or physical condition on the inside.

For others, the trauma of life events (e.g., incest and domestic violence) may have been the precipitating force behind their drug addictions. For this group of individuals, prison programs have little to offer incest survivors; they are mostly left on their own to reflect on their life experiences and support each other to heal. In such cases, inmates may gain direction and meaning for their life from the practice of religion while in prison.

Religion also provides hope for incarcerated men and women—the hope to reform from a life of crime and from a life of imprisonment may give them peace of mind or some level of personal contentment. This is especially important to the well-being of those serving long sentences (Zaitzow, 2006).

Incarcerated women and men may opt to become involved with a faith-based program to improve their self-concept. Because the core of many religious beliefs includes acceptance and love from a higher being—and from members of the faith group—those who suffer from guilt related to failures in life, remorse for criminal acts, or from the pain of a dysfunctional family background, may feel better about themselves if they practice religion while incarcerated.

Finally, some inmates have committed horrific crimes which make them outsiders within the prison world and often subject to attacks by other inmates. Participation in a faith-based program can provide them with the social support that would not otherwise be available to them in prison (Jones, 2006).

B. Practical-Material Benefits

The serious practice of religion typically involves self-discipline, self-introspection, and concern for others to follow the principles associated with one's faith. Learning and practicing such self-control helps inmates avoid confrontations with other inmates and staff that might otherwise result in a negative response. Moreover, it helps them comply with prison rules and regulations.

There are additional reasons why prisoners might become involved with prison religious programming. Depending on the prison, some may believe that membership in a religious group will provide protection from some of the negative features of prison life like physical confrontation, sexual exploitation, or blackmail. The presumed safe territory of the prison chapel may be a refuge for those who wish to escape the day-to-day frustrations associated with living in prison. Further, affiliation with religious groups may facilitate new friendships among the inmate population as well as the opportunity to meet male and female volunteers who visit the prison to conduct religious services. Moreover, such affiliations may result in access to special resources that are difficult or impossible to obtain while incarcerated. For example, food and drink that may be offered at the religious service may be an incentive for people to attend services. In addition, free goods/materials (e.g., books, music, holiday and greeting cards) may be given to inmates as a means by which they may continue their religious training after the volunteers have departed.

There are many men and women doing time in our nation's prisons and jails who do a lot of community service work so that they can heal and reconnect with the community and, perhaps atone for their crimes. They may feel remorse and hope that the community will accept their new efforts. Many are determined to contribute to society. They transcribe educational materials for the blind and read books into tapes for the blind (Prison Braille Program). They train puppies to serve as helpers for the mobility-impaired in the community (Pathways to Hope Prison Dog Project) and support a variety of community projects throughout the nation. The Jaycee program at the Minnesota Correctional Facility in Stillwater raises money to combat Muscular Dystrophy. Or during natural disasters, prisoners can often be found filling sand bags or doing other work to help save communities from flooding waterways. Sadly, we rarely hear about such positive efforts as the media is busy catering to the fast-food mentality of the citizenry and stories of pain, endurance, and redemption are not often viewed as big sellers.

As a society, we must promote and embrace policies and practices that support the reality that women and men are different and diverse but that each group's needs can be addressed during their imprisonment as well as upon their release. There is a need for networking between agencies and groups to partner with incarcerated populations and prison administrators to create pastoral and public policy reforms that address the specific needs of the incarcerated and their families.

THE POWER OF FAITH/RELIGION IN PRISON

As long as there have been prisons, religious education and training have been a staple of prison life. Religious programs for inmates are not only among the oldest but also among the most common forms of rehabilitative programs found in correctional facilities today. Previous research has focused largely on incarcerated males and traditional measures of religiosity such as participation in religious-based activities while incarcerated (Clear & Sumter, 2002). While more recent research has examined incarcerated individuals, their offenses, and religious/spiritual orientation (Fernander, Wilson, Staton, & Leukefled, 2005), there is a paucity of systematic research on the relationship between prison religious practice and key outcomes important to a rehabilitative or correctional framework for diverse populations. The limited empirical research that does exist has tended to examine the effects of religious programs in a prison setting on outcomes such as institutional behavior and recidivism. For example, an exploratory study by Sumter (2000) did examine the effect of inmate religiosity on postrelease community adjustment. Findings indicated that inmates who reported high levels of belief in the supernatural were less likely to be arrested after release. Another study by Johnson, Larson, and Pitts (1997) evaluated the impact of religious programs on institutional adjustment and recidivism rates upon release. They found that inmates who were most active in Bible studies were significantly less likely to be arrested in the following year after release.

More recently, according to one prison chaplain, recidivism is reduced by half for persons who participate in a weekly faith-based activity (Rioux, 2007). Other administrators report observable behavioral improvements among incarcerated persons with the expansion of faith-based programs. For example, in a southeastern prison, religiosity among residents was associated with reduced verbal and physical conflicts and prosocial behavior (Kerley, Matthews, & Blanchard, 2005). Clear and Sumter (2002) report that religiosity among the incarcerated is helpful in modifying behavior as well as psychological states. In their study, higher levels of religiosity were linked to enhanced psychological adjustment and fewer self-reports of disciplinary confinement. In a review by O'Connor and Perryclear (2002) of studies which examined the outcomes (e.g., prison infractions, adjustment, recidivism) of prison religious involvement, the researchers concluded that while the effects were modest, there were questions regarding methodological weaknesses that rendered the findings inconclusive.

Little is known about the process of offender rehabilitation or why some offenders desist in their criminal careers. Maruna (2001) describes a phenomenology of reform in which the individual's transformation of self entails leaving the past behind (that selfish, hedonistic, immoral criminal) and replacing it with the new self who cares for others and has new goals, aspirations and actions. Whether in the context of *finding God, being born again* or simply *finding personal peace*, the transformation process for people of all religious and spiritual beliefs involves a recasting of oneself. More research is obviously needed to explore these intriguing findings which have implications for the reintegration of formerly incarcerated people into the community and most importantly, for their reformation as law-abiding citizens.

Although religious services have long been a staple of prison life, officials across the nation are beginning to realize just how important faith can be in promoting the rehabilitation of inmates and managing the increasing numbers of people in prison. Many prison officials report that religious activities are widely popular and successful. Thus, it is not surprising that increasing theoretical attention has focused on the use of such programs in a correctional institution as well as a resource for reentry efforts (O'Connor, 2004, 2004–2005; Thomas & Zaitzow, 2006).

THE CONTINUATION OF REDEMPTION UPON RELEASE

There is an abundance of research that documents the structural impediments to postprison success resulting in numerous legal restrictions and economic difficulties (Petersilia, 2003; Richards & Jones, 2004). Roughly two thirds of all prison inmates recidivate within three years of their release from prison (Austin & Irwin, 2001). This statistic is often used as a measure of the intractability of criminal behavior or as a failure of the criminal justice system in rehabilitating criminal offenders. Two structural factors have been identified as key to the successful reentry of ex-prisoners into the free world. Those two factors are obtaining meaningful employment and maintaining a strong social support network. Although there is some empirical evidence that religious involvement may enhance inmates' adjustment and coping in prison (Clear et al., 1992), there is little research to document the role of religious commitment and participation in facilitating a successful community reentry.

Anecdotal evidence reinforces what many prison researchers have known for years—one of the greatest fears many inmates have is being released. Typically, if an inmate has no family or support group to meet them at release, the state transports them to the local greyhound station or capital city. Before the van drives away, the inmate is given approximately $100, a duffle bag with his meager personal effects, and the clothes worn on his back at the time of imprisonment. In effect, men and women are set up to fail, without any means for obtaining transportation, lodging, food, clothing, or employment. Imagine the fear and anxiety of being thrust into this situation when for the past several years of life, your schedule has been determined for you while in prison. Food, clothing, shelter, recreation, education, and even menial work responsibilities—all has been provided for you up until this time. Now you are responsible to provide those essentials of life for yourself without any knowledge or skills to do so. As simple as these everyday responsibilities are for those on the outside, it becomes a complete culture shock for the now ex-prisoner. Unfortunately, many believe they have no alternative other than the life they know how to live. Many have already been rejected by family and friends. Some are caught in a revolving door, out of prison only to go back into prison. They are powerless to change in their own strength. They go back to the same neighborhood, the same way of life, the same temptations and find their personal strength and determination fails them.

Participation in faith-based programs may strengthen social norms through the identification and reinforcement of values, attitudes, and beliefs. This, in turn, may also serve as a social support mechanism in helping men and women to overcome the challenges associated with reintegration upon release. The great need in the lives of people behind prison walls—and those who will soon return to their communities—is hope. Faith-based programming may be the means by which hope is instilled in the hearts and minds of formerly incarcerated men and women. Believers in some spiritual core, who are released from prison, need a support network of a local church body that will care enough to offer fellowship, encouragement and a way to grow in their faith, as well as help them in practical ways with physical needs. The transition period from the old way of doing things into the new way of life must be supported by the local church or organization that provides the instruction. Newly released community members need friends who will counsel and encourage them in the religious/spiritual life they feel most comfortable with and the jobs they will need to seek out to be able to provide for themselves and their family. They need to know they can make it.

The successful transition from life in jail or prison to life in the community has profound implications for increasing public safety by reducing offender recidivism. A key way to accomplish that goal is to institutionalize the cross-agency and community teamwork needed to make reentry succeed. Reentry efforts must begin in the prison and be actively carried into the community after prisoners are released. Services need to be tailored to prisoners' needs that help them reintegrate into society. Many practitioners agree that an active link between in-prison services and community services requires an involved mentor, case manager, or steering committee. Many of the prisoners that reentry initiatives work with must be taught how to interact with them. Here, religion or spirituality may serve a variety of functions that may expedite the successful reintegration of the formerly incarcerated into society.

As correctional departments face increasing costs for an expanding array of inmate needs, budgets are stretched to the maximum. In some jurisdictions, this has resulted in a reliance on faith-based organizations even though very little research has been conducted to assess offender outcomes after receipt of services by faith-based providers. A growing number of correctional administrators and community reentry experts have found that faith-based organizations can provide much-needed services to offenders through volunteers. These in-prison and community services are important because, prior to release, they may prepare prisoners to more easily use the community services that will aid in their transition after release. In addition to offering in-prison programs, faith-based organizations often help prisoners' families. Faith-based groups can provide assistance that reflects the values of the community where the offender will live upon release. Because they are part of the community, faith-based volunteers may offer invaluable knowledge and assistance to offenders who are trying to manage transportation, housing, employment assistance, and health issues.

The need for faith-based organizations to be involved in prisoner reentry initiatives is widely recognized by local, state, and federal prison systems. As criminal justice professionals continue to develop strategies to reduce recidivism, it has become more apparent that the likelihood of success without the substantial involvement of faith-based organizations is unrealistic. Nationwide, states face huge budget deficits. Spending on prisons make up the largest (or close to the largest) portion of state expenditures. In order for states to begin chipping away at looming budget deficits, it is critical to reduce spending on prisons. Reducing recidivism is a critical part of any state's formula for reducing spending.

Indeed, the desire of many states to reduce recidivism is fueled to a great degree by finances instead of compassion. Departments of correction are coming to the conclusion that in order to be successful in keeping people out of prison, they must establish real partnerships with agencies and organizations in the community, including churches, synagogues, and other faith-based organizations. Aside from the financial problems faced by states, many have come to realize that certain aspects of reentry such as family reunification are best left to faith-based and community organizations.

In response to lawsuits, federal receivership of its medical, mental health, and juvenile justice systems, and pressure from the federal courts to immediately reduce massive overcrowding, it is inevitable that reducing prison overcrowding will entail expanding community-based alternatives to incarceration. Here, it is a well-known and documented fact that religious communities, like churches and other faith-based organizations, are seen as first responders to any crisis (Oppenheimer, Flannelly, & Weaver, 2004). Faith-based groups have a significant role to play in the reentry process in their communities, since offenders and their family members often turn to them for immediate assistance and advice on accessing services. Therefore, as communities nationwide prepare to move thousands of prisoners into community reentry programs, faith-based organizations need to be prepared not only to provide services, but to actively participate in developing its capacity to impact public policy. More importantly, churches and other faith-based programs need to provide strong, supportive, welcoming, and caring environments that can help recently released prisoners (and their families), take the initial steps toward community reengagement.

Most offenders return to their communities with multiple, cross-systems levels of needs—lack of adequate job skills, safe housing, and, the number one predictor of parole success or failure, substance abuse. Relapse to drug use is common for all recovering individuals, and offenders suffer from stresses more numerous and intense than those affecting the typical treatment patient. Many offenders, even those rare few who have received some type of in-custody treatment or education and are motivated to follow aftercare recommendations, are unable to maintain abstinence when faced with a myriad of difficult decisions with little or no positive support. Successful recovery requires development of a set of positive coping skills—being able to identify triggers, organizing one's day, disengaging from negative situations—as well as strong social and family supports. This is difficult for many offenders because of weakened family ties, and long-standing psychosocial problems, which put them at greater risk for relapse by virtue of their extreme socioeconomic deficits, exposure to drug-using associates, and other high-risk situations

The benefits of engaging the faith community in both prevention and treatment of substance abuse and dependence cannot be overstated, as the spiritual model of addiction is one of the most influential in America (Galanter, 2007). Twelve-step fellowships like Alcoholics Anonymous (AA) and Narcotics Anonymous (NA), for example, and 12-step program models emphasize the importance of a spiritual path to recovery—recognizing a Higher Power (God) beyond one's self, and a desire to achieve health through a connection with that which transcends the individual. Many churches actively support spiritual recovery models by opening their facilities for meetings, maintaining lists of available community resources, or operating transitional housing programs.

Healthy, productive ex-offenders can fortify families and resurrect the fragile communities that receive them socially, politically, and economically. These same men and women also bring with them overwhelming potential public health and safety challenges if their communities and governmental agencies do not provide them with appropriate, compassionate care. Faith-based organizations have a significant role to play in reintegrating residents returning from prison. Communities that receive these residents are depending on faith-based organizations to respond to fill the void that the state has been unwilling or unable to address. Nationwide, prison officials are encouraging community and faith-based organizations to assist them in developing plans to deal with the more systemic problems of substance abuse, lack of educational/vocational skills, and housing. Local public safety officials are relying on the faith community to help keep large numbers of offenders out of the revolving door between incarceration and freedom. However, faith-based organizations cannot continue to respond effectively without an expansion of true partnership opportunities and public investment in building their capacity to provide services.

POLICY IMPLICATIONS

With unprecedented numbers of formerly incarcerated men and women expected to be released from the nation's prisons, corrections officials sought innovative ways to increase the chance that fewer of them will return. Many officials turned to faith and character-based programs aimed at rehabilitation as well as reintegration that seek to change inmates' internal motivations as well as external behaviors. George W. Bush's administration strongly supported such programs, as a key focus of its Faith-Based and Community Initiative, an effort to encourage religious charities and other nonprofits to provide social services.

Faith-based prison programs typically include training in such secular topics as life skills, including reading, managing personal finances, and dealing with family issues. Some programs also aim at character transformation, sometimes with a deeply religious component. And some groups will assist in finding employment, either through job referrals or transportation to job interviews. Among the questions about the programs is whether they are truly effective in their ultimate nonreligious goal of reducing recidivism. At this early stage of the programs' development, insufficient research exists to supply a solid answer. And, even if participation in religious programming was correlated with reduced recidivism, questions would remain on how to discern whether the reduction was based exclusively on religious participation, the secular benefits that these programs also provide, or a combination thereof. In future analyses of these programs, it will be important to try to determine which factors are most important in reentry success.

Some groups have charged that, even if the programs eventually prove to be effective, they are, nonetheless, illegal. Critics worried that the programs blur the legal line separating church and state have mounted challenges to the programs' constitutionality in courts around the country. At the heart of the legal disputes is whether the government is merely accommodating prisoners' right to freely practice their faith—a constitutional protection that must be afforded to those under its custody, who do not have usual access to religious services—or actually supporting religious indoctrination, in violation of the law. To operate within the bounds of the Constitution, prison programs must (1) be neutral, without showing preference to one faith over another, or to religious over secular programming; (2) not mandate participation but allow inmates' to choose voluntarily to attend; and (3) ensure that religious content is not financed with taxpayer money.

Addressing the crisis in corrections requires policy intervention, because the present corrections reform debate is limited largely to "inside the building" discussions between bureaucrats, legislators, and traditional public safety interests. The response to reintegration thus far has overwhelmingly been from a program perspective and few community or faith-based organizations are in a position to make investments in public policy. This imbalance hinders comprehensive reintegration efforts. Increasing the capacity of community and faith-based organizations to contribute to public policy discussions increases successful reintegration efforts, by adding a unified community voice to the discussions. An additional benefit is that ownership/buy-in of reintegration and public safety outcomes expand.

Based on existing research, we recommend the following:

1. Developing Evidence-Based Practice

To support more rigorous testing of faith-based corrections models, policy makers and corrections officials implementing faith-based initiatives need to clearly define the intended outcomes of the initiative, create benchmarks for measuring success, and implement systems for tracking and analyzing outcomes data. To facilitate evaluation, program offerings should be standardized to provide a measurable treatment that is consistent over time and across facilities. When developing programming, secular models that have been shown to be effective should be reviewed and possibly adapted to the faith-based environment.

2. Leveraging Private Resources

One of the greatest benefits of faith-based prison programming is that it brings extensive program offerings into facilities at a minimal cost. The primary costs are the expenses for a somewhat expanded chaplaincy team and the additional demands on staff time driven by increased volunteer and inmate activity, although these added demands may be balanced with reductions in behavioral problems among inmates. Local volunteers, particularly from the faith community, are a tremendous untapped resource for both faith-based and traditional prisons and a potential asset for budget-strapped systems.

3. Extending Success Beyond Release

Like all corrections programs, faith-based initiatives intended to have a long-term impact need to address the reentry process. While positive outcomes may result inside prisons (e.g., adjustment, less disciplinary issues) there is not much known about "over time" and upon release. There is a need for providing the continuity of support needed to extend program benefits beyond the prison walls. Corrections officials implementing faith-based initiatives should incorporate mechanisms for extending the support and guidance provided by the programming through release and reentry. They should also ensure that the faith-based and character-development activities are complemented with vocational training and educational opportunities that develop the concrete skills necessary for reentry success.

4. Avoiding Religious Discrimination

Faith-based efforts in public correctional facilities can successfully serve inmates from different faiths and avoid religious discrimination. Many of the most popular faith-based corrections programs such as the InnerChange Freedom Initiative are exclusively Christian and explicitly religious, and these types of programs have run into legal challenges because of their bias toward a specific creed or denomination and the blurring of lines between church and state (Henriques & Lehren, 2006). But, there may be ways to design programs to draw on the perceived benefits of a faith-based approach while avoiding some of the church-state conflicts encountered by other faith-based corrections programs. For example, having all faith-based programming provided by volunteers using private funds, including a nonreligious character-development component in the model, making participation voluntary, explicitly avoiding any form of religious test for program participation, and recruiting volunteers from both Christian and non-Christian faiths (La Vigne, Brazzell, & Small, 2007). Religious diversity could benefit other faith-based corrections initiatives.

Specific policy-related issues that should be considered include the following:

Prison Infrastructure

1. Correctional institutions should be encouraged, wherever practical, to utilize faith-based programs that address documented criminogenic needs. Evidence-based programming that has been shown to impact the offender's lives should be made available to the faith community.

2. Wardens and superintendents should be encouraged to develop programs which will facilitate a cultural change in institutions to encourage collaboration with faith-based service providers.

3. Develop a standard training program for staff, volunteers, and the community to facilitate working together at each institution. The program should include

information on the ethics of working with offenders, confidentiality issues, ensuring the safety and security of volunteers, working with volunteers, and the rules and regulations for volunteers.

4. Improvements should be made in the various corrections departments with regard to communication about programs and services between the staff and the volunteers, the staff and the community, and other parts of the criminal justice system and the community.

Institutional Programming

1. Departments of corrections should work with the faith community and volunteers to develop and expand programs within the institutions: life skills programs, financial management/budgeting programs, personal hygiene programs, and family programs including classes on parenting.

2. Involve the faith community when appropriate in the development of release plans for the offender that flow from the institution to community reentry.

Reentry Programming

1. Methods should be developed to increase and encourage the involvement of the community and the faith community in various reentry efforts and to encourage collaboration among faith groups.

2. Inform offenders of various options before leaving prison or immediately upon release. This could be accomplished through seminars, with free legal or consultation services, along with the increased involvement of the community and faith community.

3. Partner with grassroots and community organizations in an educational effort toward the general public aimed at decreasing the negative stigma of ex-offenders and making the public aware of the needs involved in the process of reentry.

Alternatives to Incarceration

1. Revise statutes to increase judicial use of community options for nonviolent offenders so that prison space can be reserved for violent offenders.

2. Encourage faith-based programs to supplement existing community and diversionary programs for offenders and provide services that are not currently available.

3. State agencies need to take a more active role in linking with the faith-based community to develop programs to meet the gaps in services to adult and juvenile offenders.

4. Expand partnership efforts to work with the employment centers and faith community to increase practical employment opportunities for offenders in the community. A job placement program should be implemented, focusing on the following: providing information on job fairs to ex-offenders, education of businesses/employers on the benefits of hiring ex-offenders, incentives for employers to hire ex-offenders (i.e. tax breaks), and the increased involvement of faith-based groups/community groups.

CLOSING REMARKS

More research on these issues is just the starting point. Action is needed to address the multitude of policies and practices that ensnare men and women in systems that are unable to recognize and accommodate their needs as individuals and members of various communities. Men and women leaving prison face so many obstacles that perhaps the spiritual side of prisoners is the missing element in bringing about rehabilitation and/or facilitating successful reintegration upon release from prison. Prison efforts such as education, vocational training, and counseling are good, but they fail to target core values. Without this concentration on basic morals, many prisoners will go on to commit other crimes. Faith-based efforts offer spiritual development to inmates by preparing them for a job, teaching how to manage finances, and instilling in them strong values. Moreover, administrators appear to be willing to allow religion-based ministries into prisons. Women and men should be supported—at the individual, family, and community level—in their efforts to attain self-sufficiency and successful lives in their communities. Supporting such a process requires understanding how poverty, trauma, and victimization (past and present) and bad choices can combine to propel human beings into criminal involvement. Assisting these individuals effectively means providing access to coordinated services that address these multiple issues simultaneously.

DISCUSSION QUESTIONS

1. What role should outside religious organizations play in corrections (prisons, jails, community corrections)? Should constitutional concerns about separation of church and state factor into this decision?

2. Critics complain that inmates may be coerced into religious programming in order to receive special benefits afforded to program participants. Is this concern relevant, and how should it be addressed by prison administration?

3. Proponents of religious programming in prison claim that their programs work in reducing recidivism. Is it religious programming that is producing the change (transformation/conversion), or is it the additional benefits that produce the change in recidivism rates?

4. An interesting aspect of many of the faith-based groups entering prison to work with prisoners is that for once, the prison has opened its doors to outsiders. This, of course, can reveal some of the negative aspects of prison life that prisons have worked hard to keep from the general public. Do you think that prisons should partner with other, outside social groups to expand its programmatic offering? If so, what concerns might this raise for prison officials?

5. Identify the factors that influence inmates' willingness to participate in religious activities. Discuss the immediate and latent (dys)functions associated with such participation for inmates and staff.

6. What prison religious/spiritual programs have the most potential to promote long-lasting individual change? Are such programs compatible with institutional policies and procedures?

7. Identify future research questions and methods of studying the role of religion and spirituality with incarcerated populations.

SUGGESTED READINGS

Dammer, H. (1992). *Piety in prison: An ethnography of religion in the correctional environment*. Ann Arbor, MI: University Microfilms International.

Maruna, S., Wilson, L., & Curran, K. (2006). Why God is often found behind bars: Prison conversions and the crisis of self-narrative. *Research in Human Development 3*(2/3), 161–184.

Mears, D. P. (2007). Faith-based reentry programs: Cause for concern or showing promise? *Corrections Today, 69*(2), 30–33). American Correctional Association.

Philips, J., & Coles, R. (2008). *Letters from the Dhamma Brothers: Meditation behind bars*. Onalaska, WA: Pariyatti Publishing.

Sullivan, W. F. (2009). *Prison religion: Faith-based reform and the constitution*. Princeton, NJ: University Press, Princeton.

REFERENCES

Austin, J., & Irwin, J. (2001). *It's about time: America's imprisonment binge*. Belmont, CA: Wadsworth/Thomson Learning.

Besen, W. (2004, January 20). Florida's faith-based prison is a dangerous idea. *Tallahassee Democrat* [Electronic version]. Retrieved March 9, 2012, from http://www.tallahassee.com/mld/democrat/news/opinion/7747872.htm

Burnside, J., Loucks, N., Adler, J., & Rose, G. R. (2005). *My brother's keeper: Faith-based units in prison*. Devon, England: Willan.

Carroll, L. (1974). *Blacks, hacks and cons: Race relations in a maximum security prison*. Lexington, MA: Lexington Books.

Clear, T., & Sumter, M. (2002). Prisoners, prison, and religion: Religion and adjustment to prison. *Journal of Offender Rehabilitation 35*(3):127–159.

Clear, T. R., Stout, B. D., Dammer, H. R., Kelly, L. Hardyman, P. L., & Shapiro, C. (1992). *Does involvement in religion help prisoners adjust to prison?* NCJ 151513. Washington, DC: U.S. Department of Justice, National Institute of Justice.

Clemmer, D. (1958). *The prison community.* New York, NY: Holt, Rinehart & Winston.

Cooper v. Pate, 378 U.S. 546 (1964).

Cruz v. Beto, 405 U.S. 319, 322 (1971).

Drowns, R. W., & Hess, K. M. (1995). *Juvenile justice* (2nd ed.). St. Paul, MN: West.

Fernander, A., Wilson, J. F., Staton, M., & Leukefled, C. (2005). Exploring the type-of-crime hypothesis, religiosity, and spirituality in an adult male prison population. *International Journal of Offender Therapy and Comparative Criminology 49,* 682–695.

Fox, J. G. (1982). *Organizational and racial conflict in maximum security prisons.* Lexington, MA: Lexington Books.

Frink, C. (2004, May 7). Breaking into prison [Electronic version]. *Christianity Today.* Retrieved March 9, 2012, from http://www.txcorrections.org/article.pdf

Fulwood v. Clemmer, 206 F.Supp 370 (1962).

Galanter, M. (2007). Spirituality and recovery in 12-step programs: An empirical model. *Journal of Substance Abuse Treatment 33,* 265–272.

Glaze, L. (2010). *Correctional populations in the United States, 2009.* NCJ 231681. U.S. Department of Justice, Bureau of Justice Statistics. Retrieved from http://bjs.ojp.usdoj.gov/index.cfm?ty=tp&tid=11#pubs

Hall, S. T. (2003). Faith-based cognitive programs in corrections. *Corrections Today 65*(7), 108–113,120,137.

Henriques, D. B., & Lehren. A. (2006, December 10). *Religion for a captive audience, with taxpayers footing the bill. The New York Times.* Available at http://www.nytimes.com/2006/12/10/business/10faith.html

Hughes, C. (2006). *Potential for widespread fallout in ruling against Iowa faith-based prison program* [Electronic version]. Retrieved March 9, 2012, from http://www.religionand socialpolicy.org/news/article.cfm?id=4384

Irwin, J. (1980). *Prisons in turmoil.* Boston, MA: Little, Brown.

Johnson, B. R. (2002). *Assessing the impact of religious programming and prison industry on recidivism: An exploratory study.* Retrieved March 9, 2012, from http://web.archive.org/web/20030408001536/http://www.txcorrections.org/article.pdf

Johnson, B. R., Larson, D. B, & Pitts, T. C. (1997) Religious programs, institutional adjustment, and recidivism among former inmates in prison fellowship programs. *Justice Quarterly 14*(1), 145–166.

Johnston, N. (1994). *Eastern State Penitentiary: Crucible of good intentions.* Philadelphia, PA: Philadelphia Museum of Art.

Johnston, G., & Van Ness, D. (2006). *Handbook of restorative justice.* Devon, England: Willan.

Jones, R. S., & Schmid, T. J. (2000). *Doing time: Prison experience and identity.* Stamford, CT: Jai Press.

Jones, R. (2006, November). *Coping with re-entry: The role of prison fellowship in the re-entry process.* Paper presented at the annual meetings of the American Society of Criminology, Los Angeles, CA.

Kerley, K., Matthews, T., & Blanchard, T. (2005). Religiosity, religious participation, and negative prison behaviors. *Journal for the Scientific Study of Religion 44,* 443–457.

La Vigne, N., Brazzell, D., & Small, K. (2007). *Evaluation of Florida's faith- and character-based institutions.* Washington, DC: Urban Institute.

Maruna, S. (2001). *Making good: How ex-convicts reform and rebuild their lives.* Washington, DC: American Psychological Association.

Mears, D. P. (2007). Faith-based reentry programs: Cause for concern or showing promise? *Corrections Today 69*(2), 30–33.

Nolan, P. (2002). Prison fellowship and faith-based initiatives. *On the Line: A Publication of the American Correctional Association 25*(5), 1–2.

O'Connor, T. P (2004). What works, religion as a correctional intervention: Part I. *Journal of Community Corrections 14*, 11–22, 27.

O'Connor, T. P. (2004–2005). What works, religion as a correctional intervention: Part II. *Journal of Community Corrections 14*, 4–6, 20–26.

O'Connor, T. P., & Pallone, N. (2002). *Religion, the community, and the rehabilitation of criminal offenders*. Binghamton, NY: Haworth Press. Also available in *Journal of Offender Rehabilitation 35* (1,2). 2002.

O'Connor, T. P., & Perreyclear, M. (2002). Prison religion and its influence on offender rehabilitation. *Journal of Offender Rehabilitation 35*, 11–33.

O'Lone v. Shabazz, 107 S.Ct. 2400 (1987).

Oppenheimer, J. E., Flannelly, K. J., & Weaver, A. J. (2004). A comparative analysis of the psychological literature on collaboration between clergy and mental-health professionals— perspectives from secular and religious journals: 1970–1999. *Pastoral Psychology 53*(2), 153–162.

Petersilia, J. (2003). *When prisoners come home: Parole and prisoner reentry*. New York, NY: Oxford University Press.

Pew Research Center. (2008). *Pew report finds more than one in 100 adults are behind bars.* [Electronic version]. Available at http://www.pewcenteronthestates.org/news_room_detail.aspx?id=35912

Richards, S. C., & Jones, R. S. (2004). Beating the perceptual incarceration machine: Overcoming structural impediments to reentry. In S. Maruna & R. Immarigeon (Eds.), *After crime and punishment: Pathways to offender reintegration* (pp. 201–232). Devon, England: Willan.

Rioux, P. (2007, January 28). A chance for a fresh start. *Times Picayune*. Available at http://www.timespicayune.com

Sumter, M. T. (2000). *Religiousness and post-release community adjustment, Graduate research fellowship–Final report*. NCJ 184508. U.S. Department of Justice, National Institute of Justice.

Sumter, M. T., & Clear, T. (2005). Religion in the correctional setting. In R. Muraskin (Ed.), *Key Correctional Issues* (pp. 86–113). Upper Saddle River, NJ: Pearson/Prentice Hall.

Sykes, G. M. (1958). *The society of captives*. Princeton, NJ: Princeton University Press.

Thomas, J., & Zaitzow, B. H. (2006). Conning or conversion? The role of religion in prison coping. *The Prison Journal 86*, 242–259.

Turner v. Safley, 482 U.S. 78 (1987).

United States Conference of Catholic Bishops. (2000). *Responsibility, rehabilitation, and restoration: A Catholic perspective on crime and criminal justice*. Washington, DC: Author.

Zaitzow, B. H. (2006, November). *Doing time: Finding one's calling and sharing a message of hope*. Paper presented at the annual meetings of the American Society of Criminology, Los Angeles, CA.

Zaitzow, B. H. (1999). Doing time: Everybody's doing it. *Criminal Justice Policy Review 9*, 13–42.

CHAPTER 12

Incarcerated Veterans

Joel Rosenthal and Jim McGuire

INTRODUCTION

Each night some 225,000 military veterans can be found in jails and prisons (correctional facilities) throughout the United States (Mumola & Noonan, 2008), representing approximately 10% of the overall inmate population.

Each year an estimated 28,900 to 56,300 veterans will be released from state and federal prisons (differing estimates based on, for example, types of offenses and time served). Many have served in wartime, and of those who were in combat, battle scars are not uncommon. Regardless of whether in combat or not, each incarcerated veteran carries with him or her a military history and a sense of service to the country. As this subgroup of the general inmate population is to be more fully understood by institutional and reentry service providers, it is evident that military or wartime background represents an important factor in the care and rehabilitation of incarcerated

Table 12.1 National Estimates, Justice-Involved Veterans

Criminal Justice Involvement	Number of U.S. Residents Incarcerated, 2007	Percent Reporting Prior Military Service	Estimated Number of Military Veterans, 2007
Local jail custody[a]	780,600	9.3%	72,600
State prison custody[b]	1,315,300	10.4%	136,800
Federal prison custody[b]	197,300	9.8%	19,300

Source: Mumola and Noonan, 2008.

[a]Local jail population counts based on Bureau of Justice's *Annual Survey of Jails, 2007*; percentage of veterans based on Bureau of Justice's *Survey of Inmates in Local Jails, 2002*.

[b]State and federal prison population counts based on Bureau of Justice's *Survey of Inmates in State and Federal Correctional Facilities, 2004*.

veterans. Additionally, clear is the array of needs that may distinguish many of these veterans from the overall inmate population.

Because this chapter will necessarily focus on incarcerated veterans, an important beginning point in the discussion of veterans and incarceration is the fact that veterans—consistent with the fact of their prosocial commitment to military service—have substantially lower rates of incarceration than nonveterans: among adult males, the incarceration rate of veterans (630 prisoners per 100,000) was less than half that of nonveterans (1,390 prisoners per 100,000), a gap that has grown consistently over time (Noonan and Mumola, 2007). While veterans do represent a significant incarcerated population, media reports of veteran violence necessarily minimize the readjustment to civilian life that most veterans make and support a one dimensional perception of the incarcerated veteran population that can impede rehabilitation.

In this chapter, distinguishing features of incarcerated veterans are identified, including among a range of factors, military experiences that may be relevant to both the reasons for, and the response to, the veteran's incarceration. The chapter revisits and updates the profile of the incarcerated Vietnam veterans detailed over 25 years ago (Pentland & Dwyer, 1985). This will be followed by a description of the veteran experience within correctional facilities throughout the country, as well as those activities and programs that have been developed to serve incarcerated veterans, including two nationwide incarcerated veterans initiatives of the U.S. Department of Veterans Affairs (VA), the Veterans Health Administration's (VHA) Healthcare for Reentry Veterans (HCRV), and Veterans Justice Outreach (VJO) programs. Multisystem responses to veterans are highlighted, outlining models that have been operationalized to promote a second chance through effective reentry. The chapter concludes with a discussion of the implications of the overlapping worlds of military experience and the criminal justice system as well as future directions of consideration, for both the veteran and the systems serving him or her.

The scope of the chapter is limited to issues of veterans incarcerated in prison or jail facilities, and does not address veterans' issues in courts, community corrections, or law enforcement, though VA's work with veterans in these domains of the larger justice system is mentioned. Though emphasis will be on veterans in jail and prison, how veterans get there and what makes a difference when they leave is included as an essential part of the discussion.

Frank's Story

Frank is a two-tour decorated Vietnam army combat veteran, with no premilitary trouble with the law. In Vietnam, Frank became increasingly involved in smoking marijuana and eventually shooting heroin—"it helped me to deal with things day to day." In spite of his efforts to adjust upon discharge from the military, he thought of himself different than before, and others noticed the changes as well. Eventually, there were a series of incidents in bars, often culminating in fights and brief stints in county jail. When the local newspaper reported that he had been charged with murder in the beating of a man outside of a bar, it was not a surprise to those who knew him. He was eventually convicted of second degree murder and sentenced to 15 years to life in state prison.

CRIMINAL BEHAVIOR AND INCARCERATION
OF VETERANS IN THE UNITED STATES

Reaction to the trauma experienced during combat has been associated in popular and clinical literature with subsequent problematic psychological or social adjustment in civilian life. Holbrook's (2010) manuscript of the effects of war provides a description of historical accounts from Homer's *Odyssey* to Shakespeare's *Henry IV*, early clinical formulations of combat reactions from *Soldier's Heart* to *Shell Shock*, as well as case law from the years following World War I through the Supreme Court's 2009 decision in *Porter v. McCollum*.

Emotional and behavioral symptoms of combat-related disorders—posttraumatic stress disorder (PTSD) in particular—have been implicated in criminal behavior (More information is available at http://www.ptsd.va.gov/professional/news letters/research-quarterly/V22N1.pdf). Focus on combat trauma and crime continues in media coverage of the current wars. Post-combat trauma's assumed relationship to criminal behavior has emerged as a defining element both in legislative initiatives addressing veterans and the justice system and in the development of a new model of treatment courts, Veterans Treatment Courts (Clark, McGuire, & Blue-Howells, 2010). Attention to PTSD has been a constructive contrast to its neglect during and after the Vietnam War, particularly the emphasis upon prevention of poor community readjustment.

The National PTSD Center concludes, however, that epidemiological research is needed to "determine the complex relationship between PTSD and crime," and that determination of any role that PTSD may play in criminal behavior needs a case-by-case appraisal (Visit this website for more information: http://www.ptsd.va.gov/professional/newsletters/research-quarterly/V9N2.pdf). The same caution may be extended to consideration of incarcerated veterans generally: there are both differences and similarities between veterans and nonveterans, and among veterans themselves in age, ethnicity, service periods, and combat exposure. In fact, as will be presented, incarcerated combat veterans and noncombat veterans do not differ on rates of violent offense or mental health problems. Though combat exposure and associated PTSD remain relevant, the broader relationship for discussion is between military experience and crime.

A substantial body of information about incarcerated veterans comes from confidential surveys conducted for the U.S. Department of Justice's Bureau of Justice Statistics (BJS). While not yet inclusive of many veterans from the current wars in Iraq (Operation Iraqi Freedom [OIF]), Afghanistan (Operation Enduring Freedom [OEF]), and the current Iraq engagement, Operation New Dawn (OND), specialized reports on veterans from these surveys have been published in 2000 (data collected in 1996 and 1997 covering state and federal prisons, and jails) and 2007 (data collected in 2004 representing state and federal prisons only) (Mumola, 2000; Noonan and Mumola, 2007). Bureau of Justice Statistics is reportedly piloting an updated survey in 2011–2012. Information from the existing surveys provides an introduction to the characteristics of the veteran population that can be used to guide rehabilitation and treatment during incarceration and in transition to the community.

CHARACTERISTICS OF INCARCERATED VETERANS

Service Branch and Era, and Combat Status

In both surveys, incarcerated veterans represented all branches of the U.S. Armed Forces, including National Guard, with the majority Army (over half), followed by Navy and Marines (one in three), and Air Force (one in ten). Wartime military service was reported by half (49%) of the state prison and three in five (61%) of federal inmates. By far, the largest wartime service era represented was Vietnam (35% state prison; 43% federal prison) (Noonan & Mumola, 2007). The prison data also found that one in five state and one in four federal veteran prison inmates saw combat duty. OEF and OIF veterans constituted just 4% of veteran prison inmates. Using the Bureau of Justice Statistics data, Greenberg, Rosenheck, and Desai (2009) found higher relative incarceration risk within service era and ethnicity: White veterans ages 35–54 were at higher risk than were White nonveterans, reflecting the disadvantaged backgrounds of recruits during the early implementation of the All-Volunteer Force from 1973 to 1980.

Military Discharge Status and Eligibility for Benefits

A common misperception among incarcerated veterans is that incarceration permanently ends eligibility for VA benefits and services. The 2000 Bureau of Justice Statistics report indicated that between 76% state prison inmates and 83% jail inmates had honorable or general under honorable condition discharges. With this, approximately 80% of veterans are potentially eligible to receive VA healthcare upon their release from incarceration. The U.S. Code of Federal Regulations does preclude provision of medical care to veterans while they are incarcerated, but incarceration (or legal history) does not alter the eligibility status for VA benefits and services once the veteran is released. The regulations for receipt of financial benefits call for a reduction in the amount received directly during incarceration, with possible return to previously awarded financial benefits upon release. Further details of this are discussed later in the chapter under "Life While Incarcerated."

Demographic and Social Characteristics

Incarcerated veterans were almost exclusively (99%) male (Mumola, 2000). Veterans prison inmates' median age was over 40 (state prison 41, and federal prison 43), and jail inmates' age was 38, both median ages 10 percentage points higher than their nonveteran counterparts. Veterans were more likely to be White (half or more), and were more likely to have been married than nonveterans. Education levels were substantially higher for veterans than for nonveterans: for example, veterans were two to three times more likely to have completed some college. Rates of unemployment prior to incarceration were lower, and incomes were higher for veterans. Homelessness in the year prior to incarceration, ranging from 5.9% (federal) to 22.7% (jail) for veterans, did not differ from nonveterans.

Psychiatric and Medical Status

The 2007 Bureau of Justice Statistics report found comparable rates of mental health symptoms and disorders between veterans and nonveterans, with approximately one of every two inmates reporting psychiatric symptoms (see Figure 12.1). Major mental disorders (mania, major depression, and psychosis) in the 12 months prior to interview were similar for veterans and nonveterans, although higher than found in community samples. Veterans were more likely than other state prisoners to report recent use of mental health services while incarcerated.

In the 2007 report, combat service was not related to recent mental health problems, and in the 1997 survey, veterans who reported seeing combat duty during their military service were no more likely to be violent offenders than other veterans.

Both veteran and nonveteran inmates reported high levels of past drug use. While the percentage of veterans using drugs is slightly lower overall than nonveterans (in both 2000 and 2007 BJS reports), the surveys found that at least three fourths

Figure 12.1	Mental Health Symptoms and Major Disorders of Veteran and Nonveteran State Prison Inmates

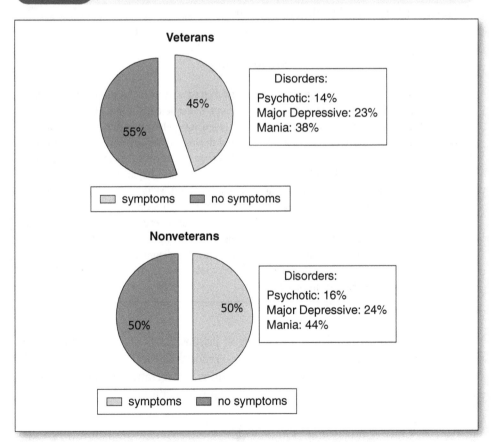

Source: Noonan and Mumola, 2007.

of veterans reported any drug use ever (marijuana/hashish, cocaine, heroin/opiates, depressants, stimulants, or hallucinogens) with almost half using drugs in the month before the instant offense, and one fourth actually using during the commission of the offense. Three fourths of veterans reported ever using marijuana/hashish, half used cocaine, at least two veterans in ten used heroin/opiates, and approximately one in three veterans used depressants, stimulants, or hallucinogens. In the 2000 report, approximately two to three in ten veterans reported being high on either marijuana/hashish, cocaine, or other drugs at the time of the offense, and, in the 2007 report, similar percentages of veteran state prison inmates reported being under the influence of alcohol at the time of the offense. No relationship was found between veteran status and alcohol use in the 2004 survey: for example, in state prison populations, veterans had an alcohol/dependence rate of 43%, nonveterans 44%.

Other issues of clinical importance not reported by Bureau of Justice Statistics have been abstracted by McGuire (2008) from the National Archive of Criminal Justice Data and are available online (http://www.icpsr.umich.edu/icpsrweb/NACJD/index.jsp[1]). Eleven percent of veteran state prison inmates in the sample (9% of federal inmates) report having been told by a mental health professional that they had posttraumatic stress disorder (PTSD). Twenty percent of veterans in state prison and 11% in federal prison had co-occurring disorders (a major mental disorder or PTSD, and either alcohol or drug dependency).

Steve's Story

After enlisting at age 18, Steve returned home from Iraq a hero, honored for his courage and accomplishment. His time in combat, however, never left his mind. He did not feel comfortable or safe—most everything raised his suspicions. He was especially tense when driving, recalling the danger on the roads traveled during his deployments. On an otherwise routine day, he noticed a car on the roadside that raised his suspicions—Steve sped ahead and through a red light. He was soon pulled over and began to experience that same edge and fear that was so prominent when deployed. *Who is this stopping me—is that uniform for real?* He began to resist the officers, though stopping when one of the officers noticed his dog tags and offered that he, too, was a veteran. Steve was taken to county jail and charged for the traffic violations, for resisting arrest, and for carrying a concealed weapon that was found in the car. In court, his diagnosed condition of PTSD was presented. He was sentenced to an additional 90 days of county time, with a plan for his further treatment also put in place.

Suicide is a serious problem for veterans in prisons: 15% of veteran state prison inmates (8% for veteran federal prison inmates) report a history of attempting suicide. For all inmates, this is a critical issue not only during incarceration (Huey & McNulty, 2005) but also in the immediate period following release during which both risk and

---

[1]Because sample sizes of veterans surveyed within the BJS studies are small, archival data reported, while representative of the sample, may not be representative of the overall incarcerated veteran population.

suicide spike. A Washington State study found that, for all inmates, suicide in the period immediately following release from prison was 3.4 times more likely than that of other state residents (Binswanger et al., 2007). Although no research has yet examined suicide among imprisoned veterans, a literature review by Wortzel, Binswanger, Anderson, and Adler (2009) suggested that the veteran in jail or prison faces a level of suicide risk beyond that conferred by either veteran status or incarceration alone.

Not addressed in the Bureau of Justice Statistics surveys is traumatic brain injury (TBI). TBI has become a major concern for veterans currently incarcerated. Those serving in the wars in Iraq and Afghanistan are known to have high rates of exposure to blasts and other sources of head injuries (Tanelian & Jaycox, 2008; Institute of Medicine, 2010). Measurement complexities have prevented the assessment of extent of dysfunction related to TBI (Belanger, Uomoto, & Vanderploeg, 2009; Hoge, Goldberg, & Castro, 2009; Chapman, Andersen, Roselli, & Meyers, 2010), although a recent meta-analysis of 20 epidemiological studies found an estimated prevalence in overall offender populations of 60.25%, apparently much more frequent than in the general population where an 8.5% prevalence is estimated (Shiroma, Ferguson, & Pickelsimer, 2010). The Centers for Disease Control (n.d.) also cites rates of four to ten times higher for incarcerated populations, research that associates TBI with perpetration of domestic and other forms of violence, and evidence of memory, attention, anger, and impulse control deficits that affect both institutional and community adjustment.

The extent and precision of identification of mental health issues in correctional settings is unclear. There is no research that documents, for prisons or jails, how systematically inmates are screened for the serious problems highlighted here as prominent veteran psychiatric problems—that is, for example, substance abuse, suicide risk, PTSD, and TBI. While suicide assessment and screening for psychiatric symptoms is embedded in intake processes such as booking and classification, there is no literature that identifies either PTSD or TBI as specific components of screening processes. The National Commission on Correctional Health Care (2008) has set standards for accreditation of correctional health care services which address screening and assessment for mental health problems. The Bureau of Justice Statistics is now collaborating with the National Center for Health Statistics on the National Survey of Prison Health Care due to be implemented in early 2012, and that survey will capture whether prison systems screen inmates for TBI, suicide risk, and general mental health problems (but not PTSD) at intake, providing a baseline for future implementation of these important screening processes.

With respect to medical problems of incarcerated veterans, data are also available in the Bureau of Justice Statistics archive files on medical problems that inmates state they currently have or ever had. For state prison veterans in the sample, the top five medical conditions among 13 current major physical illnesses that veterans reported in the 2007 report were: high blood pressure (32%), arthritis/rheumatism (29%), heart problems (17%), hepatitis (16%), and asthma (14%). Thirty-nine percent of veteran state inmates and 37% of veteran federal inmates reported two or more serious or chronic health problems. Older veterans are particularly burdened with illness or other risk factors (Williams et al., 2010).

Criminal Justice Status

Information on veteran criminal justice status comes from veteran self-report through the BJS surveys. As indicated in Figure 12.2, the 2000 Bureau of Justice Statistics report data show that state prison veterans were overall more likely to be violent offenders (57% vs. 47% for nonveterans) and less likely to be drug offenders (15% vs. 22% for nonveterans). The 2007 report indicated that veterans were overrepresented among those incarcerated for sexually violent offenses. Nearly one in four veterans in state prison were sex offenders, compared to one in ten in the nonveteran population, and with veterans, sex offences were more likely to have been committed against a known victim and without a weapon, than nonveteran offenders.

Veterans in the 2004 prison survey had a lower average number of arrests and incarcerations than nonveterans in state prison, but reported longer sentences and expected to serve more time in prison than nonveterans. While veterans were more often first-time offenders, it is also clear that a significant percentage of veterans were not first-time offenders, which suggests that there is a group of veterans with high "criminogenic risk," exhibiting characteristics that predict probability of reoffending (McGuire, 1995). In their work with incarcerated Vietnam veterans, Pentland and Dwyer (1985) drew a distinction between career (life-style) criminals and outlaw behavior, suggesting that the group of veterans with arrests and incarcerations prior to, and during and after the military, were not "hard-core sociopaths" but offenders with poor impulse control that may have been exacerbated by the Vietnam experience.

Veterans in state prisons were less likely to be recidivists: more veterans were first-time offenders and fewer veterans had lengthy criminal records (i.e., three or

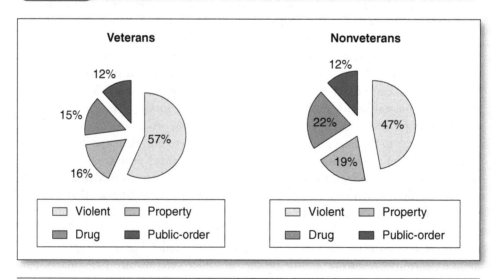

Figure 12.2 Current Offense for Veteran and Nonveteran State Prison Inmates

Source: Noonan and Mumola, 2007.

more prior sentences). In local jails and federal prisons, the criminal histories of veterans and nonveterans were more similar. A frequently cited Bureau of Justice Statistics study of criminal recidivism by Langan and Levin (2002) followed 272,111 prison inmates as they were released in 15 states and examined their rearrest and reincarceration rates over three years: 68% were rearrested within three years and 52% were returned to prison. In this study, veterans were not examined as a separate population. The study found highest rearrest rate was for offenders committing property crime (74%), followed by drug (67%), public order (62%), and violent offenses (62%). These data indicate it is possible that veterans experience differential recidivism risk based on types of conviction or offense histories, and may explain in part why overall veteran recidivism rates are lower than for nonveterans, that is, lower offense rates for property and drug crimes.

Summary: Data on Incarcerated Veterans

Despite measurement limitations and lack of more recent data, particularly for veterans in jail following the Iraq and Afghanistan wars, the Bureau of Justice Statistics survey data present the most comprehensive information available on incarcerated veterans. Incarcerated veterans are a significant subpopulation within the prisons, representing the range of branches of the military services, having generally served in the military a substantial amount of time, and an overwhelming proportion having a military discharge that makes them potentially eligible for VA healthcare benefits, with a smaller proportion eligible as well for financial benefits. Generally, while their education level better positions veterans for successful reentry in comparison to nonveterans, veterans have competing factors in the way of comparable rates of mental health problems, almost as high a rate of substance abuse problems, and data that suggest they have substantial rates of chronic health problems—estimates of one half of incarcerated veterans experiencing serious mental distress, three fourths with histories of significant substance abuse, and almost two in five reporting serious or chronic medical problems—have potential negative implications for functioning in both correctional environment and in the community after release (Malik-Kane and Visher, 2008). Veterans have lower prior arrest and incarceration rates, yet serve longer sentences, and have elevated rates of violent offenses, including sex offenses. Homelessness risk rates, as indicated by prior homelessness, are quite substantial. In short, characteristics and problems which differentiate incarcerated veterans from nonveterans suggest the importance of review of military experience as it relates to readjustment to community life following release from incarceration, to which the discussion now turns.

MILITARY CULTURE AND ITS RESIDUALS

Familiarity with military culture and prior military experience is necessary in understanding the incarcerated veteran. With this comes an associated appreciation for the strategies necessary to be responsive to individuals who have served the country.

Military Training and Justice Involvement

For each recruit, military training includes weapons training and marksmanship, and the possibility of combat involvement. For those involved in combat, training includes rationale, means of carrying out, and approach to coping with aggression (that may include the taking of lives) toward others. Even with military training in use of aggression/force only as needed, training of this nature represents a challenge to beliefs about the value of life—the value of one's own, and that of others. Training for combat involves an approach that may circumvent the individual's prohibition against killing, with combat exposure likely to have added desensitizing effect in the violation of normal social and moral prohibitions (Giardino, 2009). A soldier is trained for survival through cultivating an inner strength, and elements of survival discipline have come to be characterized by the military through the acronym, BATTLEMIND. The same tactics for survival may later contribute to the veteran's maladaptive response upon return to the community, across a range of domains as outlined in Table 12.2. Importantly, also identified on the BATTLEMIND website by the Walter Reed Army Institute of Research are specific actions a service member can take to cope with such challenges.

Table 12.2   BATTLEMIND From Combat to Community*

	Military vs. Community	Service Member (SM) in Combat	Service Member at Home
B	Buddies (cohesion) vs. withdrawal	No one understands SM's experience except your buddies who were there; your life depended on your trust in your unit	SM may prefer to be with battle buddies rather than spouse, family or friends; may assume that only those who were with SM in combat understand or are interested
A	Accountability vs. control	Maintaining control of weapon and gear is necessary for survival; all personal items are important to SM	SM may become angry when someone moves or messes with SM's stuff; may think that nobody cares about doing things right except for SM
T	Targeted vs. inappropriate aggression	Split second decisions that are lethal in highly ambiguous environments are necessary. Kill or be killed. Anger keeps SM pumped up, alert, awake and alive	SM may have hostility toward others; may display inappropriate anger, or snap at buddies or NCOs; may overreact to minor insults
T	Tactical awareness vs. hypervigilance	Survival depends on being aware of surroundings at all times and reacting immediately to sudden changes such as sniper fire or mortar attacks	SM may feel keyed up or anxious in large groups or situations where feels confined; may feel easily startled, especially when hears loud noises; may have difficulty sleeping or have nightmares

	Military vs. Community	Service Member (SM) in Combat	Service Member at Home
L	Lethally armed vs. "locked and loaded" at home	Carrying weapon at all times is mandatory and a matter of life or death	SM may feel a need to have weapons, in home and/or car at all times, believing that SM and loved ones are not safe without them
E	Emotional control vs. anger/ detachment	Controlling emotions during combat is critical for mission success and quickly becomes second nature	Failing to display emotions around family and friends will hurt relationships; may be seen as detached and uncaring
M	Mission operational security vs. secretiveness	SM talks about the mission only with those who need to know; can only talk about combat experiences with unit members	May avoid sharing any of deployment experiences with family, spouse and friends
I	Individual responsibility vs. guilt	SM's responsibility is to survive and do his/her best to keep buddies alive	May feel has failed buddies if they were killed or seriously injured; may be bothered by memories of those wounded or killed
N	Nondefensive (combat) vs. aggressive driving	Driving unpredictably, fast, using rapid changes and keeping other vehicles at a distance is designed to avoid IEDs and VBIEDs	Aggressive driving and straddling the middle line leads to speeding tickets, accidents and fatalities
D	Discipline and ordering vs. conflict	Survival depends on discipline and obeying orders	Inflexible interactions (ordering and demanding behaviors) with spouse, children, and friends often leads to conflict

*Walter Reed Army Institute of Research (WRAIR), November 21, 2005, and available at:
http://www.ptsd.ne.gov/pdfs/WRAIR-battlemind-training-Brochure.pdf
http://www.behavioralhealth.army.mil/battlemind/BattlemindTrainingII.pdf

Issues of Those Transitioning From Military Life

Veterans may have experiences in transition from the military that can increase risk for incarceration (Boivan, 1987). Transition from the military often includes such difficulties as trouble finding employment and social isolation (Card, 1983). Further, veterans may have mental health, addiction, and homelessness issues which increase risk of behaviors that can lead to incarceration. All of these are compounded by the demands and injuries experienced by those with combat experience. Though the condition was little understood at the time of the Vietnam War, many veterans returned with PTSD. Combat veterans had difficulties putting war behind them (Boivan, 1987); rather than being viewed as heroes, they encountered rage about this unpopular and controversial war (Engendorf, Laufer, Rothbart, & Sloan, 1981). Those who had served in the Vietnam theater had higher arrest rates. Both Vietnam theater and Vietnam era veterans experienced higher conviction rates, with those convicted of violent crimes receiving sentences averaging 28 months longer than nonveterans, and those with property and public offense convictions 22 months longer (Card, 1983; Kulka et al., 1990).

Almost twenty-five years ago, Boivin (1987) studying small groups of incarcerated veterans and nonveterans, and community veterans, found that the incarcerated veterans were the more likely group to have poorer interpersonal and psychological adjustment, greater distrust of and resistance to authority, and a greater sense of anomie. Since Boivin completed his work, it is clinical wisdom that this cluster of issues is frequently related to PTSD and other mental health problems, or significant alcohol or drug abuse or dependency. Veterans with PTSD struggle with a range of issues which include many interpersonal difficulties—the veteran with PTSD may find it difficult to trust and easy to react intensely and unpredictably, seemingly out of their control. Anger and rage often are just below the surface, easily triggered, with aggression a learned and possibly familiar response. Additionally, there are behavioral, judgment, and impulse implications for those with PTSD (Giardino, 2009).

Factoring in delayed onset, it is estimated that veterans of the Iraq and Afghanistan wars will have a rate of PTSD as high as 35% (Institute for Operations Research and the Management Sciences, 2009). Approximately 320,000 Global War on Terrorism (GWOT) veterans are estimated to have experienced a traumatic brain injury ranging from mild to severe (Tanielian & Jaycox, 2008), considered a signature injury of the wars in Iraq and Afghanistan. People with TBI frequently experience behavioral, decision-making, frustration tolerance, and impulse control symptoms. Giardino (2009) reports that symptoms of PTSD and TBI result in reduced abilities to appreciate the wrongfulness of one's conduct and conform one's behavior to the requirements of the law.

Recognizing that combat experience often leads to PTSD and TBI, the Departments of Defense (DOD) and VA each have increasingly worked to address these issues. Historically, assessment and treatment were primarily postmilitary discharge functions of VA and other community systems providing treatment to these veterans. With the increased understanding of PTSD and TBI has come a further dedication by both the DOD and VA to address such issues early and repeatedly. Screening and treatment now occur while on active duty, at the conclusion of deployment, with follow-up again postdeployment, and regularly for those provided care in the VA. (More information available at http://www1.va.gov/vhapublications/View Publication.asp?pub_ID=2093). Care is provided across the realm of biopsychosocial issues as will be discussed later in this chapter.

Finally, an emergent issue of concern involving trauma is military sexual trauma (MST). Although the rate of MST among incarcerated veterans is unknown, based on Veterans Health Administration (VHA) screening program data, MST prevalence rates among VHA outpatients are 21.5% for women and 1.1% for men

(Kimerling, Street, Gima, & Smith, 2008). According to a 2006 Department of Defense Workplace and Gender Relations Survey of Active Duty members, annual prevalence rate of having been the victim of sexual assault was 6.8% for women and 1.8% for men, and 9.0% and 3.0% respectively for sexual coercion (Lipari, Cook, Rock, & Matos, 2008).

The U.S. Department of Health and Human Services Substance Abuse and Mental Health Services Administration (SAMHSA) has identified trauma and its sequellae as important determinants of involvement in the justice system. Veterans' exposure to trauma suggests this is an important area of focus for services to them.

Summary: Needed Attention

Inmates in correctional facilities are in need of services while incarcerated, in preparation for release, and upon return to the community. Additionally, veterans may need support to address continuing issues related to the nature of their military experience, combat or other military trauma, or traumatic brain injury. Each of these phenomena, and in their combination, supports the increasing attention upon these services to veterans, including veteran-targeted services and programs within correctional facilities as well as those awaiting the reentering veteran upon release. Central to these efforts are the capacity of veterans to help and support one another, outlined in the following discussion of the veterans' experience in incarceration.

LIFE WHILE INCARCERATED

Once a veteran is in jail or prison, what is his or her experience like? Much of this may depend upon whether that veteran identifies himself or herself as a veteran. By doing so, the veteran is able to be served by available programs within the facility targeted to veterans, and by those service providers from outside of the correctional system, like the VA and others, providing outreach within facilities and services in the community to veterans. Additionally, self-identification as a veteran links the veteran to veterans groups within the facilities as both a source of support and as a conduit to information about veteran's benefits.

Identification of Veterans in Prisons and Jails

With the advent of VA outreach into prisons and jails, greater attention is being devoted to the identification of veterans at all points of contact with the justice system, including at the time of entry into the prisons and jails. Despite widespread initiatives to include veteran status questions as part of intake at incarceration, there continue to be large numbers of veterans whose presence in the prisons and jails is not known. Concerted future efforts for improved systematic identification of veterans throughout the justice system will insure that assistance can be provided to as many veterans as possible.

There are, however, multiple reasons veterans may not self-identify as veterans: veterans may be reluctant out of fear of loss of benefits, out of concern that they will be viewed as a threat, or based on shame. Some do not understand that they are veterans ("I did not serve in combat"). Unlike in much of American society today where veterans are honored and being a veteran is often advantageous, prison and jail settings are often perceived differently by veterans. Contact with incarcerated veterans suggests that they often feel shame regarding their criminal actions, as though they have brought disgrace to the uniform and those who serve with honor. Though this shame can be felt pervasively, it is often most prominent in concern about the opinions of the corrections officers or deputies, many of whom are veterans as well. Veteran inmates express fear they will be looked down upon, or treated more sternly, by these staff. The correctional staff is not immune to media characterizations of veterans as violent and crazy.

Veteran prison life is often characterized by the dilemma of identification. As all new inmates enter the mix of the general population, they must determine what their affiliation(s) will be. For the veteran, this includes surveying the yard to determine how veterans are perceived and treated. Again, shame may be central, as not only is there concern about the perception of the staff, but also fellow inmates. Groups and gangs are prominent in the inmate population. Operating at still another level, a veteran may withhold his or her veteran status to try to prevent VA service-connected benefits from being reduced while incarcerated. Veterans with these benefits are eligible to receive only a portion once they have been incarcerated more than 59 days. Similarly, VA pension benefits are required to be completely withheld during the period of incarceration. What veterans often may not know or may choose to ignore is that not notifying the Veterans Benefits Administration (VBA) regarding their incarceration status will result in an overpayment. Paying the money back, typically postrelease, then comes at a time when the funds are most needed to support reentry. With education about this, likely fewer veterans would choose to conceal their identification[2].

In many facilities, competing with these apprehensions to identify will be the lure of a veteran ally, and in the case of certain facilities, a veterans group. Connection with a fellow veteran may occur very naturally and easily. This often becomes the sole domain for closeness—finding someone on the yard to relate to and trust. Disclosure of veteran status may never go further—knowing and trusting one other veteran—though very often it is through these single veteran alliances that a veteran does identify himself or herself to the larger veterans group.

Peer Support Among Incarcerated Veterans

The value and benefit of others' support in an inmate's efforts toward recovery and eventual successful reentry are well described (Council of State Governments

---

[2]Further information regarding VA financial benefits adjustments and implications related to incarceration, including the possibility of reapportioning those funds to a dependent spouse or children during the time of incarceration, can be found at http://www.benefits.va.gov/warms/docs/admin21/m21_1/mr/part10/ch15/pt10_ch15.doc.

Reentry Policy Council, 2005; Davidson and Rowe, 2008). Veterans are known for reaching out to other veterans, for their camaraderie and sense of brotherhood with other veterans, and for the therapeutic value of veteran-to-veteran support (Weissman, Covell, Kushner, Irwin, & Essock, 2005; Resnick & Rosenheck, 2008). Military training itself fosters unit and task cohesion among soldiers, and what an experienced clinician describes as a type of love or bonding that enables soldiers to engage in combat to protect the military unit (Dewey, 2004). Veterans are known to value this brotherhood in civilian life following the military.

Veterans Groups

In prison settings, and to a lesser degree in jails, peer groups are central to the structure and hierarchy established on the yard, for many diverse reasons. Often these are racial, geographic, or gang related, viewed by the inmates as necessary for survival, and frequently viewed by staff and administrators as an unchangeable reality, and at times problematic (Cohn, 2006). Existing alongside these are affiliative groups viewed from a more prosocial vantage point—religious, educational, self-help. It is among the latter that veterans groups are typically thought of in prison settings. Some dating back several decades, these veterans groups exist along a continuum from highly formal and organized to those that are more informal. In order to obtain an idea of the extent of veterans groups in prisons, Boston (2010) inventoried VHA staff conducting outreach in the state and federal prisons on the presence of these groups. Table 12.3 provides information on the approximately 1,000 state and federal prisons visited regularly by the VA prison outreach specialists. Although it is likely a conservative estimate, nearly 75% of these groups were informal, yet 57 veterans groups were formally organized and identified within the state prison system.

Formal veterans groups are institutionally sanctioned with a designated sponsor, typically a veteran employee of the prison. The groups often have bylaws that define membership criteria, guidelines for functioning, and focal activities. Some are affiliated with community veterans' service organizations. Commonly there is a joint mission of wide-ranging support of one another and a compassionate community service component.

Within veterans groups, support for other veterans is first and foremost, and revolves around veteran camaraderie and encouragement to return to a life of dignity and pride. Leadership of the groups ensure that each veteran knows of benefits that

Table 12.3 Veterans Groups Inside VA-Covered Federal and State Prisons

	Formal	Informal	Total
Federal prisons	0	23	23
State prisons	57	147	204
Total	57	170	227

Source: Joel Rosenthal and Jim McGuire.

he or she may be eligible for as a result of service, and assists the veteran in pursuing benefits both while incarcerated and in anticipation of release. Many serving life sentences provide the leadership of these groups. Among them are those for whom parole is precluded, as well as those who are eligible for parole consideration. The veterans group and support of other veterans are often defining elements in providing purpose and meaning in the day to day existence of an inmate serving a life sentence.

The incarcerated veterans groups often also do community service. Though oriented toward veterans and their families, the range is far-reaching to communities more broadly and again, in a manner which may define meaning for those participating in the veterans group. Fundraisers are organized by the veterans groups to support such things as education for inmates' children, veterans programs in the community, and VA programs (e.g., OEF/OIF Polytrauma Center; Homeless Veterans homeless services program). Often the groups hold ceremonies at the prison at which the donations are presented to the families and recipient groups. Particularly inspirational are events when awards are presented during the groups' annual Veterans Day ceremonies.

As with most any formal prison group, these groups also are advisory and utilitarian to prison leadership in addressing issues of the yard. In one state, the impact of the incarcerated veterans groups was constructive to the extent that the director of the department of corrections (formerly a warden at a prison that had an active veterans group) directed the creation of a veterans group at each of the facilities in that state. According to this director, where incarcerated veterans groups exist, there are fewer problems with discipline and safety, presumably a reflection of the regimentation and deference to authority well-practiced in the military (J. Woodford, personal communication, November 10, 2011).

Well known among these are the pioneering groups of this movement. Among these are many which have affiliated with community veteran's advocacy groups such as Vietnam Veterans of America; those who have developed manualized, peer-oriented programs to address general issues as well as those unique to veterans; and those who have established themselves in the pursuit of VA financial benefits for veterans. An example of the latter are two inmates serving life sentences who are incarcerated in state prison and have established a formal Veterans Benefits Service office, staffed seven days weekly, for which they are seeking state certification status [3]. Since 2005, this unique collaboration between these two veterans and the local county Veterans Service Office has assisted in the recovery of over $5 million in disability compensation to inmates for injuries received during military service (CDCR_Star, 2011). With more than $4 million of these funds being made available to the eligible dependents of these veterans, this project has been a major success in both aiding veterans in acquiring needed financial support for their successful reentry as well as in providing essential funds for dependent family members during absences resulting from incarceration.

For those veterans who do receive VA compensation, a critical element is restarting full benefits upon release. Reprocessing times make this difficult for many veterans. As

---

[3] As indicated in the Soledad Veterans Service Office Fact Sheet, 2010.

a result, many have transitioned from prison to the community without the advantage of these monthly funds, some for extended periods of time. Historically veterans groups have attempted to assist with this. They are now aided by an organized and targeted VA effort: VBA policy now provides for notification 30 days in advance of a planned release, and restarting those full benefits at the earliest possible time subsequent to release[4]. This effort is part of a VBA outreach approach that includes a designated VBA Homeless and Incarcerated Veteran point of contact in each VBA region.

Care and Treatment While Incarcerated

The primary mission of prisons and jails is custody of the inmates in a safe and secure environment. The challenges of financing and delivery of medical care within the correctional institution context are well known in the field. For example, as noted by Wortzel and colleagues (2007), the challenge of mental health service provision in the jails is such that insufficient care precludes some inmates from achieving the competence needed to stand trial. There has been increasing attention given to the health care issue both by the courts (in California for example, *Brown v. Plata*, 563 U.S. S. Ct. 09–1233 [2011]) and by national organizations such as the National Commission on Correctional Health Care and the American Psychiatric Association (American Psychiatric Association, 2000), and promising trends appear. Even so, with recent years' federal, state, and county budget crises, correctional facilities are likely to continue to be increasingly challenged in providing needed care (Scott-Hayward, 2009).

Ultimately the life of an incarcerated veteran is significantly affected by the quality of care available to meet his or her unique treatment needs, including the specialized care for veterans who may be in need of treatment for PTSD or TBI. Given this circumstance, some veteran advocates raise the question of VA's potential role in providing the needed care to veterans while they are incarcerated. Even if correctional facilities' medical systems deemed it desirable and possible to integrate an outside treatment system with the complexities this would entail—for example, coordination and management of medications, treatment reactions, and other issues—since 1999, VA regulation 38 CFR 17.38(c)(5) has barred VA from providing hospital and outpatient care for a veteran who is either a patient or an inmate in an institution of another government agency if that agency has a constitutional duty to provide care or services.

OPPORTUNITIES WHILE INCARCERATED

Despite whatever limitations may exist in a given facility for treatment available to inmates, there are treatment opportunities in correctional facilities that address clinical needs during both incarceration and reentry. A combination of treatment

---

[4]Details of procedures for restarting of benefits may be found as well at http://www.benefits.va.gov/warms/docs/admin21/m21_1/mr/part10/ch15/pt10_ch15.doc.

and support-oriented services within correctional facilities, and in the community upon release, is critical in effectively addressing readjustment problems that frequently result in criminal recidivism (Travis, Solomon, & Waul, 2001). Review of the availability of services to veterans while incarcerated in prisons and jails begins with an overview of the types of programs and services that exist for all inmates which veterans often take advantage of to address health and other problems.

Services and Programs Offered to Inmates

Addiction-related services are commonly established in correctional facilities. They include 12-step meetings, education and awareness classes, and, to a much lesser extent, addiction treatment. The National Criminal Justice Treatment Practices (NCJTP) survey (Taxman, Perdoni, & Harrison, 2007) found that substance abuse education and awareness programs existed in 74% of prisons and 61% of jails. However, Taxman and colleagues further determined that daily access to these services was available to less than 25% of prison inmates and 10% of those in jail. It was also noted that despite increasing need for addiction treatment services, the vast majority of services being offered continue to be education and awareness oriented. An exception is a model that is utilized in which community programs contract with corrections departments to provide to inmates addiction treatment and relapse prevention (along with anger management and mental health services, including trauma-related interventions, as well as reunification, housing, and employment support upon release) (http://www.hafc-wh.org).

Employment services are frequently offered in prison facilities and to a lesser extent in jails. Very often these are work assignments for prison-level wages. The goal of work assignments is to provide inmates with skills which may serve them in pursuing employment upon release. Less common but present in some facilities are community-based work assignments and vocational training programs. One veteran-specific program provides for a work detail at three state Department of Veterans Affairs cemeteries. In this program, on work furlough each day, the inmates are responsible for landscaping and other grounds duties. In the words of one of the veterans, this type of work furlough is "one of the most redeeming things done in prison or out—honoring fallen brethren" (Daugherty, 2010, p. A5).

Prominent as well are educational classes, including those that allow completion of a GED. Taxman and colleagues (2007) reports remedial education as the most frequently available educational program in correctional facilities (89% in prisons, 60% in jails). Exemplary programs include jail facilities served by community college staff providing classes encompassing topics such as GED preparation, addiction recovery, and art.

The U.S. Bureau of Prisons, in its management and oversight of all federal prisons in the United States, has developed a comprehensive, multitiered approach to skills development offered to large numbers of its prison population. This includes nine distinct skill areas. Inmates are introduced to this by way of a dynamic assessment of all skill areas, culminating in an individualized plan for skills development and a means of monitoring progress on their plan. Targeted program linkages are identified in order to address each skill need, with collaborative partnership building with community-based agencies, including with VA, to insure that there is continuity when the inmate transitions to the community (Breazzano, 2009).

Also existing at a limited number of sites in the correctional facilities are programs which use treatments empirically demonstrated to address the issues of inmates with patterns of reoffending. These have been organized at times as state-coordinated efforts but are more typically local, facility-specific. Common to these is an approach targeting criminogenic thinking utilizing cognitive-behavioral elements such as role-plays and homework assignments to improve critical thinking, problem solving, and prosocial values. Noteworthy are such approaches as Aggression Replacement Therapy, Strategies for Self-Improvement and Change, Moral Reconation Therapy, Reasoning and Rehabilitation, Relapse Prevention Therapy, and Thinking for Change (Milkman & Wanberg, 2007). Related are interventions tailored to promote and facilitate motivation to enter treatment, notably Motivational Interviewing (Miller & Rollnick, 2002). With the demonstrated efficacy of these approaches, there is growing interest in application of these treatments in VA and community settings, including for those recently released or with chronic justice system involvement (Davis, Baer, Saxon, & Kivlahan, 2003; Wain et al., 2011).

Additional programs which veterans have been able to take advantage of in correctional facilities are designed to address issues of trauma, abuse, perpetrators, and victims, efforts which are oriented toward public safety through an emphasis on prevention of revictimization (More information available at http://www.mavcenter. org). Program components may include academic, vocational, and life skills development to include positive socialization and behavioral change. Programs such as these may also incorporate restorative justice intervention which brings victims or family members and significant others of victims together in discussion with inmates who have committed violent crimes (http://insightprisonproject.org/). Similar efforts in prison and jail facilities have addressed issues such as anger management, PTSD (general), and other content areas with interpersonal ramifications of which veterans have availed themselves.

PROGRAMS TARGETING VETERAN NEEDS

A small number of jails and prisons have developed specialized services for veterans. These efforts have typically included bringing selected veterans together to reside in a common dormitory (typically exclusively veteran inmates) and providing programming responsive to their needs and issues as veterans.

Veterans Units in Jails

In 2000, a veterans unit was established at one of the largest jail facilities in the country (Nakashima et al., 2006). VA homeless program outreach workers receive information daily regarding veterans who have entered the jail facility. VA and its community partners are able to assist with transportation from the jail to shelter care, direct entrance to rehabilitation programs, and access to the full array of VA services. The jail unit has 90 beds and veterans must meet specific medical and psychiatric stabilization criteria to be admitted to the unit. While in the unit, veterans are provided services including drug abuse and domestic violence education by staff of the local school district, and weekly services from a VBA benefits specialist. Since 2008, two additional jail facilities have established veterans units. Similar to the jail unit above, the first of these is an extension of an existing array of programs targeting special populations and issues at a large metropolitan jail which initially provided GED and art classes, then addiction classes added in the mid-1990s and by 1997 included an extensive and formal three-phase general inmate/postrelease program. The veterans program includes educational classes, and emphasis on addiction and recovery, healthy relationships, and trauma recovery.

In a neighboring county, staff of the jail facility, partners from justice and the community, and VA joined efforts in 2009, and opened a veterans unit in June, 2010. Characterized as a restorative justice therapeutic community, the program serves incarcerated and recently released veterans, as well as victims and family members. Emphasis is on the underlying issues leading to incarceration for veterans, including domestic violence, substance abuse, PTSD, lack of employment, and challenges of reintegration into the community following periods of military or combat duty.

Veterans Units in Prisons

Veterans units in prison facilities can be traced to the late 1990s. In the first of its kind in state prisons, and in contrast to past state corrections procedures which did not allow segregation of populations, veterans were placed together in multiresource hubs in three separate facilities, each housing approximately 50 veterans. Collaboration was established among staff from three VA facilities and provided veterans information and education on VA services and benefits, the state Department of Veterans Affairs providing assistance with financial benefits and exams for benefits claims, and the department of parole addressing reentry planning/support and continued monitoring upon release. A report by the state department of corrections indicated a low rate (9%) of veterans served in the hubs returning to the state prisons four years later (Canestrini, 1993).

Another prison-based unit for 106 veterans opened in 2011. Through this unit veterans are offered case management, services to support reentry, and benefits support provided by county Veterans Service Officers and the Veterans Benefits Administration (Holmes, 2011). A prominent feature is the development of a chartered American Legion chapter as part of the unit which is active in fundraising and community partnerships.

VA Services to Justice-Involved Veterans

Building on the efforts of veterans, veteran's service organizations, and VA staff over the years, national VA leadership has recognized the needs and unique issues of veterans involved in the criminal justice system. In 2006, VHA initiated formal outreach efforts focused on veterans incarcerated in state and federal prisons through implementation of the Health Care for Reentry Veterans program (HCRV). In 2009, VHA followed HCRV with a second program, Veterans Justice Outreach (VJO) that targets veterans interfacing with the front end of the justice system. With the addition of VJO, VHA's Veterans Justice Programs (VJP) now encompasses services not only to veterans incarcerated in prisons, but to veterans across the continuum, collectively designated as justice-involved veterans. The following discussion of VA efforts of outreach, reentry support, and diversion/prevention, in partnership with the justice system, complete the review of services for incarcerated veterans.

VA'S JUSTICE OUTREACH SERVICES

In recognition of the growing number of incarcerated Vietnam era veterans, veteran-focused outreach activities began in the 1970s, often by VA veteran staff members (an example is recorded in Pentland and Scurfield, 1982), in various corrections facilities around the country. Increased federal attention followed with Mumola's 2000 Bureau of Justice Statistics Report which indicated that approximately 10% of jail and prison inmates nationally were veterans. Public Law 107–95, the Homeless Veterans Comprehensive assistance Act of 2001, mandated VA and the Department of Labor (DOL) to conduct "referral and counseling for veterans transitioning from certain institutions who are at risk for homelessness." President Bush's 2004 State of the Union address announcing funding for reentry-based employment, housing, and mentoring support, legitimized and activated further VA efforts. The passage of the Second Chance Act of 2007, further strengthened national tendency to address rehabilitation through provision of $139 million for 2009 and 2010 to resource reentry initiatives.

With this as context, VA launched Health Care for Reentry Veterans (HCRV) in 2006 and—with support and assistance of the American Correctional Association, the Association of State Correctional Administrators, and the U.S. Bureau of Prisons—VA's reentry specialists were able to contact the state and federal departments of corrections as well as individual prison facilities to outline services, gain access to facilities, and identify and work with veterans. Combined with VA's initial and expanded funding that resulted in hiring and training a contingent of 44 specialists nationwide, these VA-corrections collaborations allow specialists to regularly visit and conduct outreach and reentry planning in 1,006 state and federal prisons, an estimated 78% of American prisons. Within the VA regulatory provision that prohibits VA treatment in correctional facilities, the specialists' focus is on outreach aimed at determination of eligibility for VA care, services that match reentry assessment identified needs, and linkage to resources. Working directly with the veteran and closely with corrections reentry staff, plans for reentry are developed detailing identified VA and community resources to address the array of treatment and other psychosocial needs of the veteran. VA leadership also made it clear that all VA facilities are to provide released and reentering veterans with full and timely access to residential, outpatient, and specialty care services along their treatment continuum in working toward successful veteran readjustment and prevention of recidivism.

Correctional facility access and identification of veterans are complex systems challenges at minimum, requiring educational presentations to prison leadership and staff, facilitated at times through execution of formal Memorandums of Understanding. Once facility access is established, the further challenges of travel distances and time to get to facilities, and movement within facilities once there, in order to reach as many incarcerated veterans as possible, become focal. While identification, access, travel, and time issues continue to be a VA/corrections collaboration in progress, operations to date have resulted in VHA specialists providing reentry planning services to 9,000 veterans annually in the state and federal prison systems. With the recognition of the critical nature of the transition period upon release, the role of the HCRV specialists includes time-limited case management (up to three to four months) and ongoing advocacy and systems intervention to insure that the reentry veteran continues to receive responsive services in the same manner as all other veterans.

Similar to prison outreach with its background of decades of informal outreach by community veterans, outreach to veterans in jails nationwide was officially launched by VA in 2009 as part of the larger scope VA-VJO initiative. In addition to jail outreach, the VJO mandate calls for law enforcement education and linkage to promote increased awareness of veteran-specific issues and prevention of arrest/incarceration when possible, and case management for veterans in the growing treatment court system. VJO includes support for veterans in the Veterans Treatment Courts, which are a modified version of mental health and drug treatment courts with veterans scheduled on a common court calendar, with VA and other partners present in the courtroom, insuring linkage to veteran-responsive treatment, housing, and employment services (Clark et al., 2010). Similar to HCRV, VJO's focus is on outreach and related activities to link veterans with treatment and social and ancillary services. However, with the more prominent role in the court system, VJO specialists are providing longer-term case management and, at times, direct treatment intervention not typically provided by their HCRV counterparts.

Each of 152 VA Medical Centers has a Veterans Justice Outreach Specialist, with full-time funding of 120 of those specialists currently in place. During its second year of operations (October, 2010–September, 2011), a total of 15,000 veterans were served. Veterans served in the two programs to date reflect era and gender distributions at earlier and later stages of the justice system: OEF/OIF veterans (20% in VJO compared to 4% in HCRV) and female veterans (4% in VJO compared to 1% in HCRV).

VA HEALTHCARE SERVICES

Malik-Kane and Visher (2008) found in their research on reentering inmates exiting from two large state prison systems (Texas and Ohio) that 68% of men had no health insurance following release, and that the health care received after release was episodic. VA provides a viable resource to many reentering veterans. The VA service continuum is comprehensive. It includes medical primary, specialty, and preventive care; mental health and substance dependence residential and outpatient care; specialty care such as treatment for PTSD and traumatic brain injury; and socially-based services such as housing and employment support. VA and the Department of Defense have jointly developed a series of evidence-based medical and mental health practice guidelines including separate protocols for management and treatment of bipolar, major depressive, substance use, and posttraumatic stress disorders and traumatic brain injury (TBI) (http://www.healthquality.va.gov/).

These services overall compare favorably to other healthcare systems: a RAND study found that the VA services across a spectrum of 294 measures of quality in disease prevention and medical treatment outperformed all other sectors of American health care (Asch et al., 2004). Veterans have rated their satisfaction with VA services as high as or higher than other American healthcare consumers rate their healthcare providers (Kussman, 2007; National Quality Research Center, 2006). Many veterans use VA health care. For example, a 2004 Institute of Medicine report indicated that for all American veterans who use mental health services, 41% used VA mental health services almost exclusively (Rosenheck, 2004). Finally, the importance of VA as a resource for returning service members is underscored by the fact that half (53%) of those discharged since September, 2011, have used VA services (Veterans Health Administration Office of Public Health and Environmental Hazards, 2011). With 80% of justice-involved veterans potentially eligible for VA healthcare, VA provides a quality option rated, well by veterans, that is available for the large number of justice-involved veterans who could benefit from this care.

Other VA Postrelease Transitional Programs

As efforts directed toward incarcerated veterans have evolved, intervention to address the transition from incarceration to community living and treatment in the community has been developed. VA programs that have specialized in receiving veterans as they leave prison, in particular, have found that the first two weeks after release is a critical period of reentry. Assisting veterans in structuring time and initial settlement back into the community, in navigating expected stigma and rejection, in managing impulses to make up for lost time, in asking for help, and in providing information are each important areas of initiative that must be supported in this population. This is particularly true in light of the long-term conditioning that veterans report of being told what to do in every circumstance while incarcerated. A planned short-term agenda during the first two weeks after release is essential and must be structured and logically sequenced—initially one day and one activity at a time—obtaining needed medications and health care examination, reporting to the parole officer, obtaining a state or driver's license identification and social security card, establishing a hygiene routine, setting up checking and savings accounts and other money and debt management routines, establishing housing, and participating in job readiness assessment and preparation.

VA staff working with those veterans coming out of a prison veteran's hub program developed one of the early programs of this nature. Recognizing the array of psychosocial needs and vulnerabilities of this population, a transition program was integrated into existing VA residential services. Veterans recently released, in addition to participating in the regular residential milieu, also participated in a six-week component specifically highlighting unique transition and reentry issues. This VA program developed an approach that both integrated reentry veterans into the general transitional veteran population with simultaneous support fostered through a short-term reentry veteran group.

Another VA developed a program for veterans moving directly from prison to VA residential substance abuse treatment upon release. Over time, the VA program psychology staff identified prison reentry, cognitive readjustment challenges. These clinicians formalized reentry veteran thoughts and behaviors identified into a schema that they termed *Prison Mindset* (Table 12.4), to help veterans examine and

Table 12.4 Prison Mindset and Addictive Thinking on the Road to Recovery

Thoughts	Behaviors
Work:	
Best job is the one that pays me the most money.	Takes whatever job is available regardless of its impact on recovery or toxicity
I've got to make up for lost time . . . If I stay busy I'll be OK.	Works excessive hours, gets in lots of overtime or a second job
I need to prove myself; I only have value if I'm working hard; I've got to make sure they notice me on this job; make sure they keep me around.	Does other people's work; works too fast; doesn't ask for help; has trouble following simple directions; wants to improve how job is done
I can't be expected to do a boring job.	Works in a way that mimics their drug of choice
Money:	
The more money I make, the more valuable I am.	Turns down jobs that are "beneath" them; is picky about jobs; wants to be self-employed; avoids supervision
I can spend my money anyway I want since I'm not drinking or using anymore.	Binge spending, gambling—finding ways to get rid of money
I need to have money that I can give to my kids and my partner (guilt and shame).	Gives away rent or grocery money, even savings to children or spouse

Thoughts	Behaviors
Social:	
I can't make it on my own . . . I need someone to take care of me.	Moves in with a partner who already has a house and structured lifestyle
I need to be needed.	Selects a needy caretaking partner who enables addictive behavior
Family:	
I wasn't there for them in prison . . . I have to be there for them now	Fails to recognize personal limitations (time, money, living area, belongings)
I've already missed enough time with them; this is my last chance, I have to get it right.	Cannot set boundaries or say no; insists on having parent role; often interferes with what children are doing
I've got to show my kids I've changed; I need to have their approval (guilt and shame).	Tries to get acceptance from family; makes emotional demands for recognition; upset when not forthcoming

Source: J. Hartiens & M. McCarty, March 7, 2007. *Keep Your Engines Running: Tools to Manage Addictive Thinking on the Road to Reentry.* Presentation at Defendant/Offender Workforce Development Conference, Charlotte, NC.

modify common thoughts linked to behaviors that, though intended to be solution-focused and functional within prison, become problematic in the community.

Both of these VA transitional programs, along with the VA residential programs more generally, capitalize on the camaraderie and support shown to one another by veterans. The strategy is to invoke wounded-veteran-as-healer throughout the array of groups, classes, individual support exchanges as well as in positive social and leisure activities.

Two other significant transitional service programs targeted to veterans exist. The Incarcerated Veterans Transition Program (IVTP), a long standing U.S. Department of Labor (DOL)/VA partnership program, provides transitional employment services to incarcerated veterans. DOL grantee agencies and veteran-focused state employment counselors provide prerelease and postrelease employment assessment and job placement services, and VA provides benefits and healthcare, including VA-funded transitional housing. An evaluation of the pilot of this program found a 15 percentage point, one-year rearrest difference (35% vs. 50%) between reentry veterans who received both employment and healthcare and those who did not (McGuire, 2008). Twelve sites are currently funded by DOL nationally to provide these services (http://www.dol.gov/vets/programs/ivtp/main.htm). In addition, SAM-HSA has funded 13 sites under its jail diversion and trauma recovery initiative that funds community agencies to provide trauma-informed services to veterans in the justice system, including veterans contacted in jails. Both the DOL and SAMHSA initiatives are significant collaborations with VA to assist veterans transitioning from incarceration.

POLICY IMPLICATIONS

Veterans are unique among American prison and jail populations because of their social characteristics, their military service background, and the services and benefits available to them when released. These circumstances combined with the importance of honoring and supporting those who have served, underscore the need for effective assistance to veterans both while incarcerated and upon their release (Mears, Lawrence, Solomon, & Waul, 2002). This can only be accomplished by policy and program partnership between corrections, VA, veteran's advocates and family members, community providers, and the veterans themselves.

Of concern is the need for services both within the correctional facilities and upon release that meet not only the general needs of those incarcerated but the particular needs of veterans. Especially important for veterans are medical care that includes treatment for injuries and illness related to military experiences (i.e., combat-related injuries and illnesses from exposures to toxic chemicals); mental health and addiction treatment with particular attention to co-occurring disorders; diagnosis and treatment of PTSD and other trauma-related problems including TBI; and reentry planning to address the psychosocial needs of the veteran returning to community living, with particular focus on housing and employment or other financial support. Challenges to providing this level of care in prisons and jails are daunting, fueled in part by a lack of knowledge and expertise about veteran-specific issues by corrections provider staff, and the impact of diminishing resources on care and treatment.

VA/corrections partnerships can work to fill in gaps in knowledge and in service. Within the mission and context of correctional settings, VA staff expertise can be utilized to train corrections staff, community partners, and veterans advocates, and help to engage veterans as peer supports in the provision of care uniquely needed by veterans during and following incarceration. Because of needed expertise in access to and use of VA services and linkage to postrelease services, the VA's justice outreach efforts, along with the promotion of veterans groups and units/programs in the correctional facilities, are necessary ingredients in this process. These efforts have to include effective identification of all veterans in a manner that addresses the fears and apprehensions of veterans and methods that match VA and corrections records to identify all those who have served in the military. Evaluation and research are needed to determine the impact and lessons of policies and programs designed to address these issues. Progress so far has been promising, insuring that justice-involved veterans like Frank and Steve are honored and not forgotten.

DISCUSSION QUESTIONS

1. With the growing use of prerelease assessments, what can clinicians do to help veterans make better use of treatment services both while incarcerated and after release?

2. Drug treatment studies of prison inmates demonstrate that treatment before (during incarceration) and after (in the community) release is the most effective combination and has the largest impact on reduction of recidivism. How can VA and prison clinicians help veterans engage in substance abuse prevention and treatment when veterans often may feel they have no problem because they have not used drugs while incarcerated?

3. Services such as housing, employment, and treatment for sex offenders are usually difficult to obtain in the community. What strategies and resources could better serve this veteran offender population?

SUGGESTED READINGS

Holbrook, J. G. (2010). Veterans' court and criminal responsibility: A problem-solving history and approach to the liminality of combat trauma. In D. C. Kelly, D. Gitelson, & S. H. Barksdale (Eds.), *Young Veterans: A resilient community of honor, duty, and need.* Available at http://papers.ssrn.com/sol3/papers.cfm?abstract_id=1706829

Landenberger, N. A., & Lipsey, M. W. (2005). The positive effects of cognitive-behavioral programs for offenders: A meta-analysis of factors associated with effective treatment. *Journal of Experimental Criminology, 1,* 451–476.

McGuire, J. (2007). Closing a front door to homelessness. *The Journal of Primary Prevention, 28,* 389–400.

Mumola, C. J. (2000). *Bureau of Justice Statistics Special Report: Veterans in Prison or Jail.* NCJ 178888. Available at http://bjs.ojp.usdoj.gov/content/pub/pdf/jim09st.pdf

Nakashima, J., McGuire, J., Garrow, E., Berman, S., Dalton, K., & Daniels, W. (2006). Outreach to homeless veterans in the Los Angeles County jail: The VA greater Los Angeles healthcare story. National Institute of Corrections. *LJN (Large Jail Network) Exchange,* 11–20.

Noonan, M. E., & Mumola, C. J. (2007). *Bureau of Justice Statistics Special Report: Veterans in state and federal prison.* NCJ 217199. Washington, DC: U.S. Department of Justice, Bureau of Justice Statistics. Available at http://bjs.ojp.usdoj.gov/index.cfm?ty=pbdetail&iid=808

SUGGESTED WEBSITES

- United States Department of Veterans Affairs (VA)

  http://www.va.gov

- VA Veterans Justice Outreach (outreach—law enforcement, jails, courts):

  http://www.va.gov/HOMELESS/VJO.asp

- VA Healthcare for Reentry Veterans (outreach—state and federal prisons):

  http://www.va.gov/HOMELESS/Reentry.asp

- VA Homeless Programs (homelessness prevention and housing resources):

  http://www.va.gov/HOMELESS/Programs.asp

- VA Mental Health (mental health, substance abuse, PTSD, and suicide): http://www.mentalhealth.va.gov/

- VA National Center for PTSD (PTSD and related issues): www.ptsd.va.gov

- Listings for each of the State Department of Veterans Affairs (DVAs): http://www.va.gov/statedva.htm

REFERENCES

American Psychiatric Association. (2000). *Psychiatric services in jails and prisons: A task force report of the American Psychiatric Association.* Washington, DC: Author

Asch, S. M., McGlynn, E. A., Hogan, M. M., Hayward, R. A., Shekelle, P., Rubenstein, L., Keesey, J., Adams, J., & Kerr, E. A. (2004). Comparison of quality of care for patients in the Veterans Health Administration and patients in a national sample. *Annals of Internal Medicine, 141,* 938–945.

Belanger, H. G., Uomoto, J. M., & Vanderploeg, R. D. (2009). The Veterans Health Administration system of care for mild traumatic brain injury: Cost, benefits and controversies. *Journal of Head Trauma Rehabilitation, 24,* 4–13.

Binswanger, I. A., Stern, M. F., Deyo, R. A., Heagerty, P. J., Cheadle, A., Elmore, J. G., & Koepsell, T. D. (2007). Release from prison—a high risk of death for former inmates. *New England Journal of Medicine, 356*(2), 157–165.

Boivan, M. J. (1987). Forgotten warriors: An evaluation of the emotional well-being of presently incarcerated Vietnam veterans. *Genetic, Social, and General Psychology Monographs, 113*(1), 109–25.

Boston, D. (2010). *Supportive peers in veteran reentry: A help to the reentry process.* Unpublished manuscript.

Breazzano, D. L. (2009). The Federal Bureau of Prisons shifts reentry focus to a skills-based model. *Corrections Today,* 50–57.

Canestrini, K. (1993). *Veterans program follow-up, July 1993.* Albany, NY: Department of Correctional Services.

Card, J. (1983). *Lives after Vietnam: The personal impact of military service.* Toronto, ON, Canada: Lexington Books.

Centers for Disease Control. (n.d.). *Traumatic brain injury in prisons and jails: An unrecognized problem.* Available at http://www.cdc.gov/traumaticbraininjury/pdf/Prisoner_TBI_Prof-a.pdf

CDCR_Star. (2011, July 8). *Vietnam memorial displayed at correctional training facility.* [Web log post]. Retrieved from http://inside-cdcr.blogspot.com/2011/07/vietnam-memorial-displayed-at.html

Chapman, J. C., Andersen, A. M., Roselli, L. A., & Meyers, N. M. (2010). Screening for mild traumatic brain injury in the presence of psychiatric comorbidities. *Archives of Physical Medicine Rehabilitation, 91,* 1082–1086.

Clark, S., McGuire, J., & Blue-Howells, J. (2010). Development of Veterans Treatment Courts: Local and legislative initiatives. *Drug Court Review, VII*(I), 171–208.

Cohn, E. (2006, April). The Gang Culture Continues to Grow. *Corrections Today,* 6.

Council of State Governments Reentry Policy Council. (2005). *Report of the Re-Entry Policy Council: Charting the safe and successful return of prisoners to the community.* New York, NY: Council of State Governments.

Daugherty, S. (2010, September 10). Incarcerated Vets tend cemetery through state program. *The (Annapolis) Capital,* p. A5.

Davidson, L., & Rowe, M. (2008). *Peer support within criminal justice settings: The role of forensic peer specialists.* Delmar, NY: CMHS National GAINS Center.

Davis, T. M., Baer, J. S., Saxon, A. J., & Kivlahan, D. R. (2003). Brief motivational feedback improves post-incarceration treatment contact among veterans with substance use disorders. *Drug and Alcohol Dependence, 69,* 197–203.

Dewey, L. (2004). *War and redemption: Treatment and recovery in combat-related traumatic stress disorder.* Burlington, VT: Ashgate.

Dilulio, J. J. (2008). The wacko-Vet myth: Now echoed by the New York Times. Retrieved from *Weekly Standard* http://www.weeklystandard.com/Content/Public/Articles/000/000/014/592buqao.asp?pg=2

Engendorf, C. K., Laufer, R., Rothbart, G., & Sloan, L. (1981). *Legacies of Vietnam: Comparative adjustment of veterans and their peers.* Washington, DC: Government Printing Office.

Giardino, A. E. (2009). Combat veterans, mental health issues, and the death penalty: Addressing the impact of post-traumatic stress disorder and traumatic brain injury. *Fordham Law Review, 77,* 2955–2995.

Greenberg, G. A., Rosenheck, R. A., & Desai, R. A. (2007). Risk of incarceration among male veterans and nonveterans. *Armed Forces and Society, 33*(3), 337–350.

Hartiens, J., & McCarty, M. (2007, March). *Keep your engines running: Tools to manage addictive thinking on the road to reentry.* Paper presented at meeting of National Career Development Association, Charlotte, NC.

Hoge, C. W., Goldberg, H. M., & Castro, C. A. (2009). Care of war veterans with mild traumatic brain injury—flawed perspectives. *New England Journal of Medicine, 360,* 16.

Holbrook, J. G. (2010). Veterans Court and criminal responsibility: A problem-solving history and approach to the liminality of combat trauma. In D. C. Kelly, D. Gitelson, & S. H. Barksdale (Eds.), *Young veterans: A resilient community of honor, duty, and need.* Retrieved from http://papers.ssrn.com/sol3/papers.cfm?abstract_id=1706829

Holmes, B. L. (2011, January 29). Veterans unit opens at IREF. *Hendricks County Flyer,* p. B4.

Homeless Veterans Comprehensive Assisstance Act of 2001. Public Law 107-95. 38 USC § 5(a) (1), Dec. 21, 2001, 115 Stat. 905.

Huey, M. P., & McNulty, T. L. (2005). Institutional conditions and prison suicide: Conditional effects of deprivation and overcrowding. *The Prison Journal, 85*(4), 490–514.

Insight Prison Project. San Rafael, CA. Retrieved from http://www.insightprisonproject.org

Institute for Operations Research and the Management Sciences. (2009, September 14). Iraq troops' PTSD rate as high as 35%, analysis finds. *Science Daily.* Retrieved from http://sciencedaily.com/releases/2009/090914151629.htm

Institute of Medicine. (2010). *Returning home from Iraq and Afghanistan: Preliminary assessment of readjustment needs of veterans, service members, and their families.* Washington, DC: National Academies Press.

Kimerling, R., Street, A. E., Gima, K., & Smith, M. W. (2008). Evaluation of universal screening for military-related sexual trauma. *Psychiatric Services, 59,* 635–640.

Kulka, R. A., Schlenger, J. A., Fairbank, J. A., Hough, R. L., Jordan, K., Marmar, C. R., & Weiss, D. S. (1990). *Trauma and the Vietnam war generation: Report of findings from the national Vietnam veteran's readjustment study.* New York, NY: Brunner/Mazel.

Kussman, M. J. (2007). *President's 2008 budget proposal for the Veterans Health Administration (VHA), February 14, 2007.* Retrieved March 9, 2012, from GPO http://frwebgate.access.gpo.gov/cqi-bin/getdoc.cgi?dbname=110 house hearings&docid=f:34304.wais

Langan, P. A., & Levin, D. J. (2002). *Recidivism of Prisoners Released in 1994.* NCJ 193427. Washington, DC: U.S. Department of Justice, Office of Justice Programs. Retrieved from http://bjs.ojp.usdoj.gov/index.cfm?ty=pbdetail&iid=1134

Lipari, R. N., Cook, P. J., Rock, L. M., & Matos, K. (2008). *2006 Gender Relations Survey of Active Duty Members. (Report No. 2007–002).* Arlington, VA: Department of Defense Manpower Data Center.

Malik-Kane, K., & Visher, C. (2008). *Health and prisoner reentry: How physical, mental, and substance abuse conditions shape the process of reintegration.* Washington, DC: Urban Institute Justice Policy Center. Retrieved from http://www.urban.org/Uploaded PDF/411617 health prisoner reentry.pdf

Manalive. Men Against Violence Program. Retrieved from http://www.mavcenter.org

McGuire, J. (Ed.). (1995). *What works: Reducing reoffending: Guidelines from research and practice.* Chichester, England: Wiley.

McGuire, J. (2008). *The Incarcerated Veterans Transition Program (IVTP): A pilot program evaluation of IVTP employment and enrollment, VA service use and criminal recidivism.* Report to Congress. Washington, DC: U.S. Department of Veterans Affairs.

Mears, D., Lawrence, S., Solomon, A., & Waul, M. (2002, April 1). Prison-based programming: What it can do . . . Why it is needed. *Corrections Today.*

Milkman, H., & Wonberg, T. D. (2007). *Cognitive-behavioral treatment: A review and discussion for corrections professionals.* Washington, DC: U.S. Department of Justice, National Institute of Corrections. Retrieved from http://nicic.gov/Library/021657

Miller, W. R., & Rollnick, S. (2002). *Motivational interviewing: Preparing people for change.* New York, NY: Guilford Press.

Minton, T. (2010). *Jail inmates at midyear 2009—Statistical tables.* NCJ 230122. Washington, DC: U.S. Department of Justice, Bureau of Justice Statistics. Retrieved from http://bjs.ojp.usdoj.gov/content/pub/pdf/jim09st.pdf

Mumola, C. J. (2000). *Bureau of Justice Statistics Special Report: Veterans in Prison or Jail.* NCJ 178888. U.S. Department of Justice, Office of Justice Programs. Retrieved from http://bjs.ojp.usdoj.gov/content/pub/pdf/jim09st.pdf

Mumola, C. J., & Noonan, M. E. (2008). *Justice-involved Veterans: National estimates and research resources.* Paper presented at meeting of U.S. Department of Veterans Affairs, Baltimore, MD.

Nakashima, J., McGuire, J., Garrow, E., Berman, S., Dalton, K., & Daniels, W. (2006). *Outreach to homeless veterans in the Los Angeles County jail: The VA Greater Los Angeles healthcare story.* National Institute of Corrections LJN (Large Jail Network) Exchange, 11–20.National Commission on Correctional Healthcare. (2008). Available at www.ncchc.org/resources/2008_standards/mentalhealth.html

National Quality Research Center. (2006). *The American Customer Service Satisfaction Index (ACSI).* Ann Arbor: University of Michigan Business School.

Noonan, M. E., & Mumola, C. J. (2007). *Bureau of Justice Statistics Special Report: Veterans in state and federal prison.* NCJ 217199. Washington, DC: U.S. Department of Justice,

Office of Justice Programs. Retrieved from http://bjs.ojp.usdoj.gov/index.cfm?ty=pb detail&iid=808

Pentland, B., & Dwyer, J. (1985). Incarcerated Viet Nam veterans. In S. M. Sonnenberg, A. S. Blank, & J. A. Talbott (Eds.), *The trauma of war: Stress and recovery in Viet Nam veterans* (pp. 402–416). New York, NY: American Psychiatric Press.

Pentland, B., & Scurfield, R. (1982). Inreach counseling and advocacy with veterans in prison. *Federal Probation, 36,* 21–29.

Resnick, S. G., & Rosenheck, R. A. (2008). Integrating peer-provided services: A quasi-experimental study of recovery orientation, confidence, and empowerment. *Psychiatric Services, 59*(11), 1307–1314.

Rosenheck, R. (2004). Mental and substance-use health services for veterans: Experience with performance evaluation in the Department of Veterans Affairs. In *Committee on crossing the quality chasm: Adaptation to mental health and addictive disorders improving the quality of health care for mental and substance-use conditions* (pp. 423–482). Washington, DC: Institute of Medicine.

Scott-Hayward, C. S. (2009). *The fiscal crisis in corrections: Rethinking of policies and practices.* New York, NY: VERA Institute of Justice Center for Sentencing and Corrections.

Second Chance Act. (2007). Public Law 110-199. 42 USC § 17501.

Shiroma, E. J., Ferguson, P. L., & Pickelsimer, E. E. (2010). Prevalence of traumatic brain injury in an offender population: A meta-analysis. *Journal of Correctional Health Care, 16*(2), 147–159.

Tanielian T., Jaycox, L. H. (Eds.). (2008). *Invisible wounds of war: Psychological and cognitive injuries, their consequences, and services to assist recovery.* Santa Monica, CA: RAND.

Taxman, F. S., Perdoni, M. L., & Harrison, L. D. (2007). Drug treatment services for adult offenders: The state of the state. *Journal of Substance Abuse Treatment, 32*(3), 239–254.

Travis, J., Solomon, A. L., & Waul, M. (2001). *From prison to home: The dimensions and consequences of prisoner reentry.* Washington, DC: Urban Institute. Available at http://www.urban.org/publications/410098.html

U.S. Department of Health and Human Services, Centers for Disease Control. *Factsheet: Traumatic brain injury in prisons and jails: An unrecognized problem.* Retrieved from http://www.cdc.gov/traumaticbraininjury/pdf/Prisoner_TBI_Prof-a.pdf

U.S. Department of Health and Human Services, Substance Abuse and Mental Health Services Administration. Available at http://www.samhsa.gov/nctic/trauma.asp

U.S. Department of Labor. *Incarcerated veterans transition program (IVTP).* Available at http://www.dol.gov/vets/programs/ivtp/main.htm

U.S. Department of Veterans Affairs. *VA/DOD Clinical practice guidelines.* Available at http://www.healthquality.va.gov

U.S. Department of Veterans Affairs. (2011, December 20). *Criminal behavior and PTSD.* Washington, DC: Author. Retrieved from http://www.ptsd.va.gov/public/pages/ptsd-criminal-behavior.asp

Veterans Health Administration Office of Public Health and Environmental Hazards. (2011). *Analysis of VA health care utilization among Operation Enduring Freedom (OEF) and Operation Iraqi Freedom (OIF) veterans.* Washington, DC: U.S. Department of Veterans Affairs.

Wain, R. M., Wilbourne, P. L., Harris, K. W., Pierson, H., Teleki, J., Burling, T., & Lovett, S. (2011). Motivational interview improves treatment entry in homeless veterans. *Drug and Alcohol Dependence, 115,* 113–119.

Walter Reed Army Institute of Research. (2005). *BATTLEMIND training I: Transitioning from combat to home.* Rockville, MD: Author.

Weissman, E., Covell, N., Kushner, M., Irwin, J., & Essock, S. (2005). Implementing peer-assisted case management to help homeless veterans with mental illness transition to independent housing. *Community Mental Health Journal, 41*(3), 267–276.

Williams, B., McGuire, J., Lindsay, R., Baillargeon, J., Stijacic, I., Lee, S., & Kushel, M. (2010). Coming home: Health status and homelessness risk of older pre-release prisoners. *Journal of General Internal Medicine, 25*(10), 1038–1044.

Wortzel, H. S., Binswanger, I. A., Anderson, C. A., & Adler, L. E. (2009). Suicide among incarcerated veterans. *Journal of the American Academy of Psychiatry and the Law, 37*(1), 82–91.

Wortzel, H. S., Binswanger, I. A., Martinez, R., Filley, C. M., & Anderson, C. A. (2007). Crisis in the treatment of incompetence to proceed to trial: Harbinger of a systemic illness. *Journal of the American Academy of Psychiatric Law, 35*(3), 57–63.

CHAPTER 13

Special Needs Offenders in Correctional Institutions: Death-Sentenced Inmates

Mark D. Cunningham

A comparatively small, but highly visible, portion of the American correctional system involves death-sentenced inmates. Indeed, of approximately 1.5 million inmates held in state and federal correctional institutions in 2010, only 0.002% of these faced execution. Their visibility is quite disproportionate to their number. A number of states have dedicated areas of their websites for their death row and the offenders housed there (e.g., Arizona, Florida, Oklahoma, and Texas). The general public and the popular media also have a fascination with this narrow portion of the correctional population, as reflected in films of the past two decades, including *Live! From Death Row* (1992), *Last Light* (1993), *The Green Mile* (1995), *Beyond the Call* (1996), *Dead Man Walking* (1996), *The Chamber* (1996), *Lost Highway* (1997), *The Thin Blue Line* (1998), *Last Dance* (1996), *A Letter From Death Row* (1998), *Monster's Ball* (2001), *Identity* (2003), *The Life of David Gale* (2003), *Redemption: The Stan Tookie Williams Story* (2004), *Exonerated* (2005), *The Trial* (2010), *Honk!* (2011), *Into the Abyss* (2011), and *Paradise Lost 3: Purgatory* (2011).

Much lore, if not mythology (Lyon & Cunningham, 2006), surrounds these death-sentenced offenders. Quite obviously, they are unique in a pending sanction of execution, as well as in segregated conditions of confinement that in most jurisdictions are dictated solely by this sentence. Whether these offenders have unique or "special needs" as a function of being under a sentence of death, or being held in segregated and often super-maximum conditions of confinement, or having some importation feature(s) are questions with significant correctional and public policy implications. This chapter will explore these considerations and the needs of these death-sentenced inmates.

JURISDICTIONAL FEATURES

As of January 1, 2010, there were 3,261 death-sentenced inmates nationwide, held by 35 states, the U.S. military, and the federal government (Death Penalty Information Center, 2011). This number is slowly declining, having peaked in 2000 with 3,593 death-sentenced inmates nationwide. Lower rates of death-sentencing are primarily implicated in this decline. New death sentences averaged 285 annually for 1995–1999, as compared to 124 annually for 2005–2009. The median death row is comprised of 35 inmates (Kentucky). However, this belies the broad range of death-sentenced offenders in any given correctional jurisdiction, from a single death-sentenced inmate in Wyoming to 697 awaiting execution in California. Five jurisdictions (California, Florida, Texas, Pennsylvania, and Alabama) collectively house over half (i.e., 1,855 or 51%) of death-sentenced offenders nationwide. The staff and fiscal resources directed to death-sentenced inmates, as well as the complexity of managing these prisoners, then, may be quite different from jurisdiction to jurisdiction (Hudson, 2000).

COMPARATIVE DEMOGRAPHIC CHARACTERISTICS

Sex

As with the general correctional population, the overwhelming majority of death-sentenced inmates are male. Only 61 women (1.9%) nationwide had pending executions as of January 1, 2010 (NAACP, 2010). This reflects a sharp underrepresentation of women among death-sentenced inmates, as compared to their 6.8% proportion among prisoners sentenced to more than one year in federal or state jurisdictions at year-end 2009 or 6.2% among state inmates serving sentences for murder in 2007 (West, Sabol, & Greenman, 2010). It is thus not practical in most jurisdictions to have a segregated death row for women sentenced to death.

Race

In terms of racial distribution, death-sentenced offenders generally approximate the broader correctional population, as well as offenders sentenced for homicide and violent crimes. These comparisons are reflected in Table 13.1.

Age

The mean and median age of death-sentenced inmates at year-end 2009 was 44 years old, while the modal age was 45–49. As reflected in Figure 13.1, the distribution of death-sentenced inmates is roughly a decade older than the age distribution of the general correctional population, where the modal inmate age is 25–29 years and the median age is mid-30s.

Table 13.1	Racial Distribution in Correctional Population by Type of Inmate or Offense of Conviction			

Race/ethnicity	Death-sentenced[a]	All prisoners[b]	Murder[c]	Violent offense[d]
White	0.44	0.33	0.31	0.34
Black	0.42	0.39	0.42	0.39
Hispanic	0.12	0.21	0.18	0.19
Other	0.02	0.07		

[a]Nationwide as of January 1, 2010 (NAACP, 2010).

[b]Male prisoners in state or federal jurisdiction sentenced to one year or more, as of December 31, 2009 (West et al., 2010).

[c]Includes negligent manslaughter; as of year-end 2008 (West et al., 2010).

[d]As of year-end 2008 (West et al., 2010).

Figure 13.1	Age Distribution of Death-Sentenced Inmates[a] and Total Correctional Population[b]

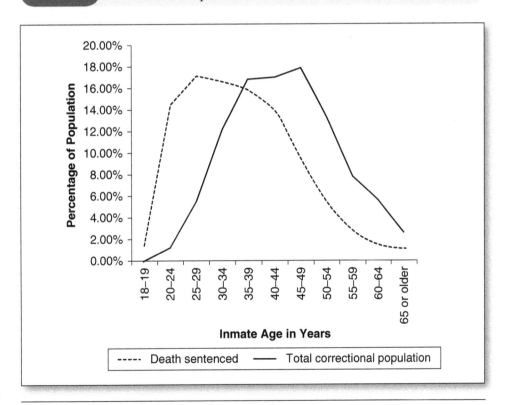

[a]As of year-end 2009 (Snell, 2010)

[b]As of year-end 2009 (West, Sabol, & Greenman, 2010)

Implications of age discrepancy

The age discrepancy between death-sentenced and other inmates has three important implications. First, one of the most well-established findings in penology is that rates of prison misconduct and inmate violence are markedly and progressively lower among older inmates. Thus, inmates in their late 30s or older demonstrate only a fraction of the institutional misconduct exhibited by inmates in their early 20s. This finding is illustrated in Figure 13.2, reflecting a large scale investigation of

Figure 13.2   Annual infraction rate for all prisoners by age categories

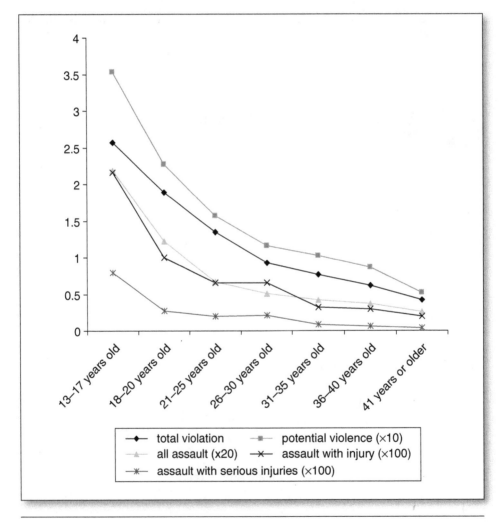

Source: Reproduced from A. Kuanliang, J. R. Sorensen, & M. D. Cunningham (2008). Juvenile offenders in an adult prison system: A comparative examination of rates and correlates of misconduct. *Criminal Justice and Behavior, 35*(9), 1186-1201. doi: 10.1177/0093854808322744

over 38,000 newly-admitted inmates in a state corrections department (Kuanliang, Sorensen, & Cunningham, 2008).

From an age factor alone, then, it is expected that death-sentenced inmates as a group would present fewer disciplinary problems and have less need for super-maximum conditions of confinement to contain misconduct or violence. An expanded discussion of the security-driven rationales for the conditions of confinement for death-sentenced inmates will follow later in this chapter.

Second, the comparatively older-age status of death-sentenced inmates suggests that they will require more intensive medical screening and treatment, particularly for age-related conditions such as elevated cholesterol, hypertension, Type II diabetes, cardiovascular disease, for example. Managing these disorders from a preventative or behavioral medicine perspective may prove to be a greater challenge than is encountered in treating these conditions among aging inmates in the general prison population, as restrictive confinement conditions inhibit opportunities for activity and exercise.

Third, much of the age difference between death-sentenced and the broader correctional population appears attributable to the longer prison tenures of death-sentenced offenders. At year-end 2009, the mean time elapsed since sentencing for inmates under a sentence of death nationwide was over 12 years (mean = 152 months, median = 146 months) (Snell, 2010). By contrast, the expected length of prison stay in 2008 among all inmates was 23.5 months and among violent offenders was 43.7 months (West et al., 2010). The extended imprisonment between admission of an inmate under a sentence of death and the carrying out, or removal, of this sentence has significant implications for what procedures and programming will support the physical and mental health of these offenders.

COMPARATIVE INTELLECTUAL CAPABILITY AND ACADEMIC ACHIEVEMENT

IQ Scores

Of 14 clinical studies (i.e., involving direct assessment or individual file review) of death-sentenced inmates (for a discussion of pre-2002 studies, see Cunningham & Vigen, 2002), 12 examined intellectual functioning, reporting mean IQ scores in the average to low average range (see Table 13.2). In the most recent of these clinical studies, Cunningham, Sorensen, Vigen, and Woods (2011) described characteristics of 111 former death-sentenced inmates in Texas, reporting a mean IQ score of 88 ($R = 60$–120) on an intelligence screening measure. The mean IQ score (M IQ=88) reported for the former death-sentenced inmates was not discrepant from the mean IQ score of 90.55 on the same instrument observed among the Texas prison population as a whole (Texas Department of Criminal Justice, 2011).

Observing that death-sentenced and general population inmates exhibit mean IQ scores in the low average to average range, however, neglects the lower tail of

Table 13.2 Clinical Studies of Death Row Inmates

Study	State	Sample	IQ Score	Education	Psychological Symptoms	Neurological Findings	History
Bluestone &	NY	$N = 19$	$37\% \leq IQ$ 79	63% < 6th grade	32% delusional		95% father absent
McGahee (1962)			$74\% \leq IQ$ 89	100% < HS grad	Pervasive maladaptive defenses		Most reared in foster/institution
Gallemore & Panton (1972)	NC	$N = 8$	$M = IQ$ 95.6 (Beta) IQ range = 76–118	$M = 9.5$ (schooling) Range = 6–12th $M = 5.6$ (achievement) Range = 1.9—8th	37% poor death row adjustment All elevated MMPI depression scale		All poverty/psych problems in family Half not reared by both parents 87% heavy ETOH abuse
Panton (1976)	NC	$N = 34$	$M = IQ$ 90.7 IQ range = 74–125	$M = 9.4$ (schooling) Range = 4–14	Higher MMPI Pa and Sc scales than general population inmates		
Panton (1978)	NC	$N = 55$	$M = IQ$ 96.5 $(SD = 12.2)$	$M = 9.8$ $(SD = 2.2)$	Higher MMPI Pa and Sc scales Symptoms subsided if commuted		
Lewis (1979)	FL	$N = 83$	Reported as similar to community distribution	$M = 9.7$ (schooling) 9.6% < 6th grade	41% diagnosed psych. disorder		42% not reared by both parents 81% intoxicated at offense
Johnson (1979)	AL	$N = 35$			Pervasive depression, mood lability, reduced mental acuity		

Study	State	Sample	IQ Score	Education	Psychological Symptoms	Neurological Findings	History
Smith & Felix (1986)	NC	N = 34	Estimated average IQ from brief mental status	58% < HS grad Range = 9–12th	Use of denial, suppression, undoing		Divorce & separation frequent Unsupportive families frequent
Lewis et al. (1986)	5 states	N = 15	M = 86.5 (WAIS-R) IQ range = 50–100	1–12th (achievement) All had islands of poor literacy	40% chronic psychosis 20% episodic psychosis 13% bi-polar	33% major impairments 47% minor neuro. signs 100% had head injuries	60% child/ adolescent psychological disorder 27% attempted suicide in child/ adolescence
Evans (1997)		N = 11				82% had abnormal EEG & neuropsych. testing	
Frierson et al. (1998)	SC	N = 18	M = IQ 90.3 IQ range = 50–122 28% ≤ borderline or MR			24% LOC head injury Half had abnormal EEG, MRI, neurological exam	78% substance abuse disorder Half intoxicated at offense
Cunningham & Vigen (1999)	MS	N = 39	M = VIQ 81.5 (WAIS-R) SD = 10.7 IQ range = 58-103 27% ≤ IQ 74	M = 9th (schooling) SD = 2.3 M = 5.1 reading comp. SD = 2.87 WIAT range = 1.2–12+	50% mod-extrem depress. (R-BDI) 71% mult PAI scale elevations > T70 43% reported depression, 30% reported anxiety 5% psychotic	46% neurological insults	57% substance abusing parent 73% substance abuse/depend.

(Continued)

Table 13.2 (Continued)

Study	State	Sample	IQ Score	Education	Psychological Symptoms	Neurological Findings	History
Freedman & Hemenway (2000)	CA	N = 16	69% ≤ borderline or MR	38% illiterate	56% psychosis with hallucinations 81% severe depression 88% posttraumatic stress disorder	75% traumatic brain injury 75% devel. or cog. impaired 19% fetal etoh syn./ effects	81% polysub abusers 88% abused physically/sexually 94% wit. family violence 94% institutional failure
Lisak & Beszterczey (2007)	Various	N = 37			95% psychiatric diagnosis or symptom	49% neurological impaired 89% school difficulties 70% cognitive/ academic problems	78% substance abusers 59% sexually abused 95% physically abused 89% verbally abused 83% witnessed violence 100% neglected
Cunningham et al. (2011)	TX	N = 111	M = IQ 88.2 IQ range = 60–120	M = 9.1 (schooling) M = 8.1 (TABE)			

Source: Adapted and updated from M. D. Cunningham & M. P. Vigen (2002). Death row inmate characteristics, adjustment, and confinement: A critical review of the literature. *Behavioral Sciences & the Law, 20* (1/2), 191-210. doi: 10.1002/bsl.473

that distribution. Cunningham and Vigen (1999) reported that 27% of Mississippi death row inmates had Wechsler Adult Intelligence Scale-Revised (WAIS-R) Verbal IQ scores below 74. If these WAIS-R scores are corrected for the progressive norm obsolescence of IQ scores, that is, the Flynn effect (Cunningham & Tassé, 2010), the proportion of Mississippi death-sentenced inmates with Verbal IQ scores below 74 increases to 43.1%. Similarly, Frierson, Schwartz-Watts, Morgan, and Malone (1998) reported that among a small sample of death row inmates in South Carolina, 28% obtained IQ scores in the borderline or mental retardation range. Cunningham et al. (2011) noted that one sixth of their sample of former death-sentenced inmates had IQ scores below 70 on a screening measure and only one-fourth obtained IQ scores > 95. By contrast, approximately 4% of inmates in the correctional population as a whole are believed to be persons with mental retardation (i.e., IQ < 75, concurrent deficits in adaptive functioning, and onset before age 18) (Petersilia, 1997).

Though it is clear that some, and perhaps a substantial minority, of death-sentenced inmates are intellectually limited, the precise contours of this proportion remain unclear. Most of the clinical studies of death-sentenced inmates suffer from small sample sizes and significant methodological problems (Cunningham & Vigen, 2002). Generalizing from the existing research may be problematic secondary to differences in death-sentenced inmates from one jurisdiction to another. These clinical studies are also increasingly dated, with most published over two decades ago. More recent research reporting larger scale comparative data relies on group-administered and/or screening measures, providing less reliable assessments.

Academic Achievement

The intellectual limitations of many death-sentenced inmates are compounded by marginal literacy capabilities. Only 41.5% of death-sentenced inmates nation-wide are high school graduates or have obtained a GED, and 13.5% have an eighth-grade education or less (Snell, 2010). Drawing conclusions regarding functional literacy from the years of schooling attended by these offenders, however, may substantially inflate their actual abilities. To illustrate, Cunningham and Vigen (1999) reported that among Mississippi death-sentenced inmates, mean schooling was reported as mid-ninth grade, while Wechsler Individual Achievement Test (WIAT) reading comprehension scores were four grades lower (i.e., $M = 5.1$ grade level). Quite consistent with this discrepancy between years of schooling and functional literacy, Gallemore and Panton (1972) reported mean school attendance at the 9.5 grade level, but mean educational achievement capabilities of only the 5.6 grade level. In more recent data from a sample of former death-sentenced inmates in Texas, years of formal education averaged 9.1, but educational achievement was at 8.1 grade level. A corresponding discrepancy has been reported for prison inmates as a whole. The Texas Department of Criminal Justice (2011) reported that among 139,316 prison inmates in custody on

August 31, 2010, 58.1% were verified to hold a high school diploma or GED, but the average educational achievement score was at 8.1 grade level.

Implications of Intellectual and Literacy Limitations

Whether the distribution of IQ or academic achievement scores is lower for death-sentenced inmates as compared to general corrections prisoners remains unclear. Some studies point to death-sentenced offenders being disproportionately compromised in these capabilities, while others suggest equivalence. From a corrections programming standpoint, the presence of any discrepancy would not seem to be the critical issue. Rather, these data indicate that death-sentenced inmates are, at best, no better suited to productively occupying themselves in intellectual or literary pursuits than other inmates. The literacy limitations of death-sentenced inmates take on additional salience in two ways. First, in considering the intersection between extended incarceration and the super-maximum confinement that typifies the custody of death-sentenced inmates in many jurisdictions (discussed subsequently), it is troubling that a substantial minority of death-sentenced inmates are unlikely to be able to successfully occupy themselves by reading or engaging in solitary intellectual pursuits. At the same time, the ability of death-sentenced inmates to constructively occupy themselves in more concrete activities such as inmate work roles, sports, and social exchange, as opposed to cell-based activities, are barred by security-based restrictions.

Second, the appellate procedures for death-sentenced inmates are more complex and more enduring than for other offenders (McDermott, 1990; Mello, 1988). This, combined with the intellectual and literacy limitations demonstrated by death-sentenced inmates, necessitates more intensive legal support services (Cunningham & Vigen, 1999).

COMPARATIVE PREVALENCE OF NEUROLOGICALLY SIGNIFICANT HISTORIES OR NEUROPSYCHOLOGICAL DEFICITS

Six of the 14 clinical studies investigated neurologically significant histories and/or neuropsychological deficits in their death row samples. A general observation that neurological abnormalities and neuropsychological deficits are frequently observed among death-sentenced inmates is supported by these findings. While this incidence is likely greater than the prevalence among inmates in general, whether it is disproportionate as compared to other violent offenders is uncertain. Fabian (2010) recently reviewed research regarding neurological and neuropsychological correlates in violent and homicidal offending, describing a recurrent association in the literature between violent offending and brain dysfunction. These conclusions are consistent with studies of murderers and violent felons, which reported a disproportionate incidence of neurological dysfunction and abnormalities among these offenders (e.g., Blake, Pincus, & Buckner, 1995; Langevin, Ben-Aron, Wortzman, Dickey, & Handy, 1987; Martell, 1992).

COMPARATIVE PREVALENCE OF PRESENTENCE DEVELOPMENTAL ADVERSITIES AND PSYCHOLOGICAL VULNERABILITIES

Clinical studies of death-sentenced inmates have reported a high prevalence of family dysfunction and childhood maltreatment in the backgrounds of death-sentenced inmates. Eight of the clinical studies of death-sentenced inmates (see Table 13.2) described frequently encountered histories among these offenders of parental abandonment, foster care and institutionalization, abuse and neglect, and parental substance abuse.

The most recent and descriptive analysis of the psychosocial histories (based on interviews of inmates and third-party sources, as well as records review) of death-sentenced inmates was provided by Lisak and Beszterczey (2007), who reviewed and rated the social histories of 37 offenders who had been sentenced to death. The jurisdictions were unspecified beyond being drawn from in a number of states. These social histories reflected near pervasive experience of family dysfunction and childhood maltreatment that would predispose these inmates to psychological disorders and reduce their coping capability. For example, 92% had families of origin characterized by substance abuse and 68% had family histories of psychological disorder. Forty-six percent had family histories of criminal activity and 51% had histories of caretaking instability. Multigenerational family dysfunction included physical abuse (54%) and sexual abuse (24%). Not surprising given the disturbances in these family systems, all of the death-sentenced inmates were identified as having been neglected and almost all (95%) had been physically abused. Almost six in ten were sexually abused and eight in ten had witnessed violence.

Reports of family dysfunction and childhood maltreatment among male state prison inmates have generally reflected a lower prevalence than reported by Lisak and Beszterczey, or other clinical studies that queried such histories. Ditton (1999) reported that 26.1% of mentally ill inmates had histories of foster or institutional care, as compared to 12.2% of other inmates. Harlow (1999), from interviews with a representative sample of male state prison inmates, reported that 13.4% of them self-described histories of physical abuse and 5.8% had histories of having been sexually abused. Notably, however, the methodology employed by Harlow relied on the inmate to characterize the childhood experience as abuse, rather than obtaining a history of conduct that was subsequently classified by mental health experts, as occurred in the data analysis of Lisak and Beszterczey. In stark contrast to the survey data detailed by Harlow, Johnson et al. (2006) reported that 59% of a male jail inmate sample self-described sexual contacts reflecting sexual abuse prior to the age of 14. Harlow's finding of sexual abuse among fewer than 6% of state prison inmates is also inconsistent with a contemporaneous study by Fondacaro, Holt, and Powell (1999) of sexual abuse histories among male prison inmates. Fondacaro and colleagues reported that 40% of their sample met standard criteria for childhood sexual abuse. Illuminative of problems inherent in Harlow's methodology, Fondacaro et al. reported that 41% of those who met criteria for childhood sexual abuse did not consider themselves to have been abused. Ditton (1999), also relying on national surveys of state prison inmates, reported that 27% of inmates with a mental condition acknowledged histories of having been physically abused and 15% reported having been sexually abused. Whether this reflects an increased incidence of childhood maltreatment among these psychologically disturbed inmates or a greater willingness to disclose is unclear.

Acknowledging the comparability problems of this literature, it is hypothesized that the histories of death-sentenced inmates reflect a greater prevalence of childhood adversity and trauma. These differences, however, may be more modest than suggested by some research.

Consistent with the association of childhood maltreatment histories with subsequent psychological disorders (Schwartz & Perry, 1994; Stein, Golding, Siegel, Burnham, & Sorenson, 1988; Widom, 2000) and substance abuse (Kilpatrick et al., 2000), Lisak and Beszterczey reported that 78% of the death-sentenced inmates had community histories of substance abuse and 95% had a history of a psychiatric diagnosis or symptoms (other than substance abuse). The prevalence of a history of substance abuse among death-sentenced inmates is quite similar to the prevalence among state prison inmates (Harlow, 1999), with 76.3% self-reporting prior regular use of illegal drugs in the community and 66.9% acknowledging preconviction regular use of alcohol. Similarly, Ditton (1999) described that 56.1% of state prison inmates acknowledged having used drugs in the month preceding their offense of conviction (see also Greenfeld, 1998).

Histories of family dysfunction, directly experienced trauma, psychological symptoms, and substance abuse would be expected to lessen resiliency and increase vulnerability to psychological disorder if subjected to enduring stressors or deprived of psychosocial supports.

COMPARATIVE PREVALENCE OF PSYCHOLOGICAL DISORDERS

Determining whether the prevalence of psychological disorder among death-sentenced inmates is higher than among the broader correctional population is problematic. No study could be identified that provided a direct comparison between death-sentenced inmates *and* the general prison population. Further, clinical studies of death-sentenced inmates are limited by small sample sizes, often reflect an earlier corrections era, and lack of comparable measures.

Among inmates in state prisons nationwide, Ditton (1999) estimated that 16.2% were mentally ill, as defined by self-report of either a mental or emotional condition or an overnight stay in a mental hospital or program. Of these, six in ten had reported receiving mental health treatment since admission to prison. Ditton also reported that inmates with mental illness histories were somewhat overrepresented among inmates serving sentences for violent offenses.

The available data demonstrate substantial rates of distressing symptoms and frank psychological disorders among death-sentenced inmates (Cunningham & Vigen, 2002), that would appear to be in excess of the prevalence in the general prison population. Such overrepresentation would be consistent with intuitive expectations of higher importation of psychological disorder among capital offenders, the psychologically arduous conditions of death row confinement, and the stress of a looming penalty of death.

Psychosis

Further complicating accurate estimates and comparative analyses, the reported incidence of severe psychological disorders among death-sentenced inmates has varied widely in the clinical studies of these offenders, particularly for rates of psychosis. These have ranged from over 50% (i.e., Freedman & Hemenway, 2000; Lewis, Pincus, Feldman, Jackson, & Bard, 1986) to only 5–20%[1] (Cunningham & Vigen, 1999). Such discrepancies appear to reflect the above noted methodological problems of small sample sizes, varying measures, and differences in operational definitions of *psychosis*. Regarding the latter, operational definitions of *psychosis* have varied in the time period of symptom occurrence. For example, Freedman and Hemenway (2000) included historical psychotic symptoms, while Cunningham and Vigen (2002) focused only on current psychotic presentation. Operational definitions have also varied in the severity of psychotic symptoms necessary to trigger this classification. Lewis, Pincus, Feldman, Jackson, and Bard (1986) noted that the symptoms of psychosis in their sample were often quite subtle. Such severity distinctions can be critical. In 2002, Cunningham and Vigen reported that four to six times as many death row inmates obtained extreme scores on the Paranoia and Schizophrenia scales of the Personality Assessment Inventory, as demonstrated by overt psychotic symptoms on clinical interview.

By comparison, the Epidemiologic Catchment Area program reported that 6.7% on prevalence of prison and jail inmates had suffered from schizophrenia at some time (Robins & Regier, 1991).

Other Psychological Disorders

Though psychosis is the most disabling, it is not the only or most common psychological disorder observed among death-sentenced inmates (see Table 13.2). Illustrating this prevalence, Cunningham and Vigen (1999) reported that 57% of Mississippi death row inmates reported symptoms of depression or anxiety on clinical interview, and half scored in the moderate-severe or severe-extreme range on the Beck Depression Inventory. Further, these death row inmates pervasively demonstrated markedly elevated scores on clinical scales of the Personality Assessment Inventory, endorsing symptoms of acute psychological disorders, characteristics of personality disturbance, and problems with anger control, suicidal ideation, stress, and lack of social support.

Importation Versus Context

One hypothesis for the arguably higher prevalence of psychological disorders among death-sentenced inmates is that as a group, they were more psychologically disturbed or vulnerable at entrance into prison. There is modest inferential support for this explanation from Ditton's (1999) observation that mentally ill inmates were somewhat more likely to have been convicted for murder (13.2%) than other inmates (11.4%).

An alternative and arguably more compelling hypothesis is that contextual factors associated with the activity restrictions and interpersonal deprivations of death row, rather than importation features of these offenders, are implicated in any over-representation of psychological disorders among death-sentenced inmates. Consideration of this hypothesis requires a review of the prevailing conditions of confinement for death-sentenced inmates nationwide.

CONDITIONS OF CONFINEMENT FOR DEATH-SENTENCED INMATES

Prevailing Conditions

Conditions of confinement for death-sentenced inmates nationwide were most recently surveyed by Babcock (2008) and previously by *Corrections Compendium* (American Correctional Association, 1999) and Hudson (2000). Little has changed over the course of this decade, with the "rigid security, isolation, limited movement, and austere conditions" that have typified death row since the beginning of the 20th century (Lombardi, Sluder, & Wallace, 1997, p. 1; for descriptive detail, see also Arriens, 1997; Johnson, 1990; Pickett, 2002; Von Drehle, 1995) continuing to be the norm. Babcock identified only two jurisdictions (Oklahoma and Missouri) where death-sentenced inmates were not confined in individual cells (aka solitary confinement). The modal time out-of-cell was only one hour daily, and in at least 13 jurisdictions, "recreation" is solitary as well. Meals in solitary confinement units are typically served through a locking metal flap in the cell door. This same "trap" is utilized in handcuffing the inmate behind his back before the cell door is opened. On such units, inmates are shackled for any out-of-cell movement. Shower and telephone access are restricted. For example, death row inmates in Pennsylvania are allowed one 15-minute telephone call weekly (Pennsylvania Department of Corrections, 2011). Babcock reported that in most jurisdictions, visitation with family or community members was "non-contact." In Texas, a radio is permitted, but not a television. Offenders currently on death row nationwide have averaged over 12 years under these conditions.

Two jurisdictions have experimented with radical departures from the prevailing norm of a super-maximum death row. The first was the 15-year work-capable program (1983–1998) in the Texas prison system. This is described by Dr. Keith Price, former Texas correctional officer and warden, in the following box. The second is the continuing procedure of the Missouri Department of Corrections of mainstreaming death-sentenced inmates at the Potosi Correctional Center.

The Texas "Work Capable" Program

By Keith Price, West Texas A&M University

In 1973, the death penalty returned to Texas (Tex. Penal Code § 19.03 Capital Murder 1973). The state had crafted a new death penalty statute (later approved by the Supreme Court in *Jurek v. Texas*, 1976) to meet the mandates of *Furman v. Georgia* (1972). *Furman* had given the states guidance on what was necessary to constitutionally sentence offenders to death under procedures known as "super due process" (Mandery, 2005). The machinery of death was again in operation, and the Texas Department of Corrections designated Cellblock J-23 of the Ellis Unit as Death Row. In the summer 1973, the Death Row count was one. It was during this same time period that I began my career as a Texas correctional officer at the Ellis Unit.

Building tenders were inmates placed in charge of a cellblock by the warden. On J-23, the warden had assigned two building tenders to keep an eye on the condemned prisoners and to keep activities on schedule. This included telling the assigned correctional officer what needed to be done. While learning the daily activities of a correctional officer, I often worked Death Row. On a routine day, the building tender would tell me to open Cell 23 to let the death row inmate go to the dayroom for recreation. After recreation, the inmate would enter the shower cell for his second daily activity. He would then return to his cell for the remainder of the day. There were no other inmates living on the cellblock except for the two building tenders. The daily routine rarely varied on Death Row. The inmate would go to the dayroom for an hour. He then was allowed to shower. He then returned to his cell. This routine continued day after day with little change.

Eventually, a second condemned inmate arrived on Cellblock J-23. The daily routine continued as before, but the schedule now had to accommodate two inmates instead of one. Additionally, the chaplain began to visit Death Row. He would talk and pray with the men during his visit. Occasionally an inmate would get a legal visit. He then had to be escorted down the hallway to the visiting room. Other than these variations, the daily schedule remained austere. As the year ended, I was promoted and sent to another prison. Before I departed, however, the first condemned prisoner committed suicide by hanging himself. The condemned count on Death Row returned to one.

Over the next months and years, Death Row grew as Texas counties utilized the new capital murder statute. Cellblock J-23 would not hold all of the condemned, and Death Row was expanded to other cellblocks. Due to the large numbers of inmates, regular schedules had to be established to deal with the growing population. Eventually, Death Row occupied almost half of the Ellis Unit's telephone pole designed building and became a major part of the security operation of the Unit. A captain was assigned as the commander of Death Row, and the operation included a cadre of selected officers, supervisors, and support staff to deal with the special needs of Death Row inmates. Occasionally, a condemned inmate would be moved from Ellis to the Huntsville Unit. It was there that the State of Texas carried out his sentence. His stay on Death Row had only been a stop over until the state executed his sentence.

In 1983, the Texas Department of Corrections was working hard to meet the demands of *Ruiz v. Estelle* (1980). One of the major issues of the litigation was how to handle segregated inmates such as those on Death Row. There was recognition that not all condemned

(Continued)

(Continued)

prisoners required maximum security segregation. Death Row began to utilize a custody risk assignment of work-capable and segregation. Inmates who behaved and posed little risk were assigned as *work-capable* and were treated as medium custody offenders. They were even allowed to work in a special garment factory that was established for these low-risk inmates (Marquart, Ekland-Olson, & Sorenson, 1994).

The disruptive inmates remained in maximum security segregation status. They were treated similarly to the growing number of gang members who were being segregated to prevent violence in the prisons. Maximum security segregation consisted of single-celled inmates who received one hour of out-of-cell recreation per day along with a shower. All other activities and interactions were curtailed or eliminated. Inmates even ate their meals in their cell.

This new operation seemed to work well. Death Row operations took on a routine that resembled other prisons. Medium security inmates worked and participated in out-of-cell activities while maximum security inmates spent most of the day in their cells. An occasional execution would take an inmate out of the population, but the rest of the operation was little different from any other prison.

On November 27, 1998, the routine of Death Row changed forever. During outdoor recreation, seven Death Row inmates escaped from the yard. Six of the inmates were stopped inside the prison perimeter by gunfire from the tower officers. The seventh inmate breached the secure perimeter and escaped into the night, although his escape was short-lived. He was found nearby several days later drowned (Lyman, [1998, November 28]: *Texas death row inmate pulls off escape*).

The escape from Death Row presented serious political considerations for the Texas Department of Corrections. A proposed move of Death Row to the Terrell Unit (later renamed the Polunsky Unit) had been postponed due to the tranquility of Death Row's operation. With the shadow of a Death Row escape hanging over the department, the move was implemented (Tomaso, 1999).

The move to Polunsky Unit Twelve Building dramatically changed the day-to-day life of Death Row inmates. The Ellis Unit cellblocks consisted of barred cells and open runs that allowed freedom of communication between inmates. The operation also had group recreation, a work program, and other group activities. These amenities were now all gone. Cells in Twelve Building had solid fronts that allowed no verbal communication. All group activities were removed. Recreation was limited to one inmate at a time, and outdoor recreation was conducted in special open air confinement cells in the same cellblock. Any time that an inmate left his cell, he moved with handcuffs, leg irons, chains, and two officer escorts. Death Row operated like all other segregation cellblocks that were filled with maximum security gang members.

Texas Death Row today remains a maximum security cellblock. Condemned inmates now spend years in isolation until the time comes for the execution of their sentence. They then take the 43 mile ride to the Huntsville Unit to enter the Death Chamber.

Keith Price, Ph.D., is an associate professor of criminal justice and sociology at West Texas A&M University. He retired from the Texas Department of Corrections/Criminal Justice in 2003 after 30 of service as an officer and warden.

Dr. Price's observation of the relative "tranquility" of the Texas death row during the work-capable era is consistent with analyses of inmate assaultive misconduct. Marquart et al. (1994) examined the disciplinary records of 421 inmates who passed through the Texas death row during the 15-year period (1974–1988) overlapping the work-capable years. Only 10.7% of these death-sentenced inmates assaulted correctional staff or other inmates, committing 63 total assaultive acts. Two inmates (0.0048) killed other death row inmates. Marquart et al. (1994) concluded:

> The majority of inmates awaiting execution on death row have served their time without major incident. Many of them work in the garment factory with objects that might serve as weapons close at hand and yet do not commit any violent assaultive acts. (p. 181)

By contrast, the rate of serious violent rule infractions among general population inmates in Texas prisons in 1986 was 11.66 per 100 inmates that year alone (Marquart, Ekland-Olson, and Sorensen, 1989).

Two conclusions emerge from the Texas work-capable program experience and its demise. First, a substantial proportion of death-sentenced inmates can be effectively managed (i.e., without disproportionate violence) with general population type programming and medium security procedures. Second, the visibility of death-sentenced inmates and a century of conventional wisdom regarding their security requirements are potent challenges to the political will to sustain enlightened policies toward these offenders.

THE MISSOURI "MAINSTREAMING" EXPERIENCE

In January 1991, the Missouri Department of Corrections closed their death row and initiated an innovative policy of mainstreaming death-sentenced inmates at the Potosi Unit, a high security prison (Cunningham, Reidy, & Sorensen, 2005; Lombardi et al., 1997; Lyon & Cunningham, 2006). Consistent with the classification policy utilized with other offenders, death-sentenced inmates subsequently would only be assigned to super-maximum conditions of confinement if their prison behavior warranted this, not in response to their sentence. Accordingly, since 1991 these mainstreamed death-sentenced inmates have typically been celled with, on units with, on the yard with, in educational programming and inmate work roles with, and at contact visitation with inmates sentenced to life or a term of years. Notably, the Potosi Unit also developed a web of incentives to motivate adaptive and compliant behavior in the inmates confined there.

The 5-year and 11-year status of mainstreaming death-sentenced inmates have been reported by Lombardi, Sluder, and Wallace (1997) and Cunningham, Reidy, and Sorenson (2005). Two primary conclusions emerge from these follow-up studies. First, when mainstreamed, death-sentenced inmates do not appear to require intensive mental health services. Of 62 death-sentenced offenders at the Potosi Unit in

January 2002, none were classified as special needs and only two were assigned to a partial treatment unit. Two additional inmates were on permanent, single-cell status, though still allowed yard and other privileges. Four death-sentenced inmates were assigned to protective custody.

Second, death-sentenced inmates do not have disproportionate security needs. Examining the first five years of mainstreaming experience, Lombardi et al. (1997) concluded that "disciplinary actions, grievances, and inmate-on-inmate violence has [sic] decreased, thus minimizing the difficulties commonly experienced by corrections staff under the old [segregated death row] structure" (p. 7).

Controlling for other factors (e.g., age, race, marital status, education, history of prior prison sentence, time at risk), Cunningham et al. (2005) reported that death-sentenced inmates had approximately half (0.6) the likelihood of assaultive misconduct as the parole-eligible inmates ($N = 2,199$) they were side-by-side with in the same facility during the same decade. Similarly reduced risk, holding other factors constant, was observed among inmates sentenced to life-without-parole for first degree murder ($N = 1,054$) as compared to parole-eligible inmates. As another metric of their institutional adjustment and security needs that were not disproportionate to other Potosi prisoners, Cunningham et al. (2005) found that 52 death-sentenced inmates (83.8%) were assigned to the three levels of general population, with a fourth of these classified to the "honor dorm." Only one death-sentenced inmate was assigned to administrative segregation at the 11-year point in Missouri's mainstreaming experience.

Taken together, data from the work-capable era of the Texas death row and from mainstreaming in Missouri strongly refute expectations that death-sentenced offenders will be super-predatory inmates because they "have nothing to lose," as well as its corollary that their institutional violence is only contained by super-maximum security procedures. The work-capable and mainstreaming experiences, however, are not the only data illuminating whether death-sentenced inmates have special security needs.

The Experience With Former Death-Sentenced Inmates

A number of studies have examined the institutional behavior of offenders who had been sentenced to death, but subsequently obtained relief from these sentences and were transferred to the general prison population to serve capital-life sentences. These former death row (FDR) samples have been drawn from various jurisdictions: nationwide (Marquart & Sorensen, 1989); Texas (Cunningham, Sorensen, Vigen, & Woods, 2011; Marquart, Ekland-Olson, & Sorensen, 1989); Indiana (Reidy, Cunningham, & Sorensen, 2001); and Arizona (Sorensen & Cunningham, 2009). Quite obviously, these studies of the postrelief behavior of these offenders cannot directly test how they would have behaved if not under the heightened security procedures of death row. However, postrelief data do illuminate whether an irrepressible proclivity for violence is endemic to these offenders, as an importation feature of the capital murders and criminal histories that resulted in their original death sentences (Cunningham, 2008). Such an inherent proclivity for violence would seem to be the only alternative rationale to "nothing to lose" in justifying the super-maximum security procedures that typify death row nationwide.

The postrelief conduct of FDR offenders provides no support for a hypothesis of inherent violence proclivity requiring uniform application of super-maximum procedures to contain. Following their removal from death row, these offenders are neither frequently nor disproportionately involved in serious violence. To illustrate with the most recent study, Cunningham et al. (2011) examined the prison files of 111 Texas FDR inmates. These offenders had been sentenced to death under a *special issue* in the Texas capital sentencing scheme, whereby their capital juries had unanimously endorsed the proposition, "whether there is a probability that the defendant would commit criminal acts of violence that would constitute a continuing threat to society." These offenders obtained relief from their death sentences between 1989 and 2008. They averaged 9.9 years on death row and 8.4 years in Texas prisons postrelief. Prevalence of serious assault among these inmates was 3.6% while on death row (many overlapping the work-capable era) and 4.5% postrelief. None of these assaults resulted in life-threatening injury to the victims. Approximately three fourths of these inmates were currently held in medium or minimum security, with only one sixth of them in administrative segregation. Comparison of these FDR inmates with offenders who had sentences to capital-life terms at entrance to Texas prisons during the same era revealed no significant differences in rates of assaultive misconduct, regardless of severity.

A steadily expanding body of direct and inferential data, from multiple jurisdictions and various time periods from the past 40 years, demonstrates that the security needs of death-sentenced are no greater than those of other inmates facing life-sentences or classified to high security prisons. In other words, death-sentenced inmates do not have special needs for heightened security as a function of their sentence or inherent violent proclivity.

EFFECTS OF SOLITARY CONFINEMENT ON PSYCHOLOGICAL WELL-BEING

The above discussion of the conditions of confinement for death-sentenced inmates, and the examination of the associated security-driven rationale for these conditions, was offered to provide a backdrop for whether any overrepresentation of psychological disorders among death-sentenced inmates was a function of unique vulnerabilities these offenders possessed at entrance into prison or were the result of the conditions of their confinement—either directly or in interaction with these vulnerabilities. In Chapter 9, by Miller and McCoy, issues of protective custody and solitary confinement are discussed in much detail. However, the attention is turned once again to these issues as they pertain also to death row inmates, and the impact on their practice on their well-being.

Because solitary confinement in prisons nationwide has not historically, and is not currently, restricted to death row inmates, a broader literature is available on the psychological impacts of this isolation (Arrigo & Bullock, 2008; Cohen, 2006;

Grassian, 2006; Haney, 2003, 2009; Haney & Lynch, 1997; Lovell, 2008; McLeod, 2009; Sharff Smith, 2009; Toch, 2001, 2003). Haney (2003) aptly characterized this literature:

> Empirical research on solitary and supermax-like confinement has consistently and unequivocally documented the harmful consequences of living in these kinds of environments. Despite some methodological limitations that apply to some individual studies, the findings are robust. Evidence of these negative psychological effects comes from personal accounts, descriptive studies, and systematic research on solitary and supermax-type confinement, conducted over a period of four decades, by researchers from several different continents who had diverse backgrounds and a wide range of professional expertise . . . To summarize, there is not a single published study of solitary or supermax-like confinement in which nonvoluntary confinement lasted for longer than 10 days, where participants were unable to terminate their isolation at will, that failed to result in negative psychological effects. (p. 132)

Associated adverse psychological reactions to solitary confinement detailed in this literature include psychotic-spectrum symptoms of paranoia and hallucinations; mood-spectrum symptoms of depression, withdrawal, appetite and sleep disturbance, fatigue and lethargy, and suicidal ideation; anxiety-spectrum symptoms of subjective distress, feelings of impending doom, somatic complaints, dissociative experience, and ruminative thoughts; affective lability characterized by irritability, rage, and aggressive impulses; and behavioral self-control symptoms of aggression, assaults, and self-mutilation.

An application of this research to the deprivations of super-maximum security on death row and their psychological impacts has been detailed (Harrison & Tamony, 2010; Lyon & Cunningham, 2006; Yuzon, 1996). Lyon and Cunningham (2006) summarized (citations omitted):

> That it is psychologically injurious to confine a human being in a small cell 23 hours a day, without social interaction or meaningful activity or varied stimulation, for years at a time, should be self-evident. Our heritage as a species is to live in social groups. This context is essential for the maintenance of psychological equilibrium and health through various mechanisms of companionship, physical contact, the reflected reality that the interaction with others provides, and associated processes. Similarly, human beings require regular meaningful activity and varied stimulation; and experience deterioration in mood, cognitive functioning, and psychological integrity in the absence of these. Though facing the ultimate sanction, death-sentenced inmates have not ceased to be human beings, nor are they somehow immune to the impact of fundamental psychological deprivations. (p. 19)

U.S. Supreme Court Decisions and Legislation Affecting the Confinement of Death-Sentenced Inmates

The application of the Eighth Amendment prohibition against cruel and unusual punishment to peneological conditions has been a process of recurrent review over the last half century. U.S. Supreme Court decisions on such conditions that may have implications for death-sentenced inmates include the following (for a discussion see Lyon & Cunningham, 2006):

Trop v. Dulles, 356 U.S. 86 (1958)

Procunier v. Martinez, 416 U.S. 396 (1974)

Wolff v. McDonnell, 418 U.S. 539 (1974)

Estelle v. Gamble, 429 U.S. 97 (1976)

Hutto v. Finney, 437 U.S. 678 (1978)

Rhodes v. Chapman, 452 U.S. 337 (1981)

Turner v. Safley, 482 U.S. 89 (1987)

Wilson v. Seiter, 501 U.S. 294 (1991)

The interested reader is also directed to legislation establishing a policy of judicial deference to the concerns of various correctional institutions—Prison Litigation Reform Act (PLRA) of 1995, Pub. L. No. 104–134, §§ 101, 801–810, 110 Stat. 1321, 1321–1377 (1996) (codified in scattered sections of U.S.C.).

As a result of U.S. Supreme Court decisions, two classes of special needs inmates are no longer subjected to the death penalty.

Atkins v. Virginia, 536 U.S. 304 (2002): regarding persons with mental retardation

Roper v. Simmons, 543 U.S. 551 (2005): regarding offenders less than 18-years-old

POLICY IMPLICATIONS

This chapter began by posing the question of whether death-sentenced inmates have special needs. Comparative data suggest that these offenders have many more shared characteristics than discrepancies when compared to the state prison populations. This equivalence supports a conclusion that their needs are consistent with those of other prisoners, particularly those facing long prison sentences.

The problem, of course, is that death-sentenced inmates are not typically afforded the inmate work roles, programming and varied activities, ample exercise opportunities, and extensive daily social interactions that support the physical and mental health of inmates serving multiyear prison sentences. In other words, the conditions of confinement that support and optimize the physical and mental health of long-term inmates are well-known. With the notable exception of Missouri's Potosi Correctional Center, the conditions of confinement of death-sentenced inmates do not reflect these lessons. This discrepancy is not benign. The integration of comparative data, clinical studies of death-sentenced inmates, the work-capable experience in Texas, the success of Missouri's innovative policy of mainstreaming death-sentenced inmates, and research on the effects of solitary confinement demonstrates that the special needs these death-sentenced offenders exhibit are largely in reaction to the restrictive/isolated conditions of confinement under which they are held, impacting on somewhat greater psychological vulnerabilities predating their capital convictions.

These data, as well as a broader body of research on rates and correlates of serious violence in prison (for recent reviews see Cunningham, 2008; Cunningham, Sorensen, & Reidy, 2009; Cunningham, Sorensen, Vigen, & Woods, 2011) further demonstrate that death-sentenced offenders as a class do not require segregation or special security measures. Rather, the solitary confinement and super-maximum activity restrictions typically applied to death-sentenced inmates are rooted in prevailing, but unfounded correctional lore; political intolerance for incidents involving death-sentenced inmates, however infrequent; and, arguably, agendas that enhanced punishment (i.e., suffering beyond confinement) should precede execution.

A troubling dilemma ensues. Addressing the special medical and psychosocial needs of death-sentenced inmates held in solitary confinement would invariably involve lessening the isolation and restrictions that are aggravating if not producing the impairments in these arenas. Though these modifications could be accomplished without disproportionate jeopardy to staff, other inmates, or the public, institutional resistance and political risk are potent counterbalancing forces to these reforms. This reality is starkly illustrated by the innovation, but subsequent retreat, in policies regarding death-sentenced offenders in Texas over the past 30 years.

Failing to directly and overtly grapple with this dilemma results in interventions that range from incongruous to bizarre: for example, prescription of antihypertensive medication for aging inmates who are allowed little opportunity for physical activity; group therapy performed with inmates in 3 ft. by 3 ft. individual steel cages arranged in a semi-circle; cell-front mental health status checks—on inmates consigned to psychologically-corrosive solitary confinement 23 hours a day; inmates who have documented intellectual limitations and marginal literacy, but who are allowed neither out-of-cell activity nor in-cell television.

Ultimately, fiscal realities may have the greatest impact on corrections policy toward death-sentenced inmates. Super-maximum confinement is resource and staff intensive, with costs that are easily 50% higher than general population classifications (Cunningham et al., 2005). As these beds are occupied by death-sentenced offenders whose prison conduct gives no indication of their requiring these resources, other inmates of demonstrated hazard to staff and other inmates remain in the general prison population. As evidence of the impact of fiscal considerations on the confinement of death-sentenced inmates, in 2011 California scuttled plans for a new $356 million death row in response to budgetary pressures and governmental priorities.

In the alternative to fully-embracing the Missouri mainstreaming model, it is recommended that corrections administrations carefully review their confinement and security policies toward death-sentenced inmates for how these might be modified to better support the physical and mental health of these offenders.

DISCUSSION QUESTIONS

1. Why is the lore associated with death-sentenced inmates so persistent in the minds of public policy makers and the public?

2. Should the public care about the conditions of confinement for death-sentenced inmates? Why or why not?

3. If sentenced to prison at the Potosi Correctional Center, would you rather be celled with a 20-year-old prison gang member sentenced for drug trafficking and armed robbery, or a 35 year-old mainstreamed death-sentenced inmate? How do you weigh research-based versus gut factors in your decision?

4. What steps and timetable might a prison administrator employ in adopting the findings of this chapter, while balancing the political risk?

5. What is the role of family dysfunction, childhood adversity, and brain dysfunction in violent offending? In capital offending?

6. In light of the contrasting agendas discussed in this chapter, how would you design a program of meaningful mental health intervention for death-sentenced offenders?

SUGGESTED READINGS

Cunningham, M. D., Sorensen, J. R., & Reidy, T. J. (2009). Capital jury decision-making: The limitations of predictions of future violence. *Psychology, Public Policy, and Law, 15*(4), 223–256. doi: 10.1037/a0017296

Cunningham, M. D., Sorensen, J. R., Vigen, M. P., & Woods, S. O. (2011). Life and death in the Lone Star State: Three decades of violence predictions by capital juries. *Behavioral Sciences & the Law, 29*(1), 1–22. doi: 10:1002/bsl.963

Cunningham, M. D., & Vigen, M. P. (1999). Without appointed counsel in capital postconviction proceedings: The self-representation competency of Mississippi death row inmates. *Criminal Justice and Behavior, 26*(3), 293–321.

Haney, C. (2009). The social psychology of isolation: Why solitary confinement is psychologically harmful. *The Prison Services Journal, 181,* 12–20.

Johnson, R. (1990). *Death work: A study of the modern execution process.* Pacific Grove, CA: Brooks/Cole.

Lyon, A. D., & Cunningham, M. D. (2006) Reason not the need: Does the lack of compelling state interest in maintaining a separate death row make it unlawful? *American Journal of Criminal Law, 33*(1), 1–30.

Snell, T. L. (2010, December). *Capital punishment, 2009—Statistical tables.* NCJ 231676. Washington, DC: U.S. Department of Justice, Bureau of Justice Statistics. Retrieved from http://bjs.ojp.usdoj.gov/content/pub/pdf/cp09st.pdf

USEFUL WEBSITES

- Death Penalty Information Center
  http://www.deathpenaltyinfo.org

- Bureau of Justice Statistics
  http://bjs.ojp.usdoj.gov

- NAACP Death Row USA
  http://naacpldf.org/death-row-usa

REFERENCES

American Correctional Association. (1999). Death row and the death penalty. *Corrections Compendium, 24*, 6–18.

Arriens, J. (Ed.). (1997). *Welcome to hell: Letters and writings from death row.* Boston, MA: Northeastern University Press.

Arrigo, B. A., & Bullock, J. L. (2008). The psychological effects of solitary confinement on prisoners in supermax units: Reviewing what we know and recommending what should change. *International Journal of Offender Therapy and Comparative Criminology, 52*, 622–640.

Babcock, S. (2008). *Time on death row.* Death Penalty Information Center. Retrieved from: http://www.deathpenaltyinfo.org/time-death-row#INTRODUCTION

Blake, P., Pincus, J., & Buckner, C. (1995), Neurologic abnormalities in murderers. *Neurology, 45*, 1641–1647.

Bluestone, H., & McGahee, C. L. (1962). Reaction to extreme stress: Impending death by execution. *American Journal of Psychiatry, 119*, 393–396.

Cohen, F. (2006). Prison reform: Commission on Safety and Abuse in Americas Prisons: Isolation in penal settings: The isolation-restraint paradigm. *The Journal of Law & Politics, 22*, 295–302.

Cunningham, M. D. (2008). Institutional misconduct among capital murderers. In M. DeLisi & P. J. Conis (Eds.), *Violent offenders: Theory, research, public policy, and practice* (pp. 237–253). Boston, MA: Jones & Bartlett.

Cunningham, M. D., Reidy, T. J., & Sorensen, J. R. (2005). Is death row obsolete? A decade of mainstreaming death-sentenced inmates in Missouri. *Behavioral Sciences & the Law, 23*, 307–320. doi: 10.1002/bsl.608

Cunningham, M. D., Sorensen, J. R., & Reidy, T. J. (2009). Capital jury decision-making: The limitations of predictions of future violence. *Psychology, Public Policy, and Law, 15*(4), 223–256. doi: 10.1037/a0017296

Cunningham, M. D., Sorensen, J. R., Vigen, M. P., & Woods, S. O. (2011). Life and death in the Lone Star State: Three decades of violence predictions by capital juries. *Behavioral Sciences & the Law, 29*(1), 1–22. doi: 10:1002/bsl.963

Cunningham, M. D., & Tassé, M. (2010). Looking to science rather than convention in adjusting IQ scores when death is at issue. *Professional Psychology: Research and Practice, 41*(5), 413–419. doi: 10.1037/a0020226

Cunningham, M. D., & Vigen, M. P. (1999). Without appointed counsel in capital post-conviction proceedings: The self-representation competency of Mississippi death row inmates. *Criminal Justice and Behavior, 26*(3), 293–321.

Cunningham, M. D., & Vigen, M. P. (2002). Death row inmate characteristics, adjustment, and confinement: A critical review of the literature. *Behavioral Sciences & the Law, 20*(1/2), 191–210. doi: 10.1002/bsl.473

Death Penalty Information Center. (2011, April 1). Facts about the death penalty. Retrieved from http://www.deathpenaltyinfo.org/documents/FactSheet.pdf

Ditton, P. M. (1999). *Mental health and treatment of inmates and probationers.* Special report. NCJ 174463. Washington, DC: U.S. Department of Justice, Bureau of Justice Statistics.

Evans, J. R. (1997). Quantitative EEG findings in a group of death row inmates. *Archives of Clinical Neurology, 12,* 315–316.

Fabian, J. M. (2010). Neuropsychological and neurological correlates in violent and homicidal offenders: A legal and neuroscience perspective. *Aggression and Violent Behavior, 15,* 209–223.

Fondacaro, K. M., Holt, J. C., & Powell, T. A. (1999). Psychological impact of childhood sexual abuse on male inmates: The importance of perception. *Child Abuse & Neglect, 23*(4), 361–369.

Freedman, D., & Hemenway, D. (2000). Precursors of lethal violence: A death row sample. *Social Science & Medicine, 50,* 1757–1770.

Frierson, R. L., Schwartz-Watts, D. M., Morgan, D. W., & Malone, T. D. (1998). Capital versus noncapital murderers. *Journal of the American Academy of Psychiatry and Law, 26,* 403–410.

Furman v. Georgia, 408 U.S. 238 (1972).

Gallemore, J. L., & Panton, M. A. (1972). Inmate responses to lengthy death row confinement. *American Journal of Psychiatry, 129,* 167–172.

Grassian, S. (2006). Prison reform: Commission on Safety and Abuse in America's Prisons: Psychiatric effects of solitary confinement. *Washington University Journal of Law & Policy, 22,* 325–383.

Greenfeld, L. A. (1998). *Alcohol and crime: An analysis of national data on the prevalence of alcohol involvement in crime.* NCJ 168632. Washington, DC: U.S. Department of Justice, Bureau of Justice Statistics.

Haney, C. (2003). Mental health issues in long-term solitary and "supermax" confinement. *Crime & Delinquency, 49*(1), 124–156.

Haney, C. (2009). The social psychology of isolation: Why solitary confinement is psychologically harmful. *The Prison Services Journal, 181,* 12–20.

Haney, C., & Lynch, M. (1997). Regulating prisons of the future: A psychological analysis of supermax and solitary confinement. *New York University Review of Law and Social Change, 23,* 477–552.

Harlow, C. W. (1999). Prior abuse reported by inmates and probationers. (Selected Findings). NCJ 172879. Washington, DC: U.S. Department of Justice, Bureau of Justice Statistics.

Harrison, K., & Tamony, A. (2010). Death row phenomenon, death row syndrome and their affect on capital cases in the U.S. *Internet Journal of Criminology.* Available at http://www.internetjournalofcriminology.com/Harrison_Tamony_%20Death_Row_Syndrome%20_IJC_Nov_2010.pdf

Hudson, D. (2000). Managing death-sentenced inmates: A survey of practices. (2nd ed.). Lanham, MD: American Correctional Association.

Johnson, R. (1979). Under sentence of death: The psychology of death row confinement. *Law & Psychology Review, 5*, 141–192.

Johnson, R. (1990). *Death work: A study of the modern execution process*. Pacific Grove, CA: Brooks/Cole.

Johnson, R. J., Ross, M. W., Taylor, W. C., Williams, M. L., Carvajal, R. I., & Peters, R. J. (2006). Prevalence of childhood sexual abuse among incarcerated males in county jail. *Child Abuse & Neglect, 30*(1), 75–86. doi:10.1016/j.chiabu.2005.08.013

Jurek v. Texas, 428 U.S. 262 (1976).

Kilpatrick, D. G., Acierno, R., Schnurr, P., Saunders, B., Resnick, H. S., & Best, C. L. (2000). Risk factors for adolescent substance use and dependence: Data from a national sample. *Journal of Consulting and Clinical Psychology, 68*, 19–30.

Kuanliang, A., Sorensen, J. R., & Cunningham, M. D. (2008). Juvenile offenders in an adult prison system: A comparative examination of rates and correlates of misconduct. *Criminal Justice and Behavior, 35*(9), 1186–1201. doi: 10.1177/0093854808322744

Langevin, R., Ben-Aron, M., Wortzman, G., Dickey, R., & Handy, L. (1987). Brain damage, diagnosis, and substance abuse among violent offenders. *Behavioral Sciences & the Law, 5*, 77–94.

Lewis, D., Pincus, J., Feldman, M., Jackson, L., & Bard, B. (1986). Psychiatric, neurological, and psychoeducational characteristics of 15 death row inmates in the United States. *American Journal of Psychiatry, 143*, 838–845.

Lewis, P. W. (1979). Killing the killers: A post-Furman profile of Florida's condemned. *Crime & Delinquency, 25*, 200–218.

Lisak, D., & Beszterczey, S. (2007). The cycle of violence: The life histories of 43 death row inmates. *Psychology of Men and Masculinity, 8*, 118–128.

Lombardi, G., Sluder, R. D., & Wallace, D. (1997). Mainstreaming death-sentenced inmates: The Missouri experience and its legal significance. *Federal Probation, 61*, 3–11.

Lovell, D. (2008). Patterns of disturbed behaviour in a supermax population. *Criminal Justice and Behavior, 35*, 985–1004.

Lyman, R. (1998, November 28). Texas death row inmate pulls off escape. *New York Times.* Available at http://www.nytimes.com/1998/11/28/us/texas-death-row-inmate-pulls-off-escape.html?scp=1&sq=&st=r

Lyon, A. D., & Cunningham, M. D. (2006). Reason not the need: Does the lack of compelling state interest in maintaining a separate death row make it unlawful? *American Journal of Criminal Law, 33*(1), 1–30.

Mandery, E. J. (2005). *Capital punishment: A balanced examination*. Sudbury, MA: Jones and Bartlett.

Marquart, J. W., Ekland-Olson, S., & Sorensen, J. R. (1989). Gazing into the crystal ball: Can jurors accurately predict dangerousness in capital cases? *Law & Society Review, 23*, 449–468.

Marquart, J. W., Ekland-Olson, S., & Sorensen, J. R. (1994). *The rope, the chair, and the needle: Capital punishment in Texas, 1923–1990*. Austin: University of Texas Press.

Marquart, J. W., & Sorensen, J. R. (1989). A national study of the Furman-commuted inmates: Assessing the threat to society from capital offenders. *Loyola of Los Angeles Law Review, 23*, 5–28.

Martell, D. (1992). Estimating the prevalence of organic brain dysfunction in maximum-security forensic psychiatric patients. *Journal of Forensic Sciences, 37*, 878–893.

McDermott, B. L. (1990). Defending the defenseless: *Murray v. Giarrantano* and the right to counsel in capital postconviction proceedings. *Iowa Law Review, 75*, 1305–1334.

McLeod, J. S. (2009). Anxiety, despair, and the maddening isolation of solitary confinement: Invoking the first amendment's protection against state action that invades the sphere of the intellect and spirit. *The University of Pittsburgh Law Review, 70,* 647.

Mello, M. (1988). Facing death alone: The post-conviction attorney crisis on death row. *American University Law Review, 37,* 513–607.

NAACP. (2010). Death row U.S.A.: Winter 2010. Criminal Justice Project of the NAACP Legal Defense and Educational Fund, Inc. Retrieved from http://www.deathpenaltyinfo .org/documents/DRUSA_Winter_2010.pdf

Panton, J. H. (1976). Personality characteristics of death-row prison inmates. *Journal of Clinical Psychology, 32,* 306–309.

Panton, J. H. (1978). Pre and post personality test responses of prison inmates who have had their death sentences commuted to life imprisonment. *Research Communications in Psychology, Psychiatry and Behavior, 3,* 143–156.

Pennsylvania Department of Corrections. (2011). Visiting rules for phase III capital case inmates. Retrieved from: http://www.cor.state.pa.us/portal/server.pt/community/death_ penalty/17351

Petersilia, J. (1997). Justice for all? Offenders with mental retardation and the California corrections system. *The Prison Journal, 77*(4), 358–380.

Pickett, Carroll. (2002). *Within these walls: Memoirs of a death house chaplain.* New York, NY: St. Martin's Press.

Reidy, T. J., Cunningham, M. D., & Sorensen, J. R. (2001). From death to life: Prison behavior of former death row inmates in Indiana. *Criminal Justice and Behavior, 28,* 62–82.

Robins, L. N., & Regier, D. A. (1991). *Psychiatric disorders in America: The Epidemiologic Catchment Area Study.* New York, NY: Free Press.

Ruiz v. Estelle, 503 F. Supp 1265 (S.D. Tex. 1980).

Schwarz, E. D., & Perry, B. D. (1994). The post traumatic response in children and adolescents. *Psychiatric Clinics of North America, 17,* 311–358.

Sharff Smith, P. (2009). Solitary confinement—History, practice, and human rights standards. *Prison Services Journal, 181,* 3–11.

Smith, C. E., & Felix, R. R. (1986). Beyond deterrence. A study of defense on death row. *Federal Probation, 50,* 55–59.

Snell, T. L. (2010, December). *Capital punishment, 2009—Statistical tables.* NCJ 231676. Washington, DC: U.S. Department of Justice, Bureau of Justice Statistics. Retrieved from http://bjs.ojp.usdoj.gov/content/pub/pdf/cp09st.pdf

Sorensen, J. R., & Cunningham, M. D. (2009). Once a killer always a killer? Prison misconduct of former death-sentenced inmates in Arizona. *Journal of Psychiatry and Law, 37*(2/3), 237–267.

Stein, J., Golding, J., Siegel, J., Burnham, M., & Sorenson, S. (1988). Long-term psychological sequalae of child sexual abuse: The Los Angeles Epidemiologic Catchment Area study. In G. Wyatt & G. Powell (Eds.), *Lasting effects of child sexual abuse* (pp. 135–154). Newbury Park, CA: Sage.

Texas Department of Criminal Justice. (2011). *Statistical report: Fiscal year 2010.* Executive Services Department. Retrieved from http://www.tdcj.state.tx.us/documents/Statistical_ Report_2010.pdf

Texas Penal Code § 19.03 Capital Murder (1973).

Toch, H. (2001). The future of supermax confinement. *The Prison Journal, 81*(3), 376–388.

Toch, H. (2003). The contemporary relevance of early experiments with supermax reform. *The Prison Journal, 83*(2), 221–228.

Tomaso, B. (1999, June 9). Death row's new home offers fewer amenities for its tenants. *The Dallas Morning News.*

Von Drehle, D. (1995). *Among the lowest of the dead: Inside death row.* New York, NY: Fawcett Press.

West, H. C., Sabol, W. J., & Greenman, S. J. (2010, December). *Prisoners in 2009.* NCJ 231675. Washington, DC: U.S. Department of Justice, Bureau of Justice Statistics.

Widom, C. S. (2000, January). Childhood victimization: Early adversity, later psychopathology. NCJ 180077. *National Institute of Justice Journal.* Available at http://www.ncjrs.gov/pdffiles1/jr000242b.pdf

Yuzon, F. J. (1996). Conditions and circumstances of living on death row—violative Texas Department of individual rights and fundamental freedoms? Divergent trends in judicial review in evaluating the "death row phenomenon." *George Washington Journal of International Law and Economics, 30,* 39–73.

CHAPTER 14

Immigrants Under Correctional Supervision: Examining the Needs of Immigrant Populations in a Criminal Justice Setting

Harald E. Weiss and Lauren M. Vasquez

I mmigration polarizes the U.S. population like few other topics. Despite its history as an immigration country, sentiments about immigration policy are split along political, racial, ethnic, and class lines. While arguments for stricter regulation of immigration focus on a number of perceived social problems, including immigrants' use of social services and costs to taxpayers, fears of immigrant crime also feature prominently in the public discourse. These fears, often exacerbated with concerns about drug-related violence and the ever-present specter of terrorism, have led the U.S. government to adopt a military paradigm in order to defend the U.S. border (Dunn, 1996; Kil & Menjívar, 2006). One unintentional consequence of this strategy is that illegal immigrants now avoid larger border towns and instead are forced to traverse desolate and dangerous territory in an attempt to enter the U.S. The new routes enable *coyotes*, human traffickers who smuggle immigrants into the country, to charge more money but cost thousands of immigrants their lives every year (Kil & Menjívar, 2006).

America's militarization of the southern border "creat(es) an image of the nation as an innocent victim and an image of undocumented immigrants as an enemy" (Kil & Menjívar, 2006, p. 169). U.S. public policy and laws governing illegal immigration have grown in tandem with the image of the new enemy. Illegal immigration, which was considered a civil offense until 2005, has now been elevated to a criminal offense, requiring prison sentences that range from months to years. These changes, together with a lack of resources to support the needs of immigrants in the U.S. criminal justice system, have led to systematic procedural victimization of immigrant defendants in high-immigration jurisdictions. The new influx of illegal immigrants into prisons, while increasing the revenue of the private prison companies that pushed for harsher laws, also overwhelms prisons and further victimizes already vulnerable immigrant prisoners. Finally, the expansion of Immigration and Customs Enforcement's ability to detain legal immigrants who have not committed a crime has led to indefinite detention for some individuals; detention in this case is not subject to the normal legal protections native-born prisoners receive. Detainees are nevertheless housed in prisons and sometimes with incarcerated native-born offenders.

This chapter discusses abuses, neglect, and violations of both legal and illegal immigrants' rights and physical/psychological needs at the hands of U.S. law enforcement, court, and prison officials. It first describes the historic and political antecedents of current immigration policies and the political and commercial reasons behind the increasingly harsh treatment of illegal immigration in U.S. law. The chapter then discusses statistics on imprisoned and detained immigrants and the procedural, physical, and psychological victimization of immigrant detainees and prisoners in U.S. criminal justice institutions in more detail. It concludes with seven policy recommendations that would improve the treatment and restore the rights of immigrant prisoners and detainees.

CURRENT U.S. IMMIGRATION POLICY AND HOW WE GOT HERE

Current immigration policy permits legal immigration into the U.S. along several pathways. Legal permanent residence is available to the foreign children and spouses of American citizens, even if the latter originally entered the U.S. as immigrants themselves. A green card, which serves as evidence of legal permanent immigrant status, is also available through employment. In the latter case, a company is the sponsor and applies for legal status on behalf of the immigrant worker. However, immigration through a family or employment sponsor is subject to quotas. In 2010, a maximum of 226,000 and 150,657 permanent immigrants could be admitted through family and employment sponsorship respectively. Refugees and asylum seekers are not subject to caps but must go through a difficult legal process that requires a lawyer. Asylum may be denied due to procedural reasons despite a very real and legitimate danger to the asylum seeker in the home country (Harvard Law Review, 1987). Other pathways to legal permanent residence are the annually held diversity lottery and a number of other smaller programs (Monger & Yankay, 2010). International students, their immediate families, temporary and seasonal workers, tourists, and diplomats generally enter the country through nonimmigrant visas. Figure 14.1 shows numbers of newly naturalized citizens (Lee, 2011), new temporary permanent residence permits (Monger & Yankay, 2010), new nonimmigrant admissions (Monger & Mathews, 2011), and overall Department of Homeland Security (DHS) estimates of the illegal immigrant population in the U.S. (Hoefer, Rytina, & Baker, 2011) between the years of 2000 and 2010. Estimates of illegal immigration for the years between 2001 and 2004 were not calculated by the Office of Immigration Statistics and are absent from Figure 14.1.

Figure 14.1   Levels of Immigration Between 2000 and 2010

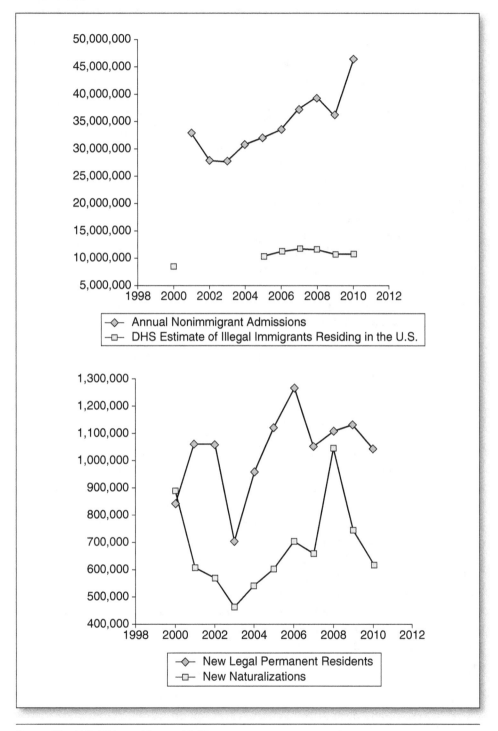

Source: Harald E. Weiss and Lauren M. Vasquez.

Because illegal immigration is a particularly contentious issue in both the public mind and in the mind of lawmakers, it bears closer examination. While it is difficult to determine exactly how many undocumented immigrants reside in the U.S., recent DHS security data suggests a number hovering between 10 and 12 million (Hoefer et al., 2011). This figure is supported by census data as well (Passel & Cohn, 2010). The number of illegal immigrants is thought to have peaked in 2007 (11.8 million) before slowly declining. By January 2010, only 10.8 million illegal immigrants remained. Most of these entered the U.S. across the southern border, although some also overstayed their visas or entered the country through other routes (Sapp, 2011).

Data on the number of apprehended undocumented immigrants suggests a decrease in illegal immigration since at least 2005; the number of illegal immigrants apprehended on our southwestern border decreased continuously from 1,171,391 in 2005 to 447,731 five years later. Illegal immigrants arrested while trying to enter the U.S. along the coast or the northern border show a similar decline, although the relative number of arrests is much smaller.

The nationality of the majority of apprehended immigrants was Mexican, followed by Guatemalans in the years between 2007 and 2010 and El Salvadorans in 2005 and 2006. Apprehended aliens also tended to be mostly male and 70% of the immigrants apprehended in the years between 2005 and 2010 were between the ages of 18 and 35 (Sapp, 2011).

However, these statistics have to be understood in the context of U.S. immigration policy. Unbeknownst to most Americans, immigration processes and policies have changed considerably over the past few decades, a development that has led to harsher treatment of immigrants as a group.

Three Decades of Immigration Policy

While immigration is a contentious issue, it is illegal immigration that is of particular concern for many Americans. Over the past three decades, public fears of terrorism, the illegal interborder trade of drugs (entering the U.S.) and guns (exiting the U.S.), and the ever-present specter of the criminal immigrant, served as justification for turning stretches of the U.S. border with Mexico into a new and technologically more sophisticated version of the Iron Curtain (Kil & Menjívar, 2006). Following congressional funding approval for 700 miles of fencing in 2006, the federal government began to install reinforced wire fences along the U.S.-Mexican border in order to keep unwanted immigration at bay. Furthermore, the border is patrolled by Immigration and Customs Enforcement (ICE) agents who rely on military-grade equipment and sophisticated computers to detect interlopers by electronic means (Kil & Menjívar, 2006).

However, current treatment of undocumented aliens, and the strategies used to apprehend them, must be understood in a historic and economic context. The contemporary militarization of our southern border began decades ago and has, contrary to some commentators, had bipartisan support from high-ranking officials throughout several administrations. Ronald Reagan, concerned about terrorist infiltration from Central American countries, began to strengthen surveillance of the

U.S.-Mexican border. He also changed U.S. laws, allowing immigration officials to detain refugees that were not clearly eligible for asylum (Simon, 1998). The administration of George H. W. Bush continued Reagan's buildup of forces and equipment and added broad legal authorities for federal law enforcement with jurisdiction over the border region (Kil & Menjívar, 2006). Under Bill Clinton, the Immigration and Naturalization Service (INS) sought to reroute illegal immigration into the desolate wilderness and away from population centers close to the border. Floodlights and large walls were installed at chokepoints along the usual immigration routes in order to force illegal immigration away from established routes. This strategy was effective in forcing illegal immigration away from urban areas but did nothing to deter illegal immigration (Kil & Menjívar, 2006). Instead, the new travelling routes improved the business opportunities of coyotes, professional immigrant smugglers who often extort thousands of dollars from already poor immigrants in order to deliver them into the U.S.[1] This INS strategy, continued by its successor, the ICE, has led to the deaths of thousands of immigrants in the deserts between the U.S. and Mexico. Kil and Menjívar (2006), citing a newspaper report, argue that "in the fiscal year 2002, the number of immigrant deaths has increased, particularly in Arizona, where 3,217 bodies were discovered" (p. 168). The buildup of this strategy continued under Clinton and under the administration of George W. Bush, and with the memories of 9/11 still looming large, still more border patrol personnel and military-grade equipment was put in place in order to capture elusive undocumented immigrants. This occurred despite the fact that the participants in the 9/11 terrorists attacks were in the U.S. legally under student visas.

Despite Arizona governor Jan Brewer's recent statements—and her lawsuit against the federal government—claiming that the current administration is neglecting its duty to protect the border, the Obama administration has continued the trend of previous administrations. Under President Obama, several thousand additional border agents have been placed along the U.S. border and military-style tactics and operations continue (Miller, 2010).

Thus, the war-like situation on our southern border has developed over decades. However, policy changes and reinterpretations of existing laws coincided with the southern buildup and led to harsher treatment of immigrants as well.

The Evolution of Federal Immigration Laws

While the U.S. has been an immigration country from its inception, its past shows a long history of intermittent bouts of anti-immigrant sentiment. Individual states passed immigration laws long before the federal government began to legislate immigration laws (Moehling & Piehl, 2009). In the early 20th century, fears about immigration led to a host of restrictive federal laws. During the 1920s, congress passed laws requiring literacy of immigrants only to be repeatedly vetoed by the president.

---

[1]One interesting side effect of making the U.S. border more impenetrable is that illegal immigrants who arrive here are less likely to leave. While previous illegal immigrants came and went, more recent immigrants have stayed in place longer because an easy way to cross the border is blocked (Massey, Durand, & Malone, 2003).

By the time congress passed literacy laws, European countries had raised their literacy standards enough to no longer make the law an effective exclusionary tool (Moehling & Piehl, 2009). Subsequent legislation, for example, the Emergency Quota Act and the National Origins Quota Act, established quotas for immigrants, including a maximum annual immigrant headcount by country of origin. The allowable number of immigrants in the latter law was based on the size of the immigrant population of specific countries that already resided in the United States. The National Origins Quota Act was instrumental in excluding immigrant groups that had not already established themselves in the U.S. and favored European immigrants to the exclusion of non-Caucasian and Hispanic individuals (Moehling & Piehl, 2009).

The decades from 1930s through the 1960s contained surprisingly little public concern about immigration, as witnessed by the absence of the topic in politics and public discourse (Moehling & Piehl, 2009). However, immigration laws again changed in 1965 with the Hart-Celler Immigration Reform Act. This new law opened U.S. borders to the most recent wave of immigrants by removing the quota system and granting free entry to immigrants, irrelevant of their national origin. The long-term effect of this legislation has been an increase in the diversity of immigrants, not only by country of origin, race, and ethnicity, but also by demographic characteristics such as religion, education, human capital, and social class (Greenwood & McDowell, 1986; Zhou, 2001).

The recent Immigration Reform and Control Act of 1985, was specifically designed to counteract illegal immigration by forcing employers to verify their employees' immigration status. The law made it illegal to knowingly employ illegal aliens, although it also provided a pathway for illegal immigrants who had been in the country to gain legal status. Nevertheless, publicity-based political maneuvering with few discernible beneficial effects has led to increasingly exclusionary laws that have expanded the group of deportable immigrants to include all noncitizens (Massey, Durand, & Malone, 2003). This change has, in turn, drastically increased Immigration and Customs Enforcement's scope of operations to a much larger population (Butcher & Piehl, 1999).

THE RECENT PUSH FOR STATE-LEVEL IMMIGRATION LAWS

Immigration management is generally thought of as a responsibility of the federal government. But recently several states have passed immigration legislation that attempts to either complement or add to the immigration enforcement function of ICE. Politicians often support the need for state-level immigration legislation by citing wide public support or the claim that the federal government neglects to protect our borders. However, one incentive for the passage of state-level immigration laws politicians neglect to mention is that the private-prison industry stands to gain greatly from state-level immigration enforcement.

Privately-owned prisons originally emerged during the 17th century in parts of Europe (Blakely & Bumphus, 2004). In the U.S., they reappeared throughout the 1960s after decades of obscurity. Companies that imprisoned people for profit grew throughout the 1970s as distrust in government and subsequent budgetary woes in some states led to increases in the role of for-profit prisons (Blakely & Bumphus, 2004). Their reemergence of this industry also coincided with get–tough-on-crime rhetoric from politicians who promised to send more people to jail for less severe offenses and longer periods. The war on drugs further strengthened the portfolio of private prison companies and increased their lobbying for more and tougher sentencing.

The war on immigration is only the most recent stage in a business plan that has greatly increased the control over prison populations for companies like the Correctional Corporation of America (CCA) and the GEO group (Cervantes-Gautschi, 2010; Feltz, 2008). Since the mid-80s an increasingly hostile anti-immigrant sentiment has combined with lobbying from private prison firms to create an exclusionary environment in which immigrants can be incarcerated or detained, often without having committed any infractions. As a consequence, more immigrants are held in prisons and detention centers; the number of noncitizens in federal prisons increased by 15% between 2001 and 2004 (U.S. Government Accountability Office, cited in Bosworth, 2010).

While this scenario has played out all over the country, the passage of the controversial Arizona immigration law, also known as Senate Bill 1070, provides a useful case-study to understand the intersection between corporate interests and public nativism.

Senate Bill 1070: Political and Commercial Factors Collude to Create an Immigrant-Hostile Legal Environment

SB 1070, Arizona's controversial new immigration law (Arizona Governor Jan Brewer signed the bill into law on April 23, 2010), is an amalgamate of approximately 40 previously proposed anti-immigration bills (Miller, 2010). The passage of SB 1070 was catalyzed through the violent murder of rancher Robert Krentz, a prominent member of Arizona's farming establishment. His death originally blamed on undocumented immigrants but later discovered to involve Mexican drug traffickers, created enough fear and rage in the native-born population to drum up support for the passage of SB 1070. Unfortunately, native-born Americans' concerns about violent victimization appear to be less noticeable when immigrants are the victims. Box 14.1. Describes a case where native-born vigilantes victimized an immigrant family. The incident caused barely a ripple in the local native-born population.

Box 14.1

At about 1 a.m. on May 30, 2009, Ms. Forde and an accomplice, Jason Bush, burst into the Flores family home, prosecutors say. First introducing themselves as law enforcement, and then quickly dropping the act, Mr. Bush is believed to have shot Mr. Flores, and then his wife, Gina Gonzalez, and their daughter, Brisenia, investigators say. As the two intruders rummaged through the home, Ms. Gonzalez retrieved a handgun that belonged to her husband and began to fire, hitting Mr. Bush in the leg, prosecutors say. The two intruders then fled.

Source: Adapted about this case of "Murder Trial in Tucson Shows Rift in Minuteman Border Movement," Joseph Goldstein. The New York Times, February 10, 2011. http://www.nytimes.com/2011/02/11/us/11minutemen.html?_r=1.

The above article from the *New York Times* describes the planned robbery, and subsequent murder, of a Mexican immigrant family in Arivaca, Arizona, a small community approximately 11 miles north of the US-Mexican border. As opposed to widely-held national fears about the illegal interborder trade of drugs, the crime was not part of the Mexican drug war. Drugs were part of the issue, but those who murdered Flores and his daughter and wounded Gonzalez, were members of Minutemen American Defense, a small anti-immigrant vigilante group. The leader of this group, and supposed mastermind behind the attack, Shawna Forde, was convicted on February 14, 2011. Prosecution suggested that Forde and her coconspirators invaded and killed the family in the hopes of finding both drugs and drug money they could use to fund their vigilante movement. Apparently, a local drug dealer had pointed Flores out as a member of the Mexican drug cartel. The expected drugs were curiously absent on the scene of the crime. Unfortunately, as opposed to the murder of Robert Krentz, the local native-born community showed little concern about these murders.

Senate Bill 1070 makes several important changes to Arizona's existing laws and "obeys the same 'zero tolerance' logic behind . . . the broader federal 'deterrence' policy that began in Arizona in 1993" (Miller, 2010, p. 3). It adds criminal trespassing charges to criminal charges imposed by federal law and requires lengthy prison sentences for which incarcerated immigrants have to bear the costs. The most contentious change in law requires law enforcement officers to stop and investigate the immigration status of individuals they suspect might be immigrants. Law enforcement officers who neglect to investigate a suspected immigrant can be sued by the public.

Considering that Arizona has one of the highest rates of illegal immigration of any state and places third by the number of arrests and incarceration of illegal immigrants (following California and Texas), it is not surprising that attempts at passing restrictive anti-immigrant legislation in the state of Arizona have existed for decades (Stana, 2005a). However, explaining SB 1070 solely through public sentiment neglects to account for both political and economic forces that have contributed to the new law.

The increasing criminalization of illegal immigration grows the private investment portfolios of some politicians who own stock in private prison corporations (Cervantes-Gautschi, 2010). While this does not necessarily mean that politicians deliberately make decisions that benefit these corporations, it is likely difficult for them to consider laws they know would hurt their financial investments. In addition to the private investment gains politicians reap from their support of anti-immigrant legislation, the recent decision by the Supreme Court to remove campaign-spending limits for corporate donors allows private prison corporations to lobby politicians more directly.

The private prison industry as a whole, and Correctional Corporation of America and GEO-group in particular, have spent millions of dollars lobbying politicians for laws that increase their business opportunities; data show that their investment has paid off. CCA, one of the leaders in private prisons, obtains approximately 40% of its annual revenue from contracts with Immigration and Customs Enforcement (Feltz, 2008), and private prison companies are seeking to increase their share of its business, including prisons and detention facilities for men, women, and children (Sullivan, 2010). Cervantes-Gautschi (2010) writes the following:

> From 2005 through 2009, for every dollar spent on lobbying the federal government, GEO received a $662 return in taxpayer-funded contracts, for a total of $996.7 million. CCA received a $34 return in taxpayer-funded contracts for every dollar spent on lobbying the federal government, for a total of $330.4 million. (p. 4)

As a consequence, Feltz (2008) estimates that the number of criminal prosecutions of illegal immigrants more than doubled from 28,000 in 2006 to 59,570 in 2008. Interestingly, despite the fact that ICE contracts funnel millions of tax dollars into private prison corporations, both the agency and the corporations are highly secretive about their details (TRAC Immigration, 2009). This secrecy inhibits any objective evaluation of these contracts, including their fiscal usefulness and the performance of private prisons.

Lobbying likely also played a role in the passage of SB 1070, as it seems to be designed to help increase private prison corporations' revenue. One difficulty the CCA and GEO's conveyor-belt approach to immigrant incarceration has faced in the past is the limited number of ICE agents who are able to arrest, detain, and refer immigrants to their facilities. Furthermore, previous enforcement strategies, which have since been replaced by the criminalization of illegal immigration in federal law, allowed illegal immigrants to remain free pending their hearing and kept potential prisoners and detainees out of the private prison system (Cervantes-Gautschi, 2010). In certain cases, undocumented aliens that had been apprehended could forego punishment if they conceded their illegal presence and left voluntarily (U.S. DHS, 2002). In the latter case, immigrants' records remained clean, allowing them to enter the U.S. legally at a later time.

SB 1070, which stands to become a legal test case for laws proposed in other U.S. states, remedies the problem of having too few ICE agents by extending the ability to arrest illegal immigrants to all law enforcement officers in the state of Arizona. In addition, the law also institutionalizes both racism and classism. Any person a law enforcement agent deems Hispanic or foreign-looking becomes a valid target for investigation; looking foreign to a law enforcement officer replaces the need for probable cause. White immigrants, and those who are of sufficiently high class standing, are effectively immune to being stopped for such investigations. Even if White or upper-class immigrants are stopped for other reasons, they may escape having their immigration status questioned as the social construction of immigration along the southern border pictures the immigrant menace as the generic poor, brown, and uneducated Mexican.

In addition to increasing the number of immigrants who can be funneled into CCA and GEO prisons by increasing the number of enforcement agents, SB 1070 also lengthens the sentences of apprehended undocumented aliens by adding state-level charges to already existing charges on the federal level (Miller, 2010). Unfortunately the great increase in immigrant arrests and incarceration, brought on by the conversion of illegal immigration from a civil to a criminal offense, has stretched the resources of courts and prosecutors. In order to continue functioning despite the unmanageable increase in prosecutions, court officials have developed a number of procedural shortcuts that curtail immigrant defendants' rights (Feltz, 2008).

ABUSES OF IMMIGRANTS IN THE U.S. CRIMINAL JUSTICE SYSTEM

Immigrants in the Criminal Justice System

Considering the recent history of immigration policy in the U.S., it is not surprising that the number of convicted immigrants held in U.S. prisons has grown. Immigrants, both legal and illegal, represent a relatively small proportion of the overall U.S. population. The Census Bureau identified 38.5 million immigrants (12.5% of the total U.S. population) living in the U.S. in 2009.[2]

Immigrants are at first glance disproportionally represented in the U.S. criminal justice system. However, it is noteworthy that there is surprising variability in criminal justice data on immigrants, depending on their source and type of data collection. The Federal Bureau of Prisons estimates that 26.4% of all federal inmates are not U.S. citizens, compared to only 8.6% in the adult U.S. population.[3] The Department of Homeland Security reports that it identified 221,000 noncitizens in U.S. jails (Camarota & Vaughan, 2009) while a Bureau of Justice Statistics report only located 94,724 (West & Sabol, 2009) immigrants under both federal and state correctional supervision in 2008. The Government Accountability Office (GAO) meanwhile located 178,512 criminal aliens in federal prisons in 2004 and approximately 48,708 of these were illegal immigrants. Many more were imprisoned in state and local institutions (Stana, 2005b). This number does not include immigrant detainees, who are awaiting deportation and have not being charged with a crime.

A second investigation of immigrant incarceration through the GAO provides further insights on immigrants' sentences. In his research based on data from 2003, Stana (2005a) investigated statistics for arrests, convictions, and the types of offenses recorded for the illegal-immigrant prison population. Overall, the GAO located 308,168 convicted criminal aliens within U.S. prisons. 46,063 of these were incarcerated in federal prisons, the remaining 262,105 in state prisons or local jails (Stana, 2005a). However, of this relatively large number of immigrant prisoners only 55,322 (representing 17.9% of the immigrant prisoner population and

---

[2]The census does not differentiate between legal and illegal immigrants, although it is likely that the presented number is an undercount. Illegal immigrants are likely unwilling to participate in government-sponsored data collections out of fear of being discovered. In order to capture elusive immigrants in their data, the census has elicited the help of community-based organizations that have better access to illegal immigrants.

[3]Data on immigrants in federal institutions is not generalizable to the population of immigrants in all U.S. prisons.

0.6% of the estimated illegal immigrant population) appeared to have entered the country illegally.[4] Stana (2005a) further reports that the illegal immigrant inmates had been arrested 459,614 times and charged with 691,890 offenses. Ninety-seven percent of the undocumented alien prison population had more than one arrest and 80% of the arrests were made in only three states: Arizona, California, and Texas.

Thirty-two percent of the illegal immigrant prison population housed in federal prisons (18,581) had been arrested for immigration violations, 24% for drug-related offenses. However, once GAO staff extended their investigation to convictions, rather than arrests, most offenses appeared to be either unfounded or were filtered out along the criminal justice process. Only 18,581 of the 267,709 offenses illegal immigrants had been arrested for (7%) led to convictions. Sixty-eight percent of these were immigration violations, 21% were drug offenses. Thus, the GAO data suggest that the vast majority of convicted immigrants are in jail for immigration violations; only a relatively small share of convictions are based on other crimes and most of these are nonviolent in nature. Other research corroborates this pattern (Bosworth, 2010) and data for the first half of 2011 show that 47% of all lead charges for criminal immigration violations were for felony reentry. Illegal entry and reentry represented 91% of all prosecutions for all immigration-related crimes (TRAC Immigration, 2011). Thus, data show that as ICE apprehended fewer undocumented immigrants (Sapp, 2011) the number of immigrants convicted as felons for reentry nevertheless rose (TRAC Immigration, 2011).

Procedural Victimization of Illegal Immigrants Through Law Enforcement

Beyond the current budgetary woes, the buildup of personnel and equipment on the southern border is significant because it symbolizes the U.S. view on immigration. Public and political fears of immigrants have led to border patrol strategies that are reminiscent of armed conflicts. The enemy, in this case, is the elusive undocumented immigrant against whom the country has to be protected at all cost (Kil & Menjívar, 2006). The *illegal-immigration-as-war* metaphor is also reflected in the success of private vigilante movements that coat extremist nativism with patriotic rhetoric. These organizations often adopt patriotic names like *American Border Patrol* and *The Minutemen* and represent themselves as concerned private U.S. citizens who, armed to the teeth, patrol the southern border in private vehicles (Kil, Menjívar, & Doty, 2009). Despite the questionable nature of this enterprise, U.S. law enforcement has not actively discouraged this vigilantism. Rather, there is evidence that law enforcement has cooperated with vigilantes, both by following vigilante's lead in choosing locations for raids and by allowing members of these movements to participate in them (Miller, 2010).

[4]The percentage of illegal immigrant prisoners in comparison to the estimated illegal immigrant population is based on the lower threshold of the DHS's projection that places 10–12 million illegal immigrants in the U.S. (Hoefer et al., 2011).

Considering the pervasiveness of the view that undocumented aliens are the enemy, it is not surprising that the current climate has led to abuses of the supposed enemy combatants. Every year, our border patrol strategy is partly responsible for hundreds of deaths as our enforcement pushed immigration paths into increasingly inhospitable terrain (Kil & Menjívar, 2006). Unfortunately, being found by U.S. border patrol agents appears often to lead to further abuse, rather than safety. While ICE maintains regulations intended to ensure the proper treatment of apprehended immigrants, ICE enforcement agents seem to disregard these rules on a regular basis. After first hearing about illegal immigrants being abused by ICE agents, members of No More Death, an organization concerned about the health and safety of undocumented immigrants, began to interview illegal immigrants about their experiences with Border Patrol. The first report issued by the organization, published in 2008, reported widespread abuses of power as well as disregard for ICE's own established regulations (No More Deaths, 2008). In the more recent follow up to the 2008 report, No More Deaths uses a representative sample to detail more than 30,000 abuses and suggests that the accountability of ICE agents has not improved since 2008 (No More Deaths, 2011).

According to the 2011 report, collected over two and a half years of interviews, ICE agents routinely withheld water and food from apprehended immigrants who were, due to their apprehension in the desert, dehydrated. The interview data show that more than 19% of males, 22% of females, 21% of teenagers, and 31% of children were either denied water or were provided with insufficient quantities of water after their arrest. The report also suggests that immigration agents used unnecessary physical violence in order to control immigrants who demanded to be treated more humanely; often these abuses were accompanied by racist language. Individuals who had a need for medical treatment were refused access to medical professionals; necessary medication, for example insulin for the treatment of diabetes, was often discarded upon arrest. Severe injuries, open wounds, and broken bones sometimes remained untreated, and immigrants were repatriated without receiving medical attention.

In addition to physical abuse and neglect, the report also details psychological abuse through ICE personnel. Detainees were threatened with death while in the custody of Border Patrol personnel. Apprehended undocumented immigrants were forced to undress and left exposed in cold weather conditions for prolonged periods of time. Women were threatened with being left alone with men they didn't know, which equates to an attempt by law enforcement agents to utilize the threat of rape in order to elicit women's cooperation.

Overall, the interviews detailed in No More Death's 2011 report are reminiscent of war-time abuses, where enemy combatants are dehumanized and treated as a lower form of life. There is currently not enough research on this topic to discern to what extent these abuses are systemic in origin. However, the fact that there was little improvement between the 2008 and 2011 reports suggests that assuring the appropriate treatment of undocumented aliens in the care of Border Patrol is not an important enough concern for ICE to institute effective safeguards.

Procedural Victimization of Illegal
Immigrants Through Court Officials

Between 1965 and 1986, migration between the U.S. and Mexico constituted "a set of delicately balanced social and economic processes that emerged gradually over many years in response to specific changes in the political economies of Mexico and the United States" (Massey et al., 2003, p. 1). Interruptions of this very finely tuned system emerged in the mid-1980s and were symbolically political, rather than pragmatic in nature. In 2005, the DHS initiated Operation Streamline, which for the first time treated illegal immigration as a crime (a misdemeanor), rather than a civil violation. Undocumented immigrants who were caught a second time now faced felony charges (Cervantes-Gautschi, 2010; Feltz, 2008). First-time offenders frequently received sentences of a few weeks to months; repeat offenders received felony sentences of months to years (Feltz, 2008).

These changes in the treatment of illegal aliens quickly filled prison cells and put considerable strain on the criminal justice system (Feltz, 2008; Finley, 2006). The zeal with which new immigration laws are enforced has risen far more quickly than the available staffing and facilities of the courts who are supposed to adjudicate undocumented aliens (Feltz, 2008). Among other things, increases in caseloads have led to shortages in the availability of public defenders.

While the well-known shortage of public defenders is problematic even for disadvantaged native-born defendants, immigrants find themselves adjudicated in large groups of one hundred or more (Feltz, 2008). In these courtrooms, public defenders satisfy the letter of criminal law but are woefully ineffectual in actually defending clients. However, the high immigrant defendant/public defender ratio does aid the quick adjudication of immigrants because defense counsel is too overwhelmed to advise any of them.

Immigrants' lack of familiarity with the U.S. criminal justice system and the language barrier is, in these cases, favorable to courts and prosecutors (Feltz, 2008). Defendants' compliance is assured by prosecutors making it clear that contesting the offered sentence will prolong immigrants' detention and keep them from their loved ones while their case is being processed. They are also told that contesting their sentence increases the possibility that they will be sentenced for a more severe offense. Once incarcerated, correctional officers and prison administrators instill the belief that immigrant inmates have no rights and that nobody, including their embassies, cares about their situation (Anonymous, 2009).[5]

The overwhelming caseload of public defenders also means that defendants' counsel cannot counter deceptive practices by law enforcement and prosecutors. Arrested undocumented immigrants are sometimes charged with exaggerated felony

---

[5]The author of this published paper notes that "[i]f the administration here finds out that I wrote this, I could be sent to segregation and be placed under 'investigation.' The threat of these measures keeps all women in fear of doing anything they might disapprove of" (Anonymous, 2009, p. 104). In order to prevent retaliation from ICE or prison officials against the incarcerated immigrant author of this publication the editors decided to withhold her name.

offenses that do not fit the facts of their crime but which help prosecutors to gain guilty pleas to a lesser offense. Feltz (2008) provides an example of such a practice. He describes an ICE raid on a meatpacking plant in Idaho that yielded a group of 697 undocumented aliens, 300 of whom were charged with "aggravated identity theft." This felony charge is generally used when an individual uses someone else's social security number, but only one of the 697 undocumented aliens was using the social security number of an existing person. The other 299 aliens used a social security number that was not tied to an individual and should therefore have yielded a misdemeanor charge of "possessing a false social security number." A court interpreter explained ICE's approach before an Iowa district court in the following way: "By handing down the inflated charge of aggravated identity theft . . . the government forced the defendants into pleading guilty to the lesser charge and accepting five months in jail" (quoted in Feltz, 2008, p. 27). An effective defense lawyer would have guarded against such abuses of power through the prosecution. Because of the unmanageable caseload of public defenders, immigrant defendants accepted the offered sentences without contention, believing that they had been lucky to avoid a felony charge.

Unfortunately, even if public defenders were able to devote adequate time to their clients, their training may not be enough to ensure appropriate counsel (Feltz, 2008). Immigration law is a specialty area within law; public defense lawyers, specializing in criminal law, are usually not familiar with immigration law; deals and legal maneuvering that would be appropriate for citizen clients introduce unwanted consequences for an immigrant defendant (Butcher & Piehl, 1999).

Current procedures also beg the question as to whether information derived from immigrants being interviewed by civil immigration authorities should be usable by prosecutors in subsequent criminal cases. Civil immigration authorities' interviews with immigrants do not require the presence of a lawyer because the matter is not criminal in nature. However, once the prosecutor makes a decision to press criminal charges against the immigrant, these previously collected statements are made available to the prosecutor, circumventing protections normally provided to criminal defendants (Feltz, 2008).

The abuses of power described here likely only constitute the tip of the proverbial iceberg. Because many of the previously described procedures have only emerged very recently, social scientists have yet to describe immigrants' victimization through the justice system in an organized manner that transcends case studies and circumstantial evidence. In addition, ICE is known to deliberately transfer immigrants if they seek public attention, in order to minimize negative publicity to the agency (Dow, 2007). However, it is likely that the misuses of power mentioned above are particularly salient in jurisdictions where the justice system is stretched to its limit by the number of immigrant arrestees and where displaying a proactive anti-immigrant stance helps judges, prosecutors, and other elected criminal justice officials keep their position secure.

Thus, the increasing severity with which illegal immigration is punished has partially been a consequence of private prison companies lobbying on both the federal and state level. If the constitutionality of state-level laws such as SB 1070 is upheld by the Supreme Court, companies such as CCA and the GEO Group stand to profit substantially from housing and controlling immigrant convicts. The public increase in anti-immigrant sentiment, immigrants' unfamiliarity with the U.S. criminal justice system, and criminal justice authorities' desire to streamline an overextended system have created a conveyor-belt criminalization system that is slated to become a major source of income for companies that are, in one way or another involved with prisons (Feltz, 2008; Sullivan, 2010). Adequate staffing of public defenders' offices and oversight of criminal cases brought before courts for illegal immigration, could make these cases more equitable. However, considering the strained financial situation of most states in the current economy, the considerable financial incentives lobbying provides to tweak the system in the direction of more corporate profit, and the fact that public defenders' offices are rarely adequately staffed, the situation is unlikely to improve any time soon.

Immigrant Vulnerability in Correctional Institutions

Immigrants are not only held in jails and prisons when they are convicted of crimes; U.S. criminal justice institutions also serve as a warehouse for individuals who are awaiting their asylum hearings and legal aliens whom ICE has marked for deportation. This has especially been the case since the Immigration Reform and Control Act of 1985 extended the group of who could be easily deported to all noncitizens. Immigrants who have not broken the law are frequently housed with convicted criminals and prison personnel treat them like criminals. Prisons are inherently dangerous places and inmates often suffer abuse and neglect at the hands of prison guards and violence at the hands of other inmates. In this context, immigrants are particularly vulnerable to violence for racial and ethnic reasons. Furthermore, language barriers make it difficult for them to make themselves understood. This can lead to abuses against immigrants and can even lead to their death.

The degree to which immigrants can come to harm is clearly visible from an ICE report (Bernstein & Williams, 2009). It lists 90 deaths of immigrants who were in the care of ICE between October 2003 and February 2009. Some of these deaths were due to illness. However, some detained immigrants also committed suicide or died after prison officials neglected to provide them with necessary medical care. Although there are considerable errors in the report, including omissions of known deaths and incorrect detention locations at the time of death, Bernstein and Williams' investigation showed that approximately a third of the deaths occurred in prisons that were operated by the Correction Corporation of America. An updated listing for the period between October 2003 and October 2011 shows 126 deaths but continues to omit some of the known deaths that were missing in the 2009 report (Immigration and Customs Enforcement, 2011).

Changes in policies that criminalize illegal immigration and give immigration officials greater powers to detain and deport legal immigrants have greatly increased the number of immigrants that are, for one reason or another, under the control of prison officials (Butcher & Piehl, 1999). The previous sections discussed the challenges immigrants face when coming into contact with the criminal justice system. While immigrants as a group are vulnerable in a prison setting, it is important to remember that, consistent with the dynamics within most groups, immigrants are not immune to differential treatment across gender and age categories. Immigrant women and children are at an even greater disadvantage than their male and adult counterparts. This section will explore the added duress the immigrants face.

SPECIAL NEEDS OF WOMEN INMATES

In the U.S. men are far more likely to be incarcerated than women. In the early 1900s women made up a mere 3.7% of all incarcerated individuals and their share of the prison population remained relatively stable until the 1980s. The incarceration boom of the mid-80s began to change this pattern so that by 2008, the percentage of women in the prison population had increased to 7.2% (West & Sabol, 2009). Criminologists have attributed this change to the increased enforcement of and harsher penalties for drug offenses within the context of the war on drugs. With the increase of women under the domain of correctional facilities, it is important to acknowledge the challenges that many native-born incarcerated women face. The changing demographics of prisons have been gradual and have not been accompanied by a change in the services and policies to accommodate this shift.

As discussed earlier by Pasko and Chesney-Lind in Chapter 3, some of the unique issues women face include healthcare, potential sexual abuse from correctional staff, problems associated with their separation from children and family support networks, and psychological programs. The latter becomes an issue when we consider that around 60% of women who are incarcerated previously reported being sexually or physically abused (Greenfeld & Snell, 1999).

When it comes to separation from their children, female inmates find themselves in a very different situation than their male counterparts. Henriquez and Gladwin (Chapter 4) further discussed the issues of motherhood behind bars. According to the Bureau of Justice Statistics, around 62% of incarcerated women have children under the age of 18 (Greenfeld & Snell, 1999). Female prisoners' separation from their children causes them added stress and places a heavy burden on the woman's family; the maternal grandmother is more often than not the person who takes the children in. Nevertheless, this childcare solution is often preferable to social services as it makes it easier to regaining custody of the children upon release. Moreover, incarcerated mothers are not just losing contact with their children; they are also often housed in facilities that are geographically distant from them. Because women are disproportionally underrepresented in the criminal justice system, most states have a larger proportion of their prisons dedicated to incarcerating men. This means that women are more likely to be bused away to a female-only prison, distancing them geographically from their social support network and family. The distance between the prison and the family also means that women find it more difficult to see their children than an incarcerated male would (see previous Chapters 3 and 4).

Immigrant Women and Children in the Criminal Justice System

Since prison represents native-born women with considerable difficulties, it is clear that incarcerated women's immigrant status further exacerbates their problems. According to the U.S. Bureau of the Census' American Community Survey of 2008, 12% of all women in the U.S. were foreign-born and they represented 49.8% of all foreign-born inhabitants of the U.S. in 2008.[6] The majority of female immigrants identified their place of birth as Mexico.

Immigrant women differ from their male counterparts in several respects. They are less likely to be proficient in English but more likely to be U.S. citizens. When compared to their native-born counterparts, immigrant women tend to be older, are less likely married, and less likely to have more than a high school education. They are also less likely to be employed and those who are heads of their household make, on average, 4% less money. By and large, single-parent immigrant women are more likely to live in high-crime neighborhoods. This not only makes them more likely to have contact with police but also puts them at a much higher risk of being victimized.

The fact that they lack proficiency in English puts immigrant women at a disadvantage when coming into contact with police and other representatives of the criminal justice system (Anonymous, 2009). Their inability to voice their disagreement within a system that is designed to minimize the rights of detained immigrants makes them particularly vulnerable to abuses through criminal justice personnel (Anonymous, 2009). As previously mentioned, prosecutors use immigrants' inexperience with U.S. laws to push them toward pleas that are not necessarily in their best interest.

Women's difficulty to communicate adds an additional layer of disenfranchisement to these proceedings; they are unable to effectively communicate with prosecutors, lawyers, and other members of the courtroom work group. As an example, while there are treaties between the U.S. and Mexico that allow incarcerated immigrants to be transferred to their home countries, immigrants' language barriers and lack of knowledge about the legal process makes it impossible for them to initiate such a transfer (Anonymous, 2009). Unfortunately, the Mexican embassy does not appear to show much interest in helping Mexicans under U.S. criminal justice control either.

The language barrier has not escaped the attention of the criminal justice system. In the Federal Court Interpreters Act of 1978, federal courts were provided interpreters for individuals whose native tongue is not English. However, there are several caveats to this act; since it was enacted at the federal level, it is does not apply to state courts and U.S. states have various certification processes for their court interpreters. It is also costly to employ an interpreter so they are rarely available in rural or impoverished areas of the country.

States that have been on the vanguard of providing interpreters in court cases include Florida, Idaho, New Jersey, and Washington State. However, these states are

---

[6]The group of the foreign-born also includes individuals who have since entering the country become naturalized citizens.

not locations where the most recent wave of immigrants enters the country. Furthermore, although translation services are becoming more and more utilized, immigrants are often forced to make plea bargains quickly before they can benefit from the services of an interpreter. Because immigrant men generally have better English skills, it is particularly the women who suffer from the shortage of interpreters.

One of the biggest issues facing incarcerated women is their separation from their children. Since 1991, the number of children with an incarcerated mother has doubled (Lincroft, 2011). Children suffer from having an incarcerated parent in several ways; they are more likely stigmatized by both their peers and adults, they are more likely to have to contend with foster care, and they are more likely to experience poverty. In order to ease mothers' separation from their children, and to better prepare them for their reunification after release, the correctional system in some states have attempted to adopt policies that focus on this issue. Incarcerated women can, for example, take parenting classes and receive mandatory phone calls from their children's caregivers (see Chapter 4). However, while many correctional systems have adopted such programs, the DHS has proven resistant.

Immigrant women are not being afforded the same services as their native-born counterparts. This is particularly worrisome since ICE routinely transfers immigrants several times during their detention, potentially separating family members over large distances (TRAC Immigration, 2009). Immigrants are also often adjudicated separately and, if they are to be deported, are repatriated separately as well (No More Deaths, 2011). These ICE procedures can lead to prolonged periods during which parents do not know each other's whereabouts. While the child often remains with the mother, the absence of the father likely leads to unnecessary stress for both mother and child.

THE PROCEDURAL VICTIMIZATION OF LEGAL IMMIGRANTS

In his survey of the 2003 prison population, Stana (2005a) found that 17.9% of the 55,322 immigrants incarcerated in the U.S. were undocumented. However, U.S. prisons also house a large number of legal immigrants who have not broken any laws and are not counted in prison statistics—detainees and asylum seekers. The legal definition of who is deportable has been broadened considerably over recent decades and now includes any noncitizen (Massey et al., 2003). In 2006, 53% of immigrants who were deported had not committed any crime at all (Finley, 2006, cited in Dow, 2007). Bosworth (2010) notes that in 2007 approximately 300,000 detainees moved through 400 institutions across the U.S.—most of them had no criminal convictions.

Many individuals detained in U.S. prisons originally came to the U.S. seeking asylum in order to escape religious and political persecution or persecution based on their sexuality (Anderson, 2010; Wood, Gibson, Ribeiro, & Hamsho-Diaz, 2010). Legislative changes in 1996 led to new opportunities to detain immigrants. The Illegal Immigration Reform and Immigrant Responsibility Act broadened the scope of who could be detained and deported to include legal immigrants who had committed a minor offense at any point in their past (Dow, 2007). A second new law, the Antiterrorism and Effective Death Penalty Act, removed immigrants' ability to petition for deportation waivers based on them having proven, often for decades, that they were upstanding legal alien residents who paid taxes, served in the U.S. military, and held down stable jobs. Being married to a U.S. citizen was also no longer a consideration in deportation decisions (Dow, 2007).

Since 1996, deportation also looms for resident aliens who entered the U.S. in their childhood and have few or no ties to their country of origin. In these cases, the country of origin may not accept the deportation and the immigrant remains in a legal limbo and in detention indefinitely. Immigrants who await deportation for minor violations of their visa or for committing a minor offense decades earlier, are joined by tens of thousands of asylum seekers from many different countries who are being detained by Immigration and Customs Enforcement pending the investigation of their case (Dow, 2007).

Publically, immigration authorities, politicians, and personnel of the criminal justice system justify the unrestricted detention without charging immigrants with a crime by arguing that detention is not punitive in nature. Rather, it serves to keep immigrants in one place until they can be deported (Dow, 2007). The U.S. Supreme Court agreed with this argument, although detainees are frequently housed in prisons with incarcerated criminals and suffer from verbal and physically abuse by both inmates and prison guards (Dow, 2007). The legality of this procedure has been debated by scholars (Capitaine, 2001; Kessler, 2009; Neeley, 2008) especially since some legal experts feel that administrative detention violates the due process clause in the Fifth Amendment of the U.S. Constitution (Capitaine, 2001). The number of detainees who struggle in such environments is not trivial. Dow (2007) estimates that "between 1995 and 2007, the average daily population of U.S. immigration detainees increased from about 6,000 to more than 27,000" (p. 535). For the 2012 fiscal year, President Obama budgeted $2,023,827,000 for detention and removal of immigrants through ICE. This equates to 33,400 detainees who can be maintained at any point in time. The U.S. House of Representatives further increased this budget to $2.75 billion. Taxpayers are spending $7.5 million daily in order to detain and deport legal immigrants, most of whom have not committed a crime and were, until ICE arrested them, productive members of U.S. society.

More importantly, immigration authorities' use of prisons for nonpunitive detention has created an incarceration system that parallels that of imprisoned native-born offenders. However, while both native-born and immigrant convicts have certain rights and grievance procedures they can use, for example, the right for legal counsel, detainees move in a legal grey-zone.[7]

Courts are hesitant to intervene in immigration-related questions, leaving ICE to act with little oversight (Dow, 2007). Even when decisions are rendered, they are rarely enforced, as Box 14.2 shows. As a consequence, thousands of immigrants

---

[7]There is evidence that guards use misinformation and immigrants' naïveté about the U.S. criminal justice system even when the latter have been convicted of a crime. Thus even immigrant convicts who have legal protections available to them are not easily able to exercise them (Anonymous, 2009).

continue to be held in prisons without ever having committed a crime; they are liable to strip searches and other invasions of privacy, to wear prison jump suits, and often to share a cell with convicted criminals.[8] However, as opposed to their convicted cellmates, immigrant detainees can be detained indefinitely for days, weeks, years, or even decades without a reason or access to review. And because their legal position makes them invisible, abuses of immigrant detainees rarely come to light (Anderson, 2010; Anonymous, 2009).

Box 14.2

While justices and administrators from Immigration and Customs Enforcement argue that administrative detention is legal and not punitive, both legal scholars and detainees themselves have argued against this view. In 2001, the U.S. Supreme Court decided on a combined lawsuit brought by two detained immigrants (*Zadvydas v. Davis*, 2010). Both aliens had been admitted to the U.S. and were to be deported. However, since ICE could not find a country willing to accept them, their temporary detention developed into indefinite administrative detention. In their lawsuit, the immigrants alleged that their indefinite detention was illegal. The Supreme Court sided with the immigrants and declared that indefinite detention violated the due process clause in the Fifth Amendment of the Constitution. Nevertheless, despite this verdict, a 2004 GAO report found that ICE continued to detain hundreds of individuals who, based on *Zadvydas v. Davis*, should have been released (GAO, 2004). The GAO report suggests that ICE does not possess a case management system that allows for timely access to information on when immigrants are due for release. While individual ICE case managers sometimes try to develop their own system to determine which cases need to be reviewed, ICE has not responded to *Zadvydas v. Davis* in a way that would systematically allow for timely review and release of detained immigrants. Thus, the lack of oversight over DHS and ICE, combined with U.S. courts' reluctance to interfere in immigration questions, has created a situation in which even immigrants who have access to legal aid have little effect on immigrants' treatment by government agencies.

Source: Harald E. Weiss and Lauren M. Vasquez.

POLICY IMPLICATIONS

While the U.S. has always been an immigration nation, Americans' acceptance of immigrants has ebbed and flowed throughout history. Recent decades can be characterized by increasing nativism and anti-immigrant sentiment. While the U.S. economy benefits from highly skilled foreign labor and low-skilled immigrants' willingness to work in jobs most native-born workers refuse (Waldinger, 1997), Americans superficially embrace the idea of diversity while fearing non-White immigration. Immigrants

---

[8]It should be noted that ICE and prison officials claim that detainees and incarcerated criminals are held separate from each other even when they share the same facility. My review of the literature suggests that while this may happen in some instances, it is far from the norm. The literature suggests that housing detainees and immigrants is so common that incarcerated individuals have, in the past, pleaded with authorities to help detainees whom they see as incarcerated innocently (Dow 2007).

who are subject to control through agents of the U.S. criminal justice system are frequently incarcerated together with convicted native-born criminals even if they have not committed any crimes. However, in addition to the abuses and problems associated with being in prison itself (see, for example, Amnesty International, 2005), immigrants' citizenship status further increases their vulnerability to abuses (Anonymous, 2009; Dow, 2007).

Lobbying by corporations who make profit from incarceration has led to harsher laws, leading to lengthy prison terms for relatively minor offenses. Because these laws seek to control a population that is already poor, undereducated, and disenfranchised, immigrants who become trapped in the U.S. criminal justice system have little opportunity to legally challenge their treatment (Anonymous, 2009; Feltz, 2008). In addition, a lack of oversight allows overly zealous enforcement officials to abuse immigrants while in their custody. While these well-supported problems should be deplored in a country that prides itself on freedom and free speech, ICE and DHS have instead chosen to keep immigrant victims quiet by removing their right to counsel or by transferring them geographically to make legal intervention unavailable (Dow, 2007). The current treatment of immigrant arrestees, prisoners, and detainees is deplorable but could be improved through a small number of tweaks to the system:

1. Removal of Overzealous Agents from Direct Contact with Immigrants

No More Deaths' (2008, 2011) reports paint an unflattering picture of ICE personnel. One of the most basic job requirements of any kind of law enforcement agent is the protection of the well-being of the offender once he or she is in custody. This is no more important than when apprehended individuals require medical care. The lack of a change in the abuse data between the 2008 and 2011 No More Deaths reports suggests that ICE does not consider immigrant abuse and neglect an important enough topic to oversee its agents. ICE should be forced to take responsibility for the immigrants in its care; an independent oversight mechanism that minimizes potential conflicts of interest should proactively interact with apprehended and detained immigrants and investigate reports of abuse and neglect. Officers who have repeatedly proven to be unable to disconnect their personal sentiments about immigrants from their sworn duties should be removed from service, or should at least no longer be permitted to have direct contact with immigrants.

2. Provide Adequate Legal Counsel to Guarantee a Fair Trial

Many legal matters immigrant defendants agree to are based on a lack of understanding of U.S. law and the absence of effective legal counsel. Public defenders in high-immigration jurisdictions should be trained in immigration law and carry appropriate caseloads. If lawmakers decide to pass harsh laws that are guaranteed to drastically increase the number of immigrants within the court system, they should also provide defendants with adequate legal counsel that guarantees that their due process rights are honored. Having adequate counsel would make it more difficult for prosecutors and ICE personnel to use scare tactics in order to extract easy plea deals. Public defenders could also limit the use of information that was derived in a legally questionable manner in an immigrant's criminal proceedings.

3. Provide Access to Legal Aid for Detainees

Access to a lawyer is vital for immigrants in administrative detention as well. The view that immigrant detainees are not eligible for legal counsel because they are not charged with a crime potentially leads to treatment that is worse than that of convicted offenders. Furthermore, while detaining immigrants who await deportation is necessary, indefinite incarceration is reminiscent of the Bastille. Because they are trapped in a legal grey-zone that denies them basic legal protection, detained immigrants are invisible and open to abuses that rarely see the light of day. Physical, emotional, and procedural abuses through agents of the criminal justice system have been known to occur and have no repercussions because immigrants have nobody to talk to (Anderson, 2010; Anonymous, 2009). Access to a lawyer provides social control over prison personnel, as potential abusive behaviors will be noticed by the detainee's legal support network.

4. Increase the Transparency of the Detention Process

Judges and administrators have to begin recognizing that even a population that is not accused of a crime needs legal recourse and protection from abuse. Making the detention process more transparent and allowing immigrants to air grievances would provide support for the claim that detention is not punitive; grievance procedures are not currently extended to immigrant detainees. The Department of Homeland Security could use regulatory reform to improve the situation for immigrants in ICE detention centers (Heeren, 2010). External oversight and program evaluations would ensure that reforms intended to improve the system have the desired effects.

5. Establish a System to Monitor Immigrants' Length of Detention

ICE does not try to keep detainees in prison indefinitely on purpose; it suffers from an inadequate information system that does not allow case managers to easily determine which immigrants are approaching the legal limit of their detention (Government Accountability Office, 2004). Thus, immigrants often remain detained beyond their legally mandated time because they got lost in the system. A restructuring of the case management system, overseen by courts or an external agency, would allow case managers to develop lists of immigrants who are approaching the legal limit of their detention. Hearings and reviews could be scheduled in a timely manner before the legal limit to detention expires.

6. Place Detainees Into an Environment That Is Not Designed to Punish

The rather fictitious claim that administrative detention is not punitive in nature must be debunked. Law enforcement removes offenders from society and incarcerates convicted criminals in institutions that were designed to punish. It is irrelevant what the disposition of judges and immigration administrators toward immigrant detainees is; institutions that were designed to punish fulfills this purpose. Since administrative detention has been performed for decades, the U.S. government has had ample time and opportunity to build detention centers that detain, rather than punish. Yet, prisons and jails are still the major locations where immigrant detainees are being held.

7. Separate Profit From the Management of Immigrants Under Criminal Justice Supervision

Most importantly, we must remove the profit motive from immigration-related incarceration and detention. Sentencing should be based on evidence of guilt and an assessment of social harm, not on an industry's profit interest. Corporations have both pushed for and benefited from the tightening of current immigration legislation.[9] Disenfranchising immigrants has become a booming business, and private prison companies stand to reap large gains from more incarceration. In addition to the social costs, U.S. taxpayers, in the end, pay the bill. While laws like SB 1070 stipulate that immigrants pay for their own incarceration, it is unlikely that illegal immigrants, who have often spent their life savings to be brought to the U.S., will be able to pay for their prison sentences. Taxpayers will invariably foot the bill, which assures private prison corporations suppliers a low-risk investment that in the current climate is guaranteed to yield record profits. Maybe the most important thing any of us can do is to publicize the relationship between Wall Street, politicians, and immigration law in the hopes that the public will begin to weigh its anti-immigrant feelings against its love for lower taxes and less government spending.

DISCUSSION QUESTIONS

1. The move toward restrictive anti-immigrant legislation has been partly supported by corporate financial incentives to lawmakers. What rules would have to be enacted to effectively disconnect politicians' decisions from corporate control while still providing businesses with input in the political process?

2. Proponents of deregulation argue that economies and the political sphere should be completely deregulated. How would immigration policy change if complete deregulation were to occur?

---

[9]Prison companies have also been important supporters of the imprisonment binge that began in the mid-80's (Irwin, 2004).

3. What powers would a new government agency require in order to assure that detained immigrants are treated well and that their cases are reviewed in a timely manner?

4. Most illegal immigrants enter the U.S. in order to earn money. What economic programs, beyond foreign aid, could the U.S. government pursue in order to reduce the stream of illegal immigrants into the country?

5. The vital difference between administrative detention and incarceration is that detainees are not being punished. What characteristics would a dedicated detention center have to have in order to not punish detainees during their stay while still fulfilling its requirement of confining immigrants awaiting deportation?

SUGGESTED READINGS

Lee, M. T., & Martinez, R. (2009). Immigration reduces crime: An emerging scholarly consensus. *Sociology of Crime, Law & Deviance, 13*, 3-16.

Massey, D. S., Durand, J., & Malone, N. J. (2003). *Beyond smoke and mirrors: Mexican immigration in an era of economic integration.* New York, NY: Russell Sage Foundation.

Perea, J. F. (1996). *Immigrants out! The new nativism and the anti-immigrant impulse in the United States.* New York, NY: New York University Press.

Reiman, J. (2001). *The rich get richer and the poor get prison.* Boston, MA: Allyn & Bacon.

Welch, M. (2002). *Detained: immigration laws and the expanding I.N.S. jail complex.* Philadelphia, PA: Temple University Press.

REFERENCES

Anderson, L. (2010). Punishing the innocent: How the classification of male-to-female transgender individuals in immigration detention constitutes illegal punishment under the Fifth Amendment. *Berkeley Journal of Gender, Law & Justice, 25*, 1–31.

Amnesty International. (2005). *Stonewalled: Police abuse and misconduct against lesbian, gay, bisexual and transgender people in the U.S.* New York, NY: Amnesty International USA.

Anonymous. (2009). Some barriers detained migrant women face. *Social Justice, 36*(2), 104–105.

Bernstein, N., & Williams, M. (2009, April 2). Immigration agency's revised list of deaths in custody. *New York Times.* Retrieved from http://www.nytimes.com/2009/04/03/nyregion/03detainlist.html

Blakely, C. R., & Bumphus, V. W. (2004). Private and public sector prisons – A comparison of select characteristics. *Federal Probation, 68*(1), 27–31.

Bosworth, M. (2010). *Explaining U.S. imprisonment.* Thousand Oaks, CA: Sage.

Butcher, K. F., & Piehl, A. M. (1999). *The role of deportation in the incarceration of immigrants* [electronic resource]. Cambridge, MA: National Bureau of Economic Research.

Camarota, S. A., & Vaughan, J. M. (2009). Immigration and crime: Assessing a conflicted issue. Center for Immigrant Studies. Retrieved from http://www.cis.org/ImmigrantCrime

Capitaine, V. C. (2001). Life in prison without a trial: The indefinite detention of immigrants in the United States. *Texas Law Review, 79*(3), 769.

Cervantes-Gautschi, P. (2010). Wall Street & our campaign to decriminalize immigrants. *Social Policy, 40*(3), 3–8.

Dow, M. (2007). Designed to punish: Immigrant detention and deportation. *Social Research, 74*(2), 533–546.

Dunn, T. J. (1996). *The militarization of the U.S.-Mexico border, 1978–1992: Low intensity conflict doctrine comes home.* Austin: University of Texas Press.

Feltz, R. (2008, November/December). A new migration policy: Producing felons for profit. *NACLA Report on the Americas, 41*(6), 26–29.

Finley, B. (2006). Migrant cases burden system. *Denver Post.* Retrieved from http://www.denverpost.com/news/ci_4428563

Goldstein, J. (2011). Murder trial in Tucson shows rift in minuteman border movement. *New York Times.* Retrieved from http://www.nytimes.com/2011/02/11/us/11minutemen.html

Greenfeld, L. A., & Snell, T. L. (1999). *Women offenders.* NCJ 175688. Washington, DC: U.S. Department of Justice, Bureau of Justice Statistics. Retrieved from https://www.ncjrs.gov/App/Publications/abstract.aspx?ID=175688

Greenwood, M. J., & McDowell, J. M. (1986). The factor market consequences of U.S. immigration. *Journal of Economic Literature, 24*(4), 1738.

Harvard Law Review. (1987). INS transfer policy: Interference with detained aliens' due process right to retain counsel. *Harvard Law Review, 100*(8), 2001.

Heeren, G. (2010). Pulling teeth: The state of mandatory immigration detention. *Harvard Civil Rights-Civil Liberties Law Review, 45*(2), 601–634.

Hoefer, M., Rytina, N., & Baker, B. C. (2011). *Estimates of the unauthorized immigrant population residing in the United States: January 2010.* Washington DC: U.S. Department of Homeland Security. Retrieved from http://www.dhs.gov/xlibrary/assets/statistics/publications/ois_ill_pe_2010.pdf

Immigration and Customs Enforcement. (2011). *List of deaths in ICE custody.* Washington, DC: Author. Retrieved from www.ice.gov/doclib/foia/reports/detaineedeaths2003–present.pdf

Kessler, B. (2009). In jail, no notice, no hearing . . . no Problem? A closer look at immigration detention and the due process standards of the International Covenant on Civil and Political Rights. *American University International Law Review, 24*(3), 571–607.

Kil, S. H., & Menjívar, C. (2006). The "war on the border": criminalizing immigrants and militarizing the U.S.-Mexico border. In R. Martinez Jr. & A. Valenzuela (Eds.), *Immigration and crime: Race, ethnicity, and violence.* New York, NY: New York University Press.

Kil, S. H., Menjivar, C., & Doty, R. L. (2009). Securing borders: Patriotism, vigilantism and the brutalization of the US American public. *Sociology of Crime, Law & Deviance, 13,* 279–312.

Lee, J. (2011). *U.S. naturalizations: 2010.* Washington, DC: U.S. Department of Homeland Security. Retrieved from www.dhs.gov/xlibrary/assets/statistics/publications/natz_fr_2010.pdf

Lincroft, Y. (2011). Children of incarcerated parents. *First Focus.* Retrieved from http://www.firstfocus.net/library/fact-sheets/children-of-incarcerated-parents

Massey, D. S., Durand, J., & Malone, N. J. (2003). *Beyond smoke and mirrors: Mexican immigration in an era of economic integration.* New York, NY: Russell Sage Foundation.

Miller, T. (2010). Arizona, the anti-immigrant laboratory. *NACLA Report on the Americas, 43*(4), 3–4.

Moehling, C., & Piehl, A. M. (2009). Immigration, crime, and incarceration in early twentieth-century America. *Demography, 46*(4), 739–763.

Monger, R., & Mathews, M. (2011). *Nonimmigrant admissions to the United States: 2010.* Washington, DC: U.S. Department of Homeland Security. Retrieved from http://www.dhs.gov/xlibrary/assets/statistics/publications/ni_fr_2010.pdf

Monger, R., & Yankay, J. (2010). *U.S. legal permanent residents: 2010.* U.S. Department of Homeland Security. Retrieved from www.dhs.gov/xlibrary/assets/statistics/publications/lpr_fr_2010.pdf

Neeley, S. (2008). Immigration detention: The inaction of the Bureau of Immigration and Customs Enforcement. *Administrative Law Review, 60*(3), 729–748.

No More Deaths. (2008). *Crossing the line.* Retrieved from http://www.nomoredeaths.org

No More Deaths. (2011). *A culture of cruelty.* Retrieved from http://www.nomoredeaths.org

Passel, J. S., & Cohn, D. V. (2010). *U.S. unauthorized immigration flows are down sharply since mid-decade.* Pew Hispanic Center. Retrieved from http://pewhispanic.org/files/reports/126.pdf

Sapp, L. (2011). *Apprehensions by the U.S. Border Patrol: 2005–2010.* Retrieved from http://www.dhs.gov/files/statistics/publications/apprehensions-border-patrol-2010.shtm

Simon, J. (1998). Refugees in a carceral age: The rebirth of immigration prisons in the United States. *Public Culture, 10*(3), 577.

Stana, R. M. (2005a). Information on certain illegal aliens arrested in the United States. GAO-05-646R. *GAO Reports* (p. 1). Washington, DC: U.S. Government Accountability Office.

Stana, R. M. (2005b). Information on criminal aliens incarcerated in federal and state prisons and local jails. GAO-05-337R. *GAO Reports* (p. 1). Washington, DC: U.S. Government Accountability Office.

Sullivan, L. (2010). Prison economics help drive Ariz. immigration law. Retrieved from National Public Radio http://www.npr.org/templates/story/story.php?storyId=130833741

TRAC Immigration. (2009). Huge increase in transfers of ICE detainees. Retrieved from http://trac.syr.edu/immigration/reports/220/

TRAC Immigration. (2011). Illegal reentry becomes top criminal charge. Retrieved from http://trac.syr.edu/immigration/reports/251/

U.S. Government Accountability Office. (2004). *Immigration enforcement: Better data and controls are needed to assure consistency with the Supreme Court decision on long-term alien detention.* GAO-04-434. Washington, DC: Author.

U.S. Department of Homeland Security. (2002). *Fiscal year 2002 yearbook of immigration statistics.* Retrieved from www.dhs.gov/xlibrary/assets/statistics/yearbook/2002/ENF2002.pdf

Waldinger, R. (1997). Black/immigrant competition re-assessed: New evidence from Los Angeles. *Sociological Perspectives, 40,* 365–386.

West, H. C., & Sabol, W. J. (2009). *Prison inmates at midyear 2008-Statistical tables.* NCJ 225619. Washington, DC: U.S. Department of Justice, Bureau of Justice Statistics. Retrieved from http://bjsdata.ojp.usdoj.gov/content/pub/pdf/pim08st.pdf

Wood, C. H., Gibson, C., Ribeiro, L., & Hamsho-Diaz, P. (2010). Crime victimization in Latin America and intentions to migrate to the United States. *International Migration Review, 44*(1), 3–24.

Zhou, M. (2001). Contemporary immigration and the dynamics of race and ethnicity. In N. J. Smelser, W. J. Wilson, & F. Mitchell (Eds.), *America becoming: Racial trends and their consequences* (pp. 200–242). Washington, DC: National Academy Press.

CHAPTER 15

Homeland Security and the Inmate Population: The Risk and Reality of Islamic Radicalization in Prison

Aaron Rappaport, Tinka Veldhuis, and Amos Guiora

Since 9/11, commentators and policy makers have expressed alarm about an emerging threat within the prison systems of the West—a threat of terrorist attacks carried out by radicalized inmates released into society. Prisons are said to be a "fertile ground for extremists" (Mueller, 2006), to offer a dangerous "intermingling" of terrorist networks and criminals (Cuthbertson, 2004, p. 15), to constitute part of an "international network of subversion, conversion, and recruitment. (Kushner, 2004, p. 41)

These concerns reflect a fear that prison inmates are particularly vulnerable to *radicalization*, a process through which individuals are exposed to, and ultimately adopt, a violent ideology justifying attacks against the state (Brown, 2009). Of course, many kinds of extremists can be found in the prison system—White supremacists, animal rights liberationists, and anarchists, to name a few. But the central concern, at least for many commentators, has been the threat of Islamic radicalization.

This may be understandable. For many, the dangers posed by Islamic terrorist groups like al-Qaeda and its associates seem far greater than any other extremist ideology. Islam is widely seen as having a particular appeal to inmates, confirmed by seemingly high rates of conversion, and thus giving Islamic radicals an entry to this literally captive audience. Radicalized prisoners, moreover, are seen as particularly dangerous agent of terror. Rupp (2006) writes, as citizens or long-term residents of the state, these individuals are intimately familiar with Western culture and

432 Special Needs Offenders in Correctional Institutions

can easily blend into the fabric of society. The fear, as one paper put it, is of "an Islamic fifth column" (p. 9).

If these fears are understandable, the public clamor over the threat of radicalization also raises its own set of concerns. This is a subject, after all, where the danger of stereotyping and overreaction seems especially high. Indeed, prison radicalization raises a host of sinister specters that play into the public's deepest and most terrifying fears.

The threat of terrorism, of course, continues to pervade the consciousness of the West's populace. But in this context, that fear is married to several others. There is the fear of prisons, which are often perceived, in the United States at least, as nearly ungoverned places of criminality (Clarke & Soria, 2010). There is the fear of gangs, which are seen as coercing individuals into illicit conspiracies. And there is a fear of Muslims, who continue to be viewed, at least by certain segments of the populace, as foreign, potentially dangerous, and not entirely trustworthy.

The issue of prison radicalization thus brings together this multiplicity of perceived threats—terrorists, prisons, gangs, and Muslim extremists—to form a mixture that can easily overflow into unthinking hysteria. Overreaction is particularly problematic in this context because efforts to monitor, disrupt, or control the conduct of Muslim inmates may implicate and perhaps trespass religious freedoms. In that way, hysteric and stigmatizing reactions can fuel radicalization among prisoners and their followers, contributing to the threat rather than managing it. In this combustible situation, it becomes particularly important to examine dispassionately the objective evidence about the risk of prison radicalization, in order to ensure that restrictions placed on Muslim prisoners are carefully justified.

This chapter makes a first step in that endeavor, exploring what we know about the risk of Islamic radicalization in prison and the kinds of policies that have been implemented to respond to that risk. Although the principal focus of this study is the United States, the approaches of several European nations—the U.K., France, Spain, and the Netherlands—are considered where relevant.

Our conclusion is a largely negative one: We know very little about the degree of risk posed by radicalization in the prison system. Much of the talk about the risk of radicalization is simply talk, unsupported by research or evidence. Indeed, the truly remarkable thing is how little is known about even the most basic details of the issue such as the number of Muslims in the prison system or their demographics. This is certainly not to suggest that the danger of Islamic radicalization in prison is nonexistent. It simply means we don't *know* if the risk is significant. It also means that the current claims that prison radicalization has reached a crisis stage are grossly premature and, at this point, mere speculation.

A similar conclusion can be made about the current policy response of governments to the perceived risk. Commentators have listed a range of options for responding to the threat of radicalization, including increased screening of Muslim chaplains in prison, restrictions on religious literature available to inmates, and the segregation of radicalized offenders. Although some of these changes may seem commonsensical, and all appear well-intentioned, there remains a significant lack of careful thinking about the rationales for many widely shared prescriptions. Just as troubling, some worry that no attempt has been made to coordinate the policy prescriptions, resulting in unintended, and in certain cases counter-productive, consequences.

Our ultimate conclusion is that a broad-based commitment is needed on the part of Western governments to gather evidence about the real risks of radicalization in prison and to formulate a coordinated response after that evidence has been gathered. This will require a national commitment on the part of the United States in particular, which has lagged behind Britain and other nations in collecting this kind of information. In light of the powerful emotions that are provoked by the fear of prison radicalization, the failure to move ahead with that kind of research effort will mean that policy will inevitably be carried along not by reason, but by the political passions inevitably at play.

To avoid misunderstanding about the scope of this analysis, three caveats must be mentioned before starting.

First, the focus of this chapter is the risk of radicalization among *Muslim* inmates. This focus does not deny that other individuals might also be at risk of radicalization. Indeed, some commentators suggested that other groups such as white supremacists pose a greater risk to the United States at least. Our analysis focuses on Islamic radicalization primarily because that has been the central concern of commentators and the public in recent years, and also because this topic raises difficult and unique issues regarding religious freedom and its possible connection with the broader fight against international terrorism. We recognize that simply by selecting Muslim radicalization as our topic, the analysis could be misinterpreted as implying that a heightened and special risk flows from this group of inmates. We hope that the substance of this chapter makes clear that we do not assert such a claim, and that we remain entirely agnostic as to the relative dangers of different inmate groups.

Second, throughout the chapter, we use the term *Islamic radicalization* to refer to extremists of Islamic orientation having a violent ideology oriented against the state. This term, however, should not be taken to mean that a single ideology is behind the radicalization of Muslim inmates. Rather, as others have pointed out (Hamm, 2007, p. 20), the forms of Islam in prison are manifold, including traditional forms of Sunni and Shia religious doctrine, as well as forms of Islam that are unique to prison (such as the so-called "prIslam"). Some of these variants are more traditional, structured, and formalized; others are contemporary, informal, and unstructured. We use the term *Islamic radicalization* simply as a convenient phrase to refer to any form of Islam that adopts the kinds of ideology that might justify violence against the sovereign nation.

Third, and finally, this chapter focuses principally on the risk of radicalization among ordinary inmates in prison. Excluded from this category are the groups of prisoners that have been convicted of terrorist offenses and are currently being held in military or civilian prisons. In the United States, for example, several hundred individuals are currently being held in Guantanamo Bay or in special prison facilities called Communications Management Units. The treatment of these inmates warrants more attention and further study. However, since these policies raise their own distinct and particularly complex questions, we do not address them here, except as they relate to the radicalization of "ordinary" criminals in prison.

The discussion proceeds in two parts. Part one examines what sorts of information exist regarding prison radicalization. It summarizes the few pieces of objective evidence that exist about terrorist plots that have been hatched in prison, and it brings together general statements from experts and commentators about the danger of prison radicalization. Although some risk certainly exists, this section argues that very little is known about the true nature and magnitude of the danger. However frequently made, claims about a crisis are based on largely unsupported assertions.

Part two focuses on how governments in the United States and other Western nations have responded to the still ambiguous risk of radicalization in prison. This part focuses on several key initiatives, including attempts to screen Muslim leaders and to isolate high-risk individuals. The analysis suggests that policies implemented so far seem reasonable, though the lack of coordinated response has led to some troubling and unintended effects.

I. RISK, RHETORIC, AND RADICALIZATION

Prison inmates are widely seen as being unusually susceptible to radicalization. That vulnerability, commentators suggest, reflects several features of the prison experience itself. Inmates, on entering the prison, are disoriented and disempowered, experiencing personal vulnerability both from prison guards and from threatening prison gangs. Fears about their personal security may make inmates open to groups offering protection. Feelings of loss and disorientation may lead to a period of reflection and reexamination. Inmates may feel drawn to belief systems, like certain forms of Islam, that offer them a feeling of importance and an identity that can give meaning to their life challenges (Brandon, 2009; Hannah, Clutterbuck, & Rubin, 2008)

Of course, a greater openness to a religion, like Islam, is not itself a cause for alarm. The concern is that the same vulnerability that leads individuals to Islam will lead them down a path to radicalization. Commentators recognize that only a small portion of Muslim inmates take that last step toward extremism. The question is: *How great is that danger?* The answer to this question, as becomes disturbingly clear from available documentation, is that we do not know how great the risk is. Even more so, we *cannot* know how great the risk is.

Simply stated, only the barest amount of data is available to assess the risk of radicalization. Incidents of radicalization and recruitment are difficult to recognize—let alone acknowledge—by prison authorities, and no integrated documentation efforts exist across prisons to keep track of such incidents. As a result, it is almost impossible to make an accurate assessment of how serious the problem is, under what circumstances inmate radicalization is likely to occur, or how often terrorist organizations try to and succeed in recruiting inmates into their cohorts.

The following sections explore what little is known about radicalization in prison, and what the evidence suggests, if anything, about the seriousness of the threat. We begin by surveying the few notable and documented cases where individuals have been radicalized in prison and then sought to carry out, or succeeded in carrying out, a terrorist attack.

The Hard Evidence of Radicalization

To date, the number of documented cases of prison radicalization is quite low. According to Jenkins (2010), from September 11, 2001, though the end of 2009, "46 publicly reported cases of domestic radicalization and recruitment to jihadist terrorism occurred in the United States" (p. 9). Based on our survey of the available documentation, only 1 out of those 46 is known to have been operationalized *in prison.*

This is the case of Kevin James, who adopted a radical version of Islam while serving time in a California penitentiary (Hamm, 2009, pp. 668–669). During the 1990s and early 2000s, James recruited other inmates to his brand of Islam, called Jam'iyyat Ul-Islam Is-Saheeh (JIS). In prison, James ultimately hatched a plan to use several newly paroled inmates to attack army recruiting stations and the Israeli consulate in Los Angeles. The plan unraveled and the entire group was arrested after one of the parolees accidentally left his cell phone at the scene of a robbery. James himself was convicted in 2009. The JIS case remains the only documented instance in the United States of a terrorist plot being organized in prison (Hamm, 2009).

To be sure, Europe has experienced additional cases, with more deadly results. Most notably, several individuals who masterminded the 2004 Madrid bombing were radicalized in prison. The mastermind of the plot, Jamal "el Chino" Ahmidan "embraced jihadist principles while serving time for immigration fraud in a Spanish detention center in 2002 (Rotella, 2004). Jose Emilio Suarez Trashorras, who also took a lead role in the plot, was "indoctrinated into radical Islam in a Spanish prison," as well (See Carlile, 2006; Rotella, 2004; Hamm, 2009, p. 668; Rupp, 2006, p. 20).

In addition to the Madrid bombing, several less well-known cases of radicalization have also occurred in European prisons. In Spain, Mohamed Achraf (also known as Abderrahmane Tahiri), convicted in 2007 of being a member of a terrorist organization, recruited others while incarcerated in Salamanca prison. In France, Safé Bourada was convicted in 2008 for planning terrorist attacks in France. Among those convicted with him were other former convicts who he had met while incarcerated (Combelles Siegel, 2006; Brandon, 2009). In Britain, Muktar Said Ibrahim, the leader in the failed "second-wave" attack on the London transport system in 2005 served time in a juvenile institution in the mid-1990s. Some reports suggest that Ibrahim was radicalized there and may have used his time to recruit others into his plot (Travis, 2005; BBC News, 2005). The RAND Corporation suggests that the Madrid bombing, along with some of the other examples, demonstrates "that contemporary violent Jihadists can and will seek out new recruits in the prison environment" (Hannah et al., 2008, p. 49).

These cases, though troubling, are relatively few in number. But do they fully account for the number of terrorist attempts originating in prison? One might argue that several other terrorist offenders should be included in this list. These are individuals who converted to Islam in prison, but only became radicalized after their release. A well-known example is Michael C. Finton, who converted to Islam while serving in an Illinois prison from 1999 to 2005 (for robbery and battery). No clear evidence exists that Finton was planning a terrorist attack at that time. However, in 2008, Finton traveled to Saudi Arabia. He was arrested the following year on terrorist charges after he parked a van that he thought was loaded with explosives outside a federal courthouse in Springfield, Illinois—the explosives were fake and were provided by an undercover FBI agent.

In a separate incident in 2009, four men were arrested in the United States and charged with various terrorist offenses after seeking to buy weapons from an FBI informant. The *New York Times* reported that all the men had served time in prison, and at least two of the men appeared to be prison converts (Walkin, 2009). At the same time, the terrorist plot appears to have been formed at a mosque in Newburgh, New York, after their release from prison (Hernandez & Chan, 2009). The implication, as James Brandon (2004) puts it, is that "prison radicalization does not mean that terrorist plots are being routinely hatched in prison" (although this has occasionally happened). More often, however, it leads to inmates adopting Islamist ideologies that may ultimately lead to terrorism after their release (p. 4).

These cases heighten concerns about prison radicalization. The worry is that, even if terrorist plots are not themselves hatched in prison, the prison experience might prime individuals to be receptive to radical ideologies *after* their release.

Whether prison really predisposes individuals to embrace radical ideologies after release remains uncertain. Nonetheless, even taking the postrelease cases into account, the documented cases of prison radicalization do not, by themselves, suggest a crisis. Yet, it is also impossible to discount the possibility of a serious threat either. The problem is that one cannot know whether the documented cases represent the full extent of the threat, or whether they are just the tip of an iceberg. Given this uncertainty, it makes sense to look at other sources of information to see if they offer additional evidence of a broader radicalization risk.

Radicalization and the Limits of Risk Assessment

One approach is to undertake a preliminary risk assessment of this inmate population—to look at features of the Muslim inmate population that might offer some indications of the magnitude of the radicalization threat. To start such an analysis, certain basic facts would be obvious and essential such as facts about the size and characteristics of the Muslim population in prison. How many Muslims are in the prison system? What is their age, background, belief system? What are their views about the government and society at large? One would expect such information would be readily available. However, for the United States at least, that expectation would be mistaken. Even the most basic facts about the Muslim inmate population in the U.S. are unknown.

Consider the total number of Muslims in the prison system. While it is widely believed that Islam is the fastest growing religion in the system, precise figures are not available and up to date for the United States. Approximately 6% of the roughly 150,000 inmates serving time in the federal prisons in 2004 were said to "seek Islamic services," according to the chief of the bureau's chaplaincy service (Office of the Inspector General [OIG], 2004a, p. 5). Several states have provided estimates as well. For examples, according to published reports, "Muslims make up about 18 percent of the 63,700 inmates in New York state prisons; 18 percent of the 41,000 state prisoners in Pennsylvania" (Zoll as cited in Hamm, 2007, p. 20). And roughly 6% of South Carolina's prison population was Muslim in 2009 (Gelinas, 2010). However, no reliable nationwide estimates currently exist.

France faces a somewhat similar situation. France does not allow its governmental institutions and agencies to collect data on race, religion, or ethnicity, which makes establishing such numbers very difficult. Nonetheless, widely quoted experts reports that "Muslims make up an astounding 80 percent of the nation's prison population (Khosrokhavar, 2004; Hamm, 2007, 2009). This number is shockingly high, especially given the fact that Muslims make up only 8% of the French population. How is the 80% figure, then, determined?

Ultimately, the figures seem to be based on secondary indicators such as observations regarding the complexion and names of inmates, their dietary practices, and whether inmates attend religious services (Khosrokhavar, 2004). Even though questions exist concerning the accuracy of these figures, the numbers are fervently copied in other publications, and several authors express fear that French prisons are hotbeds of radicalization. In 2005, the French counterterrorism agency dismantled a terrorist network of which several members had met—and were allegedly radicalized—in prison (Combelles Siegel, 2006). Quantitatively however, the threat appears to be rather limited. The French prison system contains approximately 60,000 inmates, of which only 99 are being held for terrorism-related offenses (Combelles Siegel, 2006).

Britain, in contrast to the United States and to France, has made recent efforts to collect nationwide figures for its Muslim inmate population. In 2010, the British Ministry of Justice (MoJ) undertook a comprehensive nationwide assessment of Muslims in its prison population. In that study, the Ministry concluded that, "There are around 10,300 Muslims in prisons in England and Wales" up from 9,975 in 2008. "Muslims now constitute the third largest religious group in prison, after those with no religious affiliation and Christians" (HM Chief Inspector of Prisons [HMCIP], 2010). That constitutes roughly 12% of the prison population. Worryingly to some, the percentages have been increasingly steadily, up from 5% of the prison population in 1994 and 8% in 2004 (HMCIP, 2010). For comparison, Muslims made up 2.7% of the general population in 2001.

Of course, any accurate assessment of the risk of radicalization requires much more detailed information than the total number of Muslim inmates. At a minimum, a useful risk assessment must also look at the demographics and beliefs of the Muslim inmate population. But again, such information is nearly wholly lacking.

To give a notable example, commentators have repeatedly cited one subgroup of Muslim inmates for special attention—prison converts to Islam. The concern is that this group poses a particularly high risk for radicalization. Given that concern, one would expect some assessment of the numbers of converts in the prison system. And in fact, commentators have suggested that yearly conversions to Islam in local, state, and federal correctional institutions range are significant. Dix-Richardson (2002) asserts that converts to Islam total 30,000. Waller (2003) contends the number of Muslim inmates increases by 40,000 per year, with the majority of the growth occurring through conversion. These are dramatic estimates, which suggest that as many as 300,000 have converted to Islam in prison since 9/11 (Hamm, 2007). Unfortunately, the source for these estimates is wholly unclear.

Dix-Richardson's estimate, for example, is drawn from a single sentence in a 1999 book by Jane Smith, entitled *Islam in America*. In that book, Smith writes, "while exact figures are again hard to determine, it is estimated that more than 300,000 prisoners are converts to Islam, and that the rate of conversion may be more than 30,000 per year" (p. 165). Smith herself offers no citation in support of that figure. The source for Waller's estimate of up to 40,000 converts per year is similarly uncertain.

Another common claim about converts is the widely repeated statement that 80% of all conversions in prison are conversion to Islam (Rupp, 2006; Wilner, 2010). This figure has been cited so many times in the U.S. press that it has taken on the semblance of established truth. Yet, once again, the figure appears to be based largely on the testimony of J. Michael Waller, without further empirical support (Waller, 2003).[1]

In short, for the United States at least, even basic facts about the Muslim inmate population are unavailable. But collecting such information is obviously just the start of a more sophisticated risk assessment effort. It is not enough to know, for example, how many Muslim converts are in the prison system. We need to have a broader understanding of the political, religious, and ideological views of inmates in the prison system, and an assessment of other risk factors for radicalization.

Much of what passes for understanding today is anecdotal. For example, one senior official within the FBI notes that some inmates "either feel discriminated against in the United States or feel that the United States oppresses minorities and Muslims overseas. The feeling of perceived oppression, combined with their limited knowledge of Islam, especially for converts, makes this a vulnerable population for extremists looking to radicalize and recruit" (Van Duyn, 2006, p. 24). Up to now, studies that delve in depth into the social and psychological makeup of Muslim inmates are scarce. Given the lack of information about the numbers, demographics, and beliefs of the Muslim inmate population, it can hardly be surprising that our understanding of radicalization in prison, an exceptionally complex and dynamic process in itself, is even more limited.

---

[1]Other nations in the West do not seem to have much more accurate numbers. Britain, for example, also lacks concrete data about the number of converts in its prison system. But at least to its credit, the Ministry of Justice has acknowledged as much and spoken of the need to expand its analysis of its Muslim inmate population. In a preliminary survey of 164 Muslim prisoners, Britain indicated that 30% "had converted to Islam (HM Chief Inspector of Prisons, 2010). The ministry also provides some preliminary data on the makeup of this group. As they observed, the converts—like the Muslim prisoners in general—indicated "over-representation of black Muslim prisoners compared with black Muslims in the community. . . . This was reflected in our sample of converts of whom 65% (n=32) were black, 18% (n=9) white and 16% (n=8) of mixed heritage. None were Asian. No definitive reason for this disparity emerged from our interviews." (Id at 31).

Risk and Rhetoric

Given the lack of information about even the most basic features of the Muslim population in prison, one might be surprised that influential researchers and security experts continue to make confident-sounding claims about the magnitude of the radicalization threat. A close look reveals how little evidence exists to support these specific claims. Consider two widely-reported assertions about the threat of Islamic radicalization in prison.

In testimony before the Senate in 2003, conservative writer and researcher, J. Michael Waller declared:

> Radical Islamist groups, most tied to Saudi-sponsored Wahhabi organizations suspected by the U.S. government of being closely linked to terror financing activities, dominate Muslim prison recruitment in the U.S. and seek to create a radicalized cadre of felons who will support their anti-American efforts. Estimates place the number of Muslim prison recruits at between 15–20% of the prison population. (p. 97)

Waller's estimate yields a shocking number of prison recruits. In a total prison population of nearly 1.6 million in 2010 (PEW Center on the States, 2010), this suggests that the number of radicalized felons in United States prisons is between 240,000 and 320,000. Given our previous observations about the dearth of objective evidence, one might not be surprised to discover that the basis for Waller's dire warning is wholly unclear. As Hamm (2009) writes,

> [Waller] offers no explanation for his numerical estimate; no case studies of radicalization and terrorist recruitment; no interviews with wardens, intelligence officers, chaplains or prisoners. In fact, there is no reason to believe that Waller has ever set foot inside a prison." (p. 681)

More recently, the British think tank, Royal United Service Institute (RUSI), made national news when it offered a dramatic warning that, "some 800 potentially violent radicals, not previously guilty of terrorism charges, will be back in society over the coming five to 10 years." RUSI's estimate was based on a 2008 news article, which states that "probation officers . . . believe that attempts have been made to convert one in 10 of the estimated 8,000 Muslims in the eight high-security prisons in England and Wales to the Al-Qaeda cause in the past two years" (Leppard, [2008] as cited in Clarke & Soria, 2010, p. 24–31). This figure, however, was subsequently rejected by a Ministry of Justice spokesman, who said, "There are only 6,000 prisoners in the High Security Estate, most of whom are not Muslim. The figure of 'one in ten of the 8,000 Muslims' in the High Security Estate is therefore unrecognizable" (Doyle, 2010).

The truth is, we do not know how great the risk is and, given our lack of data, we *cannot* know how great the risk is (see also Rupp, 2006, p. 6). This is not to say that the risk is nonexistent. The few documented cases of prison radicalization suggest that the threat is hardly imaginary. The vulnerability of inmates to new ideologies in prison seems commonsensical, if not yet fully proved. Additionally, some evidence exists that Al-Qaeda has been, and perhaps still is, targeting inmates for recruitment (Rupp, 2006, p. 2; Cuthbertson, 2004; Brandon, 2009, p. 43; Hannah et al., 2008, p. 32).

Notably, in 2000, an Al-Qaeda training manual was recovered during a raid on a safe house in Manchester, England, in 2000. The manual "identifies Western prisoners as candidates for conversion to Islam because they may harbour hostility towards their governments" (Hamm, 2009, p. 671; Rupp, 2006, p. 2; Cuthbertson, 2004; Brandon, 2009, p. 43). More recently, the Senate Foreign Relations Committee reported that al-Qaeda has had some success in reaching out to inmates in United States. A committee report states that "a group of as many as three dozen former criminals who converted to Islam in prison . . . moved to Yemen" (U.S. Senate Committee on Foreign Relations, 2010, p. 9). The ultimate concern is that at least some of these men might return to their home country to launch attacks against Western targets. This information is certainly worrisome and cannot be ignored. At the same time, without more specifics, it is difficult to assess the significance of these reports.[2]

Finally, apart from al Qaeda's possible activities, some anecdotal evidence exists that Muslim gangs may be gaining strength in prison and may be using that strength to coerce other inmates to convert (see for example, HMCIP, 2008, p. 43). The claim is that religious extremists congregate in gang-like formations, which systemically recruit fellow inmates and, in some cases, may have ties to terrorist entities (Hamm, 2009; Allen, 2006). Such extremist Islamist gangs, it is feared, might systematically use their connections within prison with ordinary criminal networks to plan and coordinate even more sophisticated terrorist attacks.

It is difficult to know the significance of these statements, and particularly whether they highlight isolated problems or something warranting broader concern. The few scholars or researchers who have actually studied the prison system from the inside—by interviewing prisoners, correctional staff, and Muslim chaplains—offer much more tempered and optimistic statements. Hamm (2007), for example, notes:

> There is no consensus on this issue; in fact, prison chaplains, along with a growing number of wardens and FBI agents, claim that there are few documented cases of U.S. inmates joining a terrorist group while in prison. This position has been succinctly summarized in Congressional testimony by Paul Rogers, Past-President of the American Correctional Chaplains Association. "Regarding reports of prisons being infiltrated by terrorists or terrorist organizations via prison religious programs," he said, "these have been blown way out of proportion." (p. 10)

---

[2]On the other side of the ledger, one can imagine a number of reasons Al Qaeda might be reluctant to work with inmates or ex-cons: They are already in the US criminal database, may be informants and may suffer from other problems (like drugs or mental illness). Add to these considerations the difficulties in organizing and remaining undetected in a prison setting, it seems plausible that al-Qaeda's efforts to recruit cells in civil society might be a bigger concern (Hamm, 2007, p. 32).

Similarly, in the British Ministry of Justice, HMCIP is skeptical of claims that prison radicalization has reached a crisis stage:

> There was some staff concern about conversions in dispersal and young offender establishments, but this was rarely found elsewhere. Concerns about intimidation of non-Muslims, the emergence of gangs and conversions to Islam were often linked, but were backed by little evidence. . . . Similarly, in several young offender establishments, staff raised concerns over young people who had converted to Islam while in the establishment, although there was little suggestion of bullying or forcible conversions by Muslim gangs. (p. 29)

The report warned of a different danger—that through misunderstanding and over-reaction, the prison service might "turn inmates towards extremism." One official said that, "the service tended to treat all Muslim prisoners as 'potential terrorists' and, by doing so, was pushing young men to 'embrace extremism'" (HMCIP, 2010, p. 29).

In the end, we are left with some concern about the risk of prison radicalization, with no sense of the precise magnitude of the problem. Despite the lack of evidence, government policy makers must still decide what sort of response to make to the potential danger. Should the possibility of radicalization cause government officials to impose restrictions on the types of religious literature distributed in prison? Should individuals suspected of radical beliefs be segregated? Should Muslim chaplains be carefully screened and monitored? Can these steps be taken without infringing on religious freedoms?

Like many counterterrorism issues, then, the challenge is how to make policy decisions in a realm of deep uncertainty. Part two takes a closer look at how governments have, in fact, responded to the perceived crisis. In doing so, this Part provides a preliminary analysis on the coherence and appeal of the response.

II. RADICALIZATION AND RESPONSE

Despite the uncertainty about the magnitude of risk, Western countries have responded to the fears of prison radicalization with a range of policies. Broadly stated, these policies fall into two broad categories: (1) restrictive policies, which attempt to impose limiting conditions on inmates, and (2) ameliorative policies, which attempt to improve the conditions of imprisonment. The policies have not, however, been implemented in equal measure. Purposively or not, most countries have pursued a "security first" approach, in which the emphasis appears to be primarily on the first strategy, with somewhat less attention to the second.

Perhaps that is to be expected. One can see the choice between these two options as mirroring an old debate within the criminal justice system itself—between those advocating a punitive approach to crime, and those favoring a more rehabilitative, preventive approach. The United States has long favored tough-on-crime measures. With a few notable exceptions, the country has tended to follow that same strategy in its counterradicalization policy.

Restrictions, Resistance, and Radicalization

The first category of policy responses is restrictive in nature. To address the risk of radicalization, governments have implemented an array of restrictions on inmates and prison services. This section focuses on three notable restrictions—restrictions on Muslim chaplains, on high-risk prisoners, and on certain kinds of religious literature—that have been used or contemplated by prison authorities in the West.

1. Radical Imams

Some research suggests that social relationships are one of the major factors in leading an individual toward adopting an extremist ideology (Sageman, 2004). Radical religious leaders are viewed as particularly threatening since, as one commentator put it, inmates are "a captive audience" for these extremists to target (See Cuthbertson 2004, p. 18). In fact, an enormous amount of publicity has, since 9/11, focused on the threat of radical imams infiltrating the prison system.

This issue first broke into the public eye in 2003, when the *Wall Street Journal* carried an interview with Warith Deen Umar, formerly the head Muslim chaplain in the New York State prison system. Umar had retired with commendation several years earlier, but was quoted in the *Wall Street Journal* in 2003 as affirming that, "[e]ven Muslims who say they are against terrorism secretly admire and applaud [the September 11 hijackers]." According to a subsequent report, Umar also stated that he "believed black inmates who converted to Islam in prison were logical recruits for committing future terrorist attacks against the United States" (OIG, 2004a, p. 35). The news article caused Governor Pataki to respond in a press release that Umar's statements were "outrageous and deplorable."

Umar's postretirement speech heightened fears that Muslim chaplains might be spreading extremist beliefs in prison. New York Senator Chuck Schumer expressed particular concern about Islamic groups that prior to 2001 had been used to certify and screen Muslim chaplains in the Bureau of Prisons (BOP) in the United States (Schumer, 2009). Schumer subsequently asked the Office of Inspector General (OIG) to "examine the BOP's process for selecting Muslim chaplains" (p. 1). The resulting report was highly critical of the bureau's approach, noting a series of "deficiencies in how the BOP selects and supervises Muslim religious service providers" (OIG, 2004a, p. 2). Among other things, the OIG criticized the BOP for performing inadequate supervision of religious services and religious leaders.

When the report was released, the bureau was already struggling with ways to screen and hire Muslim chaplains. Immediately after 9/11, the BOP froze hiring of new prison chaplains, and the controversy over Umar kept the ban in place. The result was that for years after 9/11, the bureau hired no new Muslim chaplains (OIG, 2004a, p. 36).

Some have argued that the danger posed by Muslim chaplains has been vastly overstated (Walkin, 2009; Rupp, 2006). Whether this is true or not, the U.S. government responded aggressively to the perceived threat. The question remains whether the response generated unintended, and possibly negative, consequences.

Perhaps most significantly, the new restrictions on prison imams means that BOP suffered from a "shortage of Muslim chaplains" (OIG, 2004a). Similar shortages have been reported in state prison facilities, as well. To address this shortfall, some prison systems have relied on volunteer chaplains or even turned to Muslim inmates to conduct services. In some cases, this appears to have made the problem worse than before.

One commentator, for example, noted that, "[o]ne state prison admitted 3,000 religious volunteers in a month, an impossible number for short-staffed prison officials to monitor effectively" (Straw, 2007: 517). Ballas (2010) in an FBI report notes:

> The shortage of qualified religious providers in prisons heightens the threat of inmate radicalization. Prisoners with little training in Islam have asserted themselves as leaders among the prison population, at times misrepresenting the faith. Prison Islam incorporates violent inmate culture with religious practice. Currently, little standardization or accreditation exists to identify persons qualified to teach Islam or lead its services in prisons. Wardens rely on local endorsing agencies or simply leave it up to inmates to choose. Prison authorities are not ensuring that religious leaders have adequate training or if they espouse radical theology. (p. 4)

According to another prison chaplain, in Hamm (2007),

> [w]e are called on by the administration to monitor [the volunteer] Muslim preachers who come into the prison. The problem is that many of these volunteers go over our heads to get credentials. Also, we get no gang intelligence down here [in the chapel]. There is no officer presence in the chapel. Yet we have to abide by the chaplain's code: We won't permit one religious group to speak negatively about another. (p. 86)

Some evidence exists that the shortage of prison imams may have even contributed to the development of the JIS terrorist plot in California prisons. In that case, the chaplain said, "inmates were disenchanted with the religious offerings they received from the institution. To avoid that problem again, we must offer inmates something they are not disenchanted with" (quoted in Hamm, 2007, p. 87). Hamm adds, "[v]olunteer clergy are not the solution to this problem because they cannot be controlled."

The challenge going forward is to ensure both that there are sufficient numbers of prison chaplains, and that these chaplains are also well-screened and vetted. Whether both goals can be met in the near term is uncertain. According to Vanyur (2007), every chaplain,

> Must meet all the requirements for employment as a Federal law enforcement officer, including a field investigation, criminal background check, reference check, drug screening, and pre-employment suitability interviews and screenings. . . . Our religious contractors and volunteers are also subject to a variety of security requirements prior to being granted access to an institution, including criminal background checks, law enforcement agency checks to verify places of

residence and employment, a fingerprint check, information from employment over the previous 5 years, and drug testing. . . . Information on contractors and volunteers (whether the contractor or volunteer is being considered to help provide religious services or not) is checked against databases supported by the FBI. (p. 65)

Whether the BOP continues to face shortages of Muslim chaplains, however, is unknown. If shortages persist in the federal or state system, the question remains whether it is better to have more imams entering prison without full screening, or to leave religious leadership to the inmates within the prison system.

2. Radical Inmates

In addition to fears of radical imams in the prison system, government officials have expressed concerns about charismatic inmates who seek to recruit other inmates into their ideology. To respond to these concerns, prison officials have imposed heightened restrictions—and in some cases extremely severe restrictions—on offenders deemed to be high-risk.

Identifying high-risk individuals is relatively straightforward when it comes to inmates who have already been convicted of terrorist offenses. The more challenging task is to identify inmates in the general prison population who might be seeking to radicalize others, or who might be vulnerable to the radicalizing influence of others. Doing so means developing stronger intelligence capacities in prison. At least in some states, those capacities seem to be woefully underresourced. In California, for example, there are 125 gang investigators for the more than 150,000 inmates in the prison system (Hamm, 2009). Lack of resources also means states must make hard choices about the kinds of intelligence activities deemed appropriate. For example, greater use of snitches in prison may provide intelligence benefits but may also alienate inmates who deem such efforts heavy-handed and duplicitous.

Even after high-risk inmates are identified, the question remains what to do with them. In the United States, the typical response has been to isolate these individuals, either in Guantanamo Bay or in special facilities called "Communications Management Units." Inmates sent to these facilities are subject to intensive monitoring and intrusive supervision (Vanyur, 2007). Needless to say, these programs have been the subject of controversy, with questions raised about whether the offenders sent to these facilities are the most dangerous, whether the conditions of confinement are humane, and whether appropriate procedures are in place to ensure a fair adjudication of individual cases.

Finally, in addition to these restrictions, some institutions have considered making institutional changes to the prison system to reduce the ability of extremist inmates to recruit other individuals. For example, one initiative in the Bureau of Prisons has "eliminated most institution-based inmate organizations with community ties to control the influence that outside entities have on Federal inmates" (Vanyur, 2007, p. 63). The British Ministry has "attempted to curb the growth of radical Islam by restricting communal prayers and the reading of the Koran during work breaks" (Leppard, 2008).

The Justice Department's Office of Inspector General (OIG) has expressed particular concerns about inmates leading religious services. Religious services are one of the few places where inmates can congregate together with relative ease. The OIG report in 2004 noted that supervision of religious services in BOP facilities was inconsistent, and in some cases "rely on chaplains to provide supervision" of inmates. Moreover, the report added, "it was apparent to us that at certain facilities the supervising correctional officers and the associate warden who oversees chaplaincy services were not familiar with chapel activities" (OIG, 2004a, p. 40). The central concern is that inmates might use the pulpit, in effect, as a platform for radicalization. As the OIG (2004a) stated:

> Inmates are radicalized primarily by other inmates. We do not believe that it is appropriate for inmates to assume leadership positions in BOP facilities, including the position of surrogate chaplain. We recommend that the BOP take steps to reduce inmate-led religious services. (p. 54)

The OIG (2004a) recommended increased supervision of religious services by correctional staff, and restrictions on inmates leading religious services, including use of audio monitoring where inmate-led services were necessary. Needless to say, these proposals must be implemented carefully and thoughtfully, as all have the potential, if imposed in an overly-broad or intrusive manner, to impinge on inmates' religious freedoms. Even if lawful, they can easily be viewed by inmates as impinging on those rights.

3. Restricting Literature in Prison

A third kind of restriction limits the kinds of reading materials available to inmates in prison. Although authorities have pursued various approaches, one particularly notable—and troubling—initiative was undertaken by the federal Bureau of Prisons in 2004. That year, the BOP decided it would sanitize its prison libraries to purge them of extremist literature. The bureau's initiative was in response to a highly critical report issued by the Department of Justice's Office of Inspector General that highlighted a series of shortcomings in the bureau's efforts to counter prison radicalization.

In addition to mentioning the bureau's lax screening of Muslim chaplains, discussed earlier, the report also highlighted the potential availability of extremist literature in the prison system. The OIG's 2004 report stated that:

> Supervision of chapel libraries is not as thorough as it should be. None of the chaplains at the facilities that we visited was able to produce an inventory of the books and videos available to the inmates, and it did not appear that these materials had been evaluated after the terrorist attacks of September 11. We recommend that the BOP undertake an inventory of chapel books and videos to confirm that they are permissible under BOP security policies. The BOP also should consider maintaining a central registry of acceptable material to prevent duplication of effort when reviewing these materials. (p. 55)

In response, the BOP indicated that it would examine library materials "for endorsement of violence [or] support for domestic or foreign terrorism" and that it would provide a list of materials appropriate for circulation, "which can be used for 'future library acquisitions." The review was to be completed by June 1, 2005 (OIG, 2004b, p. 17).

Initially, the BOP planned to review existing collections to determine which materials should be prohibited. However, according to news reports, the bureau quickly determined that this approach would be too burdensome (Banerjee, 2007). Instead, the bureau decided it would simply create a list of *approved* books, and that all books that did not appear on the list would be discarded. To avoid charges of discrimination, the lists would cover all significant religions, not just Islam.

To implement the project, the BOP called upon unidentified experts "to produce lists of up to 150 book titles and 150 multimedia resources for each of 20 religions or religious categories—everything from Baha'ism to Yoruba" (Goodstein, 2007). All other materials would be eliminated. At the same time, the bureau failed to allocate additional funds to buy books left on the list. The result was that "after the shelves were cleared of books not on the lists, few remained" (Goodstein, 2007).

One Muslim inmate in New York said that, after unapproved books were eliminated, the "only thing left on the sole shelf devoted to Islam was a Koran and a few volumes of sayings of the Prophet Muhammad" (Goodstein, 2007). A representative of a Jewish organization noted that the same prison had an "extensive library of Jewish religious books, many of them donated." After the plan was implemented, "[i]t was decimated. Three-quarters of the Jewish books were taken off the shelves" (Goodstein, 2007).

Others noted that the list of accepted materials seemed to favor certain viewpoints over others, perhaps reflecting the preferences of the list's author. Reviewing the materials, one Christian scholar concluded the lists "show a bias toward evangelical popularism and Calvinism," but apparently "lacked materials from early church fathers, liberal theologians and major Protestant denominations" (Goodstein, 2007). Two thirds of the titles on the list for Judaism were from the same Orthodox publishing house (ibid).

Once publicized, the plan triggered criticism from religious groups across the political and religious spectrum, including leading U.S. denominations (ibid). Lawsuits were also filed against the prison system claiming that the removal of reading materials absent any showing of a threat violated First Amendment guarantees of religious freedom.

The barrage of criticism seemed to take the Bureau of Prisons by surprise. Within months, the bureau declared that it would repeal its policy and return most of the materials to the prison libraries (Banerjee, 2007). Just to make sure the bureau was serious, Congress followed up with the passage of the Second Chance Act of 2007. The Act declared that the bureau must "discontinue the Standardized Chapel Library project, or any other project by whatever designation that seeks to compile, list, or otherwise restrict prisoners' access to reading materials, audiotapes, videotapes, or any other materials made available in a chapel library." The Act was signed into law by President Bush on April 9, 2008.

The ill-fated library project illustrates in rather sharp relief some of the common problems that arise when a prison institution responds to radicalization fears. Facing a possible, but not proven, concern about extremist literature in the prison system, the bureau implemented a highly intrusive and overly broad ban on religious materials, one that seemed to show little regard for the religious freedoms of individual inmates. The approach, as the head of one Christian group put it, was like "swatting a fly with a sledgehammer" (Goodstein, 2007).

Moreover, the BOP failed to ask even the most basic questions about the possible threat such as whether such materials were widely available in prison and whether they were influential. One prison chaplain questioned those basic assumptions, noting that "chaplains routinely reject any materials that incite violence or disparage, and donated materials already had to be approved by prison officials" (Goodstein, 2007).

The bureau also seemed to ignore approaches that were much more tailored, like creating a list of *prohibited* books rather than approved ones. One might even wonder whether the widespread removal of books might have actually proved counterproductive, leaving inmates angry, alienated, and bored. One final question is just as troubling: If the initiatives had not infringed the rights of mainstream denominations, would the repeal have been accomplished so quickly and easily?

Ameliorative Policies

The principal thrust of government efforts to date has been to counter the risk of radicalization by implementing restrictive policies. A different approach, however, is also feasible. Ameliorative policies focus primarily on alleviating the conditions of prison life that can make inmates more receptive to extremist influence. These ameliorative efforts range from extremely expensive and dramatic changes in the prison system, to more tailored, less ambitious reform proposals.

1. Improve Prison Conditions

Perhaps the most ambitious kind of proposal seeks to redress basic deficiencies in the conditions of prison life. Overcrowded prisons, poor health care, violence-prone facilities are all pandemic in parts of the U.S. prison system. A number of state correctional systems suffer from such widespread deficiencies that federal courts have intervened to mandate improvements.[3]

---

[3]California is a particularly dramatic example. The prison system is wildly overcrowded, currently operating at nearly 200% of capacity. It is simultaneously underfunded and neglected, yielding a system where health care and other necessities are provided in a wholly inadequate manner according to a number of federal courts. Indeed, a two-decade long period of litigation culminated with dramatic interventions by the federal courts over the past few years. In 2005, the federal courts appointed a "receiver" to take over the prison medical system and to institute needed reforms. Then, this past year, the Supreme Court ordered the release of 30–40,000 prisoners (nearly one quarter of the entire prison system). *Brown v. Plata*, 131 S.Ct. 1910 (2011).

These kinds of humiliating and inhumane conditions are widely thought to contribute to an atmosphere that allows gangs and other violent extremists to flourish. Improving the prison environment and making prison life a less depriving experience for inmates could reduce the radicalization potential among Muslim and other categories of inmates (Hamm, 2009, p. 673).

The difficulty, of course, lies in developing an effective response. In some correctional facilities, problems of overcrowding and deficient services are so pervasive that any redress will require wide-ranging structural reform in the system. At a basic level, for example, any reduction in overcrowding calls for either a significant reduction in prison populations or a significant increase in expenditures for prison. The former is widely seen as politically infeasible, the latter financially impossible. Absent extraordinary political leadership, or continued intervention by the federal courts, little improvement can be expected in the near term.

2. Expand Rehabilitation Programs

If improving basic prison conditions requires wide-ranging reform, a second set of ameliorative efforts is more focused in its objectives. These efforts attempt to address the concern that inmates leave prison lacking even basic educational and vocational skills. Without basic skills, and with the added burden of a criminal record, inmates face serious obstacles in attempting to reintegrate back into society. Subsequent failure, and the resulting alienation from society, may contribute to the possibility of radicalization after release.

One response is to expand vocational and educational opportunities for inmates in prison. Another is to expand reentry programs for high-risk offenders to help them transition to a law-abiding life upon their release. The U.S. Bureau of Prisons appears to recognize the importance of these steps in the context of its counter- radicalization efforts. In testimony before Congress, one senior bureau official, Vanyur (2007) stated:

> In addition to managing and monitoring inmates who could attempt to radicalize other inmates, we help inmates become less vulnerable to any such attempts. Experts have identified the societal marginalization of inmates as a key factor in their becoming radicalized. Our agency provides inmates with a broad variety of programs that are proven to assist in the development of key skills, thereby minimizing the likelihood of the inmates being marginalized. The programs we provide include work in prison industries and other institution jobs, vocational training, education, substance abuse treatment, religious programs, and other skills-building and pro-social values programs. (p. 64)

Though not expressly formulated as a counterradicalization program, a number of states and locales have also implemented reentry programs to assist individual offenders integrate better into society after their release, as well (American Bar Association, 2008).

Nonetheless, despite these efforts, rehabilitation initiatives face significant political headwinds. Programs that offer social services, like vocational and educational opportunities, have been deemphasized over the past two decades, as the United States has embraced an increasingly punitive ideology. Recent budgetary pressures have only exacerbated that trend. In a 2010 report, the Vera Institute of Justice found that 20 of the 37 states examined had cut rehabilitation programming in response to budgetary pressures, and nine decreased health services.

Britain appears more open to providing these kinds of rehabilitation programs. The Ministry of Justice acknowledges the importance of expanding educational and vocational training. Several local communities have developed innovative reentry programs, teaming up with local mosques to deal specifically with Muslim prisoners upon their release. For example, in the 2010 report from Ministry of Justice, HMCIP states:

> In Rochester, the chaplaincy team had set up an innovative work placement in the local mosque specifically for Muslim prisoners. It offered a frank account of life in prison to those in the community to promote understanding of prison life and to deter offending. (p. 44)

A similar program has been instituted in East London. Robin Tuddenham, the Group Director for Safer and Stronger Communities, in a report from the U.K. House of Commons, Communities and Local Government Committee 2010, described some of the lessons learned in that effort:

> You have to work very closely with the police on a risk-based approach to work with those individuals, particularly individuals coming out of prison. What I have been doing until recently in East London is developing a regional East London project for people coming out of prison who have been radicalized in prison. That is a real cause of concern. Their attitude to extremism and recruitment in prison is leading them to be very vulnerable coming into the community. I like to see it in terms of vulnerable people and the safeguarding work with particular individuals at risk. (p. 35)

Even in Britain, however, no nationwide effort has been made to evaluate these programs or to coordinate a response to inmates leaving prison. Do these programs work? How should they be structured? Should they be open to all inmates, or just to certain categories of high-risk offenders? All of those questions remain to be answered.

3. Improve Treatment of Inmates

The policies discussed thus far—improving the conditions of prison and expanding rehabilitation services—have long been part of progressive attempts to reform the prison system in the United States for all inmates. The final ameliorative proposal differs from these others because it focuses primarily on the treatment of Muslim inmates themselves. Specifically, the proposal addresses concerns that Muslim inmates may be subject to discriminatory or derogatory treatment from correctional staff, and that this conduct may fuel a movement toward extremism.

Mistreatment of Muslim inmates can occur for any number of reasons. Correctional staff, of course, reflects the values of society at large. To the extent members of the public hold negative stereotypes about Islam, one can expect similar views to be held by members of the correctional staff as well. Maltreatment can occur, as well, because of ignorance about the religious principles and requirements of the religion.

These kinds of problems may be exacerbated by the institutional demands of prison bureaucracies. By their very nature, these bureaucracies emphasize security. As a result, inmates with special needs—such as special food and religious service requirements—can be viewed as problematic and burdensome. In 2010, HMCIP emphasized this point, noting concerns that some staff members focus "solely on Muslims as potential or actual extremists" (p. 5). These problems are heightened in prisons plagued by over-crowding and violence, where staff are understaffed and underresourced. Addressing these kinds of problems will require changes in the core structure of prison administra-tion, an extremely challenging goal even in less constrained budgetary situations.

Limited data exist in the United States on the degree of staff mistreatment of Muslim inmates. But Britain has collected self-reporting data from Muslim inmates which suggests that significant issues exist. According to the Ministry of Justice's 2010 report, HMCIP states:

> Forty-nine per cent of mixed heritage Muslims said they had been victimised by staff compared with 25% of mixed heritage non-Muslims. Thirty-eight per cent of black Muslims (compared with 32% of non-Muslims), 35% of Asian Muslims (compared with 24% of non-Muslims), and 29% of white Muslims (compared with 22% of non-Muslims) said the same. (p. 38)

The Ministry of Justice report concludes that part of the problem is due to a lack of training, and to staff's limited understanding of Islam. The result, says the Ministry, is not only a failure of religious sensitivity, but also threat to public safety. Lacking a basic understanding of religious practices, the staff remains unable to recognize and confront real risks where they exist.

Addressing concerns about staff treatment of Muslim inmates has typically focused on staff training, including educating staff about the religious requirements of Islam in general and about specific signs of radicalization in particular. The hope is that such efforts will sensitize staff to the special needs and demands of the Muslim religion. In the United States, efforts of this sort are inconsistent. A few states have publicized efforts to educate their staff about the basic principles of Islam (Gelinas, 2010). In addition, the Bureau of Prisons has emphasized the impor-tance of additional staff training on how to treat Muslim inmates. However, the focus of this training seems primarily directed at recognizing and managing signs of radicalization (Vanyur, 2010). Indeed, the Office of Inspector General (2004) has specifically warned that a lack of knowledge of Islam may hinder staff's "ability to recognize radical Islamist messages that are inappropriate in BOP facilities." Thus, the Inspector General's office continues,

> We believe that the BOP should provide basic training to its staff members who supervise Muslim religious services so that they will be familiar with accepted prayer and service rituals, understand Islamic terminology, and rec-ognize messages that violate BOP security policy. (p. 54)

The Ministry of Justice, HM Prison Service, appears more proactive in developing a coordinated response to the problem:

> In 2007, the Prison Service embarked on a programme of training to help staff identify and respond to signs of radicalisation and, even though it recognised the risks of stereotyping, the effect has been to encourage a focus on Muslims as potential extremists. (p. 11)

In its recent report, the Ministry acknowledged that its efforts have not been fully adequate. But it affirmed the need for a national response to the problem:

> It is essential that the National Offender Management Service develops a strategy, with support and training, for effective staff engagement with Muslims as individual prisoners with specific risks and needs, rather than as part of a separate and troubling group. Without that, there is a real risk of a self-fulfilling prophecy: that the prison experience will create or entrench alienation and disaffection, so that prisons release into the community young men who are more likely to offend, or even embrace extremism. (p. 5)

Whether Britain moves forward with such a plan remains to be seen.

CONCLUSIONS AND IMPLICATIONS

The present chapter has examined the available data concerning the risk of radicalization among Muslims in Western prisons. The central goal has been to gain insight into the nature and magnitude of the potential threat, and to explore how various countries have responded to the perceived danger. This was done while addressing the needs of the Muslim inmate population along with their perceived radicalization propensity, and the challenges they present to the correctional facilities that houses them.

The analysis suggests that a lack of reliable information dominates research on radicalization in Western prisons. Very little is known about the degree to which radicalization occurs, about which segments of the prison population are potentially at risk, and about the severity of the threat of terrorist activity behind bars. In fact, most countries in the West know very little about their Muslim inmate population. Even basic facts, like demographic characteristics, are rarely collected. Based on the current state of the literature, it is simply impossible to make an accurate assessment of the risk of radicalization.

Similarly, there is no integrated effort at the national or international level to combat prison radicalization. In some cases, authorities have implemented—or at least considered—restrictive measures imposing limitations on available literature, increasing screening of prison imams, and isolating extremist inmates from other prisoners. However, a comprehensive rationale for implementing many of these policies seems often to be absent, as are regular evaluations of implemented policies.

The implication is that policy makers are operating with little empirical guidance as they attempt to develop a counterradicalization program in prison. As such, it is often unclear whether or which interventions are necessary. Policy development, in short, is sometimes driven not by careful analysis, but to a large extent, by prevailing sentiments and emotions. Our goal is not to blame policy makers for ineffective policies, but to raise awareness of the need for an integrated effort—both in research and policy—in order to advance the understanding of and inform the response to the threat of prison radicalization.

There are, of course, a few limitations to this study. The views presented here are formed on the basis of open and secondary sources. Little access exists to primary data so that claims cannot be assessed on the basis of qualitative, let alone quantitative, primary data. This is a general problem in terrorism studies, where the lack of evidence and concrete, objective information implies that statement should not be accepted unchallenged. It underscores the critical need for additional empirical work in this area.

RECOMMENDATIONS FOR RESEARCHERS

To address this information gap, substantial research needs to be conducted that involves both qualitative and quantitative data collection. To date, an abundance of questions remains unanswered.

Most prominently, insight is needed into the most basic facts. What are the main characteristics of our prison populations, not only in terms of demographics but also in terms of belief systems and convictions? In order to be able to gauge the risk of radicalization, researchers need to be able to assess the sociodemographic distribution of the inmate population and to examine which segments might be vulnerable to radicalization, and why. Obviously, this raises an abundance of questions about privacy and individual rights, and prison authorities might be reluctant to allow researchers into their prison to gather such information among the inmates. Although these considerations are perfectly legitimate, the problem is that without detailed information about the social and psychological well-being of prisoners, efforts to evaluate the risks posed by prison radicalization will remain practically impossible.

Moreover, fundamental research is required into the underlying processes of prison radicalization. To understand which inmates might be susceptible to radicalization or extremist influence, researchers need insight into the dynamic interplay between contributing factors operating at different levels: institutional, social, and individual. Only by understanding how the custodial setting interacts with the social and personal factors contributing to the radicalization process can attempts be made to predict who is at risk and who is not. How do these factors differ from different types of prison radicalization, including religious, nationalist, or supremacist variations? Which processes are responsible for the spread and contamination of radical beliefs among inmate populations?

A first hint at explaining the apparent ease with which extremist ideologies spread through prisons might be found in the presence—and specific characteristics—of social networks. Within a prison context, social relationships are particularly important in that they can fulfill a number of essential needs for inmates. For example, social networks can fulfill practical needs such as offering security and protection, facilitating information gathering, or helping inmates obtain difficult-to-obtain goods, including contraband. In addition, social networks can fulfill social needs, including the need to belong, to gain social status, to receive affection, and to maintain self-confidence.

Researchers also need to understand the complex ways in which social networks relate to prison radicalization. For example, it is well known that social networks can have a positive effect on people's well-being. In a sense, social networks can function as a *buffer* against negative influences in prison. For instance, social networks might be able to counteract the radicalizing effect of experiences of discrimination, marginalization, and isolation, by contributing to inmates' social and psychological well-being.

Of course, networks can also affect the radicalization potential among its members in a negative sense. They can be a source of intergroup conflict and gang violence, and they can transmit negative attitudes and criminal behaviour throughout the prison population. Understanding the factors that lead the negative features of social networks to overwhelm the positive ones will be a critical part of the research agenda, as will a more complete understanding of the special risks posed by individuals at the periphery of these groups who may not be properly embedded in any social group.

Equally important is the need to investigate the role of social networks in the transition of inmates from prison to society. For example, the question arises whether social networks established in prison can survive after an inmate is released into society. That is to say, to what extent do extremist networks cross prison walls? How easily and often do ex-felons maintain their connection with related networks outside prison? What does the answer to that question mean for the propensity to commit violent acts after detention? In general, a more comprehensive understanding about how structural characteristics of social networks affect an inmates' susceptibility to radicalization would provide an important cornerstone for the development of counterradicalization efforts.

One further focus for future research should be the dynamics of religious conversion and its relation to radicalization. Converts are often seen as particularly vulnerable to radicalization, though concrete information on the subject is virtually absent. Are converts indeed more susceptible to radicalization, and if so, why? What are the figures, what are the reasons for conversion, what determines whether converts radicalize or not? To determine whether heightened attention on converts is justifiable, a thorough understanding of this group, its social position in the prison system and its role in the spread of extremist thought will be indispensable.

POLICY IMPLICATIONS

Given the lack of information on prison radicalization today, policy makers face special challenges in understanding the dimensions of the threat and in crafting a response. As research progresses in different countries, policy makers will need to be aware how country-specific characteristics—including demographics, the socio-political climate, institutional characteristics of the penitentiary system, and cultural and historical patterns—can affect the risk of prison radicalization and appropriate responses.

Similarly, governments need to be cautious in relying on internationally established "best practices." Policies that appear to be effective in one country might produce suboptimal or counterproductive outcomes in another country. In a similar vein, policies that were successful in the past or aimed at other populations will not necessarily be successful now. Policies must be considered, in this regard, in light of the unique cultural, historic, and political characteristics of the individual national contexts.

In line with this, policy makers need to be aware of potential unintended consequences of their policy decisions in both the short and the longer run. Policies that produce favorable results in the near term might elicit negative consequences over extended periods of time. For example, imposing severely restrictive prison regimes on extremist inmates might erect barriers against recruitment efforts by these inmates, but might simultaneously contribute to shaping an environment that is conducive to radicalization.

Sensitivity to individual offender circumstances will be critical. Since only a small minority of the prison population appears to be susceptible to radicalization, standardized interventions that are aimed at large subgroups (e.g., Muslims in general) can cause resentment and run the risk of stigmatizing and unduly marginalizing groups of people. Rather, the implementation of restrictive measures should be grounded whenever possible on individual risk assessments, to temper accusations of institutionalized discrimination.

At the same time, governments and prison authorities must resist the temptation to focus wholly on restrictive measures. A balanced approach will incorporate ameliorative efforts that help to prepare inmates for their return into society. Governments should invest in developing programs that encourage extremist inmates to renounce violent ideologies and move toward more peaceful interpretations. Such interventions should start at the moment inmates enter the prison system and carry on after the inmates are released.

Additionally, a balanced approach requires prison authorities to be cognizant of the perceived or real infringements on individual or religious freedoms. Prison authorities need to be aware that imposing restrictive measures on particular groups of inmates can be met by antagonism and frustration. Authorities need to deal sensitively with inmates' complaints or accusations. Failure to do so will likely backfire by promoting protests or extremist thought.

To ensure legitimacy and broad acceptance, government policies and interventions must be thoroughly explicated. Policy subjects, goals, target populations, divisions of responsibility and expectations about policy outcomes need to be unambiguously articulated to facilitate transparency and assessment. Moreover, policies and interventions have to be evaluated on a regular basis to ensure their efficacy. Reliable indicators have to be defined according to which intended policy outcomes can be measured.

Ultimately, the nations of the West will need to develop a coordinated and integrated effort to assess the threat of prison radicalization and to develop a coherent and effective response. This will take a renewed appreciation of how little is currently known about this complex subject, and a commitment to developing policies that are nuanced, flexible, and based on facts rather than emotion.

DISCUSSION QUESTIONS

1. The chapter discusses the causes of radicalization among Muslims in prison. However, many kinds of extremists can be found in the prison system, like white supremacists, animal rights liberationists, and anarchists. Do you think that the underlying causes for these different types of radicalization are the same, or that there are differences in the factors that produce different kinds of extremism?

2. The authors argue that no coherent approach currently exists to combat radicalization in prison. In crafting an appropriate response to this possible threat, can lessons be learned from policies that deal with other kinds of special needs populations in prison? Similarly, what can be learned from rehabilitation programs for other kinds of offenders, like sexual offenders or drug addicts?

3. When confronted with the potential threat of religious radicalization in prison, governments face a pressing dilemma to maintain a delicate balance between religious rights and public safety. To what extent should the government be able to restrict the religious freedoms of inmates in order to prevent radicalization?

SUGGESTED READINGS

Brandon, J. (2009). *Unlocking al-Qaeda: Islamist extremism in British prisons.* London, England: Quilliam Foundation.

Hamm, M. S. (2007). *Terrorist recruitment in American correctional institutions: An exploratory study of non-traditional faith groups.* NCJ 220957. Washington, DC: U.S. Department of Justice, National Institute of Justice.

Hamm, M. S. (2009). Prison Islam in the age of sacred terror. *British Journal of Criminology, 49*(5): 667–685.

Hannah, G., Clutterbuck, L., & Rubin, J. (2008). *Radicalization or rehabilitation: Understanding the challenge of extremist and radicalized prisoners.* Cambridge, England: RAND Corporation.

Neumann, P. (Ed.). (2010). Prisons and terrorism. Radicalisation and de-radicalisation in 15 countries. International Centre for the Study of Radicalisation and Political Violence. Retrieved from http://icsr.info/publications/papers/1277699166PrisonsandTerrorism RadicalisationandDeradicalisationin15Countries.pdf

REFERENCES

Al Qaeda in Yemen and Somalia: A Ticking Time Bomb: A Report to the Committee on Foreign Relations (S. Rpt. 111–40), U.S. Senate, 111th Cong. (2010).

Allen, C. (2006). (Muslim) Boyz-n-the-Hood. *International Institute for the Study of Islam in the Modern World Review, 18.*

American Bar Association. (2008). *Survey on Reentry.* Washington DC: The American Bar Association Criminal Justice Section.

Ballas, D. A. (2010). Prisoner radicalization. *FBI Law Enforcement Bulletin, 79*(10), 2–5.

Banerjee, N. (2007, September 27). Prisons to restore purged religious books. *New York Times.* Retrieved from http://www.nytimes.com/2007/09/27/washington/27prison.html

BBC News. (2005, 29 July). *Do prisons radicalise inmates?* Retrieved from http://news.bbc.co.uk/2/hi/uk_news/4727723.stm

Brandon, J. (2009). *Unlocking al-Qaeda: Islamist extremism in British prisons.* London, England: Quilliam Foundation.

Brown, E. G., Jr. (2009). *Organized crime in California. 2009 annual report to the California legislature.* Sacramento: California Department of Justice, Bureau of Investigation and Intelligence. Retrieved from http://ag.ca.gov/publications/org_crime2009.pdf

Carlile, J. (2006, July 8). *Islamic radicalization of Europe's jails?* Msnbc.com. Retrieved from http://www.msnbc.msn.com/id/13733782/ns/world_news-islam_in_europe/t/islamic-radicalization-feared-europes-jails/

Clarke, M., & Soria, V. (2010, August). Terrorism: The new wave. *Royal United Services Institute Journal, 150*(4).

Combelles Siegel, P. (2006, July 28). Radical Islam and the French Muslim prison population. *The Jamestown Foundation Terrorism Monitor, 4*(15). Available at http://www.jamestown.org

Cuthbertson, I. M. (2004). Prisons and the education of terrorists. *World Policy Journal, 21*(3), 15–22.

Dix-Richardson, F. (2002). Resistance to conversion to Islam among African American women inmates. *Journal of Offender Rehabilitation, 35*(3), 107–124.

Doyle, J. (2010, August 27). Muslim inmates 'turning to terror' as think tank says convicted terrorists are radicalising fellow inmates. *Mail Online.* Retrieved from http://www.dailymail.co.uk/news/article-1306570/Muslim-inmates-turning-terror-think-tank-says-terrorists-radicalising-fellow-inmates.html

Gelinas, J. (2010). *More inmates report to be Muslim.* South Carolina Department of Corrections. Retrieved from http://www.corrections.com/news/article/23771-more-inmates-report-to-be-muslim

Goodstein, L. (2007, September 21). Prisons purging books on faith from libraries. *New York Times.* Retrieved from http://www.nytimes.com/2007/09/10/us/10prison.html?pagewanted=all

Hamm, M. S. (2007). *Terrorist recruitment in American correctional institutions: An exploratory study of non-traditional faith groups.* NCJ 220957. Washington, DC: U.S. Department of Justice, National Institute of Justice.

Hamm, M. S. (2009). Prison Islam in the age of sacred terror. *British Journal of Criminology, 49*(5): 667–685.

Hannah, G., Clutterbuck, L., & Rubin, J. (2008). *Radicalization or rehabilitation: Understanding the challenge of extremist and radicalized prisoners.* Cambridge, England: RAND Corporation.

Hernandez, J. C., & Chan, S. (2009, May 21). N.Y. bomb plot suspects acted alone, police say. *New York Times*. Retrieved from http://www.nytimes.com/2009/05/22/nyregion/22terror .html?pagewanted=all

HM Chief Inspector of Prisons. (2010). *Muslim prisoners' experiences: A thematic review*. (Online Report), HMIP. Retrieved from http://www.official-documents.gov.uk/document/ hc1012/hc14/1454/1454.pdf

Jenkins, B. M. (2010). *Would-be warriors: Incidents of jihadist terrorist radicalization in the united states since September 11, 2001*. Santa Monica, CA : RAND Corporation.

Khosrokhavar, F. (2004). *L'Islam dans les prisons*. Paris, France: Balland.

Kushner, H. (2006). In D. G. Steil (2011, May 4), *The threat to America from the south: Iran and self-propelled fully submersible watercraft*. Newport, RI: Naval War College, Joint Military Operations Department.

Leppard, D. (2008, September 28). Al-Qaeda bid to recruit inmates. *Sunday Times*. Retrieved from http://www.timesplus.co.uk/tto/news/?login=false&url=http%3A%2F%2Fwww .thetimes.co.uk%2Ftto%2Fnews%2Fuk%2Fcrime%2F

Mueller, R. (2006, June 23). *The threat of homegrown terrorism*. Remarks delivered at City Club, Cleveland, OH.

Neumann, P. (Ed.). (2010). *Prisons and terrorism. Radicalisation and de-radicalisation in 15 countries. International Centre for the Study of Radicalisation and Political Violence*. Retrieved from http://icsr.info/publications/papers/1277699166PrisonsandTerrorismRad icalisationandDeradicalisationin15Countries.pdf

Office of the Inspector General. (2004a). *A review of the federal bureau of prisons' selection of Muslim religious services providers*. U.S. Department of Justice, Office of the Inspector General.

Office of the Inspector General. (2004b). *Analysis of the response by the federal bureau of prisons to recommendations in the OIG's April 2004 report on the selection of Muslim religious services providers*. U.S. Department of Justice, Office of the Inspector General.

PEW Center on the States. (2010). *Prison count 2010—state population declines for the first time in 38 years*. Washington, DC: Author.

Rotella, S. (2004, February 23). Holy water, hashish and jihad. *Los Angeles Times*. Retrieved from http://www.latimes.com/

Rupp, E. E. (2006). *America's prisons: Radical Islam's new recruiting ground? A test of the Infiltration-Conversion-Radicalization hypothesis*. (Unpublished Dissertation). Roosevelt University, Chicago, IL.

Sageman, M. (2004). *Understanding terror networks*. Philadelphia: University of Pennsylvania Press.

Schumer, C. Quote from U.S. Congress. Hearing before the Subcommittee on Terrorism, Technology, and Homeland Security of the Committee on the Judiciary. *"Terrorism: Growing Wahhabi influence in the United States."* (2003, June 26). Available at http:// www.judiciary.senate.gov/resources/transcripts/108transcripts.cfm

Second Chance Act of 2007, Pub. L. No. 110–199, § 214, 122 STAT. 657 (2008).

Smith, J. (1999). *Islam in America*. New York, NY: Columbia University Press.

Straw, J. (2007). Prisons: Fostering extremism? *Security Management, 51*. Retrieved from http://www.securitymanagement.com/article/prisons-fostering-extremism

Travis, A., & Gillan, A. (2005, July 28). Bomb suspect 'became a militant' in prison. *The Guardian*. Retrieved from http://www.guardian.co.uk/uk/2005/jul/28/july7 .politics

U.K. House of Commons. Communities and Local Government Committee. *"Preventing violent extremism."* (2010, March 16). Available at http://www.publications.parliament .uk/pa/cm200910/cmselect/cmcomloc/65/65.pdf

U.S. Department of Homeland Security. (2007, January 11). Homeland Security Advisory Council's Future of Terrorism Task Force. Retrieved from http://www.dhs.gov/xlibrary/ assets/hsac-future-terrorism-pres-011107.pdf

U.S. Senate Committee on Foreign Relations, Majority Staff. (2010). *Al Qaeda in Yemen and Somalia: A ticking time bomb: A report to the committee on foreign relations.* (S. Rpt. 111–40). U.S. Senate, 111th Congress. Washington, DC: U.S. Government Printing Office.

Van Duyn, D. Quote from: U.S. Congress. Hearing before the Committee on Homeland Security and Governmental affairs. *"Prison radicalization: Are terrorist cells forming in U.S. cell blocks?"* (2006, September 19). Available at http://www.google.com/ search?sourceid=navclient&ie=UTF-8&rlz=1T4SKPB_enUS372US372&q=Prison+radic alization%3a+Are+terrorist+cells+forming+in+U.S.+cell+blocks%3f

Vanyur, J. M. Quote from U.S. Congress. Hearing before the Subcommittee on Intelligence, Information Sharing, and Terrorism Risk Assessment of the Committee on Homeland Security. *"Radicalization, information sharing and community outreach: Protecting the homeland from home grown terror."* (2007, April 5). Available at http://www.gpo.gov

Vera Institute of Justice. (2010). *The fiscal crisis in corrections: Rethinking policies and practices.* New York, NY: Author.

Walkin, D. J. (2009, May 23). Imams reject talk that Islam radicalizes inmates. *New York Times.* Retrieved from http://www.nytimes.com/2009/05/24/nyregion/24convert.html

Waller, J. M. Quote from U.S. Congress. Hearing before the Subcommittee on Terrorism, Technology, and Homeland Security of the Committee on the Judiciary Terrorism. *"Radical Islamic influence of chaplaincy of the United States military and prisons."* (2002, October 14). Available at http://www.judiciary.senate.gov/resources/transcripts/ 108transcripts.cfm

Wilner, A. (2010). *From rehabilitation to recruitment: Canadian prison radicalization and Islamist terrorism.* Ottawa, ON, Canada: Macdonald-Laurier Institute.

Zoll, R. (2005, June 4). American prisons become political, religious battleground over Islam. *Associated Press.*

CHAPTER 16

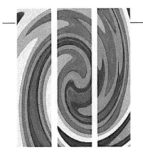

Substance Use and Addiction and American Prison and Jail Inmates[1]

Hung-En Sung, Linda Richter, Roger Vaughan, and Susan E. Foster

The United States has the highest incarceration rate in the world, driven in large part by crime linked to alcohol and other drug use and addiction. Two thirds of America's inmates meet medical criteria for the complex brain disease of addiction, yet only 11% of them receive any form of professional treatment. Both substance use and high rates of incarceration destroy lives, break up families, and devastate communities. Worse, they exacerbate and reinforce each other in a desperate cycle of addiction and social exclusion that has wreaked havoc among the most vulnerable segments of our population.

In this chapter, we report results from an exhaustive analysis of the extent to which alcohol and other drugs are implicated in the crimes and incarceration of America's prison population. We explain how despite greater recognition of the problem and potential solutions, our country has allowed the population of substance-involved inmates crowding our prisons and jails—and the related costs and crimes—to increase. And, most importantly, we set out steps our society can take to reduce crime and the taxpayer costs of prisons by addressing treatment needs of offenders while holding them accountable for their crimes.

The solution to the problem is neither complex nor financially prohibitive. America provides treatment to prisoners for other chronic disease like hypertension and diabetes. It should do so for the chronic disease of addiction, particularly because treatment offers the added benefits of significant reductions in crime and incarceration costs. What is required is for public officials to stop squandering

---

[1]This chapter is an abridged version of the report *Behind Bars II: Substance Abuse and America's Prison Population* published by the National Center on Addiction and Substance Abuse (CASA) at Columbia University, 2010, with additional commentary. The authors of this chapter were the primary staff responsible for the CASA report.

459

taxpayer dollars building more and more prisons to incarcerate men and women whose core problem is alcohol and other drug addiction.

TRENDS AND PREVALENCE OF SUBSTANCE INVOLVEMENT OF JAIL AND PRISON INMATES

Despite the unprecedented decline in violent and property crimes during the past 15 years, incarcerations linked to alcohol and other drugs have continued to grow. More substance-involved offenders are crowding our prisons and jails than ever before as our nation's criminal justice system maintains a costly loop of untreated addiction and criminal recidivism.

Between 1996 and 2006,[2] the U.S. prison population grew by 12.5% (The National Center on Addiction and Substance Abuse at Columbia University [CASA], 2010s, 2010t). In 2006, 2.3 million American adults were incarcerated in federal (0.2 million), state (1.3 million), and local (0.8 million) correctional facilities (Sabol, Couture, & Harrison, 2007)—up 32.8% from 1.7 million in 1996 (CASA, 2010h). By 2006, there were 1.9 million substance-involved offenders behind bars in America, an increase of 43.2% from 1996[3] (CASA, 2010k, 2010l, 2010o, 2010p, 2010m, 2010n, 2010h, 2010i).

Substance misuse and addiction are key factors in the continuous growth of the U.S. inmate population. Substance-involved inmates comprised 84.8% of all incarcerated offenders in federal, state, and local prisons and jails in 2006—86.2% of federal inmates, 84.6% of state inmates and 84.7% of local jail inmates—up 6.2% from 1996. The largest increase in the percentage of substance-involved inmates was in the jail population (11.3%). (Table 16.1)

Substance-involved inmates are those who either: (1) had a history of using illicit drugs regularly;[4] (2) met medical criteria for a substance use disorder; (3) were under the influence of alcohol or other drugs when they committed their crime; (4) had a history of alcohol treatment;[5] (5) were incarcerated for a drug law violation; (6) committed their offense to get money to buy drugs; (7) were incarcerated for an alcohol law violation; or (8) had some combination of these characteristics.

---

[2]CASA has used the time frame of 1996 to 2006 for purposes of analysis because 1996 was the latest year of CASA's first *Behind Bars* analysis and 2006 provided a decade interval and was the latest year in common and verified federal, state, and local data at the time of analysis.

[3]Unless otherwise noted in this chapter, percentage and numerical estimates are either drawn directly from or based on CASA's analysis of the *Survey of Inmates in Federal Correctional Facilities* (1991 and 2004), *Survey of Inmates in State Correctional Facilities* (1991 and 2004), and the *Survey of Inmates in Local Jails* (1989 and 2002) [Data files], and U.S. Bureau of Justice Statistics Reports, *Prisoners in 1996 and 2006*. Although the percentages of federal, state, and local inmates are derived from 1989 and 2002 (local jails) and 1991 and 2004 (prisons) data, these percentages are applied respectively to the 1996 and 2006 estimates of the prison population.

[4]One or more times a week for at least a month.

[5]As measured by prior participation in treatment for alcohol misuse.

| Table 16.1 | Substance-Involved Federal, State, and Local Inmates, 1996 and 2006 | | | |

	1996		2006	
	Number	Percentage	Number	Percentage
Federal Prison	84,787	80.3	164,521	86.2
State Prison	871,636	81.0	1,101,779	84.6
Local Jail	380,677	73.4	648,664	84.7
Total Substance-Involved Inmates	**1,337,099**	78.6	**1,914,964**	84.8

Source: CASA analysis of the *Survey of Inmates in Federal Correctional Facilities* (1991, 2004), *Survey of Inmates in State Correctional Facilities* (1991, 2004), *Survey of Inmates in Local Jails* (1989, 2002) [Data files], and U.S. Bureau of Justice Statistics Reports on prisoners in 1996 and 2006.

TYPES OF SUBSTANCE-INVOLVED INMATES

Of the seven categories of substance-involved inmates that we examined, the largest increase in the *number* of substance-involved inmates was found in the group who reported ever using illicit drugs regularly (Table 16.2). Among substance-involved offenders, the largest increases in the percentage of offenders in the seven categories were seen in the percentage incarcerated for alcohol or drug law violations. (Table 16.3)

Used illicit drugs regularly. The largest group of substance-involved inmates includes those who have used illicit drugs regularly—more than 1.5 million individuals. The total number of offenders in this category showed the largest increase (326,348) among categories of substance-involved offenders, growing by 27.2% from 1996 to 2006. This group makes up 67.6% of inmates; however, because of increases in other categories of offenders, the share this group represents is down from 70.6% in 1996.

Met medical criteria for substance use disorder. Almost 1.5 million (1,456,851) inmates met medical criteria for alcohol and/or drug abuse and/or dependence in the year prior to their arrest. This group constitutes 64.5% of the inmate population.[6] Seventy-six percent (76.1%) of substance-involved inmates have a substance-use disorder diagnosis.

Under the influence at time of crime. Almost one million inmates (967,046) were under the influence of alcohol or other drugs at the time of their crimes, up 37.4%

---

[6]20.3% (458,113) of the inmate population is substance involved but does not meet medical criteria for a substance use disorder.

Table 16.2   Number of Inmates Who Are Substance Involved, by Type

	1996	2006	Increase 1996–2006	Percentage of Increase
Used illicit drugs regularly	1,201,158	1,527,506	326,348	27.2
Met medical criteria for substance use disorder	N/A	1,456,851	N/A	N/A
Under the influence of alcohol or other drugs at the time of crime	703,788	967,046	263,258	37.4
History of alcohol treatment	403,384	586,490	183,106	45.4
Drug law violation	357,734	567,366	209,632	58.6
Committed crime for money to buy drugs	225,623	338,563	112,940	50.1
Alcohol law violation	53,950	99,955	46,006	85.3
Substance-Involved Inmates	**1,337,099**	**1,914,964**	**577,865**	**43.2**

Source: CASA analysis of the *Survey of Inmates in Federal Correctional Facilities* (1991, 2004), *Survey of Inmates in State Correctional Facilities* (1991, 2004), *Survey of Inmates in Local Jails* (1989, 2002) [Data files], and U.S. Bureau of Justice Statistics Reports on prisoners in 1996 and 2006.

Table 16.3   Percentage of Inmates Who Are Substance Involved, by Type

	1996	2006	Percentage of Change 1996–2006
Used illicit drugs regularly	70.6	67.6	−4.3
Met medical criteria for substance use disorder	N/A	64.5	N/A
Under the influence of alcohol or other drugs at the time of crime	41.4	42.8	+3.5
History of alcohol treatment	23.7	26.0	+9.5
Drug law violation	21.0	25.1	+19.4
Committed crime for money to buy drugs	13.3	15.0	+13.0
Alcohol law violation	3.2	4.4	+39.5
Substance-Involved Inmates	**78.6**	**84.8**	**+7.8**

Source: CASA analysis of the *Survey of Inmates in Federal Correctional Facilities* (1991, 2004), *Survey of Inmates in State Correctional Facilities* (1991, 2004), *Survey of Inmates in Local Jails* (1989, 2002) [Data files], and U.S. Bureau of Justice Statistics Reports on prisoners in 1996 and 2006.

from 1996—the second largest numerical increase (263,258) of the categories of substance-involved offenders. This group comprises 42.8% of the inmate population, up from 41.4% in 1996.

History of alcohol treatment. Among U.S. inmates, 586,490 have a history of alcohol treatment. The total number of inmates in this category jumped 45.4% between 1996 and 2006. This group comprises 26.0% of the inmate population, up from 23.7% in 1996.

Drug law violation. In 2006, 567,366 inmates were incarcerated for drug law violations, an increase of 58.6% from 1996. Drug law violations include possession or use, substance trafficking, or other unspecified substance offenses. This group comprises 25.1% of the U.S. inmate population, up from 21.0% 1996. Eighty-two percent of those incarcerated for drug law violations also have a history of alcohol treatment or regular drug use, or were under the influence of alcohol or other drugs at the time of their crimes.

Committed crime for money to buy drugs. Our nation's prisons and jails housed 338,563 inmates in 2006 who committed their crimes to get money to buy drugs, up 50.1% since 1996. This group constitutes 15.0% of inmates, increasing from 13.3% in 1996.

Alcohol law violation. Nearly 100,000 inmates (99,955) were in prison or jail in 2006 for alcohol law violations, an increase of 85.3% from 1996. Alcohol law violations include driving under the influence, drunkenness/vagrancy/disorderly conduct, and liquor law violations. This group makes up 4.4% of the inmate population, up from 3.2% in 1996.

Substance Involvement by Type of Crime

To examine the extent to which substance involvement varies by crime type, we examined the following categories of controlling offenses:[7] violent, property, substance (alcohol/other drug), other, and unspecified offenses.[8] Substance involvement is an overwhelming factor in all types of crime.

Violent Crimes. The controlling offense for more than a third (37.0%) of federal, state, and local prison and jail inmates was committing a violent crime including murder, forcible rape, robbery or aggravated assault.[9] Of these inmates, 77.5% were substance involved; that is, they were under the influence of alcohol or other

---

[7]A controlling offense is the most serious of the offenses for which the inmate has been incarcerated.

[8]Includes inmates who were being held for probation/parole violation hearings, awaiting arraignment, or waiting to stand trial on these counts. Such inmates constitute 0.6% of federal inmates, 1.4% of state inmates, and 51.9% of the local jail population.

[9]Robbery and aggravated assault account for 50.2% of incarcerations for violent crimes.

drugs at the time of the crime, committed their crime to get money to buy drugs, had a history of alcohol treatment, a history of regular drug use, or had a substance use disorder.

Substance Crimes. Federal, state, and local inmates who were incarcerated for alcohol or drug law violations make up 29.2% of inmates. By definition, all of these inmates were substance involved.

Property Crimes. Federal, state, and local inmates who were incarcerated for property crimes—burglary, larceny-theft, car theft and arson—comprise 19.2% of the inmate population. Of this group, 83.4% are substance-involved, meaning they were under the influence of alcohol or other drugs at the time of the crime, committed their crime in order to get money to buy drugs, had a history of alcohol treatment, a history of regular drug use, or had a substance use disorder.

Other Crimes. Federal, state, and local inmates incarcerated for other crimes including supervision violations,[10] public order offenses (e.g., tax law violations, antitrust, racketeering, and extortion), immigration offenses, and weapon offenses comprise 13.3% of the inmate population. Of these offenders, 76.9% are substance involved—they were under the influence of alcohol or other drugs at the time of the crime, committed their crime in order to get money to buy drugs, had a history of alcohol treatment, a history of regular drug use, or had a substance use disorder.

Inmates incarcerated for probation and parole supervision violations account for 45.5% of the category of other crimes; 83.2% of supervision violators were under the influence of alcohol or other drugs at the time of the crime, committed their crime in order to get money to buy drugs, had a history of alcohol treatment, a history of regular drug use, or had a substance use disorder.

Conviction Unspecified. For 1.3% of inmates, the controlling offense was unknown.[11] Among those inmates for whom the type of crime for which they had been convicted was not specified, 51.2% were under the influence of alcohol or other drugs at the time of the crime, committed their crime to get money to buy drugs, had a history of alcohol treatment, a history of regular drug use, or had a substance use disorder.

The Dominant Role of Alcohol

Alcohol is implicated in the incarceration of over half (56.6%) of all inmates in America. In addition to the inmates who were convicted of an alcohol law violation, 51.6% of drug law violators, 55.9% of those who committed a property crime,

---

[10]Violated the terms of their probation or parole.

[11]National data sets reported *missing*, *don't know*, or *refused* in this response category.

57.7% of inmates who committed a violent crime, and 52.0% of those who committed other crimes were either under the influence of alcohol at the time of the crime, had a history of alcohol treatment or had an alcohol use disorder.

The Role of Illicit Drugs

Illicit drugs are implicated in the incarceration of three fourths (75.9%) of all inmates in America. In addition to the inmates who were convicted of a drug law violation, 54.3% of alcohol law violators, 77.2% of those who committed a property crime, 65.4% of inmates who committed a violent crime, and 67.6% of those who either committed their crime to get money to buy drugs, were under the influence of drugs at the time of the crime, had a history of regular drug use or had a drug use disorder.

Inmates incarcerated in federal and state prisons and local jails for any marijuana charge as the controlling offense account for 2.0 percent of all inmates and 7.9 percent of all those incarcerated for drug law violations. Those incarcerated for *marijuana possession as the controlling offense* account for 1.1 percent (25,235) of all inmates and 4.4 percent of those incarcerated for drug law violations. Those incarcerated for *marijuana possession as their only offense* account for 0.9 percent (20,291) of all inmates and 2.9 percent of those incarcerated for drug law violations.

Tobacco Use

In 2005, 37.8 percent of state inmates and 38.6 percent of federal inmates smoked in the month of their arrest.[12] In contrast, approximately 24.9 percent of the population were current smokers[13] (Substance Abuse and Mental Health Services Administration [SAMHSA], 2006). State and federal inmates who met clinical criteria for substance use disorders had even higher rates of tobacco use; 66.5 percent of state inmates and 51.5 percent of federal inmates with substance use disorders smoked in the month of their arrest. Of current smokers, 19.3% of state inmates and 22.3% of federal inmates started or resumed smoking with their incarceration.

PROFILES OF SUBSTANCE-INVOLVED INMATES

Substance-involved inmates differ from those who are not substance involved in several key ways. Compared with inmates who are not substance involved, substance-involved inmates are

- Four times more likely to receive income through illegal activity (24.6% vs. 6.0%)
- Almost twice as likely to have had at least one parent misuse alcohol or other drugs (34.5% vs. 18.4%)

---

[12]No information on local jail inmate smoking patterns was available in the survey data.

[13]Age 12 and older who smoked in the past 30 days.

- 40.6% more likely to have some family criminal history (42.6% vs. 30.3%)
- 29.2% less likely to have completed at least high school (30.4% vs. 39.3%) 20.0% more likely to be unemployed a month before incarceration (32.1% vs. 26.8%)

Inmates who are substance involved also are more likely than those who are not substance involved to be: younger (average age 33.9 vs. 36.2), to have lived only with their mother during childhood (39.6% vs. 32.5%), and to have ever spent time in foster care (12.2% vs.7.3%). (See Table 16.4) Substance-involved inmates are more likely than non-substance involved inmates to have a mental health problem (34.5% vs. 25.7%) or to have been on probation or parole at the time of their arrest (44.1% vs. 28.9%).

Table 16.4 Background Characteristics of Substance-Involved and Non-Substance-Involved Inmates

	Percentage Substance Involved (1,914,964)	Percentage Non-Substance Involved (344,019)
Average age (years)	33.9	36.2
Gender		
Male	91.7	91.0
Female	8.3	9.0
Participation in religious activities[a]	56.4	58.3
Family criminal history[b]	42.6	30.3
Lived with mother in childhood	39.6	32.5
Parental substance misuse[c]	34.5	18.4
Unemployed	32.1	26.8
Income through illegal activity	24.6	6.0
Married	16.4	20.9
Completed at least high school	30.4	39.3
Ever spent time in foster care	12.2	7.3
Income through welfare/charity	5.5	4.4

Source: CASA analysis of the *Survey of Inmates in Federal Correctional Facilities* (2004), *Survey of Inmates in State Correctional Facilities* (2004), *Survey of Inmates in Local Jails* (2002) [Data files], and U.S. Bureau of Justice Statistics Reports, *Prisoners in 2006.*

[a]Had participated in religious activities such as religious services, private prayer or meditation, or Bible reading or studying in the past week.

[b]Had an immediate family member who had served time in jail or prison.

[c]Had at least one parent abusing alcohol or illicit drugs.

SUBSTANCE USE DISORDERS (SUDs)

In 2006, 64.5% (1.5 million[14]) of the 2.3 million prison and jail inmates had a substance use disorder—more than seven times the rate for the general population (9.1%)[15] (CASA, 2010x, 2010p, 2010n, 2010l, 2010i) (Table 16.5). The lowest proportion of inmates with substance use disorders was among federal inmates. In 2006, 54.8% of the federal prison population had a SUD—six times the rate of the general population. Half of federal inmates (51.8%) met criteria for substance abuse and 36.8% met criteria for substance dependence. In 2006, 65.2% of state prison inmates had a substance use disorder—more than seven and one half times the rate of the general population; 62.4% met criteria for substance abuse and 47.9% met criteria for substance dependence. Among local jail inmates, 65.8% had a substance use disorder in 2006; 64.8% met criteria for substance abuse and 43.7% met criteria for substance dependence. (Table 16.6)

 Table 16.5 Percentage With Past Year Substance Use Disorders U.S. Inmate Population and General Population Ages 12 or Over

	Inmate Population (2,258,983)	General Population (299,398,484)
Substance abuse	62.4	4.9
Substance dependence	45.5	4.7
Substance abuse AND/OR dependence	64.5	9.1

Source: CASA analysis of the *Survey of Inmates in Federal Correctional Facilities* (2004), *Survey of Inmates in State Correctional Facilities* (2004), *Survey of Inmates in Local Jails* (2002) [Data files], and U.S. Bureau of Justice Statistics Reports, *Prisoners in 2006*; CASA analysis of the *National Survey on Drug Use and Health (NSDUH)* (2006) [Data file].

CO-OCCURRING SUBSTANCE USE AND MENTAL HEALTH DISORDERS

Our analysis found that approximately one third (32.9%) of inmates have a mental health disorder.[16] An estimated one in ten individuals in the general population has such a disorder (James & Glaze, 2006). In 2005, 45% of federal inmates, 56% of

---

[14]1,456,851 inmates with SUDs.

[15]Using the most recently available national surveys of inmate populations—2004 for state and federal prisons and 2002 for local jails—CASA imputed prevalence rates for 2006 based on the weighted 2002/2004 datasets and the 2006 prison and jail population estimates published in *Prison and Jail Inmates at Midyear, 2006*, by the Bureau of Justice Statistics. CASA analyzed data from the *2006 National Survey on Drug Use and Health* to determine rates of SUDs for the U.S. population ages 12 or older.

[16]Defined as any past diagnosis of a psychiatric disorder or history of treatment.

Table 16.6   Prevalence of Substance Use Disorders in Prisons and Jails

	Federal Prison (190,844)		State Prison (1,302,129)		Local Jail (766,010)	
	Number	Percent	Number	Percent	Number	Percent
Substance abuse	96,843	51.8	813,082	62.4	496,517	64.8
Substance dependence	70,178	36.8	623,428	47.9	334,576	43.7
Substance abuse and/or dependence	104,529	54.8	848,426	65.2	504,896	65.8

Source: CASA analysis of the *Survey of Inmates in Federal Correctional Facilities* (2004), *Survey of Inmates in State Correctional Facilities* (2004), *Survey of Inmates in Local Jails* (2002) [Data files], and U.S. Bureau of Justice Statistics Reports, *Prisoners in 2006*.

state inmates, and 64% of local inmates have mental health problems[17] (James & Glaze, 2006). Inmates with mental health problems are more likely than their peers without such problems to be more entangled in the criminal justice system (James & Glaze, 2006).

A quarter of state and local inmates with mental health problems have had three or more prior incarcerations compared to a fifth of their peers without mental health problems (James & Glaze, 2006). They also are more likely than are their peers to face homelessness, unemployment, physical or sexual abuse and alcohol or other drug problems (James & Glaze, 2006).

In 2006, 24.4% (550,608) of the 2.3 million prison and jail inmates had both a substance use disorder and a co-occurring mental health disorder. Among local jail inmates, 25.5% (195,652) have co-occurring disorders as do 25.4% (330,145) of state prison inmates, and 13.0% (24,810) of federal prison inmates.

Of the inmate population, 40.1% (906,243 inmates) had substance use disorders while only 8.5% (191,249 inmates) had mental health disorders without substance use disorders. Just 27.0% (610,883 inmates) of the entire prison and jail population is free of a substance use or mental health disorder. (Table 16.7)

While mental health disorders alone rarely increase the rate or frequency of criminal behaviors, their co-occurrence with substance use disorders dramatically increases the risk of criminal activities (Junginger, Claypoole, Laygo, & Crisanti, 2006). Increased rates of re-incarceration of inmates with co-occurring mental health and substance use disorders suggest that they are not being rehabilitated under the current system and instead are cycling in and out of incarceration (McNiel, Binder, & Robinson, 2005).

---

[17]Defined by a clinical diagnosis, having received mental health treatment during the prior 12 months or experiencing sub-clinical levels of symptoms based on the DSM-IV.

Table 16.7   Percentage of Prison and Jail Inmates With Mental Health and Substance Use Disorders

	Federal Prison (190,844)	State Prison (1,302,129)	Local Jail (766,010)	Total (2,258,983)
Both mental health and substance use disorders	13.0	25.4	25.5	24.4
Mental health disorders only	6.6	9.2	7.7	8.5
Substance use disorders only	41.8	39.8	40.2	40.1
None	38.7	25.6	26.5	27.0
Total[a]	100.0	100.0	100.0	100.0

Source: CASA analysis of the *Survey of Inmates in Federal Correctional Facilities* (2004), *Survey of Inmates in State Correctional Facilities* (2004), *Survey of Inmates in Local Jails* (2002) [Data files], and U.S. Bureau of Justice Statistics Reports, *Prisoners in 2006.*

[a]Columns may not equal 100% due to rounding.

INMATES FROM MINORITY GROUPS

Blacks, Hispanics and Native Americans are overrepresented in our nation's prisons and jails. In 2006, Blacks constituted 12.3% of the U.S. adult population and 41.0% of the inmate population. Hispanics were 14.8% of the U.S. population and 18.8% of the inmate population, while Native Americans comprised 0.8% percent of the U.S. population and 3.8% of the inmate population. Whites comprised 66.4% percent of the U.S. population and 34.6% of the inmate population. (Table 16.8)

Table 16.8   Percentage of Substance-Involved Inmates by Race/Ethnicity Compared With the General Population

	Inmate Population (2,258,983)	Substance-Involved Inmates (1,914,964)	Non-Substance Involved Inmates (344,019)	U.S. Adult Population (299,398,484)
White[a]	34.6	35.4	31.2	66.4
Black[b]	41.0	40.8	42.0	12.3
Hispanic	18.8	18.4	20.5	14.8
Native American	3.8	3.9	3.4	0.8
Other[c]	1.6	1.4	2.7	5.8

Source: CASA analysis of the *Survey of Inmates in Federal Correctional Facilities* (2004), *Survey of Inmates in State Correctional Facilities* (2004), *Survey of Inmates in Local Jails* (2002) [Data files], and U.S. Bureau of Justice Statistics Reports, *Prisoners in 2006*; U.S. Census Bureau (2006).

[a]Non-Hispanic White.

[b]Non-Hispanic Black.

[c]Asian, Hawaiian, Pacific Islander and others.

In the general population, more Blacks report having been booked for a crime in the past year (21.5%) than Whites (16.5%) or the population as a whole (16.6%). Black inmates whose controlling offenses are drug charges are more likely to be non-substance using offenders than are Whites whose controlling offenses are drug charges (18.5% vs. 7.4%) (CASA, 2010x).

Between 1983 and 1997, the number of Black offenders admitted to prison for drug offenses grew more than 26 times, relative to a sevenfold increase for White offenders (Pager, 2007). As of 2008, more than 1 in every 100 adults in the U.S. were incarcerated; however, the numbers remain much higher for minority groups. One in 15 Black men (1 in 9 among Black men ages 20–34) and 1 in 36 Hispanic men were incarcerated in 2006 (Pew Center on the States, 2008).

Substance involvement does not explain this overrepresentation since Black and Hispanic inmates report lower rates of drug use in the month prior to their arrest and have lower rates of substance use disorders than White inmates. Some explanations that have been offered for the disproportionately high number of incarcerated individuals from minority groups include: the legal provision of harsher sentences for the possession and sale of crack cocaine, a drug more often used by Blacks; the law enforcement emphasis on outdoor drug sale venues more frequently found in poor and minority communities; the concentration of police resources in minority and racially-mixed neighborhoods of major urban areas; and race-specific sentencing practices by the judges (Kautt & Spohn, 2002; Beckett, Nyrop, & Pfingst, 2006; Western & Pettit, 2002).

WOMEN BEHIND BARS

Earlier in the book, Pasko and Chesney-Lind provided a description and discussion of the increasing visibility of female population as clients of the criminal justice system, stating that more than one million women are under some sort of criminal justice supervision (Chapter 3). Here we briefly focus on this population as female inmates make up 8.4% of the total inmate population—up from 7.7% in 1996 (CASA, 2010p, 2010n, 2010k, 2010m, 2010o, 2010l, 2010h, 2010i). Female inmates are more likely to have a substance use disorder than are male inmates (66.1% vs. 64.3%) (Table 16.9).

Table 16.9 Percentage of All Prison and Jail Inmates With Past Year Substance Use Disorders, by Gender

	Male (2,069,027)	Female (189,956)
Substance abuse	62.3	63.5
Substance dependence	44.9	52.6
Substance abuse and/or dependence	64.3	66.1

Source: CASA analysis of the *Survey of Inmates in Federal Correctional Facilities* (2004), *Survey of Inmates in State Correctional Facilities* (2004), *Survey of Inmates in Local Jails* (2002) [Data files], and U.S. Bureau of Justice Statistics Reports, *Prisoners in 2006*.

This holds true for both state prisons and local jails, but among inmates in federal prisons, males have higher rates of substance use disorders than do females.

JUVENILE OR YOUTHFUL INMATES[18]

In 2006, 0.7% (15,340) of the 2.3 million offenders incarcerated in state prisons and local jails were juveniles or youthful offenders who had been tried in adult court.[19]

In 2006, half (52.4%) of juvenile or youthful offender inmates in state prisons and local jails met clinical criteria for substance use disorders. The problem is particularly severe among youth incarcerated in local jails where 54.3% met such clinical criteria compared with 36.7% of juvenile inmates in state prison (Table 16.10). Juveniles behind bars were discussed in more detail earlier in this book, Chapter 2.

Table 16.10 Percentage of Inmates Convicted as Juvenile or Youthful Offenders and Confined in State Prisons and Local Jails Who Have Substance Use Disorders

	State Prison		Local Jail		Total	
	Non-Juveniles (1,300,474)	Juveniles (1,655)	Non-Juveniles (752,325)	Juveniles (13,685)	Non-Juveniles (2,052,799)	Juveniles (15,340)
Substance abuse	62.5	36.7	65.0	53.8	63.4	52.0
Substance dependence	47.9	21.2	43.9	29.2	46.5	28.3
Substance abuse and/or dependence	65.2	36.7	66.0	54.3	65.5	52.4

Source: CASA analysis of the *Survey of Inmates in State Correctional Facilities* (2004), *Survey of Inmates in Local Jails* (2002) [Data files], and U.S. Bureau of Justice Statistics Reports, *Prisoners in 2006.*

[18]The category of juvenile or youthful offenders, established by statute in some states, has an age limit usually above that of juvenile delinquents (often refers to youth ages 18 to 25). Youthful offenders are not sentenced as adults and special correctional commitments and special record-sealing procedures are made available. They are distinguished from juvenile delinquents who are youth sentenced to juvenile court. Age limitations of juvenile delinquents vary among the states from 16 to 21 years of age, with the most common upper limit being 18 years.

[19]Juvenile and youthful offenders rarely are incarcerated in federal facilities; therefore, they are not included in this analysis. CASA analysis of *Surveys of Inmates in Federal* prisons showed only 127 juvenile or youthful offenders in federal prisons in 2006.

TREATMENT NEEDS OF SUBSTANCE-INVOLVED INMATES

Of the 1.5 million inmates with substance use disorders in 2006, we estimate that only 163,196 (11.2%[20]) received any type of professional treatment, including treatment in a residential facility or unit (7.1%), professional counseling (5.2%) or pharmacological therapy such as methadone, antibuse or naltrexone (0.2%). Less than 1% (0.9%) received detoxification services. Inmates were most likely to receive the adjunct services of mutual support/peer counseling (22.7%) or education (14.2%) (Table 16.11).

Federal prison inmates with substance use disorders were more likely to receive treatment including residential services, professional counseling, or pharmaceutical therapies (15.7%) than state prison inmates (14.2%) or local jail inmates (5.2%). However, since the state prison system houses more inmates than the federal and local correctional systems, most inmates who received professional treatment did so through the state prison system.

In terms of other addiction-related services, state prisoners were more likely to receive mutual support/peer counseling (29.9%) compared with their federal (22.3%) or local jail (10.7%) counterparts. Federal prison inmates were more likely to receive substance-related education services (29.2%) than state (17.7%) or local jail inmates (5.0%).

Table 16.11	Percentage of Prison and Jail Inmates With Substance Use Disorders Receiving Treatment or Addiction-Related Servicesa Since Admission			
	Federal Prison (104,529)	**State Prison (848,426)**	**Local Jail (503,896)**	**Total (1,456,851)**
Detoxification	0.9	0.9	1.0	0.9
Any professional treatment since admission	15.7	14.2	5.2	11.2
Residential facility or unit	8.8	9.2	3.1	7.1
Counseling by a professional	7.8	6.5	2.3	5.2
Maintenance drug	0.3	0.2	0.1	0.2
Other addiction-related services since admission	39.7	36.0	13.1	28.4
Mutual support/peer counseling	22.3	29.9	10.7	22.7
Education	29.2	17.7	5.0	14.2

Source: CASA's analysis of the *Survey of Inmates in Federal Correctional Facilities* (2004), *Survey of Inmates in State Correctional Facilities* (2004), *Survey of Inmates in Local Jails* (2002) [Data files], and U.S. Bureau of Justice Statistics Reports, *Prisoners in 2006*.

[a] Participation in specific types of professional treatment or addiction-related services is not mutually exclusive.

---

[20] 7.2% of the total inmate population.

Female inmates with substance use disorders are more likely than their male counterparts to receive residential treatment (9.6% vs. 6.8%), professional counseling (6.1% vs. 5.1%), pharmacological therapies (0.6% vs. 0.2%) or detoxification services (1.6% vs. 0.9%). They also have better chances than male inmates to participate in mutual support/peer counseling (25.5% vs. 22.4%) but less likely to receive some type of addiction-related education (13.3% vs. 14.3%). With the exception of detoxification services in federal prisons, these patterns hold true among federal, state, and local jail inmates.

While White inmates have the highest rate of substance use disorders (73.1%), only 13.2% of those with such disorders receive any professional treatment; 69.5% of Native American inmates meet clinical criteria for substance use disorders and 13.1% of those with substance use disorders receive professional treatment. Among Blacks, 60.2% meet criteria for substance use disorders while 10.1% of those with such disorders receive treatment. Hispanic inmates, 58.3% of whom meet clinical criteria for a substance use disorder, are the least likely to have received treatment (8.6%).

SHORTAGE OF EVIDENCE-BASED TREATMENT SERVICES

Most correctional facilities that offer addiction-related services continue to employ approaches not grounded in research, despite a considerable body of evidence to guide effective treatment in correctional settings (National Institute on Drug Abuse [NIDA], 1999, 2006). In 2007, the *National Criminal Justice Treatment Practices* survey estimated the prevalence of evidence-based practices (EBPs) of addiction treatment services that are employed in correctional facilities.[21] The survey from Friedmann, Taxman, and Henderson (2007) included the following 13 evidence-based practices:

1) Standardized risk assessment
2) Standardized substance misuse assessment and treatment matching
3) Use of techniques to engage and retain clients in treatment
4) Use of therapeutic community, cognitive-behavioral or other standardized treatment orientation
5) A comprehensive approach to treatment and ancillary needs
6) Addressing co-occurring disorders
7) Involvement of family in treatment
8) A planned treatment duration of 90 days or longer
9) Integration of multiple systems to optimize care and outcomes
10) Use of drug testing in treatment
11) Use of graduated sanctions
12) Incentives to encourage progress

---

[21]The design consisted of a mail survey of both correctional administrators and treatment program directors, who could report up to 13 or 15 EBPs, respectively.

Of these 13 evidence-based practices, correctional administrators reported only offering an average of 5.9; in local jails the average was 1.6. Nearly two thirds (64.7%) of the surveyed prisons, jails, and probation/parole departments provided only three or fewer of the 13 possible EBPs (Friedmann, Taxman, & Henderson, 2007).

In addressing substance use disorders, behavioral approaches are the most commonly used interventions. Evidence-based behavioral interventions include cognitive therapies that teach coping and decision-making skills, contingency management therapies that encourage behavioral changes, and motivational therapies (Chandler, Fletcher, & Volkow, 2009). However, correctional facilities tend to provide alcohol and other drug education or low-intensive outpatient counseling sessions rather than evidence-based, intensive treatment (Friedmann, Taxman, & Henderson, 2007). Services in local jails are even less intensive, structured, and accessible because of the high turnover rate and short facility stay of jail inmates (Taxman, Prerdoni, & Harrison, 2007).

Only half of administrators in state and federal prisons and one third in local jails report addressing co-occurring disorders. The least prevalent evidence-based practice reported by administrators in prisons (19%) and local jails (10%) is family involvement in treatment (Friedmann et al., 2007) (Table 16.12).

Table 16.12 Percentage of Facilities Offering Evidence-Based Practices in Prison and Jail-Based Treatment Services as Reported by Correctional Administrators

Evidence-Based Practices (EBPs)	Federal/State Prisons (98)	Local Jails (41)
Standardized substance misuse assessment	60	51
Standardized assessment/treatment matching	20	12
Engagement techniques	36	24
Treatment approach	21	12
Comprehensive approach	84	90
Address co-occurring disorders	50	32
Family involvement in treatment	19	10
Planned duration greater than 90 days	54	49
System integration	53	73
Continuing care/aftercare	48	32
Drug testing	32	34
Graduated sanctions	32	27
Incentives	81	54
EBPs per correctional facility (mean)	5.9	1.6

Source: P. D. Friedmann, F. S. Taxman, & C. E. Henderson (2007).

Specialized units segregated from the general prison population such as therapeutic communities can produce better outcomes, as measured by drug use and arrests postrelease, at least in part because they prevent the "prison culture" from derailing the recovery process (Inciardi, Martin, Butzin, Hooper, & Harrison, 1997; National Institute on Drug Abuse [NIDA], 1999).[22] The existence of specialized units does not, however, necessarily mean that quality care is offered.

An analysis of national data in 2002 by the Substance Abuse and Mental Health Services Administration (SAMHSA) found that 94% of federal prisons, 56% of state prisons, and 33% of jails reported that they provided some type of treatment for substance use disorders[23] with an average daily attendance of approximately 147,000 inmates. Only a small percentage of the inmate population had access to such services on a daily basis[24] (Taxman et al., 2007; SAMHSA, 2002). In correctional facilities that provided treatment for substance use disorders, the majority delivered their services within the general population setting of their facilities (94% in federal prisons, 82% in state prisons, and 79% in local jails). In facilities that offered such services, addiction treatment was offered in specialized treatment units in 41% of federal facilities, 33% of state facilities, and 31% of local facilities (SAMHSA, 2002) (Table 16.13).

| Table 16.13 | Treatment for Substance Use Disorders by Settings Among Correctional Facilities Offering Such Services (1997a) |

	Federal Prisons (129)	State Prisons (1,183)	Local Jails (3,114)
Percentage offering within the general correctional population	94	82	79
Percentage offering in specialized units	41	33	31
Percentage offering in a hospital or psychiatric unit	6	6	8

Source: SAMHSA (2002).

[a]The most recent data provided by SAMHSA.

---

[22]To varying degrees, incarcerated offenders become socialized to the inmate subculture that values the solidarity among fellow inmates and the resistance of official correctional goals (Sykes & Messinger, 1960). The threat of peer violence and the deprivation of basic needs also force many inmates to seek protection and privileges through gang affiliation (Compton & Meacham, 2005; Kalinich & Stojkovic, 1985; Valdez, 2009). This climate is not conducive to effective treatment.

[23]Includes services such as detoxification, group or individual counseling, rehabilitation, and methadone or other pharmaceutical therapies.

[24]The *National Criminal Justice Treatment Practices* (NCJTP) survey is a nationally representative survey of correctional agencies (e.g., prisons, jails, and probation and parole) conducted in 2005 by a consortium of researchers to understand the breadth and availability of drug treatment services in the criminal justice system.

BARRIERS TO INTERVENTION AND TREATMENT

Government inertia and a failure of leadership to address the widespread problem of substance-involved offenders can be attributed to many factors: mandatory sentencing policies that eliminate the possibilities of alternative sentencing or parole, lack of a clear legal mandate to provide treatment, economic interests in prison expansion, and the failure of public policy to reflect changing public attitudes about addiction and justice.

Mandatory Sentencing

In the 1970s and 1980s, scholars and politicians alike advocated for harsher punishment and deterrence policies instead of rehabilitation (Martinson, 1974; Tonry, 2004; Wilson, 1983). Mandatory sentencing laws that compel judges to deliver fixed prison sentences to convicted offenders regardless of mitigating circumstances became very popular during the period of skyrocketing drug crime in the 1970s and 1980s (Benekos & Merlo, 1995; Tonry, 1995). Sentences under federal and state mandatory guidelines were based on the weight and type of the drugs and vary from five years to life in prison (Osler, 2007; Schiraldi, Colburn, & Lotke, 2004).

One form of mandatory sentencing is the *three strikes* laws that require lengthy incarceration of chronic offenders who have been convicted of a serious criminal offense on three or more separate occasions (Benekos & Merlo, 1995). Offenders who were substance involved disproportionately bore the burden of the increased punitive environment. A 2003 study reported that more *third strikers*[25] in California were serving such a sentence for drug possession than for second-degree murder, assault with a deadly, and rape combined (Ehlers, Schiraldi, & Ziedenberg, 2004).

Since the mid-1990s, there has been substantial movement toward eliminating this barrier to addressing the needs of substance-involved offenders. Judges and prosecutors have found ways to circumvent these mandatory provisions, departing downward from sentencing guidelines and mandatory minimum sentences in 44% of all federal drug sentences between 1999 and 2001 (U.S. General Accounting Office, 2003). Between 2001 and 2002, 20 states either proposed or had already taken steps to reduce sentences, replace prison time with drug treatment, or return some discretion to judges (Wilhelm & Turner, 2002).

In January 2005, the Supreme Court ruled that federal judges are no longer bound by mandatory sentencing guidelines but need only consult them when they punish federal criminals (*United States v. Booker*, 543 U. S. 220, 2005; U.S. Sentencing Commission, 2006). Two years later, in December 2007, the U.S. Sentencing Commission unanimously agreed to allow federal inmates serving crack cocaine sentences to seek sentence reductions retroactively. As of July 2008, 10,707 federal prisoners applied for the retroactive reduction of their sentences, and 8,147 (76.1%) were granted the approval (U.S. Sentencing Commission, 2008).

---

[25]Imprisoned for longer periods for a third felony.

The highly publicized 2009 decision of the State of New York to reform the Rockefeller Drug Laws was the next step in the growing movement to rethink how our nation deals with non-violent drug offenders. The changes in New York included the elimination of mandatory minimums and a return to judicial discretion in the sentencing of most drug cases, the expansion of drug treatment and alternatives to incarceration, and the resentencing of some incarcerated people who were serving sentences under the old Rockefeller laws (Drug Policy Alliance, 2009a; Scott, 2009). The return to judicial discretion gives judges the flexibility to link sentences to effective treatment for substance use disorders.

Lack of Clear, Legal Mandate to Provide Treatment

Federal, state, and local governments are constitutionally required to provide health care to inmates (McLearen & Ryba, 2003). In the 1950s, the American Medical Association recognized alcohol addiction as a disease (American Medical Association, 2009); nonetheless, historically there has been a debate about whether prisons and jails are constitutionally or legally required to provide treatment for mental health disorders to incarcerated offenders[26] (McLearen & Ryba, 2003).

In *Marshall v. United States* (1974), the Supreme Court determined that an inmate was not constitutionally entitled to drug treatment. The basis for this ruling was that there was no medical consensus at that time as to the efficacy of known addiction treatment methods and the prospect for the successful rehabilitation of substance-involved offenders largely was shrouded in uncertainty (*Marshall v. United States*, 414 U.S. 417, 1974; Peters & Steinberg, 2000).

Since these rulings, however, science has demonstrated that addiction is a brain disease, and that addictive substances activate and disrupt normal chemical functioning in the reward centers of our brains, and essentially "hijack brain circuits that exert considerable dominance over rational thought, leading to progressive loss of control over drug intake in the face of medical, interpersonal, occupational and legal hazards" (Dackis & O'Brien, 2005, p. 1431; NIDA, 2008). Left untreated, addiction causes and contributes to more than 70 other medical conditions requiring hospitalizations and increasing the risk of illness and death (CASA, 1993). Research has demonstrated that there are effective strategies to initiate and maintain the recovery process (NIDA, 1999), and that the criminal justice system has proved to be a competent sponsor of successful treatment (NIDA, 2006). Research has demonstrated further that incarceration for crimes committed is compatible with rigorous corrections-based treatment and that investing in treatment will yield reductions in crime and much greater social and monetary benefits to society than relying on incarceration alone (Kelley, Mueller, & Hemmens, 2004; Pallone & Hennessy, 2003).

---

[26]In the case of mental health care, the Supreme Court's rulings in *Pugh v. Locke* (1978) and *Bowring v. Godwin* (1977) specifically required the provision of psychological and/or psychiatric services, while the *Washington v. Harper* (1990) case sustained incarcerated inmates' rights to decline mental health care. No case yet identifies specific steps to assure that the guidelines set forth in these suits are followed (McLearen & Ryba, 2003).

Economic Interests in Prison Expansion

A side effect of the massive reliance on incarceration to fight the war on drugs has been the rise of the private prison industry and the economic dependence of economically disadvantaged communities on prison expansion. As the inmate population exploded following the outbreak of the crack-cocaine epidemic, prison privatization provided an expedient remedy for prison overcrowding. The period from 1984 to 1998 marked the prime of the private prison industry, whose growth has since slowed (Culp, 2005). By 2006, the proportion of all inmates in federal and state prisons housed in privately operated facilities reached 7.2% (Sabol, Minton, & Harrison, 2008). The private prison firms, including the Corrections Corporation of America and the Wackenhut Corrections Corporation, have become aggressive lobbyists for tough sentencing laws and major sources of campaign contributions in state politics (Culp, 2005; Lapido, 2009; Schlosser, 1998). The recent economic downturn adds further strength to the struggle between controlling costs in the justice system and maintaining jobs in the prison industry (Gramlich, 2009; Moore, 2009; Nisperos, 2009).

Attitudes About Addiction and Justice

The collective passion for harsh punishment over rehabilitation and the readiness of the state to incarcerate an unprecedented large number of citizens made penal populism a hallmark of American society among industrialized democracies (Tonry, 2004; Zimring, Hawkins, & Kamin, 2001). Indeed, compared with other countries, more Americans are incarcerated for nonviolent crimes such as minor property offenses and drug use (Lynch, 1995; Mauer, 2003, 2007). Prison sentences also are longer in the U.S. than in other countries (Mauer, 2003, 2007; Van Kesteren, 2009).

A national poll found that 87% of American voters favored making rehabilitative services available to offenders during incarceration, after release, or during both periods. Only 11% of voters favored a purely punitive approach. More than half of voters reported that access to job training, mental health services, family support, mentoring, and housing are very important components of a person's successful reintegration into society following incarceration. Drug treatment was cited by 79% of voters as very important as well. Less than 10% of voters believed these services were not important (Krisberg & Marchionna, 2006). In a more recent survey, 82% of Americans believed that addiction is a chronic health condition that requires long-term management and support (Lake Research Partners, 2009).

ALTERNATIVES TO INCARCERATION

The use of treatment alternatives to incarceration has gained momentum in the past decade as witnessed by a rapid expansion of drug treatment courts, prosecutorial diversion programs, and treatment interventions supervised by probation and parole; the accumulation of related evaluation studies; and the emergence of advocacy coalitions for treatment alternatives. These criminal justice innovations make treatment for substance use disorders a central component, establish collaboration between justice authorities and treatment providers, and hold the offender legally accountable for treatment compliance.

Despite the encouraging growth of diversion and treatment opportunities and evidence of their cost effectiveness, still only a fraction of substance-involved offenders have benefited from treatment alternative programs. For example, of the 1.5 million arrestees likely to have substance use disorders, the Urban Institute's Justice Policy Center estimates that just over 109,900 meet current eligibility requirements for drug court, yet there were only 55,300 available drug court slots (Bhati, Roman, & Chalfin, 2008).

Probation

Deferred, low-probability threats of severe punishment are the basis for most probation systems in the country, yet these systems tend to let repeated violations go unpunished. When punishments eventually are assigned, they tend to be lengthy and expensive sentences. In 2004, Circuit Judge Steve Alm, with the help of other criminal justice and drug treatment professionals, created Hawaii's Opportunity Probation with Enforcement (HOPE) program. The program targets offenders at risk of having their probation revoked. Program participants are informed at warning hearings that the rules of probation will be strictly enforced using immediate and high-probability threats of mild punishment, and that they will be required to submit to weekly or bi-weekly random drug tests. Probation violations and failed drug tests lead to swift arrests and short stays in jail, as little as two days. Sentence length increases for each successive violation (Hawken, 2009). Probationers who continually are unable to comply on their own are required to enter treatment. Treatment services are available to all HOPE probationers on a voluntary basis.

Preliminary results from a randomly assigned comparison showed that six months after starting the program, HOPE participants reduced their missed appointments by 85% and increased their positive urinalyses by 91%. The threat of consistent sanctions alone was enough to deter the drug use of 60% of program participants. The rearrest rate of a comparison group of probationers was three times higher than for HOPE participants, and the comparison group's arrest rate for nontechnical violations was 111% higher than HOPE participants. HOPE probationers also were significantly less likely to have their probation revoked (9% vs. 31%) (Hawken, 2009).

Prosecutorial-Based Diversion

Experience with alternatives to incarceration such as the Brooklyn Drug Treatment Alternatives to Prison Program (DTAP) shows that eligibility can safely be expanded to a broad range of offenders (CASA, 2003). The Brooklyn DTAP program is a residential drug treatment program with educational, vocational, and social support services for nonviolent, drug-addicted, repeat felony offenders. It was one of the first residential drug treatment programs directed at drug sellers who also are drug dependent. A five-year evaluation found, that on average, DTAP participants had five previous drug arrests and had spent four years behind bars (CASA, 2003).

The program originally was designed to defer prosecution but was changed to a deferred sentencing program. The defendant pleads guilty to a felony but sentencing is deferred pending completion of the DTAP program, at which point the guilty plea is withdrawn and the charges are dismissed. Failure to complete the program results in sentencing on the outstanding charges.

Evaluation found that DTAP graduates compared with a matched group at two years postprogram or postrelease had 33% lower rearrest rates (39% vs. 58%), and were 87% less likely to return to prison (2% vs. 15%) (CASA, 2003). DTAP participants also were three and a half times more likely to be employed than they were before arrest. These results were achieved at about half the average cost of incarceration.

Drug Courts

The drug treatment court movement that began in 1989 provides another sign of change in American drug policy. Drug courts were developed as alternative-to-prison programs for nonviolent substance-involved offenders that integrate treatment for substance use disorders, mandatory drug testing, sanctions and incentives, and transitional services in a judicially supervised court setting (Huddleston, Marlowe, & Casebolt, 2008). Substance-involved offenders are generally referred to these programs by judges, attorneys, or law enforcement personnel (Eighth Judicial Circuit Family Court, 2010). Participants are then put on probation while they attend treatment and regularly scheduled monitoring sessions with court and treatment staff. Upon program completion, offenders may have their charges dropped, probation rescinded, or have their original sentences reduced (National Institute of Justice, 2006). Usually program dropouts face the threat of imprisonment (King & Pasquarella, 2009).

As of 2009, there were more than 2,000 drug courts serving just under half of the counties in the United States (American University, 2009). According to an analysis by the Government Accountability Office, drug court participants are rearrested and reconvicted fewer times for fewer felonies and drug offenses than their peers. While, most drug courts resulted in higher court costs than standard criminal justice services, all the programs that tracked costs and savings from reduced criminal justice and victimization costs resulted in positive net benefits, ranging from $1,000 to $15,000 per participant (U.S. General Accounting Office, 2005).

The Multnomah County STOP drug court that has served Oregon for more than 18 years has undergone multiple comprehensive reviews and demonstrated exceptional results. During its first ten years of operation, 6,502 offenders participated in the Multnomah drug court. Five years after entering the STOP program, offenders, on average, are rearrested less often (four arrests vs. six arrests) and spend fewer days in jail (46 days vs. 75 days), prison (80 days vs. 105 days) or on probation (529 days vs. 661 days) than their peers who go through the standard adjudication process. The avoided criminal justice costs of their drug court participation totaled more than $50 million. The reductions in violent and property crime also resulted in $35 million in avoided victimization costs, bringing the total savings to $85 million (Finigan, Carey, & Cox, 2007).

California's Substance Abuse and Crime Prevention Act

One example of a statewide approach to providing alternatives to incarceration for substance-involved offenders was the passage of California's Substance Abuse and Crime Prevention Act (SACPA, also known as Proposition 36) (Drug Policy Alliance, 2010). California voters, who in 1994 initiated the three strikes movement with the passage of Proposition 184, approved SACPA by 61% in 2000 (Field Research Corporation, 2009). This Act went into effect in July 2001, with $120 million for treatment services allocated annually for five years. It allows first and second-time nonviolent, simple drug possession offenders the opportunity to receive treatment for substance use disorders instead of incarceration (Drug Policy Alliance, 2010).

The diversion of prison-bound offenders to community-based drug treatment facilities added 80,000 SACPA admissions to California's licensed treatment system during the first two years of implementation. Under such a sudden increase in treatment demand, most SACPA clients were diverted to outpatient treatment which was a more affordable but an inadequate modality of intervention for some addicted offenders such as those who are homeless or who have a co-occurring mental health disorder and require more structured care. Whereas the reliance on outpatient treatment may have allowed California's treatment system to absorb SACPA clients effectively without dramatically increasing its staffing and service capacities, researchers concluded that the availability of treatment slots for non-SACPA clients may have declined in most California counties due to the displacement of voluntary non-SACPA clients by SACPA clients (Hser et al., 2007).

While similar legislative or referendum initiatives have been considered in at least 15 other states (Rinaldo & Kelly-Thomas, 2005), they failed in many of these states. In 2009, California lawmakers cut SACPA funding by 83%, or $90 million due to growing budget constrain (Richman, 2009).

POLICY IMPLICATIONS

Overcoming these barriers will require political leadership and action on the part of federal, state and local policymakers to train criminal justice personnel to respond appropriately to substance-involved offenders. It will require screening and early detection of risky substance use and substance use disorders and providing evidence-based treatments and aftercare, either as alternatives to or in conjunction with incarceration. It also will require providing education, training and employment to offenders post release.

Training Criminal Justice Personnel

A key first step in overcoming the barriers to treatment in the justice system is to increase training of police, prosecutors, judges, and other criminal justice personnel in order to equip them to deal more effectively with substance-related crime. Educational components focusing on the prevention and treatment of addiction can be incorporated into the training curriculum of criminal justice personnel. While some progress has been made in the educational curriculum for probation and parole officers (Torres & Latta, 2000), there is no evidence of improvement in the substance-related education of corrections officers and administrators or of corrections medical staff.

In 2002, 34 states required their correctional institutions to perform both punishment and rehabilitation through formal statutes (Kelley et al., 2004); yet, the basic structure and functional goals of the corrections system largely are at odds with the goals of rehabilitation and treatment. The personnel composition, the recruitment requirements, and the physical arrangement of correctional settings almost exclusively are focused on ensuring the effective custody and control of incarcerated offenders; there is virtually no attention to treatment and rehabilitation. For example, as of 2007, 39 state correctional agencies required only a high school diploma or GED for entry-level correctional officers[27] (Corrections Compendium, 2007). If states were focused on rehabilitation and treatment as well, they could be expected also to hire individuals with more advanced training in these areas. Multistate surveys have reported that even professionals working in prison-based treatment settings experience an unusually high rate of job burnout (Garner, Knight, & Simpson, 2007).

Early Detection

The value of screenings, brief interventions, and referrals to treatment has been demonstrated in many settings (e.g., Babor, Higgins-Biddle, Dauser, Burleson, Zarkin, & Bray, 2006; Gentilello, Ebel, Wickizer, Salkever, & Rivara, 2005; Mundt, 2006; Solberg, Maciosek, & Edwards, 2008). These practices can reduce risky and costly substance misuse and identify those who need treatment. Early detection followed by appropriate interventions and treatments are key to preventing future substance-related crime (NIDA, 2006).

Drug testing also is a tool for early detection. Pretrial programs have used drug testing to predict and reduce pretrial misconduct (Visher, 1992). Although highly accurate and efficient screening methods have been developed for adult arrestees

---

[27]One state had no educational requirements, two states required only that officers pass a written exam and six states did not participate in the survey. Only two states reported that some college was required.

(Henry & Clark, 1999; Wish, Petronis, & Yacoubian, 2002), subjecting noncon-
victed adult offenders to mandatory screening or drug testing has been implemented
in only a handful of jurisdictions (Rosen & Goldkamp, 1989; Henry & Clark,
1999). This is due in part to questions raised about constitutional protections from
unreasonable search and seizure and the legal assumption of innocence (Rosen &
Goldkamp, 1989; Henry & Clark, 1999). To date, courts have upheld the constitutionality of pretrial drug testing while requiring that collection and testing procedures meet the legal test of reasonableness (Rosen & Goldkamp, 1989).

Rather than using screening or drug testing alone as deterrents, they more appropriately can be used to identify those in need of intervention or treatment and to target
services in order to reduce risky and dependent substance use, reduce prison overcrowding, and save taxpayer money (Center for Substance Abuse Treatment, 2005a).

Treatment and Aftercare

A substantial body of knowledge exists to guide the provision of effective treatment
for substance-involved offenders, assure that treatment is tailored to the race/ethnicity
and gender of inmates, address their co-occurring health and mental health problems,
and increase the chances of reentry into the community and reduce recidivism.

An example of tailored treatment is family-based treatment programs that have
proven effective for serving the special populations of substance-involved juveniles
and female offenders with children (Green, Furrer, Worcel, Burrus, & Finigan, 2007;
Hogue, Dauber, & Samuolis, 2006; Kaufman, Yoshioka, & Center for Substance
Abuse Treatment, 2004). The geographic remoteness of most correctional facilities
is an obstacle to the goal of more widespread implementation of family counseling
in prisons and jails (Van Voorhis, Braswell, & Morrow, 2000).

Alternatives to Incarceration

The use of treatment alternatives to incarceration has gained momentum in the
past decade as witnessed by a rapid expansion of drug treatment courts, prosecutorial diversion programs, and treatment interventions supervised by probation and
parole; the accumulation of related evaluation studies; and the emergence of advocacy coalitions for treatment alternatives. These criminal justice innovations make
treatment for substance use disorders a central component, establish collaboration
between justice authorities and treatment providers and hold the offender legally
accountable for treatment compliance.

Despite the encouraging growth of diversion and treatment opportunities and evidence of their cost effectiveness, still only a fraction of substance-involved offenders have
benefited from treatment alternative programs. For example, of the 1.5 million arrestees
likely to have substance use disorders, the Urban Institute's Justice Policy Center estimates that just over 109,900 meet current eligibility requirements for drug court yet there
were only 55,300 available drug court slots (Bhati, Roman, & Chalfin, 2008).

Training and Employment

Assuring that the education, training, and employment needs of offenders are met is an essential component of recovery and long-term disease management (NIDA, 2006). One promising practice is California's New Start prison-to-employment program which is based on the state's recognition that key to increasing public safety is employment of parolees. To increase the likelihood that parolees will obtain and retain jobs, the state has strengthened the link between in-prison rehabilitation programs and employment by using labor market data to determine the types of jobs that will actually be available in each county; matching training and work opportunities in prison to jobs available in communities; providing documents needed to secure employment prior to release from prison (e.g., social security card, birth certificate, selective service registration, etc.); providing essential job prerequisites such as resumes, trade certificates, licenses, trade union membership, etc.; and providing support to seek, secure, and maintain employment through a collaborative partnership with the community (California Department of Corrections and Rehabilitation, 2009).

LOOKING AHEAD

Since 2001, many state legislatures have changed their criminal sentencing policies, increasingly shifting from the tough-on-crime rhetoric and strategies to the smart-on-crime discourse and practices. The three main areas of legislative reform involve redefining and reclassifying drug offenses, strengthening alternatives to incarceration for substance-involved offenders, and reducing prison terms (Austin, 2010). While some of these approaches include the provision of treatment for substance use disorders, others do not. As a result of these practices, the number of prison inmates in state facilities declined for the first time in 38 years: as of January 2010, there were 4,777 (0.3%) fewer state prison inmates than there were in December 2008 (Pew Center on the States, 2010). This small reduction marked the first year-to-year drop in the state prison population since 1972. If this trend is to continue, it will be contingent on treating the substance use disorders of offenders to assure declines in recidivism. Several states have lowered classification levels for offenses involving possession of controlled substances and even more have reduced the severity of marijuana offenses. For example, Colorado reduced possession of Schedule I or II controlled substances from Class 3–4 to Class 4–6, increased threshold quantity demarcations for possession of controlled substances from one gram to four grams, reclassified possession of Schedule III and IV controlled substances from felonies to misdemeanors, and substantially changed offenses related to marijuana with regard to the amount required to constitute a crime and softened related punishments (Austin, 2010). Arkansas, in 2001, reduced punishment for possession, use, or distribution of drug paraphernalia from a Class C felony to a Class A misdemeanor (Bill, Briggs, Huffman, & Lubot-Conk, 2003).

Many states are moving away from the war on drugs philosophy of the 1980s and toward a public health approach to the problem of substance misuse. In states such as California and New York, a focus on treatment has culminated in mandatory drug treatment policies for drug offenders as part of their criminal sentence. A rigorous cost-benefit analysis of California's Substance Abuse and Crime Prevention Act, which allows first and second-time nonviolent, drug possession offenders the opportunity to receive treatment for substance use disorders instead of incarceration, found that the state saved over $173 million on the first-year cohort alone (Longshore, Hawken, Urada, & Anglin, 2006). Because of the 2009 reform of the Rockefeller Drug Laws in New York, which removes mandatory minimum sentences and allows judges to sentence drug offenders to treatment or to short incarcerations, nearly 1,000 fewer people went to state prison in the first 12 months (New York State Division of Criminal Justice Services, 2010). Another 327 drug felons were resentenced and released from prison.

In other cases, legislatures have increased funding for services, expanding states' capacity to provide inpatient and outpatient treatment for substance use disorders. One of the most visible cases was the Justice Reinvestment Initiative in Texas. In 2007, the Texan legislature enacted a comprehensive package to stop the prison growth and to reinvest $241 million from averted prison expansion to reinforce treatment for substance use disorders and reentry capacity of the state (Austin, 2010). Among other things, 500 beds for in-prison treatment targeting DWI offenders and 1,200 slots for intensive treatment in state jail system were added. Also, 800 inpatient beds and 3,000 outpatient slots for probationers and 1,500 inpatient beds for parolees who have violated their supervision terms were created. Evaluation findings report that Texas saved $210.5 million for the first two years of the initiative, probation revocations to prison declined by 4% and parole revocations decreased 25% (Council of State Governments Justice Center, 2009).

In the past decade, diversion programs for the treatment of substance-involved offenders have increased as effective approaches for adjudicating drug cases. With more than 1,151 drug courts established between 2000 and 2009, the institutionalization of drug courts has been accompanied by relaxed eligibility criteria and significant increases in funding (Ryan & Pasquarella, 2009). Dozens of other prosecutorial diversion programs also have been created (Sung & Belenko, 2006). Hundreds of thousands of substance-involved offenders have benefited from these judicial and prosecutorial treatment-based justice efforts.

In order to consolidate these initial gains in the control and reduction of risky substance use and substance use disorders within criminal justice populations, a number of measures need to be adopted by different levels of government. Specifically, federal, state, and local governments should:

- Require that addiction treatment be provided in criminal justice settings, that it be medically managed and that pharmacological treatments be available
- Require the accreditation of prison-based and jail-based treatment programs and providers through organizations such as the American Correctional Association (ACA), the Center for Substance Abuse Treatment (CSAT) at SAMHSA or the National Commission on Correctional Health Care (NCCHC). Such accreditation should require adherence to best practice standards and include periodic performance reviews by independent experts

- Expand federal support to states and localities for integrated evidence-based and promising practices including pretrial jail diversion programs, prosecutorial diversion options, drug courts, prison-based treatment programs, and community-based treatment and aftercare programs for released offenders upon reentry into the community; require and provide resources for the documentation of impact
- Forge partnerships between criminal justice facilities on the federal, state, and local levels and community-based health, education, and service providers and recovery support programs to increase access to effective aftercare services, including employment, for released offenders and expand use of evidence-based practices
- Provide family and social support, education and health services—including substance use prevention, intervention and treatment—to children of inmates

For the first time in four decades, our society is in a privileged position to coordinate and implement tested approaches to meaningfully disrupt the vicious cycle of addiction and social exclusion that has devastated the most vulnerable communities in America. Yet, given the current fiscal environment, there is a powerful temptation to cut not only the prison population but also programs that help prevent substance-involved crime. Providing treatment for offenders for the disease of addiction presents the greatest opportunity available to both reduce crime and its costs to society. The eventual success of this struggle will hinge on the determination of both the political leadership and of the public to maintain a society that is healthy, safe and just.

DISCUSSION QUESTIONS

1. Is substance misuse a public health crisis, criminal justice challenge, or both? How could our understanding of the problem influence our response to it?

2. What are the advantages and disadvantages of incarcerating substance-involved offenders? Do the benefits outweigh the costs?

3. How did America become the country with the largest prison population in the world? Why should we be concerned about it?

4. Should states and prison administrators be legally required to treat inmates with substance use disorders? Why?

5. How could fiscal constraints and budget crises encourage and/or undermine a rational approach to the handling of the problem of substance misuse among prison inmates? What would you tell the policy makers and the public?

6. What set of policies and practices would you implement in the area of alcohol and other drug control and sentencing to maximize public health and safety? Would your solution be both politically palatable and fiscally viable?

SUGGESTED READINGS

Center for Substance Abuse Treatment. (2005). *Substance abuse treatment for persons with co-occurring disorders. Treatment Improvement Protocol (TIP) Series 42* (DHHS Pub. No. (SMA) 05–3992). Rockville, MD: U.S. Department of Health and Human Services, Substance Abuse and Mental Health Services Administration, Center for Substance Abuse Treatment.

Center for Substance Abuse Treatment. (2005b). *Substance abuse treatment for persons with co-occurring disorders. Treatment Improvement Protocol (TIP) Series 42* (DHHS Pub. No. (SMA) 05–3992). Rockville, MD: U.S. Department of Health and Human Services, Substance Abuse and Mental Health Services Administration, Center for Substance Abuse Treatment.

Kleiman, M. A. R. (2010). *When brute force fails: How to have less crime and less punishment.* Princeton, NJ: Princeton University Press.

Kleiman, M. A. R., Caulkins, J. P., & Hawken, A. (2011). *Drugs and drug policy: What everyone needs to know.* New York, NY: Oxford University Press.

Leukefeld, C. G., Tims, F., & Farabee, D. (2002). *Treatment of drug offenders: Policies and issues.* New York, NY: Springer.

Peters, R. H., & Matthews, C. O. (2003). Substance abuse treatment programs in prisons and jails. In T. J. Fagan & R. K. Ax (Eds.), *Correctional mental health handbook.* (pp. 73–74). Thousand Oaks, CA: Sage.

Springer, D. W., McNeece, C. A., & Arnold, E. M. (2003). *Substance abuse treatment for criminal offenders: An evidence-based guide for practitioners.* Washington, DC: American Psychological Association.

Substance Abuse and Mental Health Services Administration. (2006). *Results from the 2005 National Survey on Drug Use and Health: National findings* (NSDUH Series H-30, DHHS Pub. No. (SMA) 06–4194). Rockville, MD: Office of Applied Studies, Substance Abuse and Mental Health Services Administration.

The National Center on Addiction and Substance Abuse (CASA) at Columbia University. (1998). *Behind bars: Substance abuse and America's prison population.* New York, NY: CASA.

The National Center on Addiction and Substance Abuse (CASA) at Columbia University. (2010). *Behind bars II: Substance abuse and America's prison population.* New York, NY: CASA

The National Center on Addiction and Substance Abuse (CASA) at Columbia University. (2010). *Behind bars II: Substance abuse and America's prison population.* New York, NY: CASA.

REFERENCES

American Medical Association. (2009). *American Medical Association timeline: 1941 to 1960.* [Electronic version]. Retrieved from http://www.ama-assn.org.

American University, School of Public Affairs, Justice Programs Office. (2009). *BJA Drug Court Clearinghouse Project. Summary of drug court activity by state and county. July 14, 2009.* [Electronic version]. Retrieved from http://www1.spa.american.edu.

Austin, A. (2010). *Criminal justice trends: Key legislative changes in sentencing policy, 2001–2010.* New York, NY: Vera Institute of Justice.

Babor, T. F., Higgins-Biddle, J. C., Dauser, D., Burleson, J. A., Zarkin, G. A., & Bray, J. W. (2006). Brief interventions for at-risk drinking: Patient outcomes and cost-effectiveness in managed care organizations. *Alcohol and Alcoholism, 41*(6), 624–631.

Beckett, K., Nyrop, K., & Pfingst, L. (2006). Race, drugs, and policing: Understanding disparities in drug delivery arrests. *Criminology, 44*(1), 105–137.

Benekos, P. J., & Merlo, A. V. (1995). Three strikes and you're out! The political sentencing game. *Federal Probation, 59*(1), 3–9.

Bhati, A. S., Roman, J. K., & Chalfin, A. (2008). *To treat or not to treat: Evidence on the prospects of expanding treatment to drug-involved offenders.* Washington, DC: Urban Institute, Justice Policy Center.

Bill, P., Briggs, M., Huffman, K., & Lubot-Conk, R. (2003). *Drug policy reforms: 1996–2002. A report by the Drug Policy Alliance.* New York, NY: Drug Policy Alliance.

California Department of Corrections and Rehabilitation. (2009). *Corrections moving forward.* Sacramento: California Department of Corrections and Rehabilitation, Office of Public and Employee Communications.

Center for Substance Abuse Treatment. (2005a). *Substance abuse treatment for adults in the criminal justice system. Treatment Improvement Protocol (TIP) series 44* (DHHS Pub. No. (SMA) 05–4056). Rockville, MD: U.S. Department of Health and Human Services, Substance Abuse and Mental Health Services Administration, Center for Substance Abuse Treatment.

Chandler, R. K., Fletcher, B. W., & Volkow, N. D. (2009). Treating drug abuse and addiction in the criminal justice system: Improving public health and safety. *Journal of the American Medical Association, 301*(2), 183–190.

Compton, T., & Meacham, M. (2005, March 22). Prison gangs: Descriptions and selected intervention. *Forensic Examiner,* 8.

Corrections Compendium. (2007). *Correctional officers: Hiring requirements and wages.* Lincoln, NE: CEGA Services.

Council of State Governments Justice Center. (2009). *Justice reinvestment in Texas: Assessing the impact of the 2007 Justice Reinvestment Initiative.* New York, NY: Council of Author.

Culp, R. F. (2005). The rise and stall of prison privatization: An integration of policy analysis perspectives. *Criminal Justice Policy Review, 16*(4), 412–442.

Dackis, C., & O'Brien, C. (2005). Neurobiology of addiction: Treatment and public policy ramifications. *Nature Neuroscience, 8*(11), 1431–1436.

Drug Policy Alliance. (2009a). *New York's Rockefeller drug laws: Explaining the reforms of 2009.* [Electronic version]. Retrieved from http://drugpolicy.org.

Drug Policy Alliance. (2010). *About Prop 36.* [Electronic version]. Retrieved from http://www.prop36.org.

Ehlers, S., Schiraldi, V., & Ziedenberg, J. (2004). *Still striking out: Ten years of California's Three Strikes.* Washington, DC: Justice Policy Institute.

Eighth Judicial Circuit Family Court. (2010). *Specialty courts.* [Electronic version]. Retrieved from http://www.circuit8.org.

Finigan, M. W., Carey, S. M., & Cox, A. (2007). *The impact of a mature drug court over 10 years of operation: Recidivism and costs.* Portland, OR: NPC Research.

Friedmann, P. D., Taxman, F. S., & Henderson, C. E. (2007). Evidence-based treatment practices for drug-involved adults in the criminal justice system. *Journal of Substance Abuse Treatment, 32*(3), 267–277.

Garner, B. R., Knight, K., & Simpson, D. D. (2007). Burnout among corrections-based drug treatment staff: Impact of individual and organizational factors. *International Journal of Offender Therapy and Comparative Criminology, 51*(5), 510–522.

Gentilello, L. M., Ebel, B. E., Wickizer, T. M., Salkever, D. S., & Rivara, F. P. (2005). Alcohol interventions for trauma patients treated in emergency departments and hospitals: A cost benefit analysis. *Annals of Surgery, 241*(4), 541–550.

Gramlich, J. (2009). *Tracking the recession: Prison economics.* [Electronic version]. Retrieved from http://www.stateline.org

Green, B. L., Furrer, C., Worcel, S., Burrus, S., & Finigan, M. W. (2007). How effective are family treatment drug courts? Outcomes from a four-site national study. *Child Maltreatment, 12*(1), 43–59.

Hawken, A. (2009). *HOPE: Theoretical underpinnings and evaluation findings: Testimonial prepared for the Oregon State Legislature.* [Electronic version]. Crime Victims United of Oregon. Retrieved from http://www.crimevictimsunited.org

Henry, D. A., & Clark, J. (1999). *Pretrial drug testing: An overview of issues and practices* (NCJ 176341). Washington, DC: U.S. Department of Justice, Office of Justice Programs, Bureau of Justice Assistance.

Hogue, A., Dauber, S., & Samuolis, J. (2006). Treatment techniques and outcomes in multi-dimensional family therapy for adolescent behavior problems. *Journal of Family Psychology, 20*(4), 535–543.

Hser, Y. I., Teruya, C., Brown, A. H., Huang, D., Evans, E., & Anglin, M. D. (2007). Impact of California's Proposition 36 on the drug treatment system: Treatment capacity and displacement. *American Journal of Public Health, 97*(1), 104–109.

Huddleston, C. W., Marlowe, D. B., & Casebolt, R. (2008). *Painting the current picture: A national report card on drug courts and other problem-solving court programs in the United States* (2nd ed.) (Vol. 1). Alexandria, VA: National Drug Court Institute.

Inciardi, J. A., Martin, S. S., Butzin, C. A., Hooper, R. M., & Harrison, L. D. (1997). An effective model of prison-based treatment for drug-involved offenders. *Journal of Drug Issues, 27*(2), 261–278.

James, D. J., & Glaze, L. E. (2006). *Mental health problems of prison and jail inmates* (NCJ 213600). Washington, DC: U.S. Department of Justice, Bureau of Justice Statistics.

Junginger, J., Claypoole, K., Laygo, R., & Crisanti, A. (2006). Effects of serious mental illness and substance abuse on criminal offenses. *Psychiatric Services, 57*(6), 879–882.

Kalinich, D. B., & Stojkovic, S. (1985). Contraband: The basis for legitimate power in a prison social system. *Criminal Justice and Behavior, 12*(4), 435–451.

Kaufman, E., Yoshioka, M. R. M., & Center for Substance Abuse Treatment. (2004). *Substance abuse treatment and family therapy. Treatment Improvement Protocol (TIP) series No. 39* (DHHS Pub. No. (SMA) 05–4006). Rockville, MD: U.S. Department of Health and Human Services, Substance Abuse and Mental Health Services Administration, Center for Substance Abuse Treatment.

Kautt, P., & Spohn, C. (2002). Crack-ing down on black drug offenders? Testing for interactions among offenders' race, drug type, and sentencing strategy in federal drug sentences. *Justice Quarterly, 19*(1), 1–35.

Kelley, L., Mueller, D., & Hemmens, C. (2004). To punish or rehabilitate revisited: An analysis of the purpose/goals of state correctional statutes, 1991–2002. *Criminal Justice Studies, 17*(4), 333–351.

King, R. S., & Pasquarella, J. (2009). *Drug courts: A review of the evidence.* Washington, DC: Sentencing Project.

Krisberg, B., & Marchionna, S. (2006). *Attitudes of US voters toward prisoner rehabilitation and reentry policies.* [Electronic version]. National Council on Crime and Delinquency. Retrieved from http://www.nccd-crc.org

Lake Research Partners. (2009). *New poll shows broad bi-partisan support for improving access to alcohol and drug addiction treatment.* [Electronic version]. Retrieved from http://www.soros.org.

Lapido, D. (2009). The rise of America's prison-industrial complex. *New Left Review, 7*(Jan/Feb), 109–123.

Longshore, D., Hawken, A., Urada, D., & Anglin, M. D. (2006). *Evaluation of the Substance Abuse and Crime Prevention Act SACPA, cost-analysis report (first and second years).* Los Angeles: UCLA Integrated Substance Abuse Programs.

Lynch, J. P. (1995). Crime in international perspective. In J. Q. Wilson & J. Petersilia (Eds.), *Crime.* (p. 11). San Francisco, CA: ICS Press.

Mauer, M. (2003). *Comparative international rates of incarceration: An examination of causes and trends.* [Electronic version]. Retrieved from http://www.sentencingproject.org.

Mauer, M. (2007). The hidden problem of time served in prison. *Social Research, 74*(2), 701–706.

Marshall v. United States, 414 U. S. 417 (1974).

Martinson, R. (1974). What works? Questions and answers about prison reform. *The Public Interest, 35*(Spring), 22–54.

McLearen, A. M., & Ryba, N. L. (2003). Identifying severely mentally ill inmates: Can small jails comply with detection standards? *Journal of Offender Rehabilitation, 37*(1), 25–40.

McNiel, D. E., Binder, R. L., & Robinson, J. C. (2005). Incarceration associated with homelessness, mental disorder, and co-occurring substance abuse. *Psychiatric Services, 56*(7), 840–846.

Moore, M. T. (2009). *Jobs lost as states close prisons.* [Electronic version]. *USA Today.* Retrieved from http://www.usatoday.com.

Mundt, M. P. (2006). Analyzing the costs and benefits of brief interventions. *Alcohol Research and Health, 29*(1), 34–36.

National Institute of Justice. (2006). *Drug courts: The second decade* (NCJ 211081). Washington, DC: U.S. Department of Justice, Office of Justice Programs, National Institute of Justice.

National Institute on Drug Abuse. (1999). *Principles of drug addiction treatment: A research-based guide* [Revised April 2009] (NIH Pub. No. 09–4180). Rockville, MD: U.S. Department of Health and Human Services, National Institutes of Health, National Institute on Drug Abuse.

National Institute on Drug Abuse. (2006). *Principles of drug abuse treatment for criminal justice populations: A research-based guide* (NIH Pub. No. 06–5316). Washington, DC: U.S. Department of Health and Human Services, National Institutes of Health, National Institute on Drug Abuse.

National Institute on Drug Abuse. (2008). *Drugs, brains, and behavior: The science of addiction.* [Electronic version]. Retrieved from http://www.drugabuse.gov.

New York State Division of Criminal Justice Services. (2010). *Preliminary impact of 2009 drug law reform: October 2009—September 2010.* Albany, NY: Author.

Nisperos, N. (2009). *State cuts prison rehab, hundreds of prison jobs.* [Electronic version]. Retrieved http://www.dailybulletin.com.

Osler, M. (2007). More than numbers: A proposal for rational drug sentences. *Federal Sentencing Reporter, 19*(5), 326–328.

Pager, D. (2007). *Marked: Race, crime, and finding work in an era of mass incarceration.* Chicago, IL: University of Chicago Press.

Pallone, N. J., & Hennessy, J. (2003), To punish or to treat: Substance abuse within the context of oscillating attitudes toward correctional rehabilitation. *Journal of Offender Rehabilitation, 37*(3/4), 1–25.

Peters, R. H., & Steinberg, M. L. (2000). Substance abuse treatment services in US prisons. In D. Shewan & J. B. Davies (Eds.), *Drug use and prisons: An international perspective.* (pp. 89–116). Amsterdam, The Netherlands: Harwood Academic Publishers.

Pew Center on the States. (2008). *One in 100: Behind bars in America 2008.* Washington, DC: Pew Charitable Trusts.

Pew Center on the States. (2010). *Prison count 2010: State population declines for the first time in 38 years.* Washington, DC: Pew Charitable Trusts.

Richman, J. (2009). *California cuts of Prop. 36 drug treatment funding called 'a harm that keeps on hurting.'* [Electronic version]. Retrieved from http://www.mercurynews.com.

Rinaldo, S. G., & Kelly-Thomas, I. (2005). *Comparing California's Proposition 36 (SACPA) with similar legislation in other states and jurisdictions.* Berkeley, CA: The Avisa Group.

Rosen, C. J., & Goldkamp, J. S. (1989). The constitutionality of drug testing at the bail stage. *Journal of Criminal Law & Criminology, 80*(1), 114–176.

Ryan S. K., & Pasquarella, J. (2009). *Drug courts: A review of the evidence.* Washington, DC: The Sentencing Project.

Sabol, W. J., Couture, H., & Harrison, P. M. (2007). *Bulletin: Prisoners in 2006* (NCJ 219416). Washington, DC: U.S. Department of Justice, Office of Justice Programs, Bureau of Justice Statistics.

Sabol, W. J., Minton, T. D., & Harrison, P. M. (2008). *Prison and jail inmates at midyear 2006* (NCJ 217675). Washington, DC: U.S. Department of Justice, Office of Justice Programs, Bureau of Justice Statistics.

Schiraldi, V., Colburn, J., & Lotke, E. (2004). *Three strikes and you're out: An examination of the impact of 3-strike laws: 10 years after their enactment.* [Electronic version]. Retrieved from http://justicepolicy.org

Schlosser, E. (1998, December). The prison-industrial complex. *Atlantic Monthly, 51–77.*

Scott, J. (2009). *Paterson signs Rockefeller drug law reforms.* [Electronic version]. Retrieved from http://www.nbcnewyork.com.

Solberg, L. I., Maciosek, M. V., & Edwards, N. M. (2008). Primary care intervention to reduce alcohol misuse: Ranking its health impact and cost effectiveness. *American Journal of Preventive Medicine, 34*(2), 143–152.

Substance Abuse and Mental Health Services Administration. (2002). *Substance abuse services and staffing in adult correctional facilities.* [Electronic version]. Retrieved from http://www.oas.samhsa.gov.

Sung, H. E., & Belenko, S. (2006). From diversion experiment to policy movement: A case study of prosecutorial innovation in the United States. *Journal of Contemporary Criminal Justice, 22*(3), 220–240.

Sykes, G. M., & Messinger, S. L. (1960). The inmate social system. In R. A. Cloward (Ed.), *Theoretical studies in social organization of the prison.* (pp. 5–19). New York, NY: Social Science Research Council.

Taxman, F., Prerdoni, M. L., & Harrison, L. D. (2007). Drug treatment services for adult offenders: The state of the state. *Journal of Substance Abuse Treatment, 32*(3), 239–254.

The National Center on Addiction and Substance Abuse (CASA) at Columbia University. (1993). *The cost of substance abuse to America's health care system: Report 1: Medicaid hospital costs.* New York, NY: CASA.

The National Center on Addiction and Substance Abuse (CASA) at Columbia University. (2003). *Crossing the bridge: An evaluation of the drug treatment alternative-to-prison (DTAP) program.* New York, NY: CASA.

The National Center on Addiction and Substance Abuse (CASA) at Columbia University. (2010h). *CASA Analysis of the Bureau of Justice Statistics report: Prisoners in 1996*

(Revised 7/21/97) (NCJ 164619). Washington, DC: U.S. Department of Justice, Bureau of Justice Statistics.

The National Center on Addiction and Substance Abuse (CASA) at Columbia University. (2010i). *CASA Analysis of the Bureau of Justice Statistics report: Prisoners in 2006* (NCJ 219416). Washington, DC: U.S. Department of Justice, Bureau of Justice Statistics.

The National Center on Addiction and Substance Abuse (CASA) at Columbia University. (2010k). *CASA Analysis of the Bureau of Justice Statistics report: Survey of inmates in federal correctional facilities, 1991.* Washington, DC: U.S. Department of Justice, Bureau of Justice Statistics.

The National Center on Addiction and Substance Abuse (CASA) at Columbia University. (2010l). *CASA Analysis of the Bureau of Justice Statistics report: Survey of inmates in federal correctional facilities, 2004.* Washington, DC: U.S. Department of Justice, Bureau of Justice Statistics.

The National Center on Addiction and Substance Abuse (CASA) at Columbia University. (2010m). *CASA Analysis of the Bureau of Justice Statistics report: Survey of inmates in local jails, 1989.* Washington, DC: U.S. Department of Justice, Bureau of Justice Statistics.

The National Center on Addiction and Substance Abuse (CASA) at Columbia University. (2010n). *CASA Analysis of the Bureau of Justice Statistics report: Survey of inmates in local jails, 2002.* Washington, DC: U.S. Department of Justice, Bureau of Justice Statistics.

The National Center on Addiction and Substance Abuse (CASA) at Columbia University. (2010o). *CASA Analysis of the Bureau of Justice Statistics report: Survey of inmates in state correctional facilities, 1991.* Washington, DC: U.S. Department of Justice, Bureau of Justice Statistics.

The National Center on Addiction and Substance Abuse (CASA) at Columbia University. (2010p). *CASA Analysis of the Bureau of Justice Statistics report: Survey of inmates in state correctional facilities, 2004.* Washington, DC: U.S. Department of Justice, Bureau of Justice Statistics.

The National Center on Addiction and Substance Abuse (CASA) at Columbia University. (2010s). *CASA Analysis of the Census Bureau data set website: Historical national population estimates: July 1, 1990 to July 1, 1999.* [Electronic version]. Retrieved from http://www.census.gov

The National Center on Addiction and Substance Abuse (CASA) at Columbia University. (2010t). *CASA analysis of the Census Bureau data set website: Table 1: Annual estimates of the resident population for the United States, regions, states, and Puerto Rico: April 1, 2000 to July 1, 2008* (NSST-EST2008–01). [Electronic version]. Retrieved from http://www.census.gov

The National Center on Addiction and Substance Abuse (CASA) at Columbia University. (2010x). *CASA Analysis of the National Survey on Drug Use and Health (NSDUH), 2006* (Data file). Rockville, MD: U.S. Department of Health and Human Services, Substance Abuse and Mental Health Services Administration.

Tonry, M. (1995). *Malign neglect—Race, crime, and punishment in America.* New York, NY: Oxford University Press.

Tonry, M. (2004). *Thinking about crime: Sense and sensibility in American penal culture.* New York, NY: Oxford University Press.

Torres, S., & Latta, R. M. (2000). Training the substance abuse specialist. *Federal Probation, 64*(2), 52–5750.

United States v. Booker, 543 U. S. 220 (2005).

U.S. General Accounting Office. (2003). *Federal drug offenses: Departures from sentencing guidelines and mandatory minimum sentences, fiscal years 1999–2001* (GAO-04–105). Washington, DC: U.S. General Accounting Office.

U.S. General Accounting Office. (2005). *Adult drug courts: Evidence indicates recidivism reductions and mixed results for other outcomes* (GAO-05–219). [Online]. Retrieved November 2, 2009 from http://www.gao.gov.

U.S. Sentencing Commission. (2006). *Final report on the impact of United States v. Booker on federal sentencing.* Washington, DC: United States Sentencing Commission.

U.S. Sentencing Commission. (2008). *U.S. Sentencing Commission preliminary crack cocaine retroactivity data report.* Washington, DC: U.S. Sentencing Commission.

Valdez, A. J. (2009). Prison gangs 101. *Corrections Today, 71*(1), 40–43.

Van Kesteren, J. (2009). Public attitudes and sentencing policies across the world. *European Journal on Criminal Policy and Research, 15*(1–2), 25–46.

Van Voorhis, P., Braswell, M., & Morrow, B. (2000). Family therapy. In P. Van Voorhis, M. Braswell, & D. Lester (Eds.), *Correctional counseling and rehabilitation, fourth edition.* (4th ed.) (pp. 225–248). Cincinnati, OH: Anderson Publishing.

Visher, C. A. (1992). Pretrial drug testing: Panacea or Pandora's Box? (NCJ 137057). *Annals of the American Academy of Political and Social Science, 521*(1), 112–131.

Western, B., & Pettit, B. (2002). Beyond crime and punishment: Prisons and inequality. *Contexts, 1*(3), 37–43.

Wilhelm, D. F., & Turner, N. R. (2002). *Is the budget crisis changing the way we look at sentencing and incarceration?* New York, NY: Vera Institute of Justice.

Wilson, J. Q. (1983). *Thinking about crime. Revised edition.* New York, NY: Vintage Books.

Wish, E. D., Petronis, K. R., & Yacoubian, G. S. (2002). CADS: Two short screeners for cocaine and heroin dependence among arrestees. *Journal of Drug Issues, 32*(3), 907–920.

Zimring, F. E., Hawkins, G., & Kamin, S. (2001). *Punishment and democracy: Three strikes and you're out in California.* New York, NY: Oxford University Press.

CHAPTER 17

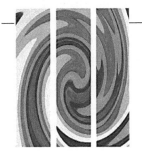

Conclusion: Assess, Progress, Success

Lior Gideon

P risons are a place of punishment and redemption. Prisons are also places where society has a unique opportunity to focus on treating offenders and preparing them to rejoin society after incarceration. By now, scholars fully acknowledge the fact that more than 90% of incarcerated inmates will be released from prisons back to their respective communities (Petersilia, 2001, 2003, 2005; Travis, 2005; Gideon, 2011). The way in which convicted and incarcerated individuals experience their incarceration will have an effect on the way in which they reenter and reintegrate with society. In light of the above, it is vital to examine how inmates with special needs experience their incarceration, and how the system addresses their needs, preparing them for reentry and successful reintegration. This is important, because when prison is perceived as unjust and excessively harsh, it may actually backfire by increasing recidivism. This effect is what Sherman (1993) calls the "defiance theory." Punishments that are perceived to be unjust, unfair, or excessive, and in the case of this discussion, punishments that violate basic rights and do not take into consideration special needs, can result in offenders becoming more defiant and rebellious, which in turn increases future criminal behavior. The public expects prison, as the ultimate form of punishment, to reduce crime and protect communities (Clear, 1994); however, if these goals are not met precisely because the harsh corrections system provokes defiance, then what good can come of it?

Incarcerated offenders experience their punishment in different ways. For example, May and Wood (2010) state that "having experienced a given sanction influences subsequent perceptions of the punitiveness of that sanction" (p. 9). Hawkins and Alpert (1989) also suggest that similar forms of punishment may impact people differently. These insights should not be taken lightly simply because society believes offenders deserve to be punished. Consequently, the argument presented in this chapter, and indeed through all the research in this book, is this: *Offenders should be punished, and at times incarcerated and segregated from society, but punishments should be differentiated according to the specific offender's needs and risk factors and their relative prospects for rehabilitation.*

Such an approach will better serve public safety and health while also signaling to offenders that they are part of society. It is within this context that a discussion of special needs offenders behind bars was introduced through the chapters of this book, with the aim to expose and familiarize readers with some of the different categories of special needs incarcerated offenders, the challenges they pose to correctional facilities and management, and how such needs and challenges should be dealt with.

The book began with the more traditional categories of those incarcerated offenders to be considered to have special needs, namely juveniles, females, elderly, and mentally ill offenders, as these categories have experienced an alarming increase in incarceration rates in recent years. The book then continue to discuss those offenders that were always in the system but received very little attention in terms of their needs and challenges, as well as the challenges they present to the management of the facilities in which they are housed. In that context, a discussion was presented about gay and lesbian inmates, inmates under protective custody, sex offenders, inmates of different religions, veterans, and inmates on death row.

The following chapters dealt with smaller populations that have become an issue only recently: illegal immigrants behind bars and the radicalization of Muslim inmates while incarcerated. These two topics have become a major focus of concern not just in the United States but worldwide, as illegal migration and terror activity are social threats to many societies. The chapter on substance-abusing inmates deals with a segment that is not at all uncommon in the correctional landscape; however, substance-abusing inmates are still increasing in numbers and are also responsible for the majority of crimes in the United States. Not surprisingly, substance-abusing inmates also comprise the majority of our prison population.

For each of the populations described and discussed, a common theme emerges: the need to assess and react to the needs and challenges each presents. Consequently, the next section will focus on developing a theoretical model that aims to incorporate the policy recommendations of previous chapters while further developing the argument set forward earlier in this chapter.

SPECIAL NEEDS OFFENDERS: ASSESS, ADDRESS, PROGRESS, AND SUCCESS

For each and every offender that is taken into correctional custody, an intake assessment must be performed. Such an assessment is essential not just for the sake of classification, but also to help correctional administrators and other correctional staff understand the needs of each offender and the risks they introduce to the system. Such knowledge is highly important especially when we acknowledge the fact that, as Dilulio (1987) suggests, it is the population that resides within an institution that defines its characteristics and dynamics, and not those who seemingly control it.

Let us now direct our attention to the different stages of the theoretical model suggested in Figure 17.1, which proposes that any success in corrections must begin with a thorough assessment. The terminology used in this model should be familiar

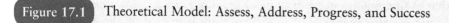
Figure 17.1 Theoretical Model: Assess, Address, Progress, and Success

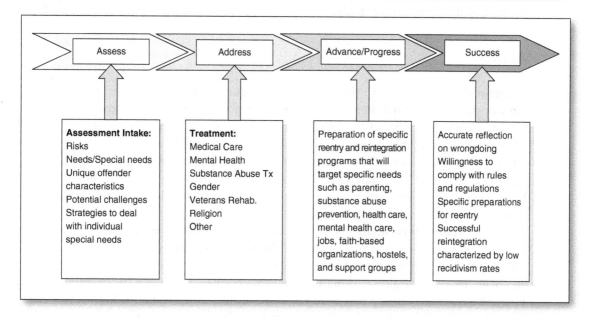

to those engaged in correctional research. Assessment has been an integral part of correctional practice for decades, and correctional treatment, rehabilitation, and recidivism are all used as measures of success. Nevertheless, it is essential to place these terms on a continuum and examine them in the context of inmates with special needs, as no two inmates are alike. Further, and as mentioned earlier, for treatment to be successful it must address the individual. A blanket treatment for all incarcerated men and women may result in very little success.

Assessment

After the risks and needs of an offender are assessed, an appropriate intervention should be prepared and offered to the inmate. It is vital that such an assessment be completed prior to admitting the offender to the institution in which he or she will be serving their sentence. Conducting the assessment at an early stage is important as it helps identify factors that may have contributed to the present offense. It is also necessary to identify health and mental health issues that may put a strain on certain facilities or pose a massive health hazard for inmates and staff. It is also recommended that additional screening and assessment be conducted by the receiving facility. This should be a more thorough intake process, in which a correctional psychologist, a member of the medical staff, and a correctional intelligence officer join forces to provide a clear portrait of the individual inmate. For the most part, this procedure is already done. However, issues of confidentiality surrounding medical issues sometimes impede the exchange of vital information that at first might not seem to be of great relevance. Such cases must be minimized, and the free exchange of information must prevail to allow a full portrait of the inmate to be made.

Address

Although all inmates must participate in an intake process, as described earlier, most of the inmates' needs are not addressed during their periods of incarceration. In fact, Gideon and Sung (2011) argue that "the lack of systematic implementation of evidence-based rehabilitation interventions in our prisons is responsible for the unacceptable fact that 67.5% of state prison inmates were rearrested within three years of their release" (p. 402). Indeed, and as evident from previous chapters in this book, many of the offenders do not receive adequate treatment, if at all, and those who do may not be receiving the sort of treatment that is research-informed to adequately address their needs. As Maile, Calkins-Mercado, and Jeglic discussed in Chapter 10, this is particularly true for sex offenders, who often fear retaliation by other inmates if their offense becomes known. It is also a problem for many veterans, who are often afraid of losing their government benefits. Many incarcerated veterans unjustifiably afraid that once the word of their incarceration is known to veterans' affairs and other related bodies, benefits will be lost. While such fear may be true for the period of incarceration, such nullification of benefits is not permanent, usually being restored after release.

One of the most outrageous paradoxes is the case of those inmates who are substance abusers, and who committed crimes because of their addiction, but who cannot break the cycle due to the lack of a substance-abuse treatment program inside prison. Females incarcerated for substance-abuse related crimes, particularly those who are pregnant and mothers of minor children, form a subset of this group, as Henriquez and Gladwin discuss in Chapter 4. Miller and McCoy (Chapter 9) point out a similar paradox in regard to inmates who are placed under protective custody, many of whom are in need of care for mental illness.

As the model in Figure 17.1 suggests, addressing the needs of offenders can be done in various ways and by introducing different types of interventions: medical care for existing illnesses such as tuberculosis; mental health treatment; sessions with a chaplain; veteran-sponsored rehabilitation initiatives such as treating of PTSD and planning for reintegration; and educational and vocational training programs. Addressing the needs of offenders will not make the sentence less punitive; readers should understand that even though incarcerated people lose their freedom, they are still entitled to basic human rights guaranteed under the U.S. Constitution. Allowing incarcerated individuals with special needs to access programs and treatment is an important part in the process of preparing them for rejoining society when their prison sentence is done. It should be clear that addressing incarcerated offenders' needs and risks should logically follow from their assessment report, and thus feedback must be present. Specifically, once initial intervention is in place, subsequent assessment should follow to chart the progress of the plan.

Advance and Progress

During their incarceration, inmates should demonstrate their advancement through the program, as well as their ability to comply with institutional rules, requirements, and regulations. Inmates should be examined and reassessed for their risk of victimization, health issues, and any progress in their mental health condition. Additionally, reentry and reintegration programs that will target specific needs—such as parenting support, substance abuse prevention, health and mental health maintenance, job coaching, faith-based support, lodging in hostels, and other support groups—should be discussed. Monitoring the advancement and progress of special needs inmates is also important for facility management, as it may affect classification levels, and consequently inmates' access to much-needed interventions. For example, not all death row inmates require maximum security and 23 hours of segregation, as Cunningham discusses in Chapter 13. Similarly, mentally ill offenders, who have a higher tendency to violate institutional rules, are often transferred to special housing units (SHUs), where access to mental care is more difficult. However, as Chapter 6 discusses, if progress is made and behavior is controlled, such offenders can be placed with the general population, where treatment is more available and psychologists can work with the inmates on their reentry and reintegration plans. Similar observations can be made for the case of prison radicalization, where intervention is highly critical to keeping inmates from being brainwashed and led astray.

Once progress is made and threat is reduced, institutional considerations of security may be changed to allow more access to the general population and to vital counseling and services. Additional referrals can be made at times of reentry. In sum, in this stage of advancement, inmates should be evaluated in the context of their assessed needs, the manner in which their needs and risks have been addressed, and what progress they made. Such progress should be weighed to determine whether needs have changed, and how such a change may affect the management of the inmate.

Success

Managing special needs offenders may be a daunting challenge. Success is in the eyes of the observer. For some correctional staff, success means they get to go home safe at the end of their shift without having to file misconduct reports. For others, success may simply be "no one died" under their shift, whereas for inmates, success can mean no special incidents, attacks, or threats—they survived another day. *Surviving* is the key word when dealing with prisons and the management of special needs offenders. Success, as Figure 17.1 indicates, can occur when prisoners display accurate reflection on wrongdoing and, despite their needs, are willing to comply with rules and regulations. Such compliance, as discussed previously in this chapter, leads to advancement that results in progress, and more exposure to available resources that will prepare the inmate for when he or she reenters society.

Success also means that incarcerated offenders are not released from prison in worse condition than when they entered. This is a very real and unfortunate possibility for many offenders who are sentenced to long periods of incarceration—a result of several fairly recent policies such as the *three strikes* laws, mandatory sentencing, and the housing of many mentally ill individuals who should be hospitalized rather than imprisoned. This is also the case for many nonviolent female offenders, particularly those who have minor children or are pregnant at the time of incarceration. For many other special needs incarcerated offenders, being segregated from society worsens their mental conditions and thus prevents them from successful reintegration. Success in those instances means that special needs must be addressed in such a way that the transition from prison to the community will be as smooth and uneventful as possible. Successful reintegration means low recidivism rates, which indicate the ability to survive in society without criminal involvement. Accordingly, successful punishment should be differentiated according to the needs of the offender and his or her relative prospects for rehabilitation and reintegration.

In sum, each stage of the theoretical model presented in Figure 17.1 leads to the other and should correspond with one another. Each stage must also be evaluated according to the stage that preceded it. As mentioned earlier, this feedback is essential for targeting not just initial needs but evolving and changing needs that are crucial for the proper management of offenders, and also for the offenders' own safety.

DISCUSSION AND CONCLUSION

Society cannot tolerate those who violate its norms and laws. It is for this reason that prisons have evolved to house those who have harmed others and violated common social norms. Indeed, punishment is a function of the moral outrage that members of society express toward those offenders who have violated the social equilibrium (Irwin, 2005). But American prisons have become warehouses, a practice that can seem inhuman to those who observe from the outside; Irwin (2005) even suggests that if aliens from another universe visited Earth, they would not understand our "barbaric" way of caging our own. This supposition seems even more plausible when one notes the diversity of inmates, all locked up under similar conditions, without any cognition of their special circumstances and unique personal needs.

Yes, offenders should be punished and pay for their wrongdoing. However, effective punishment should enable the wrongdoer to reflect on his or her actions while also offering a means of redemption. It is in this context that offenders' special needs must be acknowledged so that punishment can be tailored to be more effective. Undifferentiated punishments are counterproductive to both inmates and prison management, as they may promote higher levels of defiance (Sherman, 1993), resulting in more infractions and lack of genuine redemption and rehabilitation. Furthermore, the practice of simply locking up offenders without addressing their needs pulls us back to the dark ages in the history of prisons when people were incarcerated in harsh conditions simply because they were orphans, vagrants, paupers, mentally ill, or otherwise on the fringes of society. Years of valuable research informs us that we cannot, and should not, tolerate such practices, as they clearly have a negative effect on our communities (Clear, 1994). Ignoring the needs of the incarcerated does more harm than good. Ultimately, as prisons continue to warehouse offenders, it is society that pays the expensive bill of higher recidivism and decaying communities. Simply warehousing a person is a punishment that does not fit the crime—any crime. Differentiated punishment and incarceration, according to individual needs and risks, can be a far more productive way to deal with offenders.

Before truly effective differentiated punishment can be devised, as this book suggests, more research is needed to establish a better understanding of the scope and needs of special needs populations and how their presence in the American correctional system presents challenges to its staff and management. While some populations—females, juveniles, the elderly—have better visibility, others are less visible and need further examination. This warrants evidence) based practices that can be used as the basis for policy changes.

Although this book focuses on various categories of special needs offenders, the term *special needs* should not actually be reserved just for specific groups of incarcerated individuals. We are, after all, dealing with individual people, each with an individual set of needs that must be taken into consideration. Correctional institutions are expected to correct, not make things worse, but warehousing offenders as an undifferentiated mass and ignoring their needs does in fact make things worse. Thus it is essential to focus our attention on special needs offenders, as they are growing in presence inside our correctional system. This may strike many as a very liberal approach; however, a closer examination shows that by paying attention and addressing those needs, society will be the primary beneficiary.

REFERENCES

Clear, T. R. (1994). *Harm in American penology: Offenders, victims, and their communities.* Albany: State University of New York.

Dilulio, J. J. (1987). *A comparative study of correctional management.* New York, NY: The Free Press.

Gideon, L. (2011). Corrections in an era of reentry. In L. Gideon & H. E. Sung (Eds.), *Rethinking corrections: Rehabilitation, reentry, and reintegration* (1–17). Thousand Oaks, CA: Sage.

Gideon, L., & Sung, H. E. (2011). Conclusion: Integrative triple R theory—Rehabilitation, reentry, and reintegration. In L. Gideon & H. E. Sung (Eds.). *Rethinking corrections: Rehabilitation, reentry, and reintegration* (399–407). Thousand Oaks, CA: Sage.

Hawkins, R., & Alpert, G. P. (1989). *American prison system: Punishment and justice.* Englewood Cliffs, NJ: Prentice Hall.

Irwin, J. (2005). *The Warehouse Prison.* Los Angeles, CA: Roxbury Publishing.

May, D. C., & Wood, P. B. (2010). *Ranking correctional punishments: Views from offenders, practitioners, and the public.* Durham, NC: Carolina Academic Press.

Petersilia, J. (2001). Prisoner reentry: Public safety and reintegration challenges. *The Prison Journal, 81*(3), 360–375.

Petersilia, J. (2003). *When prisoners come home: Parole and prisoner reentry.* New York, NY: Oxford University Press.

Petersilia, J. (2005) Confronting recidivism: Inmate reentry and the second chance act. In *Reentry today: Programs, problems, & solutions* (pp. 25–34). Alexandria, VA: American Correctional Association.

Sherman, L. W. (1993). Defiance, deterrence, and irrelevance: A theory of the criminal sanction. *Journal of Research in Crime and Delinquency, 30*(4), 445–473.

Travis, J. (2005). *But they all come back: Facing the challenges of prisoner reentry.* Washington, DC: Urban Institute Press.

Name Index

503

Subject Index

About the Editor

Lior Gideon, PhD, is an associate professor at John Jay College of Criminal Justice in New York, New York. He specializes in corrections-based program evaluation and focuses his research on rehabilitation, reentry, and reintegration issues and in particular by examining offenders' perceptions of their needs. His research interests also involve international and comparative corrections-related public opinion surveys and their effect on policy. To that extent, Dr. Gideon published several manuscripts on these topics, including two previously published books on offenders needs in the reintegration process: *Substance Abusing Inmates: Experiences of Recovering Drug Addicts on Their Way Back Home* (2010, Springer), and *Rethinking Corrections: Rehabilitation, Reentry, and Reintegration* (with Hung-En Sung, 2011, Sage). Aside from the above, Dr. Gideon has published, or is in the process of completing, two books in methodology. His other works were recently published in *The Prison Journal*, the *International Journal of Offender Therapy and Comparative Criminology*, and the *Asian Journal of Criminology*. Dr. Gideon earned his PhD from the Faculty of Law, Institute of Criminology at the Hebrew University in Jerusalem, Israel, and completed a postdoctoral fellowship at the University of Maryland's Bureau of Governmental Research.

About the Contributors

Traqina Q. Emeka, PhD, is an assistant professor at the University of Houston Downtown. She serves as the assistant chair and graduate coordinator in the Department of Criminal Justice. Her research interests include juvenile delinquency, victimology, recidivism, and community corrections. She is also the coauthor of *American Victimology* and has published in the areas of child abuse, juvenile recidivism, and community corrections.

Nelseta V. Walters-Jones, PhD, is a faculty member in the Department of Justice Administration at University of Louisville in Louisville, Kentucky. She received her PhD in Juvenile Justice from Prairie View A & M University in Prairie View, Texas, in 2008. She has published in *Texas Probation Journal, Journal of Ethnicity in Criminal Justice,* and *American Journal of Criminal Justice.*

Lisa Pasko, PhD, is an assistant professor at the University of Denver in Colorado. She received her PhD from the University of Hawaii at Manoa. Lisa's primary research and teaching interests include criminology, punishment, sexualities/gender studies, as well as methodological issues in conducting studies of crime and deviance. She is coauthor of *The Female Offender* and other articles that explore issues of gender and delinquency. Dr. Pasko has published in a variety of areas, including ethnography of stripping, pathways predictors of juvenile justice involvement, a feminist analysis of restorative justice initiatives, and evaluations of two girl offender programs. Dr. Pasko teaches courses on criminology, the female offender, men and masculinities, and crime and punishment. Her current research is funded by the Colorado Division of Criminal Justice and examines the treatment of sexual minority girls in youth corrections.

Meda Chesney-Lind, PhD, is a professor of Women's Studies at the University of Hawaii at Manoa. She has served as vice president of the American Society of Criminology and president of the Western Society of Criminology. Dr. Chesney-Lind's work on women and crime, and girls in the criminal justice are nationally recognized. Her books include *Girls, Delinquency, and Juvenile Justice* was awarded the American Society of Criminology's Michael J. Hindelang Award for the "outstanding contribution to criminology, 1992." An equally important and influential book, *The Female Offender: Girls, Women, and Crime,* was published in 1997 by Sage. Her most recent book is an edited collection entitled *Female Gangs in America* and has just been published by Lakeview Press. She has also received the Distinguished Scholar Award from the Women and Crime Division of the American Society of Criminology, the Major Achievement Award from the Division of Critical Criminology, and the Herbert Block Award for service to the society and the profession from the American Society of Criminology. Finally, she has received the Donald Cressey Award from the National Council on Crime and Delinquency in 1997 for "her outstanding academic contribution to the field of criminology." Locally, she has been awarded the University of Hawaii Board of Regent's Medal for "Excellence in Research."

Zelma Weston Henriques, PhD, is a professor in the Department of Law, Police Science and Criminal Justice Administration at John Jay College, City University of New York. She was a Rockefeller Research Fellow in Human Rights at Columbia University. Her research interests are imprisoned mothers and their children; women in prison; race, class, and gender issues; and cross-cultural studies of crime. She is the author of *Imprisoned Mothers and Their Children.*

Bridget P. Gladwin, MA, is retired from a thirty-four year career in New York state and local government. Twenty-eight of those years were spent in state and local corrections. She has served as warden of three different minimum and medium security male and female New York State correctional institutions. Nine of those years were spent implementing and developing the very successful nursery program at Taconic Correctional Facility. She holds a BSW in Sociology from London University and an MSW from Rutgers University. Since her retirement, she has been an adjunct professor at Pace University, St. John's University, and currently teaches at John Jay College of Criminal Justice.

Anna Curtis, MA, is a doctoral candidate in the sociology department at the University of Massachusetts, Amherst. She is also a graduate fellow in the legal studies department at the same university. Her dissertation research focuses on incarcerated fathers, exploring the ways that fatherhood and masculinity are deployed within prison in order to control and discipline male prisoners as well as how incarcerated fathers negotiate the tensions between their masculine practices and their expectations for responsible fathering behavior.

Elizabeth Corzine Dretsch, PhD, is an assistant professor in the Department of Criminal Justice at Troy University. She earned her PhD in the administration of justice with a graduate minor in educational research from the University of Southern Mississippi. Dr. Dretsch served as the key academic advisor to the Jacksonville Reentry Center and the Jacksonville Mental Health Court in Jacksonville, Florida. Her work has been published in *Women & Criminal Justice,* the *Journal of Interpersonal Violence, International Journal of Cyber Criminology,* the *Journal of Criminal Justice and Popular Culture* and *Rethinking Corrections: Rehabilitation, Reentry, and Reintegration* (2011).

Lorie A. L. Nicholas, PhD, is a staff psychologist in the Federal Bureau of Prisons and an adjunct professor at John Jay College of Criminal Justice in the Law and Police Science Department. Her work consists of conducting suicide risk assessments and monitoring overall mental health services. Dr. Nicholas has presented at many conferences and conducted workshops and trainings on topics which include stress management, race-related concerns, the criminal justice system, substance abuse, violence, incarcerated mothers and their children, and financial stress/financial literacy. Dr. Nicholas has an extensive background working with children, youth and adults. She has been involved with numerous research projects as well.

Gerard Bryant, PhD, is the Northeast Regional Psychology Services Administrator for the Federal Bureau of Prisons. He is also currently teaching correctional psychology courses at John Jay College of Criminal Justice, which is part of the City University of New York.

Ronald H. Aday, PhD, is professor of sociology at Middle Tennessee State University. He received his PhD from Oklahoma State University, with specialties in crime, corrections and gerontology. His lifelong work on aging and health issues in the field of corrections has contributed significantly to the public policy debate on older offenders. He has published extensively on the topic including *Aging Prisoners: Crisis in American Corrections* and is coauthor of *Women Aging in Prison: A Neglected Population in the Correctional System.*

Jennifer J. Krabill, MA, is a research associate at the Tennessee Center for Gerontology and Geriatric Research. She received her MA degree in sociology from Middle Tennessee State University. A coauthor of *Women Aging in Prison: A Neglected Population in the Correctional System,* her extensive research has examined a variety of topics on aging offenders in the criminal justice system. Her most recent work focuses on religion in the lives of older female lifers.

Christopher Hensley, PhD, is an associate professor of criminal justice in the Department of Criminal Justice at the University of Tennessee at Chattanooga. He received his doctorate in sociology from Mississippi State University. His most recent publications appear in the *International Journal of Offender Therapy and Comparative Criminology* and the *Journal of Interpersonal Violence.* His research interests include the link between childhood animal cruelty and later violence toward humans, prison sexuality, and attitudes toward correctional issues.

Helen Eigenberg, PhD, is professor and department head in the Criminal Justice Department at the University of Tennessee at Chattanooga. She worked for five years at a federal, male prison both as a correctional officer and a case manager. She received her PhD in criminal justice in 1989 from Sam Houston State University. She taught and served as department head at Old Dominion University from 1988–1995 and Eastern Kentucky University from 1995–1997. She has been at UTC since 1998. Her research interests include women and crime, victimology, violence against women, institutional corrections, and male rape in prisons. She has published a book on domestic violence: *Woman Battering in the United States* (2001). She also has published over 25 articles in a wide variety of journals including: *American Journal of Police, Women and Criminal Justice, Criminal Justice Review, Journal of Criminal Justice Education, Journal of Criminal Justice, Justice Quarterly,* and *The Prison Journal.* She was the editor of *Feminist Criminology* and currently is on their editorial board. She has won several national and state awards for her innovation and success in teaching, research, and service.

Lauren Gibson, MA, is a recent graduate of the University of Tennessee at Chattanooga, where she received her master's degree in criminal justice. Her future publication will appear in *The Prison Journal.* Her research interests include prison sexuality, attitudes toward sexual assault, and LGBT prison subcultures.

Holly A. Miller, PhD, is an assistant dean of undergraduate programs and professor in the College of Criminal Justice at Sam Houston State University. She received her BA from Bethel College in St. Paul, Minnesota, and her PhD in clinical psychology from Florida State University. She teaches, consults, and conducts research in the areas of malingered psychopathology, assessment and treatment of offenders, psychopathy, sexual offenders, and diversity issues in criminal justice.

Leah A. McCoy, MA, is a doctoral student in the College of Criminal Justice at Sam Houston State University. She received her BA in psychology from West Virginia State University in Institute, West Virginia, and her MA in criminal justice and criminology from Sam Houston State University. Her research interests include gender issues in crime and criminal justice, legal issues in criminal justice, and victimology.

Christian Maile, MA, is a PhD candidate in the Clinical Forensic Psychology Doctoral Program at John Jay College of Criminal Justice, City University of New York. He is currently completing his predoctoral internship at St. Joseph's Healthcare in Hamilton, Ontario, Canada. His research interests include forensic assessment and the etiology and treatment of sex offending.

Cynthia Calkins-Mercado, PhD, is an associate professor in the John Jay College Department of Psychology. Her research aims to inform sex crime policy and sexual violence prevention through use of empirical data.

Elizabeth L. Jeglic, PhD, is an associate professor in the psychology department at John Jay College. Her research interests include the treatment and assessment of sex offenders and sex offender public policy.

Barbara H. Zaitzow, PhD, professor of criminal justice at Appalachian State University, conducts research projects in men's and women's prisons and has been involved in local, state and national advocacy work for prisoners and organizations seeking alternatives to imprisonment. Zaitzow has served on various editorial boards for nationally-recognized journals and she has published a coedited book, articles, and book chapters on a variety of prison-related topics including HIV/AIDS and other treatment needs of women prisoners and the impact of prison culture on the "doing time" experiences of the imprisoned which appear in *Criminal Justice Policy Review, International Journal of Offender Therapy and Comparative Criminology, Journal of Crime and Justice, Journal of Gang Research, Journal of the Association of Nurses in AIDS Care, Justice Policy Journal,* and *Names.*

Richard S. Jones, PhD, is an associate professor of sociology at Marquette University. He is the author of the books, *Doing Time: Prison Experience and Identity* (with Tom Schmid) and *Global Perspectives on Re-Entry* (with Ikponwosa O. Ekunwe), and has published in the areas of prison experience, social identity, and the problems of reentry faced by previously incarcerated individuals.

Joel Rosenthal, PhD, received his PhD in clinical psychology from Georgia State University in 1988 and has been a licensed practicing clinical psychologist in California since 1990. He has been employed by the U.S. Department of Veterans Affairs since 1987, currently in the position of National Training Director, Veterans Justice Programs. In this capacity, Dr. Rosenthal is responsible for development and oversight of the training and education of the over 200 VA staff responsible for outreach to justice involving veterans in prisons, jails, and courts throughout the United States. Prior to his current VA position, Dr. Rosenthal served on the staff of the VA Palo Alto Healthcare System as Coordinator of Clinical Services for Domiciliary Care, overseeing all clinical services provided in the 100-bed residential and aftercare programs serving homeless and substance dependent veterans. Dr. Rosenthal previously worked in community-based mental health in the provision of individual, adolescent, and family treatment, including serving as executive director of Iowa Runaway Service, Des Moines, Iowa.

Jim McGuire, LCSW, PhD, is a social work researcher and program administrator whose current position is National Director, VHA (Veterans Health Administration) Veterans Justice Program, which includes VA Healthcare for Reentry Veterans (HCRV) Program (prison outreach and reentry services) and VA Veterans Justice Outreach (law enforcement, jail, and court-based services for justice involved veterans). His research included: (1) longitudinal evaluations of a. VA-funded residential care outcomes for homeless veterans and b. colocation of primary care and homeless services for homeless veterans to improve access and health status; (2) outreach and treatment for incarcerated veterans reentering the community; (3) elderly homeless and incarcerated veterans; and (4) VA-community agency partnerships. Dr. McGuire has also been PI or Co-PI at VA Greater Los Angeles Healthcare System on VA's NEPEC (Northeast Program Evaluation Center) studies of Supported Employment, Seeking Safety, Critical Time Intervention (CTI), and the VA-HUD Collaborative Initiative to Help End Chronic Homelessness (CICH). Dr. McGuire was a clinician and administrator at Didi Hirsch Community Mental Health Center in Culver City, California, for 22 years prior to employment at VA. He worked in crisis intervention, substance abuse, family and child guidance, and justice treatment programs during his tenure in community mental health.

Mark D. Cunningham, PhD, ABPP, is a prolific scholar regarding death-sentenced inmates, rates and correlates of prison violence, and death penalty sentencing considerations. Dr. Cunningham's research contributions have been honored with the 2006 American Psychological Association Award for Distinguished Contributions to Research in Public Policy, the 2005 Texas Psychological Association Award for Outstanding Contribution to Science, and election as a Fellow of the American Psychological Association. He is board-certified in clinical and forensic psychology by the American Board of Professional Psychology. Dr. Cunningham's practice is national in scope and he is licensed as a psychologist in 20 states. Dr. Cunningham earned his doctorate in clinical psychology at Oklahoma State University, completed a clinical psychology internship at the National Naval Medical Center, and did postdoctoral studies at the Yale University School of Medicine. He can be contacted at: mdc@markdcunningham.com

Keith J. Price, PhD, is an associate professor of criminal justice and sociology at West Texas A&M University. He spent thirty years of employment with the Texas prison system where he served in numerous positions, including as warden of five maximum security prisons. His research interests include capital punishment and Texas prisons.

Harald E. Weiss, PhD, is assistant professor of sociology in the Department of Sociology at Mississippi State University. He earned his PhD from Ohio State University in 2008 and conducts research on the development of adolescent social capital, as well as on its protective effects on delinquency. A second focus of his research is the relationship between immigration and crime. In this area, he particularly focuses on the economic factors that may tie immigration to rates of offending in the U.S. His work has appeared in *Social Science Research, Sociological Perspectives,* and *Justice Quarterly.*

Lauren M. Vasquez, MA, is currently a doctoral student (ABD) at Mississippi State University. Her areas of interest are criminology and gender, and she is currently investigating techniques of neutralization through a gendered lens. Her past research has focused on such topics as rural crime and immigration, representations of crimes in popular media, and fear of crime management among newly married African American couples. Lauren recently completed work on a Verizon Wireless Fellowship she received last year. The fellowship allowed her to research policies and procedures on dealing with intimate partner violence and rape across several university campuses. Her work on this topic has led to several presentations that are intended to promote awareness about intimate partner violence and rape on college campuses.

Aaron Rappaport, JD, is a professor of law at the University of California Hastings College of the Law. He writes and teaches in the areas of criminal law, sentencing law, and terrorism.

Tinka Veldhuis, PhD, is a PhD Fellow and lecturer in the sociology department of the University of Groningen, the Netherlands. In addition, she is a research fellow at the

Netherlands Institute of International Relations 'Clingendael,' and at the International Centre for Counter-Terrorism (ICCT)—The Hague. Her research focuses on radicalization, violent extremism and counter-terrorism. In particular, she develops interdisciplinary research frameworks to examine detention and reintegration of violent extremist offenders and radicalization and deradicalization processes in prison. In 2010, she was involved in evaluation research commissioned by the Dutch Ministry of Security and Justice, to evaluate Dutch terrorist detention policies.

Amos N. Guiora, JD, is a professor of law at the S. J. Quinney College of Law, the University of Utah. Guiora who teaches criminal procedure, international law, global perspectives on counterterrorism and religion and terrorism incorporates innovative scenario-based instruction to address national and international security issues and dilemmas. He is a member of the American Bar Association's Law and National Security Advisory Committee; a research fellow at the International Institute on Counter-Terrorism, The Interdisciplinary Center, Herzylia, Israel; a corresponding member, The Netherlands School of Human Rights Research, University of Utrecht School of Law. He was awarded a Senior Specialist Fulbright Fellowship for the Netherlands (2008) and research grant from the Stuart Family Foundation (2011). Professor Guiora has published extensively in the U.S. and Europe on issues related to national security, limits of interrogation, religion and terrorism, the limits of power, multiculturalism, and human rights. Guiora is the author of numerous articles, op-eds and books. His recent books include *Global Perspectives on Counterterrorism*, *Fundamentals of Counterterrorism*, *Constitutional Limits on Coercive Interrogation*, *Freedom from Religion: Rights and National Security* and *Homeland Security: What Is It and Where are We Going?* He served for 19 years in the Israel Defense Forces as lieutenant colonel (retired), and held a number of senior command positions, including commander of the IDF School of Military Law, legal advisor to the IDF Home Front Command and legal advisor to the Gaza Strip. Professor Guiora received the S. J. Quinney College of Law Faculty Scholarship Award (2011).

Hung-En Sung, PhD, is professor of criminal justice at John Jay College of Criminal Justice. He specializes in offender rehabilitation, correctional health, and comparative analysis of crime and justice. His current work focuses on the diversion and treatment of chronic offenders with co-occurring disorders and the therapeutic mechanisms of faith-based recovery interventions. Dr. Sung is also examining the impact of morbidity and healthcare needs on criminal recidivism among offenders under institutional or community supervision. In 2010, the National Institute of Justice awarded him the W. E. B. Du Bois Fellowship to research on the safety and health consequences of the legal exclusion of undocumented migrants.

Linda Richter, PhD, is the associate director of the Division of Policy Research and Analysis at The National Center on Addiction and Substance Abuse at Columbia University. Dr. Richter is responsible for overseeing the preparation of all research-related proposals and products of the division which focuses on the impact of substance use and addiction on systems and populations in the United States and aims to integrate the prevention and treatment of addiction into mainstream medicine. Dr. Richter has taught in the psychology department at Barnard College and in the Department of Organization and Leadership at Teachers College of Columbia University. She received her PhD in social psychology from the University of Maryland at College Park.

Roger D. Vaughan, PhD, received his doctorate in biostatistics from the Mailman School of Public Health at Columbia University in 1997, and has been a professor there since 2003. He is currently the interim chair of the Department of Biostatistics and director of the Clinical Research Methods track. His research interests revolve around rigorous evaluation methods, methods for the analysis of data from Group Randomized Trials and of correlated data, and innovative teaching methods for the quantitative sciences. Dr. Vaughan also serves as the editor for statistics and evaluation for the *American Journal of Public Health,* and is the director of the Design and Biostatistics Resources of the Irving Institute for Clinical and Translational Research.

Susan E. Foster, MSW, is VP, Director of Policy Research and Analysis, and director of The Califano Institute at The National Center on Addiction and Substance Abuse at Columbia University (CASA Columbia). Projects under her direction have included studies of addiction prevention and treatment in the US; the impact of substance use and addiction on federal, state and local budgets, juvenile and adult corrections, schools, welfare, the family, and women; the diversion and misuse of prescription drugs; and research on the commercial value of underage and pathological drinking to the alcohol industry. She has an MSW in social policy from Rutgers University and has authored publications on a broad range of public policy issues. She is responsible for the production of CASA's first book, Women under the Influence, published by The Johns Hopkins University Press and released in February of 2006. Prior to joining CASA, she worked in local and state government, was a partner in the public policy consulting firm of Brizius & Foster, and served as Deputy Under Secretary for Intergovernmental Affairs in the U.S. Department of Health, Education, and Welfare.